MW01710899

STUDY GUIDE

Paul T. Dickinson | Gustavo Indart | E. Kenneth Grant
McGill University | University of Toronto | University of Guelph

Twelfth Canadian Edition

MACROECONOMICS

Christopher T.S. Ragan | Richard G. Lipsey

PEARSON
Addison Wesley
Toronto

Copyright © 2008, 2005, 2001, 1997 Pearson Education Canada, a division of Pearson Canada Inc., Toronto, Ontario. Pearson Addison Wesley.

All rights reserved. This publication is protected by copyright, and permission should be obtained from the publisher prior to any prohibited reproduction, storage in a retrieval system, or transmission in any form or by any means, electronic, mechanical, photocopying, recording, or likewise. For information regarding permission, write to the Permissions Department.

ISBN-13 978-0-321-45101-9
ISBN-10 0-321-45101-5

Editor-in-Chief: Gary Bennett
Developmental Editor: Maurice Esses
Production Editor: Marisa D'Andrea
Production Coordinator: Andrea Falkenberg
Copyeditor: Kelli Howey
Formatter: Nelson Gonzalez

1 2 3 4 5 11 10 09 08 07

Printed and bound in Canada.

PEARSON
Addison Wesley

CONTENTS

TO THE STUDENT

The contents of this book will help you reinforce and test your understanding of the analytical and theoretical concepts in each chapter of *Economics,* Twelfth Canadian Edition, by Professors Christopher T. S. Ragan and Richard G. Lipsey. In this new edition of the *Study Guide,* we have increased the number of questions and exercises, especially in Chapters 19–35. And we have provided explanations for the answers to many more of the Additional Multiple-Choice Questions in each chapter.

Our teaching experience has led us to believe that students often have the most trouble comprehending theoretical concepts and applying them to specific economic situations. The textbook covers a broad range of policy issues and real-world examples and applications. You will find excellent discussions of issues and policy applications in the body of the text and in the boxes entitled Applying Economic Concepts and Extensions in Theory. Consequently, the role of the *Study Guide* is twofold—to help you better understand and apply the economic concepts you will meet in the text, and to give you a means to check your understanding. Many *Study Guide* questions, therefore, stress the application of economic theory using hypothetical and often numerical examples.

Each chapter in the *Study Guide* corresponds to a text chapter and is divided into nine sections, ordered as follows. The LEARNING OBJECTIVES are identical to those appearing at the beginning of each textbook chapter. The CHAPTER OVERVIEW provides a brief overview of the important concepts and issues addressed in the chapter. The HINTS AND TIPS section provides our suggestions and tips for effective study and how you might avoid some common errors on examinations. It will be interesting for you to compare our list with yours after you have received your midterm results. Good luck!

The CHAPTER REVIEW section is divided into the same major subsections as each chapter of the textbook. Each subsection begins with a review of the main issues and concepts and then provides some multiple-choice questions which are primarily non-quantitative in nature. These questions are intended to give you quick feedback on your awareness and understanding of the basic concepts covered in the subsection. When you answer multiple-choice questions, avoid the temptation to leap at the first answer that seems plausible. There is one best answer for each question. You should be able to explain why any other answer is not as satisfactory as the one you have chosen.

The SHORT-ANSWER QUESTIONS have two functions. First, they give you practice formulating your economic reasoning in written form. We often only discover what we don't understand when we try to write an explanation. Second, the questions help you to check your understanding of the broad theoretical concepts before attempting applied questions with more technical content.

In many ways, the EXERCISES section has been the main distinguishing feature of this *Study Guide* since its first edition. We believe the greatest reinforcement to learning economics comes from doing the questions in this section. Not only do they solidify and enhance your understanding, but they also give you the tools on which to rely when memory fails in exams! We urge you not to make the mistake of avoiding the exercise questions just because your examinations may consist entirely of multiple-choice questions. Even in multiple-choice examinations you need the understanding and the ability to analyze, which you will get from doing the exercises. Wherever mathematics is used, it does not require you to know more than the basic skills you learned in Chapter 2. We firmly believe that these exercises will enhance your ability to do well on all examinations, including those consisting entirely of multiple-choice questions! Do not be discouraged if you have difficulty with certain exercises. The most effective learning often comes from seeing how and why you got the wrong answer to a problem. We have also provided some more challenging problems in the section entitled EXTENSION EXERCISES.

The ADDITIONAL MULTIPLE-CHOICE QUESTIONS section focuses on additional applications of the concepts and analysis from the textbook, and some questions require numerical or algebraic solutions. In the SOLUTIONS section, we have provided brief explanations for more than half of these questions, which are identified by an asterisk next to the question number.

Unlike other study guides, the SOLUTIONS section provides answers for all questions. Please note that the written explanations are intended to guide you through the economic reasoning only, and should not be viewed as sample answers for examination purposes. In many cases your instructors may require fuller explanations on midterm and final examinations. A full appreciation of the issues can be achieved only after you have participated in lectures, carefully read the textbook, and thought your way through the concepts and economic applications with the assistance of this *Study Guide*.

Acknowledgments

The authors appreciate the cumulative contribution to the quality and content of the current edition of two former authors, Professors Doug Auld (Loyalist College) and Bill Furlong (University of Guelph). We dedicate this edition of the *Study Guide* to Fay, Baiba, Mark, and Mara.

Paul T. Dickinson
Gustavo Indart
E. Kenneth Grant

PART 1: WHAT IS ECONOMICS?

CHAPTER 1

ECONOMIC ISSUES AND CONCEPTS

LO

LEARNING OBJECTIVES

In this chapter you will learn

1 to view the market economy as a self-organizing entity in which order emerges from a large number of decentralized decisions.

2 the importance of scarcity, choice, and opportunity cost, and how all three concepts are illustrated by the production possibilities boundary.

3 about the circular flow of income and expenditure.

4 that all actual economies are mixed economies, having elements of free markets, tradition, and government intervention.

CHAPTER OVERVIEW

This introductory chapter discusses some of the major issues that confront all economies. An economy is endowed with **scarce resources** while human wants are unlimited. Choices must therefore be made regarding **production** and **consumption**. A central element of choice is the concept of **opportunity cost,** which measures the benefit of the best forgone alternative when making a choice. An economy's opportunity cost in production is illustrated through its **production possibilities boundary**. In addition to production and consumption choices, economies must also address how to avoid unemployment and how to ensure adequate growth over time. Different types of economic systems make these choices through different processes. This chapter reviews the main features of *command* economies, *free market* economies, and *mixed* economies.

Economists focus on three sets of decision makers in a market economy: individuals (consumers), firms (producers), and government. Consumers are assumed to have the objective of maximizing their well-being (utility), while firms' decisions are made with the goal of maximizing their profits. (The objectives of government are discussed in later chapters.) The interactions between households and firms through markets are best illustrated in a diagram depicting the circular flow of income and expenditure.

One of the great economic debates of the twentieth century concerns the relative merits of **centrally planned economies** versus **free-market economies**. The pros and cons of each are reviewed, as are the main reasons why practically all communist counties have moved from command systems to mixed systems. The central lesson from this chapter is that the market economy is a self-organizing entity that coordinates millions of decentralized, independent decisions made by self-interested consumers and producers.

HINTS AND TIPS

The following may help you to avoid some of the most common errors on examinations.

✓ Understand that the opportunity cost of one commodity is the amount of other commodities you could have instead. For example, a major part of the opportunity cost of your education is the amount of income you could have earned had you not been studying.

✓ Recognize that existing resources are fully employed at all points on the production possibilities boundary (PPB), so reallocating resources to produce more of one commodity means less of other commodities must be produced. The slope of the PPB, therefore, measures the economy's opportunity cost of one commodity in terms of other commodities, and vice versa.

✓ Understand the difference between the causes and consequences of a movement along the PPB and a shift of the PPB.

CHAPTER REVIEW

The Complexity of the Modern Economy

Modern economies involve a countless number of economic decisions by self-interested individual consumers and producers. These independent decisions must be coordinated for the economy to use its scarce resources to produce the things people want to buy in the amounts that they want to purchase. This section sets the stage for subsequent study of how self-organizing free markets perform this coordination in modern economies, of the types of government actions that help or hinder efficient coordination, and of the issues that arise when economic efficiency seems to conflict with social values.

1. One of the great insights of Adam Smith was that
- (a) modern economies require central planning.
- (b) benevolence is the foundation of economic order.
- (c) the rich will get richer and the poor will get poorer in a market economy.
- (d) central coordination is required for any modern economy.
- (e) by acting in their own self-interest, people produce a spontaneous economic order.

2. Which of the following is one of the main characteristics of a market economy?
- (a) The objective of individuals is to maximize society's well-being.
- (b) Firms must meet production quotas
- (c) Sellers can sell all they want to, regardless of price.
- (d) Private property.
- (e) People ignore financial incentives.

3. Broadly speaking, a major reason why a relatively *efficient* economic order arises in a market economy is that
- (a) producers and consumers face different prices.
- (b) pricing decisions are coordinated by producers, because they have better knowledge of the availability of resources than consumers.
- (c) consumers determine the price structure, since they know best what they want.
- (d) government manipulates prices in the best interests of society as a whole.
- (e) prices respond to overall conditions of scarcity or plenty.

Scarcity, Choice, and Opportunity Cost

After studying this section you should understand the problem of scarcity, the need for choice, and why choice creates opportunity cost. You should be able to illustrate the relationships among scarcity, choice, and opportunity cost using a production possibilities boundary (PPB), to explain why growth in a country's productive capacity can be represented by an outward shift in its PPB, and why unemployment of resources can be represented by points inside a country's PPB.

4. **The fundamental problem of economics is, in short,**
   (a) too many poor people.
   (b) finding jobs for all.
   (c) the scarcity of resources relative to wants.
   (d) constantly rising prices.
   (e) the relative inefficiency that results when no single authority has control over the selfish decisions of consumers and producers.

5. **Scarcity is a problem that**
   (a) more efficient production would eliminate.
   (b) is nonexistent in wealthy economies.
   (c) exists due to finite amounts of resources and unlimited human wants.
   (d) arises when productivity growth slows down.
   (e) exists in command economies but not market economies.

6. **Which of the following is *not* an example of a factor of production?**
   (a) a bulldozer. (b) a mechanic.
   (c) a farm hand. (d) a tractor.
   (e) a haircut.

7. **Opportunity cost measures the**
   (a) different opportunities for spending money.
   (b) monetary cost of purchasing a commodity.
   (c) alternative means of producing output.
   (d) amount of one good forfeited to obtain a unit of another good.
   (e) market price of a good.

8. **If a DVD costs $20 and a videocassette costs $10, then the opportunity cost of five DVDs is**
   (a) 50 videocassettes. (b) 10 videocassettes.
   (c) 5 videocassettes. (d) 2 videocassettes.
   (e) $25.

9. **Assuming that the alternative is employment, the opportunity cost of a university education is**
   (a) tuition costs only.
   (b) tuition and book costs only.
   (c) the forgone salary only.
   (d) tuition costs plus book costs plus forgone salary.
   (e) all items in (d) plus university residence fees and the cost of cafeteria meals.

10. A downward-sloping production possibilities boundary that is also a straight line implies
(a) constant opportunity costs.
(b) zero opportunity costs.
(c) only one good is produced.
(d) rising opportunity costs.
(e) all goods are produced in equal quantities.

11. Which of the following causes an outward shift in the production possibilities boundary?
(a) A decrease in unemployment.
(b) A loss in the productive capacity of agricultural acreage caused by a prolonged drought.
(c) An increase in the productivity of all factors of production.
(d) Shifting resources away from the production of one good toward another.
(e) Both a decrease in unemployment and an increase in productivity.

12. Putting currently unemployed resources to work can be illustrated by
(a) shifting the production possibility boundary outward.
(b) a movement along a given production possibility boundary.
(c) moving from a point on the boundary to a point outside it.
(d) moving from a point inside the boundary to a point on it.
(e) moving from a point on the boundary to a point inside it.

Who Makes the Choices and How?

This section will enable you to discuss the market interactions of consumers and producers through the circular flow of income and expenditure. The fundamental concept, used throughout the text, of maximization through decisions made "on the margin" is first introduced. You will also better understand how modern economies are based on the specialization and division of labour; as well as the causes and impact of economic globalization and the areas of disagreement over its consequences.

13. In economics, the term *market economy* refers to
(a) institutions such as the Toronto Stock Exchange.
(b) a place where buyers and sellers physically meet, such as at farmers' markets.
(c) a society where individuals specialize in productive activities and enter voluntary trades.
(d) a society where most economic decisions are made by marketing analysts.
(e) an economy in which advertising is central to the marketing of goods and services.

14. In a barter economy, individuals
(a) haggle over the money price of each and every commodity.
(b) trade goods directly for other goods.
(c) use money to lubricate the flow of trades.
(d) must each produce all the goods and services he or she consumes.
(e) do not require factors of production.

15. The introduction of production lines where individuals specialize in performing specific tasks is known as

(a) the division of labour.
(b) the concentration of labour.
(c) the market economy.
(d) the advent of labour as a factor of production.
(e) lean production.

16. Economic theory assumes that individuals

(a) make choices to maximize their utility.
(b) seek to maximize profits.
(c) are the principal buyers of the factors of production.
(d) specialize their labour.
(e) are the only buyers of goods and services in a mixed economy.

17. A central assumption in economic theory regarding firms is that they

(a) are each owned by a single individual.
(b) must be incorporated.
(c) seek to maximize profits.
(d) must all be making profits.
(e) are the principal owners of the factors of production.

18. Individual consumers maximize their well-being by

(a) not wasting time making marginal decisions.
(b) comparing the total satisfaction received from one good with the total satisfaction received from another good.
(c) buying more of a good for which the marginal benefit is positive.
(d) buying more of a good for which the marginal benefit exceeds the marginal cost.
(e) comparing the average satisfaction received from various goods.

19. The two major types of markets in the circular flow of income are

(a) public markets and private markets.
(b) product markets and factor markets.
(c) free markets and controlled markets.
(d) markets for goods and markets for services.
(e) regulated markets and open markets.

20. The circular flow of income and expenditure shows the flow of

(a) goods and services from firms to consumers.
(b) payments for goods and services from consumers to firms.
(c) factor services from consumers to firms.
(d) payments for factor services from firms to consumers.
(e) All of the above.

21. The use of money when buying and selling

(a) makes exchange easier.
(b) makes barter more difficult.
(c) makes specialization of labour more difficult.
(d) increases the opportunity costs of exchange.
(e) makes the division of labour more difficult.

22. Specialization of labour leads to a more efficient allocation of resources because of
(a) more self-sufficiency.
(b) the use of barter.
(c) the principle of comparative advantage.
(d) a decrease in scarcity.
(e) both increased self-sufficiency and decreased scarcity.

23. The market in which an individual sells labour services is called a
(a) product market.
(b) factor market.
(c) foreign-exchange market.
(d) mixed market.
(e) goods market.

24. A major cause of the recent move toward globalization is
(a) international trade is a new phenomenon.
(b) a big reduction in the costs of transportation and information.
(c) a recognition that each country must produce what it consumes.
(d) increased living standards in developing countries.
(e) a growing concern about achieving equity among countries.

Is There an Alternative to the Market Economy?

This section emphasizes the remarkable achievement of the market economy in creating order out of millions of independent and decentralized decisions. After reading this section you will develop a better appreciation of the twentieth century's great economic debate on the relative merits of a market economy versus a command economy, and why practically all command economies have become mixed economies (further explained in *Lessons from History 1-1*).

25. Which of the following would be a source of similarity among alternative types of economic systems?
(a) The ownership of resources (private and public).
(b) The process for making economic decisions.
(c) The need to determine what is to be produced and how to produce it.
(d) The role that tradition plays in determining production and employment.
(e) The role of government in determining what is produced.

26. In the Canadian economy, the majority of decisions on resource allocation are made by
(a) consumers and firms through the price system.
(b) the various levels of government.
(c) negotiation between unions and firms.
(d) business firms only.
(e) legal contract.

27. Complex economic plans for many sectors of the economy are most associated with
(a) a market system.
(b) the Canadian economy.
(c) a command economy.
(d) a feudal system.
(e) a traditional economy.

28. There is general agreement among economists that government intervention in modern market economies

(a) is not needed.
(b) should be restricted to enforcing the law.
(c) creates unacceptable reductions in work incentives.
(d) is appropriate when private markets create externalities and fail to produce public goods.
(e) creates the appropriate distribution of income.

29. The failure of central planning (*Lessons from History 1-1*) was caused by

(a) production bottlenecks, shortages and gluts.
(b) lack of incentive to produce goods of high quality.
(c) a failure to protect the environment.
(d) poor incentives that didn't reward hard or efficient work.
(e) All of the above.

SHORT-ANSWER QUESTIONS

1. What was Karl Marx's basic argument against free markets? How did most centrally planned economies' attempts to address this actually contribute to their failure?

2. Explain the reasoning process that links scarcity and opportunity cost.

3. Why is the production possibilities boundary (PPB) typically drawn concave to the origin, and what does this imply for opportunity costs?

4. Outline the major conflicts between anti-globalization activists and defenders of free trade on the grounds of (a) the effect on developing countries, and (b) democracy. [*Note:* This question refers to the debate on globalization in *Applying Economic Concepts 1-2*.]

EXERCISES

1. The Key Economic Problems

Four key economic problems are identified in Chapter 1.

(1) What is produced and how? (resource allocation)
(2) What is consumed and by whom? (distribution)
(3) Why are resources sometimes idle? (unemployment)
(4) Is productive capacity growing? (economic growth)

For each of the following topics, identify which of the four types of economic problem applies. Use each classification only once.

(a) Rises in oil prices during the 1970s encouraged a switch to alternative energy sources.
(b) The standard of living in Canada, measured by real output per capita, has risen steadily over the past century.
(c) Large harvests worldwide cause lower grain prices, thereby helping consumers but hurting farmers.
(d) The unemployment rate decreased in the late 1990s.

2. The Production Possibilities Boundary (PPB)

This exercise gives you practice in constructing and interpreting a production possibilities boundary (PPB).

The economy of Islandia produces only two consumer goods, *necklaces* and *fish.* Only labour is required to produce both goods, and the economy's labour force is fixed at 100 workers. The table below indicates the daily outputs of necklaces and fish that can be produced with various quantities of labour.

Number of Workers	Daily Necklace Production	Number of Workers	Daily Fish Production (kilograms)
0	0	0	0
20	10.0	20	150
40	20.0	40	250
60	25.0	60	325
80	27.5	80	375
100	30.0	100	400

(a) Draw the PPB for this economy, using the grid in Figure 1-1. (*Hint:* The labour force is always fully employed along the PPB.)

Figure 1-1

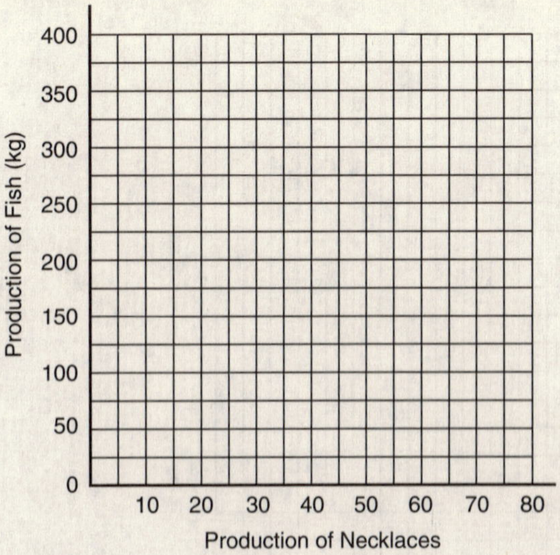

(b) What is the opportunity cost of producing the first 10 necklaces? What is the opportunity cost of producing the next 10 necklaces (i.e., from 10 to 20)? What happens to the opportunity cost of necklaces as their production is continuously increased?

(c) Suppose that actual production levels for a given period were 20 necklaces and 250 kilograms of fish. What can you infer from this information?

(d) Suppose a central planner in this economy were to call for an output combination of 35 necklaces and 150 kilograms of fish. Is this plan attainable? Explain.

(e) New technology is developed in necklace production, so that each worker can now produce double the daily amount indicated in the schedule. What happens to the PPB? Draw the new boundary on the grid. Can the planner's output combination in (d) now be met?

3. **Individual Choice and Opportunity Cost**

This exercise illustrates the concept of opportunity cost for an individual who faces fixed prices and has a fixed income.

Junior gets a weekly allowance of $10. He spends all of his allowance on only two commodities: video games at the arcade and chocolate bars. Assume that the price of a video game is 50 cents and the price of a chocolate bar is $1.

Figure 1-2

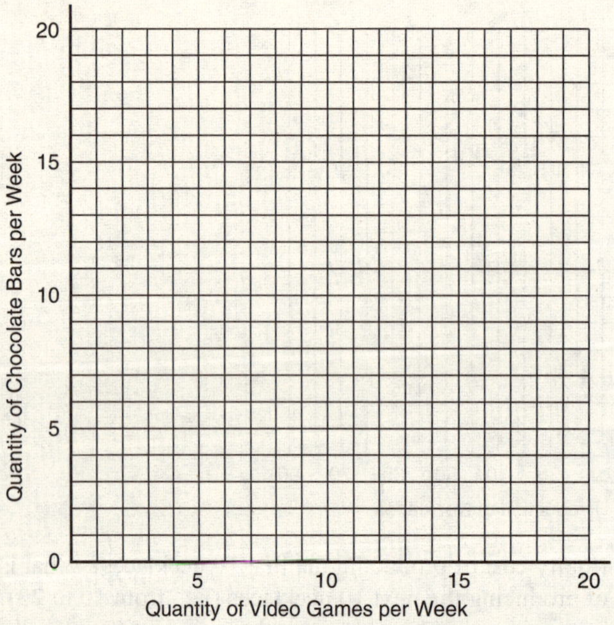

(a) Plot Junior's weekly attainable combinations of consumption.

(b) Can Junior attain the following consumption combinations?
(i) 15 video games and 2 chocolate bars
(ii) 4 video games and 8 chocolate bars
(iii) 7 video games and 7 chocolate bars

(c) What is the opportunity cost of Junior's first chocolate bar? His second? His third?

(d) By visual inspection of Junior's consumption possibility boundary, what could you say about his opportunity cost of consuming each of these commodities?

4. The Opportunity Cost of University Education

This question also explores opportunity cost but without diagrams. It is a variant of *Applying Economic Concepts 1-1.*

Pamela, a first-year student at Lakehead University, is considering whether or not to advance her studies by taking summer courses. Her monetary expenses would be tuition, $1000; books, $350; and living expenses, $1500. Her alternative is to work as a lifeguard, which would earn her $3500 for the summer. What is Pamela's opportunity cost of taking summer courses?

EXTENSION EXERCISES

E1. A Specific PPB

This exercise addresses an economy's production possibilities algebraically. In the upcoming chapters you will be asked to make more use of algebra.

An economy's production possibilities boundary is given by the mathematical expression $20 = 4A + B$, where A is the quantity of good A and B is the quantity of good B.

(a) If all resources in the economy were allocated to producing good A, what is the maximum level of production for this good? What is the maximum level of production for good B?

(b) Suppose that the production of B is increased from 12 to 16 units and that the economy is producing at a point on the production possibilities boundary. What is the opportunity cost per unit of good B? What is the opportunity cost per unit of good B if the production of this good were increased from 16 to 20?

(c) In what way is this production possibilities boundary different from that in Exercise 2 in terms of opportunity costs?

(d) In what way does the combination of four units of good A and five units of good B represent the problem of scarcity?

E2. A Conceptual PPB

This problem is conceptually challenging. The ability to solve it would reflect an excellent understanding of the production possibilities concept.

Consider the production possibilities for two totally dissimilar goods, such as apples and machine tools. Some resources are suitable for apple production and some for the production of machine tools. There is, however, no possibility of shifting resources from one product to another. In this case, what does the production possibility boundary look like? Explain and show graphically.

ADDITIONAL MULTIPLE-CHOICE QUESTIONS

***1. If the factors of production available to an economy were unlimited**

(a) the opportunity cost of producing more goods would be zero.
(b) the price of cars would be infinitely high.
(c) there would be no unemployment.
(d) scarcity would become the most serious economic problem.
(e) All of the above.

2. If a 12-month membership in a fitness club costs as much as tickets for 24 Montreal Expos baseball games, the opportunity cost of a one-month membership in the fitness club is

(a) 1/2 baseball game.
(b) 1 baseball game.
(c) 2 baseball games.
(d) 12 baseball games.
(e) 24 baseball games.

Questions 3 to 6 refer to Figure 1-3:

Figure 1-3

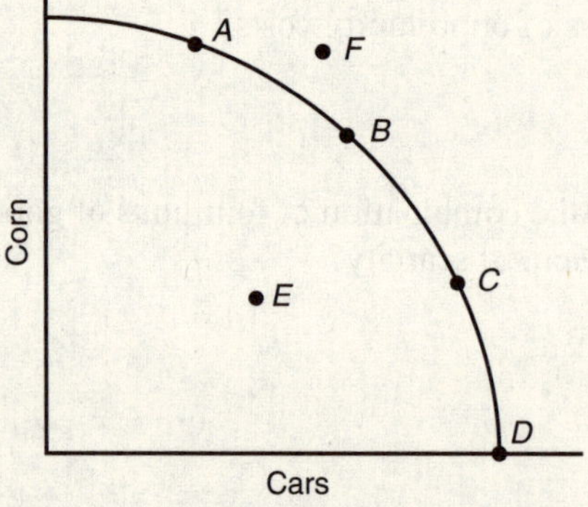

3. If the market economy moves from Point *A* to Point *C

(a) there is unemployment in the corn industry.
(b) the opportunity cost of the marginal car increases.
(c) technological change has made the production of cars more efficient.
(d) the central planner values cars more than corn.
(e) All of the above are true.

4. Point *E* represents a situation that

(a) is currently unattainable and can be expected to remain so.
(b) will be attainable only if there is economic growth.
(c) results from inefficient use of resources or failure to use all available resources.
(d) has a higher opportunity cost than points on the boundary itself.
(e) can never occur in a market economy.

*5. **With currently available resources, point *F* represents a situation that**
(a) results if resources are not fully employed.
(b) can be achieved if consumers demand fewer cars than at point *C*.
(c) is currently attainable.
(d) can be achieved if all resources were allocated to the production of cars.
(e) None of the above.

6. **Assuming the initial situation is point *B*, which one of the following represents a reallocation of resources away from car production to corn production?**
(a) point *A*. (b) point *C*.
(c) point *E*. (d) point *D*.
(e) point *F*.

Questions 7 through 14 refer to the following schedule of production possibilities for combinations of corn and beef, produced on a land tract of a given size and fertility.

Corn (bushels)	Beef (kilograms)
10 000	0
8 000	900
6 000	1 200
4 000	1 400
2 000	1 475
0	1 500

*7. **What would be the opportunity cost of producing 200 additional kilograms of beef if the current production were 4000 bushels of corn and 1200 kilograms of beef?**
(a) 6000 bushels of corn. (b) 175 kilograms of beef.
(c) 2000 bushels of corn. (d) Zero.
(e) None of the above.

8. **What would be the opportunity cost of producing 2000 additional bushels of corn if the current production were 6000 bushels of corn and 1200 kilograms of beef?**
(a) 900 kilograms of beef. (b) 1200 kilograms of beef.
(c) 300 kilograms of beef. (d) Zero.
(e) None of the above.

*9. **Which of the following combinations represent unattainable production levels with the current tract of land?**
(a) 8000 bushels of corn and 500 kilograms of beef.
(b) 8000 bushels of corn and 1200 kilograms of beef.
(c) 200 bushels of corn and 1475 kilograms of beef.
(d) 6000 bushels of corn and 1300 kilograms of beef.
(e) Both 8000 bushels of corn and 1200 kilograms of beef and 6000 bushels of corn and 1300 kilograms of beef.

*10. **The production possibilities shown for corn and beef mean**
(a) the PPB is a straight line because the change in corn is 2000 bushels all along.
(b) is concave because the total amount of beef increases as less corn is produced.
(c) is concave because the opportunity cost of beef increases as more beef is produced.
(d) is concave because the opportunity cost of corn falls as more corn is produced.
(e) The PPB is concave both because total beef increases as less corn is produced and the opportunity cost of corn falls as more corn is produced.

***11. The opportunity cost of increasing corn production from 4000 to 6000 is**

(a) the same as the opportunity cost of increasing corn production from 8000 to 10 000.
(b) the same as the opportunity cost of increasing corn production from 2000 to 4000.
(c) 0.1 kilograms of beef per bushel of corn.
(d) 1200 kilograms of beef.
(e) None of the above.

***12. Which of the following events is likely to lead to an outward shift of the production possibility boundary?**

(a) A reallocation of land use such that corn production increases from 6000 bushels to 8000 bushels while beef production decreases from 1200 kilograms to 900 kilograms.
(b) Some of the land is lost due to a flood.
(c) Twenty of the existing acres are not used for either beef or corn production.
(d) Corn prices fall relative to beef prices.
(e) None of the above.

13. The opportunity cost per bushel of corn is 0.15 kilograms of beef when

(a) corn production is increased from 8000 to 10 000.
(b) corn production is increased from 6000 to 8000.
(c) corn production is increased from 4000 to 6000.
(d) beef production is decreased from 1500 to 1475 kilograms.
(e) None of the above.

***14. Assuming that land is fully utilized and that corn production continually increases by 2000 bushels, the opportunity cost of beef**

(a) increases.
(b) decreases.
(c) is zero.
(d) remains constant.
(e) is undefined.

15. In a command economy, where to produce on the production possibility boundary is determined by

(a) the preferences of consumers, who spend their income accordingly.
(b) a central plan established by the government.
(c) traditional patterns of spending that change little from year to year.
(d) the preferences of workers, who vote to indicate their preferences.
(e) relative prices of goods.

16. Decisions regarding resource allocation are

(a) necessary only in centrally planned economies.
(b) made by central planners in traditional economies.
(c) necessary only in economies that are not industrialized.
(d) decentralized, but coordinated by the price system, in market economies.
(e) primarily determined by traditional customs in market economies.

17. In a market economy, the allocation of resources is determined by

(a) the government and its marketing boards.
(b) the various stock exchanges in the country.
(c) a central planning agency.
(d) the millions of independent decisions made by individual consumers and firms.
(e) the sobering discussions at the annual convention of the Canadian Economics Association.

***18. The main coordinating device in a self-organizing economy is**

(a) the way that government spends its tax revenues.
(b) government intervention to correct market failures.
(c) the economy's system of market-determined prices.
(d) the degree of income redistribution by government.
(e) the overall coordinated system of taxation and spending to achieve multiple objectives of government.

19. A barter economy

(a) refers to the direct trading of goods.
(b) does not require the use of money.
(c) requires a double coincidence of wants.
(d) involves costly searches for satisfactory exchanges.
(e) All of the above are true.

20. Utility-maximizing decisions of individuals are part of the study of ____________ and changes in the unemployment rate are part of the study of ____________.

(a) microeconomics; macroeconomics
(b) the theory of choice; microeconomics
(c) the production possibilities boundary; a centrally planned economy
(d) economic aggregates; the objectives of individual firms.
(e) None of the above.

SOLUTIONS

Chapter Review

1.(e) **2.**(d) **3.**(e) **4.**(c) **5.**(c) **6.**(e) **7.**(d) **8.**(b) **9.**(d) **10.**(a) **11.**(c) **12.**(d) **13.**(c) **14.**(b) **15.**(a) **16.**(a) **17.**(c) **18.**(d) **19.**(b) **20.**(e) **21.**(a) **22.**(c) **23.**(b) **24.**(b) **25.**(c) **26.**(a) **27.**(c) **28.**(d) **29.**(e)

Short-Answer Questions

1. Marx argued that although a market system would produce high total output, it could not be relied on to ensure a just distribution of that output. (He argued that the rich would get richer and the poor would get poorer.) In addressing this by measures to create a more even distribution of income (e.g., by guaranteeing complete job security), centrally planned economies did not provide the incentives for diligent and efficient work that are created by the "punishment and reward" forces of free markets.

2. Scarcity implies choice, choice means you must give up something to have something else, and what you give up is the opportunity cost of that something else. In essence, this implies that anything that has an opportunity cost is "scarce."

3. All factors of production are not equally adaptable to producing all goods. As more and more of one good is produced, the economy transfers resources from more efficient uses to progressively less efficient uses. As this happens, more and more resources must be transferred from the production of one good to get a constant increase in the amount of another good. In other words, the opportunity cost producing a good increases as more of it is produced. This is reflected in the changing slope of the PPB, which makes the PPB concave to the origin.

4. **(a)** Developing countries: Activists argue that free trade reduces the standard of living in developing countries, and does so largely at the expense of the poorest members (i.e., the poor get poorer). Defenders argue that free trade increases the average standard of living in both developed and developing countries. While there may be less disagreement that the poorest members of developing countries do get poorer, defenders may still argue that free trade at least gives developing countries the *opportunity* to internally redistribute the overall gains in a socially just way.

   (b) Democracy: Activists argue that free trade agreements are made in an undemocratic manner "behind closed doors." Defenders argue that the process is not undemocratic because the agreements must be passed by the governments of participating countries—specifically, by the *elected* bodies (parliaments) of the democratic countries.

Exercises

1. **(a)** 1 **(b)** 4 **(c)** 2—redistribution from farmers to consumers

   (d) 3—while (4) could also apply, this item is specifically talking about a fall in the proportion of the labour force (a resource) that is idle (i.e., wanting a job but not having one). It is possible for this to happen even without any economic growth.

2. **(a)** **Figure 1-4**

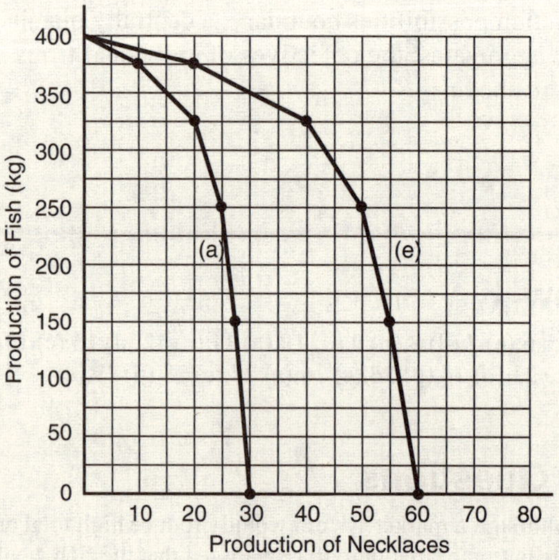

   (b) It takes 20 workers to produce the first 10 necklaces, and these 20 could have been used to increase fish production from 375 (with the other 80 workers) to 400. So the opportunity cost of these 10 necklaces is 25 (= 400 – 375) kg of fish, or 2.5 kg for each necklace (= 25/10). Similarly, the next 10 necklaces need another 20 workers, further reducing fish production from 375 to 325—an opportunity cost of 50 kg of fish, or 5 kg per necklace (= 50/10). Thus, the opportunity cost of producing necklaces is increasing (i.e., from 2.5 kg of fish per necklace to 5 kg per necklace), and if you continue transferring 20 more workers from fish to necklaces you see the opportunity cost per necklace continue rising (i.e., (325 – 250)/(25 – 20) = 15 kg, (250 – 150)/(27.5 – 25) = 40 kg, (150 – 0)/(30 – 27.5) = 60 kg). This continually rising opportunity cost per necklace is reflected in the slope of production possibilities boundary (a) in Figure 1-4 getting continually steeper as more and more necklaces (and fewer and fewer fish) are produced.

   (c) This production combination lies inside the production possibilities boundary, so some workers are unemployed or inefficiently used. In this case, using unemployment as the example, 20 necklaces should require 40 workers and 250 kilograms of fish should also require 40 workers, for a total of only 80 workers, leaving 20 of the full 100 workers unemployed.

(d) This combination is outside the production possibilities boundary and is therefore unattainable with current resources and technology. The maximum number of necklaces it is possible to make using all 100 workers is only 30. With 20 workers producing 150 kilograms of fish, the remaining 80 could produce only 27.5 necklaces (not 35).

(e) The production possibilities boundary moves to the right in the manner shown in Figure 1-4. The planner's output combination is now attainable: with 20 workers producing fish, the remaining 80 could produce 55 necklaces. The combination of 150 kilograms of fish and 35 necklaces is therefore inside the new boundary, implying that the economy would be using its resources inefficiently if it produced this combination.

3. (a) Figure 1-5

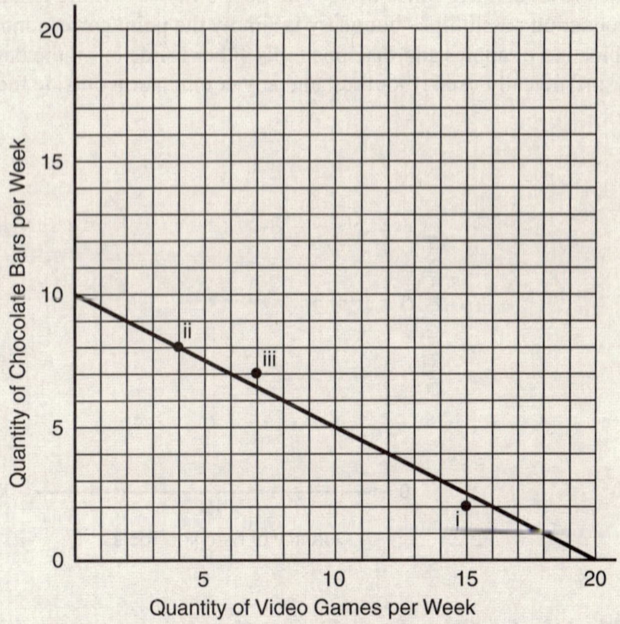

(b) (i) Yes, this combination lies inside his consumption possibilities boundary and is therefore affordable with $10. [15 videos at 50 cents each is $7.50 and 2 chocolate bars at $1 each is $2, for a total of $9.50, which is less than his $10 allowance.]

(ii) Yes, this combination is on his consumption possibilities boundary and therefore costs exactly $10. [4($0.50) + 8($1) = $10]

(iii) No, this combination costs more than his $10 allowance and therefore lies outside his consumption possibilities boundary. [7($0.50) + 7($1) = $10.50]

(c) To purchase the first chocolate bar, Junior must pay $1, which could have been used to purchase two video games. Thus, the opportunity cost of the first chocolate bar is two video games. The opportunity cost of the second and third bars is also two video games each.

(d) Since the consumption possibilities boundary is linear (i.e., a straight line), the opportunity cost is constant.

4. Pamela's opportunity cost of taking summer courses is $4850. [$1000 tuition + $350 books + forgone earnings of $3500.] Her living expenses are not counted since they would have to be incurred regardless of which alternative she chooses.

Extension Exercises

E1. (a) If all resources were allocated to the production of good *A*, there would be no production of good *B*. So, according to the mathematical expression, the maximum production of good *A* is five units. [Convert $20 = 4A + B$ to $A = 5 - 0.25B$, so $A = 5$ when $B = 0$.] If all resources were used to produce good *B*, then $B = 20$ and the production of good *A* is zero. [$B = 20 - 4A$, so $B = 20$ when $A = 0$.]

(b) The increase from 12 to 16 units of *B* requires a loss in production of good *A* of one (from two to one). An increase in *B* from 16 to 20 requires a loss in production of good *A* of one (from one to zero). Therefore, the opportunity cost *per unit* of good B is 0.25 units of *A* in each case. [From $A = 5 - 0.25B$, you see *A* changes by 0.25 whenever *B* changes by 1.]

(c) The opportunity cost is constant, whereas it was increasing in Exercise 2 above.

(d) According to the equation, four units of *A* and four units of *B* are possible. The combination of four units of *A* and five units of *B* is not feasible. Scarcity is indicated by the fact that more resources are required than are currently available.

E2. When all resources suitable to apple production are employed, the resulting apple output is *A′* in Figure 1-6. When all resources suitable to machine tool production are employed, the resulting quantity of machine tools is *M′*. Since there is no possibility of shifting resources between these two outputs, the production possibilities boundary is simply the point corresponding to the coordinates (*A′*, *M′*). Any combination of apples and machine tools either inside or on the dashed lines implies unemployed or inefficiently used resources, and any combination outside the dashed lines is unattainable.

Figure 1-6

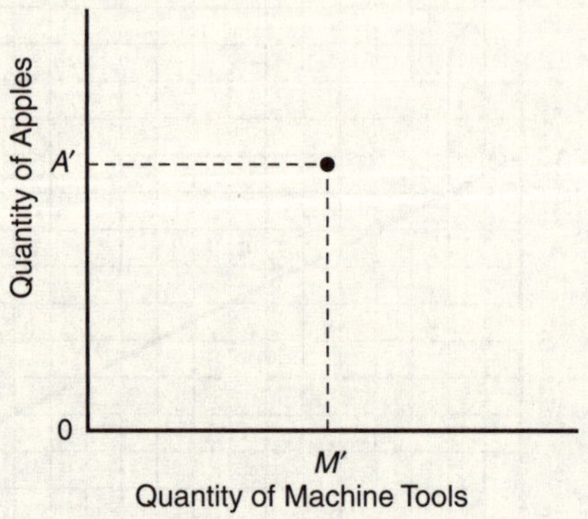

Additional Multiple-Choice Questions

1.(a) **2.**(c) **3.**(b) **4.**(c) **5.**(e) **6.**(a) **7.**(c) **8.**(c) **9.**(e) **10.**(c) **11.**(c) **12.**(e) **13.**(b) **14.**(b) **15.**(b) **16.**(d) **17.**(d) **18.**(c) **19.**(e) **20.**(a)

Explanations for the Asterisked Multiple-Choice Questions

1.(a) Unlimited resources means that having more of one good does not require having less of another, hence no opportunity cost. Since scarcity requires that there be an opportunity cost, no opportunity cost means no scarcity. Having resources available does not necessarily mean they are all used, so it does not rule out unemployment. (Indeed, technically speaking, "unlimited" means it is impossible to use them all.) Finally, in the absence of scarcity it is likely that prices would be very low rather than very high (and, again technically speaking, "infinity" can't be achieved anyway).

3.(b) The slope of the PPB (looking from the horizontal axis) shows how much corn must be given up for each extra car. The concave PPB is steeper at C than at A because more corn must be given up to get the extra car, hence a higher opportunity cost of a car. (Prove this for yourself by drawing a little right-angled triangle at each point, with equal horizontal axis and the PPB as the hypotenuse. Now compare the height of their vertical axes.) Both points are on the PPB, so there is no unemployment. Technological change would cause a shift of the PPB, not a movement along it. The relative quantities produced tells us nothing about prices, so nothing about values.

5.(e) With currently available resources, point F is unattainable.

7.(c) It is tempting to say that the opportunity cost is zero, since it is possible to produce 1400 kilograms of beef with no reduction in corn. This would be incorrect, however, since it is also possible to produce 6000 bushels of corn with no reduction in beef. The economy has a choice, and by choosing to have 200 additional kilograms of beef, it is choosing *not* to have the 2000 extra bushels of corn. Despite the fact that the economy is inside its PPB, therefore, the opportunity cost of the extra beef is the extra corn that could have been produced (i.e., another 2000 bushels, from 4000 to 6000).

9.(e) With 8000 bushels of corn the maximum amount of beef that can be produced is 900 kg, so 1200 kg, (b), is unattainable and 500 kg, (a), is attainable. At 6000 corn the maximum beef is 1200, so 1300, (d), is unattainable. At 2000 corn the maximum beef is 1475, so (c) is attainable.

10.(c) Starting from zero corn and increasing the amount of corn in constant increments of 2000 bushels, the maximum possible amount of beef falls by increasing amounts (25, 75, 200, 300, 900). Thus, the slope of the PPB keeps increasing as more corn is produced, making the PPB concave (so (a) is incorrect) because the opportunity cost of more corn keeps increasing (so (c) is correct but (d) and (e) are incorrect). While it is true that the total beef increases as more corn is produced, this would happen with any downward-sloping PPB, be it a straight line or concave or even convex (so (b) and (e) are incorrect).

11.(c) The extra 2000 bushels of corn requires giving up 200 kg of beef, so 200/2000 = 0.1 units of beef per extra unit of corn.

12.(e) Answer (a) involves a movement along the PPB. Answer (b) causes an inward shift of the PPB. Answer (c) is a point inside the PPB. Answer (d) gives an incentive to change the combination of corn and beef produced (i.e., a movement along the PPB), but does not change the combinations that it is possible to produce with current technology.

14.(b) The production of more and more corn requires moving resources out of beef production that are progressively less adaptable to the production of corn, so the quantity of beef forgone per extra unit of corn (the opportunity cost of corn) increases. If the opportunity cost of corn increases, then the opportunity cost of beef decreases. For example, if an extra 20 corn means giving up 5 beef, the opportunity cost per unit of corn is 5/20 = 0.25 units of beef and the opportunity cost per unit of beef is 20/5 = 4 units of corn. But if an extra 20 corn means giving up 10 beef instead of 5, the opportunity cost per unit of corn *increases* to 10/20 = 0.5 units of beef (i.e., up from 0.25) and the opportunity cost per unit of beef *decreases* to 20/10 = 2 units of corn (i.e., down from 4).

18.(c) All answers other than (c) refer to the actions of government which, although they may be desirable (e.g., answer (b)), are "organized" by specific individuals (politicians and civil servants) in line with the policies of the government in power. The self-organizing force in a market or even a mixed economy is the actions of masses of individuals (producers and consumers) in line with their self-interest, which in turn is heavily influenced by the prices of the various goods and services.

CHAPTER 2

How Economists Work

LO

LEARNING OBJECTIVES

In this chapter you will learn

1 to distinguish between positive and normative statements.

2 how economists use models to help them think about the economy.

3 about the interaction between economic theories and empirical observation.

4 to identify several types of economic data, including index numbers, time-series and cross-sectional data, and scatter diagrams.

5 that the slope of a relation between two variables, *X* and *Y*, is interpreted as the marginal response in *Y* to a unit change in *X*.

CHAPTER OVERVIEW

Chapter 1 provided an overview of the types of issues economists consider. Chapter 2 presents some important distinctions made by economists and discusses the approaches used to analyze economic questions.

Economists evaluate *hypotheses* that purport to explain economic behaviour. An important distinction is made between **positive statements,** which concern what is, was, or will be, and **normative statements,** which are judgments about what should be done. Disagreements over positive statements can, in principle, be settled by an appeal to the facts (i.e., they are testable). Disagreements over normative statements cannot be settled in this way.

Theories are designed to give meaning to observed sequences of events. A theory typically consists of definitions of **variables** and assumptions about how things behave. Any theory has certain logical implications that must hold if the theory is not to be rejected. These are the theory's **predictions** or **hypotheses**. Theories are tested by checking their predictions against the evidence. In economics the evidence is most often comprised of **data** drawn from the real world.

The relationships among variables in economic theories are usually presented in tables, graphs, or equations. These provide compact summaries of a large number of data observations, and play an important role in economic modelling.

HINTS AND TIPS

The following may help you to avoid some of the most common errors on examinations.

✓ Understand the difference between endogenous (dependent) and exogenous (independent) variables. Changes in the exogenous variables cause changes in the endogenous variables, not the other way around. That is, the *direction of causation* is from the exogenous variables to the endogenous variables. For example, cold weather causes more people to wear scarves, but more people wearing scarves will not cause cold weather.

✓ Recognize that assumptions must be made to create a hypothesis relevant for use in the real world, and that the predictive or explanatory powers of theory need not depend on the "accuracy" of the assumptions. Generally, it is the simplifying assumptions that give a hypothesis its ability to predict and explain major implications, rather than merely describe all possible implications.

✓ Understand how to draw and read graphs, and how to construct and solve and interpret equations. These are valuable tools which will improve your understanding of the material and, in so doing, significantly reduce the extent to which you have to rely on memory.

CHAPTER REVIEW

Positive and Normative Advice

The objective of this section is to distinguish between positive and normative statements. Positive statements are assertions of fact that can be tested, in principle even if not always in practice. Normative statements refer to what ought to be—they are based on personal opinion (i.e., on *value judgments*) and cannot be tested by appealing to facts. This section also explains why there is less disagreement among economists on many issues than may appear to be the case in public discussions.

1. Normative statements
(a) concern an individual's beliefs about what ought to be.
(b) are based on value judgments.
(c) cannot be subjected to empirical scrutiny.
(d) cannot be deduced from positive statements.
(e) All of the above.

2. "Capital punishment deters crime" is an example of
(a) a positive statement.
(b) a value judgment.
(c) a normative statement.
(d) an analytic statement.
(e) an untestable statement.

3. "Capital punishment should be reintroduced in Canada" is an example of
(a) a positive statement.
(b) a normative statement.
(c) an analytic statement.
(d) a testable hypothesis.
(e) None of the above.

4. Which of the following is probably the main reason why economists are often seen to disagree in public discussions?
(a) Economists like to stimulate debate.
(b) Different economists make different value judgments.
(c) Most economists disagree on positive statements.
(d) Economists fail to distinguish between theories and models.
(e) Economists are the only people who realize that the world is a very complex place.

Economic Theories

This section contains a non-technical discussion of the components of a theory and the role of models. After reading this section you should understand the basic structure of economic theories; the roles of variables, assumptions, and predictions in developing theories; and the purpose and usefulness of economic modelling.

5. If the assumptions imposed in an economic theory are unrealistic, then the theory
- (a) will always be refuted by the evidence.
- (b) is incorrect and should be rejected.
- (c) will not predict well and should be rejected.
- (d) will require more complex statistical techniques for testing.
- (e) may nonetheless predict better than any alternative theory.

6. The role of assumptions in theory is to
- (a) represent the world accurately.
- (b) improve understanding of a complex world by reasonably abstracting from reality.
- (c) avoid simplifications of the real world.
- (d) ensure that the theory considers all features of reality, no matter how minor.
- (e) None of the above.

7. A theory may contain all *except* which of the following?
- (a) Predictions about behaviour that are deduced from the assumptions.
- (b) A set of assumptions defining the conditions under which the theory is operative.
- (c) Hypotheses about how the world behaves.
- (d) A normative statement expressed as a functional relation.
- (e) Hypothesized relationships among variables.

8. Direction of causation refers to:
- (a) The effect of an exogenous variable on an endogenous variable.
- (b) The effect of a variable determined outside the theory on the value of a variable determined within the theory.
- (c) Whether the value of one variable rises or falls when another variable rises.
- (d) Whether an assumption increases or decreases the accuracy of a prediction.
- (e) Both (a) and (b).

Testing Theories

Economic theories adopt a scientific approach whereby hypotheses and predictions are developed and then tested against data, taking care to distinguish between a *correlation* among variables and a *causal* relationship. When the testing process shows that a theory does not give predictions that are reasonably consistent with the empirical evidence, it signals that the theory needs to be amended and/or a better alternative theory needs to be developed. The usefulness of a theory depends on how well it can predict group behaviour, not the behaviour of a particular individual in the group.

9. **The statement that the quantity produced of a commodity is positively related to its price is**
   (a) a normative statement.
   (b) a testable hypothesis.
   (c) not testable as currently worded.
   (d) a value judgment.
   (e) both a testable hypothesis and a value judgment.

10. **Statistical analysis in economics**
   (a) uses data generated in controlled laboratory experiments.
   (b) is mainly designed to prove or disprove the validity of assumptions.
   (c) must use techniques that take account of simultaneous changes in many variables.
   (d) should look only for evidence that confirms a theory.
   (e) uses correlation as proof of causality.

11. **Economic predictions are intended to**
   (a) forecast the behaviour of each consumer.
   (b) forecast the behaviour of groups of individuals.
   (c) test normative statements.
   (d) anticipate the irrational behaviour of certain odd individuals.
   (e) identify value judgments.

12. **The theory that extra-terrestrials exist and visit earth in flying saucers**
   (a) has been disproved by scientific evidence.
   (b) is inconsistent with scientific observation.
   (c) can never be disproved.
   (d) has been refuted.
   (e) has not been scientifically proved, but can't be disproved.

Economic Data

Economists use data drawn from real-world observations to test their theories. This section reviews two ways in which data can be examined: index numbers and graphs.

13. **If a particular index number in 2002 is 159 and the base year is 1999, then the index shows an increase of**
   (a) 5.9 percent between 1999 and 2002.
   (b) 59 percent between 1999 and 2002.
   (c) 159 percent between 1999 and 2002.
   (d) 0.59 percent between 1999 and 2002.
   (e) an indeterminable amount, since the value of the index in the base year is unknown.

14. **Index numbers are useful because**
   (a) identifying trends is easier using relative rather than absolute numbers.
   (b) each component can be weighted to reflect its relative importance.
   (c) they can all be given the same value in the base year.
   (d) All of the above are true.
   (e) Only (a) and (c) are true.

15. Which of the following is an example of cross-sectional data?

(a) Annual unemployment rates for Canada
(b) Vancouver housing prices for the period 1950–1999
(c) Last year's crime rates for all Canadian cities
(d) A series of this year's daily interest rates
(e) None of the above—they are all examples of time-series data.

16. Observations drawn repeatedly from successive months are

(a) cross-sectional data.
(b) time-series data.
(c) unweighted data.
(d) logarithmic data.
(e) scattered data.

17. A scatter diagram can be used to plot

(a) time-series data but not cross-sectional data.
(b) cross-sectional data but not time-series data.
(c) neither cross-sectional nor time-series data.
(d) either cross-sectional or time-series data.
(e) only endogenous variables.

Graphing Economic Theories

The relationship between schedules of numbers for two (or more) variables can be more easily seen when expressed algebraically and displayed graphically. This is an important section that reviews the basic algebraic and graphical tools used for expressing these relationships. After completing this section you should be comfortable reading functional relationships, translating equations into graphs, and interpreting graphs.

18. The slope of a straight line is

(a) always positive.
(b) calculated by dividing the value of the variable measured on the horizontal axis by the value of that measured on the vertical axis.
(c) zero.
(d) constant.
(e) increasing or decreasing, depending upon whether the slope is positive or negative, respectively.

19. Suppose that economic analysis estimates the following relationship between imports (*IM*) and national income (*Y*): $IM = 100 + 0.15Y$. This means that

(a) imports are negatively related to national income.
(b) when national income is zero, imports are zero.
(c) imports are 15 percent of national income.
(d) imports are 15 times greater than national income.
(e) other things remaining constant, for every increase of $1 in national income, imports will rise by 15 cents.

20. Still using $IM = 100 + 0.15Y$ from Question 19. The equation is graphed with IM on the vertical axis and Y on the horizontal axis; if the value of Y is 200:

(a) the line is horizontal, meeting the vertical axis at $IM = 130$.
(b) the line is vertical, meeting the horizontal axis at $Y = 130$.
(c) the line is upward-sloping, meeting the horizontal axis at $Y = 130$.
(d) the line is upward-sloping, meeting the vertical axis at $IM = 100$.
(e) because we know only one value for Y, we can't draw any line.

SHORT-ANSWER QUESTIONS

1. In each case, write P or N to indicate whether it is a positive or a normative statement.

(a) A statement of fact that is factually wrong. ________
(b) A value judgment. ________
(c) A prediction that an event will happen. ________
(d) A statement about what the author thinks ought to be. ________
(e) A statement that can be tested by evidence. ________
(f) A value judgment based on evidence known to be correct. ________
(g) A hurricane forecast. ________
(h) An opinion survey that indicates a majority of Canadians believe taxes ought to be reduced.

2. In each case, identify the direction of causality by classifying the italicized variable(s) as endogenous (EN) or exogenous (EX).

(a) *Market price and equilibrium quantity* of a commodity are determined by demand and supply. ________
(b) The number of sailboats sold annually is a function of *national income*. ________
(c) The *condition of forest ecosystems* can be affected by regional air pollutants. ________
(d) The quantity of housing services purchased is determined by the *relative price of housing, income, and housing characteristics*. ________
(e) Other things being equal, an increase in interest rates reduces *consumer expenditures*. ________

3. It is very important for theory, for empirical research, and often for economic and social policy, to identify whether a correlation between variables is also a causal relationship. State whether the correlation between *each pair* of variables is positive or negative, whether or not it is also a causal relationship, and, if causal, explain the direction of causality.

(a) Average income and the number of television sets purchased both increase.

(b) The number of people who want to go to university falls, and the income that can be earned without a university degree rises.

(c) As winter approaches in Canada, (i) more birds fly south, (ii) electricity consumption increases, and (iii) the number of trees with leaves declines. [*Hint:* There are three pairs of variables: (i) and (ii), (i) and (iii), (ii) and (iii).]

(d) During the same period, (i) more children are sent to day care, (ii) income tax deductions for day care increase, and (iii) the price of potatoes falls. [*Hint:* Again there are three pairs of variables.]

EXERCISES

1. **Constructing Index Numbers**
This exercise asks you to construct a price index for the out-of-pocket cost of attending university, and illustrates how data can be used differently to support different points of view. You may want to review the section on index numbers in the text, along with Tables 2-2 and 2-3, before doing this exercise.

The following table presents a decade's data on three components of the annual out-of-pocket expenses for the University of Northern Labrador: tuition fees, the amount it costs to live in the university's hall of residence, and the cost of a full meal plan in the residence. [*Note*: This is not a question on the opportunity cost of a university education—see *Applying Economic Concepts 1-1* in Chapter 1 of the text.]

Year	Tuition	Residence	Food
1994–95	$1374	$1710	$1660
1995–96	1518	1910	1760
1996–97	1638	2050	2000
1997–98	1770	2192	2250
1998–99	1894	2352	2400
1999–00	2026	2462	2520
2000–01	2228	2462	2600
2001–02	2451	2582	2660
2002–03	2930	2672	2670
2003–04	3223	2672	2760

(a) Using 1994–95 as the base year, construct individual price indices for each of the three expense items. [*Note*: Students familiar with a spreadsheet software program may wish to use it in answering this question.]

Year	Tuition Index	Residence Index	Food Index
1994–95			
1995–96			
1996–97			
1997–98			
1998–99			
1990–00			
2000–01			
2001–02			
2002–03			
2003–04			

(b) Which of these three items increased the most in percentage terms for the period 1994–95 to 1995–96? Over the entire decade, 1994–95 to 2003–04?

(c) What was the percentage increase in residence fees between 1997–98 and 1998–99?

The next three questions together illustrate how the same data can be used to argue for different points of view—something that often happens in the world around us.

(d) Construct an *unweighted* (i.e., equal weight) index of total out-of-pocket expenses. Put the values in the table below.

(e) Construct a *weighted* index of total out-of-pocket expenses. Put the values in the table below.
[*Note*: The text discusses a weighted index in the section on *More Complex Index Numbers,* but does not construct one. A weighted index takes account of the relative importance of each component expense, as measured by the component's percentage share of total expenses *in the base year*, 1994–95. These base-year percentages are the "weights." For subsequent years, multiply each component's index number by its base-year weight, and add the resulting three numbers to get the weighted index of total expenses for each year.]

Year	Unweighted Index	Weighted Index	Year	Unweighted Index	Weighted Index
1994–95			1999–00		
1995–96			2000–01		
1996–97			2001–02		
1997–98			2002–03		
1998–99			2003–04		

(f) Assume the university wants to increase tuition fees for 2004–05. Looking over the entire decade, if you were president of the university which of the five indices would you use to argue in favour of the fee increase? If you were president of the student council, which index would you use to argue against the fee increase? Explain.

2. Linear Relationships

This exercise gives you practice in interpreting and graphing linear relationships.

Suppose that an economist hypothesizes that the annual quantity demanded of a specific manufacturer's personal computers (Q^D) is determined by the price of the computer (P) and the average income of consumers (Y). The specific functional relationship among these three variables is hypothesized to be the expression $Q^D = Y - 4P$.

(a) Which of these variables are endogenous and which are exogenous?

(b) What does the negative sign before the term $4P$ imply about the relationship between Q^D and P? What does the implicit positive sign before the term Y tell you about the relationship between income and quantity demanded?

(c) Suppose for the moment that average income equals $8000. Write a simplified expression for the demand relationship [i.e., the relationship for $Q^D = f(P)$].

(d) Assuming that $Y = \$8000$, calculate the values of Q^D when $P = 0$, $P = \$500$, $P = \$1000$, and $P = \$2000$.

(e) Plot the relationship between P and Q^D (assuming that $Y = \$8000$) on the graph in Figure 2-1. Indicate the intercept value on each axis.

Figure 2-1

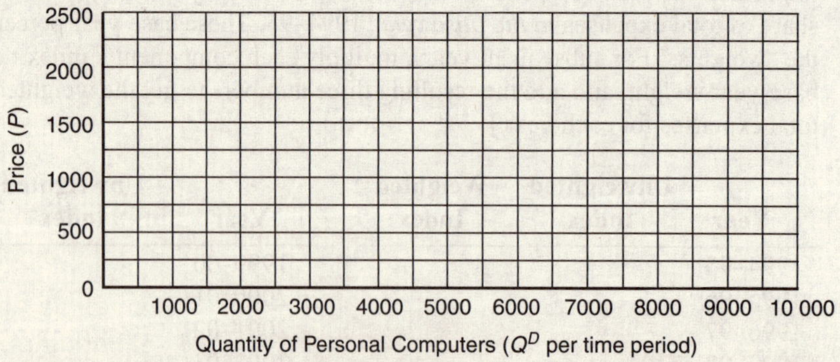

(f) Calculate the slope of the relationship in (e).

(g) Assuming that $Y = \$8000$, calculate the change in the quantity demanded when the price increases from \$1000 to \$2000. Do the same for a price increase from \$500 to \$2000. Call the change in the quantity demanded ΔQ^D and the change in the price ΔP. Determine the ratio $\Delta Q^D/\Delta P$. Is this ratio constant? (*Note:* Δ means "change in.")

(h) Now suppose that evidence indicates that in subsequent time periods, the average income of consumers changed to \$9000 per period. Plot the new relationship between P and Q^D. What are the intercept values and the slope?

EXTENSION EXERCISES

The following exercises review two methods for solving a system of linear equations. The first exercise works through the diagrammatic method while the second uses the algebraic approach. Although they are not used until Chapter 3 of the text when the demand and supply model is presented, it is useful to review these methods now while we are covering linear relationships. When you have competence in both approaches you will find that the algebraic approach is easier and takes less time than drawing scale diagrams.

E1. Using Scale Diagrams
Consider the following two linear equations:

(1) $N_1 = 5 + 0.5X$

(2) $N_2 = 55 - 0.5X$

(a) Complete the following table using the N_1 column for equation 1 and the N_2 column for equation 2.

X	N_1	N_2	N_3
0			
10			
20			
30			
40			
50			
60			

(b) Plot the relationships between X and N_1 and N_2 in the graph provided below.

Figure 2-2

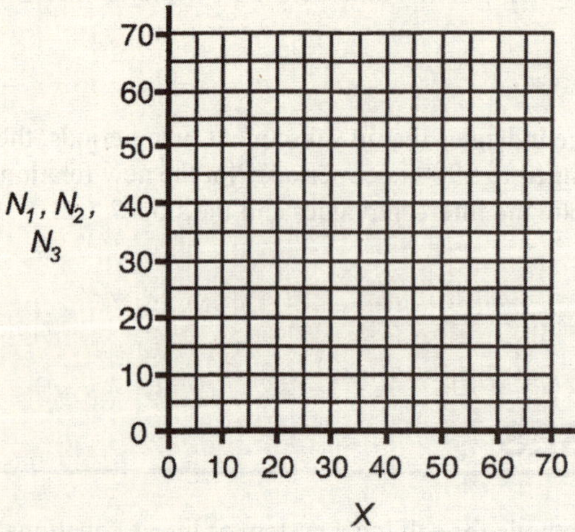

(i) The linear curve relating variables X and N_1 has a (positive/negative) _________ slope of _________.

(ii) The linear curve relating variables X and N_2 has a (positive/negative) _________ slope of _________.

(c) The equations are "simultaneously" solved at the value of X where $N_1 = N_2$ (which is where the two lines on the graph intersect). What are the values of X and N?

(d) Assume that the constant term in equation (1) increases from 5 to 25. Complete column N_3 in (a), and plot the new relationship on the graph in (b). The curve in equation (1) has shifted _________ (direction) by _________ (amount). The slope is _________.

(e) What is the new solution to this system of equations? [*Hint*: Replace N_1 with N_3 and repeat (c).]

E2. Using the Algebraic Method

This exercise takes you step-by-step through the algebraic method for solving a system of simultaneous equations. The algebraic method is extremely useful in both microeconomics and macroeconomics.

Consider two equations describing the relationships between two variables x and y

$$x_1 = \text{a} + \text{b}y, \quad (1)$$

$$x_2 = \text{c} - \text{d}y. \quad (2)$$

where a, b, c, and d are positive constants. The objective is to find values of x and y for which both equations are satisfied. First, note that there are two equations and three unknowns—the unknowns are the solution values to x_1, x_2, and y. Thus, if a unique solution exists, there is a missing equation. The missing equation to this system simply states that in the solution:

$$x_1 = x_2 \quad (3)$$

The solution procedure requires elimination of unknowns and equations by means of substitution. Each substitution reduces the system by both an unknown and an equation, until all that remains is a single unknown in a single equation.

(a) Step 1: Eliminate equation (1) and x_1 from the system by substituting equation (1) into equation (3). Write the new equation (3), and call it equation (3′). How many equations and unknowns remain?

(b) Step 2: Eliminate equation (2) and x_2 from the system by substituting equation (2) into equation (3′) you derived in (a). Write the new equation (3′), and call it equation (3″). How many equations and unknowns remain?

(c) Step 3: Solve equation (3″) you derived in (b), to create the equation for the solution value of y.

(d) Step 4: Substitute into equation (1) the expression for the solution value of y that you found in part (c). You now have the equation for the solution values of both x_1 and x_2 (since the two are the same value at the solution). [*Hint*: Check your answer by also substituting the expression for the solution value of y into equation (2). If you get the same value for x_1 and x_2 your answer is correct, but if you get different values you have the wrong answer.]

(e) Having done the exercise using the general algebraic equations, you will find it very easy to solve the system for any specific numerical values of the constants in equations (1) and (2). Let us suppose that a = 200, b = 2, c = 400, and d = 3. Repeat Steps 1 through 4 to solve for the numerical values of x and y.

ADDITIONAL MULTIPLE-CHOICE QUESTIONS

***1. Which of the following is the best example of a positive statement?**
- (a) Equal distribution of national income is a desirable goal for society.
- (b) Foreign ownership is undesirable for Canada and should therefore be eliminated.
- (c) Although free trade may cause some Canadians to lose their jobs, it will significantly increase the income of the average Canadian.
- (d) Taxes should be lowered.
- (e) Deficit reduction should be the government's priority.

***2. With respect to agriculture, weather is an example of**
- (a) an exogenous factor of production.
- (b) an endogenous input.
- (c) a dependent variable.
- (d) an induced input variable.
- (e) a positive statement.

3. **If annual per capita consumption expenditure decreases as average annual income decreases, these two variables are then said to be**

(a) negatively related.
(b) positively related.
(c) randomly related.
(d) independent of each other.
(e) None of the above.

*4. **Which of the following statements about economic theories is most appropriate?**

(a) The most reliable test of a theory is the realism of its assumptions.
(b) The best kind of theory is worded so that it can pass any test which is applied to it.
(c) The most important aspect of the scientific approach is that it uses mathematics and diagrams.
(d) We expect our theories to hold only with some margin of error.
(e) Economic theories are based upon normative statements, and can therefore never be refuted.

5. **A scientific prediction is a conditional statement because it**

(a) takes the form "if that occurs, then this will result."
(b) is conditional on being correct.
(c) is impossible to test.
(d) is true in theory but not in practice.
(e) is derived from normative statements.

6. **The term *economic model* may refer to**

(a) an application of a general theory in a specific context.
(b) a specific quantitative formulation of a theory.
(c) a particular theory or subset of theories in economics.
(d) an illustrative abstraction of some real-world phenomenon.
(e) All of the above.

*7. **Economic hypotheses are generally accepted only when**

(a) the evidence indicates that they are true with a high degree of probability.
(b) they have been proved beyond a reasonable doubt.
(c) they have been established with certainty.
(d) the evidence supports the hypotheses in all cases.
(e) Both (c) and (d) are correct.

8. **Suppose that a scatter diagram indicates that imports are, on average, positively related to national income over time. If in one year imports fall when national income increases, the observation**

(a) disproves the positive relationship between the two variables.
(b) suggests that other factors also influence the quantity of imports.
(c) proves a negative relationship between the two variables.
(d) suggests that a measurement error has necessarily been made.
(e) suggests that the two variables are independent of each other.

*9. **Which of the following equations is consistent with the hypothesis that federal income tax payments (T) are positively related to family income (Y) and negatively related to family size (F)?**

(a) $T = -733 + 0.19Y + 344F$.
(b) $T = -733 - 0.19Y - 344F$.
(c) $T = -733 + 0.19Y - 344F$.
(d) $T = +733 - 0.19Y + 344F$.
(e) None of the above.

Use the following graph to answer questions 10 to 12:

Figure 2-3

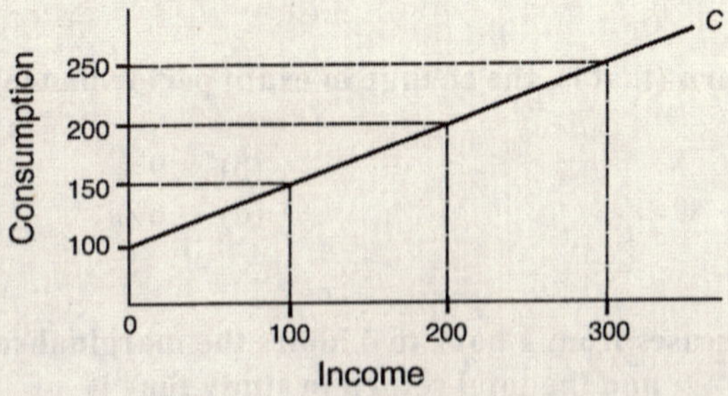

10. In the graph above, the slope of the line showing the relationship between consumption and income is

(a) –2.
(b) 0.5.
(c) 2.
(d) 2.5.
(e) 150.

11. According to the graph above, when an individual has no income, consumption is

(a) –200.
(b) –100.
(c) 0.
(d) 100.
(e) None of the above.

***12. The line showing the relationship between consumption (*C*) and income (*Y*) can be represented mathematically as:**

(a) $C = 0.5Y$.
(b) $C = 2Y$.
(c) $C = 100 + 0.5Y$.
(d) $C = 100 + 2Y$.
(e) $C = -100 + Y$.

Questions 13 to 17 refer to the following graph, which depicts the relationship between performance on an economics examination and hours spent studying late the night before the early-morning exam!

Figure 2-4

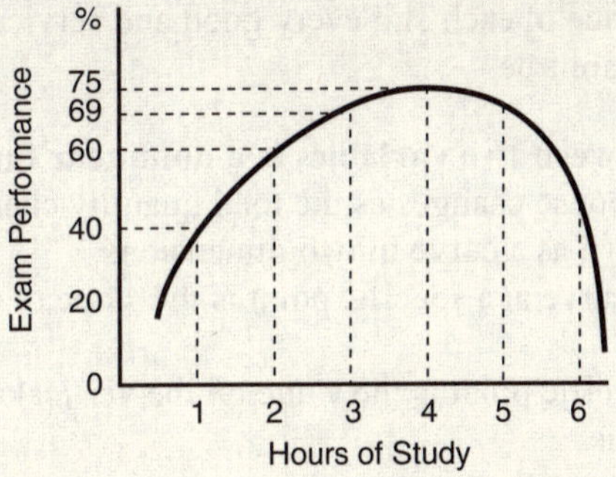

13. Exam performance is a(n) __________________ variable and hours of study is a(n) __________________ variable.

(a) nonlinear; nonlinear
(b) marginal; contour
(c) exogenous; endogenous
(d) endogenous; exogenous
(e) slope; marginal

14. The slope of this curve between 1 and 2 hours of study is calculated by

(a) 60/2.
(b) (60 – 30)/2.
(c) (60 – 40)/2.
(d) (60 – 40)/(2 – 1).
(e) (60 + 40)/(2 + 1)

15. The marginal return (that is, the change in exam performance) to the third hour of study is

(a) 69%.
(b) 9%.
(c) 23%.
(d) 6%.
(e) 3%.

***16. As study time increases from 1 hour to 4 hours the marginal return to study time is _________________ and the total return to study time is _________________.**

(a) diminishing; increasing
(b) increasing; increasing
(c) diminishing; diminishing
(d) increasing; diminishing
(e) diminishing; zero

17. At four hours of study, the marginal return to a minute of study more or less is (approximately)

(a) 75%.
(b) increasing.
(c) diminishing.
(d) zero.
(e) cannot be determined with the information provided.

***18. Due to a lack of sleep, exam performance suffers from a fifth and sixth hour of study. For this range of study hours, one can say that**

(a) total returns are diminishing.
(b) marginal returns are negative.
(c) marginal returns are diminishing.
(d) the slope of the performance curve is negative.
(e) All of the above are correct.

***19. Suppose the Consumer Price Index was 160 last year and there has since been a 2 percent price inflation. The current Consumer Price Index**

(a) is 162.0.
(b) is 163.2
(c) is 160.02.
(d) shows that the price of each and every good and service has increased by 2%.
(e) Both (a) and (d) are true.

***20. If the relationship between two variables is a nonlinear function**

(a) the marginal response changes as the total quantity changes.
(b) it can not be drawn as a curve in two dimensions.
(c) the slope of the curve at a specific point is the slope of the tangent to the curve at that point.
(d) the slope at a specific point is the value on the vertical axis divided by the value on the horizontal axis.
(e) Both (a) and (c) are true.

SOLUTIONS

Chapter Review

1.(e) **2.**(a) **3.**(b) **4.**(b) **5.**(e) **6.**(b) **7.**(d) **8.**(e) **9.**(b) **10.**(c) **11.**(b) **12.**(e) **13.**(b) **14.**(d) **15.**(c) **16.**(b) **17.**(d) **18.**(d) **19.**(e) **20.**(d)

Short-Answer Questions

1. **(a)** P **(b)** N **(c)** P **(d)** N **(e)** P **(f)** N **(g)** P **(h)** N
2. **(a)** EN **(b)** EX **(c)** EN **(d)** EX **(e)** EN
3. **(a)** Positive correlation (i.e., both move in the same direction). Probably also causal, with causality running from income (exogenous) to TV sets (endogenous)—higher income causes an increase in the number of TVs purchased.
   (b) Negative correlation (i.e., the variables move in opposite directions). Also causal, with causality running from higher alternative incomes to lower attendance—the higher alternative incomes cause lower attendance (via the increase in the opportunity cost of attending university).
   (c) Positive correlation between birds flying south and electricity consumption, negative correlation between birds flying south and trees with leaves, and negative correlation between electricity consumption and trees with leaves. There is no *causal* relationship among any of the three variables—they are all caused by a fourth variable, the fall in temperature as winter approaches.
   (d) Positive correlation between children in day care and the tax deductions, and a negative correlation between each of these and the price of potatoes. Causality runs from the size of the tax deduction to the number of children in day care, since the tax deduction reduces the cost of day care. There is no causal relationship between either of these and the price of potatoes.

Exercises

1. **(a)** For any specific year the index is found by taking the cost in that year, dividing by the cost in the base year (1994–95 in this case), and multiplying the result by 100. For example, the tuition index in year 1998–99 is (1894/1374) × 100 = 137.8 (which is rounded to 138 in the table below).

Year	Tuition Index	Residence Index	Food Index
1994–95	100	100	100
1995–96	110	112	106
1996–97	119	120	120
1997–98	129	128	136
1998–99	138	138	145
1999–00	147	144	152
2000–01	162	144	157
2001–02	178	151	160
2002–03	213	156	161
2003–04	235	156	166

   (b) The cost of residence increased by 12% for the period 1994–95 to 1995–96, while that of tuition and food increased by 10% and 6%, respectively. During the decade from 1994–95 to 2003–04, the fees for tuition, residence, and food increased 135%, 56%, and 66%, respectively.
   (c) Residence fees increased by 7.8% between 1997–98 and 1998–99. (The index increased by 10, from 128 to 138, which is 10% of the *base year* costs but only (10/128) × 100 = 7.8% of the costs in 1997–98.)
   (d) The unweighted index is obtained by taking the average of the three indexes. For example, the unweighted index for 2003–04 is (235 + 156 + 166)/3 = 186.

Year	Unweighted Index	Weighted Index	Year	Unweighted Index	Weighted Index
1994–95	100	100	1999–00	148	148
1995–96	109	109	2000–01	154	154
1996–97	120	120	2001–02	163	162
1997–98	131	131	2002–03	177	174
1998–99	140	140	2003–04	186	182

(e) The weighted index is a weighted average of the three separate indexes, with the weights being the proportions of total cost *in the base year*. In the base year 1994–95 the total fee was \$1374 + \$1710 + \$1660 = \$4744. Thus the weights are: 0.29 on tuition (\$1374 is 29% of \$4744), 0.36 on residence (\$1710 is 36% of \$4744), and 0.35 on food (\$1660 is 35% of \$4744). These weights are applied to the three indices in each year to create the single weighted average index for each year. For example, in 2003–04 the weighted index is 0.29(235) + 0.36(156) + 0.35(166) = 182. See the table above for the index values in other years.

(f) The university president would cite one of the total expenses indices in (d) to justify higher fees. The weighted index of total expenses shows that the cost of a university education increased by only 82% over the decade, and even the unweighted index shows an increase of only 86%. [*Note:* The unweighted index treats each component as one-third of total costs, while the weighted index treats tuition as only 29% of total costs, with residence and food as 36% and 35%, respectively.] The president of the student council would cite the tuition price index in (a) to argue that fees have already increased enough (or too much). This index shows tuition fees increased by 135% over the decade—far more than the 82% and 86% increases in the indices of total expenses. [Note that residence costs and food costs increased by much smaller percentages (56% and 66%, respectively) than tuition, thereby holding down the percentage increase in total expenses.]

2. **(a)** Since both price and average income affect quantity demanded, Q^D is endogenous while P and Y are exogenous. [*Note*: If you are revising after having already done Chapter 4, recall that P is exogenous in the demand curve but endogenous in the overall market for computers.]

(b) Q^D and P are negatively related; as P increases, Q^D falls. Q^D and Y are positively related; as Y increases, Q^D increases.

(c) The equation becomes $Q^D = 8000 - 4P$.

(d) $Q^D = 8000 - 4(0) = 8000$; $Q^D = 8000 - 4(500) = 6000$; $Q^D = 8000 - 4(1000) = 4000$; $Q^D = 8000 - 4(2000) = 0$.

(e) As shown in Figure 2-5, the intercept on the P axis is 2000 and the intercept on the Q^D axis is 8000. (That is, at a price of \$2000 no computers would be demanded, and if computers were free 8000 would be demanded.)

Figure 2-5

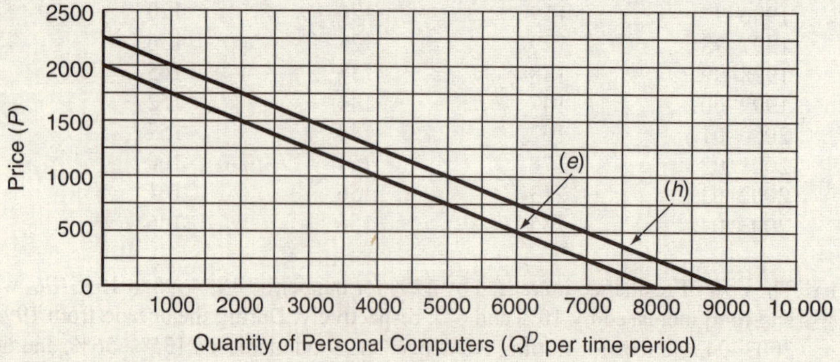

(f) The slope is calculated as $\Delta P/\Delta Q^D$; for example, –2000/8000 = –1/4. Since the relationship is linear the slope is the same all along the line.

(g) The change in quantity demanded is –4000 when P increases from 1000 to 2000. When P increases from 500 to 2000, quantity demanded falls by 6000. In both cases the ratio $\Delta Q^D/\Delta P$ is equal to –4. It is the inverse of the slope.

(h) The intercept on the P axis is \$2250, and the intercept on the Q^D axis is 9000. The slope remains –1/4 because the coefficient on P remains unchanged at 4. See Figure 2-5 above.

Extension Exercises

E1. (a)

X	N_1	N_2	N_3
0	5	55	25
10	10	50	30
20	15	45	35
30	20	40	40
40	25	35	45
50	30	30	50
60	35	25	55

(b) **Figure 2-6**

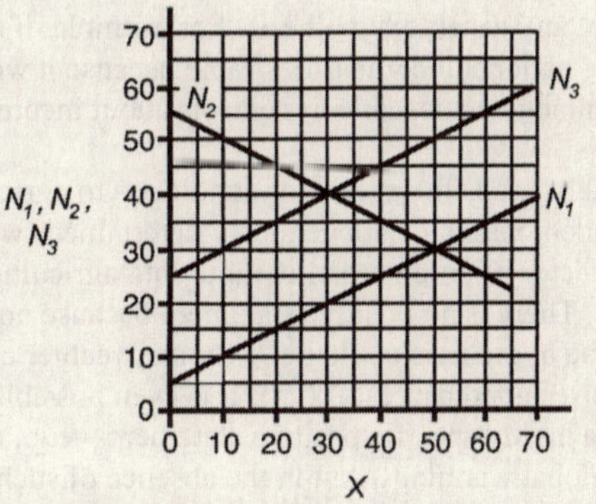

(i) positive; +1/2 (e.g., between $X = 10$ and $X = 20$, $\Delta N_1/\Delta X = +5/+10 = +1/2$)

(ii) negative; –1/2 (e.g., between $X = 10$ and $X = 20$, $\Delta N_2/\Delta X = -5/+10 = -1/2$)

(c) $N_1 = N_2$ where the two curves intersect. $N = 30$ and $X = 50$ solves this system of equations.

(d) The curve has shifted <u>leftward</u> by <u>40</u> (or equivalently, upward by 20); the slope is unchanged at +1/2.

(e) $N = 40$ and $X = 30$.

E2. (a) <u>Step 1</u>: Substitute equation (1) into equation (3) for x_1. This gives

$$a + by = x_2. \quad (3')$$

There remain two equations, (2) and (3′), and two unknowns, x_2 and y.

(b) <u>Step 2</u>: Substitute equation (2) into (3′) for x_2. This yields

$$a + by = c - dy. \quad (3'')$$

There is only one equation remaining, (3″), and only one unknown, y.

(c) <u>Step 3:</u> Rearranging terms in (3″) yields: $by + dy = c - a$, or equivalently, $(b + d)y = c - a$. Dividing both sides by $(b + d)$ yields $y^* = (c - a)/(b + d)$, which is the solution value for y.

(d) Step 4: Substitute y^* into equation (1), which yields $x_1^* = a + b(c - a)/(b + d)$
Multiply both sides by (b + d) and cancel, which gives:

$$(b + d)x_1^* = a(b + d) + b(c - a) = ab + ad + bc - ab = ad + bc$$

Divide both sides by (b + d) and cancel, giving the solution value for x_1^* (and for x_2^*, since $x_1^* = x_2^*$ from equation (3)).

$$x_1^* = (ad + bc)/(b + d).$$

(e) Inserting the numerical values gives $x_1 = 200 + 2y$ and $x_2 = 400 - 3y$
Setting $x_1 = x_2$ gives $200 + 2y = 400 - 3y$.
Rearranging gives $5y = 200$, so $y = 200/5 = 40$
Substituting $y = 40$ into $x_1 = 200 + 2y$ gives $x_1 = 200 + 2(40) = 280$
Check by substituting $y = 40$ into $x_2 = 400 - 3y$, which gives $x_2 = 400 - 3(40) = 280$

Additional Multiple-Choice Questions

1.(c) **2.**(a) **3.**(b) **4.**(d) **5.**(a) **6.**(e) **7.**(a) **8.**(b) **9.**(c) **10.**(b) **11.**(d) **12.**(c) **13.**(d) **14.**(d) **15.**(b) **16.**(a) **17.**(d) **18.**(e) **19.**(b) **20.**(e)

Explanations for the Asterisked Multiple-Choice Questions

1.(c) All other answers are statements of value judgments (as with *desirable, undesirable, should be*), none of which contain any testable hypothesis. For example, if (d) were to be reworded to say "Equal distribution of national income is desirable because it would create greater work incentives for all," it would then include a testable hypothesis about income distribution/redistribution and incentives.

2.(a) The direction of causality runs from weather conditions to agricultural production, making agriculture the dependent variable endogenously determined (within the "theory") and weather being an exogenous factor of production (an input into agricultural production and determined outside the "theory"). There is no positive statement because no testable hypothesis has been made; for example, the hypothesis could be "extreme weather causes bad harvests" (yes) or "extreme weather causes good harvests" (no). It is even possible to reverse the direction of causality by making a highly specific positive statement—e.g., changes in agricultural methods have contributed to global warming—but in the absence of such specificity the "best" answer is the one that obviously applies to the general case.

4.(d) Human behaviour, even as a group, can't be predicted with certainty. Every economic theory will predict with a margin of error, though the "best" theories will minimize that margin. The validity of a theory's assumptions is not as important as it may initially seem, since the objective is to provide reasonable explanations/predictions. For example, the ancient navigation system used by sailing ships to get from one part of the world to another was based on the (now apparent) highly unrealistic assumption that the earth was flat, and one could drop off the edge! Nevertheless, it worked (i.e., gave accurate predictions)!

7.(a) "A high degree of probability" says the hypothesis is acceptable until and unless a better one is found. "Beyond a reasonable doubt" says it is highly unlikely that a better hypothesis will be found. The two interpretations are very different.

9.(c) The positive sign on the coefficient of Y shows a direct (i.e., positive) relationship between T and Y. The negative sign on the coefficient of F shows an inverse (i.e., negative) relationship between T and F. A positive or negative sign on the constant term (733) shows only whether the intercept on the T axis on a graph is positive or negative, and says nothing about how the variables are related.

12.(c) Using $C = 100 + 0.5Y$, if $Y = 0$ then $C = 100 + 05(0) = 100$, being the intercept on the C axis. The line also shows that for each \$100 *increase* in Y (ΔY), C *increases* by \$50 (ΔC). Thus there is a positive relationship between C and Y (i.e., both move in the same direction, indicated by the "plus" sign), and the increase in C is *one-half* of the increase in Y. Thus the slope of the line (rise/run = $\Delta C/\Delta Y$) = 50/100 = 0.5.

16.(a) You will come across the relationship between marginal and total many times in your study of economics. As long as the marginal is positive, regardless of whether it is rising or falling, the total will be rising.

18.(a) Between 4 and 5 hours of study, performance falls (answer a) from about 75 to 70—a *negative marginal return* (answer b) of minus 5 to the *extra* hour of study (indicated by the negative slope of the total performance curve). Adding the 6th hour of study reduces performance even more (from about 70 to 40), and by an even greater amount than for the 5th hour (the drop of 30 marks is a bigger drop than 5 marks). Thus as you study more (beyond the 4th hour), your *marginal* returns to each extra hour diminish (answer c). [*Practical application:*
Don't stay up all night studying—you will need an active mind in your economics exams!]

19.(b) If the increase had been 2% *of the base year level,* the index would have risen from 160 to 162. In this question, however, prices rose by 2% *since last year,* when the index was 160. The index this year, therefore, is 102% of 160 = 163.2.

20.(e) For example, the extra (i.e., marginal) response can get less and less, but as long as it is positive the total response will be increasing. As the marginal gets less, the slope of the curve showing the total response gets flatter. Furthermore, the tangent to a curve at any specific point has the same slope as the curve at that point.

16.(a) [illegible]

18.(a) [illegible]

19.(b) [illegible]

20. [illegible]

PART 2: AN INTRODUCTION TO DEMAND AND SUPPLY

CHAPTER 3

DEMAND, SUPPLY, AND PRICE

LO

LEARNING OBJECTIVES

In this chapter you will learn

1. what determines "quantity demanded," the amount of some product that consumers want to purchase.
2. to distinguish between a shift in a demand curve and a movement along a demand curve.
3. what determines "quantity supplied," the amount of some product that producers want to sell.
4. to distinguish between a shift in a supply curve and a movement along a supply curve.
5. about the forces that drive market price to equilibrium, and how equilibrium price is affected by changes in demand and supply.

CHAPTER OVERVIEW

This chapter introduces you to the economic model of **demand** and **supply**, which describes how the interactions of buyers and sellers determine the **equilibrium** price and quantity exchanged in competitive markets for goods and services.

A downward-sloping **demand curve** shows the relationship between price and **quantity demanded**. From a buyer's perspective, the lower the (relative) price of a product, the more attractive it is to purchase. A **supply curve** shows the relationship between price and **quantity supplied**. From a seller's perspective, a higher (relative) price for a product makes it more attractive to sell. If quantity supplied does not equal quantity demanded (a disequilibrium situation), the model predicts that market pressures will cause changes in price, which change both quantity demanded and quantity supplied, until **quantity demanded equals quantity supplied** at the **equilibrium price**.

Using the method of **comparative statics**, the effects on equilibrium of a shift in either demand or supply can be determined. The equilibrium price and quantity exchanged respond to changes in the determinants of demand (income level and distribution, tastes, population, prices of other products, and expectations about the future) and the determinants of supply (prices of inputs, technology, government taxes or subsidies, prices of other products, expectations about the future, and the number of firms). These equilibrium responses are called the "laws" of demand and supply.

HINTS AND TIPS

The following may help you to avoid some of the most common errors on examinations.

✓ Understand the difference between changes in quantity demanded (supplied) and changes in demand (supply). A change in quantity demanded (supplied) is a response to a change in the price of the good, while a change in demand (supply) is a response to a change in some other exogenous variable.

✓ Understand how and why demand and supply curves shift in response to changes in the exogenous variables. For example, with a fall in production costs suppliers are willing to provide more at each price, so supply increases (i.e., the supply curve shifts to the right).

✓ Understand how and why a change in an exogenous variable may shift the demand in different directions depending on the type of good (normal or inferior) and the relationship between goods (substitutes or complements). For example, an increase in the price of automobile parking downtown increases the opportunity cost of driving to work. The higher opportunity cost of driving to work can increase the demand for public transportation (a substitute for driving to work) but reduce the demand for gasoline (a complement to downtown parking, because downtown parking and gasoline are linked through the use of automobiles).

✓ Practise doing freehand sketches of demand and supply diagrams to show how equilibrium price and quantity change when an exogenous variable changes. When two (or more) exogenous variables change, sketch the diagrams for each change individually and compare the results. If both sketches show (say) an increase in price you can conclude that equilibrium price will rise. But if one sketch shows an increase in price while the other shows a decrease, the net effect on equilibrium price is uncertain—it depends upon the relative magnitudes of the two changes.

CHAPTER REVIEW

Demand

Understanding the difference between the concepts of quantity demanded and demand is an important objective in this section. Remember that quantity demanded refers to the amount of a product consumers desire to purchase at a *specific price,* whereas demand refers to the *entire relationship* between price and quantity demanded. Consumers' response to a change in the product's own price is a *movement along* a demand curve, but a change in any of the other determinants of demand causes a *shift* in the entire demand curve. This section explains how and why the demand curve shifts, and the direction in which it shifts.

1. The term *quantity demanded* refers to the
- (a) amount of a good that consumers are willing to purchase at some price during some given time period.
- (b) amount of some good that consumers would purchase if they only had the income to afford it.
- (c) amount of a good that is actually purchased during a given time period.
- (d) minimum amount of a good that consumers require and demand for survival.
- (e) amount of a good that consumers are willing to purchase regardless of price.

2. **An increase in quantity demanded refers to**
   (a) rightward shifts in the demand curve only.
   (b) a movement up along a demand curve.
   (c) a greater willingness to purchase at each price.
   (d) an increase in actual purchases.
   (e) a movement down along a demand curve.

3. **The demand curve and the demand schedule**
   (a) each reflect the relationship between quantity demanded and price, *ceteris paribus*.
   (b) show the impact of changes in income or tastes.
   (c) are constructed on the assumption that price is held constant.
   (d) illustrate that in economic analysis, only two variables are taken into account at any one time.
   (e) characterize the relationship between price and actual purchases.

4. **An increase in demand means that**
   (a) consumers actually buy more of the good.
   (b) at each price, consumers desire a greater quantity.
   (c) consumers' tastes have necessarily changed.
   (d) price has decreased.
   (e) consumers buy more of the good specifically <u>because</u> its price has decreased.

5. **If goods *A* and *B* are complements, an increase in the price of good *A* will lead to**
   (a) an increase in the price of good *B*.
   (b) a decrease in the quantity demanded of good *B*.
   (c) a decrease in demand for good *B*.
   (d) no change in demand for good *B* because *A* and *B* are not substitutes.
   (e) a rightward shift in the demand for good *B*.

6. **Increased public awareness of the adverse health effects of smoking**
   (a) is a noneconomic event that cannot be incorporated into the demand and supply model.
   (b) is characterized as a change in tastes that leads to a leftward shift in the demand curve for cigarettes.
   (c) will lead to an eventual increase in the price of cigarettes due to shifts in the demand curve for cigarettes.
   (d) induces a decrease in the supply of cigarettes.
   (e) decreases the quantity demanded of cigarettes.

7. **In economics the term *inferior good* means that**
   (a) the good is of low quality.
   (b) an increase in income shifts its demand curve inward to the left.
   (c) one of its complementary goods has a significantly higher price.
   (d) demand does not change when the price of a substitute good changes
   (e) the good is of low quality <u>and</u> has many substitutes of equally low quality.

Supply

As with demand, it is important to understand the difference between quantity supplied and supply. A movement along a supply curve is a response to a change in the good's own price and is referred to as a change in quantity supplied. A shift in the entire curve is a response to a change in one of the other determinants of supply and is referred to as a change in supply. You should understand how and why the supply curve shifts, and the direction in which it shifts.

8. A shift in the supply curve may be caused by any of the following except
(a) an improvement in technology.
(b) an increase in the wage paid to labour.
(c) an increase in average consumer income.
(d) an increase in the number of firms in the industry.
(e) Both (b) and (c) are correct—neither will shift the supply curve.

9. A rightward shift in the supply curve indicates
(a) a decrease in price.
(b) an increase in demand.
(c) an increase in quantity supplied.
(d) that at each price quantity supplied has increased.
(e) an increase in consumers' desire for a product.

10. An increase in the price of an input will
(a) decrease quantity supplied.
(b) decrease quantity supplied at each price.
(c) decrease supply.
(d) cause the supply curve to shift to the left.
(e) Answers (b), (c), and (d) are all correct.

11. A movement along a supply curve could be caused by
(a) an improvement in technology.
(b) a government subsidy to producers.
(c) a change in the price of the product.
(d) a change in the number of producers.
(e) a decrease in production costs.

12. When two goods are complements *in production*
(a) a fall in the price of one will increase demand for the other.
(b) an increase in the price of one will increase the supply of the other.
(c) an increase in the production of one must be offset by a decrease in production of the other.
(d) they have identical supply curves.
(e) they must also be complements in consumption.

The Determination of Price

This section puts the demand and supply curves together to show the **market** for a product. If, at a particular market price, quantity demanded is not equal to quantity supplied, pressures are exerted on price to change until the market clears—i.e., until quantity demanded is equal to quantity supplied. You should understand **how** these pressures of **excess demand** and **excess supply** bring the market to this **equilibrium**. (*Extensions in Theory 3-2* explains how to use simultaneous equations to derive the equilibrium price and quantity.) Further, you should be able to show how equilibrium price and quantity exchanged are affected by changes in demand and supply—these are the four laws of demand and supply. [*Note: Lessons from History 3-1* explains how markets responded to recent events that changed demand and supply.] Finally, understand the important distinction between *absolute* and *relative* prices.

13. Excess demand exists whenever

(a) price exceeds the equilibrium price.
(b) quantity supplied is greater than quantity demanded.
(c) the equilibrium price is above the existing price.
(d) there is downward pressure on price.
(e) there is surplus production.

14. The "laws of demand and supply" are

(a) federal statutes and are therefore enforced by the RCMP.
(b) enshrined in the Canadian Constitution.
(c) irrefutable propositions concerning economic behaviour.
(d) basic assumptions in economic theory.
(e) predictions of economic behaviour that have tended to withstand much, but not all, empirical testing.

15. An increase in both equilibrium price and quantity exchanged is consistent with

(a) an increase in supply.
(b) a decrease in supply.
(c) a decrease in quantity supplied.
(d) an increase in demand.
(e) a decrease in demand.

16. Assuming a downward-sloping demand curve, an improvement in production technology is predicted to lead to

(a) a decrease in supply.
(b) an increase in both equilibrium price and quantity exchanged.
(c) a decrease in equilibrium price and an increase in equilibrium quantity exchanged.
(d) a decrease in equilibrium price but no change in equilibrium quantity exchanged.
(e) an increase in equilibrium price and a decrease in equilibrium quantity exchanged.

17. Comparative statics

(a) is the analysis of market equilibria under different sets of conditions.
(b) is the analysis of demand without reference to time.
(c) refers to constant equilibrium prices and quantities.
(d) describes the path by which equilibrium price changes.
(e) refers to disequilibrium prices and quantities.

18. When price exceeds its equilibrium value, the quantity actually bought and sold

(a) is the quantity demanded.
(b) is the quantity supplied.
(c) is unknown because the market is not in equilibrium.
(d) is different for consumers than for producers.
(e) is the quantity at equilibrium.

19. A change in the money price of a product, other things constant, is

(a) a change in its absolute price but not a change in its relative price.
(b) a change in its relative price but not a change in its absolute price.
(c) a change in both its relative price and its absolute price.
(d) a change in its opportunity cost.
(e) Both (c) and (d) are correct.

SHORT-ANSWER QUESTIONS

1. What is meant by equilibrium? How is it related to the concept of excess demand or excess supply being a "market force"?

2. Explain the negative slope of a demand curve in terms of the concept of opportunity cost first encountered in Chapter 1.

3. Why is the price of a product an exogenous variable in the demand and supply curves separately, but endogenous to the market as a whole?

4. In the late 1990s the prices of company shares on stock markets rose to levels which, for many firms, were much higher than warranted by the values of their assets and their profits. How can demand and supply analysis explain why this "bubble" in stock market prices was caused by expectations that share prices would continue to rise?

EXERCISES

1. **Market Equilibrium Using Demand and Supply Schedules**
The demand and supply schedules for athletic shoes sold at Trendy Shoes Inc. at the local mall are hypothesized to be as follows (in pairs of shoes per week):

(1) Price	(2) Quantity Demanded *D*	(2) Quantity Demanded *D′*	(3) Quantity Supplied	(4) Excess Demand (+) Excess Supply (–)
$120	40	____	130	____
110	50	____	110	____
100	60	____	90	____
90	70	____	70	____
80	80	____	50	____
70	90	____	30	____
60	100	____	10	____

(a) Using the grid provided in Figure 3-1, plot the demand and supply curves. Indicate the equilibrium levels of price and quantity.

Figure 3-1

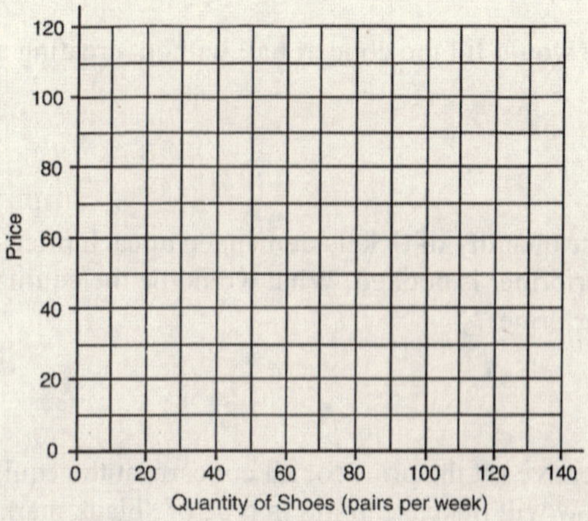

(b) Fill in column 4 for values of excess demand and excess supply. What is the value of excess demand (supply) at equilibrium?________

(c) Suppose there is a change in teenage fashion such that a substitute shoe, Block Mardens, becomes trendy. As a result, the quantity demanded of athletic shoes at Trendy Shoes Inc. decreases by 30 units per week at each and every price. Put the new quantities demanded in column (2) above, and draw the new demand curve *D′* on the grid.

(d) At the initial equilibrium price you reported in answer (b), what market pressure on price is created by this change in tastes? How does price respond to this pressure? How do quantities demanded and supplied react?

(e) After price has adjusted to the new equilibrium, what is the equilibrium price and the equilibrium quantity?

2. **"Fair Pricing" and Black Markets**

The Executive of the Students' Association at the University of Equality has recently announced that "in the interests of fairness" all seats for on-campus concerts will sell at the same price regardless of the popularity of the performer. The campus concert hall has a seating capacity of 5000. Suppose the demand schedule for tickets for a *typical* concert or performer is as follows:

Price	Quantity Demanded
$6	8000
8	5000
10	2500
12	1500
14	1000

(a) If the Executive sets a price of $10 per seat, is there an excess demand or supply of tickets for a typical concert?

(b) What price would fill the concert hall without creating a shortage of seats at a typical concert?

(c) Suppose the quantity of tickets demanded at each price doubles when a particularly popular performer is booked. What would be the equilibrium ticket price for a popular performer?

(d) If the Executive set the price for all concerts at the equilibrium price for a typical concert, how will ticket scalping (a type of "black market" where some people buy tickets at the box-office price and resell them at higher prices) affect the achievement of the "fairness" objective?

3. The Laws of Demand and Supply

Read the description of events (2nd column) in each market (1st column). Predict the impact on each market of these events by drawing the appropriate shifts of curves in the accompanying diagram. Use + and – to indicate whether there will be an increase or decrease in demand (*D*), supply (*S*), equilibrium price (*P*), and equilibrium quantity (*Q*). If there is no change, use 0. If the change can't be predicted, use *U* for uncertain. [*Note*: See "Hints and Tips" for finding the answer when two events occur simultaneously.]

Figure 3-2

	Market	Event		*D*	*S*	*P*	*Q*
(a)	Canadian wine	Early frost destroys a large percentage of the grape crop in British Columbia	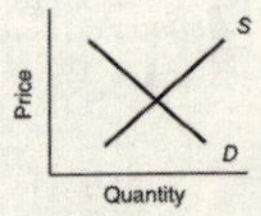	____	____	____	____
(b)	Wood-burning stoves	The price of heating oil and natural gas triples	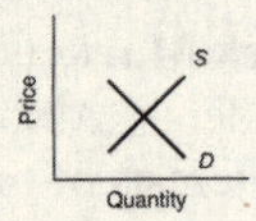	____	____	____	____
(c)	Cellular phones	Technological advances reduce the costs of producing cellular phones	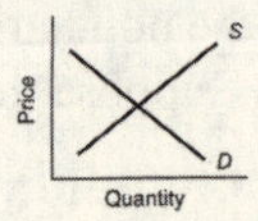	____	____	____	____
(d)	Gold	Large gold deposits are discovered in northern Ontario	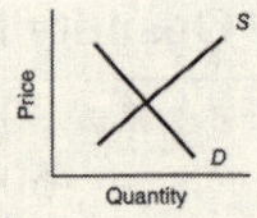	____	____	____	____

(e) Fast foods — The public show greater concern over high sodium and cholesterol in fast foods; also, there is an increase in the minimum wage

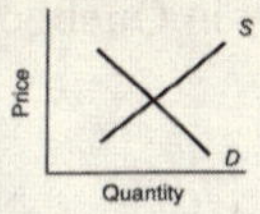

____ ____ ____ ____

(f) Bicycles — There is increasing concern by consumers about physical fitness; also, the price of gasoline falls

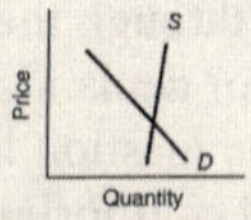

____ ____ ____ ____

(g) Beer — The population of drinking age increases; also, brewery unions negotiate a big increase in wages

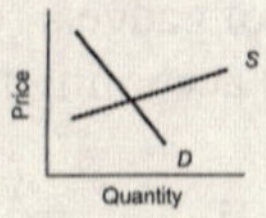

____ ____ ____ ____

(h) Housing — House prices are expected to rise significantly in the near future

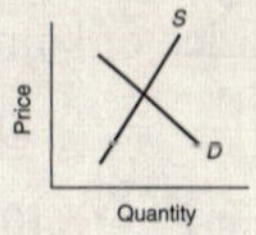

____ ____ ____ ____

4. Movements along Curves versus Shifts of Curves

For each of the following, determine if the sentence is referring to a change in demand, a change in quantity demanded, a change in supply, or a change in quantity supplied. If applicable, indicate the resulting change in equilibrium price and quantity.

(a) In August 2005, Hurricane Katrina caused an increase in the world price of oil.

(b) Prices of personal computers fall despite a substantial increase in the number sold.

(c) Apartment rental prices rise as student enrolment swells.

(d) Lower airfares reduce the number of empty seats on regularly scheduled flights. [*Hint*: There is a fixed supply of seats on regularly scheduled flights.]

(e) Increases in the price of Christmas trees cause trees to be planted on land previously used by dairy farmers. [*Note:* Answer for both the market for Christmas trees and the market for milk.]

(f) An increase in the price of Pacific salmon is linked to a reduction in fishing for Atlantic cod. [*Note:* Answer for both the market for Atlantic cod and the market for Pacific salmon.] [*Hint*: The two types of fish are substitutes in consumption.]

(g) The 1998 ice storm in Quebec affected the market for portable gas-powered generators not only in Quebec but also in other regions of Canada.

5. **Changes in Exogenous Variables**

This question demonstrates how changes in exogenous variables impact upon market equilibrium. It takes you through the process of making a scale diagram from simple functional relationships for demand and supply, and then finding equilibrium on the diagram. [*Note:* A similar question is given in *Extension Exercise E2,* using algebra instead of a scale diagram to find equilibrium.]

The quantity demanded of gadgets (Q^D) depends on the price of gadgets (P) and the price of a substitute good *(Py)* according to the following relationship.

$$Q^D = 10 - 1P + 0.5Py$$

The quantity of gadgets supplied (Q^S) is positively related to the price of gadgets and negatively related to the price of some input *(Pn)* according to

$$Q^S = 30 + 1P - 0.1Pn$$

(a) Assume initially that Py = \$40 and Pn = \$200. Substitute these values into the equations to obtain the equations for the demand and supply curves.

(b) Using the equations you obtained in (a), find Q^D and Q^S when P = \$0, and locate these quantities on the grid in Figure 3-3. Using the demand curve equation in (a), find the P at which $Q^D = 0$, and locate this price on the grid.

(c) For every \$5 increase in the price of gadgets, what is the change in Q^D and Q^S? What are the slopes of the demand and supply curves? Draw the demand and supply curves on the grid in Figure 3-3 and label them D_1 and S_1, respectively. [*Hint*: The demand and supply curves are straight lines.] What is the equilibrium price and quantity?

Figure 3-3

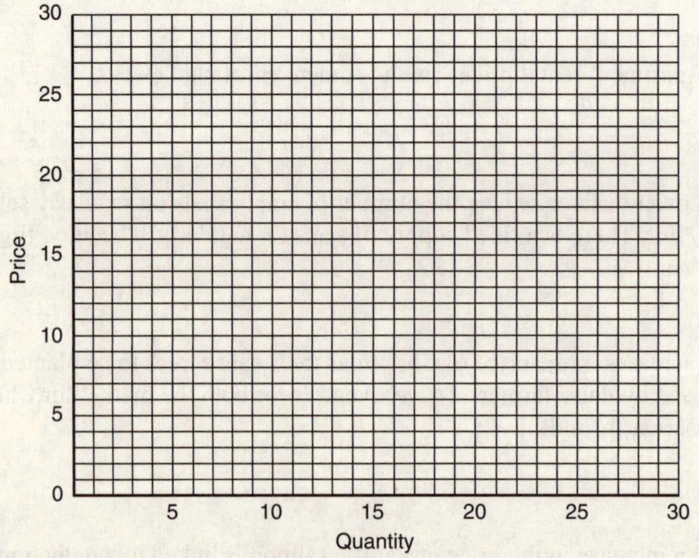

(d) Now *Py* falls from \$40 to \$20, and *Pn* rises from \$200 to \$300. What are the new equations for the demand and supply curves? Draw these new curves in Figure 3-3 and label them D_2 and S_2, respectively.

(e) By how much have equilibrium price and quantity changed as a result of the simultaneous shifts in the demand and supply curves? What do you see when you compare the change in equilibrium quantity with the horizontal shifts in the demand and supply curves? Why?

(f) What would happen to equilibrium price and quantity if *Py* fell by more than \$20? Why? What if *Py* fell by less than \$20?

6. **An Unexpected Government Budget Deficit?**

This question illustrates why it is important to take account of market reactions when calculating the cost to taxpayers of some types of government policy. [*Note:* This question is repeated as *Extension Exercise E3,* which uses algebra instead of a scale diagram.]

Figure 3-4 shows the supply curve and (private-sector) demand curve of a hypothetical market for farm machinery in Canada (with quantity in thousands of units).

Figure 3-4

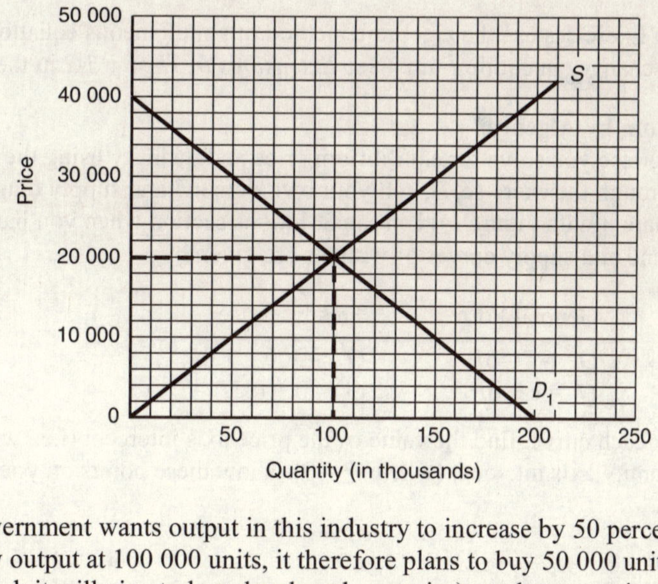

The federal government wants output in this industry to increase by 50 percent. With current industry output at 100 000 units, it therefore plans to buy 50 000 units of farm machinery (which it will give to less-developed countries) at whatever price is set by the market. Since market price is currently \$20 000 per unit, it estimates this program will cost \$1 billion (excluding administrative costs).

(a) With the government entering the market and demanding an extra 50 000 units, draw the new (private sector <u>plus</u> government) demand curve for farm machinery. What are the new equilibrium levels of price and quantity?

(b) How much does the government actually pay for the 50 000 units? What is the percentage increase in industry output? Why does this increase fall short of the government's target of 50 percent?

(c) How many units would the government have to purchase in order to meet its objective of increasing industry output to 150 000 units? How much would this cost the government?

(d) What wrong assumption did the government make about the supply of farm machinery when it predicted that buying 50 000 units would cost $1000 million and would increase production by 50 percent?

EXTENSION EXERCISES

These Extension Exercises use the algebraic method of simultaneous equations to find market equilibrium and changes in equilibrium. (See *Extensions in Theory 3-2* in the text.)

E1. Equilibrium by Algebra

In this exercise you solve for equilibrium price and quantity using the algebraic method. As you go through the exercise, sketch your own demand and supply diagram—not to scale—and compare it with Figure 3-11 in the Solutions section when you have finished.

The demand and supply curves of widgets are given by

	General Form	This Exercise
Demand:	$Q^D = a - bP$	$Q^D = 300 - 1.0P$
Supply:	$Q^S = c + dP$	$Q^S = 0 + 0.5P$

(a) For each curve, find the value of the price axis intercept (i.e., where $Q = 0$) and quantity axis intercept (where $P = 0$). Show these points on your diagram.

(b) Impose the equilibrium condition, $Q^D = Q^S$, and solve algebraically for the equilibrium price and quantity. Show the equilibrium values on your diagram.

(c) Using the values for this exercise, divide the difference between the quantity axis intercepts of the demand and supply curves (a – c) by the sum of the (absolute values) of the inverse of the slopes of the two curves (b + d). Where have you seen the resulting number before? Divide the difference between the price axis intercepts of the demand and supply curves (a/b – c/d) by the sum of the (absolute values) of the slopes of the two curves (1/b + 1/d). Where have you seen this number before?

(d) Now suppose the supply curve is unchanged, but the demand curve changes to

$$Q^D = 300 - 1.5P$$

Find the price and quantity axis intercepts for this demand curve. Add this curve to your diagram (and label it D_2).

(e) At the initial equilibrium price you found in (b), is there now any excess demand or excess supply in the market? How much? Show this on your diagram.

(f) Apply the equilibrium condition, $Q^D = Q^S$, and solve for the new equilibrium price and quantity. Show the new equilibrium values on your diagram.

(g) Repeat part (c) using the supply curve and the new demand curve. Where have you seen these numbers before?

E2. Changes in Exogenous Variables: The Algebraic Approach

This question takes you through the algebraic method of solving for the effect of changes in exogenous variables on equilibrium price and quantity.

The quantity demanded of gadgets (Q^D) depends on the price of gadgets (P) and average household income (Y) according to the following relationship:

$$Q^D = 30 - 10P + 0.001Y$$

The quantity of gadgets supplied (Q^S) is positively related to the price of gadgets and negatively related to W, the price of some input (e.g., labour) according to

$$Q^S = 5 + 5P - 2W$$

(a) Assume initially that $Y = \$40\ 000$ and $W = \$5$. Substitute these values into the equations to obtain the equations for the demand and supply curves.

(b) Now use the equilibrium condition $Q^D = Q^S$ to solve the demand and supply equations simultaneously for the equilibrium price.

(c) Substitute the equilibrium price into either the demand or supply equation to obtain the equilibrium quantity. [*Hint*: Use both the demand and the supply equations. If they do not give the same *Q*, your *P* is wrong.]

(d) Draw a diagram on the grid in Figure 3-5 showing the demand and supply curves and the equilibrium values of price and quantity. Label these curves D_1 and S_1. For each curve, show the values of the price axis intercept (where $Q = 0$) and the quantity axis intercept (where $P = 0$). [*Note:* At very low prices the supply equation gives negative quantities. Negative quantities can't be produced, so draw the supply curve as a broken line in this range.]

Figure 3-5

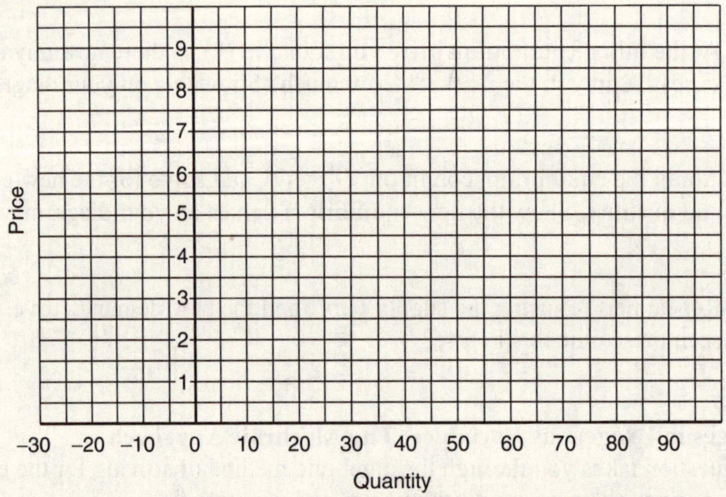

(e) Now suppose average household income increases to $55 000 but *W* remains unchanged. Derive the equation for the new demand curve and calculate the new levels of equilibrium price and quantity. Add the new curve to your diagram (label it D_2), and show the new equilibrium values.

(f) Next, assume that the input price *W* increases to $12.50. Using the demand curve you derived in (e), determine the new equilibrium price and quantity. Add the new curve to your diagram (label it S_2), and show the new equilibrium values.

E3. Government Intervention in the Market

This repeats Exercise 6 but uses the algebraic method to find equilibrium. Draw your own demand and supply diagram—not to scale—as you go along. When you have finished the question, compare your diagram with the diagram in the Solution to Exercise 6.

The government wants the output of farm machinery to increase by 50 000 units. It therefore plans to purchase 50 000 units (which it will donate to less-developed countries) at whatever price is set by the market. The supply curve and the private-sector demand curve equations (with quantity expressed in thousands of units) are

$$Q^D = 200 - 0.005P$$
$$Q^S = 0 + 0.005P$$

(a) Impose the equilibrium condition, $Q^D = Q^S$, and solve for the equilibrium price and quantity.

(b) Now the government intervenes as an additional demander, wanting to purchase 50 000 units. What is the equation for the new (private sector plus government) demand curve for farm machinery? What are the new equilibrium levels of price and quantity?

(c) By how many units does the output of farm machinery increase? Why does the increase in output fall short of the government's target? [*Hint*: How many units are now purchased by the private sector?]

(d) How many units would the government have to purchase to cause production to be 50 000 units more than before it intervened in the market? [*Hint*: Find the price at which quantity supplied would be 50 000 more than in (a), and find the quantity purchased by the private sector at this price.]

(e) Since the government expected industry output to increase by 50 000, what wrong assumption did it make about the market supply curve? What did it expect to be the total cost of purchasing 50 000 units? What is the actual total cost of the 50 000 units it purchased in (b)? What would be the total cost in (d) if government bought the number of units necessary to increase industry output by 50 000?

ADDITIONAL MULTIPLE-CHOICE QUESTIONS

***1. When the Multiple Listing Service (MLS) reports that in the month of April at an average selling price of $250 000, total sales of homes in Toronto were 2000 units, they are referring to**

(a) quantity demanded.
(b) quantity supplied.
(c) equilibrium quantity.
(d) actual purchases, which may or may not equal quantity demanded or quantity supplied.
(e) actual purchases, which must be the equilibrium quantity.

2. **A decrease in the price of iPods will result in**
(a) an increase in demand for iPods.
(b) a decrease in supply of iPods.
(c) an increase in the quantity demanded of iPods.
(d) a movement up along the demand curve for iPods.
(e) a rightward shift in the demand curve for iPods.

*3. **A decrease in the price of DVD players will cause**
(a) a leftward shift in the demand curve for videocassette tape players.
(b) an increase in demand for videocassette tapes.
(c) a rightward shift in the demand curve for DVDs.
(d) an increase in demand for DVD players.
(e) Both (a) and (c) are correct.

4. **Which of the following would *not* cause a change in demand?**
(a) A decrease in average income.
(b) An increase in the price of a substitute good.
(c) A decrease in the cost of producing the good.
(d) An increase in population.
(e) A government program that redistributes income.

5. **Which of the following would *not* cause an increase in the supply of broccoli?**
(a) A decrease in the price of broccoli.
(b) A decrease in the price of labour employed in harvesting broccoli.
(c) An improvement in pesticides, thereby decreasing the variability in broccoli output.
(d) An increase in the number of producers.
(e) An improvement in harvesting technology.

Questions 6 and 7 refer to the following diagram.

Figure 3-6

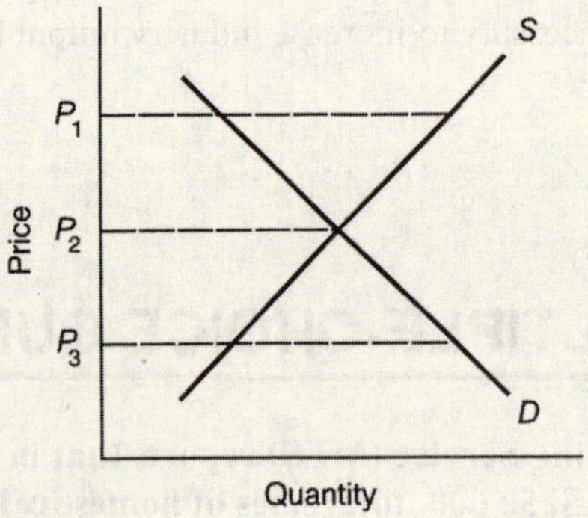

6. **At a price of P_1,**
(a) there is upward pressure on price.
(b) demand will rise to restore equilibrium.
(c) quantity supplied is greater than quantity demanded.
(d) the market has reached an equilibrium price.
(e) a shortage exists.

7. When price equals P_3,

(a) quantity exchanged equals quantity demanded.
(b) there is excess supply.
(c) there is a tendency for price to rise.
(d) the market is in equilibrium.
(e) a surplus exists.

8. As consumer preferences change in favour of organically grown vegetables, other things constant, economic theory predicts which of the following will occur in the market for these vegetables?

(a) A decrease in price and an increase in the quantity exchanged.
(b) An increase in both equilibrium price and quantity.
(c) A shift in the supply curve to the right.
(d) An increase in equilibrium price and a decrease in equilibrium quantity.
(e) A leftward shift of the demand curve.

***9. Simultaneous increases in both demand and supply are predicted to result in**

(a) increases in both equilibrium price and quantity.
(b) a higher equilibrium price but a smaller equilibrium quantity.
(c) a lower equilibrium price but a larger equilibrium quantity.
(d) a larger equilibrium quantity but no predictable change in price.
(e) a higher price, but no predicable change in equilibrium quantity.

***10. A decrease in input prices as well as a simultaneous decrease in the price of a good that is substitutable in consumption will lead to**

(a) a lower equilibrium price and a larger equilibrium quantity.
(b) a lower equilibrium price but no change in equilibrium quantity.
(c) a lower equilibrium price and an uncertain change in quantity.
(d) a lower equilibrium price and a smaller equilibrium quantity.
(e) an unpredictable change in both price and quantity.

***11. Which of the following is *not* a potential cause of an increase in the price of housing?**

(a) Construction workers' wages increase with no offsetting increase in productivity.
(b) Cheaper methods of prefabricating homes are developed.
(c) An increase in population.
(d) An increase in consumer incomes.
(e) The price of land (an input) increases.

***12. Today the price of strawberries is 60 cents a quart, and raspberries are priced at 75 cents a quart. Yesterday strawberries were 80 cents and raspberries $1. Thus, for these two goods,**

(a) the relative price of raspberries has fallen.
(b) the relative price of strawberries has fallen by 20 cents.
(c) the relative prices of both goods have fallen.
(d) relative prices have not changed.
(e) the relative price of strawberries has risen.

***13. For an inferior good, an increase in average incomes and a simultaneous increase in production costs will**

(a) increase equilibrium price and quantity

(b) decrease equilibrium price and increase equilibrium quantity

(c) increase equilibrium price but may increase or decrease equilibrium quantity.

(d) decrease equilibrium price but may increase or decrease equilibrium quantity.

(e) decrease equilibrium quantity but may increase or decrease equilibrium price.

Questions 14 to 20 refer to the following diagram of the market for hamburgers in Collegeville.

Figure 3-7

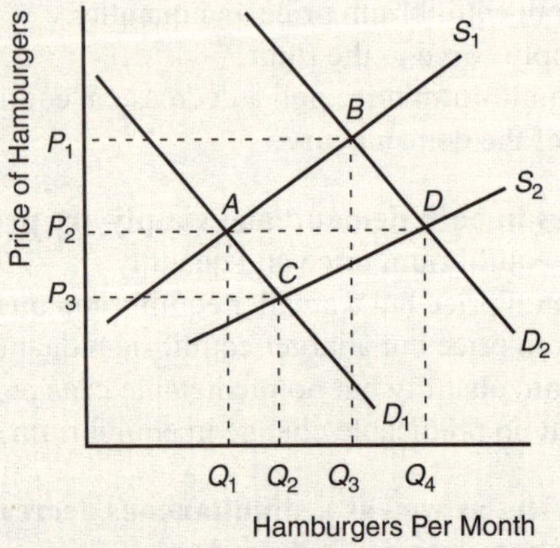

14. A change in Collegeville's market equilibrium from *A* to *B* may be caused by

(a) a decrease in wages of part-time workers.

(b) a decrease in the price of hot dogs.

(c) an increase in the student population of Collegeville.

(d) an increase in the price of hamburgers.

(e) Both (c) and (d) are correct.

15. A increase in the price of hot dogs may be depicted in the hamburger market by a change in equilibrium from

(a) *A* to *D*

(b) *A* to *C*

(c) *C* to *D*

(d) *A* to *B*

(e) Both (c) and (d) are correct.

***16. A change in equilibrium from *A* to *D* may be explained by**

(a) an increase in Collegeville's student population.

(b) a decrease in the price of beef patties.

(c) an increase in the price of hot dogs coupled with an increase in the wages of restaurant employees.

(d) a technological improvement in the production of hamburgers coupled with consumer concern about Mad Cow disease.

(e) a decrease in the price of fries (a complement to hamburgers) coupled with a reduction in the wages of restaurant employees.

17. **Which event would best explain a decrease in equilibrium quantity from Q_4 to Q_3?**
(a) An increase in the price of beef patties.
(b) A decrease in Collegeville's student population.
(c) A decrease in the price of fries (a complement to hamburgers).
(d) An increase in the supply of hamburgers due to entry of new firms.
(e) Consumer concern about the effects of a cattle disease.

18. **If equilibrium changes from *A* to *B*, one could say**
(a) there has been an increase in demand.
(b) quantity supplied has increased.
(c) price has increased.
(d) supply has not changed.
(e) All of the above are correct.

19. **A decrease in equilibrium price from P_1 to P_3 may be explained by**
(a) a decrease in supply.
(b) a decrease in quantity supplied.
(c) a decrease in demand and a decrease in supply.
(d) a decrease in demand and an increase in supply.
(e) an increase in supply and a decrease in quantity supplied.

*20. **An increase in average student incomes and an increase in the number of hamburger firms can be depicted by a change in equilibrium from**
(a) *D* to *B*.
(b) *C* to *D*.
(c) *D* to *A*.
(d) C to *B*.
(e) *A* to *D* or *B* to *C*, depending upon whether hamburgers are a normal or an inferior good, respectively.

*21. **Demand is $Q^D = 200 - 0.5P$ and supply is $Q^S = 60 + 0.5P$. In this market, equilibrium quantity is _________ units and equilibrium price is _________.**
(a) 160, \$80 (b) 105, \$90
(c) 140, \$130 (d) 130, \$140
(e) 200, \$140

*22. **In the demand function for Good X, $Q^D{}_X = 400 - 0.25P_X + 0.01P_Z - 0.001Y$, where P_Z is the price of another good and *Y* is average income,**
(a) Goods X and Z are normal goods.
(b) Good X is an inferior good and Goods X and Z are complementary goods.
(c) Good X is a normal good and Goods X and Z are substitute goods.
(d) Good X is an inferior good and Goods X and Z are substitute goods.
(e) Good X is a normal good and Goods X and Z are complementary goods.

SOLUTIONS

Chapter Review

1.(a) **2.**(e) **3.**(a) **4.**(b) **5.**(c) **6.**(b) **7.**(b) **8.**(c) **9.**(d) **10.**(e) **11.**(c) **12.**(b) **13.**(c) **14.**(e) **15.**(d) **16.**(c) **17.**(a) **18.**(a) **19.**(e)

Short-Answer Questions

1. Equilibrium is a condition of stability, with no existing pressures for change. New pressures arise from changes in the exogenous variables that shift the demand and supply curves. Such shifts create excess demand or excess supply at the old equilibrium price, which are market forces that put pressure on price and quantity until a new position of stability (i.e., equilibrium) is reached.

2. Because of the "other things constant" (i.e., *ceteris paribus*) condition, prices of other goods are constant all along a demand curve. Consequently, as the dollar price (i.e., the absolute price) of a good falls, its price relative to the price of other goods is also falling. The fall in relative price is a fall in the good's opportunity cost, to which demanders react by increasing quantity demanded (i.e., a movement along the demand curve).

3. When demanders (suppliers) move along a demand (supply) curve, they are *reacting* to a change in the product's own price, other things constant. Along the demand (supply) curve in a competitive market, therefore, quantity is endogenous and price is exogenous—neither demanders nor suppliers *by themselves* determine the price. In the market as a whole, however, both the equilibrium price and the equilibrium quantity are determined by the *interaction* of demand and supply—i.e., both price and quantity are endogenous.

4. The stock market "bubble" was an example of inflation as a *self-fulfilling prophecy*—the prices of stocks and shares rose because people expected them to rise. Expectations of higher prices shifted the demand curve for stocks and shares to the right as demanders anticipated making big capital gains (i.e., "Buy now and sell for a higher price later"). For the very same reason, the supply curve of shares offered for sale shifted to the left (i.e., "Why sell at today's prices when more money can be made by selling later at higher prices?"). Both the increase in demand and the decrease in supply created excess demand at existing prices, causing prices to rise and creating the "bubble" in the stock market. [*Note*: Eventually the bubble "burst" when expectations of rising prices changed to expectations of falling prices. Demand fell and supply increased, prices of stocks and shares plunged, and many people lost a great deal of wealth!]

Exercises

1. (a) **Figure 3-8**

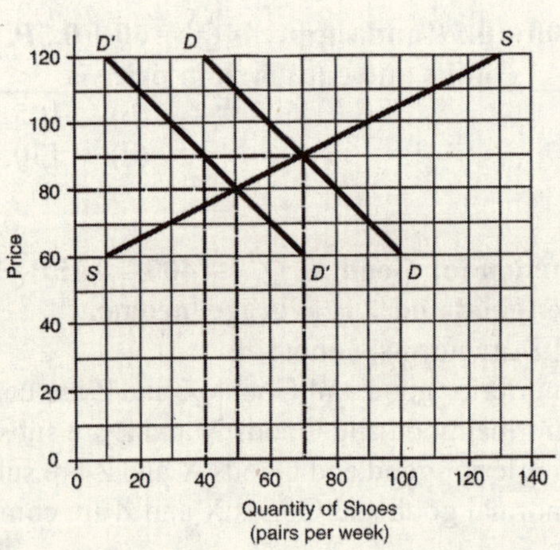

Equilibrium price is $90 and equilibrium quantity is 70 pairs per week.

(b) At each price, subtract quantity supplied from quantity demanded to get:

Price	Excess Demand (+) or Excess Supply (–)
$120	–90
110	–60
100	–30
90	0
80	+30
70	+60
60	+90

Equilibrium occurs where quantity demanded equals quantity supplied, at P = $90. There is no excess demand or excess supply in equilibrium.

(c) The change in tastes (as in "fashion") shifts the demand curve for athletic shoes to the left by 30 pairs at each price. At each price, the value in the D' column of the question's table is the value in the D column, minus 30. See Figure 3-8 in (a).

(d) After tastes change, quantity demanded at $90 is (70 – 30 =) 40 units per week. Quantity supplied remains at 70 units. There is excess supply of (70 – 40 =) 30 units per week, which puts downward pressure on price. Demanders react to the falling price by increasing the quantity of athletic shoes demanded each week (i.e., moving down D' in Figure 3-8). Trendy reacts by reducing quantity supplied (i.e., moving down S in Figure 3-8).

(e) Subtracting 30 (the fall in demand) from the excess demand/excess supply column gives zero excess demand or supply at P = $80, which is the new equilibrium price. At P = $80, the quantity in the D' column is 50 and the quantity in the S column is 50, so the new equilibrium quantity at P = $80 is 50.

2. **(a)** Excess supply of 2500 seats. (5000 seats supplied minus 2500 demanded.)

(b) At P = $8, quantity demanded equals the 5000 seats supplied.

(c) The equilibrium price for a popular performer is $10, where quantity demanded equals quantity supplied equals 5000.

(d) At the $8 equilibrium price for a typical concert, 10 000 seats are demanded for a popular performer—there is excess demand of 5000 seats. Many people are willing to pay more than $8 to see a popular performer. For example, 2000 people are willing to pay $14 to see one. If 1000 of them failed to get an $8 ticket, scalpers buying at $8 and selling at $14 would gain $6(1000) = $6000. The combination of excess demand and a box-office price (below equilibrium) that is not allowed to respond to market pressures creates a potentially lucrative "black market" for ticket scalping. As a result, some people will see the concert for $8 but others will have paid even more than the $10 market equilibrium price for a popular performer. The objective of "fairness" as defined by the Executive certainly is not achieved: not only are some (many?) students paying different prices for different concerts, but also they are not all paying the same price to see the same concert! What do you think the Executive's policy should be?

3.

	D	*S*	*P*	*Q*
(a)	0	–	+	–
(b)	+	0	+	+
(c)	0	+	–	+
(d)	0	+	–	+
(e)	–	–	U	–
(f)	U	0	U	U
(g)	+	–	+	U
(h)	+	–	+	U

Selected explanations

(e) The change in tastes (as in "concern over") reduces demand, putting downward pressure on price and quantity. Higher costs reduce supply, putting upward pressure on price and downward pressure on quantity. Both reduce quantity, but have opposing effects on price. The net effect on price, therefore, is uncertain. (The net effect depends on the relative size of the shifts in the demand and supply curves—see Exercise 5 for more on this.)

(f) The change in tastes (as in "concern about") increases demand, but the fall in price of gasoline reduces demand (because the cost of using automobiles falls). The net effect on the demand curve, and therefore on equilibrium P and Q, can't be predicted without empirical evidence on the relative size of the two effects.

(h) Expectations of higher future prices increase demand (upward pressure on P and Q) and reduce supply (upward pressure on P and downward pressure on Q). Price rises (same prediction for each event), but equilibrium quantity may rise or fall (opposing predictions for the two events).

4. (a) World supply of oil fell (a leftward shift of the supply curve). Katrina badly damaged some large oil rigs in the Gulf of Mexico, as well as the pipelines that carried oil from Gulf ports to refineries. Because most other oil producers were operating close to capacity, they did not have the flexibility to quickly increase their output to offset the reduction in supply caused by Katrina. (See *Lessons from History 3-1* for more detail.)

(b) Change (increase) in supply. The combination of a lower price and an increase in quantity sold is consistent with a rightward shift of the supply curve.

(c) Change (increase) in demand. The demand curve for apartments shifts to the right, resulting in higher rents and an increase in the quantity of apartments supplied.

(d) Lower airfares increase quantity demanded—a movement along (down) the demand curve for air travel. The supply of seats on regularly scheduled flights is unchanged (a vertical supply curve). Neither curve shifts, so the equilibrium values do not change but the market moves closer to the equilibrium.

(e) Change (increase) in quantity supplied in the market for Christmas trees. Higher prices cause a movement along (up) the supply curve, moving closer to equilibrium. Change (decrease) in supply in the market for milk. The supply curve of milk shifts left, increasing equilibrium price and reducing equilibrium quantity. (Note that the wording of the question implies that Christmas trees and milk are substitutes *in production*—if more land is used for Christmas trees, less is available for the cattle which produce milk.)

(f) Change (reduction) in supply of Atlantic cod. The supply curve of Atlantic cod shifts left, raising equilibrium price and reducing equilibrium quantity. Because Atlantic cod and Pacific salmon are substitutes *in consumption,* the higher price of cod changes (increases) the demand for salmon. The demand curve for salmon shifts right, increasing both equilibrium price and equilibrium quantity.

(g) In Quebec, the increase in demand pushed up the price and quantity sold. Because the generators are portable, generators in other parts of the country were brought to Quebec, attracted by the higher price. Thus supply also increased in Quebec, moderating the increase in price and further increasing the quantity sold (i.e., a new equilibrium caused by rightward shifts in both the demand and supply curves). The price in Quebec still increased somewhat, however, because the rightward shift of the demand curve exceeded the rightward shift of the supply curve. In other regions of the country, demand was unchanged but supply decreased as generators were diverted to Quebec, so in these regions price increased while quantity sold fell (i.e., a movement along the demand curve in these regions as the supply curve shifted leftward). (See *Lessons from History 3-1* for more detail.)

5. (a) The demand and supply curves show quantity as a function of the good's own price, other things constant (i.e., *ceteris paribus*). With Py constant at \$40, the demand equation reduces to $Q^D = 30 - 1P$ (i.e., $10 - 1P + 0.5(40) = 30 - 1P$). With Pn constant at \$200, the supply equation reduces to $Q^S = 10 + 1P$ (i.e., $30 + 1P - 0.1(200) = 10 + 1P$.) Thus the equations for the demand and supply <u>curves</u> are $Q^D = 30 - 1P$ and $Q^S = 10 + 1P$.

(b) At $P = 0$, $Q^D = 30$ and $Q^S = 10$ (the quantity axis intercepts of D_1 and S_1 in Figure 3-9). At $Q^D = 0$, $P = \$30$ (the price axis intercept of D_1).

Figure 3-9

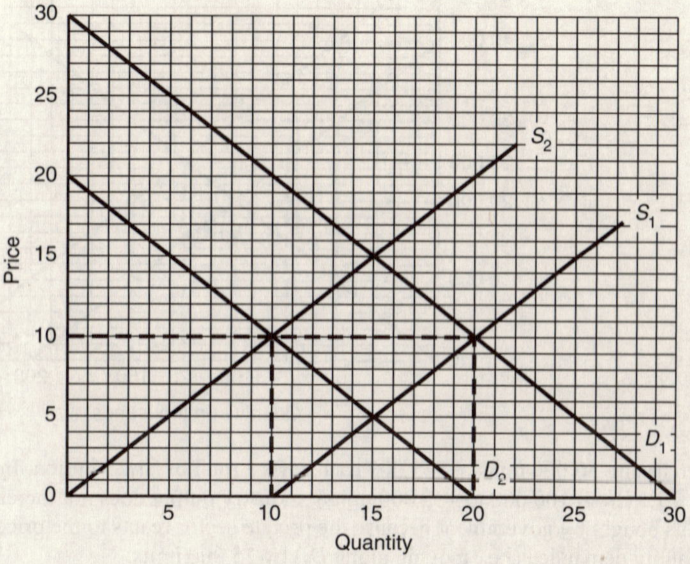

(c) For both demand and supply, every \$5 change in P changes Q by 5. Both have a slope of 1 (i.e., rise/run = $\Delta P/\Delta Q = 5/5 = 1$). [*Note*: Δ means "change in."] You now have the information needed to draw S_1 and D_1. The market is in equilibrium where S_1 and D_1 intersect, at $P = \$10$ and $Q = 20$.

(d) With *Py* constant at \$20, $Q^D = 10 - 1P + 0.5(20) = 20 - 1P$. With *Pn* constant at \$300, $Q^S = 30 + 1P - 0.1(300) = 0 + 1P$. The equations for the new demand and supply curves are $Q^D = 20 - 1P$ and $Q^S = 0 + 1P$. Repeating parts (b) and (c) using these new equations gives you the information needed to draw S_2 and D_2.

(e) S_2 and D_2 intersect (i.e., the new equilibrium) at $P = \$10$ and $Q = 10$. Thus P is unchanged and Q has fallen by 10 units (from 20 to 10). Because both curves shift horizontally by the *same amount* in the *same direction,* no excess demand or supply is created at the old equilibrium P of \$10. Consequently, the equilibrium price is unchanged and the equilibrium quantity changes by the amount of the (equal) leftward shift in the two curves.

(f) If *Py* fell by more than \$20, demand would shift left by more than 10 units. The leftward shift of D would be greater than the leftward shift of S, creating excess supply at $P = \$10$. Equilibrium price would fall and equilibrium quantity would fall by more than in (e). If *Py* fell by less than \$20, demand would shift left by less than 10 units. The leftward shift of D would be less than the leftward shift of S, creating excess demand at $P = \$10$. Equilibrium price would rise and equilibrium quantity would fall by less than in (e). [*Note*: What you see from this exercise is that when the demand and supply curves shift in the same direction, the effect on equilibrium quantity is predictable but the effect on equilibrium price depends on the relative magnitudes of the shifts. If you experiment by increasing *Py* and decreasing *Pn* you will find that, when the two curves shift in opposite directions, the outcome is reversed—the effect on equilibrium price is now predictable, but the effect on equilibrium quantity now depends on the relative magnitudes of the shifts in the demand and supply curves.]

6. **(a)** D_1 shifts to the right by the additional 50 000 units demanded by government. The new demand curve D_2 intersects the S curve (i.e., equilibrium) at $P = \$25\ 000$ and $Q = 125\ 000$ units. [*Note*: The government will buy 50 000 units at whatever price is set *by the market,* but the maximum price the private sector will pay is \$40 000. Consequently, the market price will not exceed \$40 000, so D_2 does not extend beyond $P = \$40\ 000$.]

Figure 3-10

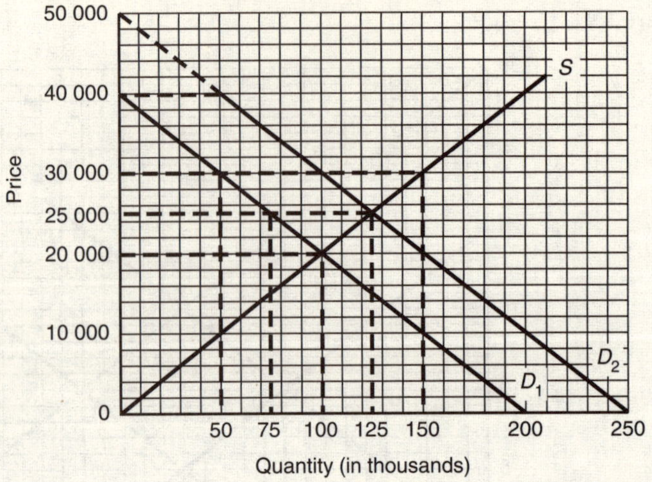

(b) Purchasing 50 000 units at $25 000 each costs a total of $1.25 billion. Industry output increases by 25% (from 100 000 to 125 000 units). Industry output does not increase by the full 50 000 units bought by government because the private sector reacts to the price increase by reducing its quantity demanded (i.e., moving along D_1) by 25 000 units.

(c) Price would have to rise to $30 000 to get Q^S = 150 000. At $30 000 the private sector would buy only 50 000 units, so the government would have to buy 100 000 units at a price of $30 000 per unit for a total cost of $3 billion—three times the initial estimate!

(d) Government erroneously assumed the supply curve of farm machinery to be horizontal at P = $20 000. Only with a horizontal supply curve would there be no increase in price when demand increased, so no fall in quantity demanded by the private sector.

Extension Exercises

E1. (a) At $P = 0$, $Q^D = 300 - 1.0(0) = 300$ and $Q^S = 0.5(0) = 0$. So $Q^D = 300$ and $Q^S = 0$ are the quantity axis intercepts for D_1 and S, respectively, in your diagram (Figure 3-11). At $Q = 0$ the demand equation solves for P = $300 and the supply equation solves for P = $0. These are the price axis intercepts for D_1 and S in your diagram.

Figure 3-11

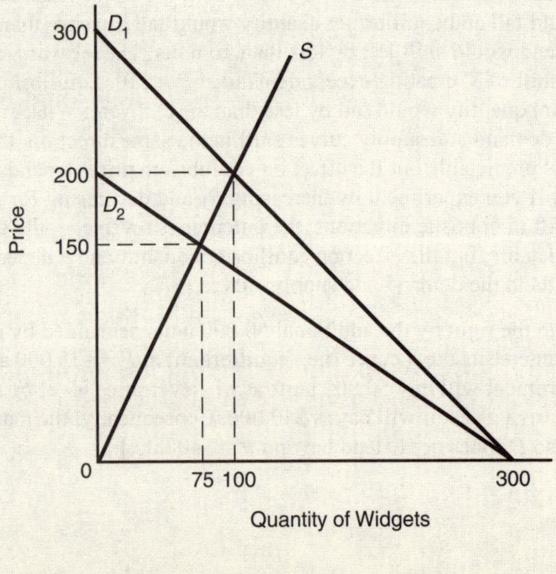

(b) Setting $Q^D = Q^S$ gives $300 - 1.0P = 0.5P$, so $1.5P = 300$ and $P = \$200$.
Putting $P = \$200$ in the demand equation gives the equilibrium quantity $Q^D = 300 - 1.0(200) = 100$. [*Note*: Putting $P = \$200$ into the supply equation also gives $Q^S = 0.5(200) = 100$. Since both Q^D and $Q^S = 100$ at $P = \$200$, you know you have the correct values for equilibrium because there is neither excess demand nor excess supply.]

(c) The equation (a – c)/(b + d) gives (300 – 0)/(1 + 0.5) = 300/1.5 = \$200. You have seen this before in part (b)—it is the equilibrium price. The equation (a/b – c/d)/(1/b + 1/d) gives (300/1 – 0/0.5)/(1/1 + 1/0.5) = 300/3 = 100. You have seen this before in part (b)—it is the equilibrium quantity. [*Note*: P = (a – c)/(b + d) is the P^* equation in *Extensions in Theory 3-2* in the text, and Q = (a/b – c/d)/(1/b + 1/d) is an alternative expression for the Q^* equation in *Extensions in Theory 3-2*.]

(d) For D_2 in the diagram, the quantity axis intercept (i.e., Q^D at $P = \$0$) remains at $Q^D = 300 - 1.5(0) = 300$. The price axis intercept (i.e., P at $Q^D = 0$) falls to $0 = 300 - 1.5P$, so $P = 300/1.5 = \$200$.

(e) At $P = \$200$, $Q^S = 0.5P = 0.5(200) = 100$, but $Q^D = 300 - 1.5P = 300 - 1.5(200) = 0$. There is excess supply ($Q^S - Q^D$) of (100 – 0 =) 100 widgets.

(f) Setting $Q^D = Q^S$ gives $300 - 1.5P = 0.5P$, so $2P = 300$ and $P = 300/2 = \$150$. Putting $P = \$150$ in the demand equation gives the equilibrium quantity $Q^D = 300 - 1.5(150) = 300 - 225 = 75$ widgets. [*Note*: Similarly, putting $P = \$150$ in the supply equation gives $Q^S = 0.5(150) = 75$.]

(g) The equation P^* = (a – c)/(b + d) gives (300 – 0)/(1.5 + 0.5) = 300/2 = \$150. The equation Q^* = (a/b – c/d)/(1/b + 1/d) gives (300/1.5 – 0/0.5)/(1/1.5 + 1/0.5) = 200/2.67 = 75 widgets. You have seen these before in part (f)—they are the new equilibrium price (P^*) and equilibrium quantity (Q^*).

E2. (a) The demand and supply curves show quantity as a function of the good's own price, other things constant (i.e., *ceteris paribus*). With Y constant at \$40 000, $Q^D = 30 - 10P + 0.001(40\,000) = 70 - 10P$. With W constant at \$5, $Q^S = 5 + 5P - 2(5) = -5 + 5P$. Thus the equations for the demand and supply <u>curves</u> are $Q^D = 70 - 10P$ and $Q^S = -5 + 5P$.

(b) Setting $Q^D = Q^S$ gives $70 - 10P = -5 + 5P$, $15P = \$75$, $P = 75/15 = \$5$.

(c) Using the demand curve equation, equilibrium $Q^D = 70 - 10(5) = 20$ gadgets.
Using the supply curve equation, equilibrium $Q^S = -5 + 5(5) = 20$ gadgets.

(d) At $P = 0$, $Q^D = 70 - 10(0) = 70$ and $Q^S = -5 + 5(0) = -5$. These are the quantity axis intercepts for D_1 and S_1 in Figure 3-12. At $Q = 0$ the demand equation solves for $P = \$7$ and the supply equation solves for $P = \$1$. These are the price axis intercepts for D_1 and S_1 in Figure 3-12.

Figure 3-12

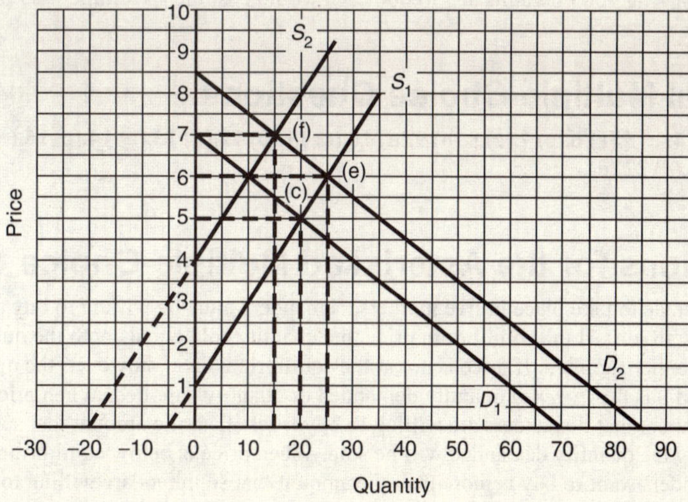

(e) With Y constant at \$55 000, $Q^D = 30 - 10P + 0.001(55\ 000) = 85 - 10P$. So the equation for the new demand curve (D_2) is $Q^D = 85 - 10P$. At $P = 0$ this equation solves for the quantity axis intercept of $Q^D = 85$. At $Q^D = 0$ it solves for the price axis intercept of $P = \$8.50$.
Setting $Q^D = Q^S$ for equilibrium gives $85 - 10P = -5 + 5P$, $15P = 90$, $P = \$6$. Setting $P = \$6$ in either the demand or supply equation solves for the new equilibrium quantity of 25.

(f) With W constant at \$12.50, $Q^S = 5 + 5P - 2(12.50) = -20 + 5P$. So $Q^S = -20 + 5P$ is the equation for the new supply curve (S_2). The price and quantity axis intercepts are \$4 and –20, respectively.
Setting $Q^D = Q^S$ for equilibrium gives $85 - 10P = -20 + 5P$, $15P = 105$, $P = 105/15 = \$7$.
Substituting $P = \$7$ into the demand curve equation gives equilibrium $Q^D = 85 - 10(7) = 15$.
[*Note*: Doing the same with the supply curve equation also gives equilibrium $Q^S = -20 + 5(7) = -20 + 35 = 15$.]

E3. Your illustrative diagram should show the curves and values in Figure 3-10 above. The note in the answer to Exercise 6.a explains why D_2 does not extend above $P = \$40\ 000$.

(a) Setting $Q^D = Q^S$ for equilibrium gives $200 - 0.005P = 0 + 0.005P$, which solves for $P = 200/0.01 = \$20\ 000$. Substituting $P = \$20\ 000$ in the supply curve equation gives equilibrium $Q^S = 0 + 0.005(20{,}000) = 100$ (i.e., 100 000 units). [*Note:* Doing the same using the demand curve equation, $Q^D = 200 - 0.005(20{,}000) = 100$.]

(b) The private-sector plus government demand is $Q^D = 200 - 0.005P + 50 = 250 - 0.005P$.
Setting $Q^D = Q^S$ for equilibrium gives $250 - 0.005P = 0 + 0.005P$, which solves for $P = 250/0.01 = \$25\ 000$—i.e., a price increase of \$5000. Substituting $P = \$25\ 000$ into either the Q^D or Q^S equation (and multiplying by 1000) gives equilibrium quantity of 125 000 units.

(c) Comparing (a) and (b) shows production of farm machinery increases by only 25 000, not the full 50 000 purchased by the government. This is because the private sector reacts to the increase in price by reducing quantity demand by 25 000 units, from 100 000 in (a) to $Q^D = 200 - 0.005(25\ 000) = 75\ 000$ in (b).

(d) Because output was 100 000 before government intervened, industry output would have to be 150 000 to meet the government's objective of a 50 000 increase. The supply curve tells us that 150 000 would be produced only when $150 = 0 + 0.005P$, which solves for $P = 150/0.005 = \$30\ 000$. At this price the private sector would purchase only $Q^D = 200 - 0.005(30\ 000) = 50$ (i.e., 50 000 units). Government would have to buy 150 000 – 50 000 = 100 000.

(e) Government erroneously assumed the supply curve of farm machinery to be horizontal at $P = \$20\ 000$. Only with a horizontal supply curve would there be no increase in price when demand increases, and so no fall in quantity demanded by the private sector. The government expected to buy 50 000 units for a total cost of \$20 000(50 000) = \$1 billion. At the new market price of \$25 000, the actual cost of 50 000 units is \$1.25 billion. To achieve its objective by purchasing 100 000 units at \$30 000 each would cost the government \$3 billion!

Additional Multiple-Choice Questions

1.(d) **2.**(c) **3.**(e) **4.**(c) **5.**(a) **6.**(c) **7.**(c) **8.**(b) **9.**(d) **10.**(c) **11.**(b) **12.**(d) **13.**(e) **14.**(c) **15.**(e) **16.**(e) **17.**(a) **18.**(e) **19.**(d) **20.**(e) **21.**(d) **22.**(d)

Explanations for the Asterisked Multiple-Choice Questions

1.(d) For a trade to take place in free markets, demanders must be willing to buy and suppliers must be willing to sell. At the equilibrium price, the quantity sold equals both the quantity demanded and the quantity supplied. If price is not at the equilibrium level, however, the quantity sold (or "traded") is the *lesser of* quantity demanded or quantity supplied. When price is above equilibrium, the amount that demanders are willing to buy is less than the amount that suppliers want to sell—so only the quantity demanded will be sold. When price is below equilibrium, the amount that demanders want to buy is more than the amount that suppliers are willing to sell—so only the quantity supplied will be sold.

3.(e) Videocassettes and DVDs are substitute goods, so a fall in the price of DVD players reduces demand for videocassettes and videocassette players. DVDs and DVD players are complementary goods, so a fall in the price of DVD players increases the demand for DVDs.

9.(d) Do this by sketching a demand and supply diagram for each change separately, starting both from the old equilibrium. In your first diagram, the increase in demand creates excess demand at the old equilibrium price, increasing both price and quantity (along the supply curve). In your second diagram, the increase in supply creates excess supply at the old equilibrium price, reducing price but increasing quantity (along the demand curve). Since both changes increase quantity, then equilibrium quantity will definitely increase. But the two changes have opposing effects on price, so the change in the equilibrium price is not predictable—it depends on the relative magnitudes of the two changes. If the (horizontal) shift in the demand curve is greater than the (horizontal) shift in the supply curve, equilibrium price will increase. If the reverse is true, equilibrium price will fall. If the two shifts are the same size, equilibrium price will remain unchanged. (Sketch a different diagram for each of these three cases.)

10.(c) Unlike Question 9, the demand and supply curves shift in *different* directions—the decrease in input prices increases supply but the fall in price of a substitute in consumption reduces demand. Follow the method suggested in the answer to Question 9—i.e., sketch a diagram for each change separately—to see that this time the direction of change in equilibrium price is predictable but the direction of change in equilibrium quantity is not. The increase in supply puts upward pressure on quantity and downward pressure on price. The decrease in demand puts downward pressure on both price and quantity. Since both changes put downward pressure on price, equilibrium price will fall. But since they put opposing pressures on quantity, the net effect on equilibrium quantity is ambiguous (it depends on which curve shifts more).

11.(b) Answers (a) and (e) increase production costs, reducing supply (i.e., a vertical upward shift of the supply curve at each Q) and raising price. Answers (c) and (d) increase demand (given that, for (d), housing is a normal good), again raising price. Answer (b), however, increases supply by reducing production costs (i.e., a vertical downward shift of the supply curve at each Q), thus reducing price.

12.(d) Yesterday the relative price of strawberries to raspberries was 0.8/1.0 = 0.8 (i.e., price of strawberries was 80% of the price of raspberries), and today it is 0.6/0.75 = 0.8—so no change. Conversely, the relative price of raspberries to strawberries went from 1.0/0.8 = 1.25 yesterday to 0.75/0.6 = 1.25 today—again no change. So while the *absolute* prices fell by different amounts (20 cents for strawberries 25 cents for raspberries), the *percentage* fall was the same for both (20/80 = 0.25 = 25% and 25/100 = 0.25 = 25%). Because each had the same percentage fall in its own price, their relative price (hence the opportunity cost) did not change

13.(e) As in Question 9, both demand and supply shift in the *same* direction (though here they shift to the left while in Question 9 they shift to the right), so the effect on equilibrium quantity is predictable but the effect on equilibrium price is uncertain. The increase in production costs shifts the supply curve to the left, putting upward pressure on price and downward pressure on quantity. The increase in average incomes shifts the demand curve *for an inferior good* to the left, putting downward pressure on both price and quantity. Both shifts cause quantity to decrease, but one shift pushes price up while other pushes price down. The net effect on equilibrium price is ambiguous (it depends on which curve shifts more—see Question 9).

16.(e) Only (a) and (e) have changes that increase demand (since a decrease in the price of beef patties increases *quantity demanded,* not demand). Only (d) and (e) have changes that increase supply. Since both demand and supply increase, the answer is (e).

20.(e) The increase in the number of hamburger firms will increase supply, shifting the curve from S_1 to S_2. This says that the initial equilibrium was on S_1 (either A or B) and the final equilibrium must be on S_2 (either C or D). The increase in average incomes will reduce demand for a normal good (shifting the curve from D_1 to D_2) but reduce demand for an inferior good (shifting the curve from D_2 to D_1). For a normal good, therefore, the initial equilibrium was on S_1 and D_1 (at point A) and the final equilibrium on S_2 and D_2 (at point D). For an inferior good, however, the initial equilibrium was on S_1 and D_2 (at point B) and the final equilibrium on S_2 and D_1 (at point C). Since the question gives no information as to whether hamburgers are normal or inferior goods, we can't say whether the equilibrium point moved from A to D (a normal good) or from B to C (an inferior good).

21.(d) Setting $Q^D = Q^S$ gives $200 - 0.5P = 60 + 0.5P$, so $P = 200 - 60 = \$140$. Putting $P = \$140$ into either the demand equation ($Q^D = 200 - 0.5(140) = 200 - 70 = 130$) or the supply equation ($Q^S = 60 + 0.5(140) = 60 + 70 = 130$) gives an equilibrium quantity of 130 units.

22.(d) The minus sign on *Y* says that an increase in income reduces the demand for X (a negative or inverse relationship), so X is an inferior good. The plus sign on *Pz* says that an increase in the price of Z increases the demand for X (a positive or direct relationship), so X and Z are substitute goods.

CHAPTER 4

ELASTICITY

LO

LEARNING OBJECTIVES

In this chapter you will learn

1 the meaning of price elasticity of demand and how it is measured.

2 about the relationship between demand elasticity and total expenditure.

3 the meaning of price elasticity of supply and how it is measured.

4 why the effect of an excise tax on equilibrium price and quantity depends on demand and supply elasticity.

5 about normal and inferior goods, and how to measure the income elasticity of demand.

6 how to measure cross elasticity of demand, and the meaning of substitute and complement goods.

CHAPTER OVERVIEW

The interaction of demand and supply was shown to determine equilibrium price and quantity in the previous chapter. The present chapter examines another important aspect of the interaction of demand and supply: the **responsiveness** of quantity demanded (or supplied) to changes in price, and the responsiveness of demand and supply to changes in other exogenous variables. **Elasticity** is the economic term for this type of responsiveness or sensitivity.

Price elasticity of demand is measured as the percentage change in quantity demanded divided by the percentage change in the commodity's own price. Demand is said to be **elastic** when the percentage change in quantity demanded exceeds (in absolute terms) the percentage change in price, and **inelastic** when the reverse holds. Demand is said to be **unit elastic** when the two percentage changes are of equal magnitude. If the price elasticity of demand for a product is known, one can predict the percentage change in quantity demanded that would result from a given percentage price change. The magnitude of a product's elasticity of demand also allows us to predict whether an increase in its price will result in an increase, a decrease, or no change in **total expenditure** on the product. An important influence on the elasticity of demand is the availability of substitute products.

Similarly, the **price elasticity of supply** is the percentage change in quantity supplied divided by the percentage change in the commodity's own price. The same classifications—elastic, inelastic, or unit elastic—also apply, again determined by the relative magnitudes of the percentage changes in quantity (supplied) and price.

Tax incidence refers to how the *burden* of a tax on goods and services is distributed between consumers and producers. This chapter shows that tax incidence is independent of whether producers or consumers *nominally* pay the tax. Rather, the distribution of the burden of a sales tax critically depends upon the relative magnitudes of the elasticities of demand and supply.

Additional elasticity measures are relevant when consumer income or the price of another good changes, the **income elasticity** and **cross-price elasticity**, respectively. The sign of the income elasticity (positive or negative) indicates whether the good is **normal** or **inferior**, while the sign of the cross-price elasticity indicates whether the goods are **substitutes** or **complements**.

HINTS AND TIPS

The following may help you to avoid some of the most common errors on examinations.

✓ Don't let the term "elasticity" overwhelm you. It is nothing more than a technical name for a measurement of responsiveness or sensitivity.

✓ The relationship between a change in price and change in total expenditure (positive or negative) on a commodity depends upon the magnitude of the *absolute value* of its price elasticity of demand. This is why the terms "more elastic" and "less elastic" refer to the absolute value of price elasticity of demand, despite the fact that it is actually a negative number on a downward-sloping demand curve (since price and quantity demanded move in opposite directions). Thus, for example, when demand has a price elasticity of –2, it is *more elastic* than when it has an elasticity of –1 (since the absolute value 2 exceeds the absolute value 1).

✓ Don't confuse slope with elasticity. For example, although a linear demand curve has a constant slope, it does not have a constant elasticity. The ratio of the *absolute* change in quantity to the *absolute* change in price is constant all along a linear demand curve, but the ratio of the *percentage* changes is not.

✓ There are different elasticities (price elasticity, income elasticity, cross elasticity) and there can be different ways of writing the formula for calculating an elasticity. It is easy to get confused if you lose sight of the fact that they are all doing the same thing. They are all comparing the percentage change in the quantity of a commodity (demanded or supplied) with the percentage change in one of the exogenous variables (the price of the commodity, income, the price of another commodity).

CHAPTER REVIEW

Price Elasticity of Demand

This section focuses on the responsiveness of quantity demanded to changes in the commodity's own price. This responsiveness can be referred to as the own-price elasticity of demand, the price elasticity of demand, or simply the elasticity of demand. Because the absolute change in price or quantity is a different percentage of the value before the change than the value after the change, elasticity takes the change as a percentage of the *average* of the two values. Depending upon its magnitude, elasticity is classified as elastic, inelastic, or unit elastic. Make certain you understand the implications of this classification for the effect of a change in the commodity's price on the change in consumers' total expenditure on the commodity, particularly along a linear (i.e., constant slope) demand curve. The section also explains why the elasticity of demand depends on the availability and closeness of substitutes, on how the "commodity" is defined, and on the length of the time span being considered.

1. The price elasticity of demand refers to a measure that shows the

(a) responsiveness of quantity demanded of a good to changes in its price.
(b) variation in prices due to a change in demand.
(c) size of price changes caused by a shift in demand.
(d) degree of substitutability across commodities.
(e) magnitude of the shifts in a demand curve.

2. The price elasticity of demand is measured by the

(a) change in quantity demanded divided by the change in price.
(b) change in price divided by the change in quantity demanded.
(c) slope of the demand curve.
(d) percentage change in quantity demanded divided by the percentage change in price.
(e) average quantity demanded divided by the average price.

3. If the percentage change in price is greater than the percentage change in quantity demanded, demand

(a) is elastic.
(b) is inelastic.
(c) is unit-elastic.
(d) shifts outward to the left.
(e) shifts to the right.

4. An increase in the price of a good and a decrease in total expenditure on this good are associated with

(a) inferior goods.
(b) substitute goods.
(c) normal goods.
(d) elastic demand.
(e) inelastic demand.

5. The price elasticity of demand for a good will be greater

(a) the less available are suitable substitutes for this good.
(b) the longer the time period considered.
(c) for a group of related goods as opposed to an element of that group.
(d) the greater is income.
(e) All of the above are correct.

6. If a 10 percent increase in the price of ski lift tickets causes a 5 percent decrease in total expenditure on lift tickets, then demand is

(a) elastic.
(b) inelastic.
(c) perfectly inelastic.
(d) normal.
(e) inferior.

7. Which of the following commodities is most likely to have an elastic demand?

(a) Toothpicks.
(b) Cigarettes.
(c) Heart pacemakers.
(d) Broccoli.
(e) Vegetables.

8. When price falls along a straight-line demand curve, the (absolute value of) elasticity

(a) first rises and then falls.
(b) is the same at all prices.
(c) first falls and then rises.
(d) continually rises as price falls.
(e) continually falls as price falls.

9. As price rises along a straight-line demand curve, total expenditure on the commodity

(a) first rises and then falls.
(b) is the same at all prices.
(c) first falls and then rises.
(d) continually rises as price falls.
(e) continually falls as price falls.

Price Elasticity of Supply

The responsiveness of quantity supplied to a change in price can also be classified as elastic, inelastic, or unit elastic. As with demand, the price elasticity of supply is calculated at the average values of price and quantity. Understand that a linear supply curve going through the origin is unit elastic throughout its whole length, regardless of slope. This section also explains why elasticity of supply is affected by the ease with which producers can shift production to other products (i.e., substitution in production, as distinct from substitution in consumption), by how costs of production change with output, and by the time span being considered.

10. A value of zero for the elasticity of supply of some product implies that
- (a) the supply curve is horizontal.
- (b) supply is highly responsive to price.
- (c) the supply curve is vertical.
- (d) the product will not be supplied at any price.
- (e) none of the above.

11. The elasticity of supply for a product will tend to be larger
- (a) the higher is the elasticity of demand for the product.
- (b) the lower is the elasticity of demand for the product.
- (c) the harder it is for firms to shift from the production of one product to another product.
- (d) the easier it is for firms to shift from the production of one product to another product.
- (e) the shorter the time period involved.

12. In the short run, a shift in demand will generally cause
- (a) the price to overshoot its long-run equilibrium value.
- (b) the price to undershoot its long-run equilibrium value.
- (c) the quantity exchanged to overshoot its long-run equilibrium value.
- (d) both price and quantity exchanged to overshoot their long-run equilibrium values.
- (e) none of the above.

13. Suppose that the short-run demand for a good is relatively more inelastic than its long-run demand. A given rightward shift in the supply curve will lead to a
- (a) smaller decrease in price in the long run than in the short run.
- (b) smaller increase in quantity in the long run than in the short run.
- (c) larger decrease in price in the long run than in the short run.
- (d) smaller decrease in both price and quantity in the long run than in the short run.
- (e) larger decrease in both price and quantity in the long run than in the short run.

An Important Example Where Elasticity Matters

This section looks at the importance of elasticity for the effects of an *excise tax* on "price." (A *sales tax* like the GST is a percentage of the price of a good or service, while an *excise tax* is the same dollar amount regardless of price. The principles of the analysis are the same in both cases, but the excise tax is easier to explain and calculate.) When government imposes a tax on a good, there is no longer a single price since the price paid by the consumer (*consumer price*) exceeds the price retained by the seller (*seller price*) by the amount of the tax. The *tax incidence,* otherwise called the *burden of the tax,* refers to the shares of the tax "paid" by sellers (via a fall in the seller price) and by consumers (via an increase in consumer price). Tax incidence depends on the relative elasticities of demand and supply, and is unaffected by whether the tax is included in the price charged by sellers, or paid by consumers as an add-on at the till. The more elastic is demand relative to supply, the smaller the consumers' share of the burden of taxation and the greater the sellers' share. This section shows why.

14. "Tax incidence" refers to
(a) who is legally responsible for paying the tax revenue to the government.
(b) the legislative process taxes must pass through.
(c) the economic costs of avoiding taxes.
(d) who ultimately bears the burden of the tax.
(e) None of the above.

15. Suppose the market supply curve for some good is upward sloping. If the imposition of a sales tax causes no change in the equilibrium quantity sold in the market, the good's demand curve must be _______, meaning that the burden of the tax has fallen completely on the _______.
(a) vertical; firms
(b) vertical; consumers
(c) horizontal; firms
(d) horizontal; consumers
(e) Not enough information is provided to answer this question.

16. Since the goods and services tax (GST) is added to the price a consumer must pay for a commodity, the
(a) entire burden of the tax is borne by consumers.
(b) consumer price increases by the amount of the tax.
(c) seller price is unaffected.
(d) entire burden is borne by sellers who must collect the tax.
(e) distribution of the burden depends upon the elasticities of demand and supply.

17. Consumers bear a greater share of the burden of the tax the more
(a) inelastic is supply.
(b) elastic is supply.
(c) inelastic is demand.
(d) elastic is demand.
(e) Both (b) and (c) are correct.

Other Demand Elasticities

The *income elasticity* of demand and the *cross-price elasticity* of demand measure the responsiveness of demand to income and to the prices of other goods, respectively. Just as price elasticity is measured holding all other exogenous variables constant (thus referring to the responsiveness of quantity demanded to price *along* a demand curve), so income elasticity and cross elasticity also hold all other exogenous variables constant, including the product's price (thus referring to how the demand curve *shifts* when income or other prices change). The sign on the income elasticity (positive or negative) shows the *direction* of the shift (i.e., whether the good is normal or inferior), and the magnitude of the income elasticity shows *by how much* the demand curve shifts when income changes. Similarly, the sign on the cross elasticity shows the *direction* of the shift (i.e., whether the two goods are substitutes or complements), and the magnitude of the cross elasticity shows *by how much* the demand curve shifts when the price of the other good changes. Review the terminology of elasticity in *Extensions in Theory 4-2* in the text to ensure a thorough understanding of the classification of the various elasticities.

18. **Which of the following pairs of commodities is most likely to have a cross elasticity of demand that is positive?**
(a) Hockey sticks and pucks.
(b) Bread and cheese.
(c) Cassettes and compact discs.
(d) Perfume and garden hoses.
(e) Hamburgers and french fries.

19. **Margarine and butter are predicted to have**
(a) the same income elasticities of demand.
(b) very low price elasticities of demand.
(c) negative cross elasticities of demand with respect to each other.
(d) positive cross elasticities of demand with respect to each other.
(e) elastic demands with respect to price.

20. **Which of the following pairs of commodities is most likely to have a cross elasticity of demand that is negative?**
(a) Cornflakes and raisin bran.
(b) Orange juice and apple juice.
(c) CD players and compact discs.
(d) Perfume and garden hoses.
(e) Hamburgers and hot dogs.

21. **Inferior commodities have**
(a) zero income elasticities of demand.
(b) negative cross elasticities of demand.
(c) negative elasticities of supply.
(d) highly elastic demands.
(e) negative income elasticities of demand.

22. **Which of the following goods is most likely to have an income elasticity of demand that is positive but less than one?**
(a) Ground beef.
(b) Microwave ovens.
(c) Perfume.
(d) Winter vacations.
(e) Sailboats.

SHORT-ANSWER QUESTIONS

1. Why is the cross elasticity of demand positive for substitute goods and negative for complementary goods?

2. If a $100 fall in the price of television sets and a $100 fall in the price of automobiles each increased quantity demanded by 50 000, would the price elasticity of demand be the same for both? Why/why not?

3. What would you expect to see when comparing the price elasticity of demand for Kit-Kat bars with the price elasticity of demand for candy as a whole? Why?

4. What does a "necessity" commonly mean in everyday language? What is the economic definition of a necessity? Can you think of a good which is a necessity according to the economic definition but not in everyday language?

The answers to the remaining questions in this section are "short," but finding them requires more thought. Also, Question 7 requires an understanding of the equation for a straight-line demand curve.

5. Mr. Quitit from Quaffalot wants to increase the sales tax on beer. He argues it would be good social policy because the price paid by consumers would increase by almost all the extra tax, which would substantially reduce purchases of beer and so leave low-income families with more money to spend on food and clothing. Can you see why Mr. Quitit's reasoning may well be inconsistent? [*Hint:* What is the condition for consumers to bear the "burden" of a tax? What is the condition for an increase in price to reduce total expenditure on a commodity?]

6. This question reviews your understanding of the relationships between elasticity of demand and total expenditure when price changes. Complete the following table:

	Price Elasticity	Change in Price	Change in Total Expenditure
(a)	2.0	up	_____
(b)	1.0	down	_____
(c)	_____	up	none
(d)	0.0	down	_____
(e)	0.6	_____	up

7. The daily demand curve facing the City Transit Authority (CTA) is given by $Q^D = 46 - 0.2P$, where quantity is in thousands of riders per day (i.e., 46 = 46 000) and price (the fare) is in cents. The current fare is \$1.30 (i.e., $P = 130$) and there are 20 000 riders per day. The CTA hires you to advise on how much it should increase the fare in order to maximize its revenues (i.e., the total expenditure of its riders). What advice will you give the CTA? [*Hint*: You do not need to actually *calculate* any elasticities. Review Figure 4-5 in the text, then find the expenditure-maximizing price from the equation.]

EXERCISES

1. **Calculating and Classifying the Price Elasticity of Demand**
   This exercise reviews your ability to calculate and classify elasticity. In each of the following scenarios, categorize the price elasticity of demand as *elastic, perfectly elastic, inelastic, perfectly inelastic,* or *unit-elastic.* Where calculations are required, use average price and quantity. [*Hint:* There are two cases where categorization is not possible with the information provided.]

   (a) The price of personal computers falls from $2750 to $2250, and the quantity demanded increases from 40 000 units to 60 000 units.

   (b) Canada Post increases the price of a stamp from 48 cents to 50 cents, but expenditure on postage stamps remains the same.

   (c) The price of a book of matches doubles from 1 cent to 2 cents, but the quantity purchased does not change.

   (d) An increase in the demand for blue jeans causes the price to increase from $45 to $55 and the amount purchased to increase from 1 million to 1.1 million.

   (e) A sudden decline in the supply of avocados leads to an increase in price by 10 percent and an accompanying reduction in quantity demanded by 20 000 units from the original level of 90 000 units.

   (f) A 5 percent decrease in the price of gasoline results in a decrease in gasoline expenditure of 5 percent.

   (g) A 10 percent increase in consumer income results in a 15 percent increase in the price of snowboards as well as a 15 percent increase in purchases.

   (h) Canadian farmers increase their output of wheat by 25 percent and there is no change in the price of wheat.

2. **Elasticity and Total Expenditure**
This exercise reviews the relationship between the price elasticity of demand and total expenditure. Two alternative demand curves are shown in the upper panels of Figure 4-1.

Figure 4-1

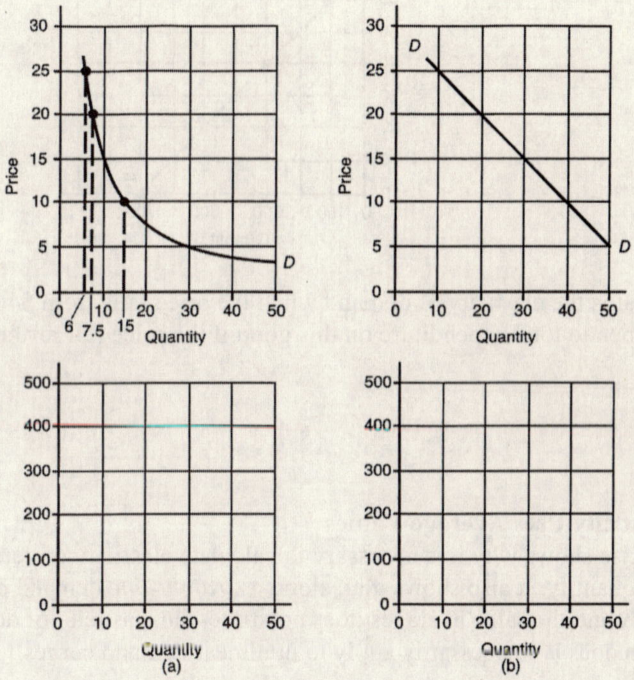

(a) Calculate the total expenditure associated with each demand curve at the following prices: $25, $20, $15, $10, and $5. Graph the respective total expenditure curves in the grids provided in the lower panels of Figure 4-1.

(b) By inspection of these expenditure curves, what can you say about the price elasticity of demand along each of the demand curves?

3. **Linear Demand and Elasticity**
This exercise establishes the point that elasticity is not constant along a straight-line demand curve. [*Note*: Extension Exercise E4 establishes the same point using a different method.]

(a) Calculate the numerical values of price elasticity along the linear demand curve in Figure 4-2, using the four price–quantity segments indicated by the dots (i.e., the arcs *A* to *B*, *B* to *C*, *C* to *D*, and *D* to *E*). Confirm that elasticity declines as price decreases even though the slope is constant.

Figure 4-2

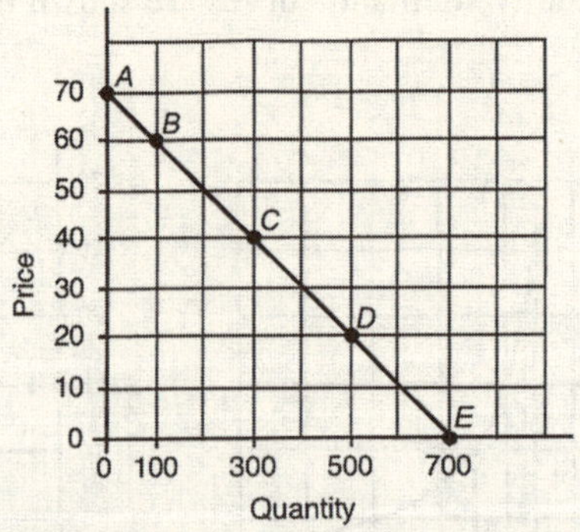

(b) What is the elasticity of demand when the price falls from $40 to $30? What would happen to total expenditure on this good if the price fell further?

4. **Why Elasticity Uses Average Values**
This exercise shows why it is necessary to calculate elasticity of demand using average price and quantity. It also shows that, along a *straight-line* demand curve, the magnitude of changes around the same averages does not affect the elasticity of demand. [*Note*: This conclusion does *not* necessarily apply to nonlinear demand curves.]

Figure 4-3

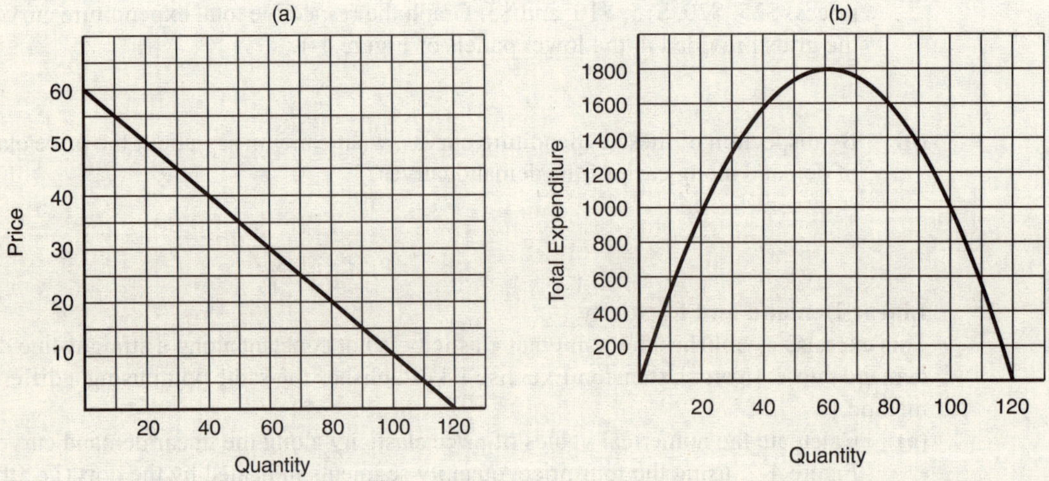

(a) What is total spending on this good at P = $40? At P = $20? Draw the prices and quantities in Figure 4-3(a) and the total expenditures and quantities in Fig. 4-3(b).

(b) What would be the elasticity between $P = \$40$ and $P = \$20$ if you calculated the change in price as a percentage of \$40 and the change in quantity as a percentage of 40 units? Would this result be consistent with the change in total spending?

(c) What would be the elasticity between $P = \$40$ and $P = \$20$ if you calculated the change in price as a percentage of \$20 and the change in quantity as a percentage of 80 units? Would this result be consistent with the change in total spending?

(d) What is the elasticity of demand between $P = \$40$ and $P = \$20$ when correctly calculated using the average price and average quantity? Is this consistent with the change in total spending? What can you conclude about the reason for using average price and quantity in the calculation of elasticity?

(e) What is total expenditure at $P = \$50$? At $P = \$10$? Draw these points in Figure 4-3. What is elasticity of demand between these two prices? Is this elasticity consistent with the change in total expenditure?

(f) Comparing what you found in (d) with what you found in (e), fill in the blanks in the following statement: On a *straight-line* demand curve, any changes that have the same __________ price and quantity give __________ elasticity.

5. **A "Quick Method" for Use with Linear Demand Curves**
This exercise teaches a quicker way to calculate elasticity once the slope of the demand curve is known. In the process you will find another way to write the formula for elasticity.

(a) In Figure 4-3(a) in Exercise 4 above, what is the elasticity of demand between $P = \$45$ and $P = \$35$?

(b) What is the slope of the demand curve (i.e., $\Delta P/\Delta Q$)?

(c) What is the ratio of price to quantity *at the mid-point* of the range between $P = \$45$ and $P = \$35$ (i.e., P_{AVE}/Q_{AVE})? Divide this ratio by the slope of the demand curve. How does the result compare with the elasticity you calculated in (a)?

Notice that in (c) you actually calculated elasticity *at a point* on the demand curve using the formula $(P/Q)/(\Delta P/\Delta Q)$. Use this formula for (d). [*Hint:* You do not have to recalculate $\Delta P/\Delta Q$ since it is constant all along a linear demand curve.]

(d) What is the elasticity of demand at $P = \$20$? Would this be the elasticity of demand if price changed from \$25 to \$15? From \$30 to \$10? Why?

6. **A Ray of Light on a Straight-Line Demand Curve**

In Exercise 5 you saw that the formula for elasticity can be written as $(P/Q)/(\Delta P/\Delta Q)$. On a diagram, P/Q is the slope of the *ray from the origin* (i.e., the line from the "zero" point) to a point on the demand curve. Since the slope of the curve $(\Delta P/\Delta Q)$ is constant all along a straight-line demand curve, the value of elasticity falls as the ray gets flatter (i.e., $(P/Q)/(\Delta P/\Delta Q)$ gets smaller as P/Q falls). This makes it very easy to see how elasticity changes along a straight-line demand curve. [Very useful in exams!]

Draw for yourself any straight-line demand curve. For each of the following questions, draw the ray from the origin to the relevant point on the demand curve and compare the slope of the ray to the slope of the curve. The answers come easily.

(a) The slope of the ray to the *mid-point* on the demand curve equals the (absolute value of) the slope of the curve. What is elasticity at the mid-point?

(b) Pick a price *above* the mid-point and draw the ray. How does the slope of the ray compare to the slope of the curve? What does this say about elasticity?

(c) Pick a price *lower* than the mid-point and draw the ray. What do you see now? What does this say about elasticity?

(d) What is the slope of the ray to the point on the demand curve where quantity demanded = 0? What is elasticity?

(e) What is the slope of the ray to the point on the demand curve at price = \$0? What is elasticity?

7. **The Elasticity of Supply**

This exercise reviews the calculation of the elasticity of supply, and compares elasticities of supply for straight-line supply curves. Find the answers by computing the elasticities between the points indicated on the supply curves in Figure 4-4.

Figure 4-4

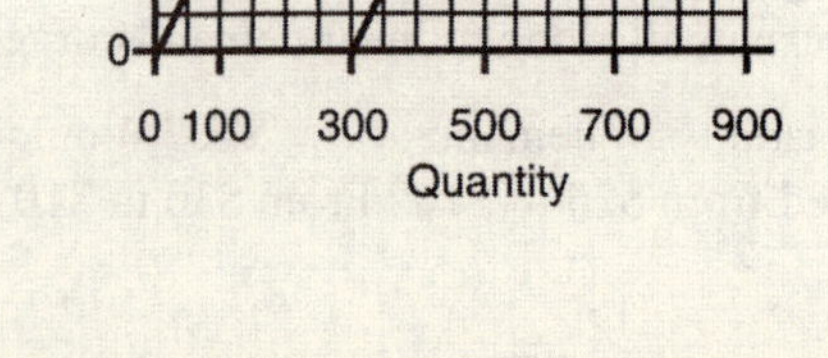

(a) Demonstrate that the elasticity of supply equals 1 all along S_1. How is this result related to the fact that this supply curve passes through the origin?

(b) Demonstrate that elasticity falls as price increases along S_2.

(c) Compare the elasticities on S_1 and S_3 between $P = \$40$ and $P = \$60$. What does this comparison tell you about the effect on elasticity when a linear supply curve takes a parallel shift to right (an increase in supply)?

(d) What does your conclusion in (c) imply about the effect on elasticity when a linear supply curve takes a parallel shift to left (a reduction in supply)?

8. **Tax Incidence**

Tax incidence depends upon the elasticities of demand and supply. This exercise illustrates the relationship. [*Note*: For the mathematically inclined, the Extension Exercise on tax incidence proves the relationship.]

The following diagrams show the demand and supply curves in the markets for beer and orange juice. Suppose a sales tax of $\$t$ per litre is imposed in each of these markets.

Figure 4-5

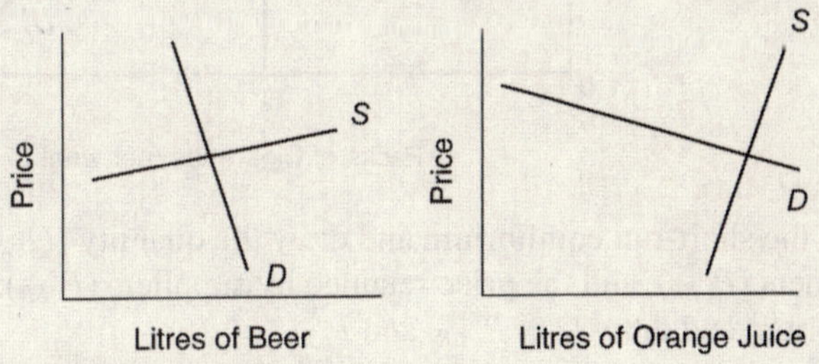

(a) Shift the appropriate curve to show the impact of the tax in each market. Label the new consumer price and seller price in the beer market P_{CB} and P_{SB}, respectively. In the market for orange juice, label them P_{CJ} and P_{SJ}, respectively.

(b) In which market is most of the burden of the tax borne by consumers? What do you see when you compare the elasticities of demand and supply in this market?

(c) In which market is most of the tax borne by producers? What do you see when you compare the elasticities of demand and supply in this market?

(d) In which market is the difference between the consumer price and the seller price greater?

9. Tax Incidence, Elasticity, and Overshooting

This exercise expands on Exercise 8 to demonstrate why policy-makers may need to take a longer-term perspective. In the example used here, the objective is to reduce smoking without reducing the standard of living of lower-income families. The exercise combines the relationship between tax incidence and elasticity with the relationship between elasticity and time.

In Figure 4-6, D_{SR} is the short-run demand curve for cigarettes and D_{LR} is the long-run demand curve. Government puts an excise tax on cigarettes of \$t per pack. Before the tax, equilibrium is at P^* per pack and Q^* packs per week.

Figure 4-6

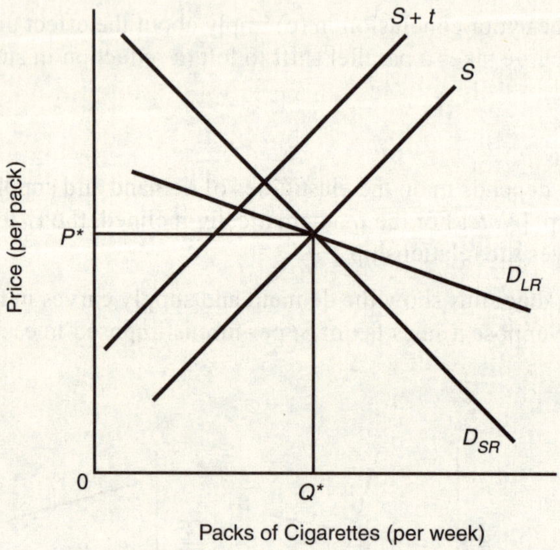

(a) Locate the short-run equilibrium and draw the quantity (Q_{SR}), the price paid by consumers (P^C_{SR}), and the price retained by suppliers (P^S_{SR}). Locate the long-run equilibrium and draw Q_{LR}, P^C_{LR}, and P^S_{LR}.

(b) How does the effect of the tax on equilibrium quantity differ between the short run and the long run? Why?

(c) How does the incidence of the tax differ between the short run and the long run? Why?

(d) How does the effect of the tax on total consumer spending on cigarettes differ between the short run and the long run? Why?

(e) Does this policy meet the policy-makers' objective in the short run? Why/why not?

(f) Does this policy meet the policy-makers' objective in the long run? Why/why not?

EXTENSION EXERCISES

E1. Elasticities and *Ceteris Paribus*

Calculating the elasticity of one variable in response to changes in another requires holding all other variables constant (i.e., *ceteris paribus*). This exercise establishes the point. [*Note*: Successful completion of this exercise would indicate that you have a very good understanding of elasticity.]

The following table provides data on income as well as prices and quantity demanded of goods x and y for five different periods (or observations). You are asked to calculate different elasticities of demand (price elasticity, income elasticity, and cross elasticity) between periods that satisfy the "other things constant" condition.

Period	Income	P_x	$Q^D{}_x$	P_y	$Q^D{}_y$
(1)	$10 000	$25	10	$10	42
(2)	10 000	28	9	10	40
(3)	10 000	28	8	15	35
(4)	11 000	28	9	15	36
(5)	11 500	34	7	20	32

(a) Why should no elasticities be calculated between periods 4 and 5?

(b) For each of the following, calculate the relevant elasticity from the changes that occur between the two appropriate periods:
price elasticity for x is ________, based upon periods _____ and _____;
price elasticity for y is ________, based upon periods _____ and _____;
income elasticity for x is ________, based upon periods _____ and _____;
income elasticity for y is ________, based upon periods _____ and _____;
cross elasticity of demand for y with respect to the price of x is ________, based upon periods _____ and _____;
cross elasticity of demand for x with respect to the price of y is ________, based upon the periods _____ and _____.

E2. Diagrammatic Features of Elasticity

The classification of elasticity can often be determined by diagrammatic features of the relevant curves. The six diagrams in Figure 4-7 represent different combinations of elasticities of demand and supply at the equilibrium price P_E. Indicate which diagrams correspond to each of the following statements. (η_d refers to elasticity of demand, and η_s refers to elasticity of supply).

(a) η_d is greater than one and η_s is unity ________

(b) η_d is unity and η_s is infinity ________

(c) η_d is unity and η_s is unity ________

(d) η_d is greater than one and η_s is zero ________

(e) η_d is zero and η_s is unity ________

(f) η_d is infinity and η_s is unity ________

Figure 4-7

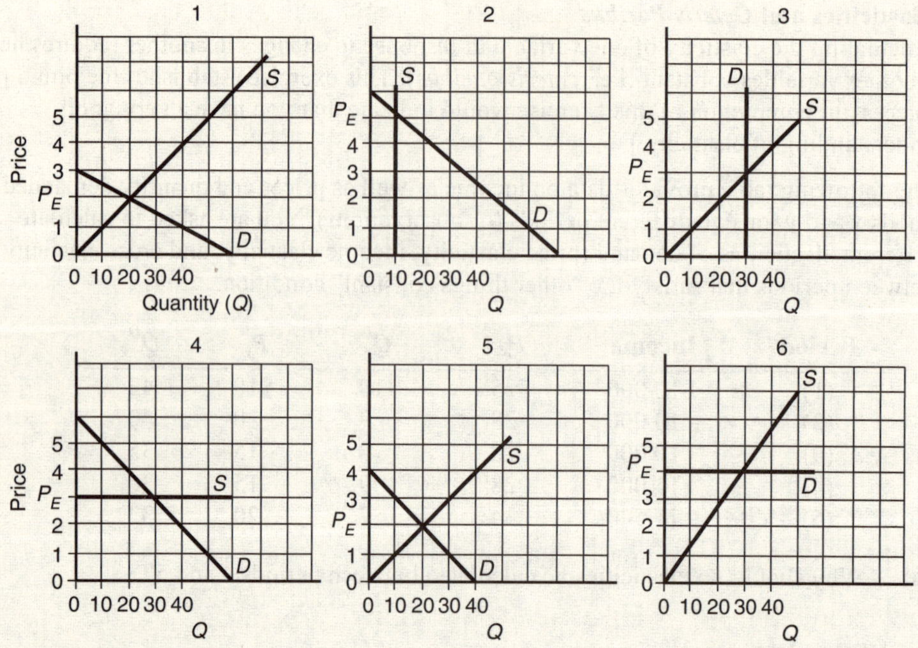

E3. Tax Incidence Using Equations

This exercise takes you step-by-step to the results of *Extensions in Theory 4-1* in the text. Draw an illustrative diagram—not a scale diagram—as you go along, to give a visual perspective on what is happening. [*Note:* This exercise is intended only for students covering *Extensions in Theory 4-1* in their course.]

(a) Using P^C for the price paid by consumers and P^S for the price retained by suppliers, the equations for the (linear) demand and supply curves are:

	General Form	This Exercise
Demand:	$Q^D = a - bP^C$	$Q^D = 200 - 0.5P^C$
Supply:	$Q^S = c + dP^S$	$Q^S = 20 + 0.25P^S$

[To draw your diagram, recall that (i) 200 and 20 are the quantity axis intercepts of the demand and supply curves, respectively, and (ii) –0.5 and 0.25 are the *reciprocals* (the inverse) of the slopes of the curves.]

At first there is no tax, so $P^C = P^S$. Calculate equilibrium price (P_E) and quantity (Q_E) with no tax.

(b) Introduce an excise tax (t) of $60 per unit sold. Now, $P^C = P^S + t$ and $P^S = P^C - t$. In the supply equation, replace P^S with $P^C - t$ and rewrite the equation to get the tax-inclusive supply function as a relationship between Q^S and P^C.

(c) Use the demand equation in (a) and the tax-inclusive supply equation derived in (b) to solve for the new equilibrium P^C. What is the change in P^C $(= \Delta P^C)$ caused by the tax? Since $P^S = P^C - 60$, what is the change in P^S $(= \Delta P^S)$? What is the tax incidence on consumers and suppliers (i.e., the change in each price as a proportion of the tax)?

(d) Put the tax-inclusive P^C from (c) in the demand equation from (a) to find the new quantity demanded. Put the after-tax P^S from (c) in the supply equation from (a) to find the new quantity supplied. Does quantity demanded equal quantity supplied? [*Hint:* If not, the prices found in (c) are wrong.] What is the change in equilibrium quantity (ΔQ_E) as a result of the tax?

You have now found *what* the effects of the tax are. The next steps show you *why*.

(e) Take the (absolute value) of the slope of the demand curve (i.e., the value of 1/b) and divide it by the sum of the (absolute values) of the demand and supply curve slopes (i.e., 1/b + 1/d). Where have you seen this number before? Multiply it by the amount of the tax (t = $60). Where have you seen this number before?

Now write the general form (i.e., using the letters instead of the numbers) of the equation for the effect of the tax on P^C. [*Hint*: It does not look the same as the equation in the text, but it means the same.]

$\Delta P^C =$

(f) Repeat section (e) using the slope of the supply curve (i.e., 1/d) as the numerator.

Write the general form of the equation for the effect of the tax on P^S.

$\Delta P^S =$

(g) How would ΔP^C and ΔP^S change if you increased the slope of the demand curve (i.e., made demand less elastic) and reduced the slope of the supply curve (i.e., made supply more elastic)?

Now fill in the blanks to complete the following statement: The less elastic is supply relative to demand, the greater is the tax incidence on __________ and the __________ it is on __________.

(h) Finally, divide the tax (t = $60) by the denominator you used in (e) and (f). Where have you seen this number before?

Write the general form of the equation for the change in equilibrium quantity.

$\Delta Qe =$

Would ΔQe change if you increased the slope of the demand curve (1/b) and reduced the slope of the supply curve (1/d) by exactly the same amount?

Fill in the spaces to complete the following statement: The effect of a sales tax on the equilibrium quantity depends solely on the amount of the tax and the _________ the slopes of the demand and supply curves, regardless of their _________ slopes.

Exercises E4 and E5 are based on material in *Additional Topics: Some Further Details about Demand Elasticity* on the text's MyEconLab website for Chapter 4. They use elasticity at a point on the demand curve (the *point elasticity* of demand) rather than the elasticity between two points (the *arc elasticity* of demand).

The point elasticity of demand is calculated as the ratio of price to quantity (P/Q) at a point on the demand curve, divided by the slope of the demand curve. On a linear demand curve, the slope ($\Delta P/\Delta Q$) is the same at all points. [*Note:* The slope is $\Delta P/\Delta Q$ because price is measured on the vertical axis and quantity on the horizontal axis.] Dividing by the slope, $\Delta P/\Delta Q$, is the same as multiplying by the reciprocal of the slope, $\Delta Q/\Delta P$. Thus:

$$\eta_d = (P/Q)/(\Delta P/\Delta Q) \quad \text{or} \quad \eta_d = (P/Q) \times (\Delta Q/\Delta P)$$

For the linear demand curve $Q = a - bP$, $\Delta P/\Delta Q = 1/b$, so the point elasticity formula is:

$$\eta_d = (P/Q)/(1/b) \quad \text{or} \quad \eta_d = (P/Q) \times b$$

E4. Point Elasticity Along a Straight-Line Demand Curve

Using the point elasticity formula and the linear demand curve equation $Q^D = 200 - 2P$, complete the table below. [An example row is done for you.] Sketch your own illustrative diagram to give a visual perspective as you go through the exercise.

				Expenditure as Price	
Price	**Quantity**	η_d	**Description**	**Falls**	**Rises**
$100					
$ 80	40	4	elastic	increases	decreases
$ 60					
$ 50					
$ 40					
$ 20					
$ 0					

E5. Point Elasticity on Different Demand Curves

This exercise again shows that elasticity is more than just slope, this time by comparing elasticities (at the same price) *between* linear demand curves rather than *along* a curve. The equations for the demand curves in Figure 4-8 are:

D_0: $Q = 30 - P$ $\quad$ D_1: $Q = 40 - 2P$ $\quad$ D_2: $Q = 60 - 2P$ $\quad$ D_3: $Q = 80 - 2P$

Figure 4-8

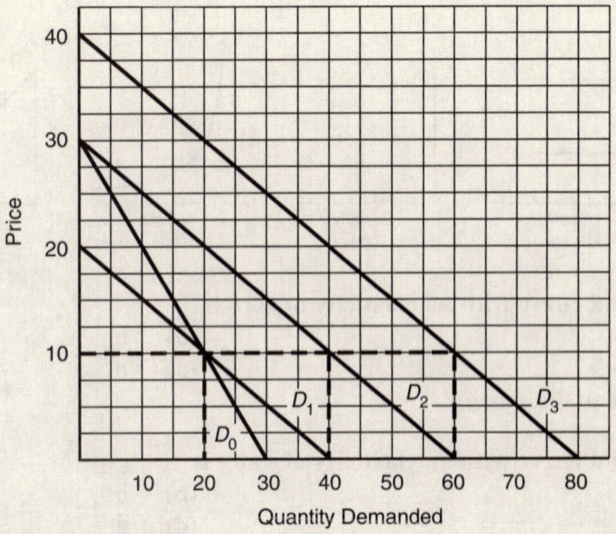

(a) Complete the following table:

Curve	Price	Quantity	Slope	Elasticity
D_0	\$10			
D_1	\$10			
D_2	\$10			
D_3	\$10			

(b) Complete the following statements using the results found in (a). In all cases the comparison is between price elasticities at *the same price* on different *straight-line* demand curves.

(i) When two demand curves intersect at a positive quantity, the one with the ________ slope is ________ elastic.

(ii) When two demand curves with different slopes have the same price–axis intercept, the elasticity of demand of the flatter curve is ________ that of the steeper curve.

(iii) When demand increases with no change in slope, elasticity ________.

(iv) When two demand curves with different slopes do not intersect at any price, elasticity on the outer curve is ________ than on the inner curve ________ slope.

ADDITIONAL MULTIPLE-CHOICE QUESTIONS

***1. If the price elasticity of demand for a good is 2 and price increases by 2 percent, the quantity demanded**

(a) decreases by 4 percent.
(b) decreases by 1 percent.
(c) decreases by 2 percent.
(d) does not change.
(e) is indeterminable with data provided.

Questions 2 through 5 refer to the four diagrams in Figure 4-9.

Figure 4-9

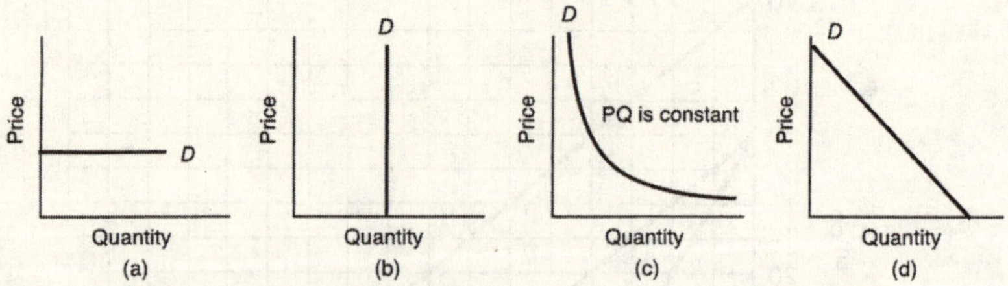

2. The demand curve with an elasticity of zero is

(a) a. (b) b.
(c) c. (d) d.
(e) None of the above.

3. The demand curve with an elasticity of unity is

(a) a. (b) b.
(c) c. (d) d.
(e) None of the above.

4. The demand curve with an elasticity of infinity is

(a) a. (b) b.
(c) c. (d) d.
(e) None of the above.

5. The demand curve with an elasticity that is variable is

(a) a. (b) b.
(c) c. (d) d.
(e) Both (c) and (d).

***6. The price elasticity of demand for snowmobiles is estimated to be 1.2; thus an increase in price**

(a) always decreases quantity demanded by 12 percent.
(b) always decreases quantity demanded by 1.2 percent.
(c) increases total expenditure.
(d) decreases total expenditure.
(e) decreases total expenditure by 1.2 percent.

***7. If the demand for some commodity has an elasticity of unity, a decrease in price**

(a) causes a 1 percent decrease in quantity demanded.
(b) induces no change in quantity demanded.
(c) results in no change in total expenditure.
(d) is matched by a unit increase in quantity demanded.
(e) Both (a) and (c) are correct.

Questions 8 to 10 refer to the following schedule. (Use average prices and quantities in your calculations.)

Price per Unit	Quantity Offered for Sale
$10	400
8	350
6	300
4	200
2	50

8. As price increases from $4 to $6, the elasticity of supply is

(a) 1.0.
(b) 50.
(c) 0.5.
(d) 5.0.
(e) 2.0.

***9. As price rises from $6 to $10 per unit, the supply response is**

(a) elastic.
(b) of unit elasticity.
(c) of zero elasticity.
(d) inelastic.
(e) infinitely elastic.

***10. The supply curve implied by the schedule is**

(a) elastic for all price ranges.
(b) inelastic for all price ranges.
(c) of zero elasticity for all price ranges.
(d) of variable elasticity, depending on the initial price chosen.
(e) of constant elasticity.

11. A perfectly inelastic demand curve means that

(a) a percentage decrease in price increases quantity demanded by the exact same percentage.
(b) an increase in price reduces quantity demanded.
(c) the price elasticity of demand is infinity.
(d) any change in price is perfectly matched by a change in quantity demanded.
(e) quantity demanded does not change in response to any price change.

12. A decrease in income by 10 percent leads to a decrease in quantity demanded by 5 percent; the income elasticity of demand is therefore

(a) –0.5.
(b) 2.0.
(c) 0.5.
(d) 50.0.
(e) 15.0.

***13. A commodity is classified as a normal good if**

(a) a decrease in consumer income results in a decrease in demand.
(b) it is consumed by a majority of the population.
(c) its price and quantity demanded are negatively related, *ceteris paribus.*
(d) an increase in its price leads to an increase in quantity supplied.
(e) a decrease in consumer income results in an increase in demand.

14. If an individual allocates $200 as monthly expenditure on compact discs and decides to spend no more and no less regardless of price, this individual's demand for compact discs is

(a) perfectly inelastic.
(b) perfectly elastic.
(c) of unit elasticity.
(d) less than one but greater than zero.
(e) of zero elasticity.

15. A shift in demand would not affect price when supply is

(a) perfectly inelastic.
(b) perfectly elastic.
(c) of unit elasticity.
(d) a straight line through the origin.
(e) of zero elasticity.

***16. The producers' share of the burden of a sales tax will be greater**

(a) the more elastic is supply.
(b) the more inelastic is supply.
(c) the more elastic is demand.
(d) the more inelastic is demand.
(e) Both (b) and (c) are correct.

***17. Suppose the market supply curve is upward sloping. If the imposition of a sales tax causes no change in the price consumers pay, the good's demand curve must be _________, implying that the burden of the tax is _______________.**

(a) vertical; entirely borne by producers
(b) horizontal; entirely borne by consumers
(c) perfectly inelastic; shared equally by consumers and producers
(d) perfectly elastic; entirely borne by producers
(e) downward sloping; shared by consumers and producers

18. If two goods have a negative cross-price elasticity of demand, we know that

(a) they are both inferior goods.
(b) they are substitutes.
(c) they are both normal goods.
(d) they are complementary goods.
(e) one is inferior and the other is normal, but we can't determine which is which.

***19. Pizza and hamburgers are likely to have**

(a) a positive cross elasticity of demand.
(b) positive income elasticities of demand.
(c) a negative cross elasticity of demand.
(d) price elasticities of demand greater than one.
(e) a cross elasticity of demand equal to zero.

***20. A commodity with an income elasticity equal to –0.5**

(a) is said to have an inelastic demand.
(b) is an inferior good.
(c) is a complementary good.
(d) has a downward sloping demand curve.
(e) has a demand curve with a constant slope of 0.5 in absolute terms.

Elasticity at a Point on the Demand Curve

Questions 21 to 24 are mainly intended for students covering material in *Additional Topics: Some Further Details about Demand Elasticity* on the text's MyEconLab website for Chapter 4. They use elasticity at a point on the demand curve (the *point elasticity* of demand) rather than the elasticity between two points (the *arc elasticity* of demand). Point elasticity is very useful for showing how elasticity changes along a straight-line demand curve (as Exercise 6), and for comparing elasticities between different demand curves (as Extension Exercise E4).

The elasticity formula in the text can be rearranged to give $\eta_d = (P/Q)/(\Delta P/\Delta Q)$, which is the price/quantity ratio at a point divided by the slope of the demand curve. It can also be written as $\eta_d = (P/Q) \times (\Delta Q/\Delta P)$, which is the P/Q ratio multiplied by the inverse of the slope.

Use the following figure to answer Questions 21 to 23.

Figure 4-10

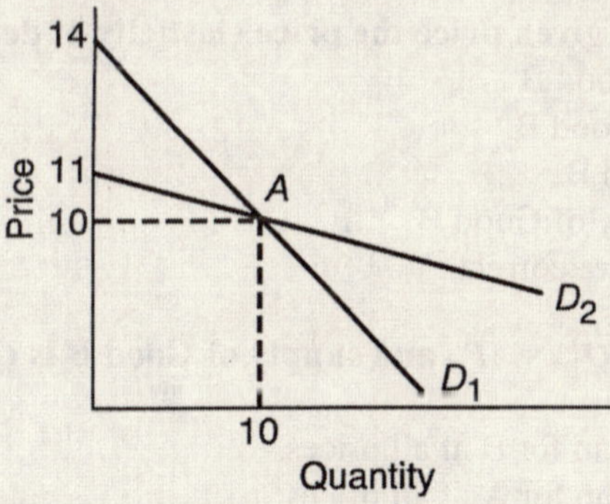

Example Question: What is the elasticity for D_1 at point A?
At A both P and $Q = 10$, so $P/Q = 1$. The constant slope along the straight-line demand curve D_1 is the change in price from \$14 to \$10 (so $\Delta P = 4$) divided by the change in quantity from 0 to 10 (so $\Delta Q = 10$) giving the slope $(\Delta P/\Delta Q) = 4/10 = 0.4$. At point A, therefore, $\eta_d = (P/Q)/(\Delta P/\Delta Q) = 1/0.4 = 2.5$.

21. The point elasticity of demand for D_2 at point A is

(a) 0.1
(b) 2.5
(c) 1.0
(d) 10.0
(e) 4.0

***22. At a price of \$10, demand curve D_1**

(a) has the same elasticity as any other point along D_1.
(b) is more elastic than at any other price below \$10.
(c) is more elastic than D_2.
(d) is inelastic.
(e) None of the above.

23. Starting from point A, a 10 percent reduction in price along D_1 will result in an increase in quantity demanded of

(a) 25 percent.
(b) 100 percent.
(c) 10 percent
(d) 1 percent.
(e) 2.5 percent.

***24. If two demand curves have the same price–axis intercept but different slopes, then at a given price**

(a) the one with the flatter slope is more elastic.
(b) they have the same elasticity.
(c) the one with the steeper slope is more elastic.
(d) they are both unit elastic regardless of price.
(e) the relative elasticities are unknown, because elasticity is different at each price.

Elasticity Using Equations

These questions are intended for courses that use equations to describe the demand and supply functions, and Questions 25 through 27 use point price elasticity (explained before Question 21 above). For demand equation $Q^D = a - bP$, the slope is 1/b and price elasticity of demand at a specific price is $\eta = (P/Q)/(1/b)$ or $\eta = (P/Q) \times (b)$. For supply equation $Q^S = c + dP$, the slope is 1/d and price elasticity of supply is $\eta = (P/Q)/(1/d)$ or $\eta = (P/Q) \times (d)$.

***25. If demand for Good A is $Q^D_A = 200 - 1P_A$ and demand for Good B is $Q^D_B = 100 - 0.5P_B$, at a given price the price elasticity of demand for Good A is**

(a) the same as for Good B
(b) greater than for Good B.
(c) less than for Good B.
(d) twice the elasticity of Good B.
(e) Both (b) and (d) are correct.

***26. If supply of Good A is $Q^S_A = 4P_A$ and supply of Good B is $Q^S_B = 2P_B$, the price elasticity of supply**

(a) is greater for A than for B at all prices.
(b) is greater for B than for A at all prices.
(c) decreases for both A and B as price rises.
(d) equals unity at all prices on both supply curves.
(e) increases for both A and B as price rises.

***27. Along the same linear demand curve, elasticity of demand (i) between P = \$10 and P = \$8, (ii) between P = \$12 and P = \$6, and (iii) at P = \$9**

(a) is the same for all three cases.
(b) is greater between P = \$12 and P = \$6 than for the other two cases.
(c) is smaller at P = \$9 than for the other two cases.
(d) is the same at P = \$9 as between P = \$10 and P = \$8, but both are greater than between P = \$12 and P = \$6.
(e) cannot be compared, because quantity demanded and change in quantity demanded are unknown.

***28. The demand function for widgets is $Q^D = a - b_1P - b_2Y - b_3P_A$, where P is the price of widgets, Y is average household income, and P_A is the price of ayogs. This function says**

(a) widgets are a Giffen good.
(b) widgets are an inferior good, and ayogs and widgets are substitute goods.
(c) widgets are a normal good, and ayogs and widgets are substitute goods.
(d) widgets are a normal good, and ayogs and widgets are complementary goods.
(e) widgets are an inferior good, and ayogs and widgets are complementary goods.

SOLUTIONS

Chapter Review

1.(a) **2.**(d) **3.**(b) **4.**(d) **5.**(b) **6.**(a) **7.**(d) **8.**(e) **9.**(a) **10.**(c) **11.**(d) **12.**(a) **13.**(a) **14.**(d) **15.**(b) **16.**(e) **17.**(e) **18.**(c) **19.**(d) **20.**(c) **21.**(e) **22.**(a)

Short-Answer Questions

1. For substitutes, price and demand move in the same direction (e.g., an increase in the price of cola increases demand for Sprite). For complements, they move in opposite directions (e.g., an increase in price of CDs reduces demand for CD players).

2. No. These are the same absolute changes but different percentage changes. $100 is a much smaller percentage change in the price of automobiles than in the price of TV sets, and 50 000 is a bigger percentage of automobile sales than of TV sales. Thus there would be a bigger percentage change in quantity demanded and a smaller percentage change in price for automobiles than TV sets, hence a larger elasticity of demand for automobiles. [*Note*: Since these numbers are purely hypothetical, so are the conclusions about relative elasticities of automobiles and TV sets in the real world.]

3. Kit-Kat bars have a significantly bigger price elasticity of demand, since there are many more close substitutes for a particular type of candy than for candy as a whole.

4. In everyday language, a necessity is something a person "can't do without." In economics, it is a commodity with an income elasticity of demand that is positive but less than unity. Likely example—eggs, or some other food staple. People can do without eggs, but the income elasticity of demand likely is quite small.

5. For consumers to bear such a high burden of the tax, demand would have to be much less elastic than supply. If demand were *inelastic* (i.e., price elasticity less than 1), spending on beer would increase, leaving *less* money to spend on food and clothing. [*Note*: The policy could work in the longer term if the long-run demand curve for beer were more elastic than the short-run demand, but this would not change the inconsistency in Mr. Quitit's reasoning.]

6. (a) down; (b) none; (c) 1; (d) down; (e) up.

7. On the demand curve $Q^D = 46 - 0.2P$, the mid-point at which elasticity = 1 and revenue is maximized is at 23 (000) riders. The revenue-maximizing price is $0.2P = 23$ cents, $P = 115$ cents ($1.15). The current fare of $1.30 is greater than $1.15, so it is on the *elastic* part of the demand curve. Raising price would reduce revenue (i.e., expenditure of riders), not increase it. You should advise the CTA to *reduce* the fare to $1.15.

Exercises

1. **(a)** $\eta = 2.0 = (20\ 000/500 \times 2500/50\ 000)$; elastic demand (i.e., >1)

(b) Elasticity of unity – constant expenditure means $\%\Delta Q = \%\Delta P$.

(c) Perfectly inelastic demand (elasticity = 0). The percentage change in Q is zero, and zero divided by anything is zero.

(d) η cannot be determined because the demand curve has shifted—i.e., other things are not constant (*ceteris paribus* condition violated).

(e) The 20 000 change (from 90 000 to 70 000) is 25% of the 80 000 average. $\eta = (\%\Delta Q/\%\Delta P) = 25/10 = 2.5$. Since 2.5 > 1, demand is elastic.

(f) Perfectly inelastic demand. For a 5% fall in price to reduce expenditure by 5%, quantity must be unchanged. $\eta = (\%\Delta Q/\%\Delta P) = 0/5 = 0$.

(g) η can't be determined because the demand curve shifts—so all other things are *not* constant (i.e., the *ceteris paribus* condition is violated).

(h) $\eta = (\%\Delta Q/\%\Delta P) = 25/0$ = infinity (undefined). Demand is perfectly elastic.

2. (a) **Figure 4-11**

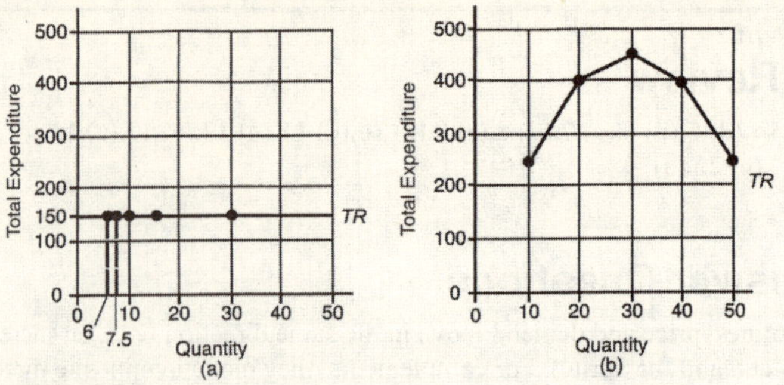

(b) Panel (a): Multiplying P by Q at each price gives the same total expenditure at every point on the demand curve. A constant expenditure means that the percentage rise in Q equals the percentage fall in P, so the price elasticity of demand ($\%\Delta Q/\%\Delta P$) must equal unity all along this demand curve.
Panel (b): Since total expenditure increases as price falls from \$25 to \$20 to \$15, demand is elastic over this range. Total expenditure is at its maximum value of \$450 when price equals \$15; this corresponds to unit elasticity. As price decreases from \$15 to \$10 and then to \$5, total revenue falls so demand is inelastic along this portion of the demand curve.

3. (a) The following measures express elasticity as $(\Delta Q/\Delta P) \times (P_A/Q_A)$, where Q_A and P_A are the average quantity and price, respectively, and $(\Delta Q/\Delta P)$ is the reciprocal (inverse) of the slope.
A–B, $\eta = (100/10)(65/50) = (10)(1.3) = 13.0$;
B–C, $\eta = (200/20)(50/200) = (10)(0.25) = 2.5$;
C–D, $\eta = (200/20)(30/400) = (10)(0.075) = 0.75$;
D–E, $\eta = (200/20)(10/600) = (10)(0.0167) = 0.167$.
[Note that in all cases the reciprocal of the slope is 10, so the slope = 1/10 = 0.1]

(b) $\eta = (\Delta Q/\Delta P)(P_A/Q_A) = (100/10)(35/350) = 1.0$. Over this price range, demand is unit-elastic so total expenditure is constant. With further reductions in price, total expenditure will decline as we move into the inelastic portion of the demand curve.

4. **Figure 4-12**

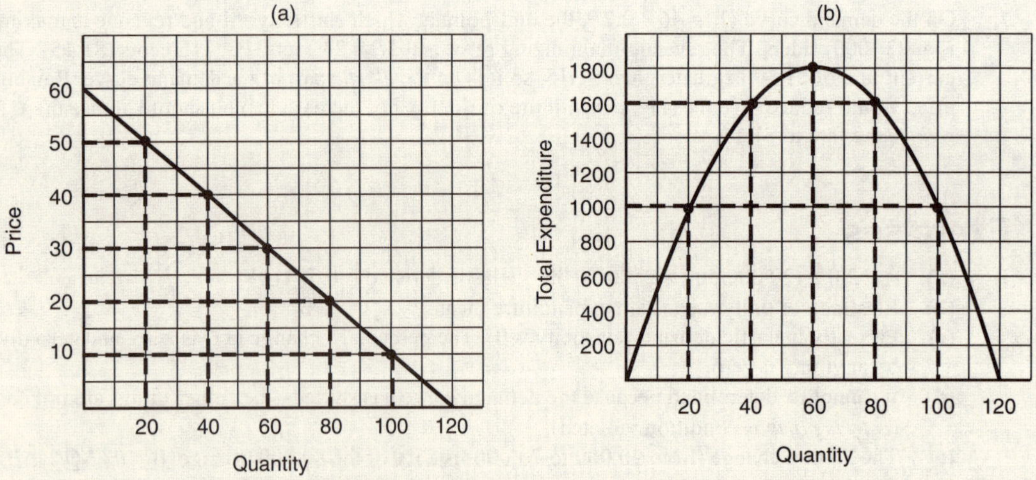

(a) At $P = \$40$ and $Q = 40$, TE $= P \times Q = 40(40) = \$1600$. At $P = \$20$ and $Q = 80$, TE $= P \times Q = 20(80) = \$1600$. [*Note*: TE is constant because the average $P = (40 + 20)/2 = 30$, and $P = \$30$ is the mid-point of the demand curve, where $\eta = 1$. Similarly, the average $Q = (40 + 80)/2 = 60$, which is the mid-point of the demand curve read from the quantity axis.]

(b) Calculating elasticity this way would give $\eta = (\Delta Q/Q)/(\Delta P/P) = (40/40)/(20/40) = 1(0.5) = 2$. This would imply an elastic demand, meaning that expenditure would increase when price fell from \$40 to \$20. But this is not consistent because expenditure remains constant at \$1600.

(c) This method would give $\eta = (\Delta Q/Q)/(\Delta P/P) = (40/80)/(20/20) = 1(0.5) = 0.5$. This would imply an inelastic demand, meaning that expenditure would decrease when price increased from \$20 to \$40. Again, this is not consistent with a constant expenditure of \$1600.

(d) In this case $\eta = (\Delta Q/Q_{AVE})/(\Delta P/P_{AVE}) = (40/60)/(20/30) = 0.67/0.67 = 1$. This says demand is unit-elastic between \$40 and \$20, meaning expenditure should remain unchanged—which it does. This is consistent. Elasticity calculated using the average values of P and Q, therefore, gives the correct prediction for the change in total expenditure.

(e) At $P = \$50$, $Q = 20$ and TE $= 50 \times 20 = \$1000$. At $P = \$10$, $Q = 100$ and TE $= 10 \times 100 = \$1000$. Total expenditure is constant, which is consistent with $\eta = (\Delta Q/Q_{AVE})/(\Delta P/P_{AVE}) = (80/60)/(40/30) = 1.33/1.33 = 1$.

(f) average; the same

5. **(a)** $\eta = (\Delta Q/Q_{AVE})/(\Delta P/P_{AVE}) = (20/40)/(10/40) = 0.5/0.25 = 2$.

(b) $\Delta P/\Delta Q = (45 - 35)/(30 - 50) = 10/-20 = (-)\,0.5$. [*Note*: The negative sign in parentheses shows the demand curve has a negative slope, but we are using absolute values for elasticity.]

(c) $P_{AVE}/Q_{AVE} = 40/40 = 1$. $(P_{AVE}/Q_{AVE})/(\Delta P/\Delta Q) = 1/0.5 = 2$. This is exactly the same as the value of elasticity calculated in (a).

(d) $(P/Q)/(\Delta P/\Delta Q) = (20/80)/0.5 = 0.25/0.5 = 0.5$. Yes: Elasticity of demand *between* \$25 and \$15, or *between* \$30 and \$10, is exactly the same as elasticity *at* \$20. This is because (i) the slope $(\Delta P/\Delta Q)$ is the same at all points on the linear demand curve, and (ii) the average price and quantity (i.e., \$20 and 80, respectively) are the same over both price ranges.

6. **(a)** Since the slope of the ray (P/Q) = the slope of the curve $(\Delta P/\Delta Q)$, elasticity $= (P/Q)/(\Delta P/\Delta Q) = 1$.

(b) Above the mid-point, the slope of the ray is greater than the slope of the curve, so $(P/Q)/(\Delta P/\Delta Q)$ is greater than unity, and demand is elastic.

(c) Below the mid-point, the slope of the ray is less than the slope of the curve, so $(P/Q)/(\Delta P/\Delta Q)$ is less than unity, and demand is inelastic.

(d) Quantity demanded is zero when price is at the value where the demand curve meets the vertical axis. Here, the ray from the origin is the vertical axis, with a slope of infinity (undefined). Dividing infinity by anything—in this case the slope of the curve—gives infinity. Demand at this point is perfectly elastic.

(e) Here, the ray from the origin is the horizontal axis, with a slope of zero. Dividing zero by anything—in this case by the slope of the curve—gives zero. Demand at this point is perfectly inelastic.

7. **(a)** Along S_1, the elasticities of supply calculated using $(\Delta Q/\Delta P) \times (P_{AVE}/Q_{AVE})$ are: (i) between $P = \$0$ and $P = \$20$, $(100/20)(10/50) = 1$; (ii) between $P = \$20$ and $P = \$40$, $(100/20)(30/150) = 1$; (iii) between $P = \$40$ and $P = \$60$, $(100/20)(50/250) = 1$. Because S_1 is a straight line through the origin, P and Q always change in the same proportion, which gives an elasticity value of 1. This is true for any straight-line supply curve through the origin.

(b) For S_2, when price rises from \$40 to \$50, the price elasticity of supply is $(\Delta Q/\Delta P) \times (P_{AVE}/Q_{AVE}) = (200/10)(45/300) = 3.0$. When price rises from \$50 to \$60, the elasticity is $(200/10)(55/500) = 2.2$. Elasticity falls as price rises along this supply curve.

(c) On S_1, elasticity = 1 (because S_1 is a straight line through the origin—see (a) above). On S_3, $(\Delta Q/\Delta P) \times (P_{AVE}/Q_{AVE}) = (100/20)(50/550) = 5(0.09) = 0.45$. Elasticity falls when the supply curve takes a parallel shift to the right.

(d) This simply reverses (c) above. Since elasticity falls when the supply curve takes a parallel shift to the right, it must increase when the supply curve takes a parallel shift to the left.

8. **(a)** **Figure 4-13**

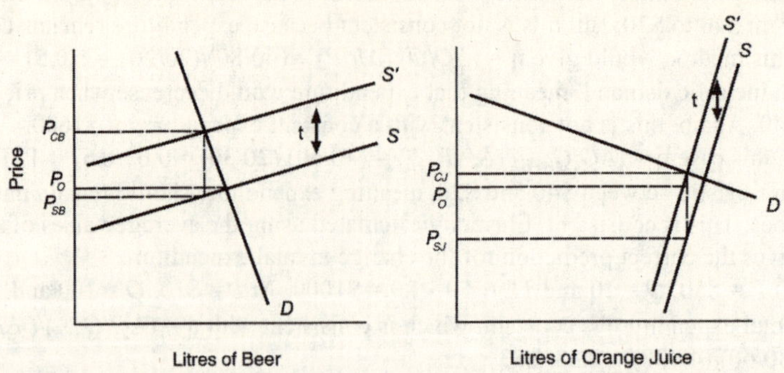

(b) The tax on beer is borne primarily by consumers. The relative slopes of the demand and supply curves in this market suggest that the demand for beer is relatively inelastic, while its supply is relatively elastic.

(c) The tax on orange juice is borne primarily by producers. Demand in this market is relatively elastic, while supply is relatively inelastic.

(d) Neither. The difference between consumer and seller prices is the same $\$t$ in each market.

9. **Figure 4-14**

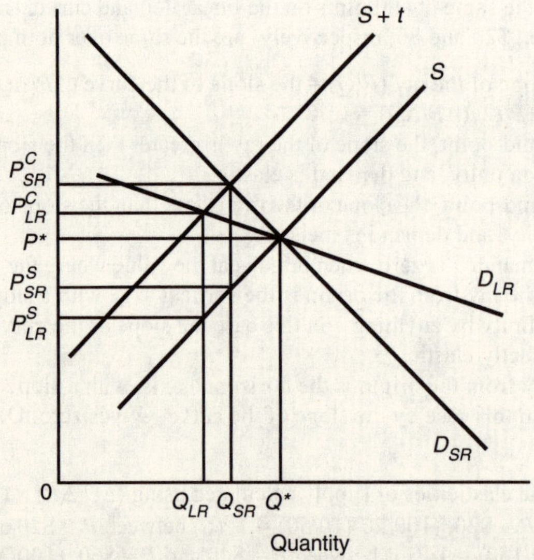

(a) See Figure 4-14.

(b) The effect on equilibrium quantity is greater in the long run, because demand is more elastic in the long run than in the short run (so quantity demanded is more sensitive to changes in price in the long run).

(c) Incidence is greater on the consumer in the short run than in the long run. Because the short-run demand curve is less elastic (or more inelastic) than the long-run demand curve, short-run prices "overshoot" their long-run equilibrium values.

(d) Because the short-run demand is inelastic over the relevant range, the increase in consumer price increases expenditure on cigarettes. The long-run demand curve is less inelastic, causing a smaller increase in consumer spending on cigarettes. If the long-run demand actually is elastic, consumer spending on cigarettes will fall (i.e., less spending on cigarettes than at the pre-tax equilibrium).

(e) No. There is a relatively small reduction in smoking, and the increase in spending on cigarettes will leave less money available to spend on other things, thereby reducing the standard of living of families with smokers.

(f) Likely it will. Because long-run demand is more elastic, there is a bigger fall in smoking and the tax incidence on consumers falls too. If the long-run demand is actually elastic (e.g., because it takes smokers some time to "kick the habit," and the higher prices deter the start of smoking among new younger generations), spending on cigarettes will fall.

Extension Exercises

E1. (a) Elasticity measures are calculated under the *ceteris paribus* assumption that other factors affecting demand are unchanged. Between periods 4 and 5, not only has income changed, but so have the prices of *x* and *y*.

(b) Periods (1) to (2), price elasticity for

$$x = -\frac{9-10}{28-25} \times \frac{(28+25)/2}{(9+10)/2} = 0.93$$

Periods (2) to (3), price elasticity for

$$y = -\frac{35-40}{15-10} \times \frac{(15+10)/2}{(35+40)/2} = 0.33$$

Periods (3) to (4), income elasticity for

$$x = \frac{9-8}{11\,000-10\,000} \times \frac{(11\,000+10\,000)/2}{(9+8)/2} = 1.24$$

Periods (3) to (4), income elasticity for

$$y = \frac{36-35}{11\,000-10\,000} \times \frac{(11\,000+10\,000)/2}{(36+35)/2} = 0.30$$

Periods (1) to (2), cross elasticity of demand for *y* with respect to the price of

$$x = \frac{40-42}{28-25} \times \frac{(28+25)/2}{(40+42)/2} = -0.43$$

Periods (2) to (3), cross elasticity of demand for *x* with respect to the price of

$$y = \frac{8-9}{15-10} \times \frac{(15+10)/2}{(8+9)/2} = -0.29$$

E2. (a) 1 and 6. **(b)** 4.
(c) 5. **(d)** 2.
(e) 3. **(f)** 6.

E3. (a) Setting $Q^D = Q^S$ makes $200 - 0.5P = 20 + 0.25P$, so $0.75P = 180$ and $P = \$240$
$Q_E = 200 - 0.5(240) = 200 - 120 = 80$, and $Q_E = 20 + 0.25(240) = 80$

(b) $Q^S = 20 + 0.25(P^C - 60) = 20 - 0.25(60) - 0.25P^C = 5 + 0.25P^C$

(c) $200 - 0.5P^C = 5 + 0.25P^C$, $0.75P^C = 195$, $P^C = 195/0.75 = \$260$
$\Delta P^C = 260 - 240 = \$20$. $P^S = P^C - t = 260 - 60 = \$200$. $\Delta P^S = 200 - 240 = (-)\$40$
$\Delta P^C/t = 20/60 = 1/3$ (incidence of tax on consumers)
$\Delta P^S/t = 40/60 = 2/3$ (incidence of tax on suppliers)

(d) $Q^D = 200 - 0.5(260) = 200 - 130 = 70$, and $Q^S = 20 + 0.25(200) = 70$. Since $Q^D = Q^S = 70$, this is the new equilibrium. The change in equilibrium quantity is $\Delta Q_E = 70 - 80 = -10$ (i.e., a reduction of 10 units as a result of the tax).

(e) (1/b)/(1/b + 1/d) = (1/0.5)/(1/0.5 + 1/0.25) = 2/6 = 1/3. You have seen this before in (c) above—it is the incidence of the tax on consumers. Multiplying by the amount of the tax gives 1/3(t) = 1/3($60) = $20. You also saw this in (c)—it is the increase in the price paid by consumers (ΔP^C). The general equation for ΔP^C is:

$$\Delta P^C = \frac{\frac{1}{b}}{\frac{1}{b}+\frac{1}{d}} \bullet t$$

(f) (1/d)/(1/b + 1/d) = (1/0.25)/(1/0.5 + 1/0.25) = 4/6 = 2/3. Multiplying by the tax gives 2/3(t) = 2/3($60) = $40. You also saw these values in (c) above: $40 is the fall in price retained by suppliers (ΔP^S), and 2/3 is the incidence of the tax on suppliers. The general form of the equation for ΔP^S is:

$$\Delta P^S = \frac{\frac{1}{d}}{\frac{1}{b}+\frac{1}{d}} \bullet t$$

(g) The easiest way to show the effect is to increase 1/b (the slope of the demand curve) and decrease 1/d (the slope of the supply curve) by exactly the same amount. Thus, the denominator in the ΔP^C and ΔP^S equations (i.e., 1/d + 1/b) is unchanged. Looking only at the numerators, therefore, the increase in 1/b increases ΔP^C and the decrease in 1/d reduces ΔP^S. The incidence of the tax on consumers rises and the incidence on suppliers falls. The blanks in the statement are: suppliers; smaller; demanders.

(h) $60/6 = 10. You saw this number in (d) above—it is the change in equilibrium quantity as a result of the tax. The general form of the equation for this change is:

$$\Delta Q_E = \frac{t}{\frac{1}{b}+\frac{1}{d}}$$

From this equation you see ΔQ_E would *not* change because 1/b + 1/d would be unchanged. The spaces in the statement should be filled in with "sum of" and "relative."

E4. $Q^D = 200 - 2P$; $\eta = (P/Q) \times 2$;

Price	Quantity	η_d	Description	Expenditure as Price Falls	Expenditure as Price Rises
$100	0	Infinite	perfectly elastic	increases	P can't rise
$ 80	40	4	elastic	increases	decreases
$ 60	80	1.5	elastic	increases	decreases
$ 50	100	1	unit-elastic	decreases	increases
$ 40	120	2/3	inelastic	decreases	increases
$ 20	160	0.25	inelastic	decreases	increases
$ 0	200	0	perfectly inelastic	P can't fall	increases

E5. D_0: $Q = 30 - P$ D_1: $Q = 40 - 2P$ D_2: $Q = 60 - 2P$ D_3: $Q = 80 - 2P$

(a) The completed table is:

Curve	Price	Quantity	Slope	Elasticity
D_0	\$10	20	1	(10/20)1 = 0.5
D_1	\$10	20	1/2 = 0.5	(10/20)2 = 1
D_2	\$10	40	1/2 = 0.5	(10/40)2 = 0.5
D_3	\$10	60	1/2 = 0.5	(10/60)2 = 0.33

b) (i) flatter; more (or steeper; less) (ii) the same as (iii) falls (iv) less; regardless of

Additional Multiple-Choice Questions

1.(a) **2.**(b) **3.**(c) **4.**(a) **5.**(d) **6.**(d) **7.**(c) **8.**(a) **9.**(d) **10.**(d) **11.**(e) **12.**(c) **13.**(a) **14.**(c) **15.**(b). **16.**(e) **17.**(d) **18.**(d) **19.**(a) **20.**(b) **Point Elasticity: 21.**(d) **22.**(b) **23.**(a) **24.**(b) **Using Equations: 25.**(a) **26.**(d) **27.**(a) **28.**(e)

Explanations for the Asterisked Multiple-Choice Questions

1.(a) Since $\%\Delta Q^D/\%\Delta P = 2$, then $\%\Delta Q^D/2 = 2$, so $\%\Delta Q^D = 2 \times 2 = 4$.

6.(d) Because 1.2 exceeds unity, demand is elastic. An increase in price reduces total expenditure when demand is elastic, because the percentage fall in quantity demanded exceeds the percentage rise in price.

7.(c) With unit elasticity the percentage increase/decrease in price equals the percentage decrease/increase in quantity demanded, so total spending on the good is unchanged—e.g., any reduction in spending attributable to the lower price is *exactly offset* by the increase in spending attributable to the increase amount demanded (so (b) is wrong). To have unit elasticity with a 1% *decrease* in quantity (answer (a)) would require both an increase in price (whereas the question says price *falls*) and that price increase also be by 1% (which the question does not specify)—so (a) is wrong for two reasons (hence (e) is also wrong). Finally, elasticity requires comparing *percentage* changes, not *unit* changes, so (d) is wrong.

9.d) The \$4 price change is 50% of the average price of \$8. The 100 increase in Q^S is 28.6% of the average of 350. So $\%\Delta Q^S/\%\Delta P = 28.6/50 = 0.57$ is less than 1, so supply is inelastic.

10.(d) The \$2 reduction in price from \$10 to \$8 is 22% of the \$9 average, and the resulting 50 fall in quantity supplied is 13% of the 375 average, for an elasticity of 13/22 = 0.59, which is less than 1 so supply is inelastic here (so answers (a) and (c) are wrong). The \$2 reduction in price from \$4 to \$2 is 67% of the \$3 average, and the resulting 150 fall in quantity supplied is 120% of the 125 average, for an elasticity of 120/67 = 1.8, which exceeds 1 so demand is elastic here (so answer (b) is wrong). Comparing the two price ranges, not only does the value of elasticity change (so answer (e) is wrong) but it varies between elastic and inelastic depending on the price range chosen (as answer (d) states).

13.(a) Income and demand move in the same direction for a normal good, so a decrease in income decreases demand. Answers (b), (c), and (d) are obviously wrong, because they refer to a change in price rather than a change in income.

16.(e) First, for a given supply curve, the more elastic (i.e., the less inelastic) is *demand* then the greater the reduction in quantity demanded as consumer price rises because of the tax. The greater reduction in quantity demanded means a bigger movement along the supply curve and so a bigger fall in the associated supplier price—i.e., *a greater "burden" of the tax on suppliers when demand is more elastic/less inelastic.* So answer (c) is correct while answer (d) is wrong. [*Note:* On Figure 4-14 in the answer to Exercise 9, see that the fall in the supplier price between the equilibrium with and without the tax is greater using the *flatter* D curve.] Next, for a given demand curve, the less elastic (i.e., the more inelastic) is *supply* then the less the reduction in quantity supplied as supplier price falls because of the tax. The smaller reduction in quantity supplied means a smaller movement along the demand curve and so a smaller rise in the associated consumer price. Since the sum of the fall in supplier price plus the rise in consumer price must equal the amount of the tax at the new equilibrium, then a smaller rise in the consumer price must also mean a bigger fall in the supplier price—i.e., *a greater "burden" of the tax on suppliers when supply is less elastic/more inelastic*. So answer (a) is wrong and answer (b) is correct. [*Note:* On Figure 4-13 in the answer to Exercise 8, see that the fall in the supplier price between the equilibrium with and without the tax is greater using the *steeper S* curve.] Thus, as answer (e) states, both answers (c) and (d) are correct. [*Note:* For students covering *Extensions in Theory 4-1,* Extension Exercise E3 gives a mathematical proof of the answer.]

17.(d) The incidence depends on the relative elasticities of demand and supply, so there are only two cases where the entire incidence is on suppliers (i.e., no change in the price paid by demanders). One case is where supply is sufficiently inelastic as to be perfectly inelastic, but this is ruled out because the question says that the supply curve is upward-sloping. The other case is where demand is sufficiently elastic as to be perfectly elastic. The combination of the upward-sloping supply curve and no change in consumer price, therefore, means demand must be perfectly elastic.

19.(a) Since the two "fast foods" are substitutes in consumption, an increase in the price of one will increase demand for the other. Since price and demand both move in the same direction, the ratio of their percentage changes is a positive number. The cross elasticities of demand between pizzas and hamburgers, therefore, are positive.

20.(b) The negative sign on the income elasticity of –0.5 says that an *increase* in income *reduces* demand for the good—i.e., it is an inferior good. "Inelastic demand" is shorthand for *price* elasticity being inelastic, so answer (a) is wrong. When *two* goods are complementary to each other they have a negative *cross elasticity* of demand, so answer (c) is wrong. A downward-sloping demand curve requires a negative *price* elasticity of demand, so answer (d) is wrong. A demand curve with a constant slope of 0.5 in *absolute* terms simply describes a *straight-line* downward-sloping demand curve, hence a negative but varying *price* elasticity, so answer (e) is also wrong. Thus, while all answers other than (b) refer to situations of *negative* elasticity, they say nothing at all about *income-elasticity* of demand.

22.(b) On a straight-line downward-sloping demand curve, the (absolute value of) price elasticity of demand falls continually as price falls, so answer (b) is correct and answers (a) and (e) are wrong. [Using $\eta_d = (P/Q)/(\Delta P/\Delta Q)$, as price falls the slope $\Delta P/\Delta Q$ is unchanged but P/Q falls, so $(P/Q)/(\Delta P/\Delta Q)$ falls.] Answer (c) is wrong because at point *A* the ratio P/Q is the same on both curves but the slope $\Delta P/\Delta Q$ is greater on D_1 than on D_2, so $\eta_d = (P/Q)/(\Delta P/\Delta Q)$ is *less* on D_1 than D_2. Finally, since D_1 is a straight-line downward-sloping demand curve, it is *price-elastic* at all points above the mid-point ($P = \$5.50$) so answer (d) is wrong. [*Note:* Practise this with Exercise 6.]

24.(b) *Additional Topics: Some Further Details about Demand Elasticity* on the MyEconLab proves that, for a straight-line downward-sloping demand curve, a "quick method" for finding the point price elasticity is to divide the price by the difference between that price and the price–axis intercept of the demand curve—i.e., at any given P_X, $\eta_d = P_X/(P_{INTERCEPT} - P_X)$. If P_X is the same on both *D* curves and $P_{INTERCEPT}$ is the same on both, then η_d is the same *regardless* of differences in slope. [*Note:* The flatter demand curve *would* be more elastic if, as in Figure 4-10, the two crossed at a *positive Q*. The flatter demand curve would then have a smaller $P_{INTERCEPT}$ than the steeper one, giving a smaller $(P_{INTERCEPT} - P_X)$ and so a bigger $P_X/(P_{INTERCEPT} - P_X)$—hence, more elastic at P_X. In Question 24, however, because the two demand curves have the same price intercept they cross at $Q = 0$. If you are confused by this, review Extension Exercise E5.]

25.(a) The two linear demand curves ($Q^D = a - bP$) have the same price–axis intercept (a/b)—i.e., 200/1 = 200 for Q^D_A and 100/0.5 = 200 for Q^D_B, and in such cases the elasticity is the same at a given price. To prove this, take any *P* and calculate both point price elasticities using $\eta = (P/Q) \times (b)$. For example, at $P = \$150$ then $\eta_A = (P/Q^D_A) \times (b) = (150/50) \times 1 = 3$ and $\eta_B = (P/Q^D_B) \times (b) = (150/25) \times 0.5 = 3$. Alternatively, applying the formula $\eta_d = P_X/(P_{INTERCEPT} - P_X)$ explained in the answer to Question 24 above, at $P = \$150$ you get $\eta_d = 150/(200 - 150) = 3$ in both cases.

26.(d) Both supply curves are straight lines through the origin (i.e., have a *zero* price–axis intercept), so price and quantity always change in the same proportion—i.e., elasticity is unity all along each curve. (See Exercise 7-a). To prove this, if you choose any *P* and apply the formula for the point elasticity of supply, $\eta = (P/Q)/(1/d)$, you will see that the ratio (P/Q) always equals the slope (1/d).

27.(a) All three cases have the same average price ($9) and, therefore, the same average quantity. Along a linear demand curve, elasticity at the average price and quantity is unaffected by the magnitude of the change around the average. Elasticity = $(\Delta Q/\Delta P) \times (P_{AVE}/Q_{AVE})$, and $\Delta Q/\Delta P$ is the same all along the straight line. Since P_{AVE}/Q_{AVE} is also the same in all three cases, then elasticity must be the same. The arc elasticities in cases (i) and (ii) are the same as the point elasticity in case (iii). (See Exercise 5.)

28.(e) The negative sign on P means that the demand curve is downward-sloping, so widgets are not a Giffen good. The negative sign on Y means that an increase in income reduces the demand for widgets, so widgets are an inferior good. The negative sign on P_A means that an increase in P_A reduces the demand for widgets, so the two are complementary goods.

PART 7: AN INTRODUCTION TO MACROECONOMICS

CHAPTER 19

What Macroeconomics Is All About

LO

LEARNING OBJECTIVES

In this chapter you will learn

1. the meaning and importance of the key macroeconomic variables, including national income, unemployment, inflation, interest rates, exchange rates, and trade flows.
2. that most macroeconomic issues are about either long-run trends or short-run fluctuations, and that government policy is relevant for both.

CHAPTER OVERVIEW

Macroeconomic aggregates result from activities in many different markets and from the combined behaviour of households, governments, and firms. Macroeconomics examines the behaviour of such broad aggregates and averages as the **price level**, **nominal** and **real national output (income)**, **output per person**, the **output gap**, **employment**, **unemployment**, **labour productivity**, the **exchange rate**, and **exports** and **imports.**

One central concept is the economy's value of total output (national product or national income), which is often measured as gross domestic product (GDP). Comparing **actual** national income to **potential** income indicates the economy's position in the business cycle and the economic and social loss from unemployment and under-utilized resources. Long-term economic growth is reflected by an increasing real GDP, which allows the material standard of living to increase.

The average price level is measured by a price index, which measures the cost of a set of goods in one year relative to its cost in a "base" year. *Applying Economic Concepts 19-2* in the textbook discusses how a Consumer Price Index is constructed. The **inflation rate** measures the rate of change of the price level. Unanticipated changes in inflation redistribute purchasing power within an economy. The rate of inflation is an important determinant of the **nominal interest rate.** The **real interest rate** is the nominal rate minus the rate of inflation.

The textbook defines the **exchange rate** as the number of Canadian dollars needed to purchase one unit of foreign currency. Hence, a fall in the exchange rate—it takes fewer units of domestic currency to purchase one unit of foreign currency—means the Canadian dollar has **appreciated.** The difference between the value of Canadian **exports** and the value of Canadian **imports** is called **net exports.**

Useful websites for Canadian data are **www.bankofcanada.ca** (Bank of Canada) and **www.statcan.ca** (Statistics Canada).

HINTS AND TIPS

The following may help you to avoid some of the most common errors on examinations.

✓ Learn the distinction between *real* (constant dollar) and *nominal* (current dollar) macroeconomic variables, and how to calculate real values from nominal data. Nominal income changes may reflect only changes in the price level and, therefore, do not necessarily imply real income changes.

✓ Understand the correct formula for the calculation of an output gap. The correct formula is actual real national income minus potential real national income. For example, when the output gap is negative, a recessionary gap is said to exist.

✓ Learn that labour productivity is the amount of real GDP produced by unit of labour employed, and also learn how changes in labour productivity affect the level of income per capita over time.

✓ Learn the correct method for calculating inflation rates from price index information (see Multiple-Choice Question 12 in the Chapter Review section for the correct method).

✓ Learn that the exchange rate is the amount of domestic currency needed to buy one unit of foreign currency. Therefore, the value of one unit of domestic currency is equal to one over the value of the exchange rate. If the exchange rate appreciates, the domestic currency depreciates.

CHAPTER REVIEW

Key Macroeconomic Variables

You should understand the issues that arise in measuring and interpreting various macroeconomic variables, especially the need to adjust for inflation to express macroeconomic variables in real (constant-dollar) terms. The distinction between real and nominal values of macroeconomic variables will continue to be critical in the material that follows.

Potential output measures what the economy could produce if all resources were employed at their "normal" levels of utilization. An output gap is defined as real national income minus real potential national income. If the gap is negative, then the economy is experiencing a recessionary gap situation. If the output gap is positive, the economy is experiencing an inflationary gap situation.

The rate of inflation is calculated from price index information. The real effects of inflation on macroeconomic behaviour depend to a great extent on whether the inflation is anticipated or unanticipated. Anticipated inflation has fewer real effects on the economy than unanticipated inflation. Inflation rates also affect nominal and real interest rates.

An exchange rate can be defined either as the amount of domestic currency (Canadian dollars) that trades for one unit of some foreign currency or the amount of foreign currency that trades for one unit of domestic currency (the Canadian dollar). The textbook adopts the convention of defining the exchange rate as the number of Canadian dollars required to purchase one unit of foreign currency. It's easy to be confused since the media do not have a common convention when reporting exchange rate information. For our purposes, a rise in the exchange rate—more Canadian dollars are required to buy one unit of foreign currency—means that the Canadian dollar has depreciated. A fall in the exchange rate—fewer Canadian dollars are required to buy one unit of foreign currency—means that the Canadian dollar has appreciated.

Currencies for some selected countries are provided for your reference. Some of the questions in the *Study Guide* refer to these currencies.

Countries and Their Currencies

Country	Currency
China	renminbi
Greece	drachma
India	rupee
Japan	yen
South Korea	won
United States	dollar
Sweden	krona
European Union	euro

1. Which of the following is classified as a macroeconomic issue?

(a) Changes in the unemployment rate.
(b) A fall in the Consumer Price Index.
(c) Historical trends in the growth of real per capita national income.
(d) Short-term fluctuations in national income around its long-run trend.
(e) All of the above.

2. Changes in real national income reflect only changes in physical quantities of output, whereas changes in current-dollar national income reflect

(a) only price changes.
(b) only changes in potential physical quantities of output.
(c) changes in neither physical quantities of output nor price.
(d) changes in both price and physical quantities of output.
(e) only changes in real purchasing power.

3. National income is *by definition* equal to

(a) the number of domestic income earners.
(b) the number of domestically owned firms.
(c) the value of national product.
(d) the number of employed workers.
(e) None of the above.

4. Real national income is also known as

(a) nominal national income.
(b) current-dollar national income.
(c) constant-dollar national income.
(d) potential national income.
(e) after-tax national income.

5. An inflationary gap

(a) occurs when actual national income exceeds potential national income.
(b) occurs when the value of the output gap is negative.
(c) occurs when resource use is lower than its normal rate of utilization.
(d) occurs when actual output is lower than potential output.
(e) is most likely observed during declining economic activity.

6. **Actual national income may exceed potential national income for a short period of time when**
   (a) the unemployment rate is high.
   (b) factors of production are employed at levels that are above normal utilization levels.
   (c) nominal national income is less than real national income.
   (d) there is a recessionary gap.
   (e) None of the above.

7. **An economy that currently has a negative output gap**
   (a) suffers a loss in output and economic well-being.
   (b) experiences less severe social problems because individuals are able to enjoy more leisure time.
   (c) has reached the peak stage of the business cycle.
   (d) must have rapidly rising prices.
   (e) has reached the peak stage of the business cycle and must have rapidly rising prices.

8. **At the peak of a business cycle**
   (a) the unemployment of resources is dominant throughout the economy.
   (b) existing capacity is used to a high degree.
   (c) labour shortages may develop.
   (d) the average price level is most likely falling.
   (e) existing capacity is used to a high degree and labour shortages may develop.

9. **The unemployment rate is measured as**
   (a) the number of unemployed people expressed as a fraction of the total population.
   (b) the number of unemployed people expressed as a fraction of the total number of employed persons.
   (c) the number of unemployed people expressed as a fraction of the labour force.
   (d) the number of unemployed people who receive employment insurance as a fraction of the total number of individuals who contribute to employment insurance.
   (e) the percentage increase in the number of unemployed people over some time period.

10. **Full employment in Canada**
   (a) implies that the measured unemployment rate is zero.
   (b) occurs when the natural rate of unemployment is zero.
   (c) occurs when the output gap is positive.
   (d) has not been achieved in the past 50 years.
   (e) occurs when the only existing unemployment is structural and frictional.

11. **An example of frictional unemployment is when**
   (a) carpenters are laid off because of a decline in housing starts.
   (b) Montreal textile workers lose jobs due to a loss in Canadian export shares of textile products in world markets.
   (c) unemployed textile workers are refused jobs since they do not have knowledge of computer software packages required by firms in another industry.
   (d) a teenager quits a job at Canadian Tire in order to search for a better-paying job at one of the three large hardware stores in the same city.
   (e) flight crews lose jobs when the airline industry restructures.

12. An inflation rate is calculated by

(a) subtracting the value of two price levels.
(b) dividing the second price level by the first.
(c) dividing the difference between two price levels by the initial price level and then multiplying by 100 percent.
(d) taking the average value between two price levels.
(e) None of the above.

13. Which of the following might cause labour productivity to increase?

(a) An increase in real GDP and an increase in population.
(b) An increase in real GDP and an increase in the labour force.
(c) A more rapid increase in real GDP than in population.
(d) A more rapid increase in real GDP than in the labour force.
(e) A more rapid increase in real GDP than in the level of employment.

14. Which of the following might explain a country's over time increase in real income per capita (i.e., per person)?

(a) The use of increasingly better physical capital in the process of production.
(b) A continuous improvement in workers' skills.
(c) A continuous increase in labour productivity.
(d) A continuous diffusion of new technologies throughout the economy.
(e) All of the above.

15. Unanticipated inflation is likely to benefit

(a) creditors who have negotiated fixed interest terms with debtors.
(b) pensioners whose monthly pension income is fixed in nominal terms.
(c) landlords who, because of rent controls, cannot raise nominal rents during the lease period.
(d) those who have large balances in chequing accounts.
(e) firms that have negotiated wage freezes in a new contract period.

16. Assume that prices increase over the year by 4 percent. Who of the following will experience a decrease in purchasing power?

(a) A creditor who negotiated an annual contract at a nominal rate of interest of 6 percent and who wanted a 2 percent real rate of return.
(b) A firm that is committed to increasing its wages by 5 percent over the year but whose prices are likely to increase only by the overall rate of inflation.
(c) A retired person whose pension is totally indexed for price inflation.
(d) A landlord who successfully negotiates a 7 percent increase in rent over the year.
(e) An entrepreneur who makes a 5 percent annual rate of return on her wealth portfolio.

17. The Consumer Price Index (CPI)

(a) is the average dollar price of all goods and services produced in the economy.
(b) shows the price of a basket of consumer goods at some specific time relative to the price of the same basket of consumer goods in some base period.
(c) must always be equal to 100 in any time period.
(d) is always greater than 100 except in the base period.
(e) None of the above.

18. **The real interest rate**
   (a) measures the burden of borrowing.
   (b) is the inflation rate minus the nominal interest rate.
   (c) measures the real return on an asset, in terms of its purchasing power.
   (d) is the price paid per dollar borrowed per period of time.
   (e) measures the burden of borrowing and also the real return on an asset in terms of its purchasing power.

19. **The textbook's definition of an exchange rate between Canadian dollars and South Korean won is**
   (a) the number of Canadian dollars required to purchase one South Korean won.
   (b) the difference between the real and the nominal interest rate.
   (c) the ratio of Canadian and South Korean interest rates.
   (d) the ratio of the price of a Canadian-produced good to the price of a Korean-produced good.
   (e) the rate at which goods are traded between South Korea and Canada.

20. **If the value of a country's merchandise imports exceeds the value of its merchandise exports by $50 million, it follows that**
   (a) it has a $50 million deficit on its merchandise trade account.
   (b) the country must also have a positive output gap of $50 million.
   (c) net exports are $50 million.
   (d) it has a $50 million deficit on its merchandise trade account, and thus net exports are $50 million.
   (e) it has a $50 million surplus on its merchandise trade account.

21. **If the exchange rate between Japanese yen and Canadian dollars rises, then**
   (a) it takes fewer Canadian dollars to buy 1 Japanese yen.
   (b) the Canadian dollar has appreciated.
   (c) it takes more Japanese yen to buy 1 Canadian dollar.
   (d) it takes more Canadian dollars to buy 1 Japanese yen.
   (e) the American dollar must have depreciated.

Growth Versus Fluctuations

The most important macroeconomic issues can be divided into two broad categories—long-run trends and short-run fluctuations. Economic growth refers to a long-run increase in real national income and generally implies a rising average living standard. Business cycles represent short-run fluctuations in economic activity such as output, employment, and inflation. Broad government policies, such as monetary policy and fiscal policy, typically play a role in both discussions.

22. **Which of the following macroeconomic issues are normally associated with economic growth?**
   (a) Increases in material living standards over a decade.
   (b) Sustained increases in output per person.
   (c) An increased stock of resources for future production.
   (d) The role of investment in generating a larger capital stock.
   (e) All of the above.

23. An upward trend in real national income is called
(a) an inflationary boom.
(b) a recessionary gap.
(c) economic growth.
(d) an inflationary gap.
(e) a positive output gap.

SHORT-ANSWER QUESTIONS

1. Explain the difference between the following pairs of concepts.
(a) Real versus nominal national income.

(b) The nominal versus the real interest rate.

(c) Actual real national income and potential real national income and their relationship with the output gap.

2. Briefly explain whether the following statement is true or false: "There are two ways to express an exchange rate between a domestic currency and a foreign currency." What does it mean when the domestic currency appreciates/depreciates?

3. Explain how each of the following events taken separately may affect average labour productivity in Canada.
(a) The expansion of wheat production to lands of less fertile soils.

(b) The adoption of internet technology for students' enrolment in university courses.

(c) An increase in the average education level of new immigrants to Canada.

4. Explain how an unanticipated increase in the price level may affect each of the following macroeconomic variables. Clearly indicate who might, in each case, be negatively and/or positively affected by this unanticipated increase in the price level.
   (a) The real rate of interest.

   (b) The real wage rate.

EXERCISES

1. **Calculation of Nominal GDP**
   An economy produces four different final goods and services within the current year. The level of production and the price per unit of each are listed here.

Item	Production Level	Price per Unit
Steel	500 000 tons	$100 per ton
Wheat	15 000 tons	$8 per ton
Haircuts	6 000	$9 each
Television sets	10 000 sets	$500 per set

   Calculate the dollar value of the economy's GDP in the current year.

2. **Real GDP, Real Potential GDP, and the Output Gap**
   Here are some historical data for Canadian national income measured in terms of gross domestic product (GDP). The data in the second column show constant dollar (real) GDP, while data in the third column refer to real potential GDP. All values are in billions of 1997 dollars.

Year	Real GDP	Real Potential GDP
1980	576.4	573.2
1981	594.1	586.1
1982	576.7	600.1
1983	592.7	615.2
1984	626.4	632.0
1985	660.3	656.8
1986	677.8	681.2
1987	705.7	705.0
1988	740.6	728.3
1989	759.8	747.1

(a) Express the 1985 real value of GDP as an index (to one decimal place) of the 1981 real value of GDP. Do the same for the 1980 real value of GDP as an index in terms of 1981.

(b) What is the value of the output gap in 1984? In 1988? Were resources fully employed in these two years?

(c) What phase of the business cycle is represented by the 1981–1982 period?

(d) In what year(s) did the economy have an output gap of approximately 0?

3. **Employment, Unemployment, and the Labour Force**
The following table provides historical information for the Canadian economy in a five-year period.

Year	Real GDP 1997 Prices (billions)	Labour Force	Unemployed (thousands)	Employed	Unemployment Rate (percent)	Population 15 yrs+ (millions)
1998	918.9	15 417		14 140	8.3	23.7
1999	969.8	15 721	1190		7.6	24.0
2000	1020.8	15 999			6.8	24.3
2001	1040.4	16 246	1170			24.6
2002	1074.5		1278	15 412	7.7	24.9

(a) Fill in the missing values in the table.

(b) Calculate the percentage change in real GDP between 1998 and 1999. Compare this value with the percentage change in employment in this period. Do the same analysis for the two-year period 2000–01.

98-99 = 5.5%, 2.8%

'00-01: 1.9%, 1.1%

(c) Does there appear to be a positive or negative relationship between real GDP and employment for these two periods?

they both increase

(d) Between 2001 and 2002 the unemployment rate increased while employment increased. How is this possible?

(e) Calculate the value of real per capita GDP (in terms of the population 15 years and over) for 1998 and 2002.

'98: $34773

'02: 543.153

4. Labour Productivity

The aggregate production function of a hypothetical economy is given by the equation $Y = A\,(K\,L)^{1/2}$, where Y is physical output (i.e., real GDP), A is the level of technology, K is units of physical capital, and L is the number of workers. Initially, the level of technology is 100, physical capital is 100 units, and the number of workers is 10 000.

(a) Calculate the initial level of labour productivity in this economy.

(b) Suppose now that the quantity of physical capital increases to 121. Calculate the new level of labour productivity in this economy. Briefly explain why labour productivity has changed.

(c) Go back to the initial situation in part (a). Suppose now that a technological improvement occurs, causing the level of technology to increase by 20 percent. What is the new level of labour productivity? Briefly explain why labour productivity has changed.

5. The Consumer Price Index and the Rate of Inflation

You are given the following Consumer Price Indexes for various years. The base year (1992) has an index of 100.

Year	Price Index	Annual Inflation Rate (percent)
1998	108.6	n.a.
1999	110.5	1.7
2000	113.5	2.7
2001	116.5	2.6

(a) Calculate the annual inflation rate (to one decimal place) for 1999 and 2000, and fill in the blanks in the third column.

(b) What was the inflation rate over the period from the base year (1992) through 2000?

$\frac{113.5}{100} \times 100 = 13.5\%$

(c) Calculate (to one decimal place) the price index for 2001.

$2.6 = \frac{x - 113.5}{113.5}(100) \quad x =$

6. The Inflation Rate and Nominal and Real Interest Rates

This problem deals with the real interest rate on five-year conventional mortgages. Suppose that the lender, a financial institution, wishes to have a 4 percent annual real rate of return on the basis of its expectations for future inflation. Consider the following data. The nominal interest rates are stated for five-year conventional mortgages beginning in 1975, 1980, and 1985.

Year	Nominal Annual Interest Rate on New Five-Year Mortgages	Annual average inflation rate: Expected	Actual	Period
1975	11.4	7.4	8.9	1975–1979
1980	14.3	10.3	8.7	1980–1984
1985	12.2	8.2	4.3	1985–1989

RIR = NIR − IR
4 = 11.4 − IR
IR = 7.4

(a) Calculate the institution's expected annual rate of inflation when it set the five-year mortgage rate in 1975. Do the same for the two other five-year periods, and complete the entries in the table.

(b) By comparing the actual annual inflation rate with the nominal interest rate, in what five-year periods did the financial institution make a real return higher than 4 percent on five-year mortgages?

80 + 85

RIR: 5.6% 7.9%

(c) Comparing nominal interest rates and actual inflation, which five-year period represented the lowest real interest rate for borrowers?

75: 2.5%

7. The Exchange Rate

The exchange rate is another important macroeconomic variable discussed in Chapter 19. The information here is intended to provide practice in interpreting exchange rate changes. The values are Canadian dollars per German mark and per Japanese yen. (Note that the German mark was replaced by the euro on January 1, 2002.)

	Exchange Rate	
Year	**Dollars per Mark**	**Dollars per Yen**
1998	$0.845	$0.01139
1999	0.810	0.01311
2000	0.707	0.01387
2001	0.709	0.01276

(a) Over the period 1998–1999, the Canadian dollar (depreciated/appreciated) relative to the German mark while the Canadian dollar (depreciated/appreciated) relative to the Japanese yen. Explain.

(b) Suppose that you paid 100 marks for a one-year asset at the end of 1998 (at an exchange rate of $0.845). How many dollars did you require to buy this asset?

$84.50

EXTENSION EXERCISE

E1. **Calculation of the Consumer Price Index**

This exercise features the construction of a Consumer Price Index, which is explained in the textbook box *Applying Economic Concepts 19-2.*

Suppose that the government's data collection agency has estimated the prices of six broad groups of consumer expenditure as well as the *average* proportions of consumers' income that is spent on these expenditure groups as follows:

	Prices (base year)	**Prices (next year)**	**Proportion of Income Consumers Spend (on average)**
Shelter	$3000	$3300	30%
Food	2500	2500	25
Transportation	5000	5000	15
Clothing	100	110	10
Entertainment	60	60	10
Other	300	330	10

(a) Compute the average price level in the base year and in the next year. (Assume that the proportions do not change.)

(b) The price index for the base year, by definition, is 100. Compute the price index for the next year.

(c) You may have noticed that the price of shelter, clothing, and other goods increased by 10 percent each. Does your answer to (b) indicate a 10 percent increase in the price index from the base year? Why or why not?

ADDITIONAL MULTIPLE-CHOICE QUESTIONS

***1.** **If real potential GDP is 893 billion and current real GDP is 890 billion, then**

(a) there is an inflationary gap of 3 billion.
(b) unemployment consists only of structural and frictional unemployment.
(c) there is an output gap of –3 billion.
(d) the output gap is positive.
(e) there is an inflationary gap of 3 billion <u>and</u> the output gap is positive.

2. **If a particular index number in 1999 is 127 and the base year is 1996, then the index shows an increase of**
   (a) 2.7 percent between 1996 and 1999.
   (b) 127 percent between 1996 and 1999.
   (c) 27 percent between 1996 and 1999.
   (d) 0.27 percent between 1996 and 1999.
   (e) an indeterminable percentage, since the value of the index in 1996 is unknown.

*3. **A price index changes from 120 to 114 over a particular time period. The percentage change in the price level was**
   (a) 6 percent.
   (b) –5 percent.
   (c) 5 percent.
   (d) –6 percent.
   (e) –5.26 percent.

4. **Suppose that a price index was 160 last month and rose by 2 percent during the current month. The price index for the current month is**
   (a) 162.0.
   (b) 163.2.
   (c) 160.02.
   (d) 198.4.
   (e) 192.

5. **Suppose that a family's income grew from $38 000 to $38 100 over the period 2001 to 2002, which saw an inflation rate of 2 percent. We can conclude that this family experienced**
   (a) an increase in both nominal and real income.
   (b) a decrease in both nominal and real income.
   (c) a decrease in nominal income but an increase in real income.
   (d) a decrease in real income but an increase in nominal income.
   (e) an increase in nominal income but no change in real income.

*6. **If inflation is 5 percent and the annual nominal interest is 8 percent, then the annual real rate of interest is**
   (a) 13 percent.
   (b) 3 percent.
   (c) –3 percent.
   (d) 40 percent.
   (e) .4 percent.

7. **Canadian nominal and real interest rates in 1998 were 4.8 percent and 3.8 percent, respectively. The rate of inflation in 1998 was therefore**
   (a) 1.0.
   (b) –1.0.
   (c) 8.6.
   (d) 3.8.
   (e) 1.3.

8. **The *Canadian Economic Observer* reported that between 1997 and 1998, one German mark increased from 79.9 Canadian cents to 84.5 Canadian cents. Hence,**
   (a) the dollar appreciated.
   (b) the exchange rate appreciated.
   (c) the Canadian dollar depreciated.
   (d) Canadians could buy more marks per dollar in 1998 than in 1997.
   (e) the exchange rate appreciated <u>and</u> the Canadian dollar depreciated.

***9. Between 2001 and 2002, the Japanese yen fell from 0.01275 Canadian dollars to 0.01255 Canadian dollars. It follows that**

(a) the Canadian dollar appreciated from 78.4 yen to 79.7 yen.
(b) the Canadian dollar depreciated.
(c) it was more expensive for Canadians to buy yen in 2001 than in 2002.
(d) it was more expensive for the Japanese to buy Canadian dollars in 2001 than in 2002.
(e) None of the above.

***10. If employment in a country was 12 million and unemployment was 1 million, the unemployment rate would be**

(a) 13 million.
(b) 7.7 percent.
(c) 8.3 percent.
(d) 9.1 percent.
(e) None of the above.

Questions 11 and 12 refer to an hypothetical economy with an aggregate production function given by the equation $Y = A\,(K\,L)^{1/2}$, where Y is physical output (i.e., real GDP), A is the level of technology, K is units of physical capital, and L is the number of workers. Initially, the level of technology is 10, physical capital is 400 units, and the number of workers is 10 000.

***11. In this economy, the productivity of labour is**

(a) 0.5.
(b) 1.
(c) 2.
(d) 4.
(e) None of the above.

12. In this economy, the productivity of (physical) capital is

(a) 5.
(b) 10.
(c) 40.
(d) 50.
(e) 400.

The following information refers to questions 13 and 14. Suppose that the demand for labour is a decreasing function of the real wage rate—i.e., as the real wage rate decreases the quantity demanded of labour increases. Further suppose that the demand for labour function is given by the equation $L = 2000 - 20\,w$, where L is the number of workers (in thousands) and w is the real hourly wage rate. [Note that the real wage rate is the purchasing power of the nominal wage rate—i.e., $w = W/P$, where W is the nominal wage rate and P is the price level.]

13. Under the expectation that the price level will not change over the next two years, employers and workers agree to a $10 nominal wage rate and sign a 2-year contract (i.e., they agree that the nominal wage rate will remain fixed at $10 during the life of the contract). If $P = 1$, what is the level of employment in this economy at the time of the signing of the contract?

(a) 1 000 000.
(b) 1 500 000.
(c) 1 800 000.
(d) 2 000 000.
(e) None of the above.

***14. Suppose now that the price level unexpectedly increases to 1.25 by the end of the first year of the contract. What is the level of employment one year after the signing of the contract?**

(a) 1 640 000.
(b) 1 760 000.
(c) 1 800 000.
(d) 1 840 000.
(e) None of the above.

SOLUTIONS

Chapter Review

1. (e) **2.**(d) **3.**(c) **4.**(c) **5.**(a) **6.**(b) **7.**(a) **8.**(e) **9.**(c) **10.**(e) **11.**(d) **12.**(c) **13.**(e) **14.**(e) **15.**(e) **16.**(b) **17.**(b) **18.**(e) **19.**(a) **20.**(a) **21.**(d) **22.**(e) **23.**(c)

Short-Answer Questions

1. **(a)** Nominal national income reflects the influences of both prices and output volume of final goods and services produced in an economy in a given time period. Hence, nominal national income will increase if prices and/or physical quantity of output increase. Real national income reflects only output volume; it has been corrected for inflation. Real income increases only if output volume increases.

(b) The nominal rate of interest is defined as the real interest rate plus the rate of inflation. Hence, the real interest rate is the nominal value minus the rate of inflation. The real interest rate measures the burden of debt and the rate of return on assets.

(c) Actual real income is what the economy actually produces. Potential output measures what the economy could produce if all resources were employed at their normal levels of utilization. Potential output is sometimes called full-employment output. The output gap is defined as actual national income minus potential income.

2. This statement is true. The textbook defines an exchange rate as the amount of domestic currency that trades for one unit of foreign currency. For example, 1.40 Canadian dollars may trade for 1 US dollar. On the other hand, we can also define an exchange rate as the amount of foreign currency that trades for one Canadian dollar. With respect to the example cited above, 0.71 US dollar trades for one Canadian dollar.

If the domestic currency depreciates, then it must take a greater amount of domestic currency to buy one unit of foreign currency. Alternatively, if the domestic currency appreciates, then Canadians pay a smaller amount of their domestic currency for each unit of foreign currency. Using the example above, if the exchange rate increases from $1.40 Canadian to $1.50 Canadian, then it follows that Americans need to give up fewer US dollars to buy one Canadian dollar (0.67 as contrasted to 0.71). Hence, the Canadian dollar relative to the US dollar has depreciated.

3. **(a)** Land productivity in the wheat industry will decline since the incorporation of lands of less fertile soils reduces the average wheat output per unit of land. However, the information provided is insufficient to allow us to indicate what will happen to labour productivity, where labour productivity in the wheat industry is defined as the wheat output per unit of labour. We know that wheat output will increase and that the level of employment in the industry will also increase, but we do not know whether output will increase faster or more slowly than the level of employment.

(b) Students' enrolment in university courses through the internet will allow production of the same output (i.e., students' enrolment) with a lower quantity of labour (hours of university administrative staff). Therefore, labour productivity will increase.

(c) Higher education levels of new immigrants will increase the average education level of the Canadian labour force. Once these new, more educated immigrants get jobs, the average education level of employed Canadian workers will also increase. A more skilled (educated) labour force is expected to be more efficient—i.e., it is expected that it will be able to produce a larger output. Therefore, labour productivity is expected to increase.

4. **(a)** The real rate of interest is defined as the difference between the nominal rate of interest and the rate of inflation. If the increase in the price level (i.e., the rate of inflation) is unanticipated, then the nominal rate of interest will not be affected (i.e., it will remain constant). Therefore, an increase in the price level with no change in the nominal rate of interest will translate into a decrease in the real rate of interest. This unanticipated decrease in the real rate of interest will affect creditors (lenders) negatively, and debtors (borrowers) positively. Those with fixed nominal incomes (e.g., pensioners) will also be negatively affected since the purchasing power of their fixed nominal incomes will decrease.

   (b) The real wage rate represents the purchasing power of the nominal wage rate. An unanticipated increase in the average price (i.e., the price level) will not affect the level of the nominal wage rate since, being unanticipated, it could not have been taken into account when employers and workers negotiated the level of the nominal wage rate. With no change in the nominal wage rate, an increase in the price level will thus translate into a decrease in the purchasing power of the nominal wage—i.e., into a decrease in the level of the real wage rate. This unanticipated decrease in the real wage rate will thus benefit employers—by increasing their profits—and harm workers.

Exercises

1. $55 174 000. (Calculate price times quantity for each item and add together the products of the four equations)

2. **(a)** For 1985: 111.1 (660.3 divided by 594.1 × 100). For 1980: 97.0 (576.4 divided by 594.1 × 100).

   (b) The output gap is defined as actual real GDP minus real potential GDP. Hence, there was a negative (recessionary) output gap of −5.6 (626.4 − 632.0) in 1984 and a positive (inflationary) output gap of +12.3 in 1988. There was unused productive capacity (less than full employment) in 1984, whereas resources in 1988 were fully employed, although their utilization was greater than normal levels.

   (c) Between the two years, real GDP fell and the output gap became negative (compare 8.0 with −23.4). This period represented a recessionary phase or a slump.

   (d) The GDP gap is approximately zero in 1987; the difference between real GDP and potential GDP is only +0.7 billion.

3. **(a)** Labour force: 2002: 16 690 (1278 + 15 412)
   Unemployed: 1998: 1277 (15 417 − 14 140); 2000: 1088 (15 999 × .068).
   Employed: 1999: 14 531 (15 721 − 1190); 2000: 14 911 (15 999 − 1088);
   2001: 15 076 (16 246 − 1170).
   Unemployment rate: 2001: 7.2% (1170/16 246 × 100%).

   (b) 1998–99; Real GDP increased by 5.5 percent while employment increased by 2.8 percent. 2000–01; Real GDP increased by 1.9 percent while employment increased by 1.1 percent.

   (c) A positive relationship.

   (d) The labour force increased more in percentage terms than did employment. That is, more of those who entered the labour force became unemployed than employed.

   (e) 1998: $38 772; 2002: $43 153.

4. **(a)** $Y = A\,(K\,L)^{1/2} = 100\,(100 \times 10\,000)^{1/2} = 100\,000$. Labour productivity is defined as the level of real GDP per worker: $Y/L = 100\,000 / 10\,000 = 10$.

   (b) $Y = A\,(K\,L)^{1/2} = 100\,(121 \times 10\,000)^{1/2} = 110\,000$. Labour productivity is now $Y/L = 110\,000 / 10\,000 = 11$. The increase in the quantity of physical capital allows total output to increase and, therefore, since the number of workers does not change, labour productivity increases.

   (c) $Y = A\,(K\,L)^{1/2} = 120\,(100 \times 10\,000)^{1/2} = 120\,000$. Labour productivity is now $Y/L = 120\,000 / 10\,000 = 12$. The increase in the level of technology allows production of a larger total output with the same quantities of physical capital and workers. Therefore, labour productivity increases.

5. **(a)** 1999: 1.7 percent (1.9 divided by 108.6 × 100 percent).
   2000: 2.7 percent (3.0 divided by 110.5 × 100 percent).

   (b) 13.5 percent.

   (c) 116.5 (113.5 × 1.026).

6. **(a)** Expected inflation: 1975: 7.4 percent (11.4 – 4.0); 1980: 10.3 percent; 1985: 8.2 percent.
(b) Mortgages in 1980 yielded annually over five years 5.6 percent in real terms (14.3 – 8.7), and mortgages in 1985 garnered a 7.9 percent real rate of return per annum.
(c) Mortgages extended over the 1975–79 period; the real rate of interest was 2.5 percent (11.4 – 8.9).

7. **(a)** Since the exchange rate between dollars and marks fell, the Canadian dollar appreciated with respect to the mark. Since the exchange rate between dollars and yen rose, the Canadian dollar depreciated with respect to the yen.
(b) $84.50.

Extension Exercise

E1. (a) Base year: $(3000 \times 0.3) + (2500 \times 0.25) + (5000 \times 0.15) + (100 \times 0.1) + (60 \times 0.1) + (300 \times 0.1) = 2321$. Next year: $(3300 \times 0.3) + (2500 \times 0.25) + (5000 \times 0.15) + (110 \times 0.1) + (60 \times 0.1) + (330 \times 0.1) = 2415$.
(b) Index = $(2415/2321) \times 100 = 104.05$.
(c) No; prices increased by approximately 4 percent. This is because shelter, clothing, and other goods are only 50 percent of total expenditures.

Additional Multiple-Choice Questions

1.(c) **2.**(c) **3.**(b) **4.**(b) **5.**(d) **6.**(b) **7.**(a) **8.**(e) **9.**(a) **10.**(b) **11.**(c) **12.**(d) **13.**(c) **14.**(d)

Explanations for the Asterisked Multiple-Choice Questions

1.(c) Since actual real GDP is less than potential current GDP, there is a recessionary gap of 3 billion. The output gap is –3 billion.

3.(b) The percentage change in the price level is obtained by dividing –6 (the difference between 114 and 120) by the original price level of 120 and multiplying by 100%. This is equal to –5%.

6.(b) The real rate of interest is measured by the nominal rate minus the inflation rate; in this case 8% – 5%, or +3%.

9.(a) Since the exchange rate between dollars and yen fell, the Canadian dollar appreciated. To calculate the yen price of dollars, divide 1 by the exchange rate. Doing this, we get 78.4 yen per dollar and 79.7 yen per dollar, which means the dollar appreciated.

10.(b) This is tricky. You must remember that the labour force is defined as employment plus unemployment. Hence, unemployment of 1 million divided by a total labour force (= 13) times 100% is 7.7 percent.

11.(c) $Y = 10\,(400 \times 10\,000)^{1/2} = 20\,000 \rightarrow Y/L = 20\,000 / 10\,000 = 2$.

14.(d) $w = W/P = 10/1.25 = 8 \rightarrow L = 2000 - 20\,w = 2000 - 20\,(8) = 1840$ (in thousands).

CHAPTER 20

THE MEASUREMENT OF NATIONAL INCOME

LO

LEARNING OBJECTIVES

In this chapter you will learn

1 how the concept of value added solves the problem of "double counting" when measuring national income.

2 the income approach and the expenditure approach to measuring national income.

3 the difference between real and nominal GDP and the meaning of the GDP deflator.

4 about the many important omissions from official measures of GDP.

5 why real per capita GDP is a good measure of average "material" living standards but an incomplete measure of overall "well-being."

CHAPTER OVERVIEW

Each firm's contribution to total output is equal to its value added. Value added equals revenue minus the costs of intermediate goods. The sum of all the values added produced domestically in an economy is the economy's total output, which is called **gross domestic product (GDP).**

GDP can be calculated from the expenditure side, from the income side, or as the sum of values added in the economy. The expenditure side gives the total value of expenditures required to purchase the nation's output, and the income side gives the total value of income claims generated by the production of that output. By standard accounting conventions, these three aggregations define the same total.

Several concepts related to GDP are discussed, including gross national product and disposable personal income. **Nominal GDP** is distinguished from **real GDP**. Real measures of national income are calculated to reflect changes in real quantities. Nominal measures of GDP are calculated to reflect changes in both prices and quantities. Appropriate comparisons of nominal and real measures yield **GDP deflators.**

GDP must be interpreted with its limitations in mind. GDP excludes illegal activities, the "underground economy," home production activities, and economic "bads." Hence, GDP does not measure everything that contributes to (or detracts from) human welfare.

HINTS AND TIPS

The following may help you to avoid some of the most common errors on examinations.

✓ The concept of value added solves the problem of including more than once the contribution of some intermediate good or process used to produce a final good. For example, the contribution of a flour mill must be counted only once, either as part of the final value of a loaf of bread or as the value of the output of the flour mill, but not both.

✓ Learn the correct method for calculating real GDP using GDP deflator information. The real value of GDP is nominal GDP divided by the GDP deflator times 100. Students often forget to multiply the ratio of nominal GDP to the GDP deflator by 100!

✓ Compile an accurate list of activities that are excluded from the official measures of GDP. Know why their omission either understates or overstates GDP and overall well-being.

CHAPTER REVIEW

National Output and Value Added

You should be aware that the concept of value added gets around the problem of "double" or "multiple" counting when measuring national income. Exercises 1 and 2 test your understanding of value added and the problem of double counting.

1. Value added in production is equal to

(a) total value of output excluding the value of intermediate goods.
(b) profits of all firms, but not other factor incomes.
(c) total value of output including intermediate goods.
(d) the total costs in producing final outputs.
(e) profits of all firms plus the total costs in producing final outputs.

2. Estimating final output (GDP) by adding the sales of all firms

(a) will overstate total output because it counts the output of intermediate goods more than once.
(b) will understate the total value of national output.
(c) is a measure of income accruing to Canadian residents.
(d) provides the same value as net national income.
(e) is the best measure of economic activity.

3. All goods and services used as inputs into a further stage of production are called

(a) value added.
(b) final goods.
(c) intermediate goods.
(d) consumption goods.
(e) investment goods.

National Income Accounting: The Basics

The circular flow of income suggests there are three different ways of computing national income—total value added, adding up the total flow of expenditure on domestic output, and adding up the total flow of income generated by the flow of domestic production. This section outlines the two basic national accounting methods of measuring national income: from the expenditure side and from the income side.

It is important that you learn the components of the four broad categories of final expenditures (consumption, investment, government expenditure, and net exports) and understand the reasons for treating them separately.

GDP accounting from the income side implies the aggregation of all factor payments (wages and salaries, profits, and interest) plus depreciation and indirect taxes. The sum of wages and salaries, interest, and profits is called *net domestic income at factor cost.*

4. To calculate GDP from the expenditure side, one must add together

(a) wages, profits, government purchases, and net exports.
(b) consumption, government purchases, and interest.
(c) wages, rent, interest, and profits.
(d) consumption, investment, government purchases, and net exports.
(e) consumption, investment, government purchases, and exports.

5. Which of the following would be included in the consumption component of aggregate expenditure?

(a) Expenditures for nondurable goods, such as prescription drugs.
(b) Exports sales.
(c) Changes in business inventories,
(d) Purchases of residential housing.
(e) Expenditures by provincial governments on civil servant salaries.

6. The term "investment" in macroeconomics means

(a) the total amount of capital goods in the country.
(b) total amount of money invested in bonds and stocks.
(c) the same thing as profits.
(d) the production of goods not for immediate consumption use such as factories, machines, residential housing, and changes in inventories.
(e) the production of goods for immediate consumption.

7. Which of the following is included in the measures of the investment component of aggregate expenditure in the national accounts?

(a) A Winnipeg family buys gold bars from a bank.
(b) A business firm buys Nortel stock.
(c) General Motors (Canada) increases its holdings of bank deposits.
(d) A construction company builds 20 new homes in Burnaby, British Columbia.
(e) A Calgary oil company sells petroleum products to China.

8. When measuring GDP through the expenditure approach, which one of the following statements about investment is correct?

(a) Net investment may be negative.
(b) Net investment includes the total of all machinery and equipment produced during the year.
(c) Gross investment must equal net investment.
(d) Gross investment plus depreciation equals net investment.
(e) Net investment is one of the components of total expenditure on goods and services.

9. Government purchases are calculated by their

(a) imputed market value.
(b) cost.
(c) labour cost.
(d) opportunity cost.
(e) actual market value.

10. **Which of the following is *not* included in measures of the government expenditure component of aggregate expenditure in the national accounts?**
    (a) Salaries of civil servants whose responsibilities include the collection of the Goods and Service Tax (GST).
    (b) The city of Edmonton's purchase of forms from a Regina printing company.
    (c) Canada pension payments to eligible residents of Sherbrooke, Quebec.
    (d) The prime minister's salary.
    (e) The government of Newfoundland's payments to a New York engineering consulting company.

11. **Gross domestic product**
    (a) is equal to net national product minus depreciation.
    (b) excludes indirect taxes but includes depreciation.
    (c) must equal gross national product since both include depreciation.
    (d) includes replacement investment or depreciation.
    (e) is equal to GNP plus depreciation.

12. **Which of the following is included in the measurement of GDP from the income side of the national accounts?**
    (a) Consumption expenditures.
    (b) Expenditures for military aircraft by the federal government.
    (c) Residential construction.
    (d) Wages and salaries.
    (e) Bond purchases by households.

13. **Referring to Table 20-2 in the textbook, we see that net domestic income at factor cost**
    (a) includes wages and salaries.
    (b) includes interest and profits.
    (c) excludes depreciation.
    (d) excludes net indirect taxes.
    (e) All of the above.

14. **Suppose a Canadian firm imports $4000 worth of sport uniforms and sells them for $5000. The net effect on Canadian GDP would be**
    (a) to decrease the value of GDP by $4000.
    (b) to increase the value of GDP by $5000.
    (c) to increase the value of GDP by $1000.
    (d) to decrease the value of GDP by $5000.
    (e) no effect on GDP since the sports uniforms were produced outside of Canada.

National Income Accounting: Some Further Issues

There are several critical issues in this section. Firstly, the distinction is made between gross domestic product and gross national product. GDP measures the total output produced in Canada. GNP measures the total amount of income received by Canadian residents, no matter where that income was generated. Secondly, the section illustrates how the GDP deflator is derived from nominal (or current-dollar) GDP and real GDP values. Real measures of national income are calculated to reflect changes in real quantities. Thirdly, this section distinguishes between per capita GDP (overall material living standards) and labour productivity (GDP divided by the total numbers of hours worked). Lastly, this section emphasizes that GDP and related measures of national income must be interpreted with limitations in mind. Specifically, you should know the various activities that are omitted from GDP measurement.

15. **Disposable personal income is**
   (a) always the same as personal income.
   (b) income that is used only for consumption.
   (c) personal income remaining after net income taxes.
   (d) exclusive of transfer payments such as employment insurance payments.
   (e) personal income minus depreciation.

16. **GNP**
   (a) measures the value of production that is located in Canada.
   (b) measures the value of income that is earned from production in Canada.
   (c) measures the income accruing to Canadian residents.
   (d) excludes Canadian government purchases.
   (e) includes the value of illegal activities in Canada.

17. **The GDP deflator**
   (a) can be used only for the expenditure side of the national accounts.
   (b) is GDP at base-period prices divided by GDP at current prices times 100.
   (c) is the index used to measure the prices of goods and services purchased by households.
   (d) is GDP at current prices divided by GDP at base-period prices times 100.
   (e) is the index used to measure the prices of goods and services, including imported ones.

18. **Real GDP is calculated by**
   (a) dividing the nominal value of GDP by the GDP deflator.
   (b) dividing the GDP deflator by the nominal value of GDP.
   (c) dividing the constant dollar GDP by the GDP deflator.
   (d) multiplying nominal GDP by the GDP deflator.
   (e) dividing the nominal value of GDP by the GDP deflator and then multiplying by 100.

19. **Measures of labour productivity include**
   (a) real GDP divided by the population.
   (b) real GDP divided by the GDP deflator.
   (c) total wage and salary income divided by the population.
   (d) real GDP divided by the total number of hours worked.
   (e) real GDP divided by the labour force.

20. **If do-it-yourself homeowners stopped building their backyard decks and instead hired self-employed university students, then national income would**
   (a) be reduced as now measured.
   (b) be unaffected if the students reported their earnings.
   (c) increase if the students reported their earnings.
   (d) be unaffected since the students are not wage earners.
   (e) include only the costs of materials, but not wages.

21. **GDP understates the total production of goods and services for all but which one of the following reasons?**
   (a) No allowances are included for rental income.
   (b) Illegal activities are not included in the GDP estimate.
   (c) Legal production in the "underground economy" is not reported for income tax purposes.
   (d) Nonmarketed household services such as gardening and cleaning performed by family members are not included.
   (e) No allowances are included for non–wage productive activities.

22. **As a measure of human well-being, GDP may be inadequate because it**
   (a) overemphasizes the inequality of the distribution of income.
   (b) overstates the value of nonmarket work, such as home do-it-yourself activities.
   (c) focuses on production, not income.
   (d) ignores the influence of government transfer programmes on household spending.
   (e) ignores the way current production methods may reduce the quality of life.

23. **If the nominal value of GDP is $400 billion and the real value of GDP is $380 billion, then the value of the GDP deflator must have been**
   (a) 105.3.
   (b) 95.0.
   (c) 100.0.
   (d) 1.05.
   (e) None of the above.

SHORT-ANSWER QUESTIONS

1. Identify the items in the statements according to the following code: C = consumption; I = investment; G = government spending on goods and services; NX = net exports ($X - IM$); and N = not a component of national accounting from the expenditure side. Explain briefly.
   (a) The Bank of Nova Scotia expands its computer facilities at its Halifax offices.
   (b) As part of her duties, the sales manager of a Saskatchewan-based company stays at the Savoy Hotel in London, England.
   (c) The U.S. buys soft lumber from B.C. firms.
   (d) Winnipeg residents purchase $200 million in newly constructed homes.
   (e) Montreal Stock Exchange sales in January are $2 billion.
   (f) Manitobans take holidays in Alberta.
   (g) The government of New Brunswick buys trucks built in Oshawa, Ontario.
   (h) Marie buys "as is" a used motorcycle from her brother Chuck.
   (i) Ford (Canada) increases its inventory holdings of glass windshields produced in Ontario.
   (j) Newfoundlanders pay their annual provincial income taxes.

2. Explain briefly the difference between the following pairs of concepts:
   (a) Net versus gross national income.

   (b) GDP versus GNP.

   (c) Transfers versus taxes.

3. Which of the following transactions (or events) will be recorded in the GDP accounts in that year? Explain.
   (a) Henri, who normally earns $20 per hour, volunteers 100 hours of his time to assist a local politician in the Quebec provincial election.

(b) The federal government increases the defence budget in order to send 2000 troops to Afghanistan in 2003.

(c) Drug smugglers, using funds from the drug trade, finance the construction of a new hotel in Saskatoon.

(d) A self-employed carpenter buys $1000 worth of nails and lumber to build a fence for one of his customers. He charges the customer $1800 but doesn't report the $800 of wages or profits to the tax authorities.

(e) The Ontario government spends $200 million on improved municipal water purification systems because of the Walkerton bacteria-infected water incident.

(f) All welfare recipients in St. John's are hired as municipal workers.

4. In February 2005, a Toyota dealership in Toronto imported 100 new-model cars from Japan at a cost of $15 000 per car. By December 31, 2005, it had sold 40 of these cars to Canadian customers at a price of $20 000 each and another 20 of these cars to American customers in the U.S. at a price of $21 000 each. The remaining cars were sold to Canadian customers in January 2006 at a price of $18 000 each.

(a) Using the value-added approach, what was the contribution of this dealership to GDP in 2005?

VA = R - C of IG

= 1,220,000 - 900000

= $320 000

(b) Using the expenditure approach, indicate the changes in the different components of total expenditure (i.e., consumption, investment, etc.) in 2005 resulting from these transactions.

C = (40)(20000) = $800 000

I = (40)(15000) = $600 000

G = $0

X = (20)(21000) = $420 000

IM = (100)(15000) = $1500 000

GDP = C + I + G + (X - IM)

= $320 000

5. Assuming everything else is equal, indicate what will happen to GDP as a result of each of the following events taken separately. Briefly explain.

(a) John's washer breaks down and he starts taking his laundry to the nearby coin-laundry shop.

(b) Mary has rented an apartment in the Annex for the last four years. She now buys this apartment and continues to live there.

(c) The Tomkin Corporation issues new shares to finance a new $100 million plant to be constructed next year.

(d) The Ontario government pays compensation to victims in the contamination of Wakerton's drinking water system.

(e) The federal government issues new bonds to finance a $10 billion infrastructure project this year.

(f) The federal government issues $10 billion in new bonds to finance the purchasing of old bonds which are maturing this year.

EXERCISES

1. **Value Added at Each Stage of Production**
The value of a product in its final form is the sum of the value added by each of the various firms throughout the production process. Using the information provided here, calculate the value of one loaf of bread that is ultimately sold to a household. In doing so, calculate the value added at each stage of production. (This example demonstrates that the value-added approach avoids multiple counting.)

Stage of Production	Selling Price to the Next Stage	Value Added
1. Farmer (production of wheat)	$0.30	0.30
2. Milling company (flour)	0.55	0.25
3. Bakery (production of wholesale bread)	0.90	0.35
4. Retailer (sale to household)	1.00	0.1
Total	$2.75	$1.00

2. **Contribution to GDP Using the Value-Added Approach**

Suppose that the total output in 2000 of the metal container industry was $11 522 million and $7938 million in intermediate inputs were purchased to produce that amount.

(a) Calculate the value added in the metal container industry in 2000.

VA $3584 millio

(b) Indicate which of the following items represent value added in the metal container industry.

- payment for an independent auditor to examine business accounts
- wages of production workers who make cans –
- profits of metal container companies –
- payments for aluminium used in producing cans
- interest paid to banks by metal container companies –

3. **Calculation of GDP Using the Income and Expenditure Approaches**

There are two national accounting methods of estimating the value of GDP—from the income side and from the expenditure side. This problem deals with the calculation of gross domestic product using these two approaches. Select only the appropriate items. (Figures are in billions of dollars.)

e Government purchases of goods and services	$58.5
i Indirect taxes less subsidies	29.0
Personal income taxes	41.5
i Wages and employee compensation (including personal income taxes)	165.5
Interest on the public debt	15.5
e Consumption expenditure	168.4
e Exports	90.9
i Capital consumption allowance (depreciation)	33.5
e Imports	93.3
e Gross investment	67.2
i Net interest income	19.0
e Statistical discrepancy (expenditure side)	+0.2
i Business profits before taxes	45.1
i Statistical discrepancy (income side)	–0.2

Calculate the following values.

(a) GDP from the income side 291.9.

(b) GDP from the expenditure side 291.9.

(c) Assuming that net payments to foreigners had been $8 billion, calculate the value of GNP 283.9.

(d) Net domestic income at factor cost 229.6.

4. **Nominal GDP, Real GDP, and the GDP Deflator**
You are given the following information about an economy over the five-year period 2001–2005. All GDP values are in billions of dollars, the population (pop'n) figures are in millions. Please note that all indices have a base year of 2000 (2000 = 100).

Year	Current Dollar GDP	GDP Deflator	Constant Dollar GDP	Pop'n	Index of Output per Person Employed
2001	551.6	104.7	____	25.6	101.9
2002	605.9	____	553.0	25.9	103.1
2003	649.9	114.8	566.1	26.2	102.4
2004	____	118.6	563.1	26.6	101.7
2005	674.4	121.8	____	27.0	102.3

(a) Fill in the missing entries in the table.

(b) Current-dollar GDP increased by 9.84 percent between 2001 and 2002. Calculate the percentage increases in constant-dollar (real) income and in the GDP deflator. Why doesn't the sum of the two percentages equal the percentage increase in nominal GDP?

(c) Calculate the growth rate in real GDP per capita for 2001–2002 and 2004–2005. Which of the two periods is likely to represent a recessionary phase of the economy?

5. **Calculation of Disposable Personal Income**
This exercise focuses on other measures of national income. You are given the following national income measures for an economy in a particular year. (Figures are in billions of dollars.)

Gross domestic product at market prices	$285
Capital consumption allowances (depreciation)	32
Undistributed corporate profits	12
Government transfers to households	30
Personal income taxes	42
Indirect taxes less subsidies	30
Consumer expenditure	168
Corporate profit taxes	12
Net foreign investment income received	5

(a) Calculate the value for disposable personal income.

(b) The definition of personal saving is disposable personal income minus consumption expenditure. What is its magnitude?

6. **Contribution to GDP and Net Domestic Income**

The Racing Motor Company had 100 motorcycles in inventory at the start of the year at an imported value of $10 000 each.

- These 100 motorcycles were sold to consumers at a price of $14 000 each ($2500 for sales commissions; $1000 for corporate profit before taxes; and $500 for indirect sales taxes).
- During the year this company imported another 500 motorcycles at an import price of $11 000 each. Of these new imports, 300 were sold to consumers for $15 000 each ($2500 for sales commissions; $1000 for corporate profits before taxes; and $500 for indirect sales taxes).
- An additional 100 were exported at $13 500 ($2000 for sales commissions and $500 for corporate profit before taxes). The final 100 were held in inventory at their imported price.

(a) Evaluate the total impact from these transactions on consumption, inventory change, imports, and exports.

(b) Evaluate the total impact from these transactions on wages, corporate profit before taxes, and indirect taxes.

(c) Compute the total change in GDP at market prices.

(d) Compute the total change in net domestic income at factor cost.

7. **Calculation of National Accounts**

Below are data from the national accounts of a hypothetical country. Assume that all relevant items you need to answer the questions have been provided.

Wages and salaries	800	Depreciation	60
Indirect taxes minus subsidies	40	Undistributed corporate profits	80
Corporate profits before taxes	300	Corporate profits taxes	170
Imports	140	Exports	130
Net unincorporated business income	50	Consumption	920
Investment	200	Interest and rental income	200

Use the above data to compute the following:

(a) Net domestic income

(b) Gross domestic product

(c) Government spending

(d) Net investment

(e) Dividends

EXTENSION EXERCISE

E1. Nominal GDP, Real GDP, and the GDP Deflator

This exercise focuses on nominal and real output and the GDP deflator outlined in *Applying Economic Concepts 20-2*. It also demonstrates that the value of the GDP deflator depends on the selection of the base year. Assume that there are only two industries in an economy. Output and unit price for each industry are shown for three years.

Year	Quantity of Industry A (tons)	Quantity of Industry B (metres)	Price in Industry A (per ton)	Price in Industry B (per metre)	Nominal Value of Output
1	4000	20 000	$20	$5	$____
2	6000	21 000	22	4	$____
3	6000	18 000	24	6	$____

(a) Calculate the nominal value of output in Industry A in each of the three years. Do the same for Industry B. Find national output in nominal terms for each of the three years by adding the two output values for A and B.

(b) Using Year 1 prices, calculate the real value of output in Industry A for each of the three years. Do the same for Industry B. What is the value of real output in the economy for each of the three years?

(c) Calculate the value of the GDP deflator (base year 1) for each of the three years.

(d) Repeat question (b) but now use Year 2 prices and calculate the real value in Industry A and B and then aggregate to determine the value of real output in the economy for each of the three years.

(e) Calculate the new value of the GDP deflator (base year 2) for each of the three years.

(f) Comment on your answers to parts (c) and (e).

ADDITIONAL MULTIPLE-CHOICE QUESTIONS

1. **Suppose that a firm sells its output for $40 000, that it pays $22 000 in wages, $10 000 for materials purchased from other firms, and $3000 in interest payments to bankers, and that it declares profits of $5000. The firm's value added is**
   (a) $18 000.
   (b) $40 000.
   (c) $30 000.
   (d) $35 000.
   (e) $27 000.

2. **Suppose that the steel industry has a total output of $63.8 billion and purchases $49.0 billion in intermediate inputs. Hence, the value added in billions of the steel industry in that period is**
   (a) $112.8.
   (b) –$14.8.
   (c) $63.8.
   (d) $14.8.
   (e) $49.0.

3. **Measured from the expenditure side, GDP equals**
   (a) $C_a + I_a + G_a + (X_a - IM_a)$.
   (b) $C_a + I_a + G_a - T_a + (X_a - IM_a)$.
   (c) $C_a + I_a + G_a - X_a + IM_a$.
   (d) GNP minus depreciation.
   (e) None of the above.

4. Company XYZ receives $50 million from a new issue of stock. It uses $30 million of the proceeds to build a new factory and uses the other $20 million to retire its debt with various banks. This transaction increases measured GDP in millions of dollars by

(a) 50.
(b) 30.
(c) 20.
(d) 100.
(e) 80.

***5. Current measures of GDP tend to overstate economic welfare because**

(a) the benefits of increased leisure time are ignored.
(b) the non-market activity of work in the home is ignored.
(c) the economic "bads" associated with production, such as pollution, are ignored.
(d) transactions such as teenage babysitting services are ignored.
(e) the tips that waiters receive are ignored.

6. According to Figure 20-1 in the textbook, what is an *injection* into the circular flow?

(a) imports.
(b) domestic production.
(c) investment.
(d) taxes.
(e) consumption.

***7. If nominal GDP is $150 and real GDP is $125, the value of the GDP deflator is**

(a) 120.
(b) 0.83.
(c) 1.2.
(d) 83.
(e) 125.

***8. If an economy's annual real GDP increases by 11 percent and its prices increase on an annual basis by 9 percent, then nominal GDP**

(a) increases by approximately 99 percent.
(b) increases by approximately 21 percent.
(c) decreases by approximately 20 percent.
(d) increases by 2.0 percent.
(e) remains constant.

***9. If nominal GDP rises from $400 billion to $408 billion and the GDP deflator rises from 125 to 127,**

(a) real GDP has risen from $3.2 billion to $3.21 billion.
(b) real GDP has risen from $500 billion to $518 billion.
(c) real GDP is unchanged.
(d) everyone is necessarily better off since nominal GDP has increased.
(e) real GDP has risen from $320 billion to approximately $321 billion.

***10. In a particular year an economy's GDP is $401 billion, net payments to foreigners are $46 billion, and indirect taxes less subsidies are $5 billion. The value of the economy's GNP is**

(a) $447 billion.
(b) $355 billion.
(c) $350 billion.
(d) $360 billion.
(e) $452 billion.

For Questions 11 to 13 use the information in the table below for a hypothetical economy that produces only two goods, A and B.

Year	Price	Quantity
2002		
Good A	$1.00	50 units
Good B	$2.00	100 units
2003		
Good A	$2.00	90 units
Good B	$3.00	160 units

11. The values of nominal GDP in 2002 and 2003 were, respectively,
(a) $150, $250.
(b) $250, $660.
(c) $800, $720.
(d) $230, $660.
(e) $660, $150.

12. The real GDP in 2003, expressed in 2002 dollars, was
(a) $660.
(b) $400.
(c) $410.
(d) $800.
(e) 250 units.

***13. The value of the GDP deflator in 2003 was approximately**
(a) 161.
(b) 165.
(c) 61.
(d) 21.
(e) 176.0.

14. Under the expenditure approach, gross domestic product includes
(a) paving of old roads.
(b) sale of used cars.
(c) sale of government bonds.
(d) sale of Air Canada shares.
(e) None of the above.

***15. Assume a dealership in Toronto bought 40 brand-new cars from the Ford Motor Company in Oakville, Ontario, at a cost of $15 000 per car in July of 2005, and by December 31, 2005 had sold 20 of these cars at a price of $20 000 each. The remaining cars were sold in January 2006 at a price of $18 000 each. The effect of these transactions on GDP in the year 2005 is**
(a) 760 000.
(b) 600 000.
(c) 400 000.
(d) 160 000.
(e) 100 000.

16. Consider a hypothetical economy where, at the start of 2005, aggregate output was $100 billion and the population was 10 million. During 2005, aggregate output increased by 5%, the population increased by 2%, and the average price level remained constant. Given this information, which of the following statements is correct?
(a) Aggregate output per capita was $1000 at the start of 2005.
(b) Aggregate output was $100.5 billion at the end of 2005.
(c) Aggregate output per capita was $10 500 at the end of 2005.
(d) The annual growth rate of output per capita was approximately 3% during 2005.
(e) None of the above.

***17. Alcan Co. produces 1000 tons of aluminium. Aluminium sells for $60 per ton. Alcan pays wages of $20 000; buys $30 000 worth of bauxite, which is the only intermediate good needed to produce the aluminium; pays dividends of $6000 to its shareholders; and pays $4000 in corporate taxes. Alcan's contribution to GDP is**

(a) $20 000.
(b) $24 000.
(c) $30 000.
(d) $56 000.
(e) $60 000.

***18. Suppose that the government collects $3 million in taxes, pays $2 million in social security benefits, pays $0.5 million in interest on the national debt, and pays workers $2 million in wages. The government contribution to GDP is**

(a) $2 million.
(b) $3 million.
(c) $4.5 million.
(d) $7.5 million.
(e) None of the above.

SOLUTIONS

Chapter Review

1.(a) **2.**(a) **3.**(c) **4.**(d) **5.**(a) **6.**(d) **7.**(d) **8.**(a) **9.**(b) **10.**(c) **11.**(d) **12.**(d) **13.**(e) **14.**(c) **15.**(c) **16.**(c) **17.**(d) **18.**(e) **19.**(d) **20.**(c) **21.**(a) **22.**(e) **23.**(a)

Short-Answer Questions

1. **(a)** *I;* the bank is investing in computer equipment to increase production efficiency and better serve its customers.

(b) *NX;* the trip to London is a business expense on a service purchased abroad. Hence, this purchase will be recorded as an import.

(c) *NX;* soft lumber sales are Canadian exports to the U.S.

(d) *I;* many students incorrectly believe that purchases of new residential homes is consumption in the national accounts. This is *not* true, because national accountants assume that most new homes are built by construction companies as investments and then sold to households.

(e) *N;* stock sales are not expenditures on goods and services. They are a form of financial saving.

(f) *C;* Manitobans purchase tourist services from Albertans—purchases of a domestically produced service.

(g) *G;* this is a straightforward example of a government expenditure.

(h) *N;* Chuck's purchase of a new motorcycle will have already been recorded. Hence, Marie's used motorcycle purchase will not be recorded in the national accounts.

(i) *I;* the textbook explains that increases in inventory holdings count as investment. Ford increased its holding of windshields to increase its ability to produce future cars.

(j) *N;* income tax payments are not components of aggregate expenditure. They are leakages from the circular flow.

2. **(a)** Net national income excludes capital consumption allowances (depreciation). Gross national income includes depreciation.

(b) GDP measures the value of output produced in Canada. GNP measures the total amount of income received by Canadian residents, no matter where that income was generated. A country that is a "net debtor" pays more in income to non-residents than it receives in income from non-residents.

(c) Transfer payments to Canadians include subsidies to businesses, Canada Pension Plan payments, and welfare payments. Tax payments by Canadian businesses and households include personal and business taxes. Net taxes are therefore defined as tax liabilities minus all transfers. Since tax liabilities are generally greater than transfer payments, net taxes are usually positive.

3. (a) This is an example of a nonmarketed activity and therefore is not included in GDP accounts. If the politician had paid Henri $2000 for his 100 hours of work, then Henri's income would have been included in the GDP accounts.

(b) This is a straightforward example of an increased government expenditure that would be recorded in the GDP accounts.

(c) Even though the funds used to purchase the hotel are from illegal activities, the actual purchase would be recorded in the investment component of the GDP accounts.

(d) The $1000 purchase of nails and lumber would be recorded in the GDP accounts. The carpenter's value added ($800) is not included since the carpenter did not report his income. The $800 represents an "underground" economy transaction.

(e) The costs ("bads") of bacteria-infected water in Walkerton would not be included, but the Ontario government's new expenditures on improved municipal water systems would be recorded in the government expenditure of aggregate expenditures.

(f) The income paid to welfare recipients is not included in the measure of GDP. However, if all were hired as municipal workers, their salaries would be included in the government expenditure component of aggregate expenditures.

4. (a) Value added is the difference between the revenue a firm generates by selling its product and the cost of intermediate goods required for the production of that product. In the case of this car dealership, the intermediate good is the car bought from the factory in Japan and the final good is the same car when sold to the public. The dealership adds value to the product (the car) by providing an intermediary service between the car producer and the final consumer of the car.

Let's examine the value added (VA) here to the 40 cars sold to Canadian customers, to the 20 cars sold to American customers, and to the remaining 40 unsold cars:

- VA to 40 cars sold to Canadian customers = 40 ($20 000 – $15 000) = $200 000.
- VA to 20 cars sold to American customers = 20 ($21 000 – $15 000) = $120 000.
- VA to 40 unsold cars = 40 ($15 000 – $15 000) = $0

Therefore, the total value added is $320 000.

(b) Let's see what changes have occurred to C, I, G, X, and IM.

$\Delta C = +800\,000$ (i.e., 40 times $20 000)

$\Delta I = +\$600\,000$ (i.e., an increase in inventory of 40 times $15 000)

$\Delta G = 0$

$\Delta X = +\$420\,000$ (i.e., 20 times $21 000)

$\Delta IM = +1\,500\,000$ (i.e., 100 times $15 000)

Therefore, the total change in GDP is:

$$\Delta GDP = \Delta C + \Delta I + \Delta G + \Delta X - \Delta IM$$
$$= \$800\,000 + \$600\,000 + \$420\,000 - \$1\,500\,000$$
$$= \$320\,000.$$

5. (a) When John used to wash his clothes himself at home, the cost of doing his laundry was not counted as part of GDP. Now that he washes his clothes at the laundry shop, the cost of doing his laundry is reported to Statistics Canada and thus GDP increases.

(b) This question is a bit tricky. First, the purchase of an old apartment is not counted as investment for GDP purposes—so investment expenditure does not change as a result of this event. Second, now Mary is no longer paying rent and thus we would be tempted to conclude that GDP decreased. However, we have seen that there is a significant degree of arbitrariness regarding which types of expenditures are included in GDP and which are not. Indeed, inclusions/exclusions of types of expenditures are determined by conventions, and conventions do not follow any strict rules. And this is one of those cases! Statistics Canada counts your rental payment as part of GDP when you rent a housing unit, but also counts it when you don't! That is, for GDP purposes, Statistics Canada counts as if you were paying rent to yourself—this is called *imputed rents to owners' occupied houses*. Therefore, GDP does not change as a result of this event.

(c) There is no change in GDP in the current year since the Tomkin Corporation raises the necessary financial resources for the investment project but it will wait until next year to make the investment. Therefore, GDP will increase next year but not in the current year.

(d) This represents a government transfer—a transfer from Ontario taxpayers to the victims of this tragedy. It's not a payment for a good or service, and thus it is not counted as part of GDP. Therefore, GDP does not change as a result of this event.

(e) The public's purchase of the newly issued bonds does not in itself affect the level of GDP since this is not considered an investment for GDP purposes. However, current GDP increases when the government spends these funds in the infrastructure project.

(f) Again, the public's purchase of the newly issued bonds does not in itself affect the level of GDP since this is not considered an investment for GDP purposes. But the government does not use the raised funds to buy goods and services—it uses these funds to pay back old debt. This transaction, therefore, represents a transfer payment from new lenders to the government to old lenders to the government and GDP does not change.

Exercises

1. (a) The market value of one loaf of bread is $1.00. This is found by the sum of the value added ($0.30 from the first stage plus $0.25 from the second stage plus $0.35 from the third stage plus $0.10 from the fourth stage). Thus, the sum of the valued added at each stage equals the value of the final product. Notice that the total $2.75 counts the contribution of the farmer four times.

2. (a) $3584 million = $11 522 – $7938.
   (b) Items that represent value added are wages of production workers, profits of metal container companies, and interest paid by metal container companies. Payments for aluminium and for an independent auditor are intermediate inputs.

3. (a) 29.0 + 165.5 + 33.5 + 19.0 + 45.1 – 0.2 = 291.9.
   (b) 58.5 + 168.4 + 67.2 + 90.9 – 93.3 + 0.2 = 291.9.
   (c) 291.9 – 8.0 = 283.9.
   (d) 291.9 – 33.5 – 29.0 + 0.2 = 229.6.

4. (a) GDP in current dollars: 2004: 667.8 (563.1 × 1.186).
   GDP deflator: 2002: 109.6 [(605.9 × 553.0) × 100].
   GDP in constant dollars: 2001: 526.8 [(551.6 × 104.7) times 100]; 2005: 553.7.
   (b) Real GDP increased by 4.97 percent while the prices increased by 4.68 percent. The increase in nominal GDP is equal to the product of the two (1.0497)(1.0468) rather than the sum of the two percentages. See footnote #3 in the textbook chapter (p. 490).
   (c) The growth rate in real GDP per capita for 2001–2002 is calculated by first determining real GDP per capita for each of the years. In 2001 per capita real GDP was $20 578 (526.8 billion × 25.6 million) and in 2002 it was $21 351; hence, the percentage increase was 3.76 percent. The percentage change in real per capita GDP between 2004 and 2005 was –3.13 percent [(20 507 – 21 169)/21 169 × 100%]. The period 2004–2005 was considered a recessionary period.

5. (a) Disposable personal income = GDP + net foreign investment income – capital consumption allowance – indirect taxes less subsidies – retained earnings – business taxes + government transfers – personal income taxes; 285 + 5 – 32 – 30 – 12 – 12 + 30 – 42 = 192.
   (b) Personal saving = disposable personal income minus consumption expenditure; in this case, S = 192 – 168 = 24.

6. (a) The initial sale of the 100 motorcycles in inventory reduces investment (i.e., inventory investment) by 100 × $10 000 = $1 000 000, and increases consumption expenditure by 100 × $14 000 = $1 400 000. The import of an additional 500 motorcycles increases imports by 500 × $11 000 = $5 500 000. The sale of 300 of these motorcycles increases consumption by 300 × $15 000 = $4 500 000. The export of an additional 100 of these motorcycles increases exports by 100 × $13 500 = $1 350 000. The remaining 100 motorcycles increases investment (i.e., inventory investment) by 100 × $11 000 = $1 100 000. Therefore, 1) consumption increases by $1 400 000 + $4 500 000 = +$5 900 000; 2) inventory changes by –$1 000 000 + $1 100 000 = +$100 000; 3) imports increase by +$5 500 000; and 4) exports increase by +$1 350 000.

(b) Wages increase by \$250 000 (i.e., 100 × \$2500) plus \$750 000 (i.e., 300 × \$2500) plus \$200 000 (i.e., 100 × \$2000) for a total of \$1 200 000. Corporate profits before taxes increase by \$100 000 (i.e., 100 × \$1000) plus \$300 000 (i.e., 300 × \$1000) plus \$50 000 (i.e., 100 × \$500) for a total of \$450 000. The collection of indirect taxes increases by \$50 000 (i.e., 100 × \$500) plus \$150 000 (i.e., 300 × \$500) for a total of \$200 000.

(c) $\Delta GDP = \Delta C + \Delta I + \Delta X - \Delta MI$
= \$5 900 000 + \$100 000 + \$1 350 000 – \$5 500 000
= \$1 850 000.

(d) The change in net domestic income is equal to the change in GDP minus the change in indirect taxes:
$\Delta NDI = \Delta GDP - \Delta(\text{Indirect Taxes})$
= \$1 850 000 – \$200 000
= \$1 650 000
Alternatively, the change in net domestic Income is equal to the change in wages plus the change in corporate profits before taxes:
$\Delta NDI = \Delta \text{Wages} + \Delta(\text{Corporate Profits})$
= \$1 200 000 + \$450 000
= \$1 650 000

7. (a) Net domestic income (NDI) = Wages & salaries (800) + Corporate profits (300) + Interest & rental income (200) + Net unincorporated business income (50) = 1350.

(b) Gross domestic product (GDP) = NDI (1350) + indirect taxes minus subsidies (40) + depreciation (60) = 1450.

(c) GDP = C + I + G + NX
G = GDP (1 450) – I (200) – C (920) – X (130) + IM (140) = 340

(d) Net investment = Investment (200) – Depreciation (60) = 140

(e) Corporate profits = Corporate profit taxes + Undistributed corporate profits + Dividends
Dividends = Corporate profits (300) – Corporate taxes (170) – Undistributed profits (80) = 50

Extension Exercise

E1. (a) Nominal value of output (in dollars)

Year	In A	In B	In Economy
1	80 000	100 000	180 000
2	132 000	84 000	216 000
3	144 000	108 000	252 000

(b) Real value

Industry A:
in year 1 = 4000 × 20 = \$80 000
in year 2 = 6000 × 20 = \$120 000
in year 3 = 6000 × 20 = \$120 000

Industry B:
in year 1 = 20 000 × 5 = \$100 000
in year 2 = 21 000 × 5 = \$105 000
in year 3 = 18 000 × 5 = \$90 000

Total Economy:
in year 1 = 80 000 + 100 000 = \$180 000
in year 2 = 120 000 + 105 000 = \$225 000
in year 3 = 120 000 + 90 000 = \$210 000

(c) year 1: 180 000/180 000 × 100 = 100.0
year 2: 216 000/225 000 × 100 = 96.0
year 3: 252 000/210 000 × 100 = 120.0

(d) Real value

Industry A:
in year 1 = 4000 × 22 = \$88 000
in year 2 = 6000 × 22 = \$132 000

in year 3 = 6000 × 22 = \$132 000

Industry B:

in year 1 = 20 000 × 4 = \$80 000

in year 2 = 21 000 × 4 = \$84 000

in year 3 = 18 000 × 4 = \$72 000

Total Economy:

in year 1 = 88 000 + 80 000 = \$168 000

in year 2 = 132 000 + 84 000 = \$216 000

in year 3 = 132 000 + 72 000 = \$204 000

(e) year 1: 180 000/168 000 × 100 = 107

year 2: 216 000/216 000 × 100 = 100

year 3: 252 000/204 000 × 100 = 124

(f) Although the ranking is the same, the values differ because relative prices are different in the two years. The relative price of A to B is 4 in year 1 but is 5.5 in year 2. Hence, output is weighted by different relative prices in the two years.

Additional Multiple-Choice Questions

1.(c) **2.**(d) **3.**(a) **4.**(b) **5.**(c) **6.**(c) **7.**(a) **8.**(b) **9.**(e) **10.**(b) **11.**(b) **12.**(c) **13.**(a) **14.**(a) **15.**(e) **16.**(d) **17.**(c) **18.**(a)

Explanations for the Asterisked Multiple-Choice Questions

5.(c) The presence of pollution and other "bads" that are not included (as negative items) in the GDP implies that GDP overstates economic welfare.

7.(a) Dividing \$150 (nominal income) by \$125, we obtain 1.2. Multiplying this value by 100 implies that the GDP deflator is 120.

8.(b) This is a tricky question because you must read footnote #3 (Chapter 20) in the textbook. Nominal income increases by the formula (1.11) times (1.09), or 1.2099), not by simply adding 9 and 11.

9.(e) Real GDP in the two years is \$320 (\$400 divided by 1.25) and \$321.3 (\$408 divided by 1.27). Hence, (e) is correct.

10.(b) Indirect taxes less subsidies are not at issue. GNP is calculated by subtracting (since we have net payments to foreigners) \$46 billion from \$401 billion.

13.(a) This is obtained by dividing \$660 by \$410 and then multiplying by 100 which equals 161 approximately.

15.(e) The effect on GDP is equal to the value added by this dealership: \$5000 per car sold and none for the cars kept in inventory at the end of the year—i.e., VA = 20 cars times \$5000 = \$100 000.

17.(c) The value added by this company is equal to the revenues generated by the production and sale of aluminium minus the cost of intermediate goods required for the production of aluminium (bauxite): VA = \$60 000 – \$30 000 = \$30 000.

18.(a) The only payment for goods and services is wages (i.e., payment for labour services); payments in social security benefits and interest on the national debt are transfer payments and are not included in GDP. Therefore, the government contribution to GDP is \$2 million.

PART 8: THE ECONOMY IN THE SHORT RUN

CHAPTER 21

THE SIMPLEST SHORT-RUN MACRO MODEL

LO

LEARNING OBJECTIVES

In this chapter you will learn

1 the difference between desired expenditure and actual expenditure.

2 the determinants of desired consumption and desired investment expenditures.

3 how to define equilibrium national income.

4 how a change in desired expenditure affects equilibrium income, and how this change is reflected by the multiplier.

CHAPTER OVERVIEW

Desired aggregate expenditure consists of desired consumption expenditure, desired investment, desired government expenditure, and desired net exports (desired exports minus desired imports). This chapter focuses on only two sources of desired demand: desired consumption and desired investment.

The next three chapters discuss how equilibrium national income is determined. This chapter imposes three simplifying conditions:

- the price level, interest rates, and the exchange rate are fixed (constant);
- the economy has no government (no net taxes and no government purchases); and
- the economy is "closed" (no foreign trade).

Recall also that factor productivity and factor supplies are assumed constant in the short run. However, factor utilization rates can change in the short run.

The chapter introduces two important distinctions: **desired versus actual expenditure** and **autonomous versus induced expenditure**. Whereas national accounts measure *actual* expenditures, national income theory deals with *desired* expenditures. Desired expenditure refers to what people would like to spend out of the resources that are at their command rather than what they actually spend. An expenditure is said to be autonomous when its level *does not* depend on the level of actual national income. Components of aggregate expenditure that change in response to changes in national income are called **induced expenditures**. Those that don't are called **autonomous expenditures**.

It is critical that students understand the meaning of the word "marginal" as it applies to economic concepts. A concept that is described as marginal means that the concept involves some aspect of change. In many cases, the economic concept involves a ratio of two variables. If the ratio is described as marginal then it involves a change in one variable over the change in another. The symbol Δ (Greek delta) is often used to denote change.

A key relationship in this chapter is the **consumption function**: the relationship between disposable income and desired consumption. The ratio of the change in desired consumption to a change in disposable income is called the **marginal propensity to consume (MPC)**. Those familiar with mathematics will quickly appreciate that the marginal propensity to consume is the slope of the consumption function.

Some macroeconomic ratios are described as "average" propensities, which means that the behaviour we are describing is the ratio of levels. For example, the ratio of the consumption level to the level of actual national income is called the **average propensity to consume (APC).**

If consumption is known, then saving is known, since disposable income must be either consumed or saved. As result, we can derive a saving function, a relationship between desired saving and actual national income. The slope of the saving function is called the **marginal propensity to save**; it measures the ratio of the change in saving to the change in national income. By way of contrast, the ratio of the level of saving to the level of national income is called the **average propensity to save**.

Desired consumption and desired investment (which is assumed to be autonomous) together determine **aggregate desired expenditure (*AE*)** in the economy, which is depicted by an aggregate expenditure function. **Equilibrium national income** is defined as that level of national income where desired aggregate expenditure equals actual national income. If desired and actual income are not equal, production will adjust eventually to create an equilibrium situation.

Changes in equilibrium occur from changes in autonomous expenditure which shift the aggregate expenditure function. The simple multiplier analysis indicates the quantitative change in equilibrium income from changes in autonomous expenditure *assuming a constant price level.* The size of the multiplier depends on the slope the *AE* curve.

HINTS AND TIPS

The following may help you to avoid some of the most common errors on examinations.

✓ Learn what is meant by "marginal" and "average" propensities and know how to calculate them. A marginal propensity denotes a ratio of changes. For example, the marginal propensity to consume is the ratio of the change in desired consumption to the change in disposable income.

✓ Understand that movements along the consumption function are caused by changes in real disposable income while changes in wealth, interest rates, and expectations shift the consumption function. If wealth decreases, the consumption function shifts downward.

✓ Purchases of financial assets (such as stocks and bonds) and households' purchases of big-tag items (such as vehicles and home appliances) are not components of investment in macroeconomic theory. Instead, components of investment expenditure are residential construction, changes in inventory, and new plant and equipment.

✓ Understand that the autonomous investment expenditure function shifts when real interest rates and business expectations change. A decrease in real interest rates shifts the investment expenditure function upward.

✓ Understand the underlying factors that shift the aggregate expenditure function versus those that cause movements along it. Only changes in actual national income cause movements along the *AE* function. Exogenous factors such as changes in wealth, interest rates, and expectations shift the *AE* function.

✓ Learn that the equilibrium condition in this simple model is $Y = C + I$.

✓ Learn the correct formula for the simple multiplier. The correct formula for the simple multiplier is $1/1 - z$ where z is the marginal propensity to spend. Note that z is equal to the *MPC* only for this chapter.

CHAPTER REVIEW

Desired Aggregate Expenditure

Households divide their disposable income (which is equal to actual income since there are no taxes and no government transfers in the simplest model) between consumption and saving. The textbook identifies four factors that influence desired consumption: (1) current disposable income, (2) wealth, (3) interest rates, and expectations about the future. Changes in current disposable income cause movements along the consumption and saving curves, while changes in wealth, interest rates, and expectations cause shifts in the consumption and saving curves. The distinction between the marginal and average propensities to consume and save is important. The slopes of the consumption and saving curves are the *marginal propensity to consume* and the *marginal propensity to save,* respectively.

Desired investment (changes in inventory, residential construction, and new plant and equipment) is assumed to be an autonomous expenditure. Make sure you understand how changes in the three most important determinants of desired investment expenditure—the real interest rate, changes in sales, and business confidence—shift the *investment curve* up or down in a parallel fashion.

1. Desired expenditure is
- (a) the level of expenditure actually made by decision makers.
- (b) what national accountants measure.
- (c) what decision makers would like to spend with the resources at their command.
- (d) always autonomous.
- (e) what decision makers aspire to spend without regard to the resources at their command.

2. Autonomous expenditures
- (a) depend on desired national income.
- (b) do not depend on national income.
- (c) are induced expenditures.
- (d) are net of taxes.
- (e) are those made by countries that are politically autonomous.

3. The consumption function
- (a) describes the relation between desired real consumption expenditure and the factors that determine it, like real disposable income.
- (b) refers to the relation between consumption expenditure and prices.
- (c) is relatively unimportant in macroeconomics, because consumption is a small component of aggregate expenditure in most economies.
- (d) is a relationship between consumption expenditure and saving.
- (e) refers to the relation between individuals' consumption and their imported purchases.

4. The marginal propensity to consume is expressed as
- (a) the change in autonomous consumption.
- (b) the change in consumption divided by disposable income.
- (c) consumption divided by disposable income.
- (d) the change in consumption divided by the change in disposable income.
- (e) consumption divided by the change in disposable income.

5. Which of the following is a basic characteristic of the textbook's consumption function?
- (a) Below the break-even level, $APC > 1$ and $MPC < 0$.
- (b) The *MPC* and *APC* are always less than unity.
- (c) As income rises, the *MPC* falls and the *APC* rises.
- (d) The *APC* is greater than zero and less than one and the *MPC* falls as income rises.
- (e) The *MPC* is greater than zero and less than one and the *APC* falls as income rises.

6. **If aggregate real disposable income rose from $20 000 to $30 000 and desired consumption expenditure rose from $19 000 to $26 000, it can be concluded that**
   (a) the average propensity to consume fell as disposable income increased.
   (b) the marginal propensity to save is 0.30.
   (c) the marginal propensity to consume is 0.70.
   (d) desired saving increased from $1000 to $4000.
   (e) All of the above are correct.

7. **Total saving divided by total income is called the**
   (a) marginal propensity to save.
   (b) saving function.
   (c) average propensity to save.
   (d) marginal propensity not to consume.
   (e) total propensity to save.

8. **An increase in households' wealth is predicted to**
   (a) shift the consumption function down.
   (b) shift the saving function up.
   (c) increase the marginal propensity to consume out of disposable income.
   (d) shift the consumption function up.
   (e) increase the marginal propensity to consume and shift the consumption function up.

9. **Canadian real per capita disposable income increased by about 16 percent between 1981 and 2005. Over this period, the share of per capita consumption expenditure in per capita disposable income increased from about 75 percent in 2001 to more than 95 percent in 2005. Which of the following statements may explain this increase in consumption expenditure as a share of disposable income?**
   (a) The increase in real per capita disposable income over the period reduced the need for saving for future consumption.
   (b) Households had negative expectations about the future state of the economy and decided to spend more while they could.
   (c) A significant decrease in asset values convinced households that saving for the future was too risky.
   (d) Real rates of interest reached historically low levels in the 1990s, thus discouraging saving and fostering higher consumption expenditure.
   (e) The average propensity to consume tends to increase as disposable income increases.

10. **Desired investment is most likely to rise when**
   (a) real interest rates rise.
   (b) sales remain constant.
   (c) sales are expected to fall.
   (d) expectations of future profits improve.
   (e) None of the above.

11. **A reduction in real interest rates**
   (a) normally reduces the mortgage payments a home buyer must make.
   (b) reduces the incentive for businesses to hold inventories.
   (c) increases the financing costs to firms that must borrow funds.
   (d) causes the investment function to shift down.
   (e) None of the above.

12. Which of the following events shifts the investment curve up?

(a) An increase in the real interest rate.
(b) An increase in the expected level of sales.
(c) An increasing expectation by firms that sales will decline.
(d) An increasing expectation by firms that actual expenditures will exceed desired expenditures.
(e) Speculation that business profits will be taxed more heavily in the future.

13. An aggregate expenditure function illustrates that as national income rises

(a) employment rises.
(b) desired expenditures on currently produced goods fall.
(c) prices rise.
(d) interest rates must also rise.
(e) desired expenditures on currently produced goods will rise by a proportion of the increase in national income.

14. The aggregate expenditure function is a relationship between

(a) actual real expenditure and real national income.
(b) desired real expenditure and nominal national income.
(c) desired real expenditure and real actual national income.
(d) real disposable income and saving.
(e) actual nominal expenditure and nominal national income.

15. In a simple macroeconomic model, with a closed economy and no government, the aggregate expenditure function is the sum of

(a) desired consumption and desired investment.
(b) saving and desired investment.
(c) consumption and disposable income.
(d) desired consumption and desired saving.
(e) actual consumption and actual investment.

16. The marginal propensity to spend

(a) falls as actual national income increases.
(b) is always equal to one.
(c) is the slope of the aggregate expenditure function.
(d) may be greater than one depending on the level of actual national income.
(e) is the ratio of the change in national income to the change in expenditure.

Equilibrium National Income

When something is in *equilibrium,* there is no tendency for it to change. In the context of national income theory, we need to specify the equilibrium conditions for national income: *desired* aggregate expenditure equals *actual* national income.

This equilibrium condition is written as $Y = C + I$. When desired aggregate expenditure is greater than actual income, actual inventory levels will fall below desired levels. Hence, there will be pressure for firms to increase production by hiring more factors of production. For any level of income at which aggregate desired expenditure is less than actual output, there will be pressure for national income to fall since actual inventory levels will increase above desired levels.

17. In a macroeconomic model that includes consumption and investment, equilibrium real national income is attained when

(a) actual real output is equal to desired real aggregate expenditure.
(b) the aggregate expenditure function intersects the 45° line.
(c) the average propensity of desired spending is unity.
(d) there is no unintended inventory accumulation or reduction.
(e) All of the above.

18. At a level of national income where aggregate desired expenditure falls short of actual national income, there will be a tendency for

(a) national income to rise.
(b) national income to fall.
(c) aggregate desired expenditure to increase.
(d) prices to rise.
(e) None of the above.

19. If desired aggregate expenditures exceed actual national income,

(a) inventories accumulate, causing national income to rise.
(b) national income will fall, because desired expenditures are less than actual expenditures.
(c) shortages of goods and reductions in inventories will cause producers to increase output and national income will rise.
(d) national income may increase or decrease, depending on the relative sizes of the average propensity to consume and the average propensity to save.
(e) there will be no change in national income.

20. On a graph depicting equilibrium national income (where desired aggregate expenditure equals actual national income), consider a level of actual national income where the vertical distance from the horizontal axis to the *AE* function is less than the vertical distance to the 45° line. At such an income level inventories are ________, and so actual national income will tend to ________.

(a) accumulating, rise
(b) equal to planned inventory accumulation, stay at that level
(c) being depleted, rise
(d) accumulating, fall
(e) being depleted, fall

21. On a graph depicting equilibrium national income (where desired saving equals desired investment), consider a level of national income where the vertical distance from the horizontal axis to the saving function is less than the vertical distance to the investment function. At this income level, inventories are ________, and so national income tends to ________.

(a) accumulating, rise
(b) accumulating, fall
(c) being depleted, rise
(d) being depleted, fall
(e) constant, remain constant

Changes in Equilibrium National Income

Shifts in the *AE* curve are central to explaining why equilibrium national income changes. An upward shift in the *AE* curve causes an increase in equilibrium national output. A downward shift in the *AE* curve decreases equilibrium output. An upward shift in the *AE* curve is caused by *increases* in autonomous expenditure.

The ratio of the change in equilibrium national income to the change in autonomous expenditure *at a constant price level* is called the *simple* multiplier, which is normally greater than one. The size of the simple multiplier depends on the slope of the *AE* function. Recall that the slope of the *AE* function is called the *marginal propensity to spend.* The multiplier is equal to $1/(1 - z)$, where z is the marginal propensity to spend. For this chapter only, the marginal propensity to spend is equal to the marginal propensity to consume.

22. Which of the following shifts the *AE* function upward in a parallel fashion?
- (a) A decrease in autonomous consumption.
- (b) An increase in real national income.
- (c) The real rate of interest falls.
- (d) The marginal propensity to spend increases.
- (e) None of the above.

23. An upward shift of the consumption function causes equilibrium income to
- (a) fall.
- (b) rise.
- (c) remain constant but its composition consists of more consumption and less investment.
- (d) remain constant but its composition consists of less consumption and more investment.
- (e) remain constant since desired aggregate expenditure has not been affected.

24. The simple multiplier describes changes in
- (a) investment induced by changes in equilibrium income.
- (b) saving caused by changes in investment.
- (c) the equilibrium level of income caused by changes in autonomous expenditure.
- (d) the rate of interest caused by increased demand for credit.
- (e) employment induced by changes in equilibrium income.

25. If the marginal propensity to spend is 0.75, then
- (a) the marginal propensity to not spend is 0.25.
- (b) the slope of the *AE* function is 0.75.
- (c) the value of the simple multiplier is 4.0.
- (d) the marginal propensity to consume is 0.75 for this simple model.
- (e) All of the above are correct.

26. If expenditure in the economy did not depend on the level of real national income, the value of the simple multiplier would be
- (a) zero.
- (b) unity.
- (c) infinite or undefined.
- (d) –1.
- (e) a positive fraction.

27. **The value of the multiplier is larger**
(a) the higher the level of autonomous expenditures.
(b) the steeper the slope of the *AE* function.
(c) the flatter the slope of the *AE* function.
(d) the steeper the slope of the saving function.
(e) the lower the value of the marginal propensity to consume.

28. **Assuming constant prices and a marginal propensity to spend of 2/3, an increase in autonomous investment of $1 million should increase equilibrium real national income by**
(a) $1 million.
(b) $3 million.
(c) $667 000.
(d) $333 000.
(e) $1.5 million.

SHORT-ANSWER QUESTIONS

1. Discuss some of the properties of a Keynesian consumption function by addressing the following issues:
(a) The value of the *APC* as actual national income increases.

(b) The value of the *MPC* as actual national income increases.

(c) The value of the *APC* at the "break-even" level of actual national income.

(d) The value of saving at the "break-even" level of actual national income.

(e) The sum of the *MPS* and the *MPC*.

2. Indicate whether or not each of the following separate events is expected to increase the equilibrium level of national income. Explain how the event would be depicted in an *AE* diagram for which the marginal propensity to spend is positive, but is less than one. Assume the economy is initially at equilibrium national income.

(a) A decrease in household wealth.

(b) A decrease in the real interest rate.

(c) A downward shift in the saving function by the same amount at every level of national income.

3. Indicate whether or not each of the following separate events is expected to cause a movement along the *AE* curve, a shift of the *AE* curve, or a change in the slope of the *AE* curve. Explain what impact, if any, these separate events are expected to have on equilibrium income. If the information provided is not sufficient to determine a possible impact on equilibrium income, explain why this might be the case. Assume the economy is initially in equilibrium.

(a) A decrease in the marginal propensity to save.

(b) An increase in the level of unemployment in the economy.

(c) An increase in the marginal propensity to spend.

(d) An announcement by the Organization of the Petroleum Exporting Countries (OPEC) that they will cut down production by one-quarter over the next few months.

4. Indicate whether or not each of the following separate events is expected to cause a change in the value of the expenditure multiplier. Explain the direction of the change, if any.
   (a) The marginal propensity to consume decreases.

   (b) Firms are optimistic about future sales and decide to increase their productive capacity.

   (c) Unexpected increases in the Toronto Stock Exchange index convince households to reduce their saving as a share of disposable income.

EXERCISES

1. **The Keynesian Consumption Function**
This question further tests your knowledge of the properties of a Keynesian consumption function. For this example, the consumption function is given by the expression, $C = 80 + 0.5Y_D$. The first two columns of the following schedule depict this functional form for various levels of disposable income. Remember, the symbol Δ refers to "change" and the symbol Y_D refers to real disposable income.

Y_D	C	S	ΔY_d	ΔC	MPC	APC
0	80	–80	n.a.	n.a.	n.a.	na
100	130	–30				1.30
			60	30	0.50	
160	160	____				1.00
			____	20	0.50	
200	180	20				____
			____	____	0.50	
400	280	120				0.70
			350	____	____	
750	455	____				____

(a) Fill in the missing values for the change in real disposable income (ΔY_D).
(b) Using the definition for the average propensity to consume (*APC*), fill in the missing values for *APC*. What did you notice happened to the value of *APC* as the level of Y_D increased?
(c) Fill in the missing values for ΔC.
(d) Using the definition for *MPC*, calculate it for the disposable income change from 400 to 750.
(e) Using the definition for saving $S = Y_D - C$, fill in the missing values in the table. Using the formula $\Delta S/\Delta Y_D$, prove that the marginal propensity to save is constant and equal to 0.5.

(f) Prove that the algebraic expression for the saving function is $S = -80 + 0.5Y_D$.

(g) What is the break-even level of real disposable income? What is the amount of saving at this level of Y_D?

(h) Plot both the desired consumption (as line *C*) and desired saving functions (as line *S*) in Figure 21-1. In addition, draw the 45° line and prove that this line intersects the consumption function at a level of Y_D for which $S = 0$.

Figure 21-1

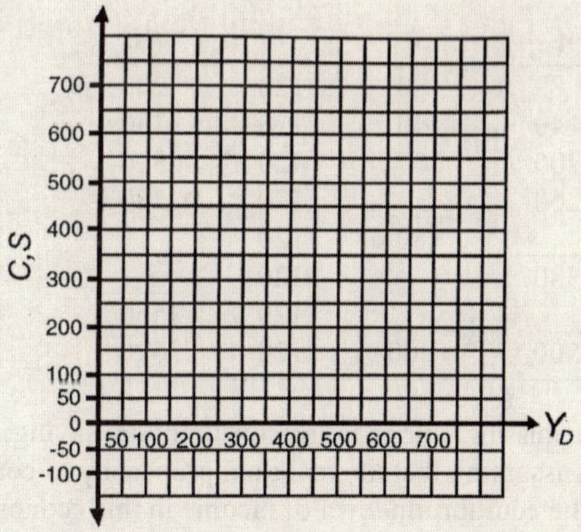

(i) Is desired consumption expenditure both autonomous and induced? Explain.

2. The Aggregate Expenditure Function and Equilibrium Income

Answer the following questions using Figure 21-2.

Figure 21-2

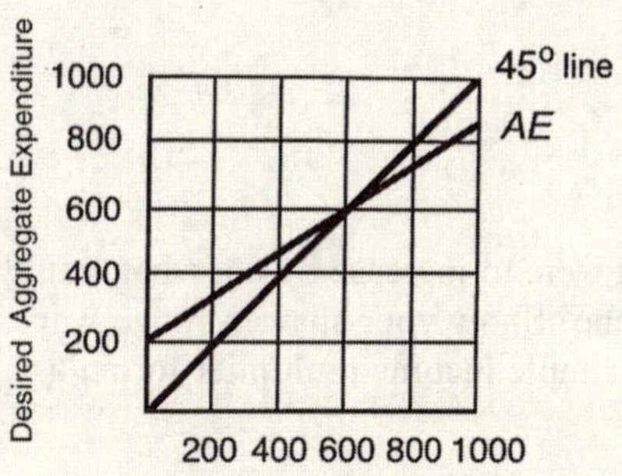

(a) When actual national income is 0, desired aggregate expenditure is ___________.

(b) When national income is 600, desired aggregate expenditure is ___________.

(c) Points on the 45° line represent situations where __________.

(d) If actual national income were 300, desired aggregate expenditure would be (less/greater) than income. Hence, inventories are likely to (fall/rise), and output and national income are likely to (expand/contract).

(e) If actual national income were 1000, desired aggregate expenditure would be (less/greater) than national income, inventories would (fall/rise), and hence output and national income are likely to (expand/contract).

(f) In this case, the marginal propensity not to spend is __________, and the marginal propensity to spend is __________.

(g) The equilibrium level of national income is __________. This is because __________.

3. The Simple Aggregate Expenditure Model

The following table summarizes desired levels of aggregate expenditure for an economy where the price level is constant. The table is based on a macro model of

$C = 80 + 0.6Y \qquad I = 120 \qquad Y = C + I$

Y	*C*	*S*	*I*	*AE*
0	80	−80	120	200
100	140	−40	120	260
200	200	0	120	320
300	260	____	120	380
400	____	+80	120	____
500	380	____	120	____
600	____	____	120	560
700	500	+200	120	620

(a) Fill in the missing entries in the consumption, saving, and aggregate expenditure columns, assuming that the marginal propensity to consume is constant.

(b) What is the equilibrium level of income in this economy? Why?

(c) Explain why an output level (*Y*) of 400 is not an equilibrium situation.

(d) What is the marginal propensity not to spend? What is the simple multiplier for this economy?

(e) If investment were to increase by 60, what would the new equilibrium level of national income become? Show your answer in two ways, by using the table above and by applying the simple income multiplier formula.

(f) If investment is 120, what is the level of *Y* at which $S = I$?

4. **The Consumption and Saving Functions**

Question 1 was based on a consumption function, $C = 80 + 0.5Y_D$, and a saving function, $S = -80 + 0.5Y_D$. Write the algebraic expression for the following cases:

(a) The consumption function that has autonomous consumption of 100 and a marginal propensity to consume of 0.5.

(b) The consumption function that has autonomous consumption of 80 and a marginal propensity to consume of 0.8.

(c) The saving function for case (b).

(d) The saving function that has autonomous saving of –50 and a marginal propensity to save of 0.6.

(e) The consumption function for case (d).

5. **Aggregate Expenditure and Equilibrium Income (I)**

Consider the following model of the economy: $C = 800 + 0.5\ Y$ and $I = 400$.

(a) What is the equation for the *AE* curve in this model?

(b) What is the equilibrium level of income?

(c) What is the value of the simple multiplier in this model?

(d) What is the level of saving when the economy is in equilibrium?

(e) What will be the change in equilibrium income if desired investment decreases by 100?

6. **Aggregate Expenditure and Equilibrium Income (II)**
This exercise involves an algebraic determination of equilibrium national income. You are given the following information about behaviour in this economy:

Equation 1, the consumption function:

$$C = 100 + 0.75Y_D$$

Equation 2, the relationship between national income and disposable income:

$$Y_D = Y$$

Equation 3, the investment function:

$$I = 50$$

(a) What does equation (2) imply?

(b) What does equation (3) mean?

(c) Aggregate expenditure is the algebraic sum of the various components. Derive the algebraic expression for *AE*.

(d) What is the marginal propensity to spend? The marginal propensity not to spend?

(e) What is the algebraic equivalent to the statement, "equilibrium is achieved when the *AE* curve intersects the 45° line"?

(f) Using your answer for part (d), solve for the equilibrium level of *Y*.

(g) What is the value of the simple multiplier?

(h) If investment increased from 50 to 55, what is the new equilibrium level of *Y*?

EXTENSION EXERCISES

E1. Investment as a Function of Income

We have seen that desired investment depends on variables such as the real rate of interest and the levels of sales. However, in our simplest model, we have been assuming these determining variables to be constant and thus their impact on investment was captured in the level of autonomous investment. Let's partially relax these simplifying assumptions and consider investment to depend on the level of income—i.e., let's assume that the level of desired investment increases as the level of income in the economy increases. Indeed, let's consider now the following model of the economy: $C = 800 + 0.5\,Y$ and $I = 400 + 0.1\,Y$.

(a) What is the equilibrium level of income?

(b) What is the level of saving when the economy is in equilibrium?

(c) If $Y = 2500$, what is the level of involuntary change in inventory?

(d) What is the value of the expenditure multiplier in this model? Why does it differ from the value you obtained in the previous exercise?

E2. The Relationship Between Wealth and the Consumption Function

Suppose that an economy has a consumption function given by $C = 60 + 0.8Y + 0.1W$. W is level of wealth, C represents desired consumption expenditure, and Y represents the level of real national income. We assume that there are no taxes and prices are constant.

(a) Given that wealth is 400, rewrite the expression for the consumption function.

(b) Fill in the missing values in columns 2 and 4 in the following schedule.

(1) Y	(2) C ($W = 400$)	(3) C ($W = 2400$)	(4) S ($W = 400$)	(5) S ($W = 2400$)
0	100	300	–100	–300
500	______	700	______	–200
1000	900	1100	100	–100
1500	______	______	______	______
2000	1700	1900	+300	+100

(c) Assume that the economy's wealth increases from 400 to 2400. Derive the new consumption function, and fill in the missing values in columns 3 and 5.

(d) As a result of the wealth increase, what happened to the consumption function? The saving function?

E3. The Aggregate Expenditure Model and the Rate of Interest

We have seen that desired investment depends on the real rate of interest (r). However, in our simplest model, we have been assuming that the rate of interest was constant and thus its impact on investment was captured in the level of autonomous investment. Let's now relax this simplifying assumption and consider the following model of the economy:

$$C = 800 + 0.5\ Y \text{ and } I = 400 - 20\ r.$$

(a) Suppose that the real rate of interest is 10 percent, i.e., $r = 10$. What is the level of equilibrium income?

(b) What is the value of the simple multiplier when $r = 10$?

(c) Suppose now that the real rate of interest falls to 5 percent, i.e., $r = 5$. What is the new level of equilibrium income?

(d) What is the value of the simple multiplier when $r = 5$? Why does or doesn't it differ from the value of the multiplier found in part (b) above?

(e) What does the vertical shift of the *AE* curve represent?

(f) Why has the level of equilibrium income changed?

ADDITIONAL MULTIPLE-CHOICE QUESTIONS

Questions 1 through 6 refer to Figure 21-3:

Figure 21-3

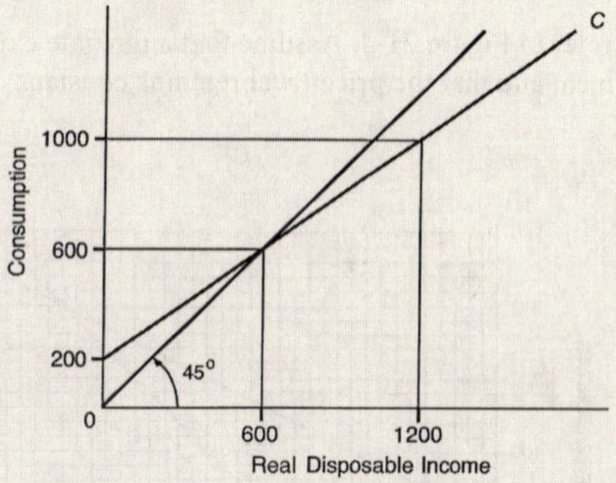

1. **The Keynesian consumption function in Figure 21-3 depicts that an economy's desired consumption expenditures are**
   (a) partially induced by increases in disposable income.
   (b) partially determined autonomously by factors other than income.
   (c) a function of disposable income in the current year rather than over a lifetime.
   (d) a declining proportion of disposable income.
   (e) All of the above.

2. **The marginal propensity to consume (*MPC*) out of disposable income according to Figure 21-3 is**
   (a) 200.
   (b) 100.
   (c) 2/3.
   (d) 1/3.
   (e) 5/6.

3. **As disposable income rises from 600 to 1200, the average propensity to consume**
   (a) rises from 1/3 to 1.
   (b) falls from 1 to 5/6.
   (c) remains constant at 2/3.
   (d) remains constant at 1.
   (e) falls from 1 to 1/3.

4. **If current disposable income was zero,**
   (a) consumption is zero.
   (b) dissaving is 200 or saving is –200.
   (c) the average propensity to consume is one.
   (d) consumption cannot be predicted.
   (e) saving is 200.

5. **When disposable income is equal to 600,**
   (a) aggregate saving is zero.
   (b) the average propensity to consume is unity.
   (c) the "break-even" level of disposable income is attained.
   (d) desired consumption is equal to actual consumption.
   (e) All of the above.

6. **When disposable income is equal to 1200,**
   (a) the marginal propensity to consume is 5/6.
   (b) there is saving of 200.
   (c) there is dissaving of 200.
   (d) desired consumption expenditures exceed actual consumption by 200.
   (e) there is saving of 200, and desired consumption expenditure exceeds actual consumption by 200.

Questions 7 through 16 refer to Figure 21-4. Assume that aggregate expenditure consists only of consumption and investment and that the price level remains constant.

Figure 21-4

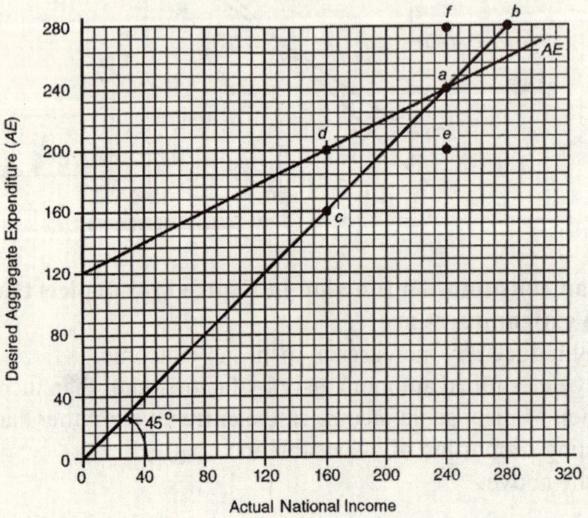

7. **According to the graph, the level of total desired *autonomous* expenditure is**
   (a) 120.
   (b) 280.
   (c) 240.
   (d) represented at point *c*.
   (e) Can't be determined.

8. **When actual national income is 160,**
   (a) desired aggregate expenditure equals 160.
   (b) desired aggregate expenditure is less than 160.
   (c) equilibrium national income is attained.
   (d) saving is zero.
   (e) None of the above.

9. **When actual national income is 280,**
   (a) there is a tendency for national income to fall.
   (b) inventories are unexpectedly decreasing.
   (c) the average propensity to spend is unity.
   (d) there is dissaving of about 20.
   (e) None of the above.

10. According to the aggregate expenditure curve labelled *AE*, the current equilibrium level of real national income is

(a) 320.
(b) 240.
(c) 120.
(d) 280.
(e) 160.

11. The *AE* curve has a slope of

(a) 0.5.
(b) 0.6.
(c) 2.0.
(d) 1.0.
(e) 0.4.

12. The value of the simple multiplier is

(a) 2.0.
(b) 0.5.
(c) 2.5.
(d) 0.
(e) 1.67.

13. The value of the marginal propensity not to spend is

(a) 0.5.
(b) 0.4.
(c) 1.0.
(d) 0.
(e) 0.6.

14. Suppose that investment expenditure decreased by 40 at *all* levels of actual national income. The aggregate expenditure curve

(a) shifts upward by 40 and intersects the 45° line at point *b*.
(b) shifts downward by 40, but its slope also decreases.
(c) shifts downward by 40, has a slope of 0.5, and intersects the 45° line at point *c*.
(d) will not shift, but adjustment involves a movement from point *a* to point *d*.
(e) will not shift, but adjustment involves a movement from point *a* to point *b*.

15. According to the new *AE* curve associated with Question 14, if output remains temporarily at 240, desired expenditure is

(a) 240 (at point *a*), and hence inventories remain unchanged.
(b) 200 (at point *e*), with the result that unplanned inventory accumulation is equal to 40.
(c) 280 (at point *f*), with the result that unplanned inventory reduction is equal to 40.
(d) 200, which is associated with point *d*.
(e) 40, which is also the level of planned saving.

16. The decrease in desired investment of 40

(a) is illustrated by a movement from point *a* to point *c*.
(b) decreases real national income ultimately by 80.
(c) decreases consumption expenditures ultimately by 40.
(d) decreases saving ultimately by 40.
(e) All of the above.

Questions 17 through 24 refer to a hypothetical economy whose behaviour is represented by the following three equations:

(1) $C = 75 + 0.6Y_D$
(2) $I = 28$
(3) $Y_D = Y$

***17. When $Y_D = 100$, the value of the average propensity to consume is**

(a) 0.6.
(b) 0.756.
(c) 0.75.
(d) 1.35.
(e) 1.03.

***18. When $Y_D = 100$, the value of desired saving (S) is**

(a) –35.
(b) 75.
(c) 1.35.
(d) –75.
(e) 35.

***19. The algebraic expression for the economy's *AE* function is**

(a) $AE = 75 + 0.6Y$.
(b) $Y = 47 + 0.6Y$.
(c) $AE = 103 + 0.6Y$.
(d) $AE = 75 + 47.6Y$.
(e) $AE = 103 + 0.4Y$.

***20. When $Y = 250$, the economy**

(a) is in equilibrium, because aggregate expenditure equals national income.
(b) has not reached equilibrium, because aggregate expenditure is less than national income.
(c) is in equilibrium, because aggregate expenditure is greater than national income.
(d) has not reached equilibrium, because aggregate expenditure is greater than national income.
(e) has not reached equilibrium, because desired saving is greater than desired investment.

***21. The economy's equilibrium level of real national income is**

(a) 250.
(b) 171.7.
(c) 187.5.
(d) 150.0.
(e) 257.5.

***22. The value of the economy's simple multiplier is**

(a) 0.6.
(b) 2.5.
(c) 1.67.
(d) 0.4.
(e) 1.0.

***23. If the investment function changed from $I = 28$ to $I = 38$, then**

(a) the economy's equilibrium income is 282.5.
(b) equilibrium national income permanently increases by 10.
(c) consumption expenditure must fall by 10.
(d) consumption expenditure must increase by 10.
(e) the economy's equilibrium income increases by 2.5.

***24. Suppose that the economy's consumption function changes from $C = 75 + 0.6Y_D$ to $C = 100 + 0.8Y_D$. Which of the following statements is correct?**

(a) The slope of the consumption function has decreased.
(b) The slope of the saving function has increased.
(c) The value of the simple multiplier has increased.
(d) The equilibrium level of Y will be less than before.
(e) Autonomous consumption has decreased.

Questions 25 through 29 refer to a hypothetical economy whose behaviour is represented by the following equations:

(1) $AE = C + I$
(2) $Y_D = C + S$
(3) $S = -100 + 0.2Y$
(4) $Y_D = Y$
(5) $I = 50$

***25. The value of autonomous consumption is**

(a) 0. (b) 20.
(c) 50. (d) 80.
(e) 100.

***26. The value of the marginal propensity to consume is**

(a) 0.2. (b) 0.5.
(c) 0.6. (d) 0.8.
(e) The information provided is not sufficient to determine the value of the marginal propensity to consume.

***27. The value of the economy's simple multiplier is**

(a) 0.5. (b) 1.2.
(c) 4.0. (d) 5.0.
(e) 5.5.

***28. The economy's equilibrium level of real national income is**

(a) 500. (b) 750.
(c) 800. (d) 1000.
(e) 1200.

***29. When Y = 1000, the involuntary change in inventory is**

(a) +50. (b) +100
(c) +250. (d) –50.
(e) –250.

***30. Suppose the function for desired saving is $S = -200 + 0.2\ Y$, and desired investment expenditure is 1000. In this economy, the equilibrium level of income is ____________ while the value of the multiplier is ____________.**

(a) 10 000, 8 (b) 10 000, 5
(c) 6000, 8 (d) 6000, 5
(e) 6000, 4

SOLUTIONS

Chapter Review

1.(c) **2.**(b) **3.**(a) **4.**(d) **5.**(e) **6.**(e) **7.**(c) **8.**(d) **9.**(d) **10.**(d) **11.**(a) **12.**(b) **13.**(e) **14.**(c) **15.**(a) **16.**(c) **17.**(e) **18.**(b) **19.**(c) **20.**(d) **21.**(c) **22.**(c) **23.**(b) **24.**(c) **25.**(e) **26.**(b) **27.**(b) **28.**(b)

Short-Answer Questions

1. (a) The slope of the line (ray vector) from the graph's origin to a point on the consumption function measures the *APC*. As actual national income increases the slope of the ray vector decreases. Hence, the value of the *APC* falls as actual national income increases. This is because the *MPC* is less than one and there is usually an autonomous level of consumption expenditure. At $Y = 0$, autonomous consumption expenditure is greater than actual national income.
   (b) The *MPC* is defined as the change in consumption divided by the change in income. This value is assumed to be greater than zero, but less than one. The textbook also assumes that the *MPC* is constant for all levels of income.
   (c) The "break-even" level of consumption is when consumption expenditure is equal to national income. Hence, the value of the *APC* is one (unity).
   (d) Saving is zero since $C = Y$.
   (e) When income changes, households change both saving and consumption expenditure. Recall that there are no taxes and no imports. Hence, $MPS + MPC$ equal unity.

2. (a) The equilibrium level of national income will fall. A decrease in wealth shifts the consumption function down and hence the *AE* function shifts downward. Inventories begin to accumulate and hence firms cut production. As a result, there is a movement down the new *AE* function as consumption expenditure is reduced. Eventually, real national income falls by a multiple of the decrease in autonomous consumption.
   (b) This event will increase equilibrium national income. A decrease in the real interest rate causes the investment function (and perhaps the consumption function) to shift up, and in turn the *AE* function shifts upward. Inventories will begin to decline and hence firms increase production. As a result, there is a movement up along the new *AE* function as consumption expenditure increases. Eventually, real national income increases by a multiple of the increase in investment (which is assumed to be autonomous expenditure).
   (c) This event will increase equilibrium national income. A downward shift in the saving function is tantamount to an upward shift in the consumption function. As a result, the *AE* function shifts upward. Inventories begin to fall and firms increase production. As a result, there is a movement up along the new *AE* function as consumption expenditure increases. Eventually, real national income increases by a multiplier of the increase in autonomous consumption (or the decrease in autonomous saving).

3. (a) A decrease in the marginal propensity to save changes the slope of the *AE* curve. Recall that the summation of the marginal propensity to save (s) and the marginal propensity to consume (c) adds to unity—i.e., $s + c = 1$ and thus $s = 1 - c$. Therefore, c increases when s decreases. Given that the marginal propensity to spend is equal to the marginal propensity to consume in our simple model, then the slope of the *AE* curve is equal to c and thus the *AE* curve becomes steeper when s decreases. As the *AE* curve becomes steeper, the economy experiences now a situation of excess demand (i.e., $Y < AE$) at the initial equilibrium level of income. Firms will experience an involuntary decrease in inventory, which will give them the signal to increase production, and thus equilibrium income will rise.
   (b) All other things equal, an increase in the level of unemployment in the economy means that the level of economic activity is falling—i.e., Y is falling toward its equilibrium level. This event, therefore, represents a movement down along the *AE* curve.
   (c) An increase in the marginal propensity to spend changes the slope of the *AE* curve—i.e., it means that the *AE* curve becomes steeper. As the *AE* curve becomes steeper, the economy moves to a situation of excess demand (i.e., $Y < AE$) at the initial equilibrium level of income. Firms will experience an involuntary decrease in inventory, which will give them the signal to increase production, and thus equilibrium income will rise.

(d) The OPEC announcement must be interpreted as an indication that the price of oil will significantly increase over the next few months. This announcement will negatively affect both households' expectations and business confidence about the future, resulting in a decrease in both autonomous consumption and autonomous investment. This event, therefore, is expected to cause a shift downward of the *AE* curve, moving the economy to a situation of excess supply (i.e., $Y > AE$) at the initial equilibrium level of income. Firms will experience an involuntary increase in inventory, which will give them the signal to decrease production, and thus equilibrium income will fall.

4. (a) Recall that the value of the multiplier is $1/(1-z)$, where z is the marginal propensity to spend (i.e., the slope of the *AE* curve). In our simple model, the marginal propensity to spend (z) is equal to the marginal propensity to consume (c). Therefore, a decrease in the marginal propensity to consume will cause the expenditure multiplier to decrease. The economic explanation is as follows: A given increase in autonomous expenditure will have a smaller overall impact on equilibrium income since households will be spending a smaller fraction of any additional dollar of income on consumption goods and services (i.e., they will be saving a larger fraction of any additional dollar of income).
(b) If firms are optimistic about future sales and decide to increase their productive capacity, then they will increase the level of desired investment at each level of national income. Given our assumption that desired investment consists only of autonomous investment, this event will translate into an upward shift of the *AE* curve but not in a change in its slope. Therefore, the value of the expenditure multiplier will not be affected.
(c) Given our assumption of fixed prices, an increase in the Toronto Stock Exchange index represents an increase in households' real wealth. Therefore, this increase in real wealth will increase households' expenditure on consumer goods and services at each level of disposable income—and thus it will reduce households' savings at each level of disposable income. This event, then, represents a shift upward of the *AE* curve and not a change in its slope (i.e., the average propensity to consume changes while the marginal propensity to consume does not). Therefore, the value of the expenditure multiplier is not affected.

Exercises

1. (a) 40, 200.
(b) 0.90, 0.61; the value of *APC* fell.
(c) 100, 175.
(d) 0.50 = 175/350.
(e) 0, 295. The marginal propensity to save is 0.50 and is constant. For an increase in Y_D from 0 to 100, saving increases from –80 to –30. The ratio of the change is 0.50.
(f) Saving is defined as $Y_D - C$, or $Y_D - (80 + 0.5Y_D)$. Hence, the saving function is,
$S = -80 + 0.5Y_D$
(g) 160, at which $S = 0$.
(h) **Figure 21-5**

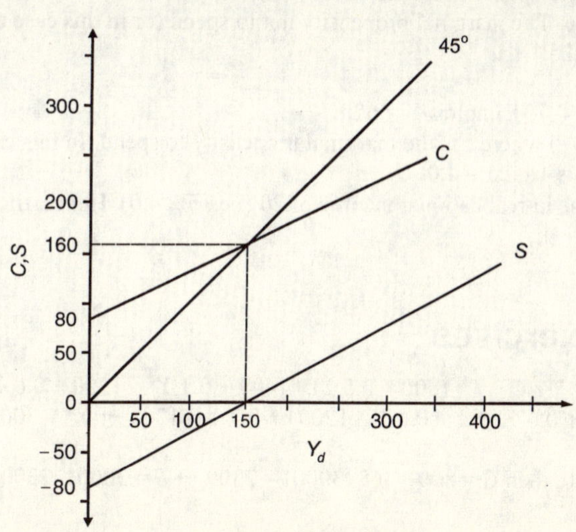

(i) Consumption expenditure is both autonomous and induced. It has an autonomous component because consumption is 80 when disposable income is zero. Since the marginal propensity to consume is 0.50, consumption is induced as well.

2. (a) 200.
   (b) 600.
   (c) Actual national income equals desired aggregate expenditure.
   (d) greater; fall; expand.
   (e) less; rise; contract.
   (f) 1/3, 2/3.
   (g) 600. Actual national income equals desired aggregate expenditure.

3. (a) *C*: 320, 440, *AE*: 440, 500, *S*: +40, +120, +160.
   (b) $Y = 500$ since $AE = Y$.
   (c) At $Y = 400$, aggregate expenditure is 440 (i.e., 320 + 120). Since desired expenditure is greater than actual expenditure, there will be unplanned inventory reductions. Firms adjust to this situation by increasing output until the economy reaches an equilibrium of 500.
   (d) $0.4 = 1 - MPC$. The simple multiplier is $K = 1/1 - z$, where *z* is the marginal propensity to spend. Hence, $K = 1/0.4 = 2.5$.
   (e) Since, the multiplier is 2.5 and investment increases by 60, the total change in real national income is 150. Hence, the new equilibrium real income level is 650 (i.e., 500 + 150). Using the schedule, the value $Y = 650$ is midpoint between 600 and 700. Hence, $C = 470$ and $I = 180$ for a total of $Y = 650$.
   (f) Saving (120) equals investment at $Y = 500$.

4. (a) $C = 100 + 0.5Y_D$.
   (b) $C = 80 + 0.8\,Y_D$.
   (c) $S = -80 + 0.2Y_D$.
   (d) $S = -50 + 0.6Y_D$.
   (e) $C = 50 + 0.4Y_D$.

5. (a) $AE = C + I = (800 + 0.5\,Y) + 400 = 1\,200 + 0.5\,Y$.
   (b) $Y = AE \rightarrow Y = 1200 + 0.5\,Y \rightarrow Y - 0.5\,Y = 1200 \rightarrow 0.5\,Y = 1200 \rightarrow Y^* = 2400$.
   (c) $\Delta Y/\Delta A = 1/(1 - z) = 1/(1 - 0.5) = 1/0.5 = 2$.
   (d) $S = Y - C$
   If $Y = 2400$, then $C = 800 + 0.5\,(2400) = 2000 \rightarrow S = 2400 - 2000 = 400$
   (e) $\Delta A = \Delta I = -100$ and the simple multiplier is $\Delta Y/\Delta A = 2$
   Therefore, $\Delta Y = (\Delta Y/\Delta A)\,\Delta A = 2\,(-100) = -200$

6. (a) Disposable income equals total income. Hence, there are no net taxes.
   (b) Since investment does not change with national income, it is autonomous.
   (c) $AE = C + I$, or $100 + 0.75Y\,(=Y_D) + 50$. Hence, $AE = 150 + 0.75Y$.
   (d) Inspecting the expression for the *AE* function, we see that the slope is 0.75, which is the marginal propensity to spend. In this case, the marginal propensity to spend is equal to the marginal propensity to consume. The marginal propensity not to spend (or in this case the marginal propensity to save) is equal to 0.25.
   (e) $AE = Y$.
   (f) $Y = 150 + 0.75Y$ implies $Y = 600$.
   (g) $K = 1/(1 - z)$ where *z* is the marginal propensity to spend. In this case, the value of the simple multiplier is $1/0.25 = 4.0$.
   (h) An increase in real national income of 20 (i.e., 5×4.0). Hence, the new equilibrium level is 620 (i.e., 600 + 20).

Extension Exercises

E1. (a) $Y = AE \rightarrow Y = C + I = (800 + 0.5\,Y) + (400 + 0.1\,Y) = 1200 + 0.6\,Y$
   $Y = 1200 + 0.6\,Y \rightarrow Y - 0.6\,Y = 1200 \rightarrow 0.4\,Y = 1200 \rightarrow Y^* = 3000$.
   (b) $S = Y - C$
   If $Y = 3000$, then $C = 800 + 0.5\,(3000) = 2300 \rightarrow S = 3000 - 2300 = 700$.

(c) If $Y = 2500$, then $AE = 1200 + 0.6\,(2500) = 1200 + 1500 = 2700$.
Therefore, at $Y = 2500$ there will be an excess demand (i.e., $Y < AE$) and inventories will decrease in an unplanned manner by 200.

(d) $\Delta Y/\Delta A = 1/(1 - z) = 1/(1 - 0.6) = 1/0.4 = 2.5$. This value differs from the one obtained in the previous exercise because now we have two components of AE that depend on the level of Y. Indeed, now a fraction of every additional dollar of income is spent on consumption and another fraction is spent on investment—i.e., now the marginal propensity to spend is the summation of the marginal propensity to consume and the marginal propensity to invest.

E2. (a) When real wealth is 400, the consumption function becomes $C = 60 + 0.8Y + 0.1(400)$ or $C = 100 + 0.8Y$.

(b) C is 500, 1300. S is 0, +200.

(c) The consumption function becomes $C = 60 + 0.8Y + 0.1(2400)$ or $C = 300 + 0.8Y$. C is 1500; S is zero.

(d) The consumption function shifted up in a parallel fashion (an increase of 200 at every level of real national income). The saving function shifted down in a parallel fashion (a decrease of 200 at every level of real national income).

E3. (a) If $r = 10$, then $I = 400 - 20(10) = 200$.
$Y = AE = C + I = 800 + 0.5\,Y + 200 = 1000 + 0.5\,Y$
$Y = 1000 + 0.5\,Y \rightarrow Y - 0.5\,Y = 1000 \rightarrow 0.5\,Y = 1000 \rightarrow Y^* = 2000$

(b) $\Delta Y/\Delta A = 1/(1 - z) = 1/(1 - 0.5) = 1/0.5 = 2$.

(c) If $r = 5$, then $I = 400 - 20(5) = 300$.
$Y = AE = C + I = 800 + 0.5\,Y + 300 = 1100 + 0.5\,Y$
$Y = 1100 + 0.5\,Y \rightarrow Y - 0.5\,Y = 1100 \rightarrow 0.5\,Y = 1100 \rightarrow Y^* = 2200$

(d) $\Delta Y/\Delta A = 1/(1 - z) = 1/(1 - 0.5) = 1/0.5 = 2$. That is, the value of the multiplier doesn't change when the real rate of interest changes since the marginal propensity to spend is not affected.

(e) The vertical upward shift of the AE curve represents the increase in autonomous AE (i.e., ΔA), which is equal to the increase in autonomous investment—i.e., the vertical shift is equal to $\Delta I = +100$.

(f) As autonomous expenditure increases when the real rate of interest falls, the level of equilibrium income increases as a result of the multiplying effect put in motion by the increase in autonomous expenditure. The increase in autonomous AE disturbs the initial equilibrium, moving the economy to a situation of excess demand (i.e., $Y < AE$). Firms will experience an involuntary decrease in inventory, which will give them the signal to increase production, and thus equilibrium income will rise.

Additional Multiple-Choice Questions

1.(e) **2.**(c) **3.**(b) **4.**(b) **5.**(e) **6.**(b) **7.**(a) **8.**(e) **9.**(a) **10.**(b) **11.**(a) **12.**(a) **13.**(a) **14.**(c) **15.**(b) **16.**(e) **17.**(d) **18.**(a) **19.**(c) **20.**(d) **21.**(e) **22.**(b) **23.**(a) **24.**(c) **25.**(e) **26.**(d) **27.**(d) **28.**(b) **29.**(a) **30.**(d)

Explanations for the Asterisked Multiple-Choice Questions

17.(d) The average propensity to consume out of disposable income is defined as the ratio of C to Y_D. First, calculate the value of C for a disposable income of 100. This value is 75 plus 0.6 times 100 (=60), or 135. Hence, the average propensity to consume out of disposable income is 135 divided by 100, or 1.35. [*Note:* Answer (a) is the value of the marginal propensity to consume.]

18.(a) Desired saving (S) is defined as Y_D minus C. Hence, $S = Y_D - [75 + 0.6Y_D]$ or $-75 + 0.4Y_D$. When disposable income is 100, then $S = -35$.

19.(c) The algebraic expression for $AE = C + I$, or in this case $75 + 0.6Y$ plus 28 (= I). Also, note that in this model $Y = Y_D$. Hence, $AE = 103 + 0.6Y$. [*Note:* Answer (a) neglects the investment component of aggregate expenditure.]

20.(d) To answer this question, you must calculate the level of aggregate expenditure when $Y = 250$. Using your answer to Question 19, the correct value of AE is 103 plus 150, or 253. Hence, desired aggregate expenditure is greater than national income (=250). The economy is not in equilibrium, and we expect national income to increase until equilibrium is reached.

21.(e) Equilibrium is attained when national income is equal to aggregate expenditure, or $Y = AE$. Algebraically this is represented by the equation $Y = 103 + 0.6Y$. Hence, $0.4Y = 103$, or $Y = 103/0.4 = 257.5$. Answer (b) is incorrect because it was obtained by dividing 103 by 0.6. Another method involves proving that $S = I$ at $Y = 257.5$. Investment expenditure is constant at 28 for every level of income. Using the expression for saving in Question 18, we obtain $S = -75 + 0.4(257.5) = 28$.

22.(b) The simple multiplier value is calculated by using the formula $1/(1-z)$ where z is the value of the marginal propensity to spend. In this model the marginal propensity to spend is the marginal propensity to consume (= 0.6). Hence, the multiplier value is 1 divided by 0.4, or 2.5. You would have been incorrect by choosing answer (c), which is calculated by dividing 1 by 0.6.

23.(a) Equilibrium national income increases by 25 = 10 (the increase in desired investment) times 2.5 (the value of the simple multiplier). Hence, adding the initial equilibrium value (257.5) will obtain a new equilibrium value of 282.5. [*Note:* Answer (b) neglects the effect of the multiplier.]

24.(c) In this model, the slope of the *AE* function is the marginal propensity to consume. Since the slope of the consumption function increased from 0.6 to 0.8, the value of the multiplier increased from 2.5 to 5.0. The new consumption function is steeper than before [hence, the saving function is flatter than before]. Moreover, autonomous consumption increased from 75 to 100. The new equilibrium will be greater than the previous case (with $I = 28$). [Can you calculate the new equilibrium value for Y?]

25.(e) Since $Y = Y_D$ and $Y_D = C + S$, $C = Y - S = Y - (-100 + 0.2Y) = 100 + 0.8Y$. Hence, autonomous consumption is 100.

26.(d) Since $C = 100 + 0.8Y$, the value of the marginal propensity to consume is 0.8.

27.(d) The simple multiplier is equal to $1/(1-z)$, where z is the marginal propensity to spend, which in this simple model is equal to the marginal propensity to consume. Therefore, the value of the simple multiplier is $1/(1-z) = 1/(1-0.8) = 1/0.2 = 5$.

28.(b) The economy is in equilibrium when $Y = AE$, and $AE = C + I$.
$\rightarrow AE = 100 + 0.8Y + 50 = 150 + 0.8Y$
$\rightarrow Y = AE \rightarrow Y = 150 + 0.8Y \rightarrow 0.2Y = 150 \rightarrow Y^* = 150/0.2 = 750$.

29.(a) When $Y = 1000$, $AE = 150 + 0.8(1000) = 950$. Since $Y > AE$, then there is an involuntary increase in inventory equal to 50.

30.(d) If the marginal propensity to save is 0.2, then the marginal propensity to consume is 0.8 (since they must add to unity). If saving is –200 when $Y = 0$, then consumption is equal to 200 when $Y = 0$ (i.e., when $Y = 0$, dissaving is 200 to allow a level of consumption of 200). Therefore, the consumption function is $C = 200 + 0.8Y$ and the desired aggregate expenditure function is $AE = C + I = 200 + 0.8Y + 1000 = 1200 + 0.8Y$. When the economy is in equilibrium $Y = AE \rightarrow Y = 1200 + 0.8Y \rightarrow 0.2Y = 1200 \rightarrow Y^* = 6000$. The multiplier is equal to $1/(1-z)$ and $z = c = 0.8$, and thus the value of the multiplier is 5.

CHAPTER 22

ADDING GOVERNMENT AND TRADE TO THE SIMPLE MACRO MODEL

LO

LEARNING OBJECTIVES

In this chapter you will learn

1 how government purchases and tax revenues are related to national income.

2 how exports and imports are related to national income.

3 how to distinguish between the marginal propensity to consume and the marginal propensity to spend.

4 why the presence of government and foreign trade reduces the value of the simple multiplier.

5 how government can use fiscal policy to influence the level of national income.

CHAPTER OVERVIEW

This chapter incorporates foreign trade and government into the national income model. The price level remains constant, and the exchange rate is assumed to be exogenous; it can change but not because national income changes.

Fiscal policy includes taxation, transfers, and government purchases. Government purchases of goods and services are part of autonomous expenditure. Net taxes (taxes minus transfers) affect national income indirectly through their influence on disposable income and hence consumption expenditure. A public saving function which incorporates net taxes and government expenditure is developed in this chapter. The slope of the public saving function is the **net tax rate**. A positive tax rate decreases the size of the simple multiplier.

Net exports, another source of aggregate expenditure, are a negative function of real national income because imports rise with real income. A larger **marginal propensity to import** increases the slope of the net export function and reduces the size of the simple multiplier.

Equilibrium national income is determined using the **aggregate expenditure** approach. The simple multiplier now incorporates the net tax rate and the marginal propensity to import.

By changing *G* and *T*, stabilization policy is intended to bring national income closer to the level of potential national income, *Y**.

HINTS AND TIPS

The following may help you to avoid some of the most common errors on examinations.

✓ Learn that net taxes *indirectly* influence aggregate expenditure by affecting disposable income and in turn consumption.

- ✓ Understand the distinction between the marginal propensity to consume out of income versus the marginal propensity to consume out of disposable income.
- ✓ Learn the correct formula for the marginal propensity to spend when the model has induced taxation and induced imports. The correct formula is $z = MPC(1 - t) - m$.
- ✓ Learn that the equilibrium condition for national income is $Y = C + I + G + NX$.
- ✓ Ensure that you understand the events that cause the net export functions to shift. Be careful! Changes in actual national income cause movements along this function.
- ✓ Learn how the government can affect the level of equilibrium income through the implementation of fiscal policy—i.e., by changing the level of taxation or the level of government purchases.

CHAPTER REVIEW

Introducing Government

It is important for you to understand that government purchases of goods and services are a component of desired aggregate expenditure, while taxes and government transfer payments are not. Net taxes (taxes minus transfers) *indirectly* affect desired aggregate expenditure (consumption) by altering disposable income. Government expenditures on goods and services are autonomous components of aggregate expenditures while net taxes depend on the level of real national income. Now, disposable income is the difference between income and net taxes.

A budget balance or public saving is the difference between net tax revenue and government purchases. If government purchases exceed net tax revenues, then a deficit budget situation exists. The public saving function is upward-sloping because net taxes increase as actual national income increases. The algebraic expression for the public saving function is given by $tY - G$, where t is the net tax rate.

1. Which of the following items would be considered a government purchase of goods and services?
(a) Quebec City pays for snow removal on its streets.
(b) British Columbia collects taxation revenue.
(c) The federal government increases employment insurance payments to unemployed fishermen when inshore fishing ports in Newfoundland are closed.
(d) Saskatoon issues welfare payments to its needy citizens.
(e) None of the above.

2. Transfer payments affect aggregate expenditure
(a) directly.
(b) indirectly through disposable income.
(c) through the 45° line.
(d) through net exports.
(e) through the government purchases curve.

3. Public saving is equal to
(a) net tax revenues minus government purchases.
(b) disposable income minus consumption expenditure.
(c) government expenditures minus net tax revenues.
(d) private saving plus government saving.
(e) $I + NX$.

4. **The slope of the public saving function is**
   (a) equal to the marginal propensity to consume.
   (b) equal to the marginal propensity to save.
   (c) equal to the net tax rate.
   (d) equal to the value of the multiplier.
   (e) flat since all components of public saving are autonomous.

5. **Suppose that *G* is 400 for all levels of income and the net tax rate is 20 percent. When *Y* equals 1000, public saving is __________, denoting a budget __________.**
   (a) 200, surplus.
   (b) 0, balance.
   (c) –200, deficit.
   (d) –200, surplus.
   (e) 200, deficit.

6. **Suppose that the public saving function is given by $0.1Y - 200$. The government budget is balanced when *Y* equals**
   (a) 1000.
   (b) 8000.
   (c) 80.
   (d) 2000.
   (e) 500.

7. **The marginal propensity to consume out of income**
   (a) shows the fraction of national income which is used for consumption.
   (b) added to the marginal propensity to save out of disposable income always equals zero.
   (c) added to the marginal propensity to save out of disposable income always equals one.
   (d) is the relationship between a change in consumer purchases and the change in income which allowed consumption to change.
   (e) declines as income declines, eventually becoming zero as income reaches zero.

Introducing Foreign Trade

Net exports (*NX*) are defined as total exports (*X*) minus total imports (*IM*). Imports purchases are usually part of every component of aggregate expenditure. For example, Canadian households consume products that have imported content such as foreign vacations, TVs, and so on. Hence, imports must be netted out of every component of aggregate expenditure in order to measure expenditure on domestically produced goods and services. The net export function relates net exports to actual national income. Exports are autonomous expenditures while imports are induced expenditures. The net export function is negatively related to actual national income since imports increase as national income increases. The slope of the net export function is the negative value of the *marginal propensity to import*. The algebraic expression for the net export function is $X - mY$, where m is the marginal propensity to import.

The net export function will shift parallel to itself upward if exports increase. Shifts in the net export function are caused by changes in foreign income and changes in relative international prices. In turn, changes in relative international prices are determined by changes in the prices of Canadian goods relative to foreign goods prices and changes in the value of the exchange rate.

Imports are induced expenditures. Anything affecting the *proportion of income* that Canadian consumers wish to spend on imports will change the *slope* of the net export function. The proportion that Canadians spend on imports will change if relative international prices change.

8. **This chapter's macroeconomic model of an open economy assumes that**
   (a) both exports and imports are autonomous.
   (b) both exports and imports are induced.
   (c) exports are exogenous and imports are induced.
   (d) exports are induced and imports are autonomous.
   (e) None of the above.

9. **Which of the following events is likely to increase an economy's export sales?**
   (a) An increase in domestic real GDP.
   (b) A decline in the exchange rate.
   (c) An increase in the domestic price level.
   (d) A decrease in the foreign price level.
   (e) An increase in the income of the economy's foreign trading partners.

10. **Which of the following events is likely to decrease import purchases into a country?**
   (a) An increase in the exchange rate.
   (b) An increase in the domestic price level.
   (c) A decrease in foreign income.
   (d) An increase in domestic GDP.
   (e) A decrease in the foreign price level.

11. **The marginal propensity to import**
   (a) is the ratio of imports to real national income.
   (b) is equal to one minus the marginal propensity to consume.
   (c) is the change in real GDP divided by the change in imports.
   (d) determines the slope of the net export function.
   (e) is usually believed to be greater than one for most developed countries.

12. **Anything that increases the proportion of income that domestic consumers wish to spend on imports will**
   (a) rotate the net export function downward and thus increase the slope of the net export function.
   (b) decrease the slope of the net export function.
   (c) cause net exports to increase at every level of real GDP.
   (d) decrease the marginal propensity to import.
   (e) shift the net export function upward in a parallel fashion.

Equilibrium National Income

Once net taxes are introduced into the macro model, net taxes (taxes less subsidies) must be subtracted from income to obtain disposable income ($Y_D = Y - T$). Desired consumption expenditure depends on the level of disposable income. Now, there are two different values for the marginal propensity to consume. The marginal propensity to consume out of *disposable income* relates the change in desired consumption to the change in disposable income while the marginal propensity to consume out of *national income* relates the change in desired consumption to changes in national income.

For macro models that have induced taxes and imports, the marginal propensity to spend is no longer equal to the marginal propensity to consume. It now incorporates the net tax rate and the marginal propensity to import, but not in a straightforward way. Specifically, the marginal propensity to spend is given by $z = MPC(1 - t) - m$.

The equilibrium condition for national income is desired aggregate expenditure equals actual income, or $Y = C + I + G + NX$.

13. Equilibrium real national income occurs when

(a) the *AE* function intersects the 45° line.
(b) the value of the average propensity to spend (*AE/Y*) is one.
(c) desired aggregate expenditure equals actual national income.
(d) $Y = C + I + G + (X - IM)$.
(e) All of the above.

14. Which of the following is *not* a component of aggregate expenditure?

(a) Investment.
(b) Government purchases on goods and services.
(c) Net exports.
(d) Consumption expenditure.
(e) Personal income taxes paid.

15. The textbook's analytical model assumes that the following items are functions of current income.

(a) Government expenditure.
(b) Consumption.
(c) Imports.
(d) Exports.
(e) Both consumption <u>and</u> imports.

16. If $Y_D = 0.8Y$ and consumption were always 80 percent of disposable income, then the marginal propensity to consume out of total income would be

(a) 0.8.
(b) 0.75.
(c) 0.64.
(d) 0.2.
(e) 1.6.

Changes in Equilibrium National Income

The value of the simple multiplier is reduced by the presence of taxes and imports since they reduce the marginal propensity to spend out of national income. The higher the marginal propensity to import, the lower the simple multiplier. The higher the net tax rate, the lower the simple multiplier.

With foreign trade and government taxation, the slope of the *AE* function is $z = MPC(1 - t) - m$. Hence the simple multiplier is $1/(1 - z) = 1/\{1 - [MPC(1 - t) - m]\}$.

Stabilization policy deals with changes in government purchases and/or net taxes that counteract output gap problems. An increase in government purchases shifts the *AE* function upward, causing an increase in equilibrium national income; a reduction in the net tax rate rotates the *AE* function upward, also causing an increase in equilibrium national income. Such policy stances would be appropriate to eliminate a recessionary gap. For changes in (autonomous) government purchases, the ratio of the change in national income to the change in expenditure is the multiplier value.

If the net tax rate changes, the relationship between national income and disposable income changes. For any given level of national income, there will be a different level of disposable income and hence a different level of consumption. This change in consumption results in a *nonparallel* shift of the *AE* function. Hence, the value of the multiplier must also change.

17. The *AE* function becomes steeper when

(a) the net tax rate increases.
(b) the marginal propensity to import increases.
(c) the marginal propensity to consume out of income decreases.
(d) the marginal propensity to save out of disposable income decreases.
(e) None of the above.

18. An increase in the net tax rate

(a) increases disposable income.
(b) decreases the slope of the *AE* function.
(c) shifts the *AE* function downward in a parallel fashion.
(d) shifts the *AE* function upward in a parallel fashion.
(e) None of the above.

19. National income is likely to increase as the result of which of the following, assuming other autonomous or exogenous variables remain constant?

(a) An increase in the net tax rate.
(b) An increase in the value of *m*.
(c) An increase in government purchases.
(d) A decrease in exports.
(e) A decrease in autonomous consumption.

20. The value of the simple multiplier becomes larger when the

(a) marginal propensity to save increases.
(b) marginal propensity to import increases.
(c) net tax rate increases.
(d) marginal propensity to spend decreases.
(e) marginal propensity to consume increases.

21. If an economy faces a negative output gap problem, then in order to eliminate the output gap, the appropriate stabilization policy is to

(a) decrease government purchases.
(b) raise the net tax rate.
(c) lower transfer payments.
(d) increase government purchases and/or lower the net tax rate.
(e) lower transfer payments <u>and</u> decrease government purchases.

Demand-Determined Output

With prices constant, equilibrium in the simple model is demand determined. This implies that firms are able and willing to produce any amount that is demanded without requiring any change in prices. This aspect of the model may be appropriate if firms have excess capacity or they are price setters. Chapter 23 considers the supply side of the economy in the short run.

When the demand side and the supply side of the economy are considered simultaneously, changes in desired aggregate expenditures usually cause both prices and real national income to change. If prices change, the simple multiplier formula no longer accurately measures the change in real income.

22. Demand-determined macroeconomic models assume that

(a) output changes do not trigger changes in the price level.
(b) the exchange rate changes when autonomous expenditure changes.
(c) changes in real GDP depend on the extent to which firms change prices and output.
(d) GDP increases must always trigger price increases.
(e) only the supply side of the economy determines the multiplier effect of an increase in autonomous expenditure.

SHORT-ANSWER QUESTIONS

1. Test your knowledge of factors that shift the *NX* function and/or change its slope. For each of the following events indicate if the *NX* curve shifts upward or downward or not at all, and indicate also if the slope of the *NX* curve increases (becomes steeper) or decreases (becomes flatter) or is not affected.
   (a) Toronto becomes a more popular destination for American tourists.

   (b) Canadian consumers increase the proportion of their income that they spend on imported goods.

   (c) The exchange rate for U.S. dollars decreases.

   (d) A booming U.S. economy increases American disposable income by 10 percent.

2. **(a)** Explain the process by which an increase in autonomous aggregate expenditure (e.g., an increase in exports or an increase in government purchases) results in an increase in the level of equilibrium national income.

   (b) Explain the process by which a decrease in autonomous aggregate expenditure (e.g., a decrease in exports or a decrease in government purchases) results in a decrease in the level of equilibrium national income.

3. **(a)** Explain the components of macreconomic behaviour that determine the slope of an *AE* function. Discuss why certain macroeconomic variables are responsive to actual real income changes.

   (b) Describe the appropriate change in fiscal policy required to eliminate a recessionary gap. Explain how the change in fiscal policy increases the equilibrium level of real income (assuming prices are constant).

4. Test your knowledge of factors that shift the *AE* curve and/or change its slope. For each of the following events indicate if the *AE* curve shifts upward or downward or not at all, and indicate also if the slope of the *AE* curve increases (becomes steeper) or decreases (becomes flatter) or is not affected. Indicate where appropriate if the value of the simple multiplier increases or decreases.

(a) The federal government reduces its net tax rate.

(b) Canadian real interest rates rise.

(c) As national income increases, Canadians increase the proportion of their import purchases from foreign countries.

(d) The foreign exchange rate changes from 1.40 Canadian dollars for every U.S. dollar to $1.50 (Canadian).

(e) The real incomes of Canada's trade partners fall.

EXERCISES

1. **Public Saving**
This exercise tests your knowledge of the concept of public saving, which in this case is represented by the equation $0.25Y - 20$.

(a) Calculate the values of public saving at $Y = 0$ and $Y = 120$. Remember, the government has a deficit budget when public saving is negative.

(b) What is the value of the net tax rate? What is the value of government purchases (G)?

(c) If the economy experiences a recession such that real national income falls from 88 to 60, what is the change in public saving, assuming government purchases and the net tax rate remain unchanged? Explain.

(d) At what level of Y will the government have a balanced budget?

(e) Suppose that the government increased its purchases by 5 at each level of real national income. Write the new expression for the public saving function and explain its relationship with the original public saving function.

(f) Suppose that the net tax rate became 30% and $G = 20$. Write the expression for this new public saving function and describe its shape relative to the public saving function in part (a).

2. **The Keynesian Consumption Function**

This question continues the analysis of the *Keynesian* consumption function. Once taxes are introduced into the macroeconomic behaviour we must deal now with the relationship of consumption to two variants of current income: real disposable income and total real income. For this exercise assume the following two behavioural equations, a consumption function of $C = 44 + 0.8Y_D$, and the relationship between income and disposable income of $Y_D = 0.7Y$.

(a) Discuss the relationship between Y and Y_D. Why is Y_D less than Y?

(b) To what does the term 44 refer?

(c) Derive the algebraic expression for the relationship between C and Y. What is the *MPC* value out of current real national income?

(d) Suppose that the marginal propensity to consume out of disposable income remains at 0.8 but that the relationship between income and disposable income becomes $Y_D = 0.6Y$. What policy change has occurred? Derive the new algebraic relationship between consumption and real national income.

3. **Net Exports**

Do you understand the properties of a net export function? Consider the following model:

$$X = 40;$$
$$IM = 0.1Y.$$

(a) Exports are assumed to be autonomous (independent of the level of Y). However, what specific relationship exists between IM (imports) and Y? What is the value of the marginal propensity to import? Identify some factors that explain the positive relationship between desired imports and real national income.

(b) Calculate the values of *net exports (NX)* for $Y = 200$ and $Y = 800$. Does the balance of trade fall (become smaller) as Y increases? At what level of Y is there a trade balance of zero?

(c) Plot the net export curve in Figure 22-1. Why is it downward sloping?

Figure 22-1

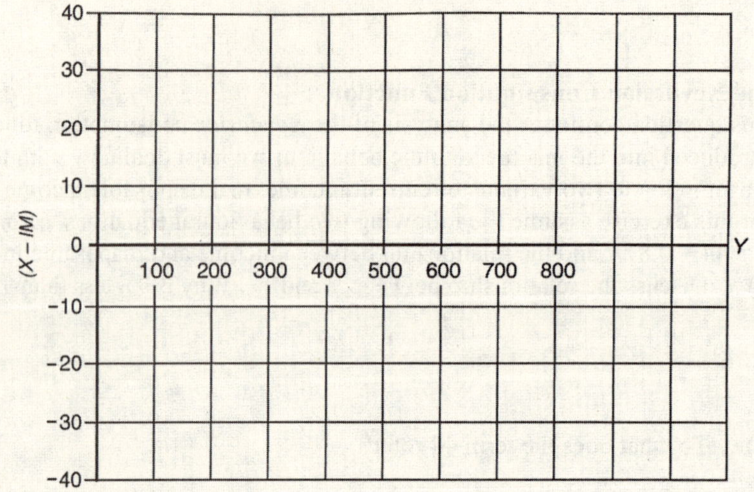

(d) Suppose that exports at each level of Y fell from 40 to 30. Derive the algebraic equation for the new net export function. Plot the new net export function in Figure 22-1.

(e) With a constant exchange rate and price level, what economic event might have led to a reduction in exports?

4. The Aggregate Expenditure Model in the Open Economy

You are given the following schedule which depicts macroeconomic behaviour in an open economy. The data in the second column are derived from the expression $C = 30 + 0.72Y$. Underlying this expression is the tax function $T = 0.2Y$. The data in the third column and in the fourth column are derived from the relationships $I = 75$ and $G = 51$, respectively. The data in the fifth column represent the net export relationship, $NX = 72 - 0.1Y$. The AE function is represented by the sixth column.

Potential real national income (Y^*) is 605.26.

Y	C	I	G	NX	AE
0	30	75	51	72	228
150	138	75	51	57	321
300	246	75	51	42	414
600	462	75	51	12	600
900	678	75	51	−18	786

(a) What is the marginal propensity to consume out of national income? What is the level of autonomous consumption (denoted as a in the textbook)? What is the algebraic relationship between consumption expenditure and real disposable income? What is the net tax rate?

(b) What is the value of the marginal propensity to import?

(c) What is the value of the marginal propensity to spend (z)? Do this two ways. First, using the data in columns 1 and 6 calculate the values for $\Delta AE/\Delta Y$ as Y changes. Then, use the correct formula for z that appears in the textbook. What is the intercept value of the AE function (when $Y = 0$)?

(d) Using the AE approach, what is equilibrium level of national income? Explain.

(e) At the equilibrium level of national income, what is the value of public saving? What is the value of private saving?

(f) What is value of the simple multiplier?

(g) What is the value of the output gap?

(h) What stabilization policy (using changes in government expenditure) is necessary to eliminate the output gap? Explain.

5. **Fiscal Policy and the Output Gap**

A newly elected government inherits an inflationary gap. Record high export sales of one of the country's manufactured goods have created an inflationary gap of 12 billion. The recently appointed minister of finance seeks advice from her advisers. After careful study, they advise her to increase taxes permanently by 3 billion, keeping government spending at its current level. Their recommendation is based on the following assumptions:

(i) The high level of export sales will continue. Potential GDP will remain at 1 trillion.
(ii) The taxation multiplier (the effect of a change in the net tax rate on national income) is 4.
(iii) Within the foreseeable future, changes in both prices and input prices are likely to be negligible.

(iv) Since the government has a large majority, policy changes can be made quickly. Moreover, the advisers are confident that the private sector will respond quickly to this policy change.

The advisers have also been told by the chief economist in the ministry that both the export and government spending multipliers are 6.0.

(a) Assuming that all information is correct, do you agree that the recommended policy will eliminate the inflationary gap? Explain.

(b) The minister accepts the advice, the tax change becomes law, and the size of the output gap begins to decrease. However, shortly after the policy change, exports of one of the country's food products fall unexpectedly by 2.5 billion due to the introduction of a cheaper and higher-quality product by a foreign competitor. Assuming that all prices are constant and that the chief economist's numbers are accurate, what will happen to the equilibrium level of GDP if no additional fiscal measures are introduced? What is the value of the output gap now?

(c) The finance minister is severely criticized in Parliament. The prime minister strongly suggests that she reverse the government's fiscal stance and restore taxes to their original levels (that is, reduce them by 3 billion). Will this reversal in fiscal policy resolve the output gap problem described in (b)? Explain.

(d) The finance minister threatens to resign. She argues that her credibility as minister is at stake. A reversal of policy would be political suicide for her. Moreover, her taxation increase was correct; unforeseen external factors caused the problem. She convinces the prime minister that the government's appropriate stance should be to retain the 3 billion increase in taxation, and also to increase government spending by 2.5 billion. Comment on this new policy stance.

6. The Aggregate Expenditure Model in a Closed Economy

Consider the following model of the economy:

$C = 90 + 0.8\ Y_D$

$I = 70$

$G = 240$

$T = 0.25\ Y$

(a) What is the equation for the AE curve in this model?

(b) What is the equilibrium level of income?

(c) What is the simple multiplier in this model?

(d) What is the level of private saving when the economy is in equilibrium?

(e) What is the level of public saving when the economy is in equilibrium?

7. The Aggregate Expenditure Model in an Open Economy

Let's add the external sector to the model described in the preceding problem. The external sector is described by the following functions:

$X = 140$

$IM = 0.14\ Y$

(a) Calculate the equilibrium level of income.

(b) Calculate the value of the multiplier in this model. Why is the multiplier smaller than the one obtained in the previous problem?

(c) Derive an expression for the trade balance, *NX*, as a function of income. What is the value of the trade balance when the economy is in equilibrium?

(d) Calculate the effect on equilibrium income and the trade balance of an increase in exports from 140 to 190.

EXTENSION EXERCISE

E1. The Aggregate Expenditure Model and Fiscal Policy

This exercise deals with an algebraic macroeconomic model. You should read the appendix to this chapter before attempting these questions. You are given the following information about behaviour in an economy that has a potential real national income (Y^*) of 300.

The consumption function is

$$C = 30 + 0.9Y_D. \tag{1}$$

The parameter 0.9 is the marginal propensity to consume out of disposable income, and we denote it as the parameter *MPC.* The value 30 represents autonomous consumption, denoted as *a* in the textbook.

The relationship between Y_D and Y is

$$Y_D = 0.8Y. \tag{2}$$

Since equation (2) implies a net tax rate (t) of 0.2, the tax function can be written as

$$T = 0.2Y. \tag{3}$$

Investment expenditure is

$$I = 40. \tag{4}$$

Government expenditure is

$$G = 20. \tag{5}$$

The net export function is

$$X - IM = 20 - 0.12Y. \tag{6}$$

The term 0.12 is the marginal propensity to import and is denoted as m.

The *AE* expenditure identity is

$$AE = C + I + G + (X - IM). \tag{7}$$

The public saving (*PS*) identity is

$$PS = T - G. \tag{8}$$

Using the *AE* approach, the equilibrium condition is

$$AE = Y. \tag{9}$$

Solving for Equilibrium Real National Income Using the AE Approach

The key to determining the equilibrium level of real national income is to derive the algebraic expression for the *AE* function. We do this step by step.

(a) Since *AE* is a relationship between desired expenditures and *Y,* it is necessary to express consumption as a function of *Y*. Hence, substitute equation (2) into (1), and form the new consumption function. Call this function equation (10). What is the marginal propensity to consume out of total income?

(b) The *AE* function is the algebraic sum of the components of desired aggregate expenditure. Substitute equations (10), (4), (5), and (6) into equation (7) and derive the algebraic expression for the *AE* function. Make sure you collect all of the autonomous terms as well as all the coefficients for the *Y* variable.

(c) The slope of the *AE* function (z) is given by, $z = MPC(1 - t) - m$, where *MPC* is the marginal propensity to consume out of disposable income. Prove that the value of z is equal to the value of the coefficient of the Y term in part (b).

(d) Using equation (9), solve for the equilibrium level of Y. What is the value of the simple multiplier? What is the value of the output gap?

(e) What is the value of public saving at the equilibrium level of GDP?

(f) What is the value of net exports at the equilibrium level of GDP?

Solving for Equilibrium Real National Income Using the Saving–Investment Approach

(g) Prove that the private saving function is the expression $S = -30 + 0.08Y$.

(h) Prove that the public saving function is the expression $PS = 0.2Y - 20$.

Fiscal Policy Issues

(i) Assume that the government wishes to eliminate the output gap. What change in government expenditures would you recommend?

(j) Eliminating the output gap by changing the tax rate is a much more difficult exercise. We use the *AE* approach to deal with this interesting policy issue. Suppose that equation (2) changed to $Y_D = 0.8367Y$. What has happened to the net tax rate? Prove that the new equation for the *AE* function is given by $AE = 110 + 0.633Y$. Using equation (9) and the new aggregate expenditure function, prove that the new equilibrium level of real national income is approximately equal to 300. Has the tax cut policy eliminated the output gap?

ADDITIONAL MULTIPLE-CHOICE QUESTIONS

Questions 1 to 9 refer to the following information about an economy. Before attempting these questions, you should calculate the values of aggregate expenditure and public saving for each of the six levels of national income *(Y)* shown in the schedule.

Y	*T*	*C*	*I*	*G*	*NX*
0	0	100	56	50	10
100	20	156	56	50	0
200	40	212	56	50	–10
300	60	268	56	50	–20
400	80	324	56	50	–30
500	100	380	56	50	–40

***1. Which of the following statements is correct?**
(a) Autonomous consumption is 100.
(b) Autonomous exports are 10.
(c) The marginal propensity to import is 0.1.
(d) The net tax rate is 0.2.
(e) All of the above.

2. The marginal propensity to consume
(a) out of disposable income is 0.56.
(b) out of total income is 0.56.
(c) out of disposable income is 0.70.
(d) out of total income is 0.70.
(e) out of total income is 0.56 and out of disposable income is 0.70.

3. Which of the following statements is correct?
(a) Desired aggregate expenditure at $Y = 200$ is 328.
(b) The marginal propensity to spend out of total income is 0.46.
(c) At $Y = 500$, there is a budget surplus of 50.
(d) At an income level of 400, exports are greater than imports.
(e) At an income level of 300, there is a government budget deficit of 10.

***4. The value of the simple multiplier is**
(a) 1.85 approximately.
(b) equal to the marginal propensity not to spend, which is 0.54.
(c) equal to the slope of the *AE* function, which is 0.46.
(d) 2.17 approximately.
(e) the reciprocal of the marginal propensity to import.

***5. The level of private saving at $Y = 400$ is**
(a) 26.
(b) –4.0.
(c) 76.
(d) 280.
(e) 156.

6. The level of public saving at $Y = 400$ is
(a) 26.
(b) 30.
(c) –30.
(d) 0.0.
(e) 50.

7. **Which of the following statements is true?**
(a) According to the *AE* approach, equilibrium national income is 400.
(b) The average propensity to spend is unity at $Y = 400$.
(c) At $Y = 400$, imports are 40.
(d) Public saving is 30 at equilibrium national income.
(e) All of the above.

8. **Which of the following statements is true?**
(a) The value of the simple multiplier is 2.1, approximately.
(b) An increase in investment from 56 to 83 will increase equilibrium national income from 400 to 450, approximately.
(c) An increase in the equilibrium value of real national income will have no effect on total taxes collected.
(d) If exports fall from 10 to 0, real national income will fall by approximately 20.5.
(e) An increase of 50 in the equilibrium value of real national income will decrease net exports by 10.

*9. **An increase in the net tax rate from 20 to 30 percent**
(a) decreases the slope of the *AE* curve.
(b) changes the value of the simple multiplier to 1.64, approximately.
(c) decreases the marginal propensity to consume out of total income to a value of 0.49.
(d) generate an equilibrium level of real national income that is less than 400.
(e) All of the above.

*10. **Suppose that current equilibrium GDP was 400 and that the target or desired level of GDP was 418.5. Which of the following stabilization policies would achieve the target value of GDP? (Use the multiplier value of 1.85.)**
(a) Government expenditures should increase by 18.5.
(b) The net tax rate should be increased from 0.20 to 0.30.
(c) Government spending should increase by 10.
(d) The government should reduce its expenditures by 18.5.
(e) None of the above.

11. **If $C = 34 + 0.7Y_D$ and $Y_D = 0.6Y$, the value of the marginal propensity to consume out of national income is**
(a) 1.3. (b) 0.1.
(c) 0.42. (d) 0.7.
(e) 0.6.

*12. **If $AE = 270 + 0.7Y$, then the equilibrium level of income would be**
(a) 385.7. (b) 270.
(c) 158.8. (d) 900.
(e) 81.

13. **According to Question 12, the economy's marginal propensity to spend is**
(a) 0.7. (b) 0.3.
(c) 1.0. (d) 1.7.
(e) Cannot be determined.

14. **If the net export function is given by the expression $NX = 100 - 0.2Y$, which of the following statements is true?**
(a) A trade balance exists at $Y = 500$.
(b) At $Y = 400$, the economy experiences a trade surplus of 20.
(c) The value of net exports declines as national income increases.
(d) The marginal propensity to import is 0.2.
(e) All of the above.

Use the following information of a hypothetical economy to answer questions 15 to 18: National income = 5200; Public saving = –150; Disposable income = 4400; Net exports = –110; and Consumption = 4100.

*15. **In this economy, net taxes are**
(a) $400. (b) $500.
(c) $600. (d) $700.
(e) $800.

*16. **In this economy, the value of government purchases is**
(a) $150. (b) $500.
(c) $650. (d) $800.
(e) $950.

*17. **In this economy, the value of private saving is**
(a) $200. (b) $270.
(c) $300. (d) $310.
(e) $390.

*18. **In this economy, the value of investment is**
(a) $250. (b) $260.
(c) $270. (d) $280.
(e) $290.

The Size of the Simple Multiplier in an Open Economy with Government

Questions 19 to 22 are based on the following table.

The table shows alternative hypothetical economies and the relevant values for the marginal propensity to consume out of disposable income (*MPC*), the net tax rate (*t*), and the marginal propensity to import (*m*). Fill in the missing values before attempting the multiple-choice questions.

Economy	*MPC*	*t*	*m*	*z*	Multiplier $K = 1/(1 - z)$
Economy A	0.80	0.1	0.02	_____	_____
Economy B	0.80	0.1	0.12	_____	_____
Economy C	0.80	0.2	0.12	_____	_____
Economy D	0.85	0.2	0.12	_____	_____

19. **What economy has the highest value of the marginal propensity to spend?**
(a) A. (b) B.
(c) C. (d) D.
(e) Both B and C.

20. The reason why A has a larger multiplier than C is that

(a) Economy C has a higher net tax rate.
(b) Economy A has a lower marginal propensity to import.
(c) Economy A has a larger marginal propensity to spend.
(d) Economy C has a larger marginal propensity not to spend.
(e) All of the above.

***21. Which economy has a multiplier value of 2.50?**

(a) A. (b) B.
(c) C. (d) C and D.
(e) D.

22. What would be the value of simple multiplier for a closed economy without government having an *MPC* value of 0.8?

(a) 0.8. (b) 1.25.
(c) 3.33. (d) 5.0.
(e) 2.5.

SOLUTIONS

Chapter Review

1.(a) **2.**(b) **3.**(a) **4.**(c) **5.**(c) **6.**(d) **7.**(d) **8.**(c) **9.**(e) **10.**(a) **11.**(d) **12.**(a) **13.**(e) **14.**(e) **15.**(e) **16.**(c) **17.**(d) **18.**(b) **19.**(c) **20.**(e) **21.**(d) **22.**(a)

Short-Answer Questions

1. (a) International trade includes the trade of both goods and services. For instance, the car industry produces a good (cars) while the tourist industry provides a service (tourist services). Therefore, sales of Canadian-made cars to the U.S. represent Canadian exports of goods to the U.S. while visits of American tourists to Toronto represent Canadian exports of services to the U.S. If Toronto becomes a more popular destination for American tourists, then Canadian exports increase and the *NX* function shifts up (i.e., *NX* increases at each level of national).

(b) If the marginal propensity to import increases, then both the *IM* function and the *NX* function become steeper. Note that the vertical intercept of the *NX* function does not change since the vertical intercept is determined by (autonomous) exports in our model.

(c) A decrease in the exchange rate for U.S. dollars increases the prices of Canadian goods relative to the prices of American goods. Therefore, American will buy less from Canada (i.e., Canadian exports will decrease) and Canadians will buy more from the U.S. (Canadian imports will increases). As a result, the *NX* function will shift down since net exports will decrease at each level of domestic income. Note that the slope of the *NX* curve could also become steeper depending on the assumptions of the model—e.g., if we assume that the proportion of income Canadians spend on imported goods increases as a result of the fall in the value of the exchange rate.

(d) Our model assumes that the level of exports is independent of the level of domestic national income, while the level of imports is positively related to the level of national income. Consequently, American imports increase when American disposable income rises, which means that Canadian exports to the U.S. increase when U.S. disposable income goes up. Therefore, the *NX* function shifts up as a result of this event.

2. (a) Starting from an initial situation of equilibrium (i.e., $Y = AE$), an increase in autonomous *AE* causes the economy to move to a situation of disequilibrium where $AE > Y$. This represents a situation where economic agents want to buy more than what the economy is actually producing (excess demand), and thus firms start to sell part of their inventories (i.e., an involuntary decrease in inventories takes place) to satisfy this greater demand. The involuntary decrease in inventories gives firms the signal that production must be adjusted upward to keep up with the increased demand. As firms increase production, Y starts to increase and the excess demand starts to decrease. This process continues until the excess demand is completely eliminated—i.e., until $Y = AE$ once again.

(b) Starting from an initial situation of equilibrium (i.e., $Y = AE$), a decrease in autonomous AE causes the economy to move to a situation of disequilibrium where $AE < Y$. This represents a situation where economic agents want to buy less than what the economy is actually producing (excess supply), and thus firms start to increase their inventories (i.e., an involuntary increase in inventories takes place) as a result of the fall in demand. The involuntary increase in inventories gives firms the signal that production must be adjusted downward to match the decrease in demand. As firms decrease production, Y starts to fall and the excess supply starts to decrease. This process continues until the excess supply is completely eliminated—i.e., until $Y = AE$ once again.

3. (a) The slope of the AE function is determined by three marginal propensities: the marginal propensity to consume out of disposable income (*MPC*), the marginal propensity to import (m), and the net tax rate (t). The slope of the AE function (z) increases if the *MPC* increases and if m and/or t decrease. As actual national income increases, induced macroeconomic variables increase such as consumption, imports, and taxes. Households want to consume more and governments and firms need more imported inputs to increase their output/services. Moreover, income tax payments vary with the level of income earned.

(b) Eliminating the recessionary gap requires government polices that increase national income. Increases in government expenditure directly shift the AE function upward. Hence, after the multiplier effect has taken place, actual national income increases by a multiple of the increase in G. Alternatively, the government could reduce its net tax rate. This has the effect of increasing the slope of the AE function (it rotates upward). Real national income will increase by a multiple. Both policies will lead to an initial situation in which desired aggregate expenditure is greater than actual national income. Firms react by increasing production and all factors of production receive more income. Hence, output and incomes will increase until a new equilibrium is reached.

4. (a) Reducing t increases disposable income. Hence, the marginal propensity to consume out of national income will increase. The AE curve will pivot up and its slope will increase. Since the marginal propensity to spend increases, the value of the simple multiplier increases.

(b) Increases in the Canadian interest rate decrease autonomous consumption and investment expenditures. As a result, the AE curve shifts downward. The slope of the AE curve is unaffected and hence the value of the simple multiplier remains unchanged.

(c) The marginal propensity to import has increased. The slope of the AE function decreases and hence it pivots downward with a smaller slope. Therefore, the value of the simple multiplier decreases.

(d) The U.S. dollar has appreciated; the Canadian dollar has depreciated. This change has two effects on the AE curve. First, exports to the U.S. are likely to increase. An increase in exports will shift the AE curve upward in a parallel fashion. Secondly, Canadians are likely to reduce the proportion of their income expended on imports. This will cause the AE curve to rotate upward and the slope of the AE curve will become steeper. Taking both effects into account, the AE curve will shift upward and its slope will increase. As a result, the multiplier value will increase.

(e) If foreign income falls, export sales (assumed to be autonomous) decrease. This shifts the AE downward in a parallel fashion. Since the slope of the AE function does not change, the multiplier value is not affected.

Exercises

1. (a) When $Y = 0$, public saving is –20 which represents a deficit situation. When $Y = 120$, public saving is 0.25×120 minus 20 which is +10, or a budget surplus.

(b) Inspecting the coefficient on the Y term, we know that the net tax rate is 25 percent. The intercept term represents autonomous government expenditure which in this case is 20. Remember, public saving is taxation revenue minus government expenditure.

(c) Public saving falls from +2 to –5 (from a budget surplus to a budget deficit). As Y falls, tax revenue falls. Since G is constant, the government's budget surplus (public saving) falls.

(d) The balanced budget occurs when public saving is zero (taxation revenue equals government expenditure). By solving the equation $0.25Y = 20$, we obtain $Y = 80$.

(e) The new public saving function is $0.25Y - 25$. The new public saving function shifts downward by 5 for every level of real national income.

(f) The new public saving function is $0.30Y - 20$. The new public saving function rotates from the intercept value (at $Y = 0$) of –20 and its slope increases from 0.25 to 0.30.

2. (a) There is a positive relationship given by the expression $Y_D = 0.7Y$. The net tax rate is 30 percent. When Y increases by \$1, disposable income increases by only 70 cents. Y_D is less than Y because taxes outweigh transfer payments; net taxes are positive and are deducted from total income.

(b) Autonomous consumption expenditure.

(c) Substituting $Y_D = 0.7Y$ into the consumption function, we obtain $C = 44 + 0.56Y$. The coefficient 0.56 is the marginal propensity to consume out of real national income.

(d) Since disposable income is now less at every level of income, the government must have increased its net tax rate. In this case, the tax rate increased from 30 to 40 percent. The marginal propensity to consume out of total real income becomes 0.48 which is equal to 0.8×0.6. The new consumption function is $C = 44 + 0.48Y$.

3. (a) Imports are positively related to national income by the expression $IM = 0.1Y$. The marginal propensity to import is 10 percent. As real national income rises, households buy more imported goods; firms, in order to produce more goods, require more imported inputs; and it is possible that governments and firms import various machines, goods, and services as part of their investment and expenditure programs.

(b) When $Y = 200$, $NX = +20\{-40 \times 0.1(200)\}$ or +20, trade surplus. When $Y = 800$, $NX = -40$, a trade deficit. A trade balance occurs at $Y = 400$.

(c) See Figure 22-2. As national income increases, import purchases increase. Hence, net exports fall.

Figure 22-2

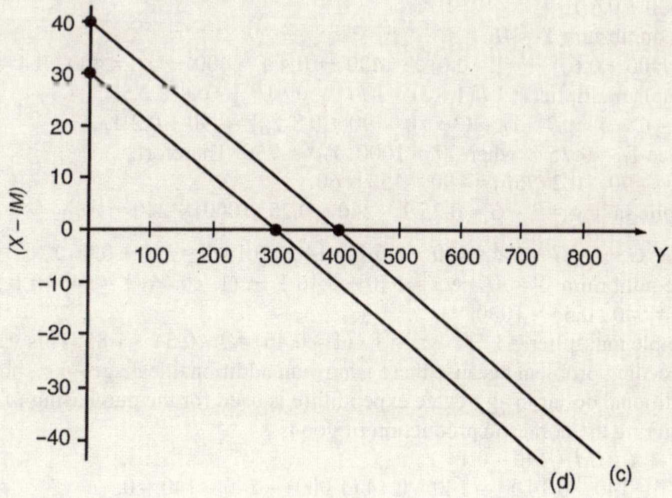

(d) The net export function becomes $30 - 0.10Y$. It will shift down by 10 for every level of real national income.

(e) There was a reduction in foreign income.

4. (a) The marginal propensity to consume out of national income is 0.72 which is the coefficient in front of the term Y in the consumption function. This can be calculated also by inspecting the schedule. When national income increases from 0 to 150 ($\Delta Y = 150$), consumption expenditure increases from 30 to 138 ($\Delta C = 108$). Hence, $\Delta C/\Delta Y = 0.72$. Autonomous consumption is the term 30 in the consumption function. The relationship between consumption and real disposable income is $30 + 0.9Y_D$. The net tax rate is 20 percent (0.2).

(b) The marginal propensity to import can be calculated from the data in the schedule or by noting the income coefficient in the net export function. In this case, $m = 0.1$.

(c) When national income increases from 300 to 600, aggregate expenditure increases from 414 to 600. Hence, $\Delta AE/\Delta Y = 186 / 300 = 0.62$. Using the textbook formula $z = MPC\,(1 - t) - m$, or in this case $[0.9(.8) - 0.1]$, we also obtain 0.62. Intercept = 228.

(d) According to the schedule, $AE = Y$ when real national income is 600.

(e) Public saving at $Y = 600$ is $0.2(600) - 51$ or $+69$. Private saving at $Y = 600$ is $18 = Y_D - C = [600 - 120] - 462$.

(f) The formula for the simple multiplier is $K = 1/(1 - z)$. We have already established that z equals 0.62. Hence, the multiplier value is 2.63.

(g) The output gap is -5.26 ($= 600 - 605.26$).

(h) The needed increase in national income is 5.26 in order to close the gap. If the government increased its expenditures by 2, then national income would increase by 5.26 with a multiplier value of 2.63.

5. **(a)** The inflationary gap of 12 will be completely eliminated if a new policy increased taxes by 3 billion since the tax multiplier is 4.

(b) GDP declines for two reasons. The increase in taxation will decrease GDP by 12 billion, and the decrease in exports will decrease GDP by 15 billion (2.5×6). The total decrease is therefore 27 billion. The economy's initial GDP level must have been 1012 billion. After the taxation and export changes, the new equilibrium level must be 27 billion less, or 985 billion. Hence the output (recessionary) gap is -15 billion.

(c) No, a taxation cut of 3 billion will increase GDP by 12 billion, leaving a recessionary gap of -3 billion ($997 - 1000$).

(d) If nothing else happens, the minister's amended policy will restore potential GDP. As was discussed before, the taxation increase will eliminate the inflationary gap. The 2.5 billion increase in government spending will counteract the 2.5 billion reduction in food exports.

6. **(a)** $AE = C + I + G$
$= 90 + 0.8\,Y_D + 70 + 240$
$= 400 + 0.8\,(Y - 0.25\,Y)$
$= 400 + 0.8\,(0.75)\,Y$
$= 400 + 0.6\,Y.$

(b) In equilibrium $Y = AE$:
$Y = 400 + 0.6\,Y \rightarrow (1 - 0.6)\,Y = 400 \rightarrow 0.4\,Y = 400 \rightarrow Y^* = 400 / 0.4 = 1000.$

(c) Simple multiplier $= 1 / (1 - z) = 1 / (1 - 0.6) = 1 / 0.4 = 2.5.$

(d) $Y_D = C + S \rightarrow S = Y_D - C = Y_D - [90 + 0.8\,Y_D] = -90 + 0.2\,Y_D.$
Since $Y_D = 0.75\,Y$, when $Y^* = 1000$, $Y_D^* = 750$. Therefore,
$S^* = -90 + 0.2\,(750) = -90 + 150 = 60.$

(e) Public saving $= T - G = 0.25\,Y - 240 = 0.25\,(1000) - 240 = 10.$

7. **(a)** $AE = C + I + G + NX = 400 + 0.6\,Y + 140 - 0.14\,Y = 540 + 0.46\,Y.$
In equilibrium: $Y = AE \rightarrow Y = 540 + 0.46\,Y \rightarrow (1 - 0.46)\,Y = 540 \rightarrow 0.54\,Y = 540 \rightarrow$
$Y^* = 540 / 0.54 = 1000.$

(b) Simple multiplier $= 1 / (1 - z) = 1 / (1 - 0.46) = 1 / 0.54 = 1.85$. This value is smaller than in the preceding problem because there is now an additional leakage—i.e., now a fraction m of every additional dollar in aggregate expenditure is used for the purchasing of imported goods and for fostering the domestic production of goods.

(c) $NX = X - IM = 140 - 0.14\,Y.$
$NX^* = 140 - 0.14\,Y^* = 140 - 0.14\,(1\,000) = 140 - 140 = 0.$

(d) An increase in exports of 50 implies an increase in autonomous expenditure of 50. Therefore, the change in equilibrium income will be equal to the simple multiplier times the change in autonomous expenditure: $\Delta Y = 1.85\,(50) = 92.5$. The new equilibrium level of income will thus be 1092.5.
The new trade balance will be: $NX^* = 190 - 0.14\,Y^* = 190 - 0.14\,(1092.5) = 190 - 152.95 = 37.05.$
That is, there will be a trade surplus of 37.05.

Extension Exercise

E1. **(a)** Equation (10) is $C = 30 + 0.72Y$. The marginal propensity to consume out of total real income is 0.72.

(b) $AE = 30 + 0.72Y + 40 + 20 + 20 - 0.12Y = 110 + 0.60Y.$

(c) $z = MPC(1 - t) - m$. $MPC = 0.9$, $t = 0.2$, $m = 0.12$. Hence, $z = 0.60$.

(d) $110 + 0.6Y = Y$ or $Y = 275$. The value of the simple multiplier is $K = 1/1\text{–}z$ or 2.5 when $z = 0.60$.
The output gap is $275 - 300$ or -25. This is a recessionary gap.

(e) $PS = 0.2 \times 275 - 20 = 35.$

(f) $(X - IM) = 20 - 0.12(275) = -13$.
(g) Private saving is equal to $Y_d - C$ or $Y - 0.2Y - [30 + 0.9(Y - 0.2Y)]$.
(h) Public saving is equal to $T - G$ or $0.2Y - 20$.
(i) The output gap is –25 (275 – 300). The government spending multiplier in this model is 2.5. Hence, government expenditure should rise by 10.
(j) The new consumption function (expressed as a function of total income is $C = 30 + (0.836 \times 0.9)Y$ or $C = 30 + .753Y$. Hence aggregate expenditure is $30 + .753Y + 40 + 20 + 20 - 0.12Y$ or $110 + 0.633Y$. Using the condition that $AE = Y$, we obtain a new equilibrium level of real national income of 299.8 (approximately 300). The output gap has been eliminated.

Additional Multiple-Choice Questions

1.(e) **2.**(e) **3.**(c) **4.**(a) **5.**(b) **6.**(b) **7.**(e) **8.**(c) **9.**(e) **10.**(c) **11.**(c) **12.**(d) **13.**(a) **14.**(e) **15.**(e) **16.**(e) **17.**(c) **18.**(b) **19.**(a) **20.**(e) **21.**(b) **22.**(d)

Explanations for the Asterisked Multiple-Choice Questions

1.(e) Autonomous consumption and exports are determined by looking along the first row of the schedule at which $Y = 0$. Consumption expenditure is 100 when $Y = 0$ and exports which do not depend on national income are 10 (since imports are 0 at $Y = 0$). The marginal tax rate is determined by inspecting the data in the first two columns of the schedule. These columns indicate that taxes rise by 20 for every 100 increase in national income. The marginal propensity to import is determined by inspecting the data in the first and last columns of the schedule. The data indicate that net exports fall by 10 for every 100 increase in national income. Since exports are autonomous, imports rise as national income increases.

4.(a) Using the formula for the marginal propensity to spend $[z = MPC(1 - t) - m]$, we obtain a value of 0.46 for z. Hence, the multiplier value is 1.85 [= 1/(1 – 0.46)].

5.(b) Private saving (S) is given by the equation $Y_D - C$. At $Y = 400$, disposable income is 320 while consumption expenditure is 324. Hence, S is equal to –4.

9.(e) By decreasing the slope of the AE function, the new AE intersects the 45° line at a lower equilibrium level of national income. The new MPC value out national income will be 0.49 [= 0.7 × 0.7], and the new z value is 0.39. The new multiplier value is 1.64 [= 1/1 – 39].

10.(c) The needed change in Y is +18.5. With a multiplier of 1.85, ΔG must be +10.

12.(d) Solve the equation $Y = 270 + 0.7Y$. Hence, $Y = 900$.

15.(e) Net Taxes = $Y - Y_D$ = \$5200 – \$4400 = \$800

16.(e) Public saving = Net taxes – $G \rightarrow G$ = Net taxes – Public saving = \$800 – (–\$150) = \$800 + \$150 = \$950.

17.(c) $Y_D = C + S \rightarrow S = Y_D - C$ = \$4400 – \$4100 = \$300

18.(b) $Y = C + I + G + NX \rightarrow I = Y - C - G - NX$ = \$5200 – \$4100 – \$950 – (–\$110) = \$260.

21.(b) Economy B has a marginal propensity to spend of 0.6 [= 0.8(0.9) – 0.12]. Hence, its multiplier is 1/0.4 or 2.5.

CHAPTER 23

OUTPUT AND PRICES IN THE SHORT RUN

LO

LEARNING OBJECTIVES

In this chapter you will learn

1. why an exogenous change in the price level shifts the *AE* curve and changes the equilibrium level of real GDP.
2. how to derive the aggregate demand (*AD*) curve and what causes it to shift.
3. the meaning of the aggregate supply (*AS*) curve and why it shifts when technology or factor prices change.
4. how to define macroeconomic equilibrium.
5. how aggregate demand and aggregate supply shocks affect real GDP and the price level.

CHAPTER OVERVIEW

The previous two chapters (21 and 22) analyzed national income determination under the assumption that the price level was fixed. Short-run macroeconomic equilibrium was demand determined. The short-run macro model in this chapter allows for changes in both real GDP and the price level. In the short run, technology and factor prices remain constant.

The transition to a variable price level is made in three steps. First, we note the effects of price level changes on the demand side of the economy. Second, we investigate the short-run aggregate supply curve—the level of output firms would like to supply. Finally, the chapter examines the concept of macroeconomic equilibrium that combines both the demand and supply sides to simultaneously determine the price level and real national income. Short-run macroeconomic equilibrium of real national income and the price level occurs at the intersection of the *AD* and *AS* curves.

A downward-sloping aggregate demand curve is developed by analyzing the effects of an exogenous change in the price level on desired aggregate expenditure. A rise in the price level lowers private-sector wealth and reduces autonomous desired consumption; this leads to a downward shift in the aggregate expenditure curve and a decrease in the equilibrium level of income. Moreover, a rise in the domestic price level shifts the net export function downward, which means a downward shift in the aggregate expenditure curve. Hence, national income equilibrium decreases.

Shifts in the *AD* function are caused only by changes in the underlying economic events that change autonomous desired aggregate expenditure.

The slope of the aggregate supply curve (*AS*) is positive, but its slope changes as real GDP changes. Although factor prices are constant for any *AS* curve, unit costs usually increase as output increases. Hence, firms usually want higher prices for increased output.

The effects of **aggregate demand shocks** on real income and the price level depend on the range of the *AS* curve in which the demand shock occurs. When the slope of the *AS* is steep, the increase in real income is small and the increase in the price level is large resulting from any increase in aggregate demand. Hence, the value of the multiplier depends on the slope of the *AS* curve.

Aggregate supply shocks shift the *AS* curve. A leftward shift in the *AS* curve, with a downward-sloping *AD* curve, causes the price level to rise and real income to fall. A rightward shift in the *AS* curve will lead to a fall in the price level, but an increase in real output.

HINTS AND TIPS

The following may help you to avoid some of the most common errors on examinations.

✓ Understand the connection between desired aggregate expenditure and aggregate demand. For example, learn that a change in the price level and changes in autonomous desired expenditure cause shifts in the *AE* curve. However, the former causes a movement along an *AD* curve while the latter cause shifts in the *AD* curve.

✓ Don't associate movements along an *AS* curve with changes in factor prices. Changes in factor prices shift the *AS* curve. Increases in factor prices shift the *AS* curve leftward/up.

✓ Remember that the equilibrium values for real GDP and the price level are determined by the intersection of the *AD* and *AS* curves. Should either (or both) curve shift, macroeconomic equilibrium will change. For example, a shift in the *AD* curve to the right causes the values of *Y* and *P* to increase.

✓ Learn that the simple multiplier formulae of the last two chapters are no longer applicable if the *AS* curve is positively sloped. The steeper the *AS* curve, the lower the multiplier value (effect on *Y*).

CHAPTER REVIEW

The Demand Side of the Economy

Understanding the relationship between *AE* and *AD* curves is crucial. An exogenous change in the price level *shifts* the *AE* curve and changes the equilibrium level of real GDP for two reasons. First, a decrease in the price level increases private-sector real wealth. Therefore, desired consumption increases shift the consumption function up. Second, a decrease in the domestic price level (foreign prices held constant) will increase exports and decrease imports. Hence, the net export function shifts up. Both factors will increase the equilibrium level of real income. These two factors explain why the *AD* curve is negatively sloped. Do not be confused; a price change causes the *AE* curve to shift, but causes a movement along the *AD* curve. The *AD* curve shifts only when some autonomous component of aggregate expenditure changes (such as investment or government expenditures). A shift in the *AD* curve is called an **aggregate demand shock.**

1. **All other things being equal, an increase in the domestic price level**
   (a) increases the value of real wealth and shifts the consumption function upward.
   (b) decreases the value of real wealth and shifts the consumption function upward.
   (c) causes the *AD* curve to shift to the left.
   (d) decreases the value of real wealth and causes the aggregate expenditure function to shift downward.
   (e) causes input prices to fall.

2. **All other things being equal, a decrease in the domestic price level shifts the net export function**
   (a) downward, thus causing the aggregate expenditure function to shift downward.
   (b) upward, thus causing the aggregate expenditure function to shift upward.
   (c) upward, thus causing the aggregate expenditure function to shift downward.
   (d) downward, thus causing the aggregate expenditure function to shift upward.
   (e) downward, thus causing the *AS* curve to shift upward.

3. **The aggregate demand (*AD*) curve relates**
   (a) real GDP to desired aggregate expenditure.
   (b) nominal national income to the price level.
   (c) equilibrium real aggregate expenditure to the price level.
   (d) consumption expenditure to the price level.
   (e) real national income to inflation rates.

4. **All other things being equal, the *AD* curve shifts to the right as a result of which of the following changes?**
   (a) Decreased government expenditure.
   (b) Increased imports.
   (c) Decreased autonomous exports.
   (d) Decreased investment expenditure.
   (e) Decreased net tax rates.

5. **All other things being equal, an increase in desired investment expenditures**
   (a) shifts the *AE* curve upward.
   (b) shifts the *AD* curve to the right.
   (c) causes the equilibrium levels of real national income and price to increase if the economy operates with a positively sloped *AS* curve.
   (d) All of the above.
   (e) None of the above.

The Supply Side of the Economy

The **aggregate supply (*AS*) curve** relates the price level to the quantity of output that firms would like to produce and sell *on the assumption that technology and the prices of all factors of production remain constant.* For a given *AS* curve, unit costs tend to rise with output because less efficient factories may have to be used, or less efficient workers may have to be hired, or existing workers may have to be paid overtime rates. Unit cost increases trigger price increases. It is assumed that the *AS* curve not only slopes up but also gets progressively steeper as real GDP increases. Hence, at low levels of GDP the *AS* curve is relatively flat, but as GDP rises the *AS* curve gets progressively steeper.

Each *AS* curve is associated with a specific set of factor prices and productivity level. Hence, the *AS* curve will shift if factor prices and/or productivity change.

6. **A positively sloped *AS* curve indicates**
   (a) firms' willingness to supply more output if the output can be produced at lower unit costs.
   (b) that expanding output means incurring higher unit costs and higher prices of output.
   (c) that expanding output means higher factor prices and therefore higher output prices.
   (d) higher output levels trigger both decreases in productivity and increases in factor prices.
   (e) higher output levels trigger increases in factor prices.

7. If the *AS* curve is horizontal, as is depicted in *Extensions in Theory 23-1*,
(a) output can be increased at a constant price level.
(b) any increase in *AD* will cause real national income and the price level to increase.
(c) output is constant but the price level is variable.
(d) the economy is most likely operating beyond its potential level of real national income.
(e) potential output varies in the short run.

8. A rightward shift in the *AS* curve is brought about by
(a) an increase in factor prices.
(b) decreases in productivity.
(c) increases in productivity and/or decreases in factor prices.
(d) decreases in factor supplies.
(e) increases in real wealth.

9. As real GDP increases, the change in the price level is greatest
(a) if the *AS* curve is relatively steep.
(b) when the unemployment rate is high.
(c) when unit costs do not change.
(d) if the *AS* curve is flat.
(e) when the economy has excess capacity.

Macroeconomic Equilibrium

The equilibrium values of real GDP and the price level occur at the intersection of the *AD* and *AS* curves. The combination of real GDP and the price level at the intersection of the *AD* and *AS* curves is called a **macroeconomic equilibrium**.

Changes in the macroeconomic equilibrium are caused by shifts in the *AD* curve and/or the *AS* curve. It is important to understand the economic factors that cause either the *AD* curve or the *AS* curve to shift and the direction of these shifts. For example, a positive demand shock associated with export increases causes the *AD* curve to shift to the right. With an upward sloping *AS* curve, the equilibrium values of both the price level and real GDP increase.

The shape of the *AS* curve has important implications on how the effects of an aggregate demand shock are divided between a change in real GDP and a change in the price level. With a positively sloped *AS* curve, the multiplier value associated with a demand shock is less than the simple multipliers outlined in Chapters 21 and 22.

Aggregate supply shocks cause the *AS* curve to shift. Aggregate supply shocks cause the price level and real GDP to change in opposite directions.

10. With a given aggregate demand curve, a shift in the *AS* curve to the left causes
(a) increases in real national income and the price level in the short run.
(b) an increase in the price level but a decrease in real national income in the short run.
(c) a decrease in the price level but an increase in real national income.
(d) a decrease in potential real national income.
(e) a movement down the *AD* curve.

11. In an *AD–AS* diagram, the simple multiplier is measured by

(a) the horizontal (for a given price level) shift of the *AD* curve in response to a change in autonomous expenditure.
(b) the vertical shift (at a given GDP level) of the *AD* curve in response to a change in autonomous expenditure.
(c) the distance moved up or down the *AD* curve in response to a change in autonomous expenditure.
(d) the distance between initial equilibrium and the new intersection of *AD* and *AS* in response to a change in autonomous expenditure.
(e) the ratio of the change in price to the change in autonomous expenditure.

12. Assume that the *AS* curve is positively sloped. After an economic shock, we observe that the equilibrium price level is lower than before but real equilibrium output has increased. Which one of the following events, by itself, could explain this observation?

(a) An increase in input prices.
(b) An increase in factor productivity.
(c) An increase in exports.
(d) A reduction in investment expenditure.
(e) A decrease in the tax rate.

13. If the current price level is below the macroeconomic equilibrium level,

(a) the desired output of firms is greater than the level of output consistent with expenditure decisions.
(b) desired aggregate expenditure is less than the amount of goods supplied in the short run.
(c) the desired output of firms is less than the level of output consistent with expenditure decisions.
(d) price will tend to adjust such that there will be movement down the *AD* curve.
(e) the price falls further.

14. The multiplier value that allows for price changes will be equal to the value of the simple multiplier if the demand shock occurs in the

(a) flat (horizontal) range of the *AS* curve.
(b) intermediate range of the *AS* curve.
(c) steep portion of the *AS* curve.
(d) range characterized by increasing unit costs.
(e) the inelastic portion of the *AD* curve.

15. Under what circumstances would a positive demand shock result in virtually no increase in real income but a large increase in the price level?

(a) If the demand shock occurred in the flat range of the *AS* curve.
(b) If the demand shock occurred in the intermediate range of the *AS* curve.
(c) If the demand shock occurred in the steep portion of the *AS* curve.
(d) If unit costs were constant before and after the demand shock.
(e) If input prices decreased.

16. If autonomous investment increased, the multiplier is zero if

(a) other autonomous expenditures also increased as a result of the fall in the price level.
(b) the demand shock occurred in the vertical range of the *AS* curve.
(c) the marginal propensity to spend was unity.
(d) the demand shock occurred in the horizontal range of the *AS* curve.
(e) net exports also increased as a result of the increase in the price level.

17. Assuming the *AS* curve is positively sloped, which of the following events would lead to a fall in both the equilibrium levels of real GDP and the price level?

(a) An increase in productivity.
(b) A decrease in government purchases.
(c) An increase in exports.
(d) A depreciation of the domestic currency in foreign exchange markets.
(e) A decrease in the marginal propensity to save.

18. Assuming the *AS* curve is horizontal, an increase in productivity would

(a) leave both equilibrium real GDP and equilibrium price level unchanged.
(b) cause equilibrium real GDP to fall and equilibrium price level to rise.
(c) cause equilibrium real GDP to rise and equilibrium price level to fall.
(d) cause both equilibrium real GDP and equilibrium price level to rise.
(e) cause equilibrium real GDP to rise but no change in equilibrium price level.

SHORT-ANSWER QUESTIONS

1. Discuss the economic reasoning for a negatively sloped *AD* curve.

2. Explain the economic reasoning for a positive and increasing sloped *AS* curve.

3. Sketch a rough, but properly labelled, *AD*/*AS* diagram that illustrates a negative demand shock causing decreases in real GDP and the price level in the short run.

4. Sketch a rough, but properly labelled, *AD/AS* diagram that depicts a positive demand shock causing a short-run increase in the price level but no change in real GDP.

5. Sketch a rough, but properly labelled, *AD/AS* diagram that illustrates the short-run effects on real GDP and the price level of a positive supply shock.

6. With the help of an *AD/AS* diagram, explain the short-run impact of the increase in oil prices in the economy of a non–oil producing country such as Spain. Assume the *AS* curve is positively sloped.

7. With the help of an *AD/AS* diagram, explain the short-run impact of the increase in oil prices in the economy of an oil-exporting country such as Canada. Assume the *AS* curve is positively sloped.

EXERCISES

1. **The Derivation of an *AD* Curve from Consumption Theory**
This exercise should improve your understanding of why an *AD* curve is downward-sloping and how it is derived. The exercise demonstrates the links among changes in price, the level of real wealth, consumption expenditure, and equilibrium real GDP.

Desired consumption (C) is shown at two different price levels, $P = 1$ and $P = 2$. The consumption function is given by the expression $C = 100 + 0.8Y + 0.1(W/P)$, where W represents the total nominal wealth in the economy and W/P represents real wealth. We assume that the value of nominal wealth is 3000. All other components of aggregate expenditure are lumped together in one column, labelled $I + G + NX$. For the purposes of this exercise only, entries in that column are assumed to be unaffected by the price level, but because imports are included in this combination, the component is a negative function of real national income.

Y	$C_1(P = 1)$	$C_2(P = 2)$	$I + G + NX$	$AE_1(P = 1)$	$AE_2(P = 2)$
0	400	250	1200	1600	1450
2500	2400	2250	700	3100	2950
2875		2550	625		3175
3250	3000	2850	550	3550	3400
3625	3300	3150	475	3775	
4000	3600		400		
4375			325	4225	4075

(a) Use the consumption equation above or apply the marginal propensity to consume that you can derive from the initial data entries. Fill in the missing values for C_1, C_2, AE_1, and AE_2.

(b) Plot the aggregate expenditure functions in the left-hand panel in Figure 23-1 and determine the equilibrium level of national income at each price level.

Figure 23-1

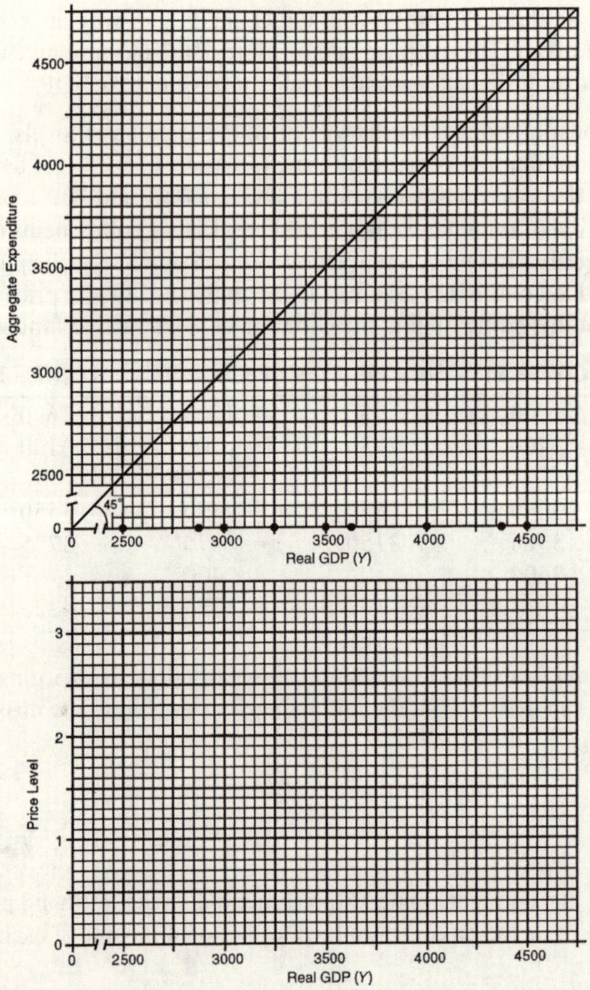

(c) What vertical shift in the *AE* function occurs as a result of a rise in the price level from $P = 1$ to $P = 2$? What is the change in the equilibrium level of national income after the change?

(d) Use the two values in (b) to plot the aggregate demand curve in the right-hand panel of Figure 23-1. Assume that a linear approximation is satisfactory. Why does the aggregate demand curve slope downward?

(e) If government purchases rise at all levels of income by 150, by how much does the equilibrium level of national income rise? Plot the new aggregate expenditure function (AE_E) in the upper graph, assuming $P = 1$, and show the new equilibrium level of income. Check your answer by determining the marginal propensity to spend, deriving the simple multiplier, and multiplying it times the autonomous expenditure change.

(f) If government purchases rise by 150, explain how that affects the position of the *AD* curve. How does your answer to (e) provide useful information regarding the size of any shift in the curve? Plot the new *AD* curve in Figure 23-1.

(g) In the examples above, if the price level falls from 2 to 1, the *AE* curve shifts up by 150, and if the government increases spending by 150, the *AE* curve shifts up by 150. Yet in one case the economy moves along the *AD* curve, and in the other case the *AD* curve shifts. Explain why these different results occur.

2. **Macroeconomic Equilibrium**
The aggregate demand function is given by $P = 40 - 2Y$, and the aggregate supply function is given by $P = 10 + Y$, where Y refers to real national income and P is the price level. These curves are drawn for you in Figure 23-2.

Figure 23-2

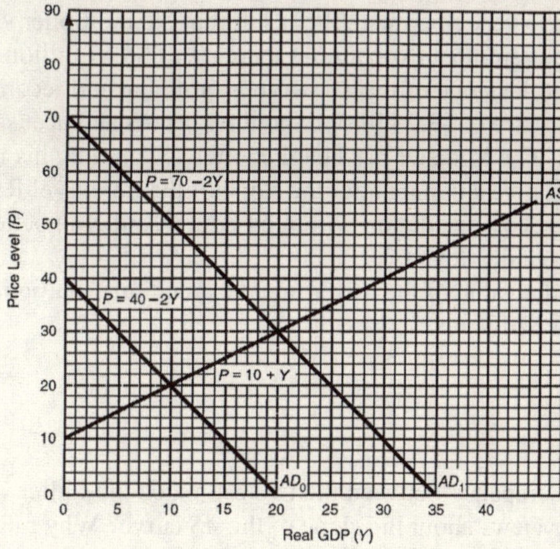

(a) Referring to the graph, what is the macroeconomic equilibrium (equilibrium levels of P and Y)? Prove algebraically that the intersection of the two equations yields these equilibrium values.

(b) Suppose that the expression for the *AD* curve became $P = 70 - 2Y$. This curve is also plotted for you in Figure 23-2. What are the new equilibrium values for P and Y? Discuss the changes that occurred to the levels of P and Y. Comment on the size of the horizontal shift in the *AD* curve (at a constant price of 20) in relation to the value of the change in the equilibrium value of real GDP.

3. **"I Don't Give a Damn about the Slope of the *AS* Curve!"**

The Finance Minister is under extreme pressure from his caucus, the public, and the opposition parties to reduce unemployment and to increase employment and real GDP. He summons his key economic advisers in the Central Bank and the Department of Finance to (1) brief him on the current situation and (2) advise him on various policy options.

After an hour's briefing, the Minister is assured that the officials from the Central Bank and his ministry have reached consensus on the following:

(1) The desired increase in real GDP is \$8 billion.
(2) Private-sector autonomous expenditures are not likely to change in the foreseeable future.
(3) Over the period of the policy change, input (factor) prices will not change.
(4) The preferred policy change is an increase in government expenditure.

The second hour of the briefing is acrimonious. The Central Bank officials argue that the slope of the *AS* curve is very steep with the result that the multiplier value is 1.2. Therefore, they recommend a government expenditure increase of \$6.67 billion. The ministry officials argue vehemently that the slope of the *AS* curve is quite flat and recommend a government expenditure increase of \$3.2 billion. Shouting occurs and accusations of incompetence are made by both parties. The Minister has heard enough! Slamming his fist on the conference table, he replies, "I don't give a damn about the slope of the *AS* curve! Resolve the issue and give me a specific policy recommendation within 24 hours. And, you better be right, or many of you will find yourselves unemployed."

(a) What is the value of the government expenditure multiplier according to the Department of Finance officials?

(b) Is the discrepancy between the two estimated multiplier values consistent with the differing views about the slope of the *AS* curve? Why might the two separate groups have differing views regarding the slope of the *AS* curve?

(c) Suppose that the views of the Department of Finance officials prevail. The Minister of Finance announces an increase in government expenditure of \$3.2 billion. After all effects of the expenditure programs have been realized in the economy, it is reported to the Minister that real national income has increased by \$3.8 billion and that the price level increase was larger than expected. The Minister is demoted by the Prime Minister to the backbenches without cabinet responsibility. What went wrong?

4. The Impact of a Change in the Price of Material Inputs

Most of the electricity required by businesses and residents of Paysandú—a small, mid-income country—is supplied by oil-burning power plants. Oil, therefore, is a very important material input for this non–oil producing country. The *AD* and *AS* curves of Paysandú are given by the following equations, respectively:

$$P = 500 - 2\,Y$$
$$P = Y - 50 - 2000 / P_{oil}$$

where P is the price level, Y is real GDP (in billions of dollars), and P_{oil} is the dollar price of a barrel of oil.

(a) What are the equilibrium values of Y and P when P_{oil} = \$25?

(b) Suppose now that conflict in the Middle East increases the price of oil to \$40 a barrel. What are the new equilibrium values of Y and P? Why and how is the *AS* curve affected by this increase in the price of oil? Explain the reasons for the specific directions of the changes in P and Y.

Suppose that significant oil reserves are discovered in Paysandú and that this country now becomes a relatively important producer and exporter of oil. The equations for the *AD* and *AS* curves of Paysandú are now, respectively:

$$P = 500 - 2\,Y + 3\,P_{oil}$$
$$P = \mathrm{Y} - 50 - 2000 / P_{oil}.$$

(c) What would be the equilibrium values of Y and P when P_{oil} = \$25? Explain why these values are different from those you obtained in part (a) above.

(d) What would be the equilibrium values of Y and P when P_{oil} = \$40? Why and how is the *AD* curve affected by this increase in the price of oil? Explain the reasons for the specific directions of the changes in P and Y.

5. **The Impact of Excise Taxes on Macroeconomic Equilibrium**

We have seen in Chapter 20 that market prices include indirect taxes such as excise taxes (taxes on production). Therefore, since excise taxes are part of the unit costs of production, changes in excise taxes will affect the position of the *AS* curve.

Suppose that the *AD* and *AS* curves of a hypothetical economy are given by the following equations, respectively:

$$P = 700 - 2\,Y$$
$$P = 2\,Y + 300 - 20\,/\,T.$$

where *P* is the price level, *Y* is real GDP (in billions of dollars), and *T* is the excise tax (in percent). Suppose that excise taxes are initially set at $T = 0.1$.

(a) What is the initial macroeconomic equilibrium?

(b) Suppose that excise taxes are reduced to $T = 0.05$. What is the size of the vertical shift of the *AS* curve?

(c) What is the new macroeconomic equilibrium after the decrease in *T*? Explain the direction of the changes in P^* and Y^*.

EXTENSION EXERCISE

E1. Multiplier Values and the Short-run Effects of Aggregate Demand Shocks

P	*AS (Y)*	AD_a	AD_b	AD_c	AD_e
1.0	0–50	50	30	70	84
1.2	70	48	28		82
1.4	80	46		66	80
1.6	85	44	24	64	
1.8	85		22		76
2.0	85	40	20	60	74

(a) Assume that the aggregate expenditure function is $AE = 30 + 0.5Y - 5P$. Derive the values for the *AD* curve by calculating the equilibrium values of national income (using $Y = 30 + 0.5Y - 5P$) at each price level. Fill in the missing values and then plot the *AD* curve in Figure 23-3, labelling it AD_a. Also, plot the *AS* curve. What are the short-run equilibrium levels of national income and the price level?

Figure 23-3

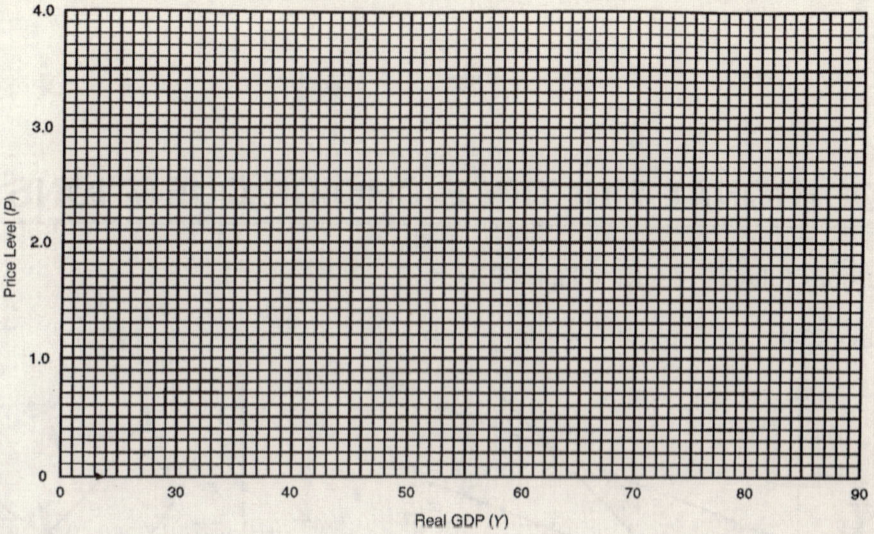

(b) Suppose that business confidence in the economy falls, so that investment declines by 10, and the *AE* function becomes $20 + 0.5Y - 5P$. Fill in the missing entries for the new *AD* curve under the column labelled AD_b, and plot it in the graph. What are the new equilibrium short-run levels of national income and the price level? What is the value of the simple multiplier?

(c) Suppose instead that business confidence rose, so that the *AE* function became $40 + 0.5Y - 5P$. Fill in the missing entries for the new *AD* curve (AD_c), and plot it in the graph. What are the new short-run equilibrium levels of national income and the price level? Comparing this result with that in part (a), what is the value of the multiplier that allows for price changes?

(d) In (b) and (c), shifts in the *AD* curve by the same amount but in the opposite direction did not result in the same change in the absolute value of output. Explain why they did not.

(e) If the economy, instead, starts from a position where $AE = 47 + 0.5Y - 5P$, determine the appropriate *AD* curve missing entries for (AD_e), plot them, and solve for the short-run equilibrium levels of income and the price level. Comparing this result with that in part (c), what is the value of the multiplier?

(f) Comment briefly on the effect of a positively sloped *AS* curve on the value of the simple multiplier.

ADDITIONAL MULTIPLE-CHOICE QUESTIONS

Questions 1 through 8 refer to Figure 23-4.

Figure 23-4

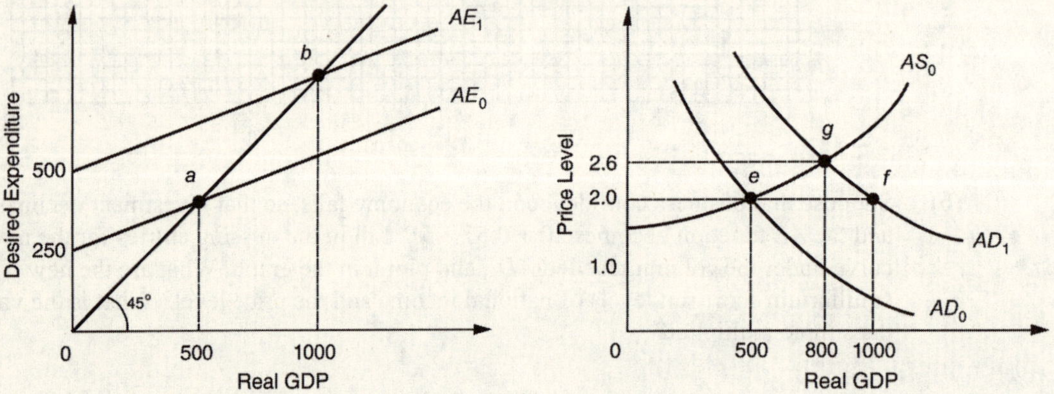

1. **According to the curves AE_0 and AD_0, the equilibrium levels of price and real national income are, respectively,**
   (a) 2.0 and 500.
   (b) 2.6 and 800.
   (c) 2.0 and 1000.
   (d) 2.6 and 1000.
   (e) None of the above.

2. **Assuming that the *AE* curve shifts upward from AE_0 to AE_1 but the price level remains constant at its initial level, we can say that**
   (a) autonomous expenditures must have increased by 250.
   (b) real national income increases by 500.
   (c) the aggregate demand curve shifts to the right so that $Y = 1000$ at the price level 2.0.
   (d) input prices must have remained constant.
   (e) All of the above.

3. **According to the diagram, the value of the simple multiplier is**
   (a) 5.0.
   (b) 0.5.
   (c) 4.0.
   (d) 1.2.
   (e) 2.0.

*4. **Given the aggregate demand curve AD_1, at the price level of 2.0,**
(a) aggregate demand is less than aggregate supply.
(b) aggregate demand is equal to aggregate supply.
(c) firms are unwilling to produce enough to satisfy the existing demand at the existing price level, and hence the price level will rise.
(d) the price level is likely to fall.
(e) input prices must rise.

5. **Given the increase in autonomous expenditure, moving from point *f* to point *g* represents the effect of an increase in the price level that**
(a) reduces both net exports and real wealth.
(b) reduces net exports but increases desired consumption.
(c) increases both net exports and real wealth.
(d) increases net exports and saving.
(e) increases input prices.

6. **The movement from point *f* to point *g* implies that the**
(a) AE_1 curve shifts downward to intersect the 45° line at an output level of 800.
(b) AE_1 curve shifts downward to intersect the 45° line at an output level of 500.
(c) economy moves along the AE_1 curve until it reaches an output of 800.
(d) economy moves along the AE_1 curve until it reaches an output of 500.
(e) economy moves along the AE_0 curve until it reaches an output of 800.

*7. **Assuming that input prices do not change, the new short-run macroeconomic equilibrium as a result of the increase in autonomous expenditure will be**
(a) at point g.
(b) at an output level of 800.
(c) at a price level of 2.6.
(d) an income that is 300 higher than the initial situation.
(e) All of the above.

8. **The value of the multiplier after allowing for a price change is**
(a) 1.2. (b) 2.0.
(c) 1.0. (d) 4.0.
(e) 0.8.

Refer to Figure 23-5 when answering Questions 9 through 13. Point *a* is the initial situation and *Y** refers to potential real national income.

Figure 23-5

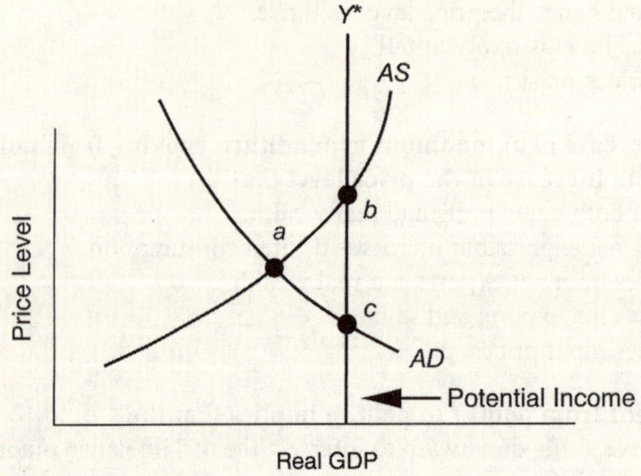

9. **When consumers become worried about the future and decide to save more out of additional income, the**
(a) *AD* curve shifts leftward, causing national income and the price level to fall.
(b) *AD* curve shifts rightward, causing national income and the price level to rise.
(c) *AS* curve shifts rightward, causing national income to rise and the price level to fall.
(d) *AS* curve shifts leftward, causing national income to fall and the price level to rise.
(e) positive output gap decreases.

***10.** **The dominant short-run effect of an increase in desired investment is to**
(a) shift the *AS* curve to the left.
(b) shift the *AS* curve to the right.
(c) shift the *AD* curve to the left.
(d) shift the *AD* curve to the right.
(e) increase the potential output level.

11. **If the *AD* curve shifts to the right, we expect**
(a) the price level to increase and output to fall.
(b) the price level to increase and output to rise.
(c) unemployment to rise.
(d) productivity to fall.
(e) input prices to increase in the short run.

12. **Rising oil prices would result in a higher price level and a lower GDP in this economy if the *AS* curve**
(a) shifted leftward, causing output and the price level to rise.
(b) shifted rightward, causing output and the price level to fall.
(c) shifted leftward, causing output to fall and the price level to rise.
(d) shifted rightward, causing output to rise and the price level to fall.
(e) intersected the *AD* curve at a higher output and price level.

***13. In order to eliminate the current output gap,**

(a) government taxes should be increased such that the *AD* curve shifts from point *a* to point *b*.
(b) net exports must increase in such a way that the *AS* curve shifts from point *a* to point *c*.
(c) input prices must increase so that the *AS* curve shifts from point *a* to point *c*.
(d) government expenditures must increase so that the new *AD* curve intersects the *AS* curve at point *b*.
(e) input prices must fall so that the new *AD* curve intersects the *AS* curve at point *b*.

Questions 14 to 17 refer to the following short-run macro model. An economy's *AD* curve is $P = 19 - 0.2Y$ and its *AS* curve is $P = 1.5 + 0.05Y$.

***14. What is the economy's current short-run equilibrium?**

(a) $P = 5.6$ and $Y = 82$.
(b) $Y = 70$ and $P = 5$.
(c) $P = 1.6$ and $Y = 92.1$.
(d) $Y = 5$ and $P = 70$.
(e) None of the above.

***15. Suppose that autonomous expenditure increased by 2 such that the *AD* curve changed to** $P = 21 - 0.2Y$. What is the value of the multiplier that allows for price increases?

(a) 4.0.
(b) 2.0.
(c) 5.0.
(d) 3.0.
(e) 10.0.

***16. Suppose that information in Question 15 applies. Providing that the *AS* curve does not change, the value of the simple multiplier that *keeps the price level at its original equilibrium value* (refer to Question 14) equals**

(a) 4.0.
(b) 2.0.
(c) 5.0.
(d) 3.0.
(e) 10.0.

17. Suppose that the *AS* curve changed to $P = 2.5 + 0.05Y$. Providing that the *AD* curve remains at $P = 19 - 0.2Y$, what are the new equilibrium levels of *P* and *Y*?

(a) $P = 5$ and $Y = 70$.
(b) $Y = 50$ and $P = 5$.
(c) $Y = 150$ and $P = 5$.
(d) $Y = 86$ and $P = 6.8$.
(e) $P = 5.8$ and $Y = 66$.

Use the following information to answer Questions 18 to 22. The *AD* and *AS* curves of a hypothetical economy are given by the following equations, respectively:

$$P = 500 - 2\,Y + 10\,F$$
$$P = 2\,Y + 200 - 20\,F - 2\,000 / P_m.$$

where *P* is the price level, *Y* is real GDP (in billions of dollars), P_m is the average price of material inputs, and *F* measures the degree of economic outlook from 0 to 10 (10 being the most optimistic outlook). Initially, $P_m = 10$ and $F = 5$.

***18. Initially, equilibrium price and equilibrium real GDP are, respectively,**

(a) 225 and \$150.0.
(b) 225 and \$162.5.
(c) 200 and \$150.0.
(d) 200 and \$205.5.
(e) None of the above.

***19. Because of turmoil in the Middle East, the price of oil—a very important production input—increases, causing P_m to rise from 10 to 20. As a result, the *AS* curve shifts**
(a) vertically up by 100.
(b) vertically down by 100.
(c) vertically down by 200.
(d) horizontally by 200.
(e) vertically up by 200.

***20. When $P_m = 20$ and $F = 5$, equilibrium price and equilibrium real GDP are, respectively,**
(a) 255 and \$137.5.
(b) 255 and \$185.5.
(c) 275 and \$137.5.
(d) 275 and \$185.5.
(e) 137.5 and \$275.0.

***21. Consumers and businesses become very optimistic about the future because of the latest macroeconomic data announced by Statistics Canada, causing *F* to reach the value of 10. As a result, the AD curve ____________ and the AS curve ____________.**
(a) shifts up; shifts up
(b) shifts up; shifts down
(c) shifts down; shifts down
(d) shifts down; shifts up
(e) shifts up; remains in the same position

***22. When $P_m = 10$ and $F = 10$, equilibrium price and equilibrium real GDP are, respectively,**
(a) 150 and \$200.
(b) 175 and \$225.
(c) 200 and \$250.
(d) 175 and \$200.
(e) 200 and \$200.

SOLUTIONS

Chapter Review

1.(d) **2.**(b) **3.**(c) **4.**(e) **5.**(d) **6.**(b) **7.**(a) **8.**(c) **9.**(a) **10.**(b) **11.**(a) **12.**(b) **13.**(c) **14.**(a) **15.**(c) **16.**(b) **17.**(b) **18.**(c)

Short-Answer Questions

1. A downward-sloping *AD* curve indicates that equilibrium levels of real GDP and the price level are negatively related. This is because exogenous price increases shift the *AE* curve downward while price decreases shift the *AE* upward. Take the case of a price level increase. A higher price level results in lower levels of private-sector real wealth and an uncompetitive situation in foreign trade markets. Hence, desired expenditure will decrease (consumption and net exports). When the *AE* curve shifts downward, a new lower GDP equilibrium is obtained.

   Hence, a higher price level is associated with a lower GDP equilibrium from a perspective of the aggregate demand side.

2. The *AS* curve relates the price level to the quantity of output that firms would like to produce and sell *on the assumption that technology and the prices of all factors of production remain constant.* To understand the positive slope of the *AS* curve, we need to see how costs are related to output and then how prices are related to output. Suppose firms wish to increase their output above current levels. In general, unit costs will rise as firms hire less efficient workers, or pay overtime rates for additional work, or use less efficient standby plants. The *law of diminishing returns* (lower productivity as output increases) implies that unit costs increase. Since unit costs increase with output increases, firms require higher prices of their product to be willing to supply more.

   The *AS* curve not only slopes up but also gets steeper as real GDP increases. At low levels of GDP, the *AS* curve is relatively flat, but as GDP rises the *AS* curve gets progressively steeper. When output is low (large recessionary gap), firms typically have excess capacity which means that output increases are achieved without much change in prices. At high levels of GDP, the *AS* curve is relatively steep (firms have no excess capacity and factors must be used beyond their normal utilization rates), and so output increases are accompanied by large increases in unit costs. Hence, price levels must rise to induce firms to supply more.

3. **Figure 23-6**

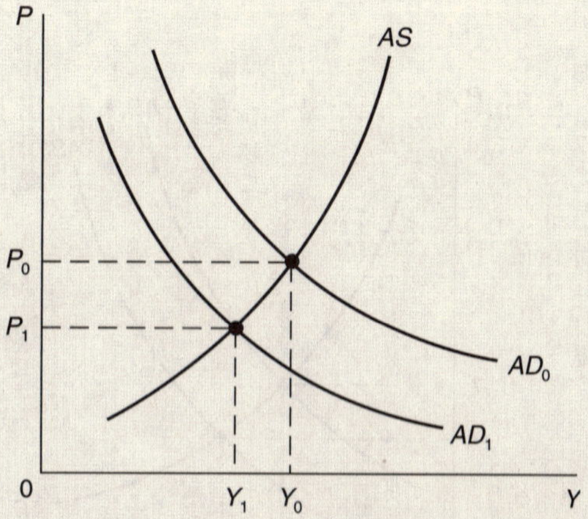

4. **Figure 23-7**

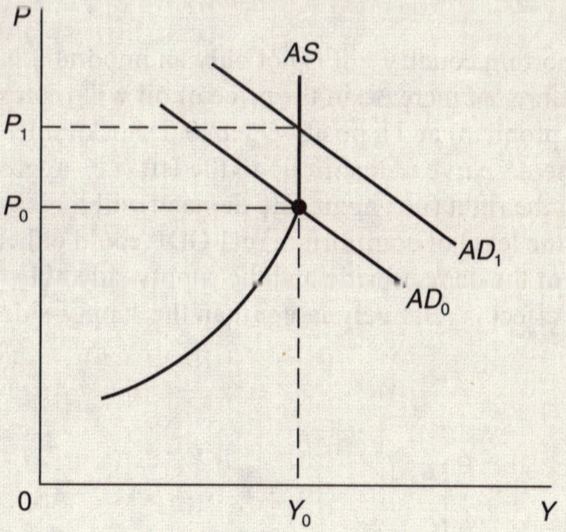

5. **Figure 23-8**

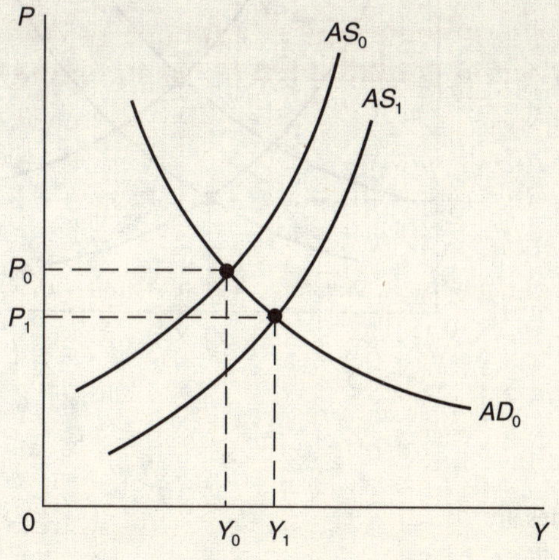

6. It is safe to assume that oil is an important input for all countries. Therefore, an increase in the price of oil will cause the unit cost of production of most goods and services to rise and the *AS* curve will shift up to the left (i.e., aggregate supply will decrease). As shown in Figure 23-9, equilibrium real GDP will fall while equilibrium price level will rise.

Figure 23-9

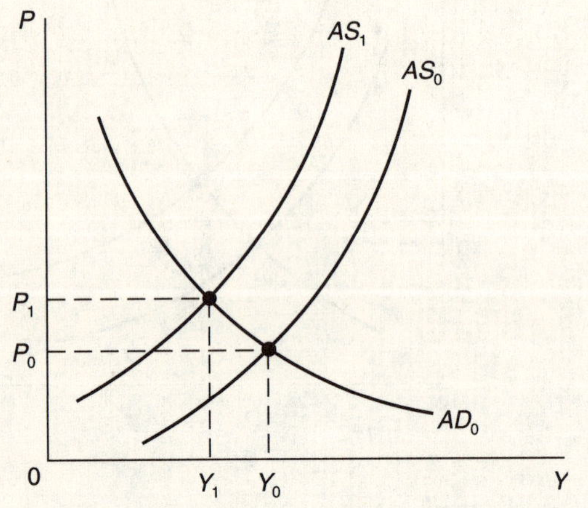

7. In the case of an oil-exporting country, oil is not only an important input used in production but also an important output. Therefore, an increase in the price of oil will represent both a negative supply shock (as shown in the preceding problem) and a positive demand shock (since the value of autonomous exports will increase). As a result, the *AS* curve will shift up to the left (i.e., aggregate supply will decrease) and the *AD* curve will shift down to the right (i.e., aggregate demand will increase). The equilibrium price level will definitely increase, but the level of equilibrium real GDP could either increase or decrease depending on the relative importance of the demand-side and the supply-side effects. Figure 23-10 depicts the situation where the demand-side effect is relatively larger than the supply-side effect and thus equilibrium real GDP increases.

Figure 23-10

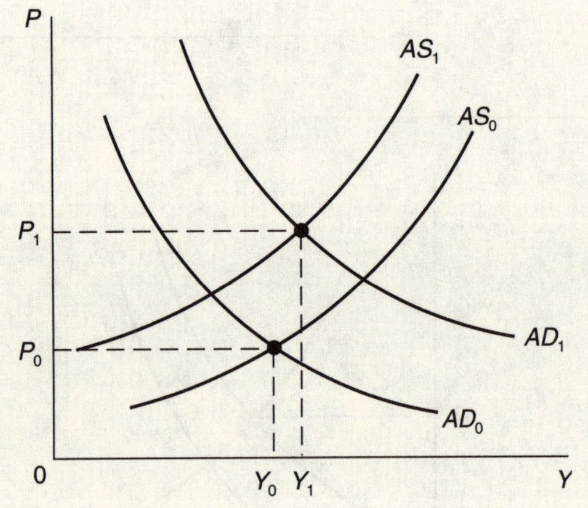

Exercises

1. (a) The missing entries are:
C_1: 2700 and 3900.
C_2: 3450 and 3750.
AE_1: 3325; 4000.
AE_2: 3625; 3850.

(b) For $P = 1$, national income is 4000. For $P = 2$, national income is 3625. See Figure 23-9 for the completed graph.

(c) *AE* shifts down by 150; national income falls by 375.

(d) The *AD* curve slopes downward because consumption is an increasing function of real wealth. As the price level increases, real wealth declines, and consumption expenditure decreases. The *AD* curves, drawn on the basis of two observations only, are approximations, because the actual relationship based on the algebraic model is non-linear, as determined by W/P.

(e) National income rises by 375. The marginal propensity to spend is 0.6 and the simple multiplier is 2.5. Note that $2.5 \times 150 = 375$.

(f) Greater government spending shifts the *AE* curve upward by 150 and the *AD* curve rightward by 375.

(g) The *AD* curve relates equilibrium national income to the price level, and therefore the change in the price level leads to a movement along the *AD* curve. The increase in government spending increases desired expenditures at all price levels, and therefore the *AD* curve shifts rightward.

Figure 23-11

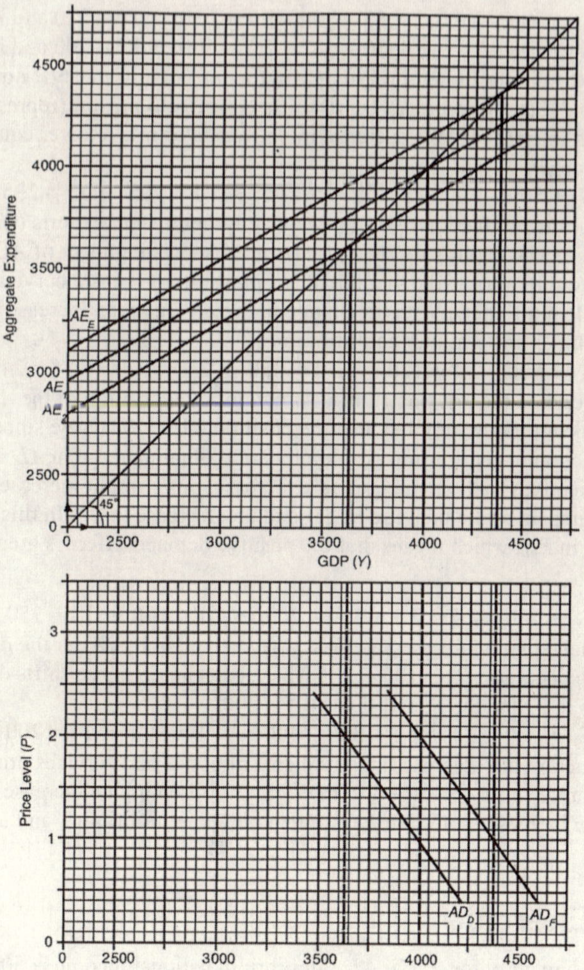

2. **(a)** Equilibrium is $P = 20$ and $Y = 10$. They can be solved algebraically by $40 - 2Y = 10 + Y$, which gives $Y = 10$. Substituting $Y = 10$ into either equation gives $P = 20$.

(b) See Figure 23-2. The new equilibrium is $P = 30$ and $Y = 20$. A demand shock has caused real income to increase by 10, but the horizontal shift in the *AD* curve is 15. Some of the stimulus from greater desired aggregate expenditures results in higher prices (a 50 percent increase) rather than greater output. This is because the expansion in output caused unit costs to increase.

3. (a) To increase GDP by \$8 billion, Finance officials believe that an increase in G of \$3.2 billion is needed. Their estimate of the multiplier value must be 2.5.

(b) Yes. A steep slope of the *AS* curve implies that any rightward shift in the *AD* curve will have a small effect on Y but a large effect on P. Hence, the multiplier value of a given increase in G will be low for the Central Bank officials. A steep slope of the *AS* curve means that Central Bank officials believe that unit costs will increase rapidly as output increases are stimulated by expenditure increases. In contrast, the Finance Department officials must believe that firms have a great deal of excess capacity and hence output increases will evoke only small changes in unit costs and the price level.

(c) Your guess is as good as ours. Several possibilities exist. First, the assumption that private-sector spending was not likely to change might have been wrong. During the period of government expenditure expansion, private-sector spending may have fallen. Second, the Central Bank officials might have been right. The slope of the *AS* curve might have been quite steep. Notice that the increase in real national income of \$3.8 billion is quite close to their predicted value of \$3.28 billion (1.2×3.2).

4. (a) $AD = AS \rightarrow 500 - 2\,Y = Y - 50 - 80 \rightarrow 3\,Y = 630 \rightarrow Y^* = 210$ and $P^* = 80$.

(b) $AD = AS \rightarrow 500 - 2\,Y = Y - 50 - 50 \rightarrow 3\,Y = 600 \rightarrow Y^* = 200$ and $P^* = 100$.
The increase in the price of oil increases the unit cost of most (if not all) goods and services produced in Paysandú, and thus the *AS* curve shifts upwards to the left (representing a decrease in *AS*). With no change in the *AD* curve, a decrease in *AS* translates into a lower equilibrium Y and a higher equilibrium P.

(c) $AD = AS \rightarrow 500 - 2\,Y + 75 = Y - 50 - 80 \rightarrow 3\,Y = 705 \rightarrow Y^* = 235$ and $P^* = 105$.
The domestic production of oil increases Paysandú's net exports (*NX*) since it no longer imports oil and now it even exports it. The increase in *NX*—a component of *AE*—causes the *AD* curve to shift upward to the right. [Note that the horizontal shift of the *AD* curve is equal to the change in *NX* times the simple multiplier.] With no change in the *AS* curve, an increase in *AD* translates into a higher equilibrium Y and a higher equilibrium P.

(d) $AD = AS \rightarrow 500 - 2\,Y + 120 = Y - 50 - 50 \rightarrow 3\,Y = 720 \rightarrow Y^* = 240$ and $P^* = 140$.
The increase in the price of oil affects not only the position of the *AS* curve (because it increases the unit costs of production), but also the position of the *AD* curve since *NX* increases. Therefore, the new macroeconomic equilibrium is a combination of an increase in *AD* and a decrease in *AS*. Consequently, P will unambiguously increase, but Y might increase or decrease depending on the relative impact of the increase in *AD* and the decrease in *AS*. In this case, Y increases as a result of the increase in P_{oil}, which means that the positive demand-effect is greater than the negative supply-effect.

5. (a) $AD = AS \rightarrow 700 - 2\,Y = 2\,Y + 300 - 200 \rightarrow 4\,Y = 600 \rightarrow Y^* = 150$ and $P^* = 400$.

(b) The initial equation for the *AS* curve was $P = 100 + 2\,Y$. After the decrease in T, the equation for the *AS* curve becomes: $P = -100 + 2\,Y$. Therefore, the *AS* curve shifts downward as a result of the decrease in T, and the size of this shift is 200.

(c) $AD = AS \rightarrow 700 - 2\,Y = 2\,Y + 300 - 400 \rightarrow 4\,Y = 800 \rightarrow Y^* = 200$ and $P^* = 300$.
The reduction in T decreases the unit cost of goods and services produced in this economy, and thus the *AS* curve shifts downward to the right (representing an increase in *AS*). With no change in the *AD* curve, an increase in *AS* translates into a higher equilibrium Y and a lower equilibrium P.

Extension Exercise

E1. (a) The missing entry for AD_a is 42. Equilibrium national income is 50 at a price level of 1.0.

(b) The missing entry for AD_b is 26. Equilibrium national income is 30 at the price level of 1.0. The value of the simple multiplier is 2.0 ($\Delta Y/\Delta I = -20/-10$).

(c) The missing entries for AD_c are 68 and 62. Equilibrium national income is a little more than 68 (68.2), and the price level is a little less than 1.2 (1.18). The multiplier value that allows for price changes is calculated by $\Delta Y/\Delta I = +18.2/+10 = 1.82$. Notice, this multiplier is less than that in part (b).

Figure 23-12

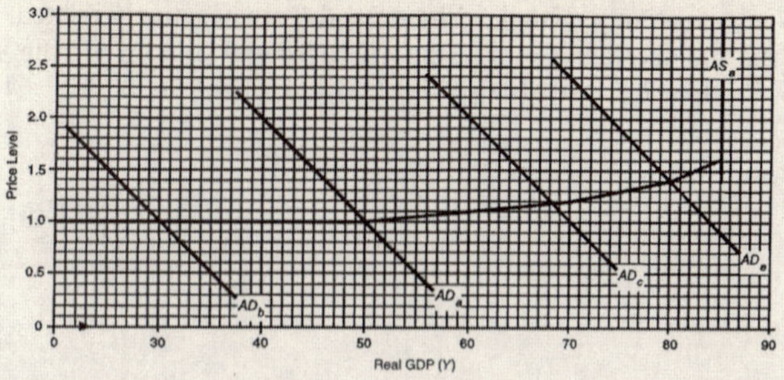

(d) When *AD* shifted leftward, the *AS* curve was horizontal and the price remained unchanged. When *AD* shifted rightward, the price level rose because the *AS* sloped upward, indicating that costs of production were higher at higher levels of output. The higher price reduces quantity demanded, and the increase in national income is smaller in absolute value than reported in (b).

(e) The missing *AD* entry is 78. Equilibrium national income is 80, at a price level of 1.4. The multiplier value ($\Delta Y / \Delta I$) is +10/+7 which is equal to 1.43.

(f) An upward-sloping *AS* curve reduces the value of the simple multiplier. As the slope of the *AS* curve increases, the value of the multiplier decreases. This is because some of the change in autonomous expenditures is absorbed by price level increases.

Additional Multiple-Choice Questions

1.(a) **2.**(e) **3.**(e) **4.**(c) **5.**(a) **6.**(a) **7.**(e) **8.**(a) **9.**(a) **10.**(d) **11.**(b) **12.**(c) **13.**(d) **14.**(b) **15.**(a) **16.**(c) **17.**(e) **18.**(b) **19.**(a) **20.**(c) **21.**(b) **22.**(e)

Explanations for the Asterisked Multiple-Choice Questions

4.(c) At point *f*, there is an excess demand for real GDP. Hence prices will eventually rise to point *g*. As the price level increases, desired aggregate expenditure decreases (consumption [lower real wealth] and net exports [fewer exports and more imports] decrease).

7.(e) If input prices do not change, the *AS* curve does not shift. The intersection of the new *AD* curve and the original *AS* curve is point *g* [$P = 2.6$, $Y = 800$]. Real GDP has increased by 300.

10.(d) In the short run, an increase in desired investment shifts the *AD* curve to the right. In the long run, the increase in investment by increasing the capital stock or improving efficiency must shift the *AS* curve to the right

13.(d) The appropriate stabilization policy involves increasing government expenditures or decreasing the net tax rate. By doing so, the *AD* curve shifts to the right. In order to eliminate the output gap, the new *AD* curve must intersect the *AS* curve at point *b*.

14.(b) Equate *AD* with *AS* and solve for *Y*; [$19 - 0.2Y = 1.5 + 0.05Y$]. Hence, $Y = 70$. Substituting $Y = 70$ into either aggregate demand or aggregate supply, we obtain $P = 5$.

15.(a) Equate $21 + 0.2Y$ to $1.5 + 0.05Y$. The new equilibrium GDP is 78. An increase in autonomous expenditure of +2 has increased real GDP by +8, yielding a multiplier of 4. The shift in aggregate demand caused a higher price level to 5.4.

16.(c) Since $P = 5$ remains constant, then using the new *AD* curve we obtain a new level of real GDP of 80. Hence, an increase in autonomous expenditure of +2 generates an increase in *Y* of +10. Therefore, the multiplier is 5.

18.(b) $AD = AS \rightarrow 500 - 2Y + 10(5) = 2Y + 200 - 20(5) - 2\,000/10 \rightarrow 4Y = 650 \rightarrow Y^* = 162.5$ and $P^* = 225$.

19.(a) Initially, the equation for the AS curve is $P = 2Y + 200 - 20(5) - 2000/10 = -100 + 2Y$, and thus the vertical intercept of the *AS* curve is –100. After the increase in P_m to 20, the equation for the *AS* curve becomes $P = 2Y + 200 - 20(5) - 2000/20 = 2Y$, and thus the vertical intercept of the *AS* curve becomes 0. Therefore, the *AS* curve shifts vertically up by 100.

20.(c) $AD = AS \rightarrow 500 - 2Y + 10(5) = 2Y + 200 - 20(5) - 2000/20 \rightarrow 4Y = 550 \rightarrow Y^* = 137.5$ and $P^* = 275$.

21.(b) *AD* and *F* are positively related, while *AS* and *F* are negatively related. Therefore, an increase in *F* will increase *AD* and decrease *AS*—i.e., the *AD* curve will shift up and the *AS* curve will shift down.

22.(e) $AD = AS \rightarrow 500 - 2Y + 10(10) = 2Y + 200 - 20(10) - 2000/10 \rightarrow 4Y = 800 \rightarrow Y^* = 200$ and $P^* = 200$

PART 9: THE ECONOMY IN THE LONG RUN

CHAPTER 24

FROM THE SHORT RUN TO THE LONG RUN: THE ADJUSTMENT OF FACTOR PRICES

LO

LEARNING OBJECTIVES

In this chapter you will learn

1 why output gaps cause wages and other factor prices to change.

2 how induced changes in factor prices affect firms' costs and shift the *AS* curve.

3 why real GDP gradually returns to potential output following an *AD* or *AS* shock.

4 why lags and uncertainty place limitations on the use of fiscal stabilization policy.

CHAPTER OVERVIEW

This chapter explains why wages and other factor prices tend to change when actual GDP differs from potential GDP. These changes in factor prices lead to changes in firms' unit costs of production and in turn to shifts of the *AS* curve. The major conclusion of the chapter is that, following aggregate demand or aggregate supply shocks, GDP eventually returns to the level of potential output. This result follows from adjustment mechanisms (changes in factor prices) that are triggered by output gaps. The macroeconomic adjustment process helps to explain how effects of shocks or policies differ in the short and long runs.

Reviewing Table 24-1 in the textbook should be very helpful in identifying the three time spans in macroeconomic analysis and understanding the underlying assumptions for each of them. Chapter 23 emphasized the short-run effects of economic shocks. However, the material in Chapter 24 focuses on what is called the **adjustment process time span** (the span between the short and the long run). The adjustment process span assumes that factor prices are flexible but that technology and factor supplies are constant (and therefore potential national income (Y^*) is constant).

Factor prices change when there is a short-run output gap (either **inflationary** or **recessionary**). An inflationary gap leads to higher factor prices (wages) and a leftward shift in the *AS* curve. The *AS* curve will continue to shift leftward, raising the price level in the process, until potential income is restored. A decrease in aggregate demand opens a recessionary gap, leading to slower wage growth or possibly lower wages. If wages fall, the *AS* curve will shift rightward, thereby generating lower prices and greater output. However, some economists believe that this adjustment process takes a very long time because wages and other factor prices tend to be "sticky" downward. This is known as the **adjustment asymmetry** (flexible wages upward, but sticky wages downward).

Students will learn the distinction between the short- and long-run effects of economic shocks. The difference between the short and long runs is the assumption regarding the flexibility of factor prices. In the long run, with flexible factor prices, the level of potential output acts like an "anchor" for the economy. For both the short run and the adjustment process phase, the level of potential output remains constant. In the long run, real GDP is determined solely by potential output. The role of aggregate demand in the long run is only to determine the price level.

Closing a recessionary gap requires discretionary **fiscal policy**—increasing government purchases, lowering taxes, or increasing transfer payments. Some changes in taxation and transfer payments occur automatically as the economy changes. They are called **automatic stabilizers**.

Fiscal policies to stabilize the economy may encounter several difficulties. There are **lags** in recognizing output gaps, making decisions to deal with them, implementing those decisions, and then reversing them when demand conditions change. Moreover, if private-sector decision makers consider the changes to be temporary rather than permanent, then some fiscal policy changes may have a limited effect on GDP.

Fiscal policy has both short-run and long-run effects on the economy. The long-run effects of fiscal policy include potential "crowding out" effects and reduced asset formation. Both can lead to a reduced rate of growth of potential output.

HINTS AND TIPS

The following may help you to avoid some of the most common errors on examinations.

- ✓ Table 24-1 is a very useful guide for learning the key characteristics of the three time spans in macroeconomic analysis. In the short run, output changes cause fluctuations of GDP around a constant value of potential GDP.
- ✓ Short-run output gaps cause changes in factor prices during the adjustment span. In the long run, factor prices have fully adjusted. Understand that factor price changes trigger shifts in the *AS* curve during the adjustment span. For example, wages fall when there is a recessionary gap and rise when there is an inflationary gap, thus changing firms' unit costs of production.
- ✓ Understand why one of the limitations of expansionary fiscal policy is the "crowding out" effect which occurs once the economy, after an increase in G, returns to the level of potential output (Y^*). Though Y^* may have not changed, its composition has—the increase in G must be equal to a decrease in $C + I + NX$. Most particularly, if I is crowded out, the future growth rate potential of Y^* will be affected.

CHAPTER REVIEW

The Adjustment Process

An output gap provides a convenient measure of the pressure on factor prices to change. An inflationary gap generates a set of conditions—high profits for firms and unusually large demand for labour—that causes **wages and thus unit labour costs** to rise. As unit labour costs rise, the *AS* curve shifts upward and to the left until potential real GDP is restored and the gap is closed. In the long run, the *AD* curve and a higher *AS* curve intersect at potential GDP. The *nominal* values of macroeconomic variables increase, but real values stay the same.

A recessionary gap generates low profits for firms and low demand for labour (factors), and hence wages and unit labour costs tend to fall. If wages fall, the *AS* curve shifts downward and to the right. Potential real GDP is restored and the recessionary gap is eliminated. However, the experience of many developed economies suggests that the downward pressure on wages during slumps (recessionary gaps) often do not occur as quickly as is the case when there are inflationary gaps. Hence, recessionary gaps can last for prolonged periods of time.

The **Phillips curve** must not be confused with an *AS* curve, although the two are related. The original Phillips curve—as developed by A. W. Phillips for the UK—depicts the relationship between the unemployment rate and the rate of change of wages. Inflationary gaps (when actual income exceeds potential GDP or the unemployment rate is less than the *natural rate of unemployment*) are associated with *increases* in wages, while recessionary gaps are normally associated with *decreases* in wages. The economy's location on the Phillips curve indicates how the *AS* curve is shifting as a result of an existing output gap. Refresh your memory by rereading *Extensions in Theory 24-1* in the textbook.

1. In an *AD–AS* diagram, a recessionary gap is shown by the
(a) *AD* and *AS* curves intersecting at an output level that is to the right of potential GDP.
(b) *AS* and *AD* curves intersecting at potential GDP.
(c) *AD* and *AS* curves intersecting at an output level that is to the left of potential GDP.
(d) horizontal distance between the *AD* and *AS* curves for any price level.
(e) vertical distance between the *AD* and *AS* curves for any output level.

2. An inflationary gap triggers
(a) factor price decreases and the *AS* curve begins to shift rightward.
(b) factor price increases and the *AS* curve begins to shift rightward.
(c) an increase in the level of potential real GDP.
(d) factor price decreases and the *AS* curve begins to shift leftward.
(e) factor price increases and the *AS* curve begins to shift leftward.

3. Assuming factor prices are flexible, a recessionary gap triggers
(a) factor price decreases and the *AS* curve begins to shift leftward.
(b) factor price increases and the *AS* curve begins to shift rightward.
(c) a decrease in the level of potential real GDP.
(d) factor price decreases and the *AS* curve begins to shift leftward.
(e) factor price increases and the *AS* curve begins to shift leftward.

4. After factor prices have fully adjusted to an output gap, we would expect
(a) potential real GDP to be restored.
(b) the new equilibrium price level to be higher after full adjustment to an inflationary gap.
(c) the new equilibrium price level to be lower after full adjustment to a recessionary gap.
(d) no further changes in price and real GDP.
(e) All of the above.

5. A movement up and along a Phillips curve starting from the *natural rate of unemployment* (U^*) means that
(a) the economy is experiencing a short-run inflationary gap.
(b) unemployment is above the *natural rate of unemployment*.
(c) wages must be decreasing.
(d) there will pressure for the *AS* curve to shift down.
(e) potential GDP must increase.

Demand and Supply Shocks

We now examine the short-run and long-run consequences of demand and supply shocks. The key when examining these issues is the extent to which factor prices (wages) are flexible upward and downward.

The short-run effect of a contractionary (negative) *AD* shock is a short-run recessionary gap. But, if wages (factor prices) are flexible downward, potential GDP is restored in the long run, albeit at a lower equilibrium price level. The story is different if wages are sticky downward. This does not mean that wages never fall, but they may do so slowly. The recessionary gap may be prolonged and unemployment can persist because of the weakness of the adjustment mechanism.

Now, consider aggregate supply shocks. A negative supply shock shifts the *AS* curve to the left. A short-run recessionary gap is created. Assuming wages are flexible, the economy's adjustment mechanism then reverses the *AS* shift and returns the economy to potential GDP. Long-run macroeconomic equilibrium will change only if the potential GDP changes.

6. **Assuming wage rates are flexible, the long-run effect of a negative demand shock is**
   (a) a restoration of potential GDP as the *AS* curve shifts left.
   (b) the creation of a permanent recessionary gap.
   (c) a permanent decrease in potential GDP.
   (d) permanently higher unemployment levels.
   (e) a restoration of potential GDP as the negative gap causes the *AS* curve to shift rightward.

7. **The short-run effect of a positive aggregate supply shock (associated with a decline in imported resource prices) is**
   (a) to shift the *AS* curve initially to the left.
   (b) the creation of a recessionary gap.
   (c) factor utilization that is beyond normal levels.
   (d) shown by a movement down the Phillips curve.
   (e) an increase in the measured unemployment rate.

8. **The economy's factor price adjustment process turns permanent shocks into**
   (a) permanent increases in potential GDP.
   (b) a situation similar to cyclical movements.
   (c) permanent output gaps.
   (d) long-term economic growth or recessions.
   (e) permanent changes in real factor prices.

9. **The long-run effect of a positive aggregate supply shock is**
   (a) an elimination of the short-run inflationary gap and the restoration of potential GDP as wage increases shift the *AS* curve to the left through time.
   (b) an increase in potential GDP, even though productivity does not increase.
   (c) a decrease in potential GDP.
   (d) an expansionary aggregate demand shock.
   (e) None of the above.

10. **The economy is in its long-run equilibrium when**
    (a) factor prices are no longer adjusting to output gaps.
    (b) the intersection of the *AD* and *AS* curves occurs at $Y = Y^*$.
    (c) the level of output that firms produce is independent of the price level.
    (d) real GDP is determined solely by potential output while the role of aggregate demand is only to determine the price level.
    (e) All of the above.

11. **The vertical Y^* line in a long-run *AD* and *AS* model depicts that**
    (a) potential real income is compatible with any price level.
    (b) real GDP is determined solely by the level of aggregate demand.
    (c) equilibrium real national income is indeterminate.
    (d) the price level is determined solely by aggregate supply.
    (e) The *AS* curve is also a vertical line.

12. **In the long run, an expansionary fiscal policy that creates a short-run inflationary gap may**
(a) expand investment and net exports.
(b) cause the price level to fall permanently.
(c) crowd out private-sector expenditure such as consumption and net exports.
(d) increase national asset formation.
(e) None of the above.

13. **Which of the following conditions is satisfied when the economy is in long-run equilibrium?**
(a) There is cyclical unemployment.
(b) Both frictional and structural unemployment are zero.
(c) The labour market is in equilibrium with full employment.
(d) *AD* shocks change the level of GDP but not its composition.
(e) Nominal wage rates might be rising or falling.

Fiscal Stabilization Policy

Discretionary fiscal policy (changes in tax rates, transfers, or government purchase of goods and services) can be used to stabilize output at Y^* by shifting the *AD* and the public saving functions. Aspects of the taxation and transfer system act as automatic stabilizers. As real national income changes, so do tax liabilities and claims on transfers. In the short run, increases in desired saving on the part of firms, governments, and households lead to reductions in real GDP. This phenomenon is called the *paradox of thrift.* In the long run the paradox of thrift does not apply.

Fiscal policy has different effects in the short and long runs. In the short run, a fiscal expansion created by an increase in government purchases increases real GDP. In the long run, the rise in G crowds out private spending and reduces the rate of asset formation, thus reducing the growth rate of potential output.

Make sure you understand the various limitations of discretionary fiscal policy because of **decision and execution lags**. The efficacy of a tax reduction also depends on whether the tax cut is viewed as long lasting or transitory. In the long run, if the tax reduction leads to more investment and work effort, there will be a positive effect on the level and growth rate of potential output.

14. **If there is currently an inflationary gap, an appropriate fiscal policy would be to**
(a) increase taxes.
(b) increase government purchases of goods and services.
(c) decrease taxes.
(d) increase transfer payments.
(e) reduce the budget surplus.

15. **The appropriate fiscal policy to eliminate a recessionary gap is to**
(a) increase taxes.
(b) increase government purchases of goods and services.
(c) decrease transfer payments.
(d) increase the budget surplus.
(e) decrease government purchases of goods and services.

16. Which of the following are potential limitations of discretionary fiscal policy?

(a) There may be long decision lags.

(b) The change in fiscal policy may overshoot its target because factor prices may be working simultaneously to eliminate the gap problem.

(c) Private-sector decision makers may view the policy to be short-lived and hence do not change their expenditure plans.

(d) All of the above.

(e) None of the above.

17. Which one of the following is a potential long-run effect of tax reductions?

(a) By stimulating investment and work effort, Y^* increases.

(b) The composition of GDP must remain unchanged.

(c) The aggregate demand curve shifts up.

(d) A permanent inflationary gap is generated.

(e) Disposable income falls permanently.

18. The paradox of thrift suggests that

(a) increased saving directly generates economic growth in the short run.

(b) increased saving reduces aggregate demand and increases unemployment in the short run.

(c) by providing larger funding sources for investment expenditure, increased domestic saving fosters economic growth in the long run.

(d) Both (b) and (c).

(e) Increased thrift has no effect on the economy either in the short or long run.

SHORT-ANSWER QUESTIONS

1. Explain the relationship between output gaps and the adjustment of factor prices.

2. What are the similarities and differences of the short run and the adjustment process span in a macroeconomic model? What is meant by the long run?

3. Comment on the following statement: "An increase in government purchases (G) is usually a more effective policy than a decrease in net taxes when the government wants to eliminate a recessionary gap."

4. Explain what is understood by "crowding out" effect?

EXERCISES

1. Short-Run and Long-Run Adjustments

Explain and also show graphically in the four panels of Figure 24-1 the short-run and long-run adjustments that you expect from the following economic changes. Assume that the economy starts from an equilibrium position where actual GDP equals potential income. Indicate what type of short-run output gap is created by the event. Assume that the level of potential GDP (Y^*) is not affected by these events.

Figure 24-1

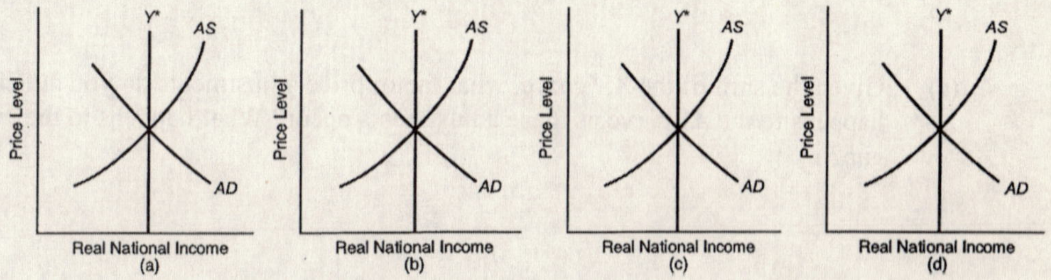

(a) Greater optimism over future economic prospects increases planned desired investment expenditure.

(b) A maturing of the baby-boom generation increases the savings rate.

(c) Political instability in major oil-producing regions increases the price of imported oil.

(d) A domestic economy experiences a decrease in its export sales of raw materials.

2. The Short-Run and Long-Run Effects of a Demand Shock

An economy's *AS* function, $P = 1 + 0.01Y$, is presented below in schedule form, where P is the price level and Y is the level of real national income. Potential real GDP is constant at 1000. Two schedules for the *AD* curve are presented, with Case I being the initial situation.

				AD			
AS		**Potential GDP**		**Case I**		**Case II**	
Y	*P*	*Y*	*P*	*Y*	*P*	*Y*	*P*
0	1.0	1000	1.0	0	111.0	0	116.5
500	6.0	1000	6.0	500	61.0	500	66.5
1000	11.0	1000	11.0	1000	11.0	1000	16.5
1050	11.5	1000	11.5	1050	6.0	1050	11.5

(a) Taking Case I for the *AD* curve, what are the equilibrium levels of *P* and *Y*? What is the value of the output gap?

(b) Assume that the *AD* curve shifts right, represented by Case II. If the *AS* curve does not change immediately, what are the new short-run equilibrium values for *P* and *Y*? What type of gap exists, and what is its magnitude?

(c) Given the shift of the *AD* curve, what factor price adjustments do you anticipate? What happens to the *AS* curve as these adjustments occur? What happens to the inflationary gap?

(d) What long-run levels of *P* and *Y* would you anticipate?

3. **The *AD/AS* Model and Fiscal Policy**
The combination of $Y = 480$ and $P = 1.0$ in Figure 24-2 depicts the initial equilibrium situation in an economy.

Figure 24-2

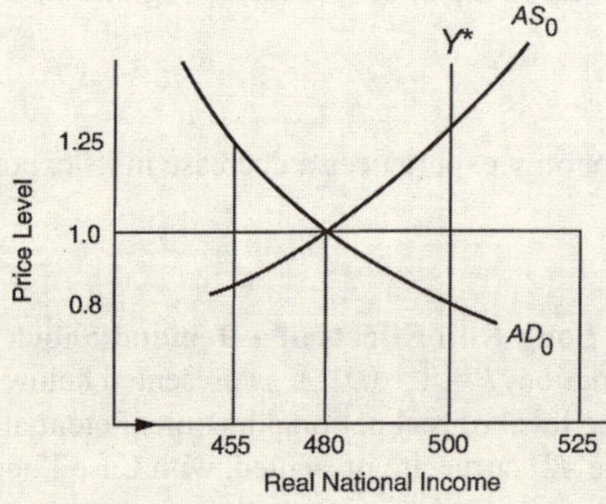

(a) The initial equilibrium reflects what type of output gap?

(b) If the government chose to wait for factor price changes to eliminate the current gap, what predictions would you make for future values of *Y* and *P*, assuming the appropriate factor price adjustments occur?

(c) The government is concerned that the policy stance associated with part (b) will take too long. Thus, the government considers eliminating the gap by increasing its expenditures by 8. It has arrived at this number by knowing that the value of the simple multiplier is 2.5. Show this policy stance in the diagram above. [*Hint*: Draw the new *AD* curve parallel to AD_0.] Will this policy change eliminate the output gap? Explain.

(d) Demonstrate the consequences of a fiscal policy that expands government expenditures by 18. Draw the corresponding *AD* curve on the diagram (again, parallel to AD_0) and explain whether you would expect this equilibrium to change in the long run.

(e) What was the value of the multiplier for the policy stance in part (c)? Explain why this multiplier value is less than the simple multiplier.

4. **The Problems Associated with the Formulation of Fiscal Policy**
A newly elected provincial premier inherits the economic situation depicted in Figure 24-3 Current potential real income is constant at 1800.

Figure 24-3

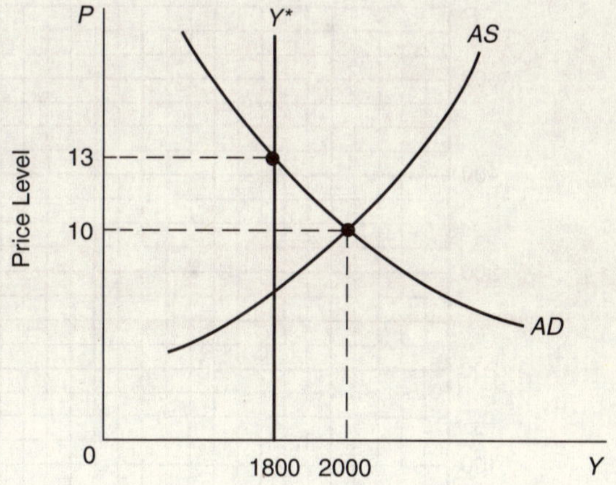

(a) Describe the economic situation that she inherited from the previous government.

(b) If the government does nothing, what is likely to happen to real national income and the price level in future time periods? Assume that aggregate demand (from the private sector) does not change.

(c) The new premier believes strongly that appropriate tax policies can increase investment and capital stock in the long run. Her government initiates tax changes to affect potential GDP. Describe the general nature of the tax changes, and explain what this policy action is attempting to do.

(d) The leader of the opposition in the parliamentary assembly vehemently objects to the government's policy. What arguments might he muster?

5. Output Gap, Fiscal Policy, and Potential Output

This is a more challenging problem that will test your knowledge of the theory presented in Chapter 24 as well as your familiarity with the more technical part generally associated with the study of economics.

Suppose that the *AD* and *AS* curves of a hypothetical economy are given by the following equations, respectively:

$$P = 500 - 8\,Y$$
$$P = 50 + 2\,Y$$

where *P* is the price level and *Y* is real GDP (in billions of dollars). The level of potential output (Y^*) is 60.

Figure 24-4

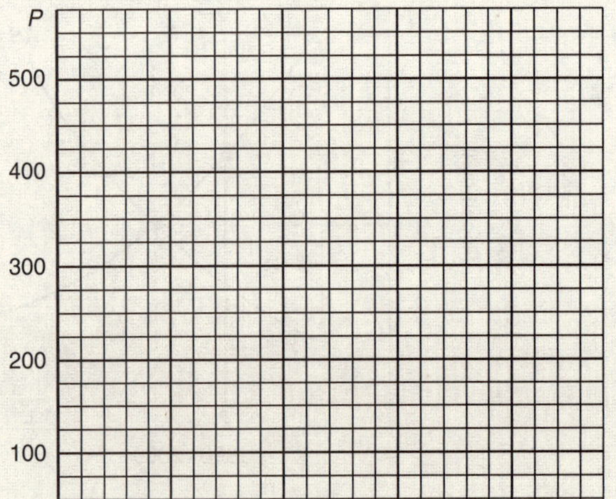

(a) What are the equilibrium values of *Y* and *G* for this economy? What is the size of the output gap?

(b) In the diagram above, sketch the *AD* and *AS* curves and label them AD_0 and AS_0, respectively. Clearly indicate all the relevant points (e.g., the vertical intercepts). Draw the line representing Y^*.

(c) Suppose the government decides to implement expansionary fiscal policy in order to eliminate the output gap. Draw in the diagram above the new *AD* curve that would allow for the elimination of the output gap and label it AD_1.

(d) What will the value of the price level be once the economy is back to long-run equilibrium as a result of the increase in *G*?

(e) What is the equation for the AD_1 curve? [*Hint:* The general equation for all parallel *AD* curves is $P = A - 8\ Y$, where *A* is the value of the vertical intercept. So you must find the value of *A* for the new curve.]

(f) What is the size of the horizontal shift of the *AD* curve from AD_0 to AD_1? Assuming the simple multiplier is equal to 3, what is the size of the increase in *G* that will move the economy to long-run equilibrium?

(g) Given the increase in *G* you have determined in part (f), what is the size of the multiplier once we take into account the impact of the increase in *P* on *AE*? [*Note:* You must recall from Chapter 23 that this multiplier is smaller than the simple multiplier.]

6. Output Gap, Factor Prices Adjustment, and Potential Output

This exercise deals with the adjustment process leading the economy toward potential output equilibrium in the absence of any government intervention.

Suppose that a hypothetical economy is initially in long-run equilibrium. The *AD* and *AS* curves of this economy are given by the following equations, respectively:

$$P = 600 - 6\ Y$$
$$P = 4\ Y$$

where *P* is the price level and *Y* is real GDP (in billions of dollars).

Figure 24-5

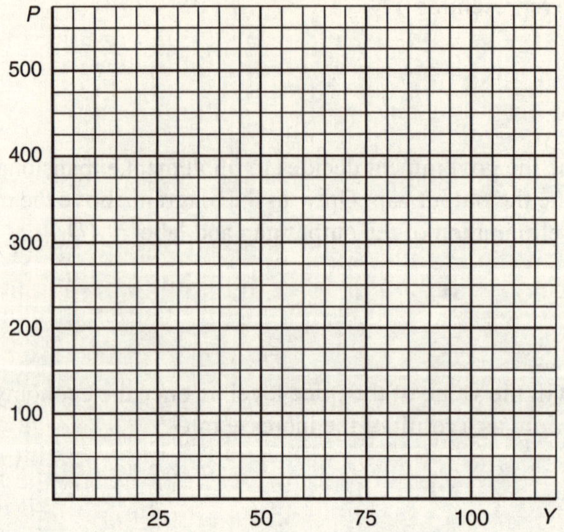

(a) What are the long-run equilibrium values of *Y* and *G* for this economy?

(b) In the diagram above, sketch the *AD* and *AS* curves and label them AD_0 and AS_0, respectively. Clearly indicate all the relevant points (e.g., the vertical intercepts). Draw the line representing *Y**.

(c) Suppose now that a decrease in autonomous exports causes the *AD* function to change to $P = 450 - 6\ Y$. What are the new short-run equilibrium values of *Y* and *P* for this economy? Sketch the new *AD* in the diagram above and label it AD_1.

(d) Explain the process by which, in the absence of any government active intervention, the economy will move back toward *Y** in the long run.

(e) Show in the diagram above the new long-run equilibrium once this process of adjustment is completed. Draw in the diagram above any new curve as needed. What is the new long-run equilibrium price level?

(f) What is the equation for the new curve you have drawn in part (e) above?

(g) If the economy will restore long-run equilibrium without any active government intervention, why do governments implement active fiscal policy?

EXTENSION EXERCISE

E1. Fiscal Policy and the Output Gap

This exercise deals with the role of fiscal policy in eliminating any output gap. It is a challenging exercise that will further test your theoretical knowledge and your expertise in using basic algebra to solve economic problems.

Suppose that the expression for the *AE* curve of a hypothetical closed economy is given by the equation:

$$AE = 100 + 0.8\ Y_D + G + 4950 / P$$

where *P* is the price level, *G* is government purchases (in billions of dollars), and Y_D is disposable income (in billions of dollars). Disposable income is equal to the difference between national income (*Y*) and the net tax function (*tY*), and $t = 0.25$.

(a) What is the function for the *AD* curve in this economy? [*Note:* You should express *Y* as a function of *G*, and *P*.]

(b) Suppose that this economy's *AS* function is $Y = 5\ P$. Given the expression for the *AD* function that you obtained in part (a), what are the equilibrium values of *Y* and *P* in this economy when $G = 200$? [*Note:* You will obtain two values for *P*—one positive, and one negative. However, since *P* cannot be negative, only the positive value counts.]

(c) What is the public saving function for this economy? Given the macroeconomic equilibrium determined in part (b), what is the level of public saving (government budget balance)?

(d) Potential output (Y^*) is estimated to be 900. What would be the value of *P* if the economy were to be producing at Y^*?

(e) Under great pressure to reduce the current high rate of unemployment, the government has decided to implement expansionary fiscal policy to eliminate the output gap. You are a close economic adviser to the Minister of Finance and the Minister asks you to determine the size of an increase in G that will eliminate the recessionary gap. What will be your advice to the Minister? What will be the new government budget balance?

(f) What is the size of the simple multiplier? What is the size of the multiplier that takes into account the effect of the accompanied change in P?

ADDITIONAL MULTIPLE-CHOICE QUESTIONS

Questions 1 through 6 refer to Figure 24-6. The curves with the subscript 0 refer to the initial situation.

Figure 24-6

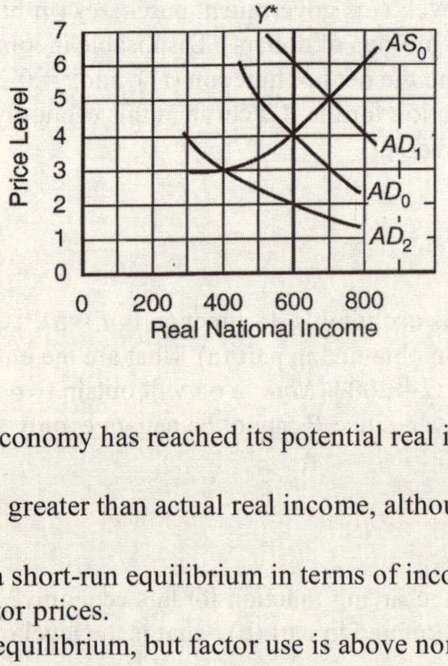

1. **At the initial situation**
   (a) we know that the economy has reached its potential real income level, and the price level is 4.
   (b) potential income is greater than actual real income, although the equilibrium price level is 4.
   (c) the economy is at a short-run equilibrium in terms of income and the price level, but not in terms of factor prices.
   (d) the economy is in equilibrium, but factor use is above normal levels.
   (e) the economy is at its utmost limit of productive capacity.

2. **Suppose that the *AD* curve shifts to AD_1 as government purchases rise. In the short run,**
   (a) potential national income increases to 700 and the price level rises to 5.
   (b) real national income increases by 100 and the price level increases to 5 due to wage increases.
   (c) an inflationary gap of 100 occurs, unit costs increase even though factor prices are constant, and the price level increases to 5.
   (d) real national income increases by 200, factor prices remain constant, and the price level remains at 4.
   (e) real national income remains constant, but the price level increases to 6.

*3. **As a result of the short-run inflationary gap caused by the *AD* shock indicated in the preceding question,**
   (a) factor prices begin to fall.
   (b) factor prices begin to rise.
   (c) the *AS* curve shifts to the right.
   (d) potential GDP increases.
   (e) the *AD* curve shifts to the left as real wealth falls.

*4. **The economy's long-run equilibrium after this demand shift is**
   (a) a real income level of 600, higher nominal factor prices, and a price level of 6.
   (b) a real income level of 400 and a price level of 3.
   (c) a price level of 6 and real income of 800, due to an induced rightward shift of the *AD* curve.
   (d) potential and real income equal to 700 and a price level of 6.
   (e) a real income level of 800, and a price level of 4.

*5. **Suppose instead that the *AD* curve had shifted from AD_0 to AD_2 because of a decline in investment expenditure. The short-run impact of this negative aggregate demand shock is**
   (a) a recessionary gap of 200.
   (b) lower unit costs because of a reduction in output.
   (c) an equilibrium price level of 3.
   (d) an increase in unemployment.
   (e) All of the above.

6. **Given the investment decline, the situation described in Question 5 will persist, possibly for a long period of time, if**
   (a) some other autonomous expenditure component increases.
   (b) factor prices remain constant or decrease very slowly.
   (c) factor prices fall rapidly.
   ((d) increases in government expenditure shift the *AD* curve to the right.
   (e) None of the above.

Questions 7 to 10 refer to the economy described below.

The initial AS equation: $P = 0.05Y$.
The initial AD equation: $P = 80 - 0.03Y$.
Potential GDP is constant at 1000.

7. With respect to the economy's short-run equilibrium situation, which of the following statements are true?

(a) $Y = 1000$ and $P = 50$.
(b) There is a recessionary gap of 900.
(c) There is an inflationary gap of 7000.
(d) In view of the initial gap situation, factor prices will rise.
(e) There is an inflationary gap of 7000 and factor prices will rise.

***8. If the *AD* equation changed to $P = 100 - 0.03Y$ with the *AS* curve unchanged, which of the following statements are true about the new short-run equilibrium situation?**

(a) An inflationary gap of 25.
(b) $Y = 1000$ and $P = 62.5$.
(c) An inflationary gap of 20.
(d) An inflationary gap of 250.
(e) A recessionary gap of 250.

9. In view of the new short-run equilibrium situation outlined by question 8, the adjustment process time span is likely to be characterized by

(a) falling factor prices until potential GDP is restored.
(b) the *AS* curve shifting rightward.
(c) rising factor prices until potential GDP is restored.
(d) increases in the level of potential GDP.
(e) a new equilibrium of $Y = 1000$ and $P = 62.5$.

***10. The long-run values of the price level and real GDP with the new aggregate demand curve are**

(a) $Y = 1000$ and $P = 70$.
(b) $Y = 1250$ and $P = 62.5$.
(c) $Y = 1000$ and $P = 62.5$.
(d) $Y = 1000$ and $P = 5$.
(e) Indeterminant.

***11. An increase in excise taxes will increase the unit costs of production of most firms in the economy. As a result,**

(a) the *AD* curve will shift up.
(b) the *AD* curve will remain in the same position but the *AS* curve will shift up.
(c) the *AD* curve will shift down while the *AS* curve will shift up.
(d) the *AS* curve will shift down while the *AD* curve will remain in the same position.
(e) both the *AD* and the *AS* curves will shift up.

12. If an increase in excise taxes is accompanied by an increase in subsidies to factors of production, which of the following outcomes would most likely occur?

(a) Both *Y* and *P* would rise.
(b) *Y* would definitely increase while *P* would definitely fall.
(c) *Y* would increase, but *P* could increase or decrease.
(d) *P* would increase, but *Y* could increase or decrease.
(e) Both *Y* and *P* could either increase or decrease, but each moving in opposite directions.

***13. An increase in government purchases accompanied by an equal increase in net taxes will**

(a) leave *Y*, *P*, and the government budget balance unchanged.
(b) cause *Y* to rise and *P* to fall while leaving the government budget balance unchanged.
(c) cause both *Y* and *P* to rise and the government budget balance to deteriorate.
(d) cause *Y* to rise and the government budget balance to deteriorate.
(e) cause *Y* and *P* to rise while leaving the government budget balance unchanged.

*14. **Suppose that equilibrium income is below potential output and that the government wants to eliminate the recessionary gap without affecting the price level. Which of the following policy mixes should the government implement?**
(a) Increase *G* and net taxes by the same amount.
(b) Increase *G* and decrease net taxes.
(c) Increase net taxes and introduce subsidies to key factors of production.
(d) Increase *G* and introduce subsidies to key factors of production.
(e) Decrease both *G* and net taxes.

15. **Suppose that equilibrium income is above potential output and that the government wants to eliminate the inflationary gap without affecting the budget balance. Which of the following policy mixes should the government implement?**
(a) Increase *G* and net taxes by the same amount in order to leave the government budget balance unchanged.
(b) Decrease *G* and net taxes by the same amount in order to leave the government budget balance unchanged.
(c) Decrease net taxes and introduce subsidies to key factors of production.
(d) Decrease net taxes and reduce subsidies to factors of production in order to leave the government budget balance unchanged.
(e) Decrease *G* and introduce subsidies to factors of production in order to leave the government budget balance unchanged.

SOLUTIONS

Chapter Review

1.(c) **2.**(e) **3.**(d) **4.**(e) **5.**(a) **6.**(e) **7.**(c) **8.**(b) **9.**(a) **10.**(e) **11.**(a) **12.**(c) **13.**(c) **14.**(a) **15.**(b) **16.**(d) **17.**(a) **18.**(d)

Short-Answer Questions

1. Output gaps provide a useful measure of the pressure for factor prices to change. Take the example of a recessionary gap characterized by high unemployment, excess capacity, and an excess supply of factors such as capital and labour. Hence, a recessionary gap leads to reductions in factor prices and a reduction in unit costs. As factor prices fall, the *AS* curve begins to shift right. Assuming wages are fully flexible downward, the recessionary gap will be closed and potential real GDP will be restored. When the recessionary gap has been closed, factor prices will not change. Some economists believe that factor prices are slow to adjust during a recessionary gap.

2. The short run assumes that aggregate demand and supply shocks can change equilibrium levels of national income and the price level. Short-run models usually assume that potential GDP, factor prices, and technology and factor supplies are constant. Hence, short-run models explain business cycles around potential GDP.

   The adjustment process span assumes that potential GDP and technology and factor supplies are constant. However, factor prices can change if output gaps are created by either positive or negative aggregate demand and supply shocks. When factor prices change so too can short-term levels of national income and the price level—yet another explanation for business fluctuations. However, factor adjustments will eventually restore potential GDP but at different price levels than existed before the short-term gap was created.

   This chapter has assumed that factor supplies and productivity remained constant. But, in the long run both these economic considerations can change. Hence, potential real GDP can also change.

3. If there is a recessionary gap, then we can conclude that *AD* is insufficient. Therefore, the government would be wise to implement policy conducive to increasing *AD*, in order to restore equilibrium in the economy at the level of potential output (Y^*). The government, for instance, could increase its expenditure on goods and services (G) or decrease the level of taxation (T)—the two possibilities indicated in the statement. Which of these options is more effective with respect to changing the level of Y? G, on the one hand, is one component of *AE*, and thus an increase in G will increase *AD* directly. T, on the other hand, is not a component of *AE*. A decrease in T will affect the level of *AE*—and thus also the level of *AD*—only indirectly, through the impact that an increase in disposable income (Y_D) might have on consumption expenditure (C). But there is no certainty that consumers will immediately increase their level of expenditure because their disposable income has increased. Depending on their expectation about the state of the economy, consumers might decide to save the additional disposable income now in order to spend it at some point in the future. If this were the case, then the objective of the government would not be achieved—at least not in the short run. Therefore, the above statement seems correct: an increase in G is usually more effective than a decrease in T if the government wants to eliminate a recessionary gap.

4. A "crowding out" effect occurs when an increase in one component of *AE* causes some other component of *AE* to decrease. For instance, if an increase in G causes *NX* to decrease, then we say that G has crowded out *NX*. The crowding out effect could be *complete* (total) or *partial*. In our example, a *complete* crowding out effect would take place if *NX* were to decrease by exactly the same absolute amount as the original increase in G—and in this case *AE* would not change, but its composition would, and Y would not change either. A *partial* crowding out effect would take place if the decrease in *NX* were to be (in absolute value) smaller than the increase in G—and thus *AE* would increase and its composition change as well, and Y would also increase. However, when considering the long run and assuming everything else equal, an increase in G will cause a complete crowding out effect since Y^* would remain unchanged—thus implying that $C + I + NX$ have decreased by the same amount as G has increased.

Exercises

1. **(a)** The *AD* curve shifts rightward in the short run, resulting in greater output and higher prices. A short-run inflationary gap is created and exerts pressure on factor prices to rise. Over time the *AS* curve shifts to the left, thus restoring the initial level of potential income but at a higher price level. When the gap is closed, factor prices no longer change.

   (b) The *AD* curve shifts leftward and rotates to become steeper as a result of an increase in the marginal propensity to save. A recessionary gap puts downward pressure factor prices. If wages decline, the *AS* curve shifts to the right, restoring the initial level of potential income at a lower price level. Due to asymmetric adjustments in the labour market, the recessionary gap may remain for a considerable time. The question assumes that Y^* is not affected by the short-run increase in saving.

   (c) The *AS* curve shifts left, resulting in higher prices and lower national income. The recessionary gap exerts downward pressure on wages and prices. If wages decline, the *AS* curve shifts to counteract the oil price increase, and the economy may eventually restore potential national income. If factor prices are slow to fall, then the recessionary gap may last for a long period of time.

   (d) The *AD* curve shifts left, resulting in lower prices and lower national income. A short-run recessionary gap situation is created. Downward pressure is put on all factor prices, including wages. If wages fall, the *AS* curve shifts to the right through time. The economy returns to its long-run potential income but has a lower price level than before.

2. **(a)** The equilibrium levels are $P = 11.0$ and $Y = 1000$. The output gap is 0.

   (b) The new equilibrium levels are $P = 11.5$ and $Y = 1050$. The output gap is a positive value (+50). This is known as an inflationary gap.

   (c) Since the economy now tries to operate beyond its potential level, unusually high demand for factors trigger increases in factor prices. As a consequence, the *AS* curve shifts leftward. As the AS curve shifts leftward, the inflationary gap is closed.

   (d) Potential income will be restored at $Y = 1000$ with a price level of 16.5.

3. **(a)** The initial situation reflects a recessionary gap, since output of 480 is less than potential output of 500, which is depicted in Figure 24-2.
(b) The *AS* curve shifts down to the right. There is a movement along the aggregate demand curve until potential income is reached ($Y^* = 500$) at a price level of 0.8.
(c) An increase in government expenditure of 8 will shift the *AD* curve to the right by 20. The new *AD* curve intersects the curve at $P = 1$ and $Y = 500$, but it intersects the *AS* curve at a level of output less than potential output. Although the size of the recessionary gap has been reduced, a recessionary gap still remains. It is possible that the remaining gap will be eliminated if factor prices decrease thereby shifting the *AS* curve down.
(d) If the government expands its purchases by 18, the new *AD* curve will shift to the right and pass through the point $P = 1$ and $Y = 525$. If the new *AD* curve has the same slope as the initial one, it will also pass through the point $P = 1.25$ and $Y = 500$. There will be no need for factor prices to adjust in the long run since the recessionary gap has been eliminated.
(e) The multiplier is calculated by dividing 20 by 18 which is equal to 1.11 and is considerably lower than the simple multiplier value, 2.5. When unit costs and prices rise some aggregate expenditures are reduced. Specifically, real wealth decreases and hence some consumption expenditure is reduced. Moreover, as the domestic price increases, net exports are likely to fall.

4. **(a)** The premier has inherited an inflationary gap of 200. Current equilibrium levels of real national income and price are 2000 and 10, respectively.
(b) If the government does nothing, the economy will adjust by itself. Factor prices will most likely increase, thereby shifting the *AS* curve upward and to the left until it intersects the curve at $Y = 1800$ and $P = 13$. As a result, the economy will have an even higher price level, but the inflationary gap will have been eliminated.
(c) The premier's policies should involve lower net tax rates, which stimulate more investment expenditure, which increases the capital stock. Thus, potential real income is affected in the long run. If these policies are totally successful potential GDP will increase, perhaps to $Y = 2000$ or beyond. Since equilibrium real national income equals the new potential level (2000), the inflationary gap has been eliminated, and there will be no pressures for the *AS* curve to shift to the left.
(d) The opposition should base their arguments on the fact that tax reductions will stimulate increases in *AD*. In the short run, there will be even higher pressures for prices and factor prices to increase. Moreover, the added pressures caused by *AD* increases may prevail for some time. Finally, the opposition could argue that tax reductions may take a very long time to increase the capital stock and potential GDP.

5. **(a)** $AD = AS \rightarrow 500 - 8Y = 50 + 2Y \rightarrow 10Y = 450 \rightarrow Y_1 = 45$ and $P_1 = 140$. The size of the deflationary gap is $Y^* - Y_1 = 60 - 45 = 15$.
(b) See Figure 24-7.

Figure 24-7

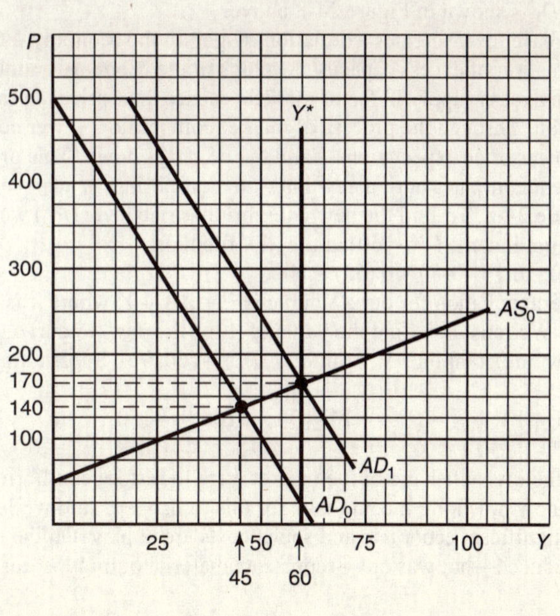

(c) See Figure 24-7.

(d) We must plug the value $Y^* = 60$ in the equation for the AS curve in order to find P^*:
$P^* = 50 + 2\ (60) = 170$.

(e) The equation for the AD_1 curve is $P = A_1 - 8\ Y$, and we have the values of one point on this line: point $(Y^*, P^*) = (60, 170)$. Plugging these values in the equation for the AD_1 curve we obtain the value for A_1:
$P^* = A_1 - 8\ Y^* \rightarrow A_1 = P^* + 8\ Y^* = 170 + 8\ (60) = 650$.
Therefore, $P = 650 - 8\ Y$.

(f) To find the size of the horizontal shift of the AD curve we must find the value of Y at the point on the AD_1 where $P = 140$:
$P = 650 - 8\ Y \rightarrow 140 = 650 - 8\ Y \rightarrow 8\ Y = 510 \rightarrow Y_2 = 63.75$.
Therefore, the horizontal shift of the AD curve is $63.75 - 45 = 18.75$, and if the value of the simple multiplier is 3, then $3\ \Delta G = 18.75$ and $\Delta G = 18.75 / 3 = 6.25$.

(g) Given that $\Delta G = 6.25$ and the deflationary gap is 15, the size of the multiplier is: $15 / 6.25 = 2.4$.

6. (a) $AD = AS \rightarrow 600 - 6\ Y = 4\ Y \rightarrow 10\ Y = 600 \rightarrow Y^* = 60$ and $P^* = 4\ Y^* = 4\ (60) = 240$.

(b) See Figure 24-8.

Figure 24-8

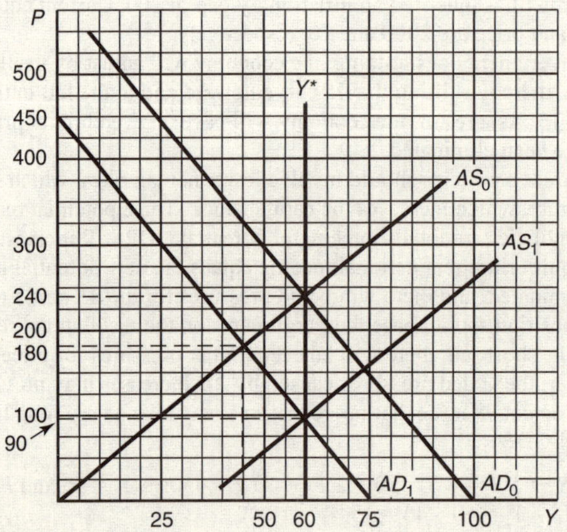

(c) $AD = AS \rightarrow 450 - 6\ Y = 4\ Y \rightarrow 10\ Y = 450 \rightarrow Y^* = 45$ and $P^* = 4\ Y^* = 4\ (45) = 180$.
Curve AD_1 is shown in Figure 24-8 above.

(d) The decrease in AD creates a deflationary gap in the economy—GDP falls below potential output, i.e., a situation of excess capacity develops in the economy and the rate of unemployment rises. The short-run excess supply in factor markets causes their prices to fall, thus reducing firms' unit costs of production. Through the process of market competition, lower costs of production translate into firms' lower price expectations—and the AS shifts down. This process of factors and goods price adjustment continues until a new long-run equilibrium is achieved.

(e) See Figure 24-8. To find the new equilibrium price level (P^*) we must plug the value of long-run equilibrium income ($Y^* = 60$) in the AD_1 function:
$P^* = 450 - 6\ Y^* = 450 - 6\ (60) = 90$.

(f) The general equation for our AS curve is $P = A + 4\ Y$, where A is the vertical intercept (initially equal to zero). We must now find the value of A for the new AS curve (AS_1).
We know one point on AS_1, point $(Y^*, P^*) = (60, 90)$. Substituting in the above equation, we solve for A:
$P^* = A + 4\ Y^* \rightarrow A = P^* - 4\ Y^* = 90 - 4\ (60) = -150$.
$AS_1 \rightarrow P = -150 + 4\ Y$.

(g) Even if the invisible hand of the market were to restore equilibrium at the level of potential output, we do not know how long it could take for this to happen. And while actual output is below potential output, significant economic and social costs are at play. On the one hand, any output that could have been produced—but was not—represents material output lost for ever. This is an important economic cost. On the other hand, one of the unused resources during periods of recession is labour—which implies unemployment, a significant social cost for those out of work. If the government were able to restore full-employment equilibrium faster through the implementation of expansionary fiscal policy and thus reduce these implicit social and economic costs, then it could be argued that government intervention is justified.

Extension Exercise

E1. (a) $AE = 100 + 0.8\,Y_D + G + 4950 / P$
$= 100 + 0.8\,(Y - tY) + G + 4950 / P$
$= 100 + 0.8\,(1 - t)\,Y + G + 4950 / P$
$= 100 + 0.8\,(1 - 0.25)\,Y + G + 4950 / P$
$= 100 + 0.8\,(0.75)\,Y + G + 4950 / P$
$= 100 + 0.6\,Y + G + 4950 / P$

To derive the equation for the *AD* curve we must equate *Y* and *AE*:
$Y = 100 + 0.6\,Y + G + 4950 / P$
$(1 - 0.6)\,Y = 100 + G + 4950 / P$
$(0.4)\,Y = 100 + G + 4950 / P$
$\mathbf{Y = 250 + 2.5\,G + 12\,375 / P}$

(b) $AD = AS \rightarrow 250 + 2.5\,(200) + 12\,375 / P = 5\text{P} \rightarrow 5P - 750 - 12\,375 / P = 0$
$\rightarrow P - 150 - 2475 / P - 0 \rightarrow P^2 - 150\,P - 2475 = 0$
$P_1 = [150 \pm (22\,500 + 9\,900)^{1/2}] / 2$
$= [150 \pm (32\,400)^{1/2}] / 2$
$= (150 \pm 180) / 2$
$= 165$ and -15 [Since *P* cannot be negative, then $\mathbf{P_1 = 165}$.]
$\mathbf{Y_1 = 5\,P_1 = 5\,(165) = 825}$.

(c) Public saving = Net taxes – Government purchases = $tY - G$
Government budget balance = 0.25 (825) – 200 = 206.25 – 200 = **6.25** (i.e., the government would be running a surplus of $6.25 billion).

(d) We plug $Y^* = 900$ in the *AS* function to find P*:
$Y^* = 5\,P^* \rightarrow P^* = Y^* / 5 = 900 / 5 = 180$.

(e) After the increase in *G* (ΔG), the equation for the new the *AE* curve becomes:
$AE = 300 + 0.6\,Y + \Delta G + 4950 / P$.
And the equation for the *AD* curve becomes:
$Y = 750 + 2.5\,\Delta G + 4950 / P$.
Since this curve goes through the point $(Y^*, P^*) = (900, 180)$, we plug this value in the *AD* function in order to find ΔG:
$Y^* = 750 + 2.5\,\Delta G + 12\,375 / P^*$
$2.5\,\Delta G = Y^* - 750 - 12\,375 / P^*$
$2.5\,\Delta G = 900 - 750 - 12\,375 / 180 = 81.25$
$\mathbf{\Delta G = 81.25\,(2.5) \approx 203}$.
The government budget balance would be now:
Budget balance = 0.25 (900) – 403 = 225 – 403 = – **178** (i.e., the government would be running a deficit of about $178 billion).

(f) The equation for the new *AD* curve is:
$Y = 750 + 2.5\,\Delta G + 4950 / P$
$= 750 + 2.5\,(203) + 4950 / P$
$= 750 + 507.7 + 4950 / P$
$= 1\,257.5 + 4950 / P$.
The horizontal shift of the *AD* curve resulting from the increase in *G* is:
ΔY = (simple multiplier) ΔG,
and thus we must find the value of ΔY.
In order to find this value of ΔY we must find the value *Y* at the point on the *AD* curve when $P = 165$:
$Y_2 = 1\,257.5 + 4\,950 / P_2 = 1\,257.5 + 4\,950 / 165 = 1\,257.5 + 30 = 1\,287.5$.
Therefore, $\Delta Y = 1\,287.5 - 825 = 462.5$ and the simple multiplier is:
Simple multiplier = $\Delta Y / \Delta G = 462.5 / 203 =$ **2.28**.

The multiplier that takes into account the impact of the change in P is equal to the change in Y that would eliminate the recessionary gap divided by the change in G responsible for the change in Y: Multiplier = 75 / 203 = **0.37**.

Additional Multiple-Choice Questions

1.(a) **2.**(c) **3.**(b) **4.**(a) **5.**(e) **6.**(b) **7.**(a) **8.**(d) **9.**(c) **10.**(a) **11.**(b) **12.**(e) **13.**(e) **14.**(d) **15.**(e)

Explanations for the Asterisked Multiple-Choice Questions

3.(b) An inflationary gap triggers factor prices to rise. They will rise until the inflationary gap is closed.

4.(a) The intersection of AD_1 and a higher AS curve will intersect at $Y^* = 600$ and $P = 6$.

5.(e) The downward shift of the AD curve (without any factor price adjustment) intersects the original AS curve at $Y = 400$ and $P = 3$. A recessionary gap of 200 has been created and undoubtedly unemployment will increase.

8.(d) Equating $100 - 0.03Y$ to $0.05Y$, we obtain $Y = 1250$. This situation represents an inflationary gap of 250.

10.(a) There are several ways to solve this problem. One way, is to solve for the long-run price level using the new AD curve for $Y = 1000$. We obtain a new price level of 70 using the equation $P = 100 - 0.03Y$ and noting that $Y = 1000$. Now, define the higher AS curve as $P = x + 0.05Y$, where x is a new intercept term. Since $Y = 1000$ and $P = 70$, x is equal to 20. Hence, the equation for the new AS curve is $P = 20 + 0.05Y$. You may also refer to Figure 24-9.

Figure 24-9

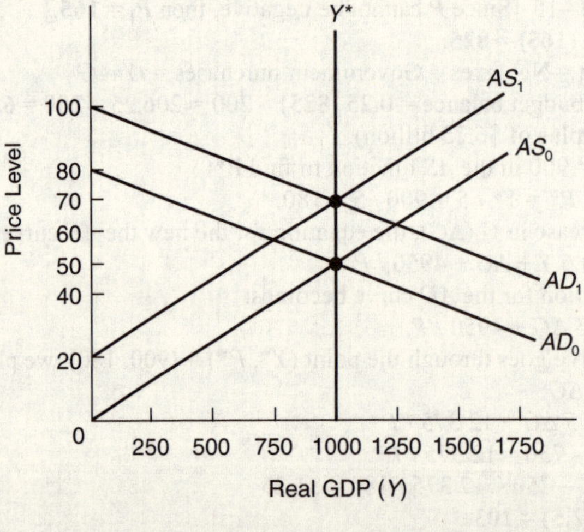

11.(b) Excise taxes are taxes on production, and thus an increase in excise taxes will increase unit costs of production and shift the AS curve upward—firms will require a higher price at each level of output to cover this increase in unit costs. Of course, the position of the AD curve is not affected by the increase in excise taxes.

13.(e) On the one hand, an increase in G accompanied by a similar increase in taxes leaves the government budget balance unchanged. On the other hand, while smaller than the simple multiplier, the balance budget multiplier is still greater than zero and thus AE increases and the AD curve shifts up. Therefore, both Y and P will increase while the government budget balance will remain unchanged.

14.(d) On the one hand, expansionary fiscal policy (e.g., an increase in G) would increase Y but also P. On the other hand, the introduction of subsidies to key factors of production would reduce unit costs and cause the AS curve to shift downwards—thus causing Y to increase and P to fall. Therefore, a proper combination of an increase in G and the introduction of subsidies to factors of production would accomplish the goal of increasing Y without affecting P.

CHAPTER 25

The Difference Between Short-Run and Long-Run Macroeconomics

LO LEARNING OBJECTIVES

In this chapter you will learn

1. why economists think differently about short-run and long-run changes in macroeconomic variables.
2. that any change in real GDP can be decomposed into changes in: factor supply, the utilization rate of factors, and productivity.
3. why short-run changes in GDP are mostly caused by changes in factor utilization, whereas long-run changes in GDP are mostly caused by changes in factor supplies and productivity.
4. that macroeconomic policies will only have a long-run effect on output if they influence factor supplies or productivity.

CHAPTER OVERVIEW

This chapter focuses on the difference between short-run and long-run macroeconomic change. Aggregate demand or supply shocks can lead to short-term deviations of real GDP from Y^*—**short-run fluctuations. Long-term trends** involve changes in potential GDP—economic growth. The equation, **accounting for GDP change**, explains how changes in three fundamental components (**factor supplies, productivity, and utilization rates of factors**) change GDP.

Since factor supply and productivity tend to be constant in the short run, short-term movements (fluctuations) in GDP are mostly accounted for by changes in factor utilization (measured by the ratio of employed factors to total available factor supplies). Since **factor utilization rates** eventually return to their "normal" levels, long-run **changes in potential GDP** are mostly accounted for by changes in **factor supplies** and **productivity** (measured by the GDP to employed factors ratio).

The difference between the short run and long run forces economists to think differently about macroeconomics relationships that exist over a few months as compared to those that exist over several years. Moreover, the effects of monetary and fiscal policy are usually different in the short run as compared to the long run. Monetary and fiscal policies have long-term effects only if they lead to change in potential GDP.

HINTS AND TIPS

The following may help you to avoid some of the most common errors on examinations.

✓ Understand the processes that create short-term changes compared to long-run changes in macroeconomic variables.

✓ Learn and apply the equations that explain GDP accounting [25-1 and 25-2]. For example, equation 25-1 indicates that long-run real GDP is influenced by changes in factor supplies and productivity, while short-run GDP fluctuations are caused by changes in factor utilization rates such the unemployment rate.

CHAPTER REVIEW

Two Examples

In response to an economic shock or a change in government policy, the economy behaves differently over several months (the short run) than it does over several years (the long run). The short run is a time period over which changes in economic conditions tend to cause changes in output and employment, with relatively small changes in prices or wages. The long run is a time period over which wage and price adjustments take place and potential GDP changes. Policy changes can have both short-run and long-term effects. The chapter talks about the relationship between inflation and the level of interest rates in the short run and in the long run. Japan's economic growth experience is related to changes in saving behaviour. Both short-term and long-term implications are explained.

1. Changes in national income in the short run

(a) are primarily supply determined.
(b) are primarily due to changes in factor productivity.
(c) must equal changes in its potential level according to the GDP accounting equation.
(d) are primarily caused by shocks in aggregate demand and supply.
(e) will reflect price and wage adjustments.

2. The short-run effect of an increase in the interest rate is likely to be

(a) adjustments in prices and wages.
(b) increases in planned expenditures.
(c) decreases in GDP and employment.
(d) an increase in potential GDP.
(e) an inflationary gap.

Accounting for Changes in GDP

To better understand the issues associated with the short run as compared to the long run, it is important for you to comprehend the GDP accounting equation (identity). GDP is created by three components: available factors, factor utilization rates, and productivity. Make sure you know the correct definition for each component, understand why each component can change, and identify within a short-run versus long-run taxonomy when the component is mostly likely to change.

3. Long-run increases in real GDP are usually associated with

(a) increases in the size of output gaps.
(b) increases in factor supply.
(c) increases in factor utilization.
(d) increases in real interest rates.
(e) decreases in capital accumulation.

4. **Everything else equal, which of the following can decrease real GDP?**
   (a) Decreases in the capital stock of the country.
   (b) Decreases in labour participation rates.
   (c) Decreases in land productivity.
   (d) Increases in mortality rates.
   (e) All of the above.

5. **Which of the following increases an economy's supply of labour?**
   (a) An increase in emigration.
   (b) A decrease in the labour-force participation rate.
   (c) A decrease in the birth rate.
   (d) An increase in the mortality rate.
   (e) More immigration.

6. **Changes in factor supplies are**
   (a) expressed by the term *GDP/employed factors* in the GDP accounting equation.
   (b) fixed, since factor prices don't vary in the long run.
   (c) very important for explaining short-run fluctuations in national output.
   (d) the primary explanation of GDP gaps.
   (e) important determinants of long-term economic growth.

7. **A low factor utilization rate**
   (a) describes an inflationary gap situation.
   (b) describes excess supply in the factor market.
   (c) implies that unemployment is also low.
   (d) would tend to lead to increases in factor prices such as wage rates.
   (e) implies that the ratio of employed factors to total factor supply is high.

8. **Which of the following is likely to explain short-term movements of GDP around its potential level?**
   (a) Productivity changes.
   (b) Economic growth.
   (c) Changes in labour supplies.
   (d) Changes in utilization rates of factors of production.
   (e) Both productivity changes <u>and</u> changes in labour supplies.

9. **When short-run actual GDP is above potential GDP,**
   (a) there is an excess supply of factors.
   (b) factor prices will tend to fall in the long run.
   (c) utilization rates of factors are above "normal" levels.
   (d) unemployment is high.
   (e) potential GDP will increase in the long run

Policy Implications

Fiscal and monetary policies affect the short-run level of GDP because they alter the level of demand. But unless they are able to affect the level of potential output, they will have no long-run effect on GDP.

10. The consensus among economists is that monetary policy

(a) affects real macroeconomic variables only in the long run.
(b) should concentrate on taxation and government expenditure programs.
(c) affects potential GDP in the short run.
(d) affects nominal macroeconomic variables in the long run.
(e) affects both real and nominal macroeconomic variables in the long run.

11. Economists, when thinking about business cycles, focus on

(a) understanding why actual GDP deviates from potential GDP.
(b) changes in labour supply, especially immigration.
(c) why potential GDP changes in the short run.
(d) productivity changes.
(e) the reasons why utilization rates are constant during the cycles.

12. To have long-term effects on the economy, monetary and fiscal policies must

(a) alter short-run aggregate supply.
(b) alter short-run aggregate demand.
(c) affect the level of potential output.
(d) smooth fluctuations in economic activity over business cycles.
(e) None of the above.

13. Which of the following policy initiatives would contribute to both the reduction of a recessionary gap *and* the increase of potential output?

(a) A reduction in immigration levels.
(b) Expansionary monetary policy.
(c) An increase in private saving.
(d) Increases in government spending on health and education.
(e) Increasing government efficiency through the elimination of redundant jobs in the public sector.

SHORT-ANSWER QUESTIONS

1. What did you learn from the textbook's discussion of the relationship between Japan's saving rate and its record of short-term business fluctuations and long-term economic growth?

2. Explain how an increase in labour participation rates may contribute to increasing both the rate of unemployment in the short run and the level of potential output in the long run.

3. If, as recent studies suggest, a child's early years are the most important in creating abilities and motivations that affect learning and behaviour throughout life, how might a government-funded early childhood development program contribute to increasing both potential GDP and the material standard of living of average Canadians?

EXERCISES

1. **Actual and Potential GDP**

The information below reflects time series of real actual GDP and potential GDP for a hypothetical economy over a seven-year period.

Year	Actual GDP	Potential GDP
1999	1000	1100
2000	1105	1105
2001	1120	1110
2002	1125	1115
2003	1000	1117
2004	1180	1120
2005	1205	1205

(a) What type of output gap existed in 1999 and what is its magnitude? What type of gap existed in 2005 and what is its magnitude?

(b) In 2001 was there an excess supply of or an excess demand for factors? Are utilization rates of resources lower or higher than "normal levels"? Do you expect factor prices to eventually fall or rise?

(c) In 2003 was there an excess supply of or an excess demand for factors? Are utilization rates of resources lower or higher than "normal levels"? Do you expect factor prices to eventually fall or rise?

(d) According to the textbook, the time period between what two years is appropriate to measure long-run changes in output? Explain. Calculate the percentage change in long-run growth. Provide two possible explanations of why there was long-run growth in real national income.

2. **Short- and Long-Run Effects of a Tax Cut**
Consider a debate between two economics professors about the effects of personal and business income tax cuts on an economy which currently has no output gap. Professor Dove argues strongly that tax cuts do not affect potential GDP. Professor Hawk argues that tax cuts can contribute to long-run growth in GDP. [*Hint:* You might want to reread the textbook section entitled *Inflation and Interest Rates in Canada* before you attempt this exercise.]
   (a) Analyze the short-run effects of tax cuts on real output, factor prices, and the price level because of increased consumer buying and business investment. Identify the type of output gap that is likely to be created.

   (b) Analyze Professor Dove's long-run predictions for real output, factor prices, and the price level because of the tax cuts.

   (c) What would have to happen in the economy for Professor Hawk to be correct?

3. **Short- and Long-Run Objectives of Government Policy**
Consider an economy where equilibrium income is currently below potential GDP. You are a senior economic adviser to the Minister of Finance and the Deputy Minister asks you to suggest some policy that would contribute to reduce the recessionary gap in the short run and increase potential GDP in the long run. What would be your policy advice?

ADDITIONAL MULTIPLE-CHOICE QUESTIONS

1. **Referring to the data in Exercise 1, we observe in 2004**
   (a) an inflationary gap of 60.
   (b) an excess demand for resources.
   (c) utilization rates above normal levels.
   (d) unemployment most likely lower than the natural rate of unemployment.
   (e) All of the above.

***2. If actual real GDP was 240 and potential GDP was 250, then**

(a) an inflationary gap of 10 exists.
(b) there is an excess demand for factors.
(c) current utilization rates are below normal levels.
(d) we would expect factor prices to rise in the long run.
(e) long-run growth in output will fall.

3. Which of the following is likely to decrease potential GDP?

(a) A decrease in taxes.
(b) A decrease in productivity.
(c) A decrease in the rate of factor utilization.
(d) A decrease in emigration.
(e) An increase in the participation rate of persons willing to work.

4. Which of the following is most likely to explain the creation of a short-run inflationary gap?

(a) An increase in labour productivity.
(b) An increase in factor supplies.
(c) A decrease in import purchases.
(d) A decrease in government purchases.
(e) An increase in personal saving.

5. Which of the following is most likely to occur in the long run when an economy has an initial short-run recessionary gap situation?

(a) Factor prices will fall.
(b) The rate of factor utilization will fall.
(c) Productivity will fall.
(d) Unemployment will increase permanently.
(e) None of the above.

***6. According to the data in Figure 25-2 in the textbook**

(a) Canadian labour productivity has steadily declined.
(b) the most important cause of long-term economic growth in Canada has been sustained growth in employment rates.
(c) the Canadian labour force has steadily increased.
(d) Canada has experienced more short-term volatility in labour productivity than it has for employment rates.
(e) the volatility of productivity changes is a major factor explaining short-term business fluctuations.

Questions 7 to 10 are based on five-year data, presented below, for a hypothetical economy. You should review textbook equation 25-2 and its definitions.

Historical Data for a Hypothetical Economy

Year	Real GDP (billions of real dollars)	Labour Force (millions of people)	Employment (millions of people)
1990	265	2.4	2.00
1995	300	2.7	2.20
2000	340	3.0	2.80
2005	375	3.3	3.05

***7. As defined by equation 25-2, labour productivity between 2000 and 2005**

(a) increased from 113.3 to 113.6.
(b) increased by 8.9 percent.
(c) increased from 121.4 to 123.0.
(d) increased by 9.1 percent.
(e) increased by 10.3 percent.

***8. Between 1990 and 2005, economic growth was**

(a) 41.5 percent.
(b) 37.5 percent.
(c) 52.5 percent.
(d) 37.5 percent.
(e) 26.5 percent.

9. Between 1995 and 2000, the employment rate

(a) increased by 12 percent.
(b) increased by 0.12 percent.
(c) increased by 10 percent.
(d) increased from 0.81 to 0.93.
(e) cannot be determined from these data.

***10. Which of the following will most likely increase potential GDP?**

(a) An increase in the money supply.
(b) An increase in government transfer payments.
(c) An introduction of an export subsidy.
(d) An increase in mortality rates.
(e) A decrease in high school drop-out rates.

***11. If the economy is in long-run equilibrium, which of the following will most likely contribute to the emergence of a deflationary gap?**

(a) A decrease in the rate of interest.
(b) A decrease in private saving.
(c) A change in consumers' tastes that reduces the level of imports.
(d) An increase in public saving.
(e) An increase in labour participation rates.

SOLUTIONS

Chapter Review

1.(d) **2.**(c) **3.**(b) **4.**(e) **5.**(e) **6.**(e) **7.**(b) **8.**(d) **9.**(c) **10.**(d) **11.**(a) **12.**(c) **13.**(d)

Short-Answer Questions

1. The Japanese example is interesting because it demonstrates the differences in the short-run and long-run effects of an increase in the saving rate. In the short run, increased saving created an economic slump. Hence, the short-run changes in the Japanese economy can be characterized as demand-determined. However, the short-run effect of saving is different from its long-run effect. Increases in saving can lead to reductions in the interest rate and represent sources of finance for more investment and asset formation in the long run. Hence, growth in Japan's capital stock was enhanced. These are important determinants of long-term economic growth. The important key for students is the need to distinguish short-run from long-run effects when important macroeconomic variables change.

2. Increases in labour participation rates—e.g., as a result of the elimination of the mandatory retirement age—will translate into increases in the size of the labour force—i.e., into increases in labour supply. On the one hand, given the short-run assumption of constant factor prices, an excess supply will materialize in the labour market as a result of an increase in labour participation rates, thus increasing the rate of unemployment in the short run. On the other hand, increases in labour or other factor supplies allow for the production of larger outputs once the process of factor price adjustments is completed in the long-run—i.e., increases in labour supply cause potential GDP to rise.

3. A government-funded early childhood development program would contribute to increasing potential GDP in two ways: (1) by allowing a greater number of mothers of young children to enter the labour market, thus increasing labour participation rates and the size of the labour force; and (2) by increasing the quality of the labour force and thus improving labour productivity. At the same time, higher labour productivity implies higher GDP per capita and—*ceteris paribus*—a potentially higher material standard of living for average Canadians.

Exercises

1. **(a)** In 1999, there was a recessionary gap of –100 (= 1000 – 1100). There was a zero gap in 2005.
   (b) There was an inflationary gap of 10 in 2001, which means there is excess demand in the factor market. Since actual real GDP exceeds real potential GDP, factor utilization is higher than normal levels. In the long run, we would expect factor prices to rise.
   (c) In 2003, actual real GDP was less than potential GDP (a recessionary gap of –117). Factor utilization was lower than normal levels, and in the long run we would expect factor prices to fall.
   (d) The textbook views long-run changes in GDP to be measured by changes in potential GDP, with no change in the output gap. The data in the table indicate that both 2000 and 2005 had zero output gaps. Hence, long-run growth in GDP is measured between 2000 and 2005, which in this case is 1205 – 1105 divided by 1105 times 100 percent, which equals 9.0 percent. Productivity and/or factor supply increased.

2. **(a)** Tax cuts increase disposable income for consumers and profits for firms. Both consumption and investment are likely to increase. An inflationary gap is created in the short run since potential GDP does not change. The demand for factors of production will increase and output will rise. Factor utilization will be higher than normal levels. In the short run factor prices and prices may be stable.
   (b) Professor Dove would argue that the excess demand for factors in the short run will trigger increases in factor prices with the result that the price level starts to rise as firms pass factor price increases on to consumers. The rise in factor prices will eliminate excess demand, and the economy's real GDP level will be restored at its potential level (the zero output gap is restored).
   (c) Professor Hawk must believe that potential GDP is increased in the long run. Tax cuts must affect real variables such as the willingness of individuals to supply factor services. Moreover, increases in investment may increase the capital stock in the long run. Thus, long-run productivity may increase. Both factors can increase potential GDP in the long run. But, there is a catch: if tax cuts cause interest rates to rise, then private spending will be "crowded out." Professor Hawk is on somewhat dangerous ground!

3. If there is currently a recessionary gap, you might conclude that *AD* is insufficient and thus expansionary fiscal or monetary policy (or a combination of both) might be called for. But you must now decide which of expansionary fiscal policy or expansionary monetary policy might be the best alternative.

   You realize that the impact of expansionary monetary policy on *AD* might take some time to be felt and, since the Deputy Minister wants results as soon as possible, you conclude that expansionary fiscal policy is the best alternative.

   Next you must decide whether to suggest a reduction in taxes or an increase in government purchases. Again, you conclude that the impact of a decrease in taxes on *AD* must also take some time to be realized and decide that an increase in government purchases is the best alternative—but what type of government purchases?

   You know that any type of government purchases will increase *AE* right away and through the multiplying effect will also cause *AE* to increase further quite rapidly, but you want to suggest an increase in some type of government spending that will also contribute to expand potential GDP. Then, what type of government spending?

You know that it must be a type of government spending that will increase the quantity or quality of factors of production, but also a type of expenditure that will not need to be maintained once the economy goes back into full gear (which might otherwise require a reduction in some other type of government spending to prevent moving into an inflationary gap).

You first consider an increase in government expenditure on health and education (which would increase the quality of the labour force in the long run), but soon realize that this is not a type of expenditure that could be easily cut back once the economy is once again at full employment.

You then conclude that an increase in government expenditure in infrastructure will increase the capital stock of the country, and that this type of expenditure will be reduced once the investment project is finalized.

You thus suggest to the Deputy Minister that an increase in public investment in infrastructure—e.g., investment to build a new power plant in Ontario to reduce the expected shortage in electricity—will contribute to both decreasing the current deflationary gap in the short run and increasing potential GDP in the long run.

Additional Multiple-Choice Questions

1.(e) **2.**(c) **3.**(b) **4.**(c) **5.**(a) **6.**(c) **7.**(c) **8.**(a) **9.**(d) **10.**(e) **11.**(d)

Explanations for the Asterisked Multiple-Choice Questions

2.(c) There is a recessionary gap of 10. Since Y is less than Y^*, utilization rates of factors are below their normal levels.

6.(c) As Figure 25-2 illustrates, productivity has steadily increased over time. Employment rate changes have been more volatile than productivity changes. The growth in the Canadian labour force has been a major contributor to Canada's economic growth.

7.(c) Labour productivity is defined as real GDP divided by employment. In 2000 labour productivity is calculated by 340/2.8 = 121.4. In 2005, labour productivity was 375/3.05 = 123.0.

8.(a) Economic growth is measured by the percentage change in real GDP. For this example, economic growth is calculated by (375 – 265)/265 times 100 percent or 41.5 percent.

10.(e) We have seen in this chapter that potential GDP would increase if there was an increase in factor supplies, factor participation rates, or factor productivity. An increase in money supply will reduce short-run interest rates and accelerate the rate of investment in the short run but not total investment in the long run. An increase in government transfer payments might increase consumption in the short run but not potential GDP. An export subsidy will increase *AD* and GDP in the short run but not the factors determining potential GDP. An increase in the mortality rate will reduce population and the size of the labour force. But a decrease in high school drop-out rates will improve the quality of the labour force, and thus increase labour productivity and potential GDP.

11.(d) A deflationary gap will emerge if there is a decrease in *AD* or an increase in *AS* in the short run. A decrease in the rate of interest will increase investment and boost *AD* in the short run. A decrease in private saving means an increase in consumption expenditure and thus an increase in *AD*. A decrease in imports will also boost *AD* in the short run. An increase in labour participation rates will increase unemployment and eventually contribute to a fall in wage rates, but not to a decrease in *AD*. Finally, an increase in public saving (e.g., as a result of a decrease in *G* or an increase in taxes) will reduce *AD* and contribute to the emergence of deflationary gap.

CHAPTER 26

LONG-RUN ECONOMIC GROWTH

LO

LEARNING OBJECTIVES

In this chapter you will learn

1 about the costs and benefits of economic growth.

2 the four fundamental determinants of growth in real GDP.

3 the main elements of Neoclassical growth theory.

4 about new growth theories based on endogenous technical change and increasing returns.

5 why resource exhaustion and environmental degradation create challenges for public policy directed at sustaining economic growth.

CHAPTER OVERVIEW

Economic growth is the single most powerful engine for generating long-term increases in material living standards. This chapter considers economic theories of how and why economies grow and material living standards increase over time. Factors that affect the rate of economic growth include the quantity of labour and physical capital; the stock and quality of human capital; and technological improvement. These are the factors emphasized by Neoclassical growth theory. The importance of ideas, knowledge, and new technology is the focus of other theories of economic growth.

The chapter discusses the **costs and benefits of economic growth**. One of the potential costs of economic growth is that current consumption might be diverted to capital formation. The distinction between economic growth and material living standards (measured by per capita output) is discussed.

Saving and investment behaviour are clearly important for discussions of economic growth. The chapter discusses the long-run connection between savings and investments and their roles in determining the real rate of interest.

Neoclassical growth theory, using an **aggregate production function**, stresses **diminishing returns** to a variable factor, **constant returns to scale**, **balanced growth**, and embodied technological change. Other growth theories emphasize the possibility of historical **increasing returns to investment** because of fixed costs, knowledge, and **endogenous technological change**. The chapter concludes by discussing the limits to economic growth (**resource depletion and pollution**).

HINTS AND TIPS

The following may help you to avoid some of the most common errors on examinations.

✓ Learn why potential social costs (e.g., greater pollution) might be incurred in order to obtain the social benefits of higher economic growth.

✓ Understand how growth in the labour force, human capital, and physical capital and improvements in technology affect economic growth.

✓ Learn that the long-run connection between saving and investment involves two relationships in a loanable funds diagram—the demand for loanable funds derives from investment activity and the supply of loanable funds is determined by national saving.

✓ Understand that changes in the real interest rate cause movements along the demand for and supply of loanable funds curves while other economic considerations cause the curves to shift. For example, a decline in government expenditure shifts the supply curve for loanable funds to the right.

✓ Learn the features and implications of a Neoclassical aggregate production function on GDP and living standards. Review your understanding of microeconomic concepts of marginal productivity, diminishing marginal productivity, and constant returns to scale.

✓ Learn why the production of ideas might ensure boundless economic growth—what economists call *knowledge-driven growth*.

CHAPTER REVIEW

The Nature of Economic Growth

Higher economic growth may render some machines obsolete and also leaves the skills of some workers partly obsolete. Moreover, economic growth has opportunity costs of forgone current consumption. The powerful and **cumulative effect** of constant growth rates on the level of real GDP over time is demonstrated. You would profit by learning two equations. The first calculates the value of real GDP at a constant growth rate after N years. Specifically, real GDP after N years equals $Y_0 (1 + g)^N$, where Y_0 is the initial value of GDP and g is the constant rate of growth. If you have a scientific calculator, you can easily calculate $(1 + g)^N$ by using the y^x key. The second equation is the famous *rule of 72*. The approximate time taken for a variable to double in value is calculated by dividing 72 by the growth rate. For example, if the growth rate is 10 percent per year you divide by 10, which means the variable doubles in value in about 7.2 years.

1. Economic growth is best defined as
- (a) a rise in real national income as unemployment is reduced.
- (b) fluctuations of GDP around its potential level.
- (c) ongoing increases in the level of real potential GDP.
- (d) increases in current real GDP as structural unemployment decreases.
- (e) a reduction in the inequality of income.

2. What of the following is a potential cost of economic growth?
- (a) Workers become less educated.
- (b) Rising average living standards.
- (c) The rapid adjustments which can cause much upset and misery to some of the people affected by it.
- (d) The need to increase consumption and decrease saving over time.
- (e) Countries become more self-sufficient in food production.

3. According to the "rule of 72," a growth in population of 2 percent per year means that population will double in approximately
- (a) 2 years.
- (b) 144 years.
- (c) 72 years.
- (d) 260 years.
- (e) 36 years.

4. **What is the approximate value of $100 that grows at 5 percent per year after 6 years?**
   (a) $130.
   (b) $105.
   (c) $134.
   (d) $630.
   (e) None of the above.

5. **Which of the following might be an undesirable result of economic growth?**
   (a) Higher living standards.
   (b) More wealth concentrated in the hands of a few citizens.
   (c) Ease in achieving some types of income redistribution.
   (d) Technological changes that produce substitutes for dwindling resource stocks.
   (e) A higher quality of life.

6. **For the economy as a whole, the primary opportunity cost of economic growth is**
   (a) the reduction in GDP per capita in future time periods.
   (b) the widespread environmental deterioration that inevitably results from economic growth.
   (c) the loss of current consumption opportunities.
   (d) increased unemployment in the short run.
   (e) a greater inequality of income within a country that might result from economic growth.

Established Theories of Economic Growth

The four fundamental determinants of growth of total output are (1) *growth in the labour force,* (2) *growth in human capital,* (3) *growth in physical capital,* and (4) *technological improvement.*

Neoclassical growth theory connects the four forces of economic growth by the aggregate production function, which has three important properties: (1) diminishing marginal productivity of a variable factor, (2) constant returns to scale, and (3) exogenous technological change. [*Note:* Students who have not taken microeconomics may wish to answer Exercise 2 before attempting the multiple-choice questions in this section.] The implications of these properties on growth in GDP and on material living standards are also explained.

This section also explains the long-run connection between saving and investment. Saving in this case is national saving, which is the sum of private saving and public saving. The demand for and supply of loanable funds are related to the real interest rate, assuming that GDP is at its potential level (Y^*). The national saving curve is upward-sloping because an increase in the real interest rate leads households to reduce their current consumption. In keeping with empirical evidence, the national saving curve (in relation to the real interest rate) is steep because household consumption responds only moderately to changes in the real interest rate. A downward-sloping investment demand curve represents the demand for loanable funds. All components of desired investment are negatively related to the real interest rate because investment is typically financed by borrowing and the real interest rate reflects the cost of borrowing. In the long run, the real interest is determined by the intersection of the investment demand and the national saving curves.

Some growth theories stress the endogenous nature of technological change with economic causes and the possibility of increasing returns to investment.

7. **The law of diminishing returns implies that successive increases in one factor to a fixed stock of other factors of production cause**
   (a) output to increase at a constant rate.
   (b) output to decrease at an increasing rate.
   (c) output to increase at a decreasing rate.
   (d) output to increase at an increasing rate.
   (e) output to decrease at a constant rate.

8. **Which of the following could increase the real interest rate in the long run?**
   (a) An increase in the marginal propensity to save.
   (b) A decrease in government purchases.
   (c) An increase in desired investment.
   (d) A short-run inflationary gap.
   (e) Both an increase in the marginal propensity to save and a decrease in government purchases.

9. **In the long run, all else equal, an increase in saving in a country is likely to**
   (a) cause the aggregate demand curve to shift to the left.
   (b) cause real national income to fall because of inadequate aggregate demand.
   (c) increase economic growth because more investment expenditure can be financed from these funds.
   (d) reduce structural unemployment and therefore increase potential GDP.
   (e) increase the reliance on foreign capital to finance investment.

10. **Increases in material living standards are determined largely by**
   (a) increases in GDP.
   (b) increases in *per capita* output.
   (c) the distribution of physical capital among domestic households.
   (d) population increases for a given stock of physical capital.
   (e) the accumulation of physical capital.

11. **For neoclassical theories of growth that assume unchanging technology, increases in population**
   (a) eventually decrease long-run living standards as measured by *per capita* real output.
   (b) generate a constant rate of growth in GDP per capita.
   (c) increase output per worker at an increasing rate.
   (d) have no effect on GDP in the short run or the long run.
   (e) have no effect on the material standard of living in the long run.

12. **The neoclassical assumption of constant returns to scale**
   (a) predicts that economic growth occurs with reduced material living standards.
   (b) cannot explain rising material living standards in the long run.
   (c) forecasts falling material living standards over time.
   (d) implies that technological innovation is embodied.
   (e) None of the above.

New Growth Theories

Two new strands of growth models emphasize endogenous technological change and increasing marginal returns. These models view technological change to be responsive to economic signals as prices and profits; in other words, technological change is endogenous to the economic system. The models that feature endogenous technological change stress learning by doing and knowledge transfer. The theories based on increasing marginal returns argue that each new increment of investment is more productive than previous increments. The notions of fixed costs and knowledge are important elements of this set of growth models.

13. **Which of the following is a feature of the increasing returns theory of economic growth?**
   (a) Firms that first develop new investment opportunities receive high initial rates of return because of low fixed costs.
   (b) Investors who follow "pioneer" investors face lower investment costs and therefore higher rates of return.
   (c) Once a technological breakthrough has been made, initial investors garner high rates of return since this technology is usually unavailable to others.
   (d) The acceptability of new products takes a "learning by using" process by producers.
   (e) Investors who follow "pioneer" investors usually face higher investment costs and also higher rates of return.

14. **Which of the following is a feature of the endogenous technological change theories?**
   (a) Technological change is viewed as independent of economic events.
   (b) The diffusion of technology is costless.
   (c) Innovation is discouraged by a strongly competitive environment and encouraged by monopoly practices.
   (d) Shocks can sometimes provide a spur to innovation.
   (e) Technological change is unresponsive to such economic signals as prices and profits.

15. **Which of the following is a feature of knowledge-driven growth theory?**
   (a) New ideas can be used only by their original developers.
   (b) New knowledge provides the input that allows investment to produce increasing marginal returns.
   (c) New ideas cannot prevent investment to be subject to diminishing marginal returns.
   (d) Income per capita becomes constant in the long run.
   (e) Capital and labour increase at the same rate in the long run.

Are There Limits to Growth?

Although resource exhaustion is a general concern, modern growth theory stresses the historical record of continual technological change and increasing resource stocks. However, the management of pollution has become a pressing matter.

16. **Which of the following statements accurately reflects an issue related to economic growth?**
   (a) There is no evidence that technological change may require fewer inputs to produce a given level of output.
   (b) The capacity of the earth's natural processes to cope with the pollution created by a growing population cannot be sustained.
   (c) The benefits of technological advances are distributed across all nations too quickly.
   (d) All nations share equally in the benefits of economic growth.
   (e) Sustainable growth is best generated by using natural resources at a faster rate.

SHORT-ANSWER QUESTIONS

1. Explain briefly how a Neoclassical aggregate production function helps to explain the causes of economic growth and changes in long-run material living standards.

2. Briefly describe the views of Neoclassical growth theory and endogenous growth theory on technological change.

3. Explain the concepts of *diminishing marginal returns* and *constant returns to scale* characterizing Neoclassical growth theory.

EXERCISES

1. **The Expansion of Potential GDP**

Suppose that an economy's current GDP is 100. Economists have estimated that the country's potential national income could grow by either 1 percent, 2 percent, or 6 percent, depending on the economy's policies with respect to promoting savings and investment, providing education, allowing free international trade, and protecting the environment. You are asked to determine the economic implications of the alternative growth scenarios.

(a) Calculate, to one decimal, the missing values in the following table. Use your calculator to estimate values for the compound growth formula, $Y_0(1 + g)^N$, where Y_0 is current GDP, g is the annual rate of growth, and N is the number of compounding periods. If you don't have this type of calculator, find the answers to part (a) in the Solutions section and then answer the rest of this question.

Estimated GDP at Various Growth Rates

Year	1 percent	2 percent	6 percent
0	100	100	100
1	101.1	102.0	106.0
10	110.5	______	179.1
12	112.7	126.8	______
36	143.1	204.0	814.7
72	204.7	416.1	6 637.8
100	______	724.5	33 930.2

(b) What is the effect on GDP of a doubling of the annual growth rate from 1 percent to 2 percent after 1 year? After 10 years? After 100 years?

(c) What is the effect on GDP of a trebling of the annual growth rate from 2 percent to 6 percent after 1 year? After 10 years? After 100 years?

(d) Use your calculations to illustrate the *rule of 72* by filling in the following blanks. Refer to the Mathematical Note at the back of the textbook. At 1 percent annual growth, GDP doubles after about _________ years; at 2 percent annual growth, GDP doubles after about _________ years; at 6 percent annual growth, GDP doubles after about _________ years.

(e) What additional information would you need to determine how living standards change in the three scenarios?

2. Changes in Factors of Production and Real GDP

Consider the following aggregate production function, $Y = T \times (KL)^{1/2}$, where

Y is real GDP
T is the state of technology
K is the capital stock
L is the amount of labour
The term $(KL)^{1/2}$ is the square root of the product KL

For parts (a) to (c), we assume that the aggregate production function takes on a specific functional form:

$$Y = 3(KL)^{1/2}$$

(a) The table below represents the case where labour use changes but all other factor supplies and technology are constant. Fill in the missing values in the table for values of real GDP.

Labour (L)	Capital (K)	Technology (T)	Real GDP (Y)
10	20	3	42.4
15	20	3	
20	20	3	
25	20	3	

(b) The marginal productivity of labour is defined as the change in real GDP divided by the change in labour use. What is the marginal productivity when labour use increases from 10 to 15? From 15 to 20? From 20 to 25? What do you observe?

(c) As labour use increases, what happens to the living standard as measured by the value of real output per unit of labour (worker)?

Parts (d) and (e) have the same functional form for the aggregate production function but different data. Specifically, labour and capital increase by the same proportion, 50 percent, but technology remains constant.

Labour (*L*)	Capital (*K*)	Technology (*T*)	Real GDP (*Y*)
10	20	3	42.4
15	30	3	
20	40	3	
25	50	3	

(d) Fill in the missing value for *Y*. What do you observe happens to changes in *Y* for successive, proportional increases in labour and capital?

(e) What happens to the standard of living as measured by real output per worker?

Part (f) assumes that technology changes. The value of *T* increases from 3 to 4, but factor use remains constant.

Labour (*L*)	Capital (*K*)	Technology (*T*)	Real GDP (*Y*)
20	20	4	

(f) Calculate the value of real GDP for this case. Compare this value with the value in row 3 for part (a). What do you conclude?

3. The Opportunity Cost of Growth

This exercise focuses on the opportunity costs of growth. Suppose that real GDP of an economy was 100 in year 0, consumption expenditure was 85, and investment expenditure was 15. The growth of real national income on an annual basis is expected to be 2 percent. The current government urges the citizens of this nation to pursue practices that increase the growth rate to 4 percent on an annual basis.

Economic forecasters suggest that by reducing consumption to 70 (increasing saving by 15) and by increasing investment expenditure to a level of 30, (1) consumption expenditure 7 years hence will be equal to that level of consumption without these policies (with the economy growing at 2 percent); and (2) the aggregate level of consumption in 20 years will be *double* the level associated with a 2 percent growth rate.

In Year	Annual Level of Consumption 2 Percent Growth	4 Percent Growth	Cumulative (loss) or Gain
0	85.0	70.0	(15.0)
1	86.7	72.8	(28.9)
2	88.4	75.7	(41.6)
3	90.2	78.7	(53.1)
4	92.0	81.9	(63.2)
7	97.6	92.1	(84.4)
8	99.6	95.8	(88.2)
9	101.6	99.6	(90.2)
10	103.6	103.6	(90.2)
17	119.0	136.4	(23.7)
18	121.4	141.8	(3.3)
20	126.3	153.4	47.8
30	154.0	227.0	
40	187.7	336.1	
50	228.8	497.5	

Your task is to confirm the accuracy of the government's economic forecasts by answering the following questions.

(a) Prove that the value of consumption after 10 years is equal to 103.6 for both a growth rate of 2 percent and for 4 percent. Using a calculator, apply the formula, $C = C_0 (1 + g)^N$.

(b) What is the loss in consumption in year 4 because of the government's growth policy? What is the cumulative loss after four years?

(c) In what year will the level of consumption with a 4 percent growth rate equal the level of consumption with a 2 percent growth rate? Compare your answer with the government's assertion.

(d) In what year does this economy recoup all of the cumulative losses in forgone consumption? This is called the "break-even" year. [*Hint:* Refer to Figure 26-1 in the textbook.]

(e) Is the government's assertion that this society will double its consumption level in 20 years correct?

4. **Changes in Labour Productivity**

The aggregate production function of a hypothetical economy is given by the equation $Y = A\,(K\,L)^{1/2}$, where Y is real GDP, A is the level of technology, K is units of physical capital, and L is the number of workers. Initially, the level of technology is 100, physical capital is 225 units, and the number of workers is 8100.

(a) Calculate the initial level of labour productivity in this economy.

(b) Suppose now that the quantity of physical capital increases to 256. Calculate the new level of labour productivity in this economy.

(c) Go back to the initial situation in part (a). Suppose now that a technological improvement occurs, causing the level of technology to increase by 10 percent. What is the new level of labour productivity?

EXTENSION EXERCISE

E1. **Marginal Returns to Factors of Production and Returns to Scale**

The production function of a hypothetical economy is given by the equation $Y = (K\,L)^{1/2}$, where Y is real GDP, K is units of physical capital, and L is the number of workers. Initially, physical capital is 100 units, and the number of workers is 400. The marginal product of labour (MP_L) and the marginal product of capital (MP_K) are given by the following expressions, respectively:

$$MP_L = 0.5\,(K/L)^{1/2} \text{ and } MP_K = 0.5\,(L/K)^{1/2}$$

(a) Fill out the blanks in the following table:

L	K	Y	MP_L	MP_K
400	100	200	0.250	1.00
400	121	____	____	____
400	____	40	____	____
441	100	210	0.238	1.05
____	100	____	____	1.10

(b) Does labour exhibit diminishing marginal returns? Does capital exhibit diminishing marginal returns? Explain.

(c) Suppose that initially $L = 400$ and $K = 100$. If labour (L) and capital (K) both increase by 10 percent, by what percentage will output (Y) increase? Does the aggregate production function exhibit increasing, decreasing, or constant returns to scale? Explain.

ADDITIONAL MULTIPLE-CHOICE QUESTIONS

Questions 1 through 4 refer to the following data for an economy with a constant technology:

Labour	Capital	Output
10.0	10	10.0
10.0	15	11.8
10.0	20	13.2
15.0	15	15.0
22.5	15	19.1

1. The marginal product of capital (extra output per extra unit of capital input, labour use unchanged)
(a) is 1.8 when capital rises from 10 to 15.
(b) is 0.14 when capital rises from 15 to 20.
(c) rises when progressively more capital is used.
(d) demonstrates the principle of increasing returns to scale.
(e) is 0.36 when capital rises from 10 to 15.

***2. The marginal product of labour (extra output per extra unit of labour input, capital use unchanged)**
(a) is 0.55 (approximately) when labour rises from 15 to 22.5.
(b) is 4.1 when labour rises from 15 to 22.5.
(c) is 1.8 when labour rises from 10 to 15.
(d) cannot be estimated in this table.
(e) demonstrates the principle of increasing returns to scale.

3. This economy operates under constant returns to scale if
(a) increasing capital inputs has a constant positive effect on output.
(b) increasing labour and capital inputs by 50 percent increases output by 50 percent.
(c) increasing labour inputs has a constant positive effect on output.
(d) both marginal productivities are positive and constant.
(e) decreasing labour and capital inputs by 30 percent increases output by 30 percent.

***4. When labour (workers) increases from 15.0 to 22.5 and capital remains at 15,**
(a) living standards per worker increase because marginal productivity is positive.
(b) output per worker stays constant because capital is constant.
(c) living standards per worker decrease even though marginal productivity is positive.
(d) the average productivity of labour (workers) is 0.55 approximately.
(e) living standards per worker increase because average productivity of labour increases.

5. Suppose that two countries initially have the same per capita output. Country *A* has an annual economic growth rate of 6 percent, while country *B* grows at 3 percent per year. According to the rule of 72, country *A* will have a per capita output four times as large as country *B*'s in
(a) 12 years.
(b) 36 years.
(c) 24 years.
(d) 48 years.
(e) 72 years.

***6. Ken and Bill begin the same job with a first-year salary of $28 000. If Ken's salary grows at 3 percent each year and Bill's grows at 2 percent per year, then after 8 years**

(a) Ken's yearly salary will be about $2664 more than Bill's.
(b) Ken's yearly salary will be about $34 720.
(c) Ken's yearly salary will be about 1 percent higher than Bill's.
(d) Bill's yearly salary will be about $32 480.
(e) Ken's and Bill's salaries are still equal.

7. Which of the following cases associated with the Neoclassical theory would increase a country's standard of living?

(a) Capital accumulates over time, but other factor uses are constant.
(b) Labour supply increases over time, but other factor uses are constant.
(c) All factors increase over time by the same proportion.
(d) Technological improvements result in increased production with less or the same amounts of all inputs.
(e) All factor supplies decrease over time with technology constant.

Questions 8 to 11 assume an aggregate production function of $Y = K \times L^{1/2}$. The term $L^{1/2}$ is the square root of L.

8. What is the value of *Y* when *K* = 2 and *L* = 4?

(a) 4. (b) 8.
(c) 2.8. (d) 5.7.
(e) None of the above.

***9. What is the value of *K* when *Y* = 7.35 and *L* = 6?**

(a) 1.23. (b) 10.4.
(c) 4.2. (d) 1.73.
(e) 3.

10. What is the value of *L* when *K* = 4 and *Y* = 11.31?

(a) 32.0. (b) 5.66.
(c) 2.38. (d) 8.
(e) 2.83.

11. Comparing your answers to Questions 9 and 10, it appears that this production function conforms to that suggested by

(a) the Neoclassical theory which features constant returns to scale.
(b) recent growth theories that emphasize increasing returns to scale.
(c) recent growth theory that stresses endogenous technological change.
(d) the Neoclassical theory which features exogenous technological change.
(e) Professor Solow's measure of technological change.

Use the following information to answer Questions 12 and 13. When the quantity of labour is 10 and the quantity of capital is 6, output is 20. When the quantity of labour is 15 and the quantity of capital is 9, output is 35.

***12. From the above information we can infer that**

(a) the marginal product of labour is 15.
(b) the marginal product of labour is 3.
(c) the marginal product of capital is 5.
(d) the marginal product of labour is 3 *and* the marginal product of capital is 5.
(e) None of the above.

***13. From the above information we can infer that**

(a) the production function exhibits constant returns to scale.
(b) the production function exhibits increasing returns to scale.
(c) the production function exhibits decreasing returns to scale.
(d) this economy employs labour-intensive technologies.
(e) capital is more productive than labour.

14. The marginal product of an input is

(a) total output divided by the quantity of the input used to produced this output.
(b) the percentage increase in output resulting from using one more unit of an input, while holding all other inputs constant.
(c) the quantity of the input used to produce a given output divided by this output.
(d) the increase in output resulting from using one more unit of an input, while holding all other inputs constant.
(e) the increase in output resulting from using one more unit of each input.

15. The law of diminishing returns assumes that

(a) all inputs are changed in the same proportion.
(b) all inputs are held constant.
(c) additional inputs are added in increasingly smaller amounts.
(d) only one other input is held constant when the quantity of an input increases.
(e) all other inputs are held constant when the quantity of an input increases.

***16. Increasing returns to scale means that**

(a) output increases when all inputs are increased.
(b) more than twice as much of all inputs is required to double output.
(c) more than twice as much of one input is required to double output.
(d) less than twice as much of all inputs is required to double output.
(e) less than twice as much of one input is required to double output.

Questions 17 to 19 are based on following equations for long-run national saving (*NS*) and the long-run investment demand (*I*) functions. Both functions depend on the real interest rate denoted as *i*. If the real interest rate is 10 percent, $i = 10$. Also, both curves assume that the economy is at its potential level (Y^*).

$$NS = 2 + 0.5i \text{ and}$$
$$I = 22 - 2i.$$

[*Note:* The textbook labels the horizontal axis in Figure 26-3 as "loanable funds." National saving is the supply of loanable funds and the investment demand curve is the demand for loanable funds.]

***17. Which of the following statements is true?**

(a) If the real interest rate decreases from 10 percent to 8 percent, national saving (loanable funds) decreases from 7 to 5.
(b) The equilibrium long-term real interest rate is 8 percent.
(c) If the real interest rate increases from 5 percent to 7 percent, desired investment increases from 12 to 36.
(d) National saving is more responsive to real interest rate changes than is desired investment.
(e) The intercept term, 2, in the national saving equation would increase in value if government purchases increased.

***18. Which of the following would cause the national saving to shift right in the long run?**
(a) A decrease in the proportion of disposable income that households save.
(b) An increase in government purchases, assuming net taxes don't change.
(c) An increase in business expectations of higher future returns on physical capital investments.
(d) A decrease in the marginal propensity to consume.
(e) A recessionary gap.

19. If the desired investment function changed to 26 – 2*i* while the national saving function did not change, we would predict
(a) the long-run equilibrium real interest rate would increase to 13 percent.
(b) the new long-run equilibrium real interest rate would increase to 9.6 percent.
(c) no change in the long-run real interest rate.
(d) a permanent long-run inflationary gap.
(e) a permanent decrease in the long-run interest rate to 4 percent.

SOLUTIONS

Chapter Review

1.(c) **2.**(c) **3.**(e) **4.**(c) **5.**(b) **6.**(c) **7.**(c) **8.**(c) **9.**(c) **10.**(b) **11.**(a) **12.**(b) **13.**(b) **14.**(d) **15.**(b) **16.**(b)

Short-Answer Questions

1. The simplest Neoclassical aggregate production function features three economic considerations that influence long-run real GDP growth: labour, capital, and technology. Most Neoclassical functions assume that technology is exogenously determined. As more labour is used, with a fixed amount capital, output increases at successively smaller increments. The same is true for increments in capital with a fixed labour force. Hence, one of the features of the Neoclassical production function is diminishing marginal returns. Notice that living standards as measured by per capita real output will fall through time. The Neoclassical function also features a property known as constant returns to scale. If all factors of production increase by a proportion x, real output will also increase by x. Although the Neoclassical function explains constant growth in real GDP, it cannot explain increases in living standards. Therefore, changes in technology are major determinants of explaining economy growth and long-run increases in living standards.

2. On the one hand, Neoclassical growth theory assumes technological change to be an exogenous variable—i.e., not explained by the model itself. The theory recognizes that technological change has a profound effect on economic variables but it cannot explain how technological change itself might be impacted by economic variables. This is one of the main shortcomings of Neoclassical growth theory, since technological change is one of the main determinants of long-run improvements in material standards of living. On the other hand, endogenous growth theory considers technological change to be an endogenous variable—i.e., a variable responsive to economic signals such as prices and profits. If the price of some particular factor of production were to increase, R&D would be directed to altering the production function to economize on this input—i.e., this process, therefore, would involve the development of new technologies in response to changes in relative prices.

3. The marginal return to a factor of production is its marginal product—it measures the increase in output resulting from the addition of one unit of this factor to the process of production while keeping the quantities of all other factors constant. For instance, in a two-factor model (capital and labour), the marginal return to labour measures the increase in output resulting from using one more unit of labour (one worker or one hour) in the process of production while keeping the quantity of capital constant. Similarly for capital: The marginal return to capital measures the increase in output resulting from using one more unit of capital in the process of production while keeping the quantity of labour constant. *Diminishing marginal returns* to labour (or capital) means that each additional unit of labour (or capital) increases total

output by less than the previous unit—i.e., it increases total output at a decreasing rate. Similar definitions can be advanced for constant or increasing marginal returns to a factor of production.

Returns to scale measures the percentage change in output relative to the percentage change in inputs, where inputs change all in the same proportion. Returns to scale could be constant, increasing, or decreasing. *Constant returns to scale* refers to the situation where the percentage change in output is equal to the percentage change in all inputs. For example, if capital and labour both increase by 10 percent and as a result output also increases by 10 percent, then we say that the production function exhibits constant returns to scale.

Exercises

1. If you have a scientific calculator this is an easy exercise! Take an example. The value of $1.02 percent compounded over 72 years is found by entering 1.02 and then pressing the y^x and then entering 72. The answer is $4.161.

- **(a)** $100(1.01)^{100} = 270.5$; $100(1.02)^{10} = 121.9$; $100(1.06)^{12} = 201.2$.
- **(b)** After 1 year, GDP is about 1 percent more; after 10 years, GDP is 11.4 more or about 10 percent more; after 100 years, GDP is 168 percent greater (454 more).
- **(c)** After 1 year, GDP is 4 percent more; after 10 years, GDP is about 47 percent more (57.2 more); after 100 years, GDP is almost 46 times more.
- **(d)** 72 years; 36 years; 12 years.
- **(e)** We would need population information because if we are interested in improved living standards, we are concerned with increasing GDP per capita. If we are concerned with a broader definition of economic welfare, factors such as health and environmental standards might also be considered. The actual distribution of income, rather than its average value per person, may also interest us.

2.
- **(a)** Real GDP = 52.0, 60.0, 67.1.
  The value 67.2 is obtained by taking the square root of 25 times 20 which is equal to 22.4 and multiplying by 3.
- **(b)** When labour increases from 10 to 15, output increases by 9.6. Hence $MP_L = 1.9$.
  When labour increases from 15 to 20, output increases by 8.0. Hence $MP_L = 1.6$.
  When labour increases from 20 to 25, output increases by 7.1. Hence $MP_L = 1.4$.
  There are diminishing returns to labour.
- **(c)** Real per worker output continually falls; Average output per worker = 4.2, 3.5, 3.0, 2.7.
- **(d)** $Y = 63.6, 84.9, 106.1$. Output increased by 50 percent, which is the same proportionate increase as occurred to labour and capital. Take for example the effect on output when labour increased from 10 to 15 and capital increased by 20 to 30. Both of these represent 50 percent increases. Output increased from 42.4 to 63.6. This also represents a 50 percent increase.
- **(e)** GDP per worker remains constant at 4.2. Hence, the standard of living has not changed.
- **(f)** Real GDP is 80. The equivalent case is in part (a) where GDP was 60.0. Hence, a technological improvement increases output by 20 units without any increased usage of labour or capital. This constitutes growth in the standard of living.

3.
- **(a)** C after 10 years at $g = .02$ is $85(1.02)^{10} = 103.6$. C after 10 years at $g = .04$ is $70(1.04)^{10} = 103.6$.
- **(b)** The loss in consumption is 10.1 (92.0 – 81.9); 63.2 is the cumulative loss.
- **(c)** According to the schedule, consumption (C) at 4 percent growth will equal C at 2 percent growth in year 10. This is substantially longer than suggested by the government.
- **(d)** Sometime between the eighteenth and nineteenth year. Note that we have treated all gains and losses the same, regardless of the year in which they occur.
- **(e)** No; it is much later. According to the schedule, C at 4 percent growth is double C at 2 percent growth in approximately 45 years.

[*Note:* All calculations assume annual compounding.]

4.
- **(a)** $Y = A\,(K\,L)^{1/2} = 100\,(225 \times 8100)^{1/2} = 135\,000$. Labour productivity is defined as the level of real GDP per worker: $Y/L = 135\,000 / 8100 = 16.7$.
- **(b)** $Y = A\,(K\,L)^{1/2} = 100\,(256 \times 8100)^{1/2} = 144\,000$. Labour productivity is now:
  $Y/L = 144\,000 / 8100 = 17.8$.
- **(c)** $Y = A\,(K\,L)^{1/2} = 110\,(225 \times 8100)^{1/2} = 148\,500$. Labour productivity is now:
  $Y/L = 148\,500 / 8100 = 18.3$.

Extension Exercise

E1. **(a)**

L	K	Y	MP_L	MP_K
400	100	200	0.250	1.00
400	121	220	0.275	0.91
400	144	240	0.300	0.83
441	100	210	0.238	1.05
484	100	220	0.227	1.10

(b) Both labour and capital exhibit diminishing marginal returns. If we increase the quantity of labour while keeping the quantity of capital constant, the MP_L decreases—e.g., as labour increases from 441 to 484 while keeping capital constant at 100, MP_L decreases from 0.238 to 0.227. Similarly, if we increase the quantity of capital while keeping the quantity of labour constant, the MP_K also decreases—e.g., as capital increases from 100 to 121 while keeping labour constant at 400, MP_K decreases from 1.00 to 0.91.

(c) If L and K increase to 440 and 110 respectively, Y increases to $[(110)\ (440)]^{1/2} = 220$. Therefore, Y also increases by 10 percent. Since Y increases by the same percentage as K and L, then we can conclude that the production function exhibits constant returns to scale.

Additional Multiple-Choice Questions

1.(e) **2.**(a) **3.**(b) **4.**(c) **5.**(d) **6.**(a) **7.**(d) **8.**(a) **9.**(e) **10.**(d) **11.**(b) **12.**(e) **13.**(b) **14.**(d) **15.**(e) **16.**(d) **17.**(b) **18.**(d) **19.**(b)

Explanations for the Asterisked Multiple-Choice Questions

2.(a) When labour use increases from 15 to 22.5 [an increment of +7.5], output increases from 15 to 19 [an increment of +4.1]. Hence, the marginal productivity of labour is 4/7.5 = +0.55.

4.(c) As we saw in Question 2, the marginal productivity of labour was +0.55 when labour increased from 15 to 22.5. However, *per capita* real output falls from [15/15] = 1 to [19.1/22.5] = 0.85.

6.(a) Ken's salary is \$28 000(1.2668) = \$35 470. Bill's salary is \$28 000(1.1717) = \$32 806. The difference is \$2664.

9.(e) Solving the equation $Y = KL^{1/2}$ for the values in this question, we obtain $7.35 = K(2.45)$ or $K = 3.0$.

12.(e) In order to measure the marginal product of an input we must hold all other inputs constant while allowing this input to change. The information provided refers to changes in output as a result of both labour and capital changing simultaneously, and thus we cannot make any inference regarding the marginal products of either input.

13.(b) The information provided shows that when both labour and capital are increased by 50 percent, output increases by more than 50 percent. Therefore, we can infer that the production function exhibits increasing returns to scale.

16.(d) Increasing returns to scale means that when all inputs are increased in a certain proportion, output increases in an even greater proportion.

17.(b) Equating $2 + 0.5i$ and $22 - 2i$, we obtain $i = 8$ (= 8 percent). If the real interest rate increases from 1 to 2 [1 percent to 2 percent], national saving increases by only 0.5 to 1. However, desired investment increases by 2. Hence, the desired investment curve is more response to real interest rate changes.

18.(d) A decrease in the *MPC* means that the marginal propensity to save increases. Hence, for every real interest rate, there is a larger supply of loanable funds.

PART 10: MONEY, BANKING, AND MONETARY POLICY

CHAPTER 27

MONEY AND BANKING

LO

LEARNING OBJECTIVES

In this chapter you will learn

1. about the various functions of money, and how money has evolved over time.
2. that modern banking systems include both privately owned commercial banks and government-owned central banks.
3. how commercial banks create money through the process of taking deposits and making loans.
4. the various measures of the money supply.

CHAPTER OVERVIEW

This is the first of three chapters that discuss the role of money and monetary policy. This chapter discusses the functions of money, the evolution of money as a medium of exchange from gold to paper to chequable deposits, how commercial banks create money through the process of taking deposits and making loans, and various measures of the Canadian money supply.

The largest component of the money supply is deposits created by commercial banks. The **banking system** in Canada consists of two main elements: the **Bank of Canada** (which is Canada's central bank) and the commercial banks. The Bank of Canada is a publicly owned corporation that is responsible for the day-to-day conduct of monetary policy and provides banking services to commercial banks and the federal government. Commercial banks are profit-seeking institutions that allow their customers to transfer deposits from one bank to another by means of cheques.

When the banking system receives a new cash deposit, it can create new deposits to some multiple of this amount. The amount of new deposits created depends on the banks' **target reserve** ratio, the amount of the cash drain to the public, and whether the banks choose to hold **excess reserves**.

The chapter concludes by distinguishing among various kinds of deposits. By doing so, different measures of the **money supply** can be identified. The distinctions between money, **near money**, and **money substitutes** are also discussed.

HINTS AND TIPS

The following may help you to avoid some of the most common errors on examinations.

✓ Learn the major components of a bank's assets and liabilities and where each is recorded (left side or right side) on the bank's balance sheet. Remember, if one side of a bank's (T-account) balance sheet changes, the other must change by an equal amount.

- ✓ Learn the differences between the terms *actual* versus *excess* (or deficient) reserve positions. Excess reserves are said to exist when actual reserves exceed target reserves. Holding high levels of excess reserves is normally a costly practice for banks in terms of forgone profits.
- ✓ When the banking system receives excess reserves, banks can expand loans and deposits by a multiple. When the banks experience deficient reserves, they will tend to contract loans and deposits by a multiple. Create a list of the important assumptions that are required for monetary expansion/contraction.
- ✓ Do not confuse the expenditure multiplier with the formula for multiple expansions/contractions of deposits equation, $[1/(v + c)]$. Learn how changes in v and/or c affect the value for this monetary "multiplier."

CHAPTER REVIEW

The Nature of Money

Money has been usually defined as any generally accepted *medium of exchange*. Money also serves as a *store of value* and a *unit of account*. Different kinds of money vary in the degree of efficiency with which they fulfill these functions. By far, the largest component of modern money is *deposit* money; money held by the public in commercial banks, some of which is chequable or can be withdrawn on demand.

1. For currency money to serve as an efficient medium of exchange, it must have all but which of the following characteristics?
(a) General acceptability.
(b) Must be convertible into gold or silver.
(c) High value relative to its weight.
(d) Divisibility.
(e) Very difficult to counterfeit.

2. The value of money depends primarily on
(a) the gold backing of the currency alone.
(b) the gold backing of both currency and deposits.
(c) its purchasing power.
(d) who issues it.
(e) a government decree.

3. To be a satisfactory store of value, money must have
(a) a relatively stable value.
(b) a direct relationship to national income.
(c) a highly volatile value over time.
(d) no interest payments for holding it.
(e) the backing of a precious metal, typically gold.

4. "Debasing" metal coinage had the effect of
(a) causing prices to fall in the economy.
(b) changing relative prices.
(c) increasing the purchasing power of each coin.
(d) creating a loss for the person issuing the coins.
(e) causing inflation.

5. **A fractionally backed paper money system exists when claims against banks' reserves**
   (a) have 100 percent backing in precious metals such as gold.
   (b) exceed the value of actual reserves.
   (c) have a direct relationship to national income.
   (d) have a fixed relationship to the quantity of coinage.
   (e) are less than the value of actual gold reserves.

6. **Today, paper money in Canada is issued by**
   (a) all chartered banks.
   (b) the federal Department of Finance.
   (c) all commercial banks.
   (d) Canada's central bank (the Bank of Canada).
   (e) the Privy Council.

7. **All Canadian currency (coins and paper notes) is**
   (a) fractionally backed by gold reserves.
   (b) totally backed by gold.
   (c) interest-bearing.
   (d) fiat money.
   (e) backed by deposits in the commercial banks.

The Canadian Banking System

To understand banking practices and the functions of banks, you should understand certain balance sheet (or "T-account") entries and transactions. A balance sheet has a left hand and a right hand side. By convention, assets are listed on the left-hand side and liabilities on the right-hand side. For the very simple balance sheets used in the textbook, the sum of all assets must be equal to the sum of all liabilities. If one side changes, the other must also change by exactly the same magnitude!

As a banker to the commercial banks, the Bank of Canada accepts commercial bank deposits (these are called *reserves*). Reserves are assets to the commercial banks, but are liabilities to the Bank of Canada. As a banker to the federal government, the Bank of Canada accepts government deposits and occasionally buys government bonds. The bonds held by the Bank of Canada are its assets, while deposits of commercial banks and the federal government at the Bank are its liabilities. The Bank of Canada also regulates the money supply by changing two of its liabilities: reserves and currency (notes in circulation).

Banks are private firms that seek to make profit. They receive revenue (interest and service charges) from their principal assets: the securities they own and the loans they make to individuals and to businesses. Costs originate from their principal liabilities: the costs of servicing deposit accounts the banks accept from individuals, businesses, and governments. Although the banks receive no return for holding reserves (cash plus deposits at the Bank of Canada), they hold them to ensure that their customers are able to meet day-to-day requirements for cash and to settle accounts with other banks.

A bank's **reserve ratio** is the fraction of deposit liabilities that is held in the form of reserves. A bank's **target reserve ratio** is the fraction of its deposits that a bank *wishes* to hold as reserves. The target reserve ratio is determined by the banks themselves. There is no longer a legally imposed reserve ratio by the central bank. If actual reserves are greater than a bank's target values, the bank is said to have excess reserves. These excess reserves earn no profit for banks. If actual reserves are less than target values, the bank might have to make up for any reserve deficiency by borrowing reserves from the central bank.

8. **Which of the following is a liability of a commercial bank?**
(a) Foreign currency holdings.
(b) Reserves.
(c) Loans.
(d) Government of Canada securities.
(e) Deposits.

9. **The reserve ratio is the fraction of a bank's**
(a) deposits that it must hold in the form of currency.
(b) deposits that it holds as reserves either in currency or as deposits at the Bank of Canada.
(c) assets that it holds in the form of reserves.
(d) reserves that it is required to hold in the form of deposits at the Bank of Canada.
(e) None of the above.

10. **Which one of the following is a function of the Bank of Canada?**
(a) Providing banking services for municipal governments.
(b) Acting as a lender of last resort to large corporations.
(c) Controlling the demand for money.
(d) Lending to business firms.
(e) Regulating and supporting financial markets.

11. **The deposits of banks at the Bank of Canada, which constitute one component of bank reserves, appear as**
(a) a liability on the Bank of Canada's balance sheet.
(b) an asset on the Bank of Canada's balance sheet.
(c) a liability on the balance sheet of the banks.
(d) an asset on the balance sheet of the banks.
(e) a liability on the Bank of Canada's balance sheet <u>and</u> as an asset on the balance sheet of the banks.

12. **If Marie Swayne transfers $400 (Canadian) from a Michigan bank to a Toronto Dominion branch in Winnipeg, then the TD branch's balance sheet will show**
(a) only an increase in reserves of $400.
(b) only an increase in deposits of $400.
(c) no change, since the increase in reserves of $400 is cancelled by the increase in deposits of $400.
(d) an increase in reserves and deposits of $400 each.
(e) only an increase in assets of $400.

13. **Which of the following is a liability of the Bank of Canada?**
(a) Government of Canada deposits.
(b) Government of Canada securities.
(c) Advances to banks.
(d) Foreign currency holdings.
(e) None of the above.

14. **If a bank currently holds $600 million in deposits and $40 million in reserves and has a target reserve ratio of 6 percent, this bank has**
(a) excess reserves of $36 million.
(b) a reserve deficiency of $4 million.
(c) target reserves of $2.4 million.
(d) target reserves of $40 million.
(e) excess reserves of $4 million.

Money Creation by the Banking System

Deposit money is the major component of Canada's money supply. This section shows that when one bank receives more reserves, because it attracts *new net deposits* to the banking system, the banking system can increase Canada's money supply by a multiple. If v is the target reserve ratio, the ultimate effect on the deposits of the banking system of a new deposit will be $1/v$ times the new deposit, assuming there is no *cash drain*. If there is a cash drain and c is the ratio of cash to deposits that the public wants to maintain, then the ultimate effect on the deposits of the banking system will be $1/(c + v)$ times the new deposits. When banks lose reserves because of a loss in deposits, the money supply is likely to contract by a multiple providing that there were no excess reserves to begin with.

15. An example of a "new" deposit is when

(a) one bank convinces a customer of another bank to transfer his or her deposit to it.
(b) deposits from banks outside Canada are transferred to Canada.
(c) the federal government transfers a deposit from one bank to another.
(d) a customer of a bank switches money from a chequing to a savings account.
(e) None of the above.

16. A reduction in domestic bank reserves because of payments to foreign banks

(a) always causes a multiple contraction in deposits.
(b) causes a multiple contraction in deposits only if banks maintain the same target reserve ratio at all times.
(c) never affects domestic deposits.
(d) always causes a multiple expansion in domestic deposits.
(e) never affects GDP in the short run.

17. Suppose a bank has a target reserve ratio of 4 percent. Over the next week, the bank unexpectedly loses $10 million of its initial deposits of $100 million. Which of the following statements is true?

(a) To maximize profits, the bank must have been holding initially $40 million in reserves.
(b) After the loss in deposits, target reserves are $4 million.
(c) After the loss in deposits, the bank has deficient reserves.
(d) After the loss in deposits, the bank has excess reserves.
(e) To maximize profits, the bank initially had more than $40 million in reserves.

18. Assuming a fixed target reserve ratio (v) of 10 percent in a banking system and no cash drain out of the banking system, a banking system that receives $1.00 in new deposits can ultimately create an expansion in deposits of

(a) $10.00, which is $1/v$ times $1.00.
(b) 10 cents, which is 10 percent of $1.00.
(c) approximately $1.11, which is determined by the formula $1/(1 - v)$.
(d) $1.10, which is $(1 + v)$ times $1.00.
(e) $0.90, which is $(1 - v)$ times $1.00.

19. The existence of a currency drain from the banking system will, other things being equal,

(a) reduce the ability of the banking system to expand or contract the money supply.
(b) have no effect on the ability of the banking system to contract the money supply.
(c) have no effect on the ability of the banking system to expand the money supply.
(d) increase the ability of the banking system to expand or contract the money supply.
(e) increase the marginal propensity to save.

20. **The multiple expansion of deposits triggered by a $1 new deposit into the banking system will be reduced if**
(a) the cash drain falls at every stage of the process.
(b) every bank increases its target reserve ratio.
(c) every bank lowers its target reserve ratio.
(d) the Bank of Canada reduces its holding of Banks of Canada notes.
(e) None of the above.

21. **Assume that commercial banks do not keep excess reserves and that they all have a target reserve ratio of 5 percent. Suppose that Ashley deposits $100 in Canadian currency in her bank account. As a result, which one of the following statements is correct?**
(a) Bank reserves would increase by $100 and the M1 money supply would increase by $100.
(b) Bank reserves would increase by $100 and the M1 money supply would increase by $2,000.
(c) Bank reserves would decrease by $100 and the M1 money supply would decrease by $100.
(d) Bank reserves would decrease by $100 and the M1 money supply would decrease by $2,000.
(e) None of the above.

The Money Supply

The measurement of the money supply varies with the type of deposits that are included. Three money supply measurements are outlined, the most narrowly defined is called **M1**. M1 (currency plus chequable commercial bank deposits) concentrates on the medium-of-exchange function of money. Assets that fulfill adequately the store-of-value function and are readily converted into a medium of exchange but are not themselves a medium of exchange are called **near money**, and they are included in **M2 and M2+**. Instruments that serve as media of exchange but are not a store of value are usually called *money substitutes*.

22. **Different measures of the money supply include different types of deposits. The narrowly defined money supply, called M1, includes currency and**
(a) term deposits.
(b) chequable deposits at commercial banks.
(c) all deposits at commercial banks.
(d) personal savings and term deposits at all credit unions and trust companies.
(e) foreign currency deposits.

23. **A money substitute is something that serves as a**
(a) store of value.
(b) unit of account.
(c) medium of exchange but not as a store of value.
(d) medium of exchange and also as a store of value.
(e) medium of exchange and a unit of account.

24. **Which of the following would qualify as "near money"?**
(a) A chequable deposit at a commercial bank.
(b) A Bank of Canada note.
(c) A term deposit.
(d) A credit card.
(e) A loonie coin.

SHORT-ANSWER QUESTIONS

1. What are commercial bank reserves? Why do Canadian commercial banks hold them? How do banks react when their actual reserves are less than target values? Why do banks avoid holding excess reserves over prolonged periods?

2. Which of the following might be regarded in Canada as money, as near money, or as neither? Explain your answers briefly.
   (a) One equity share in Toyota (Canada).

   (b) A $10 Bank of Canada note.

   (c) A Canada Savings Bond maturing in 2008.

   (d) A bank note issued by a Saskatchewan bank in 1897.

   (e) A customer's gold bar held in the vault of a Canadian bank for security.

   (f) A term deposit account at a credit union.

   (g) A Visa card issued by the Royal Bank of Canada.

3. Consider a hypothetical bank—the Farmers Bank—that has been serving southern Ontario for more than 100 years. This bank has served well various generations of clients and, as a result, its clients have come to feel a very strong sense of loyalty toward the Farmers Bank. Other banks are also operating in the region, but none has amassed such a large number of satisfied customers.
   (a) Suppose that the largest client of the Farmers Bank goes suddenly bankrupt, and the news is spread that this client was the recipient of close to 50 percent of the bank's loan portfolio. In the absence of a bank deposit insurance system, what would be the most likely reaction of the bank's other clients? Would they still feel very loyal to the Farmers Bank?

(b) Consider the same situation as in part (a) but suppose now that the government-owned Canada Deposit Insurance Corporation provides bank deposit insurance up to $100 000 to each client of the Farmers Bank. What do you think the most likely reaction of the bank's other clients would be now? Would they remain loyal to the Farmers Bank?

(c) What are the benefits of having a deposit insurance system? What are the costs?

(d) Suppose that despite the existence of a deposit insurance system, the Farmers Bank were to fail. Who would be the main losers in this situation?

4. Briefly explain the impact of each of the following events, taken separately, on the bank reserves and the money supply.
   (a) The banks increase their target reserve ratio and continue keeping neither excess nor deficient reserves.

   (b) The banks decrease their target reserve ratio and continue keeping neither excess nor deficient reserves.

   (c) You increase your desired cash-deposit ratio and banks continue keeping neither excess nor deficient reserves.

EXERCISES

1. **The Functions of Money**
   Indicate which of the three functions of money is demonstrated in each of the following transactions. Use the appropriate number: **(1)** medium of exchange, **(2)** store of value, **(3)** unit of account.
   (a) Farmer Stankowski stores currency under his bed mattress.
   (b) Storekeeper Cohen adds up the total sales for the day.
   (c) Plumber O'Hara makes $1000 per week.
   (d) Travelling salesperson Desai pays $100 by cash per week for gasoline.
   (e) The Furfanos purchase by cheque an oriental rug with the thought that it will keep its value for a long time.

2. The Balance Sheet of a Commercial Bank

Can you identify the components of a bank's balance sheet? Confirm your understanding by arranging the following items on the proper side of a commercial bank's balance sheet.

(a)	Demand deposits	2 000 000
(b)	Savings and time deposits	4 080 000
(c)	Currency in vaults	60 000
(d)	Deposits at the Bank of Canada	1 000 000
(e)	Loans to the public	4 000 000
(f)	Security holdings (Canadian government, provincial, municipal, and other)	1 500 000
(g)	Bank building and fixtures	360 000
(h)	Shareholders' equity	920 000
(i)	Foreign currency assets	80 000

Assets	**Liabilities**

3. The Effect of International Capital Outflows on the Banking System

This exercise deals with a *multiple contraction of deposits* triggered by a loss in domestic deposits to foreign banks abroad. Suppose that Bank A, a Canadian bank, begins with the T-account shown here. The target reserve ratio is assumed to be 10 percent for all domestic banks, and there is no cash drain by the public. Joe Doe, a holder of a deposit in Bank A, withdraws $1000 and deposits this amount in a commercial bank in a foreign country (an example of an international capital outflow). Thus, $1000 has been taken out of the Canadian banking system.

Bank A (initial situation)		**Bank A (after the withdrawal)**	
Reserves: $10 000	Deposits: $100 000	Reserves: $	Deposits: $
Loans: $90 000		Loans:	

(a) Initially, what were Bank A's target reserves? Did it have excess reserves initially?

(b) Show the immediate effect of the withdrawal from Bank A.

(c) What is the status of Bank A's reserves now?

(d) Bank A reacts by calling in a loan that it had made to Mary Poulos equal to the amount of its reserve deficiency. Mary repays the loan by writing a cheque on her account in Bank B, another Canadian bank that also has a fixed target reserve ratio of 10 percent. Bank B's initial T-account is shown below. Fill in the T-accounts for the effects of Bank A's receiving the payment from Mary and of Bank B's loss of Mary's deposit.

Bank B (initial situation)		**Bank B (after losing Mary's deposit)**	
Reserves: $ 5 000	Deposits: $50 000	Reserves: $	Deposits: $
Loans: $45 000		Loans:	

Bank A (after receiving loan repayment)	
Reserves: $	Deposits: $
Loans:	

(e) After this transaction, does Bank A have deficient reserves? Does Bank B?

(f) In fact, Bank B has a deficiency of reserves. It reacts by calling in a loan made to Peter Chang equal to the amount of the deficiency. Peter cashes in a deposit that he held in Bank C; that is, Bank C loses a deposit and Peter repays Bank B. Bank C's initial situation is shown next; its target reserve ratio is also 10 percent. Fill in the T-accounts for the effects of Bank B's receiving the loan repayment and Bank C's loss of Peter's deposit.

Bank C (initial situation)		**Bank C (after losing Peter's deposit)**	
Reserves: $ 7 000	Deposits: $70 000	Reserves: $	Deposits: $
Loans: $63 000		Loans:	

Bank B (after receiving loan repayment)	
Reserves: $	Deposits: $
Loans:	

(g) After this transaction, does Bank B have deficient reserves? Does Bank C?

(h) After this transaction, the reduction in the money supply has been Joe's original withdrawal plus $______________ in other deposits. Loans have been reduced by $______________.

(i) Assuming a 10 percent target ratio for all banks, the process will continue until the total reduction in the money supply will be $______________. The total reduction in loans will be $______________.

4. **The Multiple Expansion of the Money Supply**
Suppose that a foreign company withdraws money from its account in a foreign country, buys \$1 million of Canadian currency, and deposits this sum into the Canadian banking system. This is an example of an international capital inflow. The target reserve ratio for each Canadian bank is assumed to be 8 percent, and there is no currency drain from the banking system. The initial situation in the Canadian banking system is depicted as follows:

All Banks			
Reserves:	\$ 72 million	Deposits:	\$900 million
Loans:	\$728 million		
Securities:	\$100 million		

(a) According to the initial scenario, target reserves are \$_____________ and excess reserves are \$_____________.

(b) After the \$1 million deposit, target reserves are \$_____________ and excess reserves are \$_____________.

(c) Assuming that all excess reserves are used to expand loans, the final (increase, decrease) in the money supply will be times the new \$1 million deposit, which is equal to_____________.

(d) The final (increase, decrease) in loans will be \$_____________.

5. **Deposit Creation with Some Complicating Factors**
Star Bank, a Canadian commercial bank that currently has \$300 million in deposits, has been operating with a target reserve ratio of 8 percent. Judy Kupferschmidt has just inherited the equivalent of \$1 million Canadian from a relative living in Florida and deposits this sum in Star Bank.

(a) If Star Bank continued to operate on an 8 percent target reserve basis, what is the magnitude of its excess reserves after Judy's deposit? [Assume Star Bank had no initial excess reserves]

(b) If other Canadian banks also had 8 percent target reserve ratios and there was no cash drain from the banking system, what might be the final change in the Canadian money supply?

(c) Suppose that Star Bank considers the risk of extending new loans from the excess reserves created by Judy's deposit to be too high. It decides to hold all of Judy's deposits in reserves. What is its new target reserve ratio, approximately? Will a multiple expansion in bank deposits occur?

(d) Assume that the scenario in (a) holds; Judy deposits \$1 million in Star Bank. All Canadian banks, including Star, have a constant target reserve ratio of 8 percent. However, the Canadian public normally holds 2 percent of its money holdings in the form of currency (Bank of Canada notes and coins). If all banks used all of their excess reserves to extend loans, what would be the maximum possible change in the Canadian money supply?

6. **The Money Supply and the Money Multiplier**

You are given the following information about the banking system of a hypothetical economy. The commercial banks have deposits of $300 million from the public. Their reserves are $15 million, two-thirds of which are in deposits with the central bank. The total currency in the economy is $30 million.

(a) What is the amount of currency in circulation (i.e., held by the public)?

(b) What is the money supply?

(c) What is the money multiplier?

(d) Set out the consolidated balance sheet of all commercial banks. Supply any missing numbers using your knowledge of the fact that total assets equal total liabilities.

7. **The Banks' Reserves and the Money Supply**

Suppose the Canadian banking system is characterized as follows: 1) there is only one commercial bank; 2) the target reserve ratio is 10 percent against chequable deposits; 3) the commercial bank does not hold any reserves above the desired level; 4) the public's currency–deposit ratio is 15 percent. Considering only the M1 definition of money supply, answer the following questions:

(a) What is the value of the money multiplier?

(b) Now assume that the public already has any cash it wants, and that any extra cash is re-deposited in the individuals' chequing accounts. For any additional change in the bank's reserves, what is the value of the money multiplier now?

(c) Suppose that the bank's deposits at the Bank of Canada increase by $100 million. What is the change in the money supply? In your answer, show all the changes in the balance sheets of the public and the commercial bank.

EXTENSION EXERCISE

E1. **Target Reserve Ratio, Currency-Deposit Ratio, and the Money Multiplier**

The banking system of a hypothetical economy consists of only one commercial bank, and this commercial bank does not hold any reserves above the desired level. The public also holds money in the desired ratio between currency and chequable deposits. The balance sheets (T-accounts) of the public and this commercial bank look as follows:

Public				Commercial Bank			
Currency	150	Loans	800	Currency	100	Deposits	1000
Deposits	1000	Equity	1700	Deposit at B of C	100	Equity	200
Other assets	1350			Loans	800		
				Other assets	200		

[*Note:* Public "Deposits" refers to chequable deposits only, and "Deposit at B of C" represents the deposits that this commercial bank holds at the Bank of Canada.]

Given the information in the above balance sheets and considering only the M1 definition of money supply, answer the following questions:

(a) What is the value of the bank's target reserve ratio?

(b) What is the public's desired currency–deposit ratio?

(c) What is the value of the money multiplier?

(d) Suppose that the bank's deposits at the Bank of Canada increase by $100 million as a result of the bank selling $100 worth of government bonds to the Bank of Canada. Show all the changes in the balance sheets of the public and the commercial bank—i.e., show the new final values for all items.

Public		Commercial Bank	
Currency	Loans	Currency	Deposits
Deposits	Equity	Deposit at B of C	Equity
Other assets		Loans	
		Other assets	

(e) What is the final change in the bank's reserves?

(f) What is the final change in the money supply?

ADDITIONAL MULTIPLE-CHOICE QUESTIONS

Questions 1 through 4 refer to the following information about a banking system. Make the following assumptions:

(a) There is a banking system in which each bank has a fixed target reserve ratio of 5 percent.
(b) There is no currency drain from the banking system, and all banks are assumed to hold no excess reserves for a prolonged period of time.
(c) Banks experiencing excess (deficient) reserves respond by increasing (decreasing) loans.
(d) The current status of the balance sheet of all banks is as follows:

All Banks

Assets		Liabilities	
Reserves:	$________	Deposits:	$300 million
Loans:	$270 million		
Securities:	$________		

***1. If all banks initially had no excess reserves,**
(a) the reserves of the banks must have been $30 million.
(b) the holdings of securities by the banks must have been $15 million.
(c) the reserves of the banks must have been 5 percent of loans, or $13.5 million.
(d) the reserves of the banks must have been $300 million.
(e) the reserves of the banks must have been 5 percent of securities.

2. If all banks initially had $16 million of actual reserves, then
(a) excess reserves are $15 million.
(b) the banks have $1 million in deficient reserves (negative excess reserves).
(c) excess reserves are $1 million.
(d) target reserves are equal to actual reserves.
(e) the banks must borrow from the Bank of Canada.

***3. Assuming that the banking system begins with no excess reserves, a loss of $1 million of deposits from the system will ultimately lead to**
(a) a reduction in the money supply of $20 million.
(b) a reduction in the money supply of $500 000.
(c) an increase in the money supply of $20 million.
(d) deposit liabilities in the banking system of $280 million.
(e) an increase in the money supply of $19 million.

4. **Assuming that the banking system begins with no excess reserves, a gain of $1 million of deposits will ultimately lead to**
   (a) increased deposits of $19 million.
   (b) increased loans of $20 million.
   (c) increased loans of $1 million.
   (d) a $5 million increase in the money supply.
   (e) increased deposits of $20 million.

Questions 5 to 7 are based on the following monetary aggregates (billions of dollars).

Chequable deposits in commercial banks	93.9
Saving deposits at commercial banks	406.5
Currency outside banks	36.7
Deposits at non-bank financial institutions	125.0
Money market mutual funds	113.1

5. **The value of M1 at this date was (in billions)**
   (a) 93.9.
   (b) 36.7.
   (c) 537.1.
   (d) 775.3.
   (e) 130.6.

*6. **The value of M2 at this date was (in billions)**
   (a) 93.9.
   (b) 537.1.
   (c) 238.1.
   (d) 348.1.
   (e) 775.3.

7. **The difference(s) between M2+ and M2 at this date (in billions) was (were)**
   (a) 36.7.
   (b) 125.0.
   (c) 406.5.
   (d) 113.1.
   (e) Both (b) and (d).

Questions 8 to 16 differ in their assumptions about the values of v and c in a banking system. Assume initially that the banking system in a particular country has no excess reserves before it receives $50 million in new deposits. For each question, determine the final change in deposits.

8. **If $v = 0.10$ and $c = 0.10$, then the final change in the money supply will be**
   (a) +$500 million.
   (b) +$5 million.
   (c) +$55.6 million.
   (d) +$250 million.
   (e) +$62.5 million.

*9. **If $v = 0.10$ and $c = 0.05$, then the final change in the money supply will be**
   (a) +$500 million.
   (b) +$333.3 million.
   (c) +$1 billion.
   (d) +$58.8 million.
   (e) +10 billion.

10. **If $v = 0.10$ and $c = 0.15$, then the final change in the money supply will be**
   (a) +$200 million.
   (b) +$66.7 million.
   (c) +500 million.
   (d) –$1 billion.
   (e) +$333.3 million.

11. By comparing your answers to questions 8, 9, and 10, you have observed that when the cash drain increases, the final change in the money supply from an increase in new deposits

(a) decreases.
(b) is not affected.
(c) reverts from an overall expansion to an overall contraction.
(d) increases.
(e) depends on the difference between v and c.

12. If $v = 0.05$ and $c = 0.10$, then the final change in the money supply will be

(a) –$1 billion.
(b) +$333.3 million.
(c) +$58.8 million.
(d) +$10 billion.
(e) +500 million.

13. If $v = 0.20$ and $c = 0.10$, then the final change in the money supply will be

(a) +$250 million.
(b) +$500 million.
(c) +$71.4 million.
(d) +$166.7 million.
(e) +$2.5 billion.

14. By comparing your answers to questions 8, 12, and 13, you have learned that when the target reserve ratio increases, the final change in the money supply from an increase in new deposits

(a) decreases.
(b) is not affected.
(c) reverts from an overall expansion to an overall contraction.
(d) increases.
(e) depends on the difference between the cash drain ratio and the target reserve ratio.

***15. If $c = 0.1$, then chequable deposits as a share of total money supply is**

(a) 9.1 percent.
(b) 10.0 percent.
(c) 90.0 percent.
(d) 90.9 percent.
(e) None of the above.

***16. If $c = 0.2$ and the money supply increases by $100 million, the public's holding of currency will increase by ____________ and chequable deposits by ____________.**

(a) $20 million / $80 million
(b) $80 million / $20 million
(c) $16.7 million / $83.3 million
(d) $83.3 million / $16.7 million
(e) None of the above.

Questions 17 and 18 refer to the following information. Suppose that total currency in the economy is $25, money supply is $100, currency held by the banks is $10. All figures are in billions.

***17. The public's deposits at the commercial banks are**

(a) $100.
(b) $90.
(c) $85.
(d) $75.
(e) None of the above.

***18. If $v = 0.2$, the deposits of the commercial banks at the Bank of Canada are**
(a) $20.
(b) $17.
(c) $10.
(d) $7.
(e) None of the above.

***19. Suppose that the target reserve ratio in the banking system is 20 percent, there is no cash drain, and all excess reserves are lent out. If Sam deposits a $100 bill in his bank account, then the money supply (M1) will**
(a) decrease by $100.
(b) increase by $100.
(c) remain unchanged.
(d) increase by $400.
(e) increase by $500.

Questions 20 to 23 test your knowledge of balance sheet entries for various bank transactions. Assume for simplicity that a bank's balance sheet has only three items: reserves, the combination of loans and securities, and deposits to customers. A (+) refers to an increase and a (–) refers to a decrease. Remember, a balance sheet must always balance. Consider only the initial changes.

***20. If you deposited the total amount of your paycheque of $2000 at your bank, the bank's balance sheet would change by**
(a) +$2000 in deposits only.
(b) +$2000 in loans only, since you are lending the bank $2000.
(c) +$2000 in deposits and +$2000 in loans and securities.
(d) +$2000 in deposits and +$2000 in reserves.
(e) +$2000 in reserves only.

21. If a bank sells $2000 in securities to the Bank of Canada to replenish its reserves, the bank's balance sheet would change by
(a) –$2000 in loans and securities and –$2000 in deposits.
(b) –$2000 in loans and securities and –$2000 in reserves.
(c) +$2000 in reserves only.
(d) +$2000 in loans and securities and +$2000 in reserves.
(e) –$2000 in loans and securities and +$2000 in reserves.

***22. If a bank makes a loan of $2000 to Harry Gupta, a local restaurant owner, and credits $2000 to his chequing account, the bank's balance sheet would change by**
(a) –$2000 in reserves and +2000 in deposits.
(b) +$2000 in loans and securities and +2000 in deposits.
(c) –$2000 in reserves and +2000 in loans in securities.
(d) +$2000 in loans and securities only.
(e) +$2000 in deposits only.

***23. If a commercial bank sells $2000 of its securities to the Bank of Canada and receives $2000 of reserves in the Bank of Canada, the commercial bank's balance sheet would change by**
(a) +$2000 in loans and securities and +$2000 in deposits.
(b) –$2000 in loans and securities and +$2000 in deposits.
(c) –$2000 in loans and securities and +$2000 in reserves.
(d) –$2000 in loans and securities only.
(e) None of the above.

SOLUTIONS

Chapter Review

1.(b) **2.**(c) **3.**(a) **4.**(e) **5.**(b) **6.**(d) **7.**(d) **8.**(e) **9.**(b) **10.**(e) **11.**(e) **12.**(d) **13.**(a) **14.**(e) **15.**(b) **16.**(b) **17.**(c) **18.**(a) **19.**(a) **20.**(b) **21.**(e) **22.**(b) **23.**(c) **24.**(c)

Short-Answer Questions

1. Bank reserves consist of vault currency plus deposits with the Bank of Canada. Reserves are held by the banks to satisfy the daily currency needs of their customers and to protect themselves against bank runs. If banks have too few reserves they can borrow from the Bank of Canada at a cost. Actual reserves are what appear on the bank's balance sheet. Target reserves are the amount of reserves they want to hold to satisfy their customers' needs and to protect themselves against cash runs. If actual reserves are less than target reserves, they will have to liquidate assets, reduce outstanding loans by reducing their deposit liabilities, or borrow temporarily from the Bank of Canada. Banks avoid holding excess reserves for prolonged periods since they forgo profits. Reserves yield no financial return for banks.

2. (a) neither; it is neither a medium of exchange nor a unit of account.
(b) money; fiat money issued by the Bank of Canada.
(c) near money; it is easily convertible to money.
(d) neither; once money but now a collector's item.
(e) neither and considered by some to be a good store of value.
(f) near money because it is easily convertible to money.
(g) neither; a Visa card is a money substitute.

3. (a) The Farmers Bank will incur very large losses equal to close to 50 percent of its loan portfolio. This means that the assets of the bank will be significantly reduced while its liabilities will remain unchanged. The bank, therefore, will not be able to cover all its liabilities—including its clients' deposits. Knowing the bank is overexposed, clients will rush to withdraw their money since those who come late will not be able to recover it at all. Loyalty, therefore, appears to be a virtue limited for good times.
(b) If deposit insurance were in place, then clients would not be too worried that they would not be able to recover their money if the bank were to fail—unless their deposits were in excess of $100 000. Therefore, most likely most clients would remain loyal to the Farmers Bank and not transfer their deposits to another bank.
(c) The main benefit of having deposit insurance is that the possibility of a run on a bank is reduced—thus giving an opportunity to the bank to recover from bad times. Another important benefit is that if a bank were to fail, depositors would not lose their money. The main cost is implicit in the previous benefit—i.e., since a client will not lose his/her deposit under any circumstances, he/she will be less careful choosing a good, prudent bank. At the same time, knowing that the chances of experiencing a run are minimal or nil, a bank would be less risk averse than otherwise—thus increasing the possibility of becoming overexposed.
(d) If the bank were to fail, then the bank's assets would not be sufficient to cover all liabilities—particularly clients' deposits. Therefore, the Canada Deposit Insurance Corporation would have to pay the banks' clients for their deposits up to $100 000. The losers here—in addition to the bank's shareholders—would be the taxpayers who would foot the bill.

4. (a) If the bank increases its target reserve ratio, then the reserves it is actually holding will not be sufficient. Therefore, it will recall loans in order to reduce deposits until the ratio of reserves to deposits is equal to the new target level. Therefore, the bank reserves will not change, while the money supply will decrease.
(b) If the bank decreases its target reserve ratio, then the reserves it is actually holding will be in excess of the target. Therefore, it will make new loans while trying to reduce the excess reserves, and by doing so it will increase deposits. As deposits increase, the reserve ratio decreases and this process will continue until the new target reserve ratio is attained. Therefore, the bank reserves will not change, while the money supply will increase.

(c) If I want to have a larger cash–deposit ratio, I will withdraw money from my account in order to have more cash at hand. The bank's reserves will decrease by the cash I'm withdrawing—that is, the bank's currency reserves will be reduced by this amount. This will cause the bank to have deficient reserves, and thus the bank will recall loans—and deposits will decrease thus reducing the money supply. Therefore, bank reserves will decrease, and money supply will decrease as well.

Exercises

1. **(a)** 2; **(b)** 1 and 3; **(c)** 3; **(d)** 1; **(e)** 1, and the rug serves as function 2.

2.

Currency in vaults	$60 000	Demand deposits	$2 000 000
Deposits in Bank of Canada	$1 000 000	Savings deposits	$4 080 000
Loans to public	$4 000 000		
Security holdings	$1 500 000		
Bank buildings and fixtures	$360 000		
Foreign currency assets	$80 000	Shareholders' equity	$920 000
	$7 000 000		$7 000 000

3. **(a)** Target reserves = $10 000; no.
(b) Deposits –$1000 to $99 000; reserves –$1000 to $9000.
(c) Target reserves =$9900; actual reserves =$9000; hence, its reserves are deficient by $900.
(d) Bank A: reserves +$900, loans –$900; Bank B: reserves –$900 to $4100; deposits –$900 to $49 100.
(e) Bank A does not, but Bank B has a deficiency of $810.
(f) Bank B: reserves +$810, loans –$810; Bank C: reserves –$810 to $6190; deposits –$810 to $69 190.
(g) No, but Bank C has a deficiency of $729.
(h) –$900 + (–$810) + (–$729) = –$2439; loans down by $1710.
(i) $10 000; $9000.

4. **(a)** $72 million (0.08 × $900 million); 0.
(b) $72.08 million (0.08 × $901 million); $920 000.
(c) increase; 12.5 (1/0.08); $12.5 million.
(d) increase; $11.5 million (12.5 – 1.0).

5. **(a)** $920 000.
(b) $12.5 million (= 1/0.08 × $1 million).
(c) Its initial reserve holdings were $24 million. After Judy's deposit, reserves are $25 million and total deposits are $301 million. Therefore, the new target reserve ratio is 8.3 percent. No; Star has no excess reserves to lend out. Thus, no other bank receives new additional reserves.
(d) $10 million increase. This is obtained by multiplying $1 million by 1/(0.08 + 0.02). The value 0.08 is the target reserve ratio and 0.02 is the cash drain.

6. Let's call M the money supply, CU the total currency in the economy, CU_P the currency held by the public, CU_B the currency held by the banks, D the public's chequable deposits, D_{CB} the deposits of the banks at the central bank, and R the total bank reserves. Recall that $M = CU_P + D$, $R = CU_B + D_{CB}$, and $CU = CU_P + CU_B$.
(a) Since R totals $15 million and two-third of this is kept in D_{CB}, D_{CB} totals $10 million and the remaining $5 million is kept in CU_B. Therefore, if the banks are holding $5 million in CU_B and the CU is $30 million, then CU_P is the remaining $25 million.
(b) $M = CU_P + D$ = $25 million + $300 = $325.
(c) $mm = 1 / (c + v)$, where $c = CU_P / D = 25 / 300 = 1 / 12$ and $v = R / D = 15 / 300 = 1 / 20$. Therefore, $c + v = 1/12 + 1/20 = 2/15$ and $mm = 1/(2/15) = 15/2 = 7.5$.
(d)

All Commercial Banks

CU_B	5	D	300
D_{CB}	10		
Loans	275		

7. Let's call M the money supply, CU the total currency in the economy, CU_P the currency held by the public, CU_B the currency held by the banks, D the public's chequable deposits, D_{CB} the deposits of the banks at the central bank, and R the total bank reserves. Recall that $M = CU_P + D$, $R = CU_B + D_{CB}$, and $CU = CU_P + CU_B$.
   (a) $mm = 1 / (c + v) = 1 / (0.15 + 0.10) = 1 / 0.25 = 4$.
   (b) If $c = 0$ for any additional change in the bank's reserves, then $mm = 1 / v = 1 / 0.10 = 10$.
   (c) $\Delta M = mm \, \Delta R = 10 \, \Delta R$ and $\Delta R = \Delta CU_B + \Delta D_{CB}, = +100$.
   Therefore, $\Delta M = 10 (+100) = +1000$.
   Recall that $\Delta M = \Delta CU_P + \Delta D$ and $\Delta CU_P = 0$, and therefore $\Delta M = \Delta D = +1000$.

Note that the bank will increase loans by $1000 in order to increase D by $1000.

Public				Commercial Bank			
ΔD	+1000	Δ Loans	+1000	ΔD_{CB}	+100	ΔD	+1000
				Δ Loans	+1000		
				Δ Other assets	−100		

Extension Exercise

E1. (a) The target reserve ratio is equal to the ratio between bank's desired reserves and public's deposits. The balance sheet of the commercial bank shows that the bank's desired reserves are $200—i.e., $100 in cash and $100 in deposits at the Bank of Canada. The balance sheets also show that the public's deposits are $1000. Therefore, the target reserve ratio is $v = \$200 / \$1000 = 0.2$ or 20 percent.

(b) The public's currency–deposit ratio is equal to the ratio between public's currency holdings and chequable deposits. The public's balance sheet shows that the public is holding $100 in currency and $1000 in chequable deposits, and thus the currency–deposit ratio is $c = \$100 / \$1000 = 0.10$ or 10 percent.

(c) The money multiplier is equal to $1 / (c + v) = 1 / (0.1 + 0.15) = 1 / 0.25 = 4$.

(d) If the bank's deposits at the Bank of Canada increase by $100 million, then the value of other assets—which includes the value of any bank's holdings of government bonds—will decrease by this amount.

The bank is now holding excess reserves and will start the process of money creation by increasing loans to the public—the money supply will increase by the end of the multiplying process by $400 since the value of the multiplier is 4. How much of this $400 will represent an increase in the public's chequable deposits and how much an increase in the public's currency holding?

From (c) above we know that $c = 0.10$—i.e., Currency / Deposits = 0.10 and thus Currency = 0.10 Deposits. Therefore,

$$\Delta \text{ Currency} = 0.10 \, \Delta \text{ Deposits}. \tag{1}$$

We also know that $\Delta M = \Delta$ Currency + Δ Deposits and $\Delta M = \$400$—i.e.,

$$\$400 = \Delta \text{ Currency} + \Delta \text{ Deposits}. \tag{2}$$

Substituting (1) into (2) we obtain:

$$\$400 = 0.10 \, \Delta \text{ Deposits} + \Delta \text{ Deposits} = 1.10 \, \Delta \text{ Deposits}.$$

And thus Δ Deposits = $400 / 1.10 = $363.6 and Δ Currency = 0.10 ($363.6) = $36.3.

Note that since the public holds $36.3 more in currency—i.e., the public has withdrawn $36.3 in currency from the commercial bank—the bank is holding $36.3 less in currency in its vault.

Public				Commercial Bank			
Currency	186.3	Loans	1200.0	Currency	63.7	Deposits	1363.7
Deposits	1363.7	Equity	1700.0	Deposit at B of C	200.0	Equity	200.0
Other assets	1350.0			Loans	1200.0		
				Other assets	100.0		

(e) Recall that the bank's reserves consist of the currency it holds in its vault and deposits it has at the Bank of Canada. Therefore, currency held by the bank has decreased from $100 to $63.7 while deposits at the Bank of Canada have increased from $100 to $200, and thus the bank's reserves have increased from $200 to $263.7.

(f) We have already seen that the money supply would increased by $400—i.e., from $1150 to $1550—i.e., currency held by the public increased from $150 to $186.3 and the public's chequable deposits increased from $1000 to $1363.7.

Additional Multiple-Choice Questions

1.(b) **2.**(c) **3.**(d) **4.**(e) **5.**(e) **6.**(b) **7.**(e) **8.**(d) **9.**(b) **10.**(a) **11.**(a) **12.**(b) **13.**(d) **14.**(a) **15.**(d) **16.**(c) **17.**(c) **18.**(d) **19.**(d) **20.**(d) **21.**(e) **22.**(b) **23.**(c)

Explanations for the Asterisked Multiple-Choice Questions

1.(b) This is a tricky question. A bank's balance sheet must always balance. If the bank was holding no excess reserves, then its reserve holdings are 5 percent of $300 million of deposits (= $15 million). Combined with $270 million in loans, security holdings must also have been $15 million. The left-hand side sums to $300 million, as does the right-hand side of the balance sheet.

3.(d) Since there is no cash drain, the money expansion equation [1/*v*] implies that deposits decrease eventually by $20 million.

6.(b) M2 = M1 + $406.5 = $130.6 + $406.5 = $537.1 billion.

9.(b) $+50 million times 1/(.10 + .05) = $333.3 million.

15.(d) Let's call CU_P the currency held by the public and D the value of chequable deposits.
Given that $c = CU_P / D = 0.1 \rightarrow CU_P = 0.1\ D$.
And since $M = CU_P + D = 0.1\ D + D = 1.1\ D \rightarrow M = 1.1\ D \rightarrow D / M = 1 / 1.1 = 0.909$ or 90.9 percent.

16.(c) Given that $c = \Delta\ CU_P / \Delta\ D = 0.2 \rightarrow \Delta\ CU_P = 0.2\ \Delta\ D$.
And since $\Delta\ M = \Delta\ CU_P + \Delta\ D = 0.2\ \Delta\ D + \Delta\ D = 1.2\ \Delta\ D \rightarrow \$100 = 1.2\ \Delta\ D \rightarrow \Delta\ D = \$100 / 1.2 =$ $83.3 and $\Delta\ CU_P = \$100 - \$83.3 = \$16.7$.

17.(c) Let's call CU the total currency in the economy, CU_P the currency held by the public, CU_B the currency held by the commercial banks, and D the value of chequable deposits.
Since $CU = CU_P + CU_B$, $CU_P = CU - CU_B = \$25 - \$10 = \$15$.
Therefore, since $M = CU_P + D \rightarrow D = M - CU_P \rightarrow D = \$100 - \$15 = \$85$.

18.(d) If $v = 0.2$ and since $D = \$85$, bank's reserves are 0.2 ($85) = $17.
Bank reserves are equal to CU_B + deposits at the Bank of Canada, and thus
Deposits at the Bank of Canada = Bank reserves – $CU_B = \$17 - \$10 = \$7$.

19.(d) The money multiplier is $1 / v = 1 / 0.2 = 5$. A new deposit of $100 will cause total deposits by $500, and since $\Delta\ M = \Delta\ CU_P + \Delta\ D = -100 + 500 = +400$.

20.(d) The bank's assets (reserves) increase by $2000. Its liabilities (deposits) increase by $2000.

22.(b) The bank's loans increase by $2000 while its liabilities (deposits) increase by $2000.

23.(c) Only items on the bank's asset side change. Bank securities fall by $2000 but reserves increase by $2000. The net effect is zero.

CHAPTER 28

MONEY, INTEREST RATES, AND ECONOMIC ACTIVITY

LO

LEARNING OBJECTIVES

In this chapter you will learn

1 why the price of a bond is inversely related to the market interest rate.

2 how the demand for money is related to the interest rate, the price level, and real GDP.

3 how monetary equilibrium determines the interest rate in the short run.

4 about the transmission mechanism of monetary policy.

5 the difference between the short-run and long-run effects of monetary policy.

6 when monetary policy is most effective in influencing real GDP in the short run.

CHAPTER OVERVIEW

This chapter focuses on how money affects the economy. The chapter begins by explaining the relationships among the **present value** of a bond, its **market price**, and its **yield**. Also, the textbook explains the relationship between market interest rates and bond yields.

An important chain of causation is as follows: a decrease in the money supply causes an initial disequilibrium in the money and bond markets, which leads to an increase in the equilibrium level of the interest rate. A higher (real) interest rate causes a decrease in desired investment expenditure (a movement up the **desired investment demand curve, I^D**) as well as in desired consumption expenditure. As a result, the aggregate demand curve shifts leftward. The chapter assumes that real and nominal interest rates are the same since the expectation of inflation is zero.

In an open economy, there is another channel by which monetary shocks influence *P* and *Y* in the short run. A decrease in the money supply will increase domestic interest rates. Higher domestic interest rates attract more international capital (and generate lower international capital outflows). The exchange rate depreciates (the domestic currency appreciates) and hence net exports fall. The decline in net exports shifts the *AD* curve to the left. Hence, in the short run, real GDP and the price level fall.

The chapter discusses three reasons for holding money. The relationship between the desired money holdings, on the one hand, and the interest rate, level of real GDP, and price level, on the other hand, is called the **demand for money function (M_D)**. Bonds represent the other asset that can be held in one's wealth portfolio.

The chapter concludes by demonstrating the short-run and long-run effects of a change of the money supply on real income and the price level in an *AD*–*AS* framework. The strength of monetary forces with respect to the quantitative impact on *Y* and *P* depends on the response of the quantity demanded for money and the quantity change in desired investment to changes in the interest rate. Moreover, the slope of the *AS* curve determines the extent by which a shift in the *AD* curve (caused by a change in the money supply) changes *Y* and *P* in the short run. In the long run, money is neutral; that is, money shocks influence only the price level.

HINTS AND TIPS

The following may help you to avoid some of the most common errors on examinations.

✓ Learn how to calculate the present value of a bond from information about its coupon rate, its maturity, the sequence of the annual cash flows including the repayment of principal, and the interest rate. Know how a change in each of these factors affects present value. The negative relationship between the interest rate and present value is a critical concept for you to understand.

✓ Understand the meaning of monetary equilibrium and the adjustments that occur to resolve disequilibrium situations. An excess demand for money is said to exist if, *at a particular interest rate,* quantity demanded for money is greater than quantity supplied. Hence, interest rates will rise and the price of bonds will fall.

✓ Review textbook Figures 28-6 and 28-7, which outline the various elements of the monetary transmission mechanism in a closed and an open economy. In an open economy, the transmission mechanism includes the effects of changes in the domestic interest rate on the exchange rate and a country's net exports.

CHAPTER REVIEW

Understanding Bonds

For simplicity, the chapter assumes that all wealth is held in either money or bonds. Money, as a medium of exchange, has a low or zero rate of return. In our model we assume that money has a zero rate of return. Bonds are not media of exchange, but they are interest-bearing assets. It is important for you to understand that the present value (or equilibrium market price) of a bond is negatively related to its yield. Reread *Applying Economic Concepts 28-1* to understand how bond prices and yields are affected by risk, the bond's maturity date, and coupon rates.

1. In equilibrium, the market price of a bond will be

(a) the present value of the income stream it produces.
(b) unaffected by changes in the interest rate.
(c) the sum of the annual returns, compounded to their value at the end of the asset's useful life.
(d) positively related to its yield.
(e) the same as its face value.

2. A rise in the market price of a bond with a specified income stream

(a) has no effect on the bond's yield.
(b) is equivalent to a reduction in the present value of the bond.
(c) is equivalent to an increase in the bond's rate of return.
(d) will not affect the present value of the bond.
(e) implies a decrease in the bond's yield.

3. A bond promises to pay $1000 one year from now. At an interest rate of 8 percent, the bond's present value is $__________. If the interest rate were 10 percent, the market value of the bond would be $__________.

(a) $926; $909
(b) $1000; $1000
(c) $920; $900
(d) $1080; $1100
(e) $556; $500

4. **If the price of a bond is below the bond's present value, then**
(a) we expect the bond price to fall further.
(b) the lack of demand causes the bond price to fall.
(c) the abundance of demand causes the bond price to rise.
(d) the bond's present value falls.
(e) None of the above.

5. **The present value of a bond that matures in two years and has a face value of $500, an annual coupon rate of 9 percent, and a yield of 11 percent is**
(a) $450.45. (b) $442.33.
(c) $590. (d) $482.87.
(e) $73.05.

The Demand for Money

The amount of money balances everyone in the economy wishes to hold is called the *demand for money*. The opportunity cost of holding money balances is the interest rate that could have been earned if wealth had been held in bonds. The total demand for money balances holding has three components: the transactions demand, the precautionary demand, and the speculative demand. The total demand for money is negatively related to the interest rate and is positively related to the price level and real GDP. If the interest rate falls, the quantity of money demanded increases (and the demand for bonds falls). This is represented by a movement down the money demand curve. If GDP or the price level change, the money demand curve (M_D) shifts.

6. **The opportunity cost to firms and households of holding money balances is**
(a) zero, since all economic transactions require the use of money.
(b) the forgone interest that could have been earned on other assets.
(c) low when interest rates are high.
(d) the purchasing power of that money balance.
(e) zero, since the Bank of Canada pays no interest for holding commercial bank reserves.

7. **The desired amount of money for transaction balances**
(a) varies positively with national income.
(b) varies positively with interest rates.
(c) varies negatively with the value of national income.
(d) varies negatively with the price level.
(e) will be zero if there are interest-bearing assets.

8. **Precautionary balances increase if**
(a) business transactions became more uncertain.
(b) interest rates increased.
(c) people were expecting securities prices to rise.
(d) national income fell.
(e) the market prices of bonds fall.

9. **Firms' speculative demand for money balances**
(a) applies to bonds but not to other interest-earning assets.
(b) varies positively with national income.
(c) assumes that the opportunity cost of holding cash balances is zero.
(d) suggests that firms hold money in order to avoid or reduce the risk associated with increases in future interest rates and future decreases in bond prices.
(e) deals with the uncertainty of future payments and receipts.

10. An increase in the price level

(a) decreases the demand for money.
(b) increases the demand for money.
(c) has no effect on the demand for money.
(d) causes a movement up the M_D curve.
(e) causes a movement down the money demand curve.

11. Which of following causes the M_D curve to shift up and to the right?

(a) An increase in the interest rate.
(b) A decrease in the price level.
(c) A decease in the interest rate.
(d) An increase in GDP.
(e) A recessionary gap.

Monetary Equilibrium and National Income

This section outlines the monetary transmission mechanism of monetary shocks on *Y* and *P* in the short run and the long run. First, you need to understand the condition for monetary equilibrium. Simply stated, monetary equilibrium occurs when the demand for money is equal to the money supply: the intersection of the M_D function and the money supply curve (M_S). The money supply curve is vertical; the textbook assumes that the supply of money does not depend on the interest rate. Monetary equilibrium determines the equilibrium interest rate. In a disequilibrium situation where the demand for money exceeds supply (an excess demand situation), wealth holders sell bonds in order to obtain more money. By doing so, the price of bonds falls and the yield rate on bonds (and the market interest rate) increases. The equilibrium level of the interest rate changes if either the M_D curve or the money supply curve shifts. The money supply curve shifts leftward if the central bank decreases reserves in the banking system, or the commercial banks decide to reduce lending.

A monetary expansion causes the equilibrium rate of interest to fall. There are two possible channels by which the monetary expansion affects real GDP and the price level in the short run. First, the quantity of desired investment and desired consumption increases. Second, the lower domestic interest rate triggers net capital outflows that cause the exchange rate to rise (domestic currency depreciates). Hence, a domestic economy experiences more net exports (more exports and fewer imports).

12. If there is an excess supply of money, households and firms will

(a) sell bonds and add to their holdings of money, thereby causing the interest rate to fall.
(b) purchase bonds and reduce their holdings of money, thereby causing the interest rate to rise.
(c) purchase bonds and reduce their holdings of money, thereby causing bond yields to fall and bond prices to rise.
(d) purchase bonds and reduce their holdings of money, thereby causing the price of bonds to fall.
(e) sell bonds and add to their holdings of money, thereby causing the price of bonds to fall.

13. Changes in interest rates caused by money supply contractions or expansions

(a) are usually of little consequence in influencing economic activity in the short run.
(b) will not affect the market prices of bonds.
(c) cause the money demand function to shift if the price level remains constant.
(d) cause the investment demand function to shift.
(e) provide the link between changes in the money supply and changes in aggregate expenditure and aggregate demand in the short run.

14. Other things being equal, a decline in the interest rate causes
(a) a shift in the I^D function to the left.
(b) a shift in the I^D function to the right.
(c) a movement down the I^D function.
(d) a movement up the I^D function.
(e) the market price of bonds to fall.

15. The investment demand curve illustrates the
(a) positive relation between the quantity of desired investment and the (real) rate of interest.
(b) negative relation between the quantity of desired investment and the (real) rate of interest.
(c) negative relation between the quantity demand for bonds and the rate of interest.
(d) positive relation between the quantity supply of bonds and the rate of interest.
(e) positive relation between the demand for bonds and GDP.

16. A transition from an excess demand for money balances situation to a monetary equilibrium
(a) tends to increase aggregate demand.
(b) has an unpredictable effect on aggregate demand.
(c) tends to decrease aggregate demand.
(d) will affect aggregate demand but not the interest rate.
(e) will increase the demand for bonds.

17. If the Bank of Canada increases the money supply, we would expect the
(a) interest rate to fall, the *AE* curve to shift upward, and the *AD* curve to shift to the left.
(b) interest rate to fall, the *AE* curve to shift downward, and the *AD* curve to shift to the right.
(c) interest rate to rise, the *AE* curve to shift upward, and the *AD* curve to shift to the left.
(d) interest rate to fall, the *AE* curve to be unaffected, and the *AD* curve to become flatter.
(e) interest rate to fall, the *AE* curve to shift upward, and the *AD* curve to shift up.

18. Increases in Canadian interest rates relative to those in the rest of the world will
(a) increase Canadians' demand for foreign bonds.
(b) decrease foreigners' demand for Canadian bonds.
(c) decrease Canadians' and foreigners' demand for Canadian bonds.
(d) increase Canadians' and foreigners' demand for Canadian bonds.
(e) increase Canadians' demand for foreign bonds and decrease foreigners' demand for Canadian bonds.

19. If Canadian interest rates rise relative to those in other countries, the
(a) demand for Canadian dollars in international exchange markets will increase.
(b) demand for Canadian dollars in international exchange markets will fall.
(c) exchange rate will rise.
(d) Canadian dollar will appreciate.
(e) demand for Canadian dollars in international markets will increase and the Canadian dollar will appreciate.

20. With reference to your answer to Question 19, you would therefore expect
(a) net exports to increase and the *AD* curve to shift to the left.
(b) the *AD* curve to shift to the right.
(c) net exports to decrease and the *AD* curve to shift to the left.
(d) net exports to decrease and equilibrium levels of *Y* and *P* to increase.
(e) None of the above.

21. We have seen in Chapter 23 that an increase in autonomous aggregate expenditure—e.g., an increase in government purchases—would cause the *AD* curve to shift up and equilibrium income to rise. We see now in Chapter 28 that an increase in real GDP would cause the demand for real balances to increase and the real rate of interest to rise, which in turn would negatively affect desired investment expenditure and desired consumption expenditure—two other components of aggregate expenditure. Therefore, an increase in government purchases would have a greater short-run impact on equilibrium income

(a) the greater the sensitivity of the demand for money to changes in real GDP.
(b) the greater the sensitivity of the demand for money to changes in the rate of interest.
(c) the greater the sensitivity of desired investment expenditure to changes in the rate of interest.
(d) the smaller the sensitivity of desired consumption expenditure to changes in real GDP.
(e) the smaller the sensitivity of desired consumption expenditure to changes in the rate of interest.

The Strength of Monetary Forces

In the long run, monetary shocks are neutral. They influence nominal values but not the real sector of the economy such as real GDP. This is because monetary shocks create only short-run output gap situations. Factor prices adjust over time, thereby restoring potential real GDP, albeit at a different nominal price level. This result reflects the long-run neutrality of money (no effects on real macroeconomic variables).

In the short run, the extent to which the *AD* curve shifts depends on the sensitivity of money demand and desired investment to changes in the interest rate. The steeper the M_D function, the greater the change in the equilibrium interest rate when the money supply changes. Moreover, the steeper the investment demand curve (I^D), the lower the change in desired investment expenditures to changes in interest rates. The debate between Keynesians and monetarists focuses on the slopes of these two functions.

22. Starting from an initial equilibrium, the short-run impacts of a monetary contraction are

(a) a creation of a short-term recessionary gap.
(b) an increase in the rate of interest.
(c) a reduction in the level of desired investment expenditure.
(d) an appreciation of the domestic currency in the exchange market.
(e) All of the above.

23. The long-run impacts of a monetary expansion assuming factor prices adjust are

(a) an elimination of the short-run recessionary gap.
(b) no change in potential real GDP.
(c) higher factor prices.
(d) a higher equilibrium price level.
(e) All of the above.

24. The monetary transmission mechanism will eliminate a short-run inflationary gap by

(a) raising interest rates, reducing investment, and increasing aggregate expenditure.
(b) lowering interest rates, increasing investment, and increasing aggregate expenditure.
(c) raising interest rates, reducing investment, and moving upward along the *AD* curve.
(d) raising interest rates, reducing investment, and shifting the *AD* curve to the left.
(e) causing an appreciation of the exchange rate.

25. A given change in the money supply will exert a larger effect on real national income in the short run

(a) the flatter the D_M curve and the steeper the I^D curve.
(b) the flatter both the D_M and I^D curves.
(c) the steeper both the D_M and I^D curves.
(d) the steeper the D_M curve and the flatter the I^D curve.
(e) if the economy operates in the steep portion of the *AS* curve.

26. The short-run impact of a decrease in the money supply on real national income will be large when

(a) the economy operates in the steep portion of its *AS* curve.
(b) the demand for money curve is horizontal.
(c) the I^D curve is vertical.
(d) if international capital flows are completely insensitive to interest rate changes.
(e) None of the above.

SHORT-ANSWER QUESTIONS

1. Explain and illustrate graphically an excess demand for money, and predict the effects on the interest rate and the price of bonds.

Figure 28-1

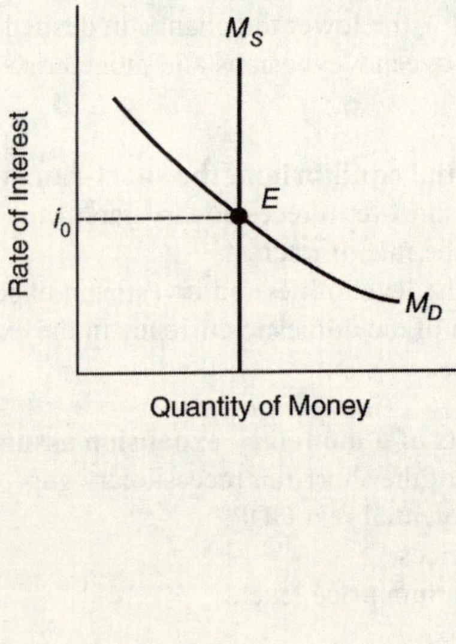

2. Explain and illustrate graphically an excess supply of money, and predict the effect on the interest rate and the price of bonds.

Figure 28-2

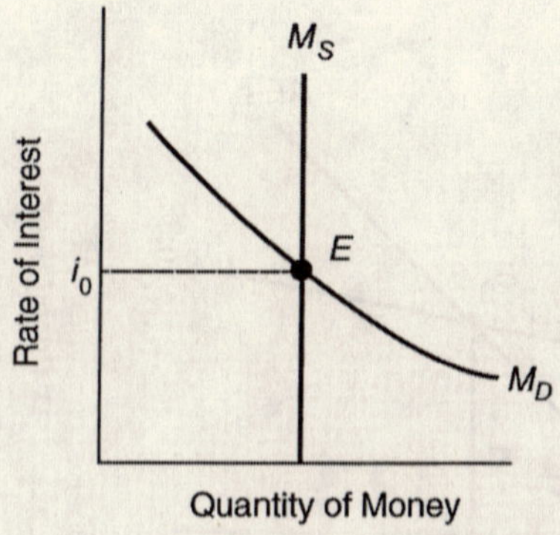

3. Analyze the effects of an increase in the money supply by the Bank of Canada on the rate of interest and desired investment expenditure. Initial equilibrium is MS_0, i_0, M_D^0, and I_0. Ignore the effect of a change in GDP on the demand for money.

Figure 28-3

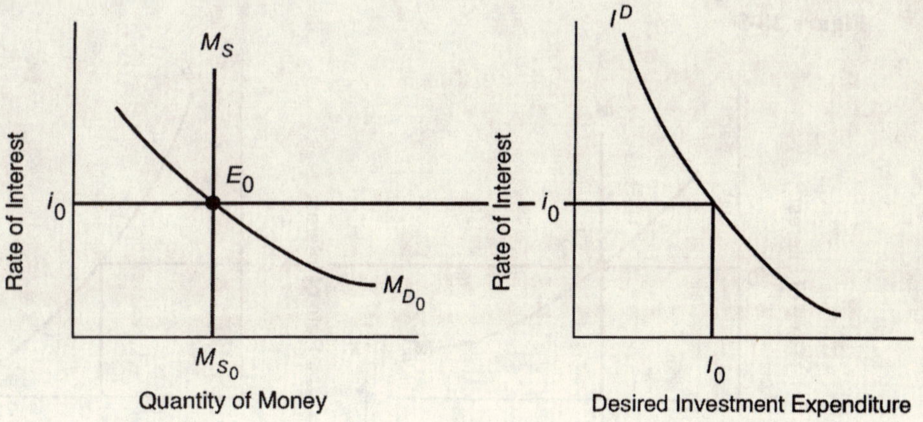

4. Assuming a price level of P_0 remains constant, show the effect of an increase in desired expenditure on the equilibrium level of real national income. Initial equilibrium is E_0 in both graphs.

Figure 28-4

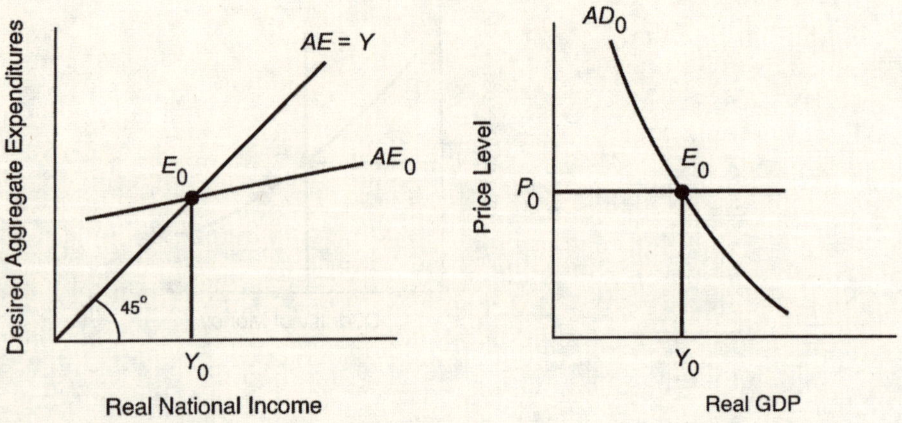

5. Show the effect of an increase in the price level, other things being equal, on the rate of interest and investment expenditure in Figure 28-5. Start from equilibrium at E_0, i_0, and I_0, and assume that the supply of money remains constant.

Figure 28-5

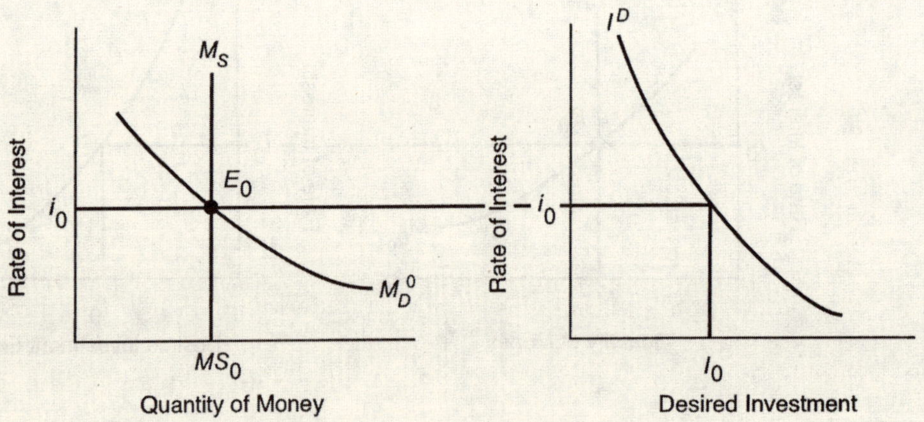

6. Consider an economy with only two financial assets: money and only one type of (government) bond. Money holdings do not generate any return, while bond holdings do. The diagram below shows the initial equilibrium in the money market and the bonds market, where both the supply of money and the supply of bonds are fixed.

Figure 28-6

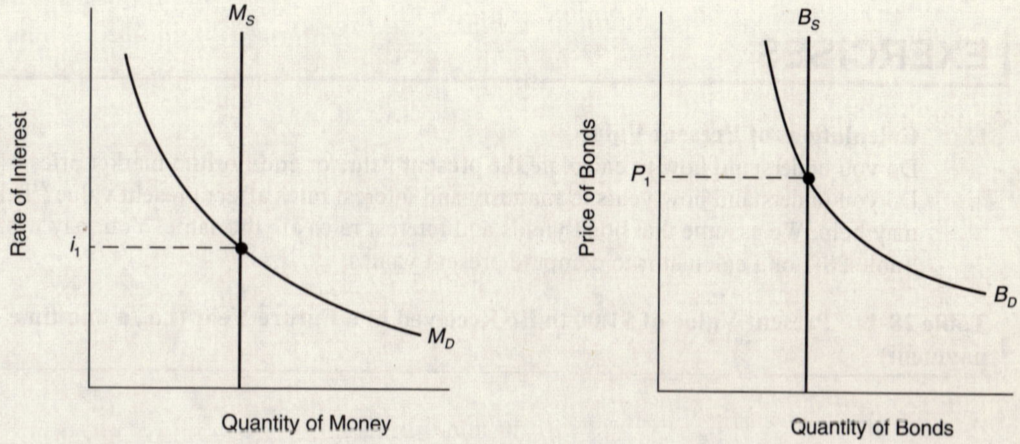

(a) What would happen to the rate of interest if the price of bonds were to fall?

(b) Suppose now that individuals and businesses believe that the price of bonds might significantly fall in the near future. Show in the diagram above how this expected drop in the price of bonds would affect equilibrium in both the money and the bonds markets. Briefly explain.

(c) Suppose now that individuals and businesses believe that the interest rate might significantly fall in the near future. Show in the diagram below how this expected drop in the price of bonds would affect equilibrium in both the money and the bonds markets. Briefly explain.

Figure 28-7

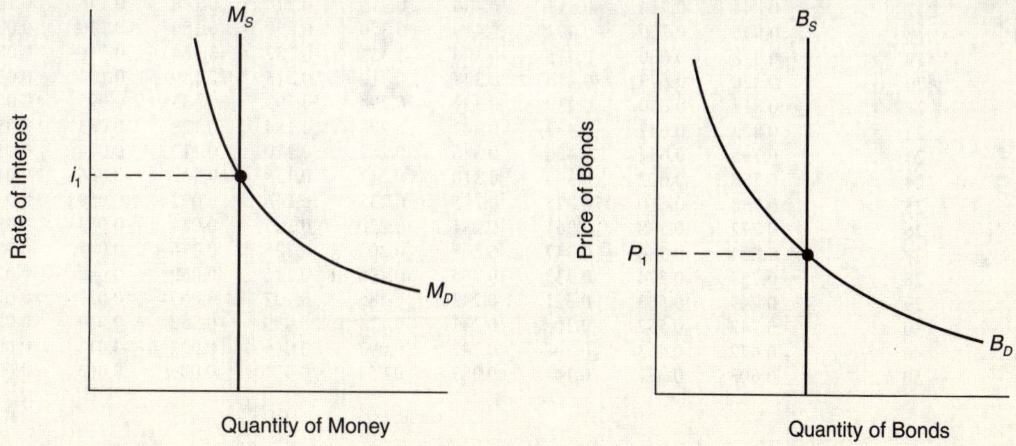

(d) What happens when individuals and businesses act upon their expectations?

EXERCISES

1. Calculations of Present Value

Do you understand how to calculate the present value or equilibrium market price of a bond? Do you understand how years to maturity and interest rates affect present value? This exercise may help. We assume that bond yields and interest rates are the same. You may wish to use Table 28-1 or a calculator to compute present values.

Table 28-1 Present Value of $1.00 to Be Received in a Future Year (i.e., a one-time payment)

$$PV = \frac{1}{(1+i)^n}$$

(*Note:* Numbers rounded to three decimal places)

	Market Rate of Interest									
Years Hence (*n*)	**1%**	**2%**	**4%**	**5%**	**6%**	**8%**	**10%**	**12%**	**14%**	**15%**
1	0.990	0.980	0.962	0.952	0.943	0.926	0.909	0.893	0.877	0.870
2	0.980	0.961	0.925	0.907	0.890	0.857	0.826	0.797	0.769	0.756
3	0.971	0.942	0.889	0.864	0.840	0.794	0.751	0.712	0.675	0.658
4	0.961	0.924	0.855	0.823	0.792	0.735	0.683	0.636	0.592	0.572
5	0.951	0.906	0.822	0.784	0.747	0.681	0.621	0.567	0.519	0.497
6	0.942	0.888	0.790	0.746	0.705	0.630	0.564	0.507	0.456	0.432
7	0.933	0.871	0.760	0.711	0.665	0.583	0.513	0.452	0.400	0.376
8	0.923	0.853	0.731	0.677	0.627	0.540	0.467	0.404	0.351	0.327
9	0.914	0.837	0.703	0.645	0.592	0.500	0.424	0.361	0.308	0.284
10	0.905	0.820	0.676	0.614	0.558	0.463	0.386	0.322	0.270	0.247
11	0.896	0.804	0.650	0.585	0.527	0.429	0.350	0.287	0.237	0.215
12	0.887	0.788	0.625	0.557	0.497	0.397	0.319	0.257	0.208	0.187
13	0.879	0.773	0.601	0.530	0.469	0.368	0.290	0.229	0.182	0.163
14	0.870	0.758	0.577	0.505	0.442	0.340	0.263	0.205	0.160	0.141
15	0.861	0.743	0.555	0.481	0.417	0.315	0.239	0.183	0.140	0.123
16	0.853	0.728	0.534	0.458	0.394	0.292	0.218	0.163	0.123	0.107
17	0.844	0.714	0.513	0.436	0.371	0.270	0.198	0.146	0.108	0.093
18	0.836	0.700	0.494	0.416	0.350	0.250	0.180	0.130	0.095	0.081
19	0.828	0.686	0.475	0.396	0.331	0.232	0.164	0.116	0.083	0.070
20	0.820	0.673	0.456	0.377	0.312	0.215	0.149	0.104	0.073	0.061
21	0.811	0.660	0.439	0.359	0.294	0.199	0.135	0.093	0.064	0.053
22	0.803	0.647	0.422	0.342	0.278	0.184	0.123	0.083	0.056	0.046
23	0.795	0.634	0.406	0.326	0.262	0.170	0.112	0.074	0.049	0.040
24	0.788	0.622	0.390	0.310	0.247	0.158	0.102	0.066	0.043	0.035
25	0.780	0.610	0.375	0.295	0.233	0.146	0.092	0.059	0.038	0.030
26	0.772	0.598	0.361	0.281	0.220	0.135	0.084	0.053	0.033	0.026
27	0.764	0.586	0.347	0.268	0.207	0.125	0.076	0.047	0.029	0.023
28	0.757	0.574	0.333	0.255	0.196	0.116	0.069	0.042	0.026	0.020
29	0.749	0.563	0.321	0.243	0.185	0.107	0.063	0.037	0.022	0.017
30	0.742	0.552	0.308	0.231	0.174	0.099	0.057	0.033	0.020	0.015
40	0.672	0.453	0.208	0.142	0.097	0.046	0.022	0.011	0.005	0.004
50	0.608	0.372	0.141	0.087	0.054	0.021	0.009	0.003	0.001	0.001

Case I: Bonds with One Payoff Period

Consider two bonds, *A* and *B*. Bond *A* promises to pay $120 one year hence, and bond *B* promises to pay $120 two years from now.

(a) Calculate the present value for bond *A* when the interest rate is 8 percent. Calculate the present value for interest rates of 10 percent and 15 percent. What happened to the (present value) market price when interest rates rose?

(b) If you were told that the market price (present value) of bond *A* increased, what is happening to the yield on bond *A*?

(c) Calculate the present value for bond *B* at interest rates of 10 percent and 15 percent.

(d) Which of the two bonds had the larger percentage change in its price when the interest rate rose from 10 to 15 percent?

(e) If the current rate of interest on both bonds were 15 percent, which bond would currently be selling for the higher market price? Why?

Case II: A Bond Having a Sequence of Payoff Periods

Consider a four-year bond that promises to repay the face value of $500 in 4 years, but will also pay an 8 percent coupon payment of $40 at the end of each of the four years that the bond is held. How much is this bond worth now if the market interest rate is 5 percent?

2. The Demand and Supply of Money

Two demand for money curves are illustrated in Figure 28-8.

Figure 28-8

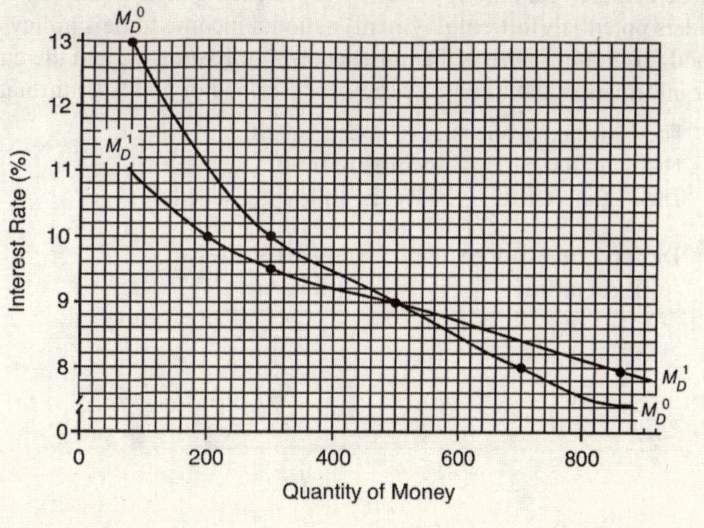

(a) Using your knowledge of the demand for money, explain why the quantity of money demanded falls when the interest rate rises.

(b) If the money supply is 500 and constant at all levels of interest rates, what interest rate is associated with monetary equilibrium? Plot the money supply function (M_S) in Figure 28-8 and indicate the monetary equilibrium interest rate.

(c) Suppose that the monetary authority decreased the money supply from 500 to 300. At an interest rate of 9 percent, what kind of situation exists in the money market? Would households and firms tend to buy or sell bonds? Explain. Predict what is likely to happen to bond prices and interest rates.

(d) As interest rates rise, what happens to the quantity of money demanded? Predict the new equilibrium level of interest rates first using D_M^0 and then using D_M^1.

(e) What increase in the money supply (from 500) would be necessary to achieve an equilibrium interest rate of 8 percent if M_D^0 applies? If M_D^1 applies?

3. Monetary Policy in Action

Suppose that the economy is currently experiencing high unemployment. The central bank considers potential (full-employment) national income to be a policy objective. The economy's demand for money curve is that labelled M_D^0 in Exercise 2 and the current money supply is 500. Other information about the economy is described in points (i) through (vii).

(i) The marginal propensity to spend is 0.50.
(ii) The potential national income is 1600.
(iii) The I^D function is given by the following schedule:

Desired Investment Expenditure	Interest Rate (percent)
160	13
180	11
200	9
210	8

(iv) Aggregate expenditures are depicted by the following schedule:

Y	*C*	*I*	*G*	*NX*	*AE*
1520	912	200	300	138	1550
1540	924	200	300	136	1560
1560	936	200	300	134	1570
1580	948	200	300	132	1580
1600	960	200	300	130	1590

(v) The M_D curve is not influenced by changes in the level of national income for the purposes of this problem.

(vi) The *AS* curve is horizontal at a price level of 2.0 for all levels of national income less than potential national income (1600), at which level it becomes vertical.

(vii) International capital flows are completely insensitive to interest rate changes.

(a) Explain the relevance of assumptions (v) to (vii).

The central bank sets its research department to work in order to establish accurate information about the current situation and to suggest what it should do in order to eliminate high unemployment.

(b) Referring to the M_D^0 curve in Figure 28-8, what is the current equilibrium level of the interest rate?

(c) Given the interest rate, what is the level of desired investment expenditure according to the I^D schedule?

(d) What is the current equilibrium value of real national income? What is the value of the output gap?

(e) What is the value of the simple multiplier? What change in autonomous expenditure is required for the economy to achieve the potential national income level without creating any price increases?

Based on the information in (a) through (e), the research department is in a position to recommend policy changes for the central bank.

(f) Should the money supply be increased or decreased in order to achieve the appropriate change in the interest rate?

(g) An interest rate change will change the level of investment. How much must investment be increased from its current level in order to achieve potential national income?

(h) To achieve this higher level of investment, what is the required level of the interest rate? (Refer to the I^D schedule.)

(i) Given the required level of the interest rate, what money supply is required to achieve equilibrium in the money market at that interest rate? Refer to the $M_D{}^0$ curve in Exercise 2. What change in the current money supply is necessary?

Now suppose that the central bank is successful in lowering the interest rate and increasing investment by the appropriate magnitudes. It follows that real national income should increase by a multiple and attain a level of 1600.

(j) Calculate the new level of consumption expenditure and calculate the aggregate level of expenditure at $Y = 1600$. Is this an equilibrium situation?

4. "Failures of the Monetary Transmission Mechanism"

Question 3 was based upon many assumptions that affect the strength of the monetary transmission mechanism to eliminate gap situations. We review some of them as separate cases in this question.

(a) Suppose that the demand for money curve was flat at an interest rate of 9 percent instead of those illustrated in Figure 28-8. What are the implications for the transmission mechanism's ability to eliminate the recessionary gap of 20?

(b) Now suppose that the $M_D{}^0$ curve in Figure 28-8 applies but that the I^D schedule [assumption (iii)] changes to one that indicates that investment expenditure remains at 200 regardless of the interest rate. Explain what this means and comment on the effectiveness of a monetary expansion to eliminate the recessionary gap of 20.

(c) Let us change assumption (vii). Suppose that a lower domestic interest rate created by the monetary expansion causes large capital outflows. Further, assume the exchange rate appreciates (and the domestic currency depreciates). Will the exchange rate change help or hinder the effectiveness of the monetary transmission mechanism?

5. Government Expenditure and the Crowding-Out Effect
This exercise shows how increases in government purchases could increase the level of equilibrium GDP while crowding out investment.

The following data describes a hypothetical closed economy:

$$C = 200 + 0.6\,Y$$
$$I = 450 - 30\,i$$
$$G = 300$$
$$M_D = 2\,Y - 600\,i$$
$$M_S = 1\,000$$

Assume that the price level is fixed. The level of potential GDP is 2300.

(a) Given the information above, fill in the blanks in the following table:

Y	C	I	G	AE	M_D	M_S	i
1100	____	____	300	____	____	____	2
1400	1040	____	____	____	____	____	____
1700	____	____	____	____	____	____	____
2000	____	300	____	____	1000	1000	____
2300	____	____	____	2150	____	____	____

(b) What are the equilibrium levels of Y and i in this economy?

(c) Suppose the government decides to use expansionary fiscal policy to move the economy to the level of potential GDP. By how much must government purchases be increased? What will be the effect on investment?

(d) Suppose now that the government decides instead to use expansionary monetary policy to move the economy to the level of potential GDP. By how much should the Bank of Canada increase M_S?

EXTENSION EXERCISE

E1. The Impact of a Change in the Price Level
Note: It will help to read *Interest Rates and the Slope of the* AD *Curve* in *Additional Topics* on the MyEconLab before attempting this exercise. This question focuses on the shape of the aggregate demand curve and the monetary transmission mechanism.

The following two tables show the effects of changes in the price level on desired investment.

The Demand for Money Schedule

	Quantity of Money Demanded	
Interest Rate	$P = 1$	$P = 2$
4	80	100
6	70	90
8	60	80
10	50	70
12	40	60
14	30	50

I^P Schedule

Rate of Interest	Desired Investment Expenditure
10%	180
11	179
12	177
13	174
14	170

Assume that the supply of money is fixed at a value of 50.

(a) Assume that the price level is 1.0; what is the equilibrium interest rate? What is desired investment expenditure?

(b) Assume that the price level becomes 2.0. For a given level of real national income, what will happen to the demand for money? What will happen in the bond market? Explain.

(c) Using the D_M schedule for $P = 2$, determine the new equilibrium interest rate.

(d) Given this change in the interest rate, what is the new level of desired investment expenditure?

The following table shows the effects of changes in desired investment (*I*) on real national income (*Y*).

Y	*C*	*I* (*i* = 10%)	*AE* (*i* = 10%)	*AE* (*i* = 14%)
340	170	180	350	____
350	175	180	355	____
360	180	180	360	____
370	185	180	365	____

(e) What is the equilibrium level of real national income (Y) associated with an interest rate of 10 percent and a price level of 1.0?

(f) The interest rate increased because of a doubling of the price level, and resulted in lower desired investment (from 180 to 170). Fill in the values for the new level of aggregate expenditure. What is the new equilibrium level of Y?

Now we synthesize the relationship between P and Y.

(g) Graph the *AD* curve in Figure 28-9, plotting the negative relationship between P and Y for this exercise. Use your answers to (e) and (f).

Figure 28-9

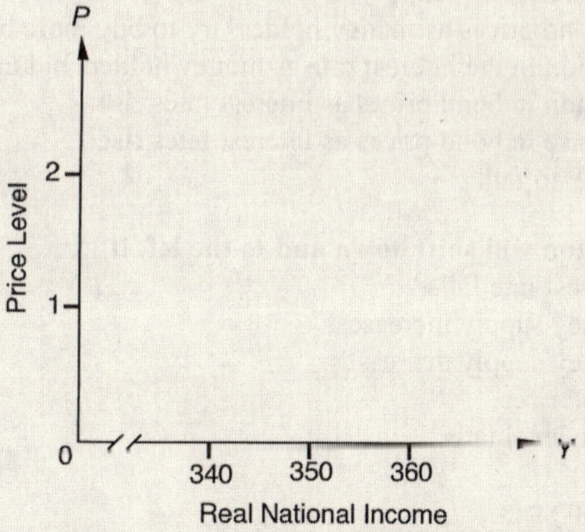

ADDITIONAL MULTIPLE-CHOICE QUESTIONS

To answer Questions 1 to 5, use Table 28-1 or your calculator. Your calculator will produce more accurate values than those in Table 28-1.

1. The present value of a bond that promises to pay $100 one year from now and that has an interest rate of 5 percent is

(a) $105. (b) $98.
(c) $94.30. (d) $78.40.
(e) $95.24.

2. The current market value of a bond that promises to pay $100 three years from now and that has a constant annual interest rate of 2 percent is

(a) $98. (b) $94.23.
(c) $96.10. (d) $97.10.
(e) $288.40.

***3. The present value of an asset that pays $100 after one year and $100 after two years and that has an annual interest rate of 10 percent is**

(a) $200. (b) $181.80.
(c) $220. (d) $173.55.
(e) $77.20.

***4. A bond that pays $100 three years from now and that currently sells for $88.90 has an annual interest rate of**

(a) about 13 percent.
(b) 12.5 percent.
(c) 11.1 percent.
(d) 4 percent.
(e) about 6 percent.

5. With a given stock of wealth, if bond holders attempt to sell bonds in order to increase their money holdings, then we would expect the

(a) price of bonds and rate of return on them to increase.
(b) price of bonds and the interest rate to fall.
(c) price of bonds to fall and the interest rate to rise.
(d) price of bonds to rise and the interest rate to fall.
(e) exchange rate to appreciate.

6. With a constant money supply, a shift to the left of the M_D function will cause

(a) lower bond prices as money holders try to buy more bonds.
(b) a reduction in the interest rate as money holders bid up the prices of bonds.
(c) a reduction in bond prices as interest rates rise.
(d) an increase in bond prices as interest rates rise.
(e) real GDP to fall.

***7. The M_D function will shift down and to the left if**

(a) the interest rate falls.
(b) the money supply increases.
(c) the money supply decreases.
(d) real GDP rises.
(e) the price level falls.

8. A steep M_D curve

(a) reflects the fact that money holders are extremely responsive to interest rate changes.
(b) is consistent with the views of Keynesian economists.
(c) leads to very large changes in the interest rate when the money supply changes.
(d) reflects the fact that investment expenditures are extremely unresponsive to interest rate changes.
(e) would lead to a very small change in short-run real GDP if the money supply increased.

Questions 9 through 13 refer to Figure 28-10. An initial equilibrium at point *a* is changed by an increase in the money supply. The new short-run equilibrium is shown by point *b*.

Figure 28-10

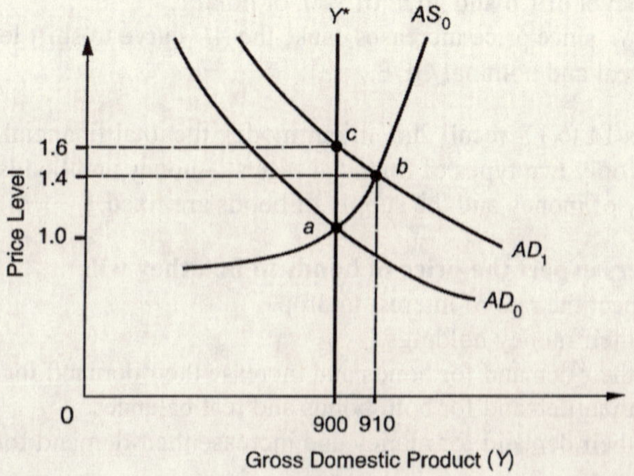

9. **Point *b* represents**
   (a) an inflationary gap of 10, but constant factor prices.
   (b) a recessionary gap of 10, but higher unit costs.
   (c) a negative output gap of 10, but higher factor costs.
   (d) long-run equilibrium, since input prices will never change.
   (e) higher factor prices than at point *a*.

*10. **An increase in the money supply shifted the *AD* curve to the right because**
   (a) an excess demand for money was created in the money market; thus interest rates and investment expenditure will both increase.
   (b) consumption expenditure increased as real GDP increased.
   (c) real wealth decreased.
   (d) a decline in interest rates stimulated more investment expenditures.
   (e) the exchange rate depreciated.

*11. **For an open economy, an increase in the money supply is also likely to shift the *AD* curve to the right because**
   (a) lower interest rates lead to larger capital inflows and a depreciated exchange rate.
   (b) higher interest rates lead to lower net exports.
   (c) an appreciation of the domestic currency and higher net exports.
   (d) lower interest rates lead to higher capital outflows, an appreciated exchange rate, and increased net exports.
   (e) None of the above.

*12. **The gap situation depicted at point *b* is likely to cause further longer-term adjustments. Specifically, we would expect**
   (a) factor prices to rise.
   (b) the *AS* curve to begin shifting leftward.
   (c) the price level to increase beyond 1.4.
   (d) a movement upward along AD_1.
   (e) All of the above.

13. As long as factor prices change completely to offset the price change, the long-run impact of the monetary expansion will be

(a) at point *b*, since real wages do not change.
(b) increases in both real GDP and the price level.
(c) a price level of 1.6 and GDP of 900, or point *c*.
(d) at point *a*, since price increases cause the *AD* curve to shift leftward to its initial position.
(e) higher real and nominal GDP.

To answer Questions 14 to 17, recall that, in our model, the total financial wealth of individuals and businesses is kept in only two types of financial assets—money and bonds—and that, at any point in time, both the supply of money and the supply of bonds are fixed.

***14. If bond holders expect the price of bonds to fall, they will**

(a) also expect the rate of interest to drop.
(b) reduce their money holdings.
(c) reduce their demand for bonds and increase their demand for money.
(d) reduce their demand for both bonds and real balances.
(e) reduce their demand for money and increase their demand for bonds.

***15. If the demand for bonds increases, then**

(a) the demand for money will also increase.
(b) the supply of money will increase and the rate of interest will drop.
(c) the demand for money will decrease and the rate of interest will fall.
(d) the supply of bonds will increase to restore equilibrium in the bonds market.
(e) the supply of money and the supply of bonds will both increase to restore equilibrium in the assets market.

***16. If bond holders attempt to sell bonds in order to increase their money holdings, at the end of the process of adjustment**

(a) the money held by individuals and businesses will increase by the same amount as their bond holdings will decrease.
(b) the money held by individuals and businesses will decrease by the same amount as their bond holdings will increase.
(c) individuals and business will reduce their bond holdings but will keep their money holdings unchanged.
(d) economic agents will keep both their total money holdings and their total bond holdings unchanged.
(e) individuals and business will reduce both their bond holdings and their money holdings by the same amount.

17. If the commercial banks decide to increase their loans to individuals and businesses, then

(a) the money supply will increase and thus both total money holdings and total bond holdings will increase in the economy.
(b) individuals and businesses might decide to increase their money holdings and the rate of interest will increase.
(c) individuals and businesses will increase their money holdings while keeping their bond holdings unchanged.
(d) individuals and businesses will increase their money holdings and decrease their bond holdings.
(e) individuals and businesses will sell bonds and the price of bonds will fall.

SOLUTIONS

Chapter Review

1.(a) **2.**(e) **3.**(a) **4.**(c) **5.**(d) **6.**(b) **7.**(a) **8.**(a) **9.**(d) **10.**(b) **11.**(d) **12.**(c) **13.**(e) **14.**(c) **15.**(b) **16.**(c) **17.**(e) **18.**(d) **19.**(e) **20.**(c) **21.**(e) **22.**(e) **23.**(e) **24.**(d) **25.**(d) **26.**(e)

Short-Answer Questions

1. At an interest rate below point *E* (say, *i*), there is an excess demand for money. Interest rates should begin to rise to equilibrium at i_0 and *E* as individuals and firms sell bonds. As firms and households sell bonds to obtain more money, the price of bonds falls and the yield on them increases.

Figure 28-11

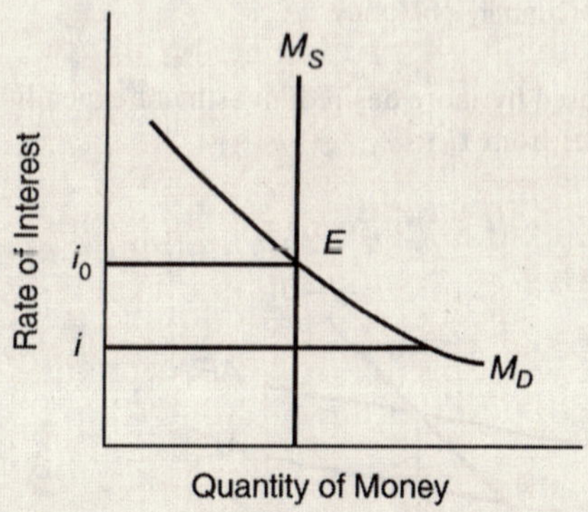

2. At an interest rate above point *E*, there is an excess supply of money at *i*. As firms and households get rid of money balances and buy more bonds, interest rates should fall to equilibrium at i_0 and *E*. This process increases bond prices and lowers the interest rate.

Figure 28-12

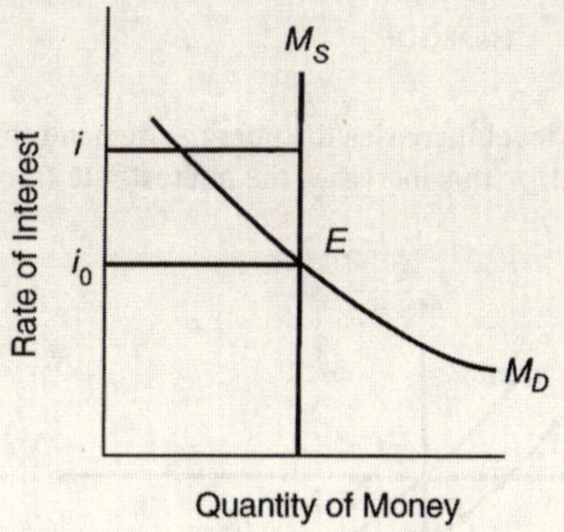

3. Interest rate drops from i_0 to i_1; investment expenditures rise from I_0 to I_1.

Figure 28-13

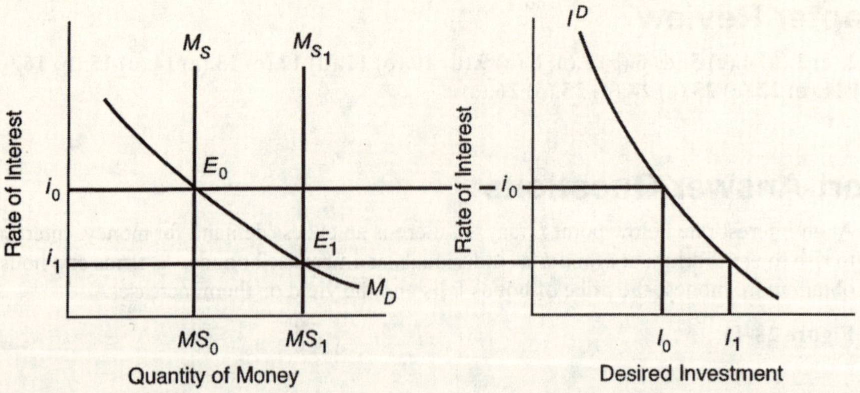

4. Upward shift in *AE* caused by more desired investment expenditure, also shifting *AD* rightward; equilibrium income rises from Y_0 to Y_1.

Figure 28-14

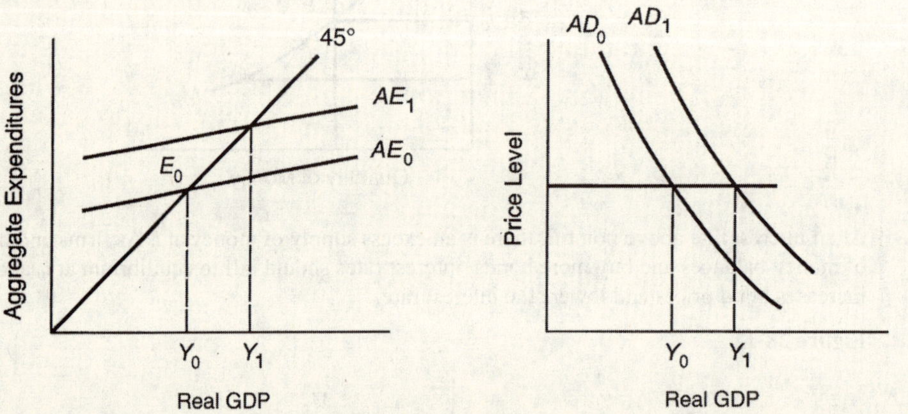

5. An increase in the price level increases the nominal demand for money (for transactions purposes primarily) from M_D^0 to M_D^1; this increases the interest rate from i_0 to i_1 and lowers investment from I_0 to I_1.

Figure 28-15

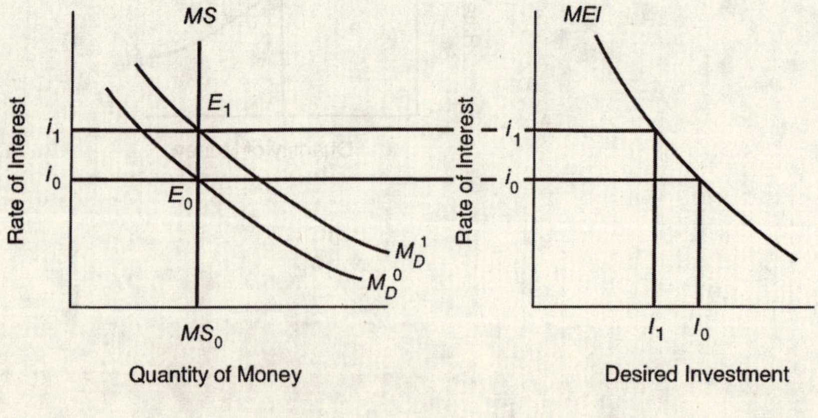

6. **(a)** The rate of interest and the price of bonds are inversely related. Therefore, the rate of interest would rise when the price of bonds fell.

(b) If the price of bonds is expected to fall, then bond holders will attempt to reduce their bond holdings and increase their money holdings. Since total financial wealth is constant, an increase in the demand for money must be met by a similar decrease in the demand for bonds. Therefore, the demand curve for bonds will shift down and the demand curve for money will shift up—thus decreasing the price of bonds and increasing the rate of interest.

Figure 28-16

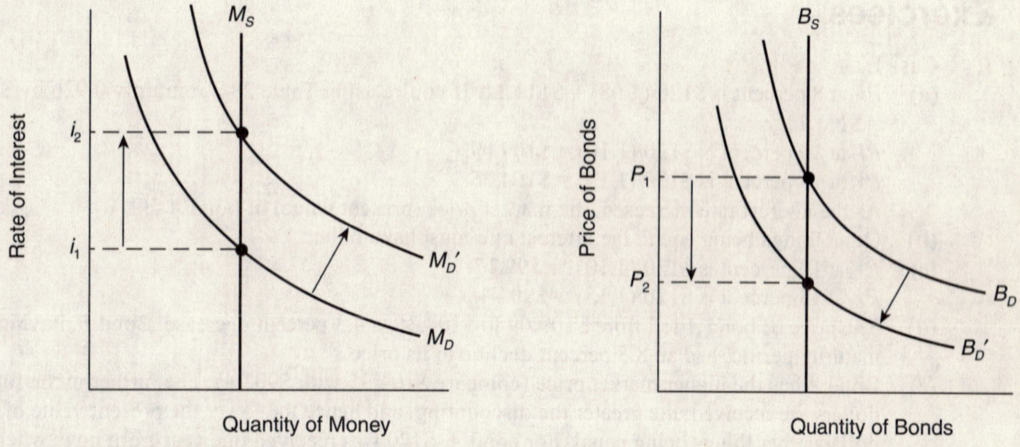

(c) If the rate of interest is expected to fall, then this is the same as saying that the price of bonds is expected to rise. Therefore, individuals and businesses will attempt to increase their bond holdings now while bond prices are low and to reduce their money holdings. Since total financial wealth is constant, an increase in the demand for bonds must be met by a similar decrease in the demand for money. Therefore, the demand curve for bonds will shift up and the demand curve for money will shift down—thus increasing the price of bonds and decreasing the rate of interest.

Figure 28-17

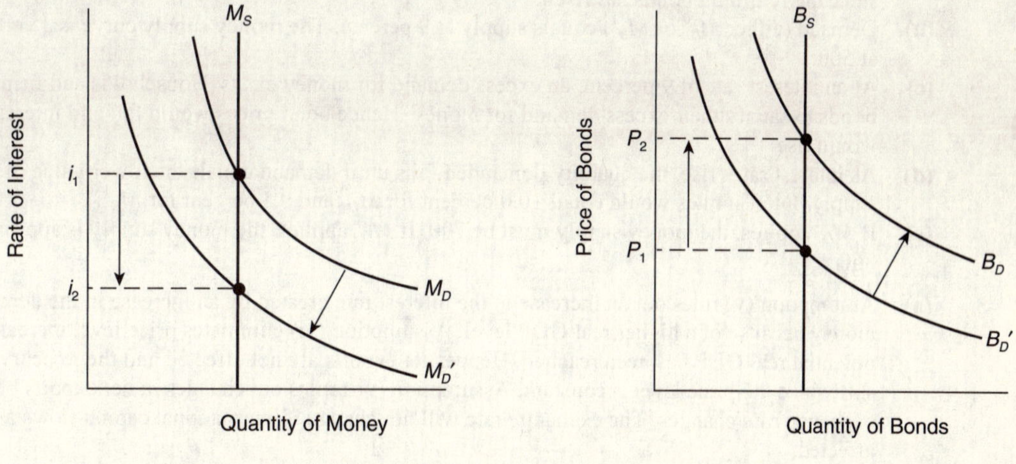

(d) The situations analyzed in parts (b) and (c) are examples of what is called "self-fulfilling prophecy"—something is expected to happen, economic agents act upon that expectation, and the expectation is realized. Indeed, when individuals and businesses expect the price of bonds to fall, they will act upon this expectation and sell bonds while their price is high. In this way, there will be more sellers than buyers at the initial equilibrium price and price will fall. Similarly, when individuals and businesses expect the rate of interest to fall—and thus the price of bonds to rise—they will act upon this expectation and buy bonds while their price is low. In this way, there will be more buyers than sellers at the initial equilibrium price and price will rise.

Exercises

1. **Case I:**

(a) PV at 8 percent is \$120/(1.08) = \$111.11. If you're using Table 28-1, multiply 0.926 by \$120 = \$111.11.
PV at 10 percent is \$120/(1.10) = \$109.09.
PV at 15 percent is \$120/(1.15) = \$104.35.
As the interest rate increased, the market price (present value) of bond A fell.

(b) Other things being equal, the interest rate must have fallen.

(c) PV at 10 percent is \$120/$(1.10)^2$ = \$99.17.
PV at 15 percent is \$120/$(1.15)^2$ =\$90.74.

(d) The price of bond A fell from \$109.09 to \$104.35, a 4.3 percent decrease. Bond B, having a longer maturity period, had an 8.5 percent decline in its price.

(e) Bond A has the higher market price (compare \$104.35 with \$90.74). The further in the future that dollars are received, the greater the discounting, and hence the lower the present value of those dollars other things being equal. For bond A, \$120 was received one year from now, whereas bond B paid \$120 two years from now.

Case II:
The formula for PV at a market interest rate of 5% is \$40/(1.05) + \$40/$(1.05)^2$ + \$40/$(1.05)^3$ + \$540/$(1.05)^4$. Using the values in Table 28-1, we obtain \$40 times 0.952 = \$38.08 plus \$40 times 0.907 = \$36.28 plus \$40 times 0.864 = 34.56 plus \$540 times 0.823 = \$444.42. The sum is \$553.34. Notice that the superscript on the term (1.05) represents the time period that the payment was received.

2. **(a)** As the opportunity cost of money rises, households and firms will tend to economize on their demand for money balances. In addition, firms are prepared to take more risk (and therefore buy more bonds) since the return on bonds has risen.

(b) Demand (either M_D^0 or M_D^1) equals supply at 9 percent. The money supply curve is a vertical line at 500.

(c) At an interest rate of 9 percent, an excess demand for money exists. Households and firms would sell bonds to satisfy their excess demand for money. Hence bond prices would fall and interest rates would rise.

(d) As interest rates rise, the quantity demanded falls until demand equals the lower value of the money supply. Interest rates would equal 10.0 percent for M_D^0 and 9.5 percent for M_D^1.

(e) If M_D^0 applies, the money supply must be 700. If M_D^1 applies, the money supply is approximately 860.

3. **(a)** Assumption (v) rules out an increase in the interest rate created by an increase in the demand for money because of a higher real GDP level. Assumption (vi) eliminates price level increases until potential real GDP has been reached. Hence, net exports are not affected and the M_D curve does not shift since the price level is constant. Assumption (vii) rules out changes in net exports because of exchange rate changes. The exchange rate will not change if international capital flows are not affected.

(b) 9 percent, at which demand is equal to supply.

(c) 200.

(d) When Y = 1580, AE = Y. The output gap (recessionary gap) is 1580 – 1600 = –20.

(e) 2.0. Autonomous expenditure must increase by 10 to achieve an increase in Y of 20.

(f) The money supply must increase in order to decrease interest rates.

(g) 10.

(h) The interest rate must fall from 9 percent to 8 percent.

(i) According to Figure 28-8, the money supply must increase from 500 to 700, an increase of 200.

(j) Consumption now equals 960, an increase of 12 (20 × *MPC* of 0.6). When $Y = 1600$, $C = 960$ and $AE = Y$. This is equilibrium.

4. (a) The monetary transmission is totally ineffective since any change in the money supply has no effect on the interest rate. Since investment is not affected, the multiplier process does not come into play.

(b) The I^D is perfectly inelastic with respect to the interest rate. Presumably firms are not at all sensitive to the interest rate when making investment decisions. Thus, even though interest rates change with monetary policy, investment is constant. The multiplier process will not occur (including any change in investment).

(c) An appreciation of the exchange rate increases net exports. The expansionary effects of the money supply increase will be helped by the increase in net exports.

5. (a) *C* depends on *Y*, and thus for each value of *Y* we find the corresponding value of *C*. *G* is independent of *Y*, and thus *G* is constant. *I* depends on *i*, and thus we must find the value of *i* corresponding to each value of *Y*. We find the value of *i* by equating M_D and M_S, where M_S is fixed and M_D depends on *Y*.

Y	*C*	*I*	*G*	*AE*	M_D	M_S	*i*
1100	**860**	**390**	300	**1550**	**1000**	**1000**	2
1400	1040	**360**	**300**	**1700**	**1000**	**1000**	**3**
1700	**1220**	**330**	**300**	1850	**1000**	**1000**	**4**
2000	**1400**	300	**300**	**2000**	1000	1000	**5**
2300	**1580**	**270**	**300**	2150	**1000**	**1000**	**6**

(b) The economy is in equilibrium when what economic agents would like to purchase (*AE*) is equal to what the economy has produced (*Y*). Therefore, equilibrium *Y* is 2000 and the corresponding equilibrium interest rate is 5.

(c) *AE* must be 2300 when $Y = 2300$ in order for the economy to be in equilibrium at the level of potential GDP. The table above shows that when $Y = 2300$, $C = 1580$ and $I = 270$, therefore *G* must be equal to 450 in order for *AE* to be equal to 2300. The required increase in *G* is then 150. The increase in *Y* causes M_D to increase, and *i* rises to 6. In turn, the increase in *i* causes *I* to decrease from 300 to 270. This decrease in *I* represents the crowding out effect of the increase in *G*.

(d) *AE* must be 2300 when $Y = 2300$ in order for the economy to be in equilibrium at the level of potential GDP. The table above shows that when $Y = 2300$, $C = 1580$, and $G = 300$, *I* must therefore be equal to 420 in order for *AE* to be equal to 2300. Given the investment demand equation ($I = 450 - 30i$), for *I* to be equal to 420, the rate of interest must be

$$420 = 450 - 30i \rightarrow 30i = 30 \rightarrow i = 1.$$

When $Y = 2300$ and $i = 1$, $M_D = 2Y - 600i = 2(2300) - 600(1) = 4000$, and since in equilibrium $M_D = M_S$, then $M_S = 4000$. Therefore, the Bank of Canada should increase M_S by 3000.

Extension Exercise

E1. **(a)** Demand equals supply (50) at an interest rate of 10 percent. Desired investment expenditure is therefore 180.

(b) If price increases, the M_D curve shifts upward or rightward (the nominal demand for money increases at every interest rate). Hence, bonds will be sold thereby lowering their price. As a consequence, the interest rate increases.

(c) The new equilibrium interest rate is 14 percent.

(d) The new level of investment is 170 for all levels of *Y*.

(e) $Y = AE$ at 360 (10 percent interest rate and $P = 1.0$).

(f) *AE*: 340, 345, 350, 355. The new equilibrium level of national income is 340.

(g) See Figure 28-18.

Figure 28-18

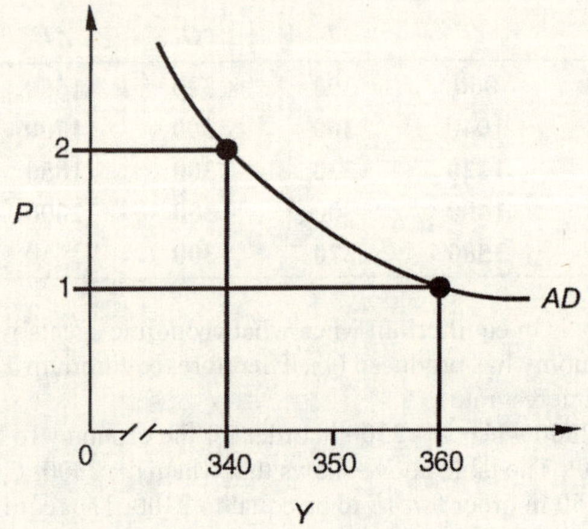

Additional Multiple-Choice Questions

1.(e) **2.**(b) **3.**(d) **4.**(d) **5.**(c) **6.**(b) **7.**(e) **8.**(c) **9.**(a) **10.**(d) **11.**(d) **12.**(e) **13.**(c) **14.**(c) **15.**(c) **16.**(d) **17.**(c)

Explanations for the Asterisked Multiple Choice Questions

3.(d) $PV = \$100/(1.10) + \$100/(1.10)^2 = \$90.91 + \$82.64 = \$173.55$ (by calculator).

4.(d) $\$88.90 = \$100/(1 + i)^3$. Using Table 28-1, the interest rate is 4 percent.

7.(e) A lower price level generates a decreased demand for money.

10.(d) An increase in the money supply lowers the interest rate. This triggers an increase in desired investment which shifts the *AD* curve rightward.

11.(d) An increase in the money supply lowers the domestic interest rate. This leads to international capital outflows and a depreciation in the domestic currency. Net exports should increase.

12.(e) Point *b* represents a short-run inflationary gap. Hence, factor prices will begin to rise and the *AS* curve will begin to drift leftward. Increases in factor prices cause the price level to increase beyond 1.4 and the economy will move up the *AD* curve.

14.(c) If the price of bonds is expected to fall, then bond holders will attempt to sell bonds now while their price is high. Therefore, they will try to reduce their bond holdings and increase their money holdings—which means that they will reduce their demand for bonds and increase their demand for money.

15.(c) The total financial wealth of an individual is given at any point in time, and thus the individual can only decide in which form she will keep her total wealth—i.e., how much in the form of bonds, and how much in the form of money. Therefore, if she decides to hold more of her wealth in the form of bonds—i.e., if her demand for bonds rises—then she is also deciding to hold less of her wealth in the form of money—i.e., her demand for money falls. Given that the money supply is fixed, the rate of interest will fall.

16.(d) The supply of money and the supply of bonds are both fixed (exogenous variables). Therefore, individuals could change the combination in which they keep their total financial wealth, but if some individuals decide to increase the proportion of money holdings in their total wealth (and thus decrease the proportion of bond holdings in their total wealth), then other individuals will decide right the opposite at the same time—i.e., to decrease the proportion of money holdings in their total wealth (and thus increase the proportion of bond holdings in their total wealth). Changes in the price of bonds and in the rate of interest will ensure this outcome, but the total money holdings of all individuals and businesses will not change and neither will the total bond holdings of all individuals and businesses since the supplies of both money and bonds are fixed.

CHAPTER 29

MONETARY POLICY IN CANADA

LEARNING OBJECTIVES

In this chapter you will learn

1. why the Bank of Canada chooses to set interest rates rather than directly influence the money supply.
2. how changes in the Bank of Canada's target for the overnight interest rate affect longer-term interest rates.
3. why many central banks have adopted formal inflation targets.
4. how the Bank of Canada's policy of inflation targeting helps to stabilize the economy.
5. why monetary policy affects real GDP and the price level only after long time lags.
6. about the main economic challenges that the Bank of Canada has faced over the past three decades.

CHAPTER OVERVIEW

This chapter examines the Bank of Canada's **monetary policy**. Monetary policy can be implemented either by influencing the money supply or by influencing the interest rate—but not both.

The Bank of Canada cannot control the money supply, though it can influence it *directly* by changing the amount of cash reserves in the banking system. The Bank can change the amount of cash reserves in the banking system through open-market operations—i.e., through the Bank's purchase or sale of government bonds in the open market. More recently, the Bank of Canada has chosen to implement monetary policy by influencing the interest rate *directly* rather than by trying to influence the money supply. The Bank of Canada influences interest rates by setting a target for the *overnight interest rate*—i.e., a target for the rate of interest that commercial banks charge each other for overnight loans.

Over the last few decades, central banks the world over came to the conclusion that high and uncertain inflation leads to arbitrary income redistributions and also undermines the efficiency of the price system. Therefore, as a way of controlling inflation the Bank of Canada adopted a formal system of *inflation targeting* in the early 1990s.

The chapter outlines the reasons why there may be long and variable lags to monetary policy. By the time that monetary policy takes effect, the Bank's policy may be destabilizing. The chapter concludes by outlining 30 years of monetary policy in Canada.

HINTS AND TIPS

The following may help you to avoid some of the most common errors on examinations.

- ✓ Understand why the Bank of Canada cannot attempt to control both the money supply and the short-term interest rate simultaneously.
- ✓ Learn why during the last few decades the Bank of Canada has chosen to implement monetary policy by influencing the interest rate directly rather than by trying to influence the money supply directly.
- ✓ Ensure that you know what is meant by the *bank rate* and the *overnight rate of interest*, and how they are determined.
- ✓ Learn why and how the Bank of Canada tries to enforce an inflation target band.

CHAPTER REVIEW

How the Bank of Canada Implements Monetary Policy

The Bank of Canada can implement monetary policy by influencing the money supply or by influencing the market rates of interest. Changing the level of reserves in the banking system is the most common monetary policy instrument used by central banks to affect the money supply. The Bank of Canada can change the amount of cash reserves in the banking system through open-market operations—i.e., through the Bank's purchase or sale of government bonds in the open market. Over the last two decades the Bank of Canada has chosen not to implement monetary policy by influencing the money supply for three reasons: (1) while it can control the amount of cash reserves in the banking system it cannot control the process of deposit expansion carried out by the commercial banks; (2) there is uncertainty about the *slope* of the M_D curve and thus there is uncertainty about the change in the interest rate that would result from any given change in the supply of money; and (3) the Bank is also unable to predict accurately the *position* of the M_D curve at any given time.

Since the 1980s the Bank of Canada has chosen to implement monetary policy by influencing the interest rate directly. This approach of implementing monetary policy has some important advantages: (1) while the Bank of Canada cannot control the money supply, it *can* control a particular market interest rate—the *bank rate* (see below); (2) the Bank's uncertainty about the slope and position of the M_D curve is not a problem because the Bank chooses instead to influence the interest rate directly; and (3) the Bank can more easily *communicate* its policy actions to the public by setting the interest rate than by setting the level of reserves in the banking system.

What policy instrument does the Bank of Canada use to influence the market rates of interest? Eight times a year the Bank sets the **bank rate**—the interest rate that the Bank of Canada charges commercial banks for loans. At the same time, the Bank sets the rate of interest it pays to commercial banks for their deposits at the Bank of Canada—a rate 0.5 percentage points below the bank rate. In this way, the Bank of Canada sets the target range for the **overnight interest rate**—the rate of interest that commercial banks charge each other for overnight loans. Therefore, the Bank's target for the overnight interest rate can be seen as the mid point of this target interest rate range.

When the Bank of Canada changes its target for the overnight rate, the change in the actual overnight rate happens almost instantly. Changes in other market interest rates also happen very quickly. As these rates adjust, firms and households begin to adjust their borrowing behaviour, but these changes take considerably longer to occur. When demand for loans gradually adjusts to changes in interest rates, commercial banks find themselves in need of changing their cash reserves. When this occurs, banks will change their cash reserves through open-market operation—buying or selling government bonds from or to the Bank of Canada in the open market.

If the Bank of Canada wants to stimulate the level of aggregate demand, it will implement *expansionary* monetary policy—i.e., it will reduce the target for the overnight interest rate. Similarly, if the Bank wants to reduce the level of aggregate demand, it will implement *contractionary* monetary policy—i.e., it will increase the target for the overnight interest rate.

1. **Which of the following must be satisfied in order for the Bank of Canada to be able to directly control the money supply?**
   (a) The precise slope of the M_D curve must be known.
   (b) The exact position of the M_D curve must be known.
   (c) The Bank of Canada must have direct control over the process of deposit expansion in the banking system.
   (d) The Bank of Canada must control the amount of cash reserves in the banking system.
   (e) All of the above must be satisfied.

2. **Open-market operations are**
   (a) purchases and sales by the Bank of Canada of government securities in financial markets.
   (b) purchases and sales among the commercial banks of securities in financial markets.
   (c) sales of government securities by commercial banks to their customers.
   (d) total purchases and sales of government securities in the bond market.
   (e) government sales of government securities in financial markets.

3. **If the Bank of Canada purchases bonds in the open market,**
   (a) bank reserves decrease.
   (b) bank reserves increase.
   (c) the money supply will fall by a maximum of $1/(v + c)$ times the value of the purchase (v is the reserve ratio and c is the cash drain).
   (d) interest rates increase.
   (e) bond prices fall.

4. **If the Bank of Canada sold $10 million of securities to the public in the open market,**
   (a) reserves and securities in the banking system each rise by $10 million.
   (b) deposits and reserves of banks initially fall by $10 million.
   (c) the money supply eventually increases by $1/v$ times the value of the sale (v is the reserve ratio).
   (d) deposits in the banking system initially rise by $10 million.
   (e) the prices of bonds rise.

5. **If the Bank of Canada purchases bonds in the open market,**
   (a) the price of bonds falls and the interest rate rises.
   (b) both the price of bonds and the interest rate rise.
   (c) both the price of bonds and the interest rate fall.
   (d) the price of bonds rises and the interest rate falls.
   (e) reserves in the banks fall.

6. **The bank rate is defined as the interest rate**
   (a) charged to preferred customers by a bank.
   (b) charged by banks for overdrafts of large corporations.
   (c) on credit card accounts.
   (d) on three-month treasury bills.
   (e) at which the Bank of Canada lends to the commercial banks.

7. **Since the 1980s the Bank of Canada has been implementing monetary policy by**
   (a) changing the amount of cash reserves in the banking system.
   (b) changing the position and/or the slope of the M_D curve.
   (c) directly controlling the money supply.
   (d) influencing the market interest rates directly.
   (e) directly changing the level of deposits in the banking system.

8. **If the Bank of Canada sets the bank rate at 3.0 percent, then**
   (a) commercial banks can borrow any amount from the Bank of Canada at a 2.5 percent rate of interest.
   (b) commercial banks will receive a 3.0 percent interest on their deposits at the Bank of Canada.
   (c) commercial banks will lend excess reserves to each other at a rate of interest of 3.0 percent or higher.
   (d) the target for the overnight interest rate is 2.5 percent.
   (e) the target for the overnight rate of interest is 2.75 percent.

9. **When the Bank of Canada changes the bank rate, its impact on the economy is not felt immediately because**
   (a) it takes time for commercial banks to adjust the overnight rate of interest.
   (b) it usually takes more than a month for the different market interest rates to also change.
   (c) borrowers are usually unable to see interest rate changes right away.
   (d) individuals need time to adjust their demand for money to the new market interest rates.
   (e) All of the above are correct.

10. **When the Bank of Canada decreases its target for the overnight rate of interest, over time**
   (a) the public reacts by reducing the volume of deposits in the banking system.
   (b) commercial banks react by reducing the volume of loans to their customers.
   (c) commercial banks find themselves with excess reserves and increase the volume of loans to their customers.
   (d) commercial banks find themselves with too little reserves and sell government securities to the Bank of Canada.
   (e) commercial banks find themselves with too little reserves and recall some of the loans from their customers.

11. **The money supply is said to be an *endogenous* variable because it is determined by the economic decisions of**
   (a) households, firms, commercial banks, and the Bank of Canada.
   (b) households and firms but not those of the commercial banks and the Bank of Canada.
   (c) households, firms, and commercial banks but not those of the Bank of Canada.
   (d) the Bank of Canada.
   (e) the Bank of Canada and the federal government.

Inflation Targeting

Over the last few decades, central banks the world over came to the conclusion that high and uncertain inflation leads to arbitrary income redistributions and also undermines the efficiency of the price system. Many economists and central bankers also agree that monetary policy is the most important determinant of a country's long-run rate of inflation. Not surprisingly, central banks have come to focus their attentions on the reduction and control of inflation. In the early 1990s, the Bank of Canada adopted a formal system of *inflation targeting* to help to stabilize the economy. The Bank's target is expressed as a 2-percentage-point band, in recognition of the fact that modest fluctuations in the inflation rate are inevitable and thus it is unrealistic to expect the Bank to keep the inflation rate at a single, precise value. At the present, the Bank of Canada conducts monetary policy with the objective of keeping inflation within the range of 1 to 3 percent.

There are two complications in pursuing an inflation-targeting policy. Some components of the CPI are quite volatile and have world-determined prices. These price increases/decreases have little to do with the level of excess demand in Canada and thus have little implication for what policy should be followed by the Bank of Canada. A similar argument can be made for Canadian indirect taxes such as the GST or excise taxes. Hence, the "core" inflation rate is a better measure for the Bank to target. Another complication involves changes in the exchange rate. Care must be taken by the Bank to identify the cause of the exchange-rate change before taking corrective action.

12. **The measure of "core" inflation**
    (a) includes all items in the Canadian CPI.
    (b) excludes rental housing prices.
    (c) includes indirect taxes such as provincial sales taxes.
    (d) includes energy prices.
    (e) excludes food and energy prices as well as indirect taxes.

13. **When would it be appropriate for the Bank of Canada to use a contractionary monetary policy?**
    (a) During a recessionary gap.
    (b) To increase interest rates.
    (c) To prevent the Canadian dollar from appreciating because of an increase in the demand for Canadian assets.
    (d) When interest rates begin to rise above the Bank's target.
    (e) When actual inflation is at or below the Bank's lower band of targeted inflation.

14. **The Bank of Canada adopted a system of *inflation targeting* because it considered that**
    (a) inflation benefited only individuals with fixed nominal incomes.
    (b) expected inflation led to an undesirable reallocation of resources between workers and firms.
    (c) expected inflation led to an undesirable reallocation of resources between borrowers and lenders.
    (d) the uncertainty generated by inflation was damaging to the economy.
    (e) All of the above are true.

15. **At the present time, the Bank of Canada inflation target is in the**
    (a) 2–3 percent range.
    (b) 2–4 percent range.
    (c) 3–5 percent range.
    (d) 0–2 percent range.
    (e) 1–3 percent range.

16. **When a demand shock threatens to increase the rate of inflation above its target, the Bank of Canada will**
    (a) directly decrease the money supply.
    (b) directly increase the market rates of interest.
    (c) increase the bank rate.
    (d) reduce the overnight rate.
    (e) buy government securities from the commercial banks.

17. If the Bank of Canada were committed to maintain an inflation target at all costs, it would react to a negative *supply* shock (e.g., an increase in the price of oil) by
(a) increasing the target for the overnight rate.
(b) decreasing the bank rate.
(c) buying government securities from the commercial banks.
(d) implementing expansionary monetary policy.
(e) All of the above are true.

Long and Variable Lags

The role of adjustment lags in the real sector to monetary shocks is a key component of the debate between Keynesians and Monetarists. Monetary policy used for stabilization purposes actually can be destabilizing if there are long and variable lags in adjustment. There are three reasons why a change in monetary policy does not affect the economy instantly. First, firms take time to change their investment plans when interest rates change. Second, changes in interest rates affect the exchange rate but changes in exchange rates take time to affect net exports. Third, the multiplier takes time to work itself through once there have been changes in expenditures. By the time the full effects of monetary policy occur, forces in the economy may have changed. Hence, the change in monetary policy may be destabilizing.

18. An important implication of long and variable lags associated with monetary policy is that
(a) national income fluctuations are easily fine-tuned with open-market operations.
(b) monetary policy is never capable of eliminating an inflationary gap.
(c) monetary policy may prove to be destabilizing.
(d) monetary policy cannot affect the price level in the long run.
(e) monetary policy never has short-run effects on GDP.

19. Which of the following are examples of lags associated with monetary policy?
(a) The time interval between changes in bank reserves and the final impact on the money supply.
(b) The time period in which business firms react to changes in interest rates with respect to investment intentions.
(c) The time taken for the full multiplier effect to affect real GDP.
(d) All of the above.
(e) None of the above.

30 Years of Canadian Monetary Policy

This section outlines the stances of the Bank of Canada and the underlying economic circumstances for the Bank's actions during various time intervals since the early 1980s. A key aspect for you to consider is the differences in the Bank's policies that were essentially short-term stabilization stances versus those that focused on long-run targets.

20. What was the Bank of Canada's immediate concern about the severe downturn in the stock market of 2001?
(a) To match the U.S. Federal Reserve's policy of high interest rates.
(b) Wealth changes could trigger increases in domestic consumption.
(c) To increase interest rate differentials *vis a vis* the United States.
(d) To provide enough liquidity to the banking system to prevent a recession.
(e) Whether a contractionary policy should be pursued by the Bank of Canada.

21. **The Asian crisis beginning in 1997 produced a complicated combination of forces on the Canadian economy including**
   (a) higher Canadian inflation because of an increased demand for Canadian raw-materials exports to Thailand and South Korea.
   (b) a positive *AS* effect from the lower-price inputs for Canadian manufacturing firms.
   (c) a negative *AD* effect from the decrease in the U.S. demand for Canadian goods.
   (d) an overall inflationary gap which caused an acceleration in the Canadian inflation rate.
   (e) a major increase in unemployment.

SHORT-ANSWER QUESTIONS

1. Use Figure 29-1 to illustrate the effects of the following Bank of Canada monetary policies and then answer the questions.

Figure 29-1

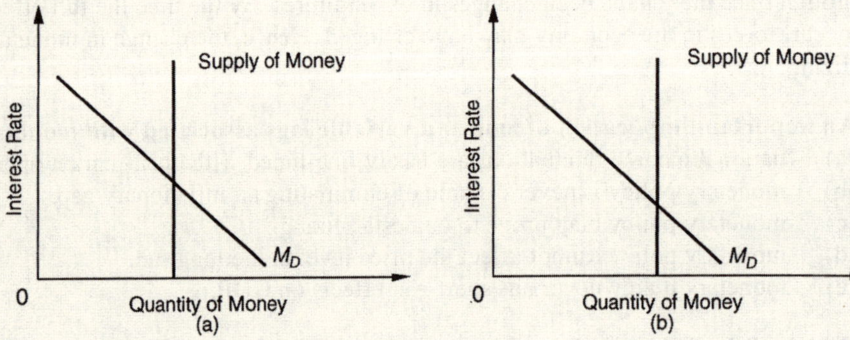

(a) Use graph (a) for this question. The Bank of Canada sells government securities to the commercial banks.
Total commercial bank reserves (increase, decrease) ____________.
The money supply curve should shift to the (right, left) ____________.
This policy is (expansionary, contractionary) ____________.
The equilibrium interest rate (rises, falls) ____________.

(b) Use graph (b) for this question. The Bank of Canada increases its target for the overnight interest rate.
Initially the (interest rate, money supply) ____________ will (increase, decrease) ____________.
The commercial banks' cash reserves will become (excessive, insufficient) ____________.
The commercial banks will (sell, buy) ____________ government securities from the Bank of Canada in order to (decrease, increase) ____________ their cash reserves.
The commercial banks will (increase, decrease) ____________ the volume of loans to their customers and the money supply curve will shift to the (right, left) ____________.
This policy is (expansionary, contractionary) ____________.

2. Explain why the Bank of Canada's inflation targeting helps to stabilize the economy when economic shocks occur.

EXERCISES

1. **An Open Market Purchase**

Suppose that each bank in the banking system has achieved its target reserve position. Now the Bank of Canada purchases a total of $300 million in government securities from the commercial banks.

(a) Show the effect of this transaction in the following balance sheets. Use + for an increase and – for a decrease.

Bank of Canada		Banking System	

(b) Is the policy designed to combat a recessionary or an inflationary gap situation? Explain.

(c) If the target reserve ratio is 5 percent, what is the possible *final* change in the money supply? What would be the final change in the money supply if the target reserve ratio is 5 percent and the cash drain is 5 percent?

(d) Discuss the factors that determine the time it takes for the change in the money supply to eliminate the output gap problem.

2. **Changes in the Demand for and the Supply of Money**

Suppose that the demand for money function was $M_D = 2Y - 20i$ where M_D is the quantity of money demanded, i is the rate of interest (an interest rate value of 5 means 5 percent in this problem), and Y is real national income which currently is 100. The supply of money is 100. The price level does not change in this problem.

(a) What is the equilibrium value for the interest rate?

(b) Suppose, because of expansion in the economy, real national income increases from 100 to 160. Derive the new expression for the demand for money function. If the supply of money remained at 100, what situation exists in the money market at the initial interest rate? What is likely to happen to the equilibrium level of the interest rate in the future? Be specific.

(c) Given the circumstances described in (b) and assuming that the Bank of Canada was determined to maintain an interest-rate target of 5 percent, what change in the money supply would be required? Be specific.

(d) What type of open-market operations would be appropriate for the change in the money supply discussed in (c)?

(e) Is this type of open-market operation likely to encourage or curtail economic expansion?

3. Control of the Rate of Interest by the Bank of Canada

Figure 29-2 shows the initial monetary equilibrium in the Canadian economy. Assume the price level is fixed in this problem.

Figure 29-2

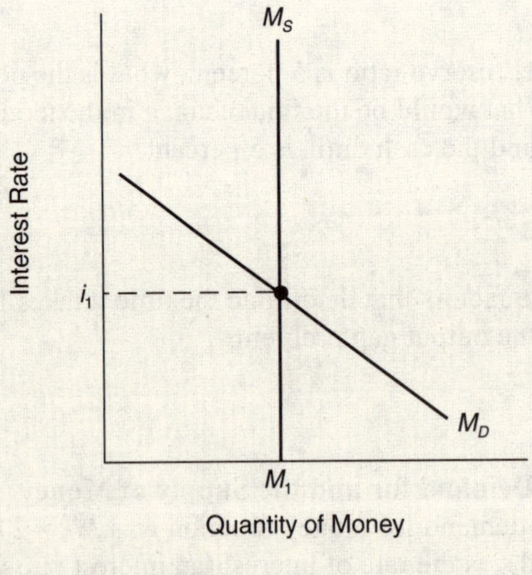

(a) Suppose that real income increases in Canada. In the absence of any change in monetary policy, show the new monetary equilibrium in the diagram above. What happens to the demand for money? What happens to the quantity demanded of money?

(b) Suppose now that the Bank of Canada decides to keep the rate of interest constant. What policy instrument will the Bank of Canada most likely use? Will the commercial banks experience a situation of excess cash reserves or of too little cash reserves?

(c) What will the commercial banks do to eliminate excess/insufficient cash reserves? What will happen to the supply of money?

4. **Targeting the Rate of Interest and Changes in Bank Reserves**

Suppose that the demand for money function was $M_D = 4\,Y - 1000\,i$ where M_D is the quantity of money demanded, *i* is the rate of interest (an interest of 5 means 5 percent in this problem), and *Y* is real national income which currently is 1500. The supply of money is 1000, currency in circulation outside the banking system is 100, the target reserve ratio is 10 percent, there is no cash drain in the banking system, and the recessionary gap is 250. The price level does not change in this problem.

(a) What is the equilibrium value for the interest rate? What is the level of cash reserve of the banking system?

(b) Suppose that the Bank of Canada estimates that a reduction of the rate of interest to 4 percent would move the economy to full employment. Given this estimate, what would be the quantity of money demanded at full employment?

(c) Suppose the Bank of Canada reduces the target for the overnight rate, prompting commercial banks to reduce the market rate of interest to 4 percent. Are the commercial banks experiencing a situation of excess cash reserves or of too little cash reserves? What is the size of this excess/insufficient cash reserve when $Y = 1500$?

(d) What will the commercial banks do to eliminate excess/insufficient cash reserves? By how much should the level of cash reserves of the banking system change for the economy to move to full employment?

5. **Monetary Policy in Action**

You are an adviser to the governor of the central bank of the country of Montand. The governor has committed the Bank of Montand to a policy of zero inflation. The situation in the recent past is depicted by point *a* in Figure 29-3. Now, quite unexpectedly, real national income and the price level rise to point *b*. Your research indicates that this situation is likely to prevail for some time. The governor asks you to outline some of the policy options open to her. The governor is known to prefer controlling the money supply rather than the rate of interest.

Figure 29-3

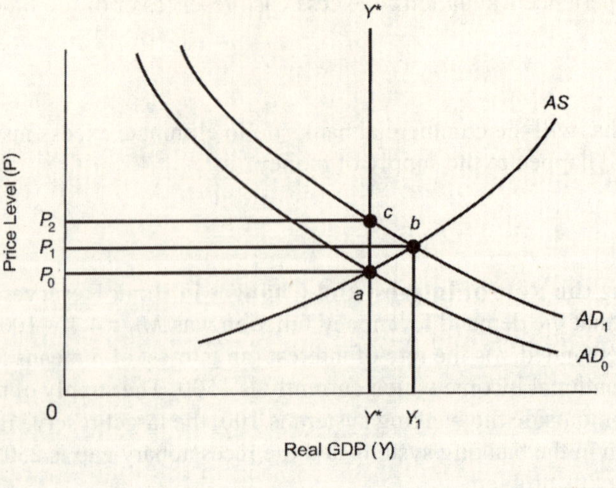

(a) Policy option I: Reverse the trend and return the economy back to point *a*. What policy recommendations would you make? What reservations might you express to the governor?

(b) Policy option II: No central bank intervention. What arguments would you make to support this stance? If this "policy" is pursued, what reservations would you express to the governor?

6. "On the One Hand—But On the Other..."

The central bank governor, Ford, requests you to brief him concerning the appropriate monetary policy to deal with an ongoing appreciation of the domestic currency. He becomes quite irritated when your advice is indecisive and includes the statement, "Well, on the one hand it might be appropriate to increase the money supply, but on the other hand circumstances might dictate a contraction of the monetary supply." He barks, "Why can't I find a one-handed economist at this bank?"

Why might your advice have been indecisive? What economic research should you have conducted before the briefing?

ADDITIONAL MULTIPLE-CHOICE QUESTIONS

Answer Questions 1 to 6 by assuming that the Bank of Canada decides to purchase $100 million of government securities from commercial bank customers. Assume that the public holds all of their money balances in deposits, and that the target reserve ratio for all banks is 0.10.

1. The initial impact of this policy stance on the Bank of Canada's balance sheet is recorded by
(a) government deposits in the banks and bank reserves, increasing both by $100 million.
(b) only bond holdings by the Bank, increasing by $100 million.
(c) commercial bank reserves in the Bank of Canada and security holdings by the Bank, increasing both by $100 million.
(d) deposits of the public in the Bank of Canada and bond holdings by the Bank of Canada, increasing both by $100 million.
(e) only deposits of the public in the Bank of Canada, increasing by $100 million.

***2. The initial impact of this policy stance on the commercial banks' balance sheets will be**
(a) bond holdings of the banks and deposits of the public will increase both by $100 million.
(b) increases in both the deposits of the public in banks and the reserves of the banks by $100 million.
(c) deposits of the public in banks and bank reserves will decrease both by $100 million.
(d) only an increase in banks' reserves by $100 million.
(e) increases in bond holdings of the bank and government deposits at the commercial banks both by $100 million.

3. The purchase of bonds by the Bank of Canada from the public
(a) creates excess reserves of $90 million.
(b) creates deficit reserves of $100 million.
(c) has no effects on the reserves of the banks since the Bank of Canada purchased bonds from the public.
(d) creates deficient reserves of $90 million.
(e) creates excess reserves of $100 million.

***4. This policy stance by the Bank of Canada would be appropriate if**
(a) the Bank wishes to eliminate an inflationary gap.
(b) the Bank intends to increase interest rates.
(c) the Bank intends to promote more international capital flows into Canada.
(d) more investment is considered important for increased economic activity.
(e) the Bank wishes the Canadian dollar to appreciate.

5. If the target reserve ratio is 10 percent and there is no cash drain, the final change in deposits in the banking system generated by this policy change is
(a) +$100 million.
(b) –$110 million.
(c) –$110 million.
(d) +$1 billion.
(e) –$1 billion.

***6. If the money supply changed by the predicted amount, we expect**
(a) an initial excess supply of money in the money market and subsequent increases in the interest rates.

(b) an initial excess supply of money in the money market and subsequent increases in bond prices.
(c) an initial excess demand for money in the money market and subsequent increases in bond prices.
(d) an initial excess demand for money in the money market and subsequent reductions in the interest rate.
(e) banks to increase interest rates on loans to the public.

Answer Questions 7 through 10 by referring to Figure 29-4.

Figure 29-4

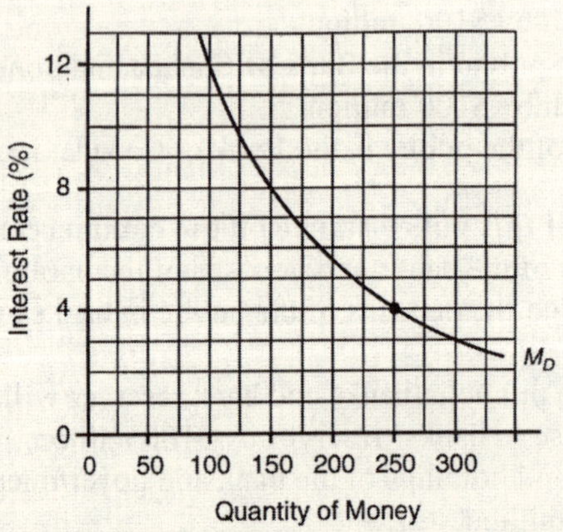

7. If the central bank chose an interest rate target of 12 percent,
(a) both the money supply and the quantity of money demanded must be 100.
(b) an adjustment in the money supply is not needed.
(c) a money supply of 150 would create an excess supply of bonds at an interest rate of 12 percent.
(d) a money supply of 250 would create an equilibrium situation at 12 percent.
(e) Both (a) and (c).

8. If the money supply were set at 150 and the central bank's interest rate target were 12 percent, the central bank
(a) need do nothing since a money supply of 150 achieves its interest-rate target.
(b) must sell bonds in the open market, thereby lowering bond prices.
(c) will lower the bank rate to indicate its intentions to decrease the supply of money.
(d) must increase government deposits in the banks in order to increase their reserves.
(e) must buy bonds in the open market.

***9. If the central bank set a monetary supply target of 150, then according to the M_D curve**
(a) there would be an excess supply of money at an interest rate of 12 percent.
(b) there would be an excess supply of bonds at an interest rate of 4 percent.
(c) the equilibrium interest rate must be 8 percent.
(d) All of the above.
(e) None of the above.

10. If the central bank reduced its interest rate target from 12 percent to 8 percent
(a) it should sell bonds in the open market.
(b) the money supply must increase from 100 to 150.
(c) the overnight rate must increase first.

(d) the actual inflation rate exceeds the Bank's targeted inflation rate.
(e) it should transfer government deposits from the commercial banks to itself.

Answer Questions 11 through 14 by referring to Figure 29-5. The current situation is depicted at point *a*. Assume that both the *AS* and *Y** do not change for the period under consideration.

Figure 29-5

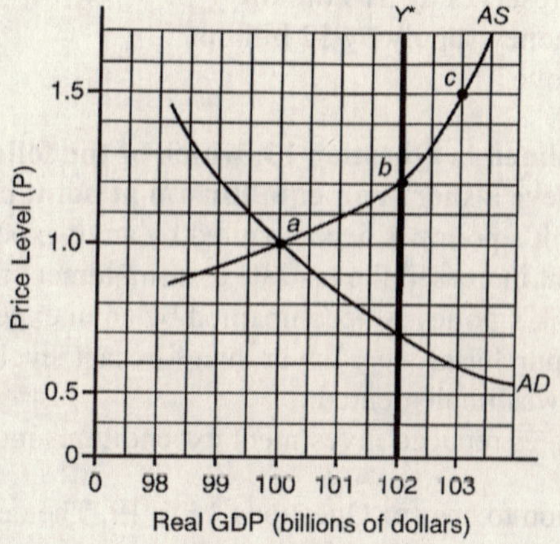

11. **Suppose the current short-run situation is depicted as point *a*. Which of the following statements is correct?**
    (a) There is an inflationary gap of 2.0.
    (b) The economy has reached its potential level of GDP.
    (c) The price level is 1.0 and GDP is 100.
    (d) The equilibrium price level is 1.2.
    (e) The price level is 0.7 and GDP is 102.

12. **Suppose that central bank policy is designed to eliminate the current output gap. Its monetary policy involves**
    (a) a policy tradeoff, since the elimination of the output gap is accompanied by a decrease in the price level.
    (b) a decrease in its interest-rate target.
    (c) decreasing the reserves of the banking system.
    (d) selling government securities to the commercial banks.
    (e) increasing the bank rate.

***13. Information concerning the strength of the monetary transmission mechanism indicates that every $500 million increase in the money supply increases real GDP by $1 billion. If the reserve ratio is 10 percent, the output gap will be completely eliminated if the commercial bank**

(a) increases their reserves by $100 million.
(b) increases the money supply by $500 million.
(c) increases their reserves by $10 billion.
(d) increases the money supply by $2 billion.
(e) None of the above.

***14. Given the policy outlined in Question 13, which of the following might explain why the economy might achieve a short-run equilibrium at point *c* rather than point *b*?**

(a) The central bank's policy is accompanied by an unexpected increase in household saving.
(b) The government increased the tax rate to complement the central bank's policy.
(c) The central bank's policy is accompanied by an unexpected decline in export sales.
(d) Actual import purchases were lower than forecast levels when the required change in the money supply was implemented.
(e) High interest rates reduced investment expenditures more than was anticipated.

Use the following information to answer Questions 15 to 19. The demand for money function is $M_D = 3Y - 900\,i$ where M_D is the quantity of money demanded, i is the rate of interest (an interest of 5 means 5 percent in this problem), and Y is real national income which currently is 1500. The supply of money is 900, the target reserve ratio is 5 percent, there is no cash drain in the banking system, and the recessionary gap is 150. The price level does not change in this problem.

***15. The equilibrium value of the interest rate is**

(a) 6.0 percent.
(b) 5.5 percent.
(c) 5.0 percent.
(d) 4.5 percent.
(e) 4.0 percent.

***16. The level of cash reserves of the banking system is**

(a) 90.
(b) 75.
(c) 55.
(d) 45.
(e) None of the above.

***17. Suppose that the central bank reduces its target for the overnight rate and the commercial banks decrease the market interest rate to 3.0 percent. As a result, an excess (demand, supply) ____________ equal to ____________ will develop in the money market.**

(a) demand / 2700
(b) demand / 1800
(c) demand / 900
(d) supply / 1800
(e) supply / 900

18. At the level of full employment income, the quantity demanded of money will be

(a) 2700.
(b) 2500.
(c) 2250
(d) 2000.
(e) 1800.

19. At full employment income, the level of cash reserves of the banking system is

(a) 125.0.
(b) 118.5.
(c) 112.5.
(d) 110.5
(e) 105.0

SOLUTIONS

Chapter Review

1.(e) **2.**(a) **3.**(b) **4.**(b) **5.**(d) **6.**(e) **7.**(d) **8.**(e) **9.**(d) **10.**(d) **11.**(a) **12.**(e) **13.**(b) **14.**(d) **15.**(e) **16.**(c) **17.**(a) **18.**(c) **19.**(d) **20.**(d) **21.**(b)

Short-Answer Questions

1. **(a)** decrease; left; contractionary; rises.
(b) interest rate; increase; excessive; buy; decrease; decrease; left; contractionary.

2. If the Bank of Canada is committed to keeping the rate of inflation near the midpoint of the target band, positive shocks that create an inflationary gap and threaten to increase the rate of inflation will be met by contractionary monetary policy. The Bank will increase interest rates by reducing reserves in the banking system and shifting the *AD* curve to the left. This policy pushes the rate of inflation back down toward the midpoint of the target band. Similarly, if a negative shock creates a recessionary gap and threatens to reduce the rate of inflation, the central bank, committed to its inflation target, will respond with an expansionary monetary policy—reduce interest rates (by increasing reserves) and shift the *AD* curve to the right.

Exercises

1. **(a)**

Bank of Canada		Banking System	
Gov't sec. +300	Bank reserves +300	Gov't Sec. −300 Bank reserves +300	

(b) Since the Bank of Canada's policy increases reserves in the banking system, the policy is directed to increasing economic activity, which is anti-recessionary policy. Assuming a stable demand for money function, interest rates will fall and investment will rise.

(c) The final increase in the money supply will be \$6 billion. This is equal to \$300 million times 1/0.05, where the value 0.05 is the target reserve ratio. With a cash drain of 5 percent, the increase would be \$3 billion. This is equal to \$300 million times 1/01, where the value 0.1 is the summation of the target reserve ratio (0.05) and the cash drain (0.05).

(d) An increase in the money supply decreases the interest rate. Firms would not necessarily revise their investment expenditures immediately. Moreover, when investment does increase, the effects on the induced components of aggregate expenditure may not be instantaneous; that is, the final effect of the multiplier process is achieved only after several time periods have elapsed.

2. **(a)** Equating demand with supply, we obtain an equilibrium level of the interest rate of 5 percent.

(b) The new demand for money function M_D^1 is $320 - 20i$. At an interest rate of 5 percent, there is now an excess demand for money. Firms and households sell their bonds, thereby reducing bond prices and increasing the interest rate on bonds. Equating the new demand function with the money supply, we find that the new equilibrium level of the interest rate is 11 percent.

(c) Since an excess demand for money exists at $i = 5$ percent with the new demand for money function, it follows that the Bank of Canada must increase the money supply in order to maintain its interest-rate target of 5 percent. Using the function $D_M = 320 - 20i$ and the fact that i must be equal to 5 (percent), M_D must equal 220. Since the demand for money must equal the supply of money, it follows that the supply of money must be increased from 100 to 220, an increase of 120.

(d) The Bank of Canada should buy bonds in the open market to provide additional reserves for banks.

(e) Given the increase in the demand for money with a fixed supply of money, the resulting interest-rate increase would have reduced some investment expenditure, thereby curtailing some of the economic expansion. However, with the Bank of Canada's interest-rate target policy and the expansionary open-market operation, economic expansion would be sustained or perhaps increased.

3. (a) As real income increases, the demand for money also increases and the M_D curve shifts up (to M_D' in Figure 29-6). The new monetary equilibrium is established at a higher rate of interest (i_2 in Figure 29-6). Since the supply of money remains unchanged, the quantity demanded of money does not change either (M_1 in Figure 29-6).

Figure 29-6

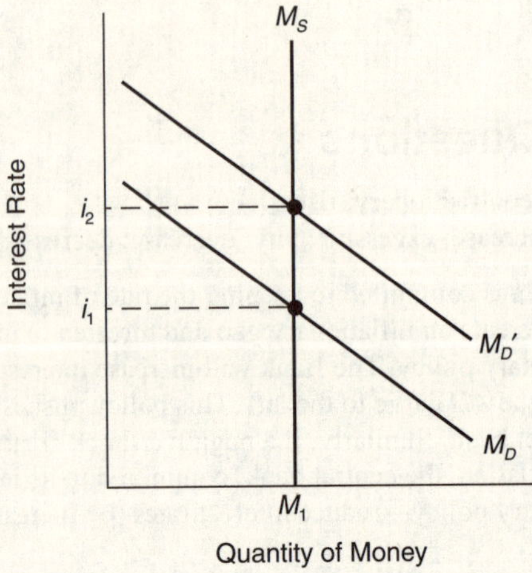

(b) If the Bank of Canada decides to keep the rate of interest constant, it will keep its target for the overnight rate unchanged. Given the increase in the demand for money resulting from the increase in real income, an excess demand for money will arise in the money market. Commercial banks would like to increase the level of loans to their customers but, given the desired reserve ratio, they encounter a situation of too little cash reserves.

(c) To increase their cash reserves to the desired level, the commercial banks will sell government securities to the Bank of Canada. As the cash reserves increase, the banks increase the level of loans to their customers. Therefore, deposits in the banking system rise and so does the supply of money.

4. (a) $M_D = 4\,Y - 1000\,i \rightarrow 1000 = 4\,(1500) - 1000\,i \rightarrow 1000\,i = 5000 \rightarrow i = 5$. Since the money supply is 1000 and currency held by the public is 100, the level of the public's deposits in the banking system is 900. Therefore, given the target reserve ratio of 10 percent—that is, 10 percent of the public's deposits of 900—the level of cash reserves is 90.

(b) $M_D = 4\,Y - 1000\,i = 4\,(1750) - 1000\,(4) = 3000$.

(c) $M_D = 4\,Y - 1000\,i = 4\,(1500) - 1000\,(4) = 2000$. Since at a 4-percent rate of interest the quantity demanded of money is 2000, banks will increase loans by 1000 to satisfy this increase in demand, i.e., the money supply will increase by 1000. Therefore, the banks are now experiencing a situation of too little reserves given their target reserve ratio of 10 percent. Since there is no cash drain in the banking system, the increase of 1000 in the supply of money represents an increase of 1000 in the level of the public's deposits in the banking system, i.e., the public's deposits increase from 900 to 1900. Given the target reserve ratio of 10 percent, the desired level of reserves of the banks is now 190 and the size of the insufficient cash reserves is thus 100.

(d) The commercial banks will sell government securities to the Bank of Canada in order to increase their cash reserves. Since at $Y = 1750$ the quantity demanded of money is 3000, the money supply must increase by 2000 which implies that the cash reserves of the banking system should increase by 200.

5. (a) The *AD* curve must be shifted leftward from point *b* back to point *a*. Such a change requires a contractionary monetary policy consisting of selling bonds in the open market or transferring government deposits from the commercial banks to the Bank of Montand. As a result, reserves of the commercial banks will fall. There are several reservations that you might express, but we discuss only three. First, the governor must be warned that this policy stance involves reducing real national income. Some workers will lose their jobs and some firms will lose profits in the process. The governor is bound to be criticized by these groups. Second, the transmission mechanism may be slow in achieving the Bank's goal. Will banks react by reducing loans; will interest rates rise; will firms and perhaps consumers downsize their expenditures; how long will the multiplier process take to reduce real national income by the value of the output gap? Third, you hope that neither the *AS* curve

nor the *AD* curves shift unexpectedly while the transmission mechanism is in operation. Otherwise, your recommended reduction in bank reserves may be overkill or inadequate.

(b) Policy option II requires that the Bank of Montand does not change the nominal money supply and that private market forces eliminate the inflation gap. The inflationary gap should trigger factor price increases. Hence, the *AS* curve will shift upward until it reaches point *c*. Critics are sure to point out that the change in the price level is higher than before (compare $P_2 - P_0$ with $P_1 - P_0$). As real national income falls back to its potential level, the governor must be warned to avoid the temptation to increase the nominal supply of money. Notice, that the movement from point *b* to point *c* involves rising prices and falling real output (*stagflation*). Critics are likely to notice the inactivity of the central bank. They may perhaps not appreciate that in time the inflationary gap will be eliminated ultimately by the reductions in real wealth, higher interest rates, and lower net exports (a movement up along AD_1).

6. The appropriate policy advice depends on the causes for the appreciation of the domestic currency, which you should have investigated before briefing Mr. Ford. One cause could have been large increases in net exports. The appropriate policy is for the central bank to tighten its monetary policy. The increase in demand for this country's goods adds directly to aggregate demand. If this shock persists, it will therefore add to domestic inflationary pressures. Hence, an appropriate action by the central bank offsets the positive demand shock by tightening its monetary policy. On the other hand, the domestic currency may have appreciated because large capital inflows were attracted by higher domestic interest rates. Hence, the central bank should pursue an expansionary policy and reduce domestic interest rates.

Additional Multiple-Choice Questions

1.(c) **2.**(b) **3.**(a) **4.**(d) **5.**(d) **6.**(b) **7.**(a) **8.**(b) **9.**(d) **10.**(b) **11.**(c) **12.**(b)**13.**(a) **14.**(d) **15.**(e) **16.**(d) **17.**(c) **18.**(c) **19.**(c)

Explanations for the Asterisked Multiple-Choice Questions

2.(b) When the Bank buys \$100 million of securities from commercial bank customers, bank customers deposit their cash receipts into the banks. Hence, commercial deposits and reserves increase by \$100 million.

4.(d) Having increased commercial bank reserves, the Bank of Canada wants to decrease the interest rate which stimulates more investment activity.

6.(b) An increase in the money supply, with no change in the quantity demanded for money, causes an excess supply of money. Money holders begin to buy bonds with their excess cash. Hence, bond prices rise and yields fall.

9.(d) The equilibrium interest rate is 8 percent when the money supply is 150. At an interest rate of 12 percent, the quantity supplied of money is greater than the quantity demanded. At an interest rate of 4 percent, there is an excess demand for money, or an excess supply of bonds.

13.(a) With a target reserve ratio of 0.10, every \$1 increase in reserves triggers an increase of \$10 in the money supply. The needed change in GDP is \$2 billion, and you were told that every \$500 million increase in the money supply stimulated a \$1 billion increase in GDP. Hence, the needed increase in reserves is \$100 million. This stimulates a \$1 billion increase in the money supply which in turn creates a \$2 billion increase in GDP.

14.(d) A short-run equilibrium at point *c* represents an inflationary gap situation. Hence, the *AD* shift to the right was excessive. Perhaps import purchases were lower than anticipated.

15.(e) $M_D = 3Y - 900\,i \rightarrow 900 = 3\,(1500) - 900\,i \rightarrow 900\,i = 3600 \rightarrow i = 4$.

16.(d) The money multiplier is 20 since the target cash reserve ratio is 0.05. Therefore, if the money supply is 900 the cash reserve must be 900/20 = 45.

17.(c) A decrease in the rate of interest will increase the quantity demanded of money and an excess demand will arise in the money market. The quantity of money demanded is now:
$M_D = 3\,(1500) - 900\,(3) = 4500 - 2700 = 1800$. Therefore, the excess demand for money is
$M_D - M_S = 1800 - 900 = 900$.

PART 11: MACROECONOMIC PROBLEMS AND POLICIES

CHAPTER 30

INFLATION AND DISINFLATION

LO

LEARNING OBJECTIVES

In this chapter you will learn

1 that wages change in response to both output gaps and inflation expectations.

2 how a constant rate of inflation is incorporated into the basic macroeconomic model.

3 how aggregate demand and supply shocks affect inflation and real GDP.

4 what happens when the Bank of Canada validates demand and supply shocks.

5 the three phases of a disinflation.

6 how the cost of disinflation is measured by the sacrifice ratio.

CHAPTER OVERVIEW

Inflation is a rise in the average level of prices. What causes inflation? How can it be eliminated? Chapter 24 illustrated how output gaps caused changes in factor prices (in particular, wages) and shifts in the *AS* curve. This chapter adds two more sources of wage and price inflation: inflationary expectations and supply shocks from non-wage factor price changes. Wage rate demands can be conditioned by expected inflation, and the chapter discusses two alternative ways that expectations are formed: backward-looking expectations and forward-looking expectations (a strong version is the *rational expectations theory*).

Inflationary shocks that are not validated by the central bank tend to be self-correcting, although the length of adjustment may be long. However, inflationary shocks that are validated can create sustained inflation. Validated inflation may also trigger expectations of sustained inflation, including accelerating inflation.

The process used by governments, particularly the monetary authority, to eliminate sustained inflation is extremely difficult. There are no quick fixes. The text outlines three important phases that are required to eliminate a sustained (or entrenched) inflationary situation.

The consequences of inflation are both real and monetary. The textbook introduces a measure of the real costs of disinflation, the *sacrifice ratio*. In the short run demand-shock inflation tends to increase real income above its potential level, whereas supply-shock inflation is accompanied by a decrease in real income below its potential level. In the long run, inflation is a purely monetary phenomenon.

HINTS AND TIPS

The following may help you to avoid some of the most common errors on examinations.

✓ Understand how inflationary expectations lead to upward shifts in the *AS* curve.

✓ Learn how the central bank validates an inflationary process. Validation by the central bank requires changes in the money supply. This is shown diagrammatically by shifts in the *AD* curve.

✓ Learn that in the short run, demand-shock inflation tends to be accompanied by an increase in real GDP above its potential. Without monetary validation, demand shocks cause temporary inflationary gaps that are removed as raising factor prices push the *AS* curve upward, returning real GDP to its potential level but at a higher price level.

✓ Understand that in the short run, supply-shock inflation tends to be accompanied by a decrease in real GDP below its potential level. Without monetary validation, negative supply shocks cause temporary bursts of inflation that are accompanied by recessionary gaps. The gaps are removed as factor prices fall, restoring real GDP to its potential and the price level to its initial level.

✓ Learn that only with continuing monetary validation can inflation initiated by either supply or demand shocks continue indefinitely.

CHAPTER REVIEW

Adding Inflation to the Model

Previous chapters examined how temporary inflationary periods were explained in the *AD–AS* framework. By introducing inflationary expectations in this chapter, the *AD–AS* model is able to explain the existence of sustained inflation. The expectation of some specific inflation rate creates pressure for wages to rise/fall by that rate. Hence, the *AS* curve shifts up and to the left or down and to the right depending on the level of expected inflation. Learn the differences between backward- and forward-looking expectations models. In order for a pure expected inflation to continue, the central bank must validate the expectations by constantly increasing the money supply.

1. **When the measured unemployment rate is below the NAIRU rate,**
   (a) current national income is less than potential national income.
   (b) there is a recessionary output gap.
   (c) frictional and structural unemployment are zero.
   (d) there will be pressure for factor prices to increase.
   (e) the Phillips curve analysis predicts negative percentage changes in wage rates.

2. **Expectations of inflation influence workers' demands for money wage changes. Hence, an expectation of future inflation causes**
   (a) the *AD* curve to shift up and to the right.
   (b) the *AS* curve to shift down and to the right.
   (c) the *AD* curve to shift down and to the left.
   (d) an inflationary gap in which measured unemployment is less than the NAIRU.
   (e) a stagflation as the *AS* curve shifts up and to the left.

3. **According to *Applying Economic Concepts 30-1*, which of the following is a characteristic or implication of backward-looking expectations?**
   (a) Backward-looking expectations tend to change quickly.
   (b) If inflation has been 5 percent for several years in the past, people will expect it to stop in the future.
   (c) People form expectations based on forecast future circumstances.
   (d) People continue to make persistent, systematic errors in forming expectations.
   (e) None of the above.

4. **If there is no supply-shock inflation, expectations of future inflation of 1.5 percent, and an excess-demand inflation of 4 percent, the overall change in actual wages and prices will likely be**
   (a) 1.5 percent.
   (b) 4.0 percent.
   (c) 5.5 percent.
   (d) 2.5 percent.
   (e) None of the above.

5. **A constant inflationary process is said to be *validated* when**
   (a) at least two federal government departments agree on the magnitude of the price increase.
   (b) the initial cause of the inflation was an expansion of government expenditure.
   (c) the Bank of Canada shifts the *AD* curve rightward by reducing the money supply by a constant amount.
   (d) the central bank increases the money supply at such a rate that the expectations of inflation are correct.
   (e) the *AS* curve shifts leftward because of inflationary expectations.

6. **A constant inflation rate is produced when**
   (a) actual inflation is equal to a constant expectation of inflation.
   (b) excess-demand inflation is zero.
   (c) the economy operates at its potential level of GDP.
   (d) the central bank increases the money supply at the same rate as the expected and actual inflation rates such that the *AD* curve shifts rightward.
   (e) All of the above are correct.

7. **Since Canada is both an important consumer and an important exporter of oil, an increase in the international price of oil will cause the Canadian**
   (a) *AD* curve to shift up and to the right while leaving the *AS* curve unchanged
   (b) *AS* curve to shift up and to the left while leaving the *AD* curve unchanged.
   (c) *AD* curve to shift up and to the right and the *AS* curve down and to the right.
   (d) *AD* curve to shift down and to the left and the *AS* curve up and to the left.
   (e) *AD* curve to shift up and to the right and the *AS* curve up and to the left.

Shocks and Policy Responses

This section identifies four different inflation scenarios: demand shocks with and without monetary validation and supply shocks with and without monetary validation. Without validation, demand and supply shocks produce only temporary inflation. With continuing monetary validation, inflation initiated by either supply of demand shocks can continue indefinitely. Hence, in the long run sustained inflation is a monetary phenomenon.

The *acceleration hypothesis* states that when the central bank engages in whatever rate of monetary expansion is needed to hold the inflationary gap constant, the actual inflation rate will accelerate because of the development of inflationary expectations. The effects of introducing inflationary expectations into the Phillips curve framework are discussed in *Extensions in Theory 30-1*.

8. **Which one of the following is not the initiating cause of a demand-shock inflation?**
   (a) An increase in the prices of imported goods and services.
   (b) An increase in exports.
   (c) An increase in the money supply.
   (d) A decrease in tax rates.
   (e) An increase in investment expenditures.

9. **Without monetary validation or expectation effects, which of the following does *not* describe the effects of a positive demand shock?**
   (a) At the initial stage, Y rises above Y^* and the price level increases.
   (b) When an inflationary output gap is created, the *AS* curve begins to shift rightward.
   (c) As the *AS* curve shifts leftward, Y begins to fall back to Y^*.
   (d) As the *AS* curve shifts leftward, P rises more.
   (e) In the long run, real income will not change and the price level, although higher than before, will be stable.

10. **Which of the following does *not* describe the effects of a positive demand shock with monetary validation but without expected inflation?**
   (a) At the initial stage, Y rises above Y^* and the price level increases.
   (b) Money wages increase because of the excess-demand inflation.
   (c) As the *AS* curve shifts leftward, the monetary authority increases the money supply to prevent real GDP from decreasing.
   (d) With monetary validation, the excess-demand inflation is maintained and hence the *AS* curve continues to shift leftward.
   (e) In the long run, real income is restored at Y^* and stable prices will be obtained even though monetary validation continues.

11. **A negative supply-shock inflation is caused by**
   (a) a rise in the price of imported raw materials.
   (b) an increase in government purchases.
   (c) the opening up of a new source of imported materials.
   (d) a decrease in the GST and/or provincial sales taxes.
   (e) an increase in the money supply.

12. **Without monetary validation or expected inflation, which of the following does *not* describe a negative supply-shock inflation?**
   (a) As the *AS* curve shifts upward, prices rise.
   (b) As the *AS* curve shifts upward, the actual unemployment rate decreases below the NAIRU.
   (c) Initially output falls, but as wages fall in response to the recessionary gap, output begins to increase back to its potential level.
   (d) The initial phase is described as stagflation.
   (e) In the initial phase, there is a movement along the *AD* curve.

13. **The reason why the central bank may choose to counteract a negative supply shock by increasing the money supply is**
   (a) to avoid a prolonged recessionary output gap situation.
   (b) to reward workers whose productivity has risen because of the supply shock.
   (c) to reduce expected inflation.
   (d) to counteract the leftward shift in the *AD* curve that will occur when prices rise.
   (e) to avoid an increase in prices.

14. **Which one of the following statements about inflation is true?**
   (a) Price level increases must eventually come to a halt, unless monetary expansion occurs.
   (b) Inflations that are not validated are always of short duration.
   (c) A temporary inflation occurs only with a monetary expansion.
   (d) Assuming that actual national income was initially at its potential level, demand-shock inflation never can have short-run effects on real national income.
   (e) From a long-run equilibrium standpoint, inflation is never sustained.

15. The acceleration hypothesis holds that

(a) inflation will accelerate even if central banks do not engage in validation.
(b) inflation rates will increase without expected inflation.
(c) the *AD* and *AS* curves shift by a constant amount over time.
(d) when the central bank engages in whatever rate of monetary expansion is needed to hold the inflationary gap constant, the rate of actual inflation will accelerate.
(e) the percentage change in nominal wealth must be equal to the inflation rate.

16. Expected inflation

(a) will create a recessionary gap unless it is validated by the central bank.
(b) will generate lower prices if the central bank validates the expected inflation.
(c) will create a long-lasting inflationary gap problem.
(d) means that workers are not sensitive to the effects of unanticipated inflation on their wages.
(e) will cause the *AD* curve to shift up and to the right.

Reducing Inflation

Disinflation means a reduction in the rate of inflation when an inflationary process has been sustained. The policy associated with disinflation imposes costs (reduced real GDP and cyclical unemployment). The textbook delineates three critical phases involved in disinflation. Economists have derived a simple measure of the costs of disinflation based on the depth and length of recession and on the amount of disinflation. This measure is called the *sacrifice ratio*.

17. Which of the following is a characteristic of Phase 1 of breaking a sustained inflation?

(a) The *AS* curve continues to shift upward and to the right.
(b) The inflationary gap increases in size.
(c) The central bank stabilizes the *AD* curve.
(d) A recessionary gap is generated.
(e) Expectations of future inflation increase.

18. Which of the following does the textbook identify as a characteristic of Phase 2 of breaking a sustained inflation?

(a) Slowing the rate of monetary expansion below the current rate of inflation.
(b) An initial demand and expected inflation becomes expected inflation.
(c) Productivity rises more than wages.
(d) At the end of the stagflation, unit costs fall, thus shifting the *AS* curve downward.
(e) At the end of the stagflation, the central bank may increase the money supply to shorten the recessionary gap phase.

19. The duration of the recession that develops when a central bank stops validating a sustained inflation

(a) depends on whether inflationary expectations are backward- or forward-looking.
(b) is determined by coincidental leftward shifts of the *AD* curve.
(c) will typically be very short according to Keynesians.
(d) will typically be very long according to Monetarists.
(e) must be extremely short if expectations are backward-looking.

20. **The cost of disinflation**
(a) is the cost of the recession that is needed to dampen inflationary tendencies.
(b) depends on the size and duration of the recession that is generated.
(c) is greater if inflationary expectations are highly backward-looking.
(d) depends on the extent to which inflation must decrease.
(e) All of the above.

21. **The sacrifice ratio is defined as**
(a) the extent to which inflation redistributes income from the poor to the rich.
(b) the cumulative loss in real GDP due to inflation.
(c) the extent to which potential GDP declines because of inflation.
(d) the cumulative loss in real GDP expressed as a percentage of potential GDP divided by the number of percentage points by which inflation has fallen.
(e) the number of percentage points by which inflation has fallen divided by the cumulative loss in GDP.

SHORT-ANSWER QUESTIONS

1. Explain briefly what is meant by the following.
(a) Demand inflation versus supply inflation.

(b) Monetary validation inflation versus no monetary validation.

(c) Constant versus accelerating inflation.

2. Briefly explain each concept and illustrate it in a graph. Assume *no* expected inflation and that neither potential GDP nor the NAIRU is influenced by the actual path of changes in national income or unemployment
(a) A negative supply shock that is validated thereafter by the central bank.

Figure 30-1

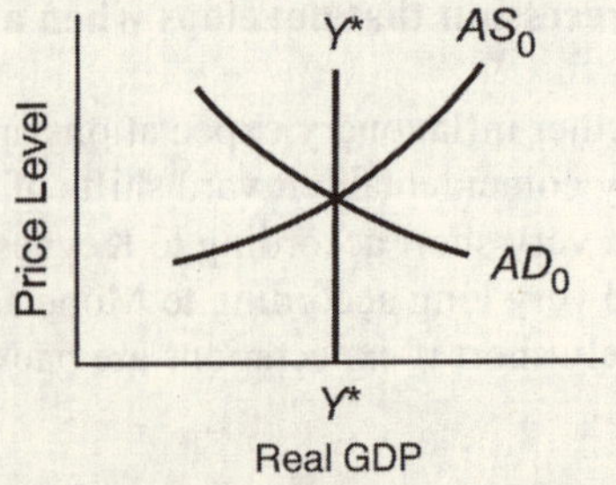

(b) A negative supply shock with no monetary validation by the central bank.

Figure 30-2

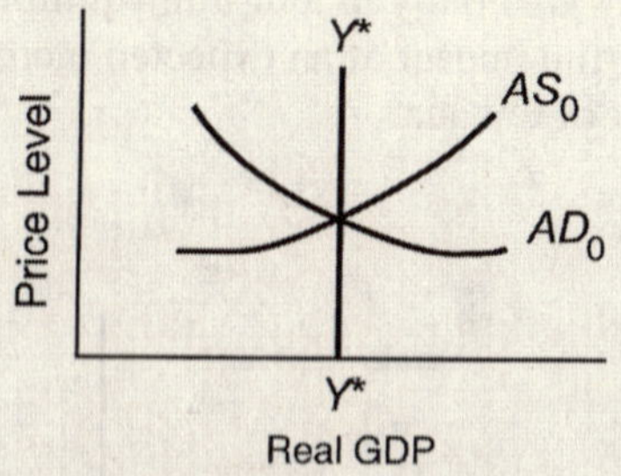

(c) A positive demand shock with no monetary validation.

Figure 30-3

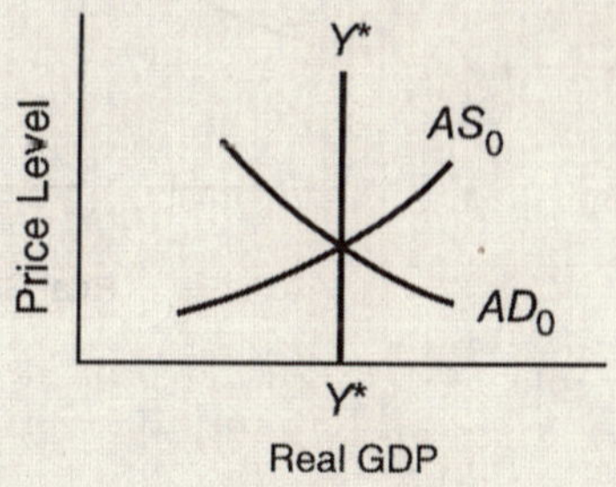

(d) A positive demand-shock inflation that is validated thereafter.

Figure 30-4

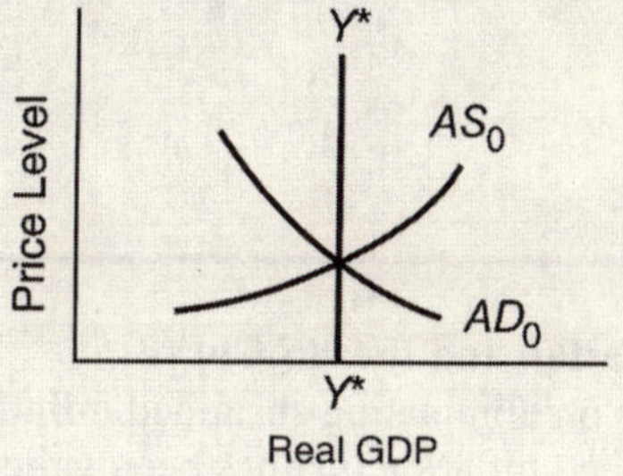

3. Explain briefly what is meant by the following:

(a) Output gap inflation.

(b) Supply-shock inflation.

(c) Expected inflation.

(d) Forward-looking expectations

(e) Backward-looking expectations.

4. Assuming the economy is initially in long-run equilibrium ($Y = Y^*$), briefly explain and graph the short-run and long-run impact of an expected increase in prices. Assume no monetary validation by the Bank of Canada.

Figure 30-5

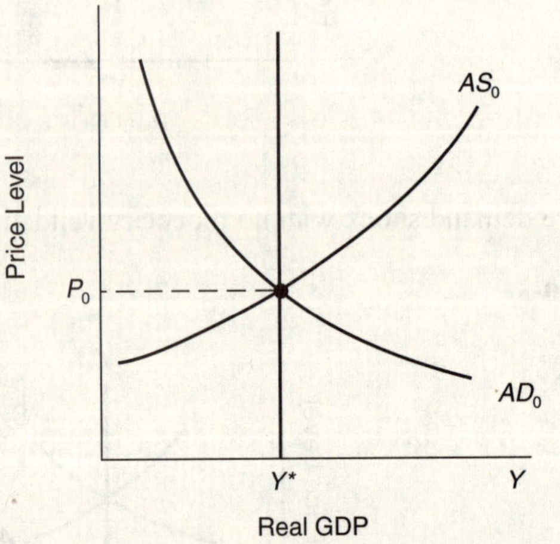

EXERCISES

1. **Expectations of Inflation and the *AS* Curve**
This exercise focuses on eliminating sustained inflation. Suppose that an economy has been experiencing entrenched inflation that has been validated by monetary policy. The starting point for this example is point *A* in Figure 30-6.

(a) If the central bank stops expanding the money supply, what do you predict will happen during Phase 1 to the levels of real national income and the price level? What will happen to the *AS* curve?

(b) During Phase 2, inflationary expectations are still present such that the *AS* curve shifts to AS_2. Indicate the new (temporary) equilibrium point on the graph. What is the value of the recessionary gap? What are the values for real national income and the price level?

Figure 30-6

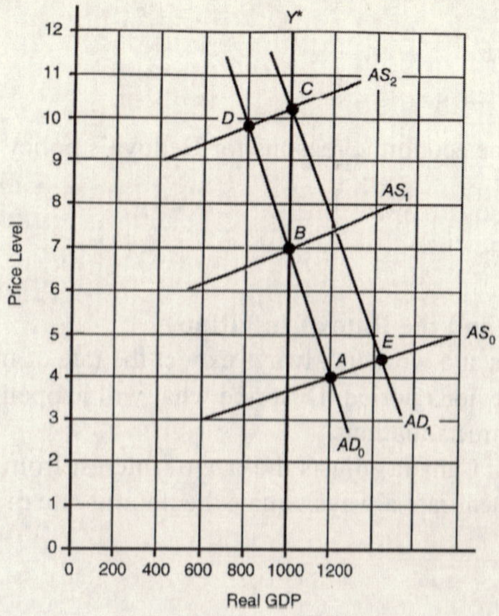

(c) After inflationary expectations are reversed, and assuming no changes in the money supply (*AD* remains at AD_0), what are your predictions for the equilibrium levels of real national income and price?

(d) Suppose that the economy is in short-run equilibrium at point *D* and that the central bank increases the money supply sufficiently to shift the *AD* curve to AD_1. What will be the equilibrium levels of real national income and price?

2. The Impact of Supply Shocks

A country has been experiencing sustained inflation and an increasing unemployment rate above the NAIRU. Fred C. Dobbs, the finance critic of the opposition party in Parliament, rises in his place and asks the finance minister, Al Bedoya, to explain the situation and to indicate what the government intends to do. The minister responds that the problem has been caused initially by continual supply shocks of higher prices of imported intermediate goods that the domestic economy cannot produce. Bedoya is pleased to announce that no further supply shocks are anticipated and assures Dobbs that his government has been quite responsible by keeping its expenditures and the nominal money supply increases at appropriate levels. To be thorough, he expresses his concern that wages have been rising because of the supply shocks.

Dobbs, an avid Monetarist, jumps to his feet once again and demands that Bedoya instruct the central bank to decrease immediately the nominal stock of money. The minister responds that he is not prepared to do any such thing. Hopefully, with the elimination of these supply shocks, the economy will adjust back to full employment with price stability. He also alludes to the fact that he is prepared to consider increasing the money supply to speed up the process to full employment.

From across the floor of Parliament, Dobbs yells to Bedoya, "Shame, resign!"

(a) Explain why wages are rising.

(b) Comment on why Dobbs believes that a decrease in the nominal money supply is an appropriate policy stance.

(c) Provide some economic reasons for Bedoya's policy stance.

3. Monetary Policy and the Rate of Inflation

Suppose that firms and workers always expect the rate of inflation to be equal to the rate of inflation in the previous period. Describe what will happen to the inflation rate over time in each of the next three situations.

(a) The Bank of Canada adjusts the rate of interest from year to year so that the unemployment rate always equals the natural rate of unemployment.

(b) The Bank of Canada adjusts the interest rate from year to year in order to keep the unemployment rate 1 percentage point below the NAIRU.

(c) The Bank of Canada adjusts the interest rate from year to year in order to keep the unemployment rate 1 percentage point above the NAIRU.

EXTENSION EXERCISES

E1. Expectations of Inflation

This problem illustrates how backward-looking expectations might be generated. A simple equation is presented that describes how individuals form inflationary expectations for next year by looking at the central bank's inflation target and current inflation rates. You should reread *Applying Economic Concepts 30-1* before you attempt this exercise.

The expectation of inflation equation is given by

$\pi^*_{t+1} = \theta\pi^T + (1 - \theta)\,\pi_t$, where

π^*_{t+1} is the expected inflation rate for year t + 1 as estimated in year t.

π^T is the central bank's announced target rate.

π_t is the actual inflation rate in year t.

θ (Greek letter theta) represents a weight; $0 < \theta < 1$.

Suppose inflationary expectations are estimated over an eight-year period. The table below shows values for both the central bank's target inflation and actual inflation.

Year (t)	π_t	π^T	π^*_{t+1} $\theta = 0.4$	π^*_{t+1} $\theta = 0.9$
1	10	2		
2	9	2		
3	6	2		
4	3	2		
5	2	2		
6	2	2		
7	2	2		
8	2	2		

(a) Using the expectations formula and $\theta = 0.4$, estimate the values of expected inflation for each year in column 4.

(b) If θ had been equal to 0.9, what would have been the value of π^*_3? Remember, expectations in year 3 are based on values in year 2. Do the same for π^*_4.

(c) Which of the two weights represents "more" backward-looking expectations? Explain.

(d) Given the different speed of adjustment of inflationary expectations, predict which disinflation is more costly in terms of lost output, $\theta = 0.4$ or $\theta = 0.9$. Recall that the textbook makes the point that the costs of disinflation depend on the size and duration of recessionary gaps that are needed to eliminate inflationary expectations.

E2. The Determination of Equilibrium Income and the Price Level

Consider the *AD–AS* model of the economy where the expressions for the *AD* and *AS* curves are, respectively:

$$P = 600 - 0.5\,Y$$
$$P = P_{-1} + 0.5\,(Y - Y^*),$$

where *Y* is real income, *Y** is full-employment income, and P_{-1} is the price level in the previous period. The economy is originally in long-run equilibrium—i.e., real income is equal to full employment income in period 0 and $P_{-1} = 100$.

(a) What is the value of *Y** in this economy? What is the initial equilibrium value of *P*?

(b) Suppose that in period 1 there is a permanent increase in aggregate demand, and the expression for *AD* becomes $P = 800 - 0.5\,Y$. What are the short-run equilibrium values of *Y* and *P* in period 1?

(c) Explain what happens to the *AS* curve in period 2. What are the short-run equilibrium values of *Y* and *P* in period 2?

(d) Explain what happens to the *AS* curve in subsequent periods. What will be the new long-run equilibrium values of *Y* and *P*?

ADDITIONAL MULTIPLE-CHOICE QUESTIONS

Questions 1 through 4 refer to Figure 30-7.

Figure 30-7

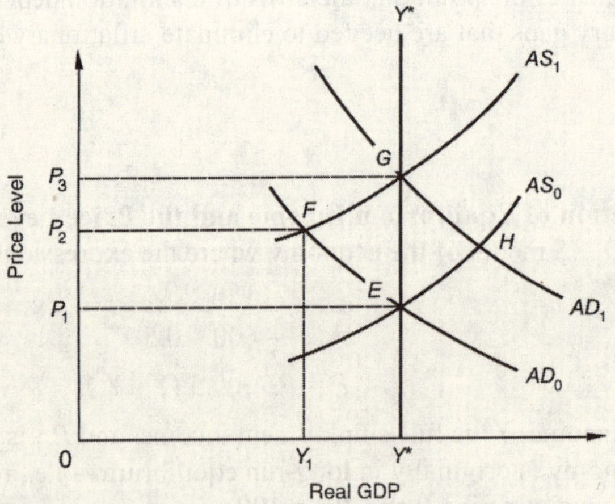

***1. Starting from equilibrium at point *E* and assuming no monetary validation, a supply shock that shifts the *AS* curve from AS_0 to AS_1 results in**

(a) a recessionary output gap puts downward pressure on wages and prices, slowly shifting the *AS* curve back downward to AS_0 (point *E*).
(b) an aggregate demand increases from AD_0 to AD_1.
(c) a long-run equilibrium at point *G*.
(d) a long-run equilibrium at point *F* if wage increases are less than productivity changes.
(e) a long-run equilibrium at point *F* since the potential GDP must decrease.

2. **Starting from equilibrium at point *E*, if the short-run aggregate supply curve shifts from AS_0 to AS_1 and there is complete monetary validation,**
   (a) real national income temporarily falls to Y_1, then is stabilized at Y^*.
   (b) the aggregate demand curve shifts to the right and passes through point *G*.
   (c) the price level rises to P_3, assuming that no inflationary expectations are generated.
   (d) in the long run, inflation is a monetary phenomenon; that is, real macroeconomic variables are not affected.
   (e) All of the above.

3. **Starting from equilibrium at point *E*, the aggregate demand curve shifts from AD_0 to AD_1. If there is no monetary validation, long-run equilibrium is at**
   (a) point *H*, if no inflationary expectations are generated.
   (b) point *E*, because the *AD* curve shifts leftward when the price level rises.
   (c) point *G*, if no inflationary expectations are generated.
   (d) point *F*, because the *AD* curve shifts leftward if inflationary expectations are generated.
   (e) point *H*, where actual output exceeds potential output.

4. **Starting from equilibrium at point *E*, the aggregate demand curve shifts from AD_0 to AD_1. If there is no monetary validation,**
   (a) the price level may temporarily increase to more than P_3 because of inflationary expectations.
   (b) a recessionary gap may be temporarily created because of inflationary expectations.
   (c) long-run equilibrium will be at point *G*, even though short-run inflationary expectations have been created.
   (d) the actual unemployment rate may be above the NAIRU temporarily if price expectations cause a recessionary gap.
   (e) All of the above.

*5. **If supply-shock inflation is –2.6 percent and expected inflation is 3.0 percent, then**
   (a) the *AS* curve shifts to the left and actual inflation is 3.0 percent.
   (b) the *AS* curve shifts to the right and actual inflation is 3.0 percent.
   (c) the *AS* curve shifts to the left and actual inflation is 0.4 percent.
   (d) an inflationary gap situation is created.
   (e) the *AD* curve shifts to the right and actual inflation is 0.4 percent.

*6. **If the economy is initially in long-run equilibrium, what is the value of the sacrifice ratio if the accumulated loss in real GDP is $120 million, potential GDP is $600 million, and the needed reduction in price inflation is 4 percentage points?**
   (a) 4. (b) 30.
   (c) 5. (d) 150.
   (e) 1.25.

7. **The interpretation of a sacrifice ratio of 3 is that**
   (a) the central bank's inflation target must have been 3 percent.
   (b) the Phillips curve must have shifted by 3 percent.
   (c) the output gap must have been 3 percent of the nation's potential GDP.
   (d) it costs 3 percent of real GDP for each percentage point of inflation that is reduced.
   (e) real GDP will fall by a multiplier effect of 3 if inflation is reduced by 1 percentage point.

***8. According to the material in *Extensions in Theory 30-1* an "augmented" Phillips curve**
(a) is one which incorporates the level of the government's budget surplus.
(b) is identical to a vertical line representing potential real GDP.
(c) demonstrates how the Phillips curve's position is determined by various levels of price expectations.
(d) illustrates that changes in price expectations have no role in determining the rate at which money wages (and prices) change.
(e) shows clearly that the NAIRU is influenced by inflationary expectations.

9. The key point about constant, purely expected inflation is that
(a) no excess-demand effect is present.
(b) wages rise at the expected rate of inflation.
(c) the labour shortages that accompany an inflationary gap are absent.
(d) the labour surpluses that accompany a recessionary gap are absent.
(e) All of the above are correct.

In answering Questions 10 to 12, assume that the economy is initially in long-run equilibrium—i.e., that output is at the full-employment level and that the actual and the expected rate of inflation are equal.

***10. In the absence of monetary validation, a permanent increase in aggregate demand will**
(a) cause both output and the price level to increase in the long run.
(b) cause the price level to increase in the short run but not in the long run.
(c) cause the price level to increase while leaving output unchanged in the long run.
(d) leave both output and the price level unchanged in the long run.
(e) cause the price level to increase more in the short run than in the long run.

***11. If the Bank of Canada responds to a negative supply shock by implementing expansionary monetary policy, then**
(a) inflation will accelerate even more.
(b) the inflation rate and the rate of unemployment will further increase.
(c) firms will further increase their product prices and cut their production.
(d) cost of production will be reduced and the *AS* curve will shift back to the right.
(e) inflation will slow down but unemployment will increase even more.

12. If expectations are backward-looking and in the absence of monetary validation, a positive supply shock will
(a) permanently increase the price level.
(b) permanently reduce the level of output.
(c) increase the price level in the short run but not in the long run.
(d) reduce the price level in the short run but not in the long run.
(e) reduce the level of output in the short run but not in the long run.

SOLUTIONS

Chapter Review

1.(d) **2.**(e) **3.**(d) **4.**(c) **5.**(d) **6.**(e) **7.**(e) **8.**(a) **9.**(b) **10.**(e) **11.**(a) **12.**(b) **13.**(a) **14.**(a) **15.**(d) **16.**(a) **17.**(c) **18.**(b) **19.**(a) **20.**(e) **21.**(d)

Short-Answer Questions

1. (a) Inflation that is caused by a rightward shift in the *AD* curve is called *demand inflation*. The shift in the *AD* curve could have been caused by a reduction in taxes, by an increase in autonomous expenditure, or by an increase in the money supply. Any rise in the price level originating from increases in firms' costs that are not caused by excess demand in the market for factors of production is called *supply inflation*. An example of a supply shock is a rise in the costs of imported raw materials. Another example is a rise in wages not created by excess demand in the labour market. The rise in wages may be caused by expectations of future inflation.

(b) When the central bank increases the money supply at such a rate that the expectations of inflation become correct, it is said to be validating the expectations. In addition, if the central bank increases the money supply that sustains a supply-shock inflation (and avoids stagflation or the need for wages/prices to fall), the central bank is said to be validating the supply-side inflation. We can also speak of the central bank validating demand-shock inflation.

(c) Constant inflation represents a sustained percentage increase in the price level. Decision makers anticipate a constant annual percentage increase in the price level. However, when the central bank engages in whatever rate of monetary expansion is needed to hold the inflationary gap constant, according to the acceleration hypothesis, the actual inflation rate will accelerate—the inflation rate increases at an increasing rate.

2. (a) Monetary validation of a single supply shock causes input costs, the price level, and money supply all to move in the same direction. The negative supply shock is represented as a leftward shift of the *AS* curve. Monetary validation shifts the *AD* curve rightward. Equilibrium shifts from E_0 to E_2.

Figure 30-8

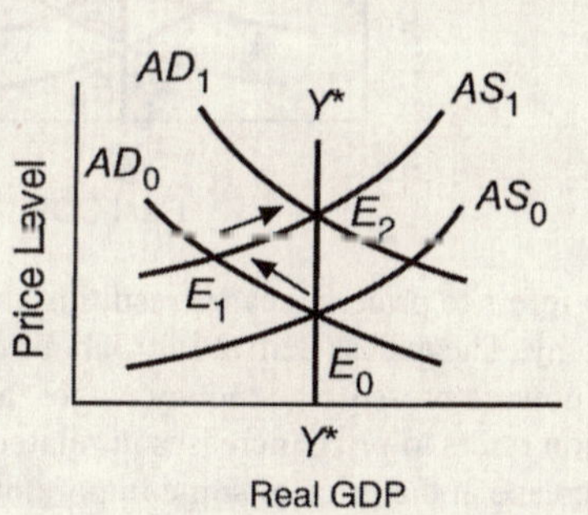

(b) The supply curve shifts to the left as a result of the supply shock, but without monetary validation unemployment puts downward pressure on wages and costs, shifting the *AS* curve back to AS_0.

Figure 30-9

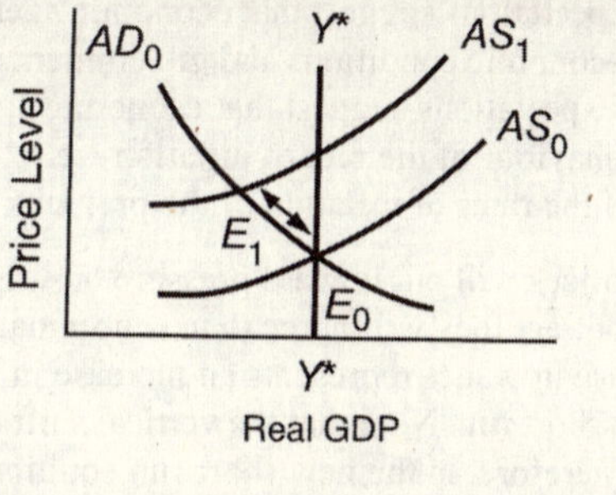

(c) The demand shock shifts the *AD* curve and creates an inflationary gap; this causes wages to rise, shifting the *AS* curve to the left. The monetary adjustment mechanism causes a movement along the *AD* curve, with the rise in price level eliminating the inflationary gap (at E_2).

Figure 30-10

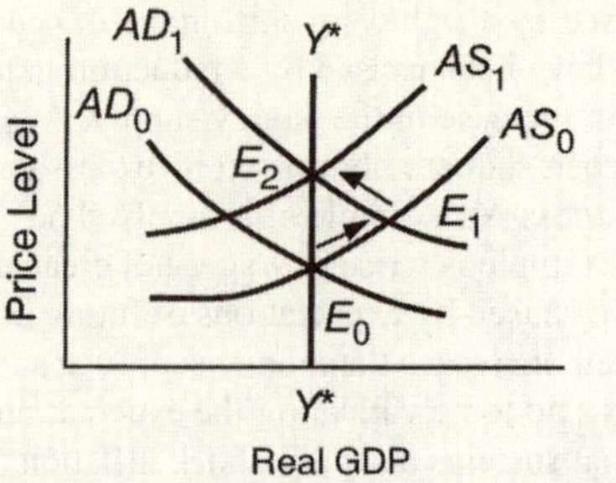

(d) The adjustment process in (c) is frustrated with monetary validation; increases in the money supply shift the *AD* curve to the right, and inflation is sustained. The economy moves along the vertical path indicated by the arrow.

Figure 30-11

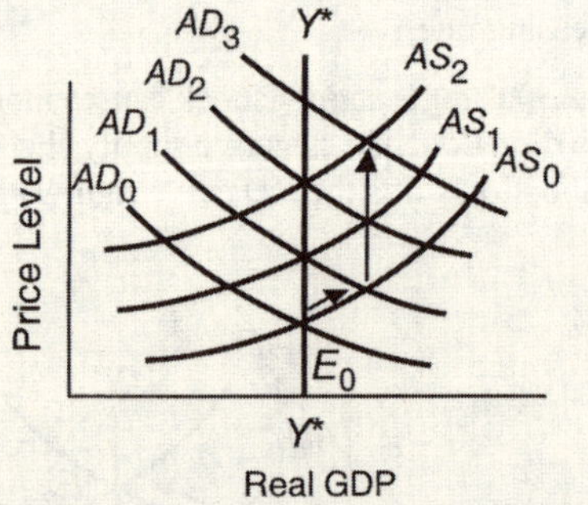

3. (a) Output-gap inflation refers to price increases resulting from wage increases caused by an excess demand in the economy. The excess demand for labour that is associated with an inflationary output gap ($AD > AS$) puts upward pressure on money wages, and thus also on prices.

(b) Supply-shock inflation refers to price increases unrelated to wage increases—e.g., to price increases resulting from an increase in the price of some important material input. This increase in costs of production is also transferred to buyers of final goods and services in the form of higher prices for these goods and services.

(c) Expected inflation refers to price increases resulting from wage increases caused by expectations of future inflation. When firms and workers negotiate wages, expectations of inflation put upward pressure on wages in the same way as an excess demand for labour does.

(d) Forward-looking expectations suggest that economic agents form their expectations about inflation based on expected economic conditions and government policies, and not on past inflation rates.

(e) Backward-looking expectations suggest that economic agents form their expectations about inflation based on the past behaviour of the rate of inflation—e.g., the expected rate of inflation could be some weighted average of the rates of inflation of the previous *n* periods.

4. An expected increase in prices will put upward pressure on wages. Indeed, when firms and workers negotiate a new labour contract they will agree to new nominal wages that will reflect these expectations. The corresponding increase in wages represents an increase in costs of production and thus the AS_0 curve will shift up to AS_1 in the short run. Note that the vertical shift of the *AS* curve at $Y = Y^*$ represents the expected increase in *P*. Therefore, in the new short-run equilibrium, *P* will be higher than before but *Y* will be below Y^*—i.e., the economy will experience stagflation. Also note that the *actual* increase in *P* is less that the initially *expected* increase in *P*.

Assuming backward-looking expectations and given that *P* increased by less than expected in period 1, firms and workers will agree now to a lower nominal wage when they negotiate a new labour contract in period 2. This represents a decrease in costs of production and the *AS* curve will shift down—and thus *P* will fall and *Y* will increase. This process will continue period after period until a new long-run equilibrium is achieved once the *AS* curve has shifted all the way back to its initial position (AS_0). In the long run, therefore, expectations of inflation will have no impact on either *P* or *Y* if there is no monetary validation by the Bank of Canada.

Figure 30-12

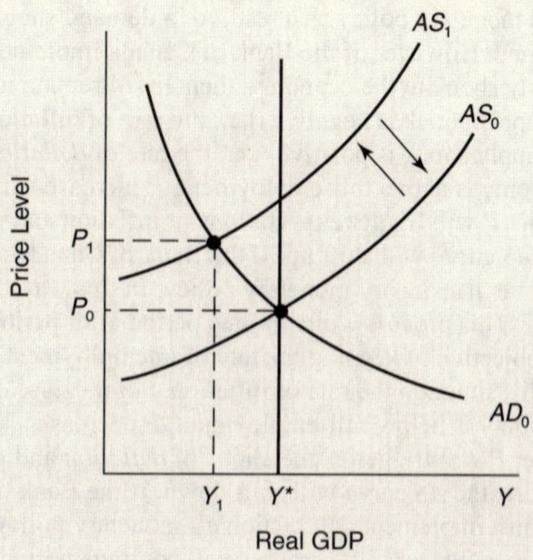

Exercises

1. (a) Under the combined influence of an inflationary gap and expectations of continued inflation, wages continue to rise and hence the *AS* curve continues to shift. In terms of the graph, the *AS* curve shifts leftward to AS_1 and intersects potential GDP at point *B*. At this point, real national income is at its potential level (1000) and the price level is 7.
   (b) Continuing price expectations shift the *AS* curve to AS_2. This curve intersects AD_0 at point *D*. A recessionary gap of 200 has been created. Real national income is 800, and the price level is approximately 10.
   (c) The recessionary gap is likely to reduce inflationary expectations and wage rates. Hence, the *AS* curve will tend to shift rightward (slowly) to point *B* (AS_1). There will be a movement along AD_0 from point *D* to point *B*, at which the price level is 7 and the economy is producing at its potential level.
   (d) This question differs from (c) in that the central banking authority increases the money supply, perhaps to speed up the process of attaining potential national income. The *AD* curve shifts rightward with monetary expansion. The new equilibrium point is point *C*, at which the price level is approximately 10 and real national income is 1000.

2. (a) The repeated supply shocks that increased domestic prices likely have generated cost of living increases and possibly expectations of future inflation. To protect the level of real wages, workers have been demanding higher money wages.
   (b) We suspect that Dobbs believes a decreased money supply will dampen inflationary expectations at a faster rate. Moreover, the contractionary money policy would certainly increase the value of the recessionary gap and workers might be more prone to lower their wages. Thus, although unemployment would be higher than before, the speed at which the economy adjusts back to price stability at potential output may be increased.
   (c) Bedoya does not want to increase the recessionary gap as Dobbs suggests. Perhaps he believes that prices will soon fall as workers lower their wage demands when supply shocks stop. Alternatively, when he is convinced that inflationary expectations have subsided and that wages are falling, he may be prepared to speed up the process to full employment by increasing the money supply. During the monetary expansion, prices will rise as the *AD* curve shifts to the right. Hopefully, the price increases will not rekindle inflationary expectations.

3. **(a)** In order to keep the economy always at full employment, the Bank of Canada must implement expansionary monetary policy every time a situation of excess supply develops and contractionary monetary policy every time a situation of excess demand develops. If the Bank of Canada implements countercyclical monetary policy as a result of a demand shock to the economy, both *P* and *Y* will remain unchanged. However, if the Bank of Canada implements countercyclical monetary policy as a result of a supply shock to the economy, then *Y* will remain unchanged but *P* will either increase further if the supply shock is negative (i.e., the rate of inflation will increase over time), or decrease further if the supply shock is positive (i.e., the rate of *deflation* will increase over time).

(b) When the economy is above full-employment, *P* increases. In turn, if expectations are backward-looking, a higher *P* will trigger expectations of inflation and put upward pressure on nominal wages. Therefore, the *AS* curve will shift up. If the Bank of Canada doesn't want *Y* to decrease toward *Y**, it must implement expansionary monetary policy. In this way, *Y* will be kept above *Y**, but *P* will increase further. This process will continue period after period as long as the Bank of Canada maintains the objective of keeping the rate of unemployment 1 percentage point below the NAIRU. Therefore, in this situation the rate of inflation will increase over time.

(c) When the economy is below full-employment, *P* decreases. In turn, if expectations are backward-looking, a lower *P* will trigger expectations of *deflation* and put downward pressure on nominal wages. Therefore, the *AS* curve will shift down. If the Bank of Canada doesn't want *Y* to increase toward *Y**, it must implement contractionary monetary policy. In this way, *Y* will be kept below *Y**, but *P* will decrease further. This process will continue period after period as long as the Bank of Canada maintains the objective of keeping the rate of unemployment 1 percentage point above the NAIRU. Therefore, in this situation the rate of *deflation* will increase over time.

Extension Exercises

E1. (a) π^*_{t+1} $(\theta = .4) = 6.8, 6.2, 4.4, 2.6, 2.0, 2.0, 2.0, 2.0$.

(b) $\pi^*_3 = .9\,(2) + .1\,(9) = 2.7$.

$\pi^*_4 = .9\,(2) + .1\,(6) = 2.4$.

(c) $\theta = 0.4$ is the more backward-looking expectation. It puts more weight on this year's inflation rate and less weight on the central bank's target.

(d) When $\theta = 0.9$, expected inflation approaches the central bank's target much faster. Hence, the recession's duration will be shorter. It follows that the costs of disinflation will be higher for $\theta = 0.4$ than for $\theta = 0.9$.

E2. (a) If the economy is in long-run equilibrium, then $Y = Y^*$ and, given the equation for the *AS* curve, $P^* = P_{-1}$.

Therefore, given the equation for the *AD* curve:

$P^* = 600 - 0.5\,Y^* \rightarrow 100 = 600 - 0.5\,Y^* \rightarrow 0.5\,Y^* = 500 \rightarrow Y^* = 1000$.

(b) $AD = AS \rightarrow 800 - 0.5\,Y = 100 + 0.5\,(Y - 1000) \rightarrow Y = 1200$ and

$P = 800 - 0.5\,Y = 800 - 0.5\,(1200) = 200$.

(c) Assuming backward-looking expectations, wages will increase when firms and workers negotiate a new labour contract in period 2 since *P* increased in period 1. Therefore, costs of production increase and the *AS* curve shifts up in period 2. The equation for the *AS* curve in period 2 is

$P = P_{-1} + 0.5\,(Y - Y^*) = 200 + 0.5\,(Y - 1000)$,

and equilibrium *Y* and *P* in period 2 are

$AD = AS \rightarrow 800 - 0.5\,Y = 200 + 0.5\,(Y - 1000) \rightarrow Y = 1100$

$P = 800 - 0.5\,Y = 800 - 0.5\,(1100) = 250$

(d) Since *P* increased again in period 2, wages will increase once again when firms and workers negotiate a new labour contract in period 3. Therefore, cost of production increase further and the *AS* curve shifts up again in period 3. This process will continue period after period as long as *P* keeps increasing.

A new long-run equilibrium will be reached when $Y = Y^* = 1000$ once again—i.e., when the *AS* intersects the *AD* curve at $Y = 1000$.

The value of *P* in this new long-run equilibrium will be

$P = 800 - 0.5\,Y = 800 - 0.5\,(1000) = 300$.

Additional Multiple-Choice Questions

1.(a) **2.**(e) **3.**(c) **4.**(e) **5.**(c) **6.**(c) **7.**(d) **8.**(c) **9.**(e) **10.**(c) **11.**(a) **12.**(d)

Explanations for the Asterisked Multiple-Choice Questions

1.(a) The supply shock shifts the *AS* curve upward, creating a recessionary gap. The negative output gap puts pressure on wages and prices to fall. As they do, the *AS* curve begins to shift rightward until the equilibrium at *E* is restored (and GDP is at its potential level).

5.(c) Supply shock inflation plus expectation inflation equal +0.4 percent inflation. Hence, the *AS* curve shifts leftward.

6.(c) The sacrifice ratio is the cost in percentage terms of real GDP to reduce inflation for each percentage point. In this case, the cumulative loss is 20 percent of potential GDP and the needed reduction in inflation is 4 percentage points. Hence, the sacrifice ratio is 20/4 = 5.0.

8.(c) The Phillips curve is a relationship between the unemployment rate and the rate of change of wages. An augmented Phillips curve is one which incorporates the rate of expected inflation. The Phillips curve shifts upward by the amount of the expected inflation.

10.(c) An increase in *AD* will cause both *P* and *Y* to rise in the short run. Assuming backward-looking expectations, the increase in *P* will cause wages to rise when firms and workers renegotiate them in the next period, and thus the *AS* curve will shift up in the next period. This process will continue period after period until a new long-run equilibrium is achieved when *Y* is once again equal to *Y** but *P* is higher than before.

11.(a) A negative supply shock will cause the *AS* curve to shift up and to the left. In the absence of any government policy, *P* will thus increase and *Y* will decrease in the short run. If the Bank of Canada implements expansionary monetary policy—i.e., decreases its target of the overnight rate of interest—to prevent the fall in *Y*, then the *AD* curve will shift up and to the right. Therefore, if the Bank of Canada is successful *Y* will not change but *P* will increase even further—i.e., the rate of inflation will accelerate even more.

CHAPTER 31

UNEMPLOYMENT FLUCTUATIONS AND THE NAIRU

LO LEARNING OBJECTIVES

In this chapter you will learn

1 how employment and unemployment change over the short and long runs.

2 the difference between the New Classical and New Keynesian views of unemployment fluctuations.

3 the causes of frictional and structural unemployment.

4 the various forces that cause the NAIRU to change.

5 about policies that might be used to reduce unemployment.

CHAPTER OVERVIEW

This chapter examines employment and unemployment in Canada. In the short run there can be large gross flows into and out of employment and unemployment. Several kinds of unemployment are discussed. Cyclical unemployment changes when there are short-term fluctuations in economic activity around potential level of GDP. Structural unemployment that occurs from the need to reallocate resources due to changing patterns of demand and supply, and frictional unemployment that occurs as people move from job to job as a normal part of labour turnover are two long-run components of the NAIRU. These distinctions are important in deciding what policies should be used to reduce the unemployment rate.

The chapter outlines the opposing views of the New Classical and New Keynesian schools concerning the flexibility of wages to adjust to cyclical unemployment and the existence of involuntary unemployment. The efficiency wage theory also explains why firms might choose to pay wages higher than the minimum amount that would induce workers to work for them. The chapter concludes by explaining the determinants of the size of the NAIRU and the potential policies to reduce the NAIRU.

HINTS AND TIPS

The following may help you to avoid some of the most common errors on examinations.

✓ Learn that if an economy operates at its NAIRU, its measured unemployment rate is greater than zero because of the existence of frictional and structural unemployment.

✓ Learn the determinants of cyclical, frictional, and structural unemployment.

✓ Learn the key differences in assumptions and predictions associated with the New Classical and New Keynesian explanations for short-run cyclical unemployment. Sticky or rigid wages are a key feature of the New Keynesian theory. It would be useful for you to review the textbook's Table 31-1 for a comparison of the two explanations.

✓ Learn the distinctions between stocks and flows and gross and net flows in the labour market. Stocks are measured at a point in time; flows occur over time. Review the figure in the textbook box *Applying Economic Concepts 31-1,* as well as the matrix approach introduced in the Chapter Review section of the *Study Guide,* below.

CHAPTER REVIEW

Employment and Unemployment

The importance of stocks and flows in the labour market is outlined in the textbook box *Applying Economic Concepts 31-1.* To better understand the issues related to flows and stocks among three "states" of the labour force (employed E, unemployed U, and not in the labour force N) between two time periods, t and t+1, you might find the following matrix helpful. There are questions in the *Additional Multiple-Choice Questions* section that further test your comprehension of labour market flows and stocks.

	E_{t+1}	U_{t+1}	N_{t+1}
E_t	EE	EU	EN
U_t	UE	UU	UN
N_t	NE	NU	NN

The element UE is the *flow* of persons who were unemployed in period t and who became employed in period t+1. The element NU is *flow* of individuals who were not in the labour force in period t who entered the labour force in t+1, but who did not find work. In summary, the flows are represented by a two-digit code. The first digit is labour-force status in period t, while the second digit refers to labour-force status in period t+1. The *stock* of employed workers in period t is the sum of the elements EE and EU and EN.

Questions 1 to 7 refer to the above matrix.

1. Which element of the matrix represents cases where employed workers lost their jobs or quit their jobs and became unemployed between t and t+1?

(a) UE.
(b) NU.
(c) EU.
(d) UU.
(e) EE.

2. The elements NU and NE represent flows of individuals between t and t+1 who are

(a) entering the labour force in t+1.
(b) leaving the labour force in t +1.
(c) entering the labour force in t.
(d) leaving the labour force in t.
(e) unemployed individuals finding jobs in t+1.

3. The flow of new entrants to the labour force between the two time periods who do not find work in t+1 would appear in element

(a) UE.
(b) UN.
(c) EN.
(d) NU.
(e) UU.

4. **The flows *out of unemployment* between the two time periods are represented by the elements**
(a) UN and UE. (b) UU and EE.
(c) NU and EU. (d) UU.
(e) EU.

5. **The flows *into unemployment* between the two time periods consist of**
(a) individuals who were employed and who become unemployed.
(b) workers who were employed and who exited from the labour force.
(c) workers who entered the labour force and became employed immediately.
(d) the element NU.
(e) Both (a) and (d) are correct.

6. **If the flows *into unemployment* exceed the flows *out of unemployment*, the stock of unemployed workers will**
(a) not be affected.
(b) increase.
(c) equal the stock of employed workers.
(d) decrease.
(e) decrease because the labour force increases.

7. **The total stock of unemployed persons in period t is**
(a) UE + UU + UN. (b) UU.
(c) EU + UU + NU. (d) UN.
(e) NN + EE.

8. **The measured unemployment rate will rise if**
(a) the percentage increase in employment is greater than the percentage increase in the labour force.
(b) the percentage increase in total unemployment is less than the percentage change in the labour force.
(c) with a constant labour force, the number of new jobs created is fewer than the number of jobs lost.
(d) actual income rises temporarily from its potential level.
(e) more discouraged, unemployed workers leave the labour force.

9. **Which of the following is a potential cost of unemployment?**
(a) The potential output of valuable resources is wasted.
(b) Workers who would like to work at prevailing wages may stay out of the labour force.
(c) The unemployed may contribute to social unrest in some societies.
(d) Workers who are unemployed for prolonged periods miss job training opportunities.
(e) All or any of the above.

Unemployment Fluctuations

Cyclical unemployment occurs when fluctuations in aggregate demand cause real output to fluctuate around its potential level. It is the difference between the actual level of unemployment and the NAIRU. If all labour markets had fully flexible wage rates, we would observe cyclical fluctuations in employment and in the wage rate but no changes in the amount of cyclical unemployment. Hence, the key issues around the creation of involuntary unemployment are the reasons why wages may decline slowly during recessionary output gap situations.

The New Classical theories cannot explain involuntary unemployment or the existence of cyclical unemployment in the short term. These theories seek to explain employment as the outcome of voluntary decisions made by individuals. Cyclical fluctuations in employment can occur because of changes in technology that lead to changes in the demand for labour. Moreover, changes in the willingness of individuals to work lead to changes in the supply of labour, and thus to fluctuations in the level of employment and real wages.

New Keynesian theories stress that people react in ways that do not cause markets to clear at all times. Sticky or rigid wages are a key feature of New Keynesian models. These models offer the theoretical framework of long-term employment relationships, efficiency wages, and union bargaining to explain slow or weak reactions of wages to macroeconomic shocks and the creation of involuntary unemployment during short-term recessionary gaps.

The sharp contrast between New Classical and New Keynesian models applies only to the short-run behaviour of the economy. In the long run, even the staunchest New Keynesians accept the proposition that wage and prices adjust to eliminate output gaps, and thus return GDP to its potential level and the unemployment rate to the NAIRU.

10. Which of the following is an aspect of the New Classical theories?

(a) Short-run fluctuations in aggregate demand cause changes in involuntary unemployment.
(b) Nominal wages do not adjust during cyclical fluctuations.
(c) Union bargaining explains the downward stickiness of real wages.
(d) With flexible wage rates employment, not unemployment, fluctuates in the short run.
(e) None of the above.

Answer Questions 11 through 13 by referring to Figure 31-1, which depicts aggregate labour demand and supply in an economy: The initial equilibrium situation is point *a*.

Figure 31-1

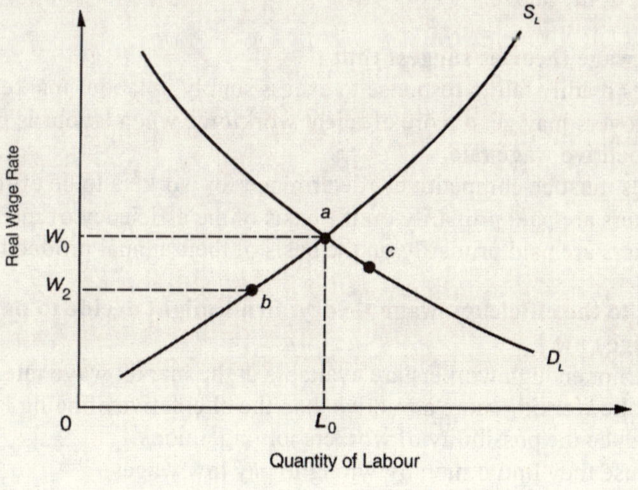

11. Which of the following statements is true?

(a) At wage rates above w_0, there is an excess demand for labour.
(b) Unemployment at point *a* consists of structural and frictional unemployment.
(c) If the wage rate is fully flexible, involuntary unemployment occurs when the wage is below w_0.
(d) At wage rates less than w_0, there is an excess supply of labour.
(e) All of the above.

12. **If the labour demand curve shifts leftward and intersects the labour supply curve at point *b*,**
(a) all of the laid-off workers are involuntarily unemployed when the wage rate falls to w_2.
(b) there will be involuntarily unemployed workers if the wage rate remains at w_0.
(c) cyclical unemployment will increase.
(d) the economy is currently encountering an inflationary gap situation.
(e) at w_2 there will be an excess demand for labour.

13. **Assuming that the real wage rate is fully flexible and that the labour supply curve shifts rightward and intersects the labour demand curve at point *c*, then**
(a) both employment and involuntary unemployment increase.
(b) both employment and involuntary unemployment decrease.
(c) both employment and involuntary unemployment remain constant.
(d) employment increases, but there is no involuntary unemployment at point *c*.
(e) voluntary unemployment decreases and employment increases.

14. **New Keynesian theories regarding the persistence of short-run involuntary unemployment**
(a) stress the importance of adverse supply shocks.
(b) start with the observation that wage rates do not respond quickly to changes in demand and supply in labour markets.
(c) imply that most unemployment is caused by fluctuations in the willingness of people to supply labour.
(d) are based on the premise that all unemployed workers cannot be retrained.
(e) None of the above.

15. **Efficiency wage theories suggest that**
(a) wages readily fall in response to excess supply in labour markets.
(b) employers may get a more efficient workforce when labour is paid more than the competitive wage rate.
(c) wages must be competitively determined for workers to be efficient.
(d) workers are paid primarily on the basis of the efficiency of management and supervisors.
(e) workers are paid primarily on the basis of their annual productivity increases.

16. **According to the efficiency-wage theory, firms might decide to pay wages above the market wage rate**
(a) since not enough workers are available at the market wage rate.
(b) to make working more attractive than the alternative of being laid off.
(c) to reduce the possibility of workers joining unions.
(d) because they find it morally wrong to pay low wages.
(e) to reward skilled workers over unskilled workers.

What Determines the NAIRU?

The NAIRU is the unemployment rate that exists when the economy's national income is at its potential level. The NAIRU is composed of structural and frictional unemployment rates. Make sure you understand the factors that can cause the NAIRU to change over time. Also, you should understand the term *hysteresis*—the possibility that the size of the NAIRU is influenced by the size of the actual current rate of unemployment.

17. **Unemployment that occurs as a result of the normal turnover of labour as people move from job to job is called**
(a) involuntary unemployment.
(b) structural unemployment.
(c) cyclical unemployment.
(d) frictional unemployment.
(e) efficiency-wage unemployment.

18. **The existence of structural unemployment means that**
(a) there is an inadequate number of jobs in the economy.
(b) construction workers, particularly those in structural steel, are suffering high rates of unemployment.
(c) the composition of the demand for labour does not match the composition of available supply.
(d) cyclical unemployment must also be present.
(e) all unemployment is voluntary.

19. **Search unemployment**
(a) may be a form of voluntary frictional unemployment.
(b) will tend to increase if search costs are low.
(c) occurs when members of the labour force look for more suitable jobs.
(d) occurs because workers have imperfect knowledge of job availability.
(e) All of the above.

20. **Which of the following does *not* usually explain the creation of structural unemployment?**
(a) Firms change their production techniques.
(b) Changes in the composition of the labour force.
(c) The composition of the demand for goods changes.
(d) Contractionary monetary policy.
(e) New labour force entrants possess inadequate training or skills for vacant jobs.

21. **If an economy has achieved its NAIRU, it follows that**
(a) the measured unemployment rate is necessarily zero.
(b) the economy operates in a recessionary gap.
(c) the economy's GDP is equal to its potential level.
(d) there is neither structural nor frictional unemployment in the economy.
(e) all unemployment is involuntary.

22. **Which of the following will increase the NAIRU?**
(a) An improvement in the educational attainment of the labour force.
(b) A slowdown in the pace at which the structural demand for labour is changing.
(c) Fewer barriers for the flow of labour from a declining to an expanding labour sector.
(d) A decrease in the speed at which labour adapts to structural changes in labour demand.
(e) The Bank of Canada buys bonds in the open market.

23. **Which of the following is *not* correct?**
   (a) Employment insurance likely increases search unemployment.
   (b) Trying to reduce the measured unemployment rate to zero is both impractical and undesirable.
   (c) Frictional unemployment in a diverse economy such as Canada's is inevitable.
   (d) Long-term relationships between employers and workers help to explain the lack of wage adjustments during economic downturns.
   (e) The NAIRU in Canada has been constant over the last half-century.

24. ***Hysteresis* means that an increase in cyclical unemployment may**
   (a) decrease the level of frictional unemployment.
   (b) increase the probability that new labour-force participants will receive job training during and after a recession.
   (c) increase the level of the NAIRU.
   (d) decrease the level of structural unemployment.
   (e) lead to the creation of new jobs in certain economic regions.

Reducing Unemployment

Different economic factors determine the three types of unemployment discussed in the textbook. It follows that policy selection should be centred on the causes of each.

25. **Which of the following policies would be appropriate for reducing the level of cyclical unemployment in Canada?**
   (a) The Bank of Canada sells large quantities of government bonds in the open market.
   (b) The federal government increases personal and corporate income taxes.
   (c) The province of Alberta cuts back on its expenditures to education.
   (d) The city of Moncton increases its expenditures on road and sewer construction.
   (e) The Bank of Canada increases its target for the overnight rate.

26. **Which of the following policies would be appropriate for reducing structural unemployment in the long run?**
   (a) More effective job-training programs.
   (b) Increases in minimum wages in all provinces.
   (c) Tax policies that promote more labour-saving technological change.
   (d) More strongly enforced interprovincial regulations that restrict labour migration.
   (e) Increased government subsidies for inefficient and declining industries.

SHORT-ANSWER QUESTIONS

1. Briefly explain what is understood by the following:
   (a) Cyclical unemployment.

   (b) Frictional unemployment.

(c) Structural unemployment.

(d) The NAIRU.

2. Classify the following situations as frictional, structural, search unemployment, or cyclical unemployment, and briefly explain your choice.

(a) An auto assembly worker is laid off because auto sales decrease during a slowdown in overall economic activity.

(b) An electrical engineer refuses a job offer and decides to look for another job that has a higher rate of remuneration or improved working conditions.

(c) A social worker is laid off because the city of Saskatoon downsizes one of its social welfare programs.

(d) A brewery worker in London, Ontario is laid off when the firm shifts its production from London to Toronto.

(e) Bookkeepers are laid off as Vancouver firms introduce computerized accounting software packages into their office operations.

(f) Systems analysts in Brandon, Manitoba lose their jobs as firms curtail information technology projects because of slumping sales.

3. Explain briefly how the New Keynesian theories explain the causes of cyclical unemployment.

EXERCISES

1. **The Effect of a Supply Shock**

   Consider an economy that begins with real GDP equal to its potential level. There is a sudden increase in the prices of raw materials, which shifts the *AS* curve leftward.

   (a) Roughly sketch the immediate effect of the supply shock in an *AD–AS* diagram.

   (b) Suppose that wages and prices in this economy adjust instantly to shocks. Describe what happens to unemployment in this economy. Explain.

   (c) If wages and price adjust only slowly to shocks, what happens to unemployment? Explain.

2. **Unemployment and Government Policy**

   What specific government policy would you recommend for each of the following types of unemployment? Explain briefly.

   (a) Structural unemployment caused by changes in the composition of labour demand.

   (b) Cyclical unemployment with downward sticky wage rates.

   (c) Longer search unemployment caused by more generous employment insurance benefits.

   (d) Frictional unemployment caused by a greater willingness of workers to seek better and improved job opportunities.

3. **The Rate of Unemployment**

   Suppose that in the month of January there were 2850 employed people and 150 unemployed people in a hypothetical economy (all figures in thousands). Further suppose that this economy was in long-run equilibrium in January.

(a) What was the rate of unemployment for this economy in January? What is the NAIRU for this economy?

(b) Suppose that in February 20 percent of those who were unemployed in January were able to find employment, while 2 percent of those who were employed lost their jobs. What is the rate of unemployment for this economy in February? What was the rate of cyclical unemployment in February?

(c) Suppose that in March, 20 percent of those who were unemployed in February were able to find employment, while 2 percent of those who were employed lost their jobs. What was the rate of unemployment for this economy in March? If the number of unemployed people as a result of cyclical unemployment was estimated to have been 33 in March, what happened to the NAIRU for this economy?

(d) The economy started to recover in April and the number of those who were unemployed in March and found employment was equal to the number of those who were employed and lost their jobs. In April, however, this economy received 200 new immigrants of working age. Although all of these 200 immigrants sought employment, only half of them were able to find employment by the end of April. What was the rate of unemployment for this economy in April?

EXTENSION EXERCISE

E1. Short- and Long-Run Equilibrium

Consider the *AD–AS* model of a hypothetical economy where the expressions for the *AD* and *AS* curves are, respectively:

$$P = 800 - 0.25\,Y$$
$$P = P_{-1} + 0.75\,(Y - Y^{*}),$$

where Y is real income (in millions of dollars), Y^* is full-employment income, and P_{-1} is the price level in the previous period. The economy is originally in long-run equilibrium—i.e., real income is equal to full employment income in period 0, and $P_{-1} = 50$. Further suppose that the production function for this economy is $Y = 10\,E$, where E is the number of employed workers (in millions). The size of the labour force is 320 (in millions).

(a) What is the value of Y^* in this economy? What is the initial equilibrium value of P?

(b) What is the NAIRU for this economy?

(c) Suppose that in period 1 there is a negative supply shock, and the expression for AS becomes $P = P_{-1} + 100 + 0.5\,(Y - Y^*)$. What are the short-run equilibrium values of Y and P in period 1?

(d) What is the rate of unemployment in period 1? What is the level of cyclical unemployment in period 1?

(e) In the absence of any countercyclical policy, what will be the new long-run equilibrium values of Y and P?

ADDITIONAL MULTIPLE-CHOICE QUESTIONS

Questions 1 to 8 refer to the following labour-market-status matrix for a hypothetical economy. The entries represent flows between two time periods, say, 2005 and 2006. The columns refer to 2006 and the rows refer to 2005.

	E_{06}	U_{06}	N_{06}
E_{05}	260	15	5
U_{05}	22	20	8
N_{05}	3	10	20

***1. What is the value of stock of the labour force in 2005?**
(a) 200.
(b) 280.
(c) 220.
(d) 330.
(e) 317.

***2. What is the unemployment rate in 2005?**
(a) 15.2 percent.
(b) 14.3 percent.
(c) 13.6 percent.
(d) 12.7 percent.
(e) None of the above.

3. The participation rate is the percentage of the adult population who are in the labour force. What is the participation rate in 2005?
(a) 87.3 percent.
(b) 96.1 percent.
(c) 90.9 percent.
(d) 100 percent.
(e) 83.3 percent.

4. **What was the total new flow *into unemployment* from 2005 to 2006?**
(a) 20. (b) 25.
(c) 15. (d) 20.
(e) 10.

5. **What was the total new flow *out of unemployment* from 2005 to 2006?**
(a) 22. (b) 8.
(c) 10. (d) 30.
(e) 20.

*6. **On the basis of your answers to Questions 4 and 5, what do you predict will be the stock of unemployment in 2006?**
(a) Higher than 2005.
(b) Lower than 2005.
(c) Equal to 50.
(d) Equal to the 2005 stock of unemployment.
(e) Equal to 20.

*7. **Comparing the 2005 flows of employed and unemployed workers who left the labour force in 2006 to those who entered the labour force in 2006, we observe that**
(a) the inflow was greater than the outflow.
(b) the outflow was greater than the inflow.
(c) the labour force increased over the one-year span.
(d) the labour force decreased over the one-year span.
(e) the labour forces were the same in the two years.

8. **The unemployment rate in 2006 is**
(a) 15.2 percent. (b) 10.6 percent.
(c) 13.6 percent. (d) 12.9 percent.
(d) 10 percent.

9. **Which of the following are aspects of the New Keynesian theory of long-term employment relationships?**
(a) Wage rates adjust quickly in excess labour demand and excess labour supply situations.
(b) Any market clearing that occurs during short-term fluctuations focuses on the volume of employment rather than on wages.
(c) As the productivity of older workers falls over time, wages for them are adjusted downward.
(d) Long-term labour contracts provide a great deal of flexibility to firms that wish to lower or increase wage rates.
(e) Fringe benefits with one firm are easily transferred to another firm when a worker moves from one job to another.

10. **One aspect of the efficiency wage hypothesis is that**
(a) firms pay a wage premium so that workers are reluctant to shirk their responsibilities and duties.
(b) it is relatively easy for employers to monitor workers' performance.
(c) workers easily transfer wage premiums paid by one firm to others.
(d) paying a wage premium to workers will increase the incidence of quit rates and absenteeism because they want more non-work activity.
(e) unions bargain payment-for-performance provisions for their members.

11. **New Keynesian economists**
   (a) believe that wages adjust quickly to short-run gap situations.
   (b) argue that short-run recessionary gaps cannot last for long.
   (c) stress wage adjustments rather than employment adjustments.
   (d) agree with New Classical economists that the actual unemployment rate is equal to the NAIRU in the long run.
   (e) reject the possibility of search unemployment.

Questions 12 to 15 refer to Figure 31-2. The economy begins at E_0, where real GDP equals potential GDP (Y^*). The unemployment rate at Y^* is assumed to be 7 percent.

Figure 31-2

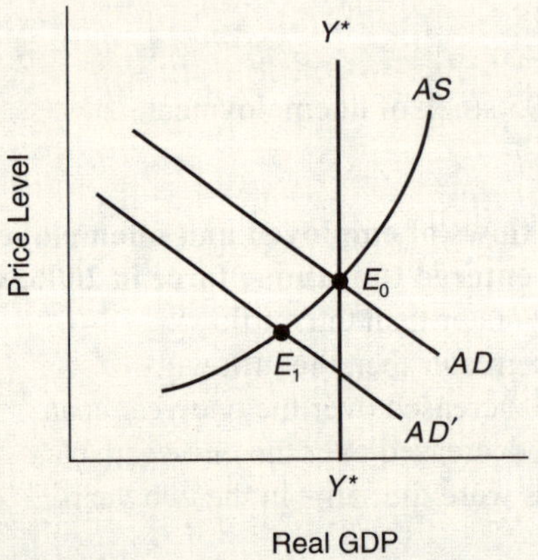

*12. **At E_0, what type of unemployment exists?**
   (a) Cyclical unemployment of 7 percent.
   (b) Involuntary unemployment of 7 percent.
   (c) There is no unemployment since the economy operates at its potential level.
   (d) Structural and frictional unemployment equal to 7 percent.
   (e) Only frictional unemployment exists, since structural unemployment is a concern only during economic slumps.

*13. **A negative aggregate demand shock now shifts the *AD* curve to *AD′*. At E_1 the measured unemployment rate is 8.7 percent. What is the level of cyclical unemployment?**
   (a) 1.7 percent.
   (b) 7 percent.
   (c) 15.7 percent.
   (d) 8.7 percent.
   (e) It cannot be determined because the combined levels of structural and frictional unemployment have not been provided.

14. **Assuming the *AS* curve does not change, which of the following would be appropriate stabilization policies to eliminate the output gap?**
   (a) Shift the *AD* curve by selling government bonds in the open market.
   (b) Increase income-tax rates.
   (c) Shift the *AD* curve to the right by transferring government deposits from the central bank to the commercial banks.
   (d) Use monetary policy to quickly reduce structural unemployment.
   (e) Increase the government's budget surplus.

15. If monetary and fiscal policies are not used, market adjustments would eliminate the output gap in the long run by

(a) shifting the *AS* curve to the left as wage rates fall.
(b) shifting the *AD* curve to the left as the price level falls.
(c) shifting the *AD* curve to the right as the price level falls.
(d) shifting the *AS* curve to the right as wage rates fall.
(e) None of the above.

Use the following information to answer Questions 16 to 18. The number of employed people in a hypothetical economy is initially 5700 and the number of unemployed people is 300 (all figures in thousands). Assume that this economy is initially in long-run equilibrium.

***16. Given that this economy is initially in long-run equilibrium,**

(a) the rate of frictional unemployment is approximately 5.3 percent.
(b) the rate of cyclical unemployment is approximately 5.3 percent.
(c) the rate of cyclical unemployment is 5.0 percent.
(d) the NAIRU is approximately 5.3 percent.
(e) the rate of cyclical unemployment is 0 percent.

***17. If the number of unemployed people as a result of structural unemployment is 120,**

(a) the rate of frictional unemployment is 4.0 percent.
(b) the rate of cyclical unemployment is 1.0 percent.
(c) the number of unemployed people as a result of frictional unemployment is 180.
(d) the number of unemployed people as a result of cyclical unemployment is 180.
(e) the rate of structural unemployment is 3.0 percent.

***18. If the NAIRU remains constant but the labour force increases by 10 percent and the number of unemployed people increases to 450,**

(a) the rate of unemployment is now 6.3 percent.
(b) the rate of cyclical unemployment is now 1.3 percent.
(c) the number of unemployed people as a result of cyclical unemployment is now 150.
(d) the number of unemployed people as a result of cyclical unemployment is now 120.
(e) the rate of cyclical unemployment is still 0 percent since the NAIRU has not changed.

SOLUTIONS

Chapter Review

1.(c) **2.**(a) **3.**(d) **4.**(a) **5.**(e) **6.**(b) **7.**(a) **8.**(c) **9.**(e) **10.**(d) **11.**(b) **12.**(b) **13.**(d) **14.**(b) **15.**(b) **16.**(b) **17.**(d) **18.**(c) **19.**(e) **20.**(d) **21.**(c) **22.**(d) **23.**(e) **24.**(c) **25.**(d) **26.**(a)

Short-Answer Questions

1. (a) Cyclical unemployment is the unemployment resulting from deviations of real GDP from the level of potential output.
(b) Frictional unemployment is the unemployment resulting from turnover in the labour market as workers move between jobs or enter the labour force.
(c) Structural unemployment is the unemployment resulting from the mismatch in skills, industry, or location between available jobs and unemployed workers.
(d) The NAIRU is the rate of unemployment that exists when the economy is producing at the level of potential output. At the level of potential output there is only frictional and structural unemployment, and thus the NAIRU only measures these types of unemployment.

2. (a) Cyclical, because of the slowdown in economic activity.
(b) Search or voluntary frictional unemployment. The engineer refused a job because of the expectation of finding another job with a higher rate of remuneration or better working conditions.
(c) Frictional if short-term, structural if the social worker is unable to find work after a prolonged search.
(d) Frictional if short-term, structural if the brewery worker with his or her current skills cannot find work in London or refused, when offered, to be relocated to the firm's Toronto plant.
(e) Structural if bookkeepers have to undergo retraining in order to acquire skills required for computerized accounting software or for other types of occupations. It would be frictional if the bookkeepers could find non-computerized office work elsewhere.
(f) If the reduction in sales is a result of a general economic recession, cyclical unemployment exists. Conversely, the sales reduction may be due to a sectoral shift away from these firms, in which case the unemployment is frictional if the system analysts find work elsewhere easily, or structural if their existing skills lead to long-duration unemployment.

3. Cyclical unemployment decreases when GDP is above its potential level. Cyclical unemployment increases when GDP is below its potential level. Consider the case when cyclical unemployment increases because there is a reduction in aggregate demand. The immediate effect is the creation of a recessionary gap (GDP falls and the price level falls). If wages and prices were fully flexible, then the *AS* curve should begin to shift downward until potential GDP (and the NAIRU) is restored. However, New Keynesian models argue that wages and prices are slow to adjust in the short term. These models stress that because of union bargaining techniques, efficiency wages, long-term employment relationships, menu costs, and wage contracts, wages and prices are sticky downward. Hence, the recessionary gap can be prolonged. During this time, cyclical unemployment increases while employment declines. In the long run, New Keynesian models would concede that wages and prices will adjust, and hence cyclical unemployment should be eliminated.

Exercises

1. **(a)** The *AS* curve shifts leftward creating a recessionary gap. Employment falls and cyclical unemployment increases.

Figure 31-3

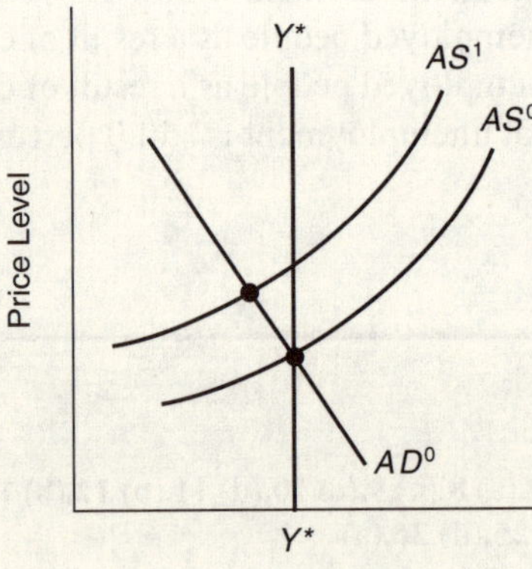

(b) The short-run recessionary gap puts pressure on wages and the price level to fall. Employment and output begin to increase and cyclical unemployment begins to fall. Equilibrium will occur when Y^* and the NAIRU are restored. Notice that we observe cyclical fluctuations in cyclical employment and unemployment only in the short run.
(c) The recessionary gap will be prolonged. Measured unemployment will go above its NAIRU level and will stay that way until prices and wages eventually fall or government initiates stabilization policy.

2. **(a)** Retraining and relocation grants to make movement of labour easier. Policies to improve information about existing and (possibly) future employment opportunities.
(b) Expansionary fiscal and monetary policies.

(c) Any policy changes are bound to be controversial. Current provisions may be enforced more strictly, or you may recommend changes in employment insurance provisions such as reduced weeks or lower weekly benefits.

(d) Improving information that workers have about market opportunities could reduce frictional unemployment. Also, the government might provide workers with relocation subsidies.

3. **(a)** Let's call U the number of persons who are unemployed, E the number of persons employed, and LF the number of persons in the labour force, where $LF = E + U$. Let's call u the rate of unemployment and u^* the NAIRU.

$LF = E + U = 2850 + 150 = 3000$.

$u = U/LF = 150/3000 = 0.05$ or 5%.

Since this economy is in long-run equilibrium ($Y = Y^*$), then $u = u^* = 5\%$.

(b) The increase in U is the net result of two opposite forces: those who lose their jobs and enter the ranks of the unemployed (2% of 2850 = 57) minus those who find jobs and leave the ranks of the unemployed (20% of 150 = 30). Therefore, U increases by 27 to a total of 177 in February, and u is now 177/3000 = 5.9%. And since $u^* = 5.0\%$, the rate of cyclical unemployment is 0.9%.

(c) At the beginning of March, $U = 177$ and $E = 2\,823$. Those who lost their jobs and entered the ranks of the unemployed in March were 2% of 2823 = 56.46, and those who found jobs and left the ranks of the unemployed in March were 20% of 177 = 35.4, and thus U increased by 56.46 – 35.4 = 21.06 to a total of 198.06. Therefore, in March u was equal to 198.02/3000 = 6.6%.

Since $U = 198$ and cyclical unemployment was now estimated to be 33, the summation of frictional and structural unemployment was 198 – 33 = 165, and $u^* = 165/3000 = 5.5\%$. The NAIRU increased because either frictional unemployment or structural unemployment or both went up.

(d) $LF = 3000 + 200 = 3200$; $U = 198 + 100 = 298$; and $E = 2802 + 100 = 2902$.

$u = U/LF = 298/3200 = 9.3\%$.

Extension Exercise

E1. **(a)** If the economy is in long-run equilibrium, then $Y = Y^*$ and, given the equation for the AS curve, $P^* = P_{-1} = 50$.

Therefore, given the equation for the AD curve:

$P^* = 800 - 0.25\ Y^* \rightarrow 50 = 800 - 0.25\ Y^* \rightarrow 0.25\ Y^* = 750 \rightarrow Y^* = 3000$

(b) Let's call U the number of persons who are unemployed, E the number of persons employed, and LF the number of persons in the labour force, where $LF = E + U$. Let's call u the rate of unemployment and u^* the NAIRU.

$Y = 10\ E \rightarrow E = Y/10 = 3000/10 = 300$.

$U = LF - E = 320 - 300 = 20$.

$u = U/LF = 20/320 = 6.25$

Since the economy is initially in long-run equilibrium, $u = u^*$, and thus $u^* = 6.25$.

(c) AS $\rightarrow P = 50 + 100 + 0.75\ (Y - 3000) = 150 + 0.75\ Y - 2250 = -2100 + 0.75\ Y$.

AD = AS $\rightarrow 800 - 0.25\ Y = -2100 + 0.75\ Y \rightarrow Y = 2900$.

And $P = 800 - 0.25\ Y = 800 - 0.25\ (2900) = 800 - 725 = 75$.

(d) What is the rate of unemployment in period 1? What is the level of cyclical unemployment in period 1?

$E = Y/10 = 2900/10 = 290$.

$U = LF - E = 320 - 290 = 30$.

$u = U/LF = 30/320 = 9.37$.

Since $U = 30$ and $U^* = 20$, cyclical unemployment is 10.

(e) In the absence of any countercyclical policy, in the long run the economy will move back to its initial long-run equilibrium $\rightarrow Y^* = 3000$ and $P^* = 50$. As long as $Y < Y^*$—and thus $u > u^*$—wages will keep dropping period after period, thus reducing costs of production and shifting the AS curve downward. This process will continue until $Y = Y^*$ once again, and $P = P^*$ as before.

Additional Multiple-Choice Questions

1.(d) **2.**(a) **3.**(c) **4.**(b) **5.**(d) **6.**(b) **7.**(e) **8.**(c) **9.**(b) **10.**(a) **11.**(d) **12.**(d) **13.**(a) **14.**(c) **15.**(d) **16.**(e) **17.**(c) **18.**(d)

Explanations for the Asterisked Multiple-Choice Questions

1.(d) The labour force is defined as the number of employed plus the number of unemployed. For 2005, the number employed is 260 + 15 + 5 and the number of unemployed is 22 + 20 + 8. The sum is 330. Hence, the labour force is found by adding all elements of row 1 with all elements of row 2.

2.(a) The unemployment rate is defined as the number of unemployed divided by the total labour force. The number of unemployed is 50 and the labour force is 330. Hence, the unemployment rate is 15.2 percent.

6.(b) Question 4 indicates that the total flow into unemployment is 25 and Question 5 indicates that the flow out of unemployment is 30. Hence, one would expect the stock of unemployment in 2006 is lower than that in 2005.

7.(e) The number of individuals who left the labour market equals 13 (5 + 8) and this is matched by the number who entered the labour force (13).

12.(d) Point E_0 equilibrium GDP is at its potential level. Since cyclical unemployment is zero, then total unemployment is structural and frictional (= 7 percent).

13.(a) Point E_1 represents a recessionary gap situation. Hence, cyclical unemployment is greater than zero. If the measured unemployment rate is 8.7 percent and the NAIRU is 7 percent, then cyclical unemployment must be 1.7 percent.

16.(e) If the economy is in long-run equilibrium, then $Y = Y^*$ and $u = u^*$. Therefore, cyclical unemployment is zero and so is the rate of cyclical unemployment.

17.(c) If the economy is in long-run equilibrium, then total unemployment consists only of frictional unemployment and structural unemployment. If total unemployment is 300 and structural unemployment is 120, then frictional unemployment is 180.

18.(d) The labour force now is 6600 and u^* is still 5%, then the summation of frictional and structural unemployment is 5% of 6600 = 330. Since total unemployment is 450, then cyclical unemployment is 120.

CHAPTER 32

GOVERNMENT DEBT AND DEFICITS

LEARNING OBJECTIVES

In this chapter you will learn

1. how the government's annual budget deficit (or surplus) is related to its stock of debt.
2. about the cyclically adjusted deficit and how it can be used to measure the stance of fiscal policy.
3. how budget deficits may crowd out investment and net exports.
4. why a high stock of debt may hamper the conduct of monetary and fiscal policies.
5. why legislation requiring balanced budgets may be undesirable.

CHAPTER OVERVIEW

The government's budget constraint means that government expenditures must be equal to tax revenue plus borrowing. The government's **budget deficit** is equal to government expenditure (including debt-service payments) minus government revenue. Since the government must borrow to finance any shortfall in its revenues, the annual deficit is equal to the amount borrowed by the government during the course of a year. Whenever the deficit is positive, the stock of government debt is growing. Conversely, a budget surplus reduces the stock of debt.

There are two components of government expenditure: purchases of goods and services (G), and debt-service payments ($i \times D$) where D is the outstanding stock of government debt and i is the interest rate. Net taxation revenue is tax revenues minus transfer payments (T). The primary budget deficit is equal to the excess of the government's program spending over total net tax revenues. The primary deficit shows the extent to which net tax revenues are able to finance the discretionary part of total government purchases.

The actual value of the budget deficit is a poor measure of the stance of fiscal policy since its value fluctuates during various phases of the business cycle. Changes in the value of the **cyclically adjusted deficit (CAD)** reflect changes in the stance of fiscal policy. A rise in the cyclically adjusted budget deficit reflects expansionary fiscal policy.

Changes in the debt-to-GDP ratio depend on the real interest rate, the growth rate of real GDP, and the size of the primary budget deficit. If the real interest rate exceeds the growth rate of real GDP, then stabilizing the debt-to-GDP ratio requires that the government run a primary budget surplus.

Three possible effects of government debt and deficits are discussed: "crowding-out" effects, the potential harm of government debt to future generations, and limitations that debt puts on the conduct of economic policy. There are two possible crowding-out effects in an open economy: private-sector investment is reduced if government borrowing increases the interest rate, and net exports are reduced because increased domestic interest rates cause an appreciation of the domestic currency.

The chapter concludes by discussing different concepts of balanced budgets: annually balanced budgets and cyclically balanced budgets.

HINTS AND TIPS

The following may help you to avoid some of the most common errors on examinations.

✓ Learn the definition of government's budget constraint equation, $G + i \times D = T +$ Borrowing. G is the government's purchase of goods and services, i is the interest rate, D is the stock of government debt, T is net taxation revenue (taxes minus transfers).

✓ Understand why the equation for changes in the debt-to-GDP ratio (Δd) depends on the value of the primary deficit as a percentage of GDP (x), the real rate of interest (r), the growth in real GDP (g), and the debt-to-GDP ratio (d). For example, a rise in r increases the debt-to-GDP ratio.

✓ Learn that movements along a government budget deficit function are caused by cyclical fluctuations in GDP while shifts in this curve represent discretionary fiscal policies such as changes in government purchases and net tax rates. For example, an increase in government expenditure shifts the budget deficit function upward (a larger deficit).

CHAPTER REVIEW

Facts and Definitions

Any excess of government spending over net tax revenues must be financed by government borrowing, which adds to the stock of outstanding government debt. Alternatively, any excess of tax revenues over government spending might be used to retire debt. The distinction between overall and primary budget deficits is important for you to understand. And, it would be useful for you to have a general idea of the recent record of budget deficit policies and trends in the debt-to-GDP ratio both at the federal and provincial levels in Canada.

1. The value of the Canadian federal debt as a share of GDP in the late 1990s and in the early years of the new millennium, has been

(a) steadily decreasing.
(b) about the same as it was in the 1960s.
(c) greater than its value during World War II (1939–45).
(d) equal to the value of the federal government deficit as a share of GDP.
(e) slightly increasing.

2. Which one of the following statements is true?

(a) An overall budgetary deficit implies a primary budget deficit.
(b) A budgetary deficit means that government borrowing does not change.
(c) Higher real interest rates imply lower debt-service payments.
(d) A budgetary deficit necessitates an increase in government borrowing.
(e) Transfer payments are not a part of a government's budget constraint.

3. The primary budget deficit is defined as the

(a) overall budget deficit minus the value of outstanding debt.
(b) total budgetary deficit generated by transfer payments to primary industries.
(c) total budgetary deficit excluding debt-service payments.
(d) deficit that exists at potential national income.
(e) budgetary deficit attributable to debt-service payments.

4. **Which of the following equations is correct?**
   (a) $\Delta D = T + (G + i \times D)$.
   (b) Primary budget deficit: $G + i \times D$.
   (c) Government budget constraint: $G - T = Borrowing$.
   (d) Primary budget deficit: $G - T$.
   (e) $\Delta D = G - T$.

5. **In the fiscal year 1996–97, the federal government had an overall budget deficit of $13.7 billion while debit-service payments were $45.2 billion. Hence, in that year**
   (a) the primary budget deficit was $58.9 billion.
   (b) the government did not need to borrow.
   (c) the primary budget deficit was $31.5 billion.
   (d) tax revenues were more than sufficient to cover program expenditures.
   (e) the primary budget surplus was $31.5 billion.

Two Analytical Issues

The stance of fiscal policy (contractionary or expansionary) is best judged by changes in the value of the cyclically adjusted deficit (*CAD*) since some changes in budget deficits (surpluses) occur even when there has been no change in fiscal policy. The key to understand this issue is the budget deficit function. Changes in deficits caused by changes in real GDP are represented by movements along a budget deficit function. The budget deficit function is negatively related to real GDP. Shifts in the budget deficit function are caused by changes in tax rates and government spending. For each budget deficit function, the value of the cyclically adjusted deficit is measured at potential real GDP (Y^*).

To fully understand the equation that explains changes in the debt-to-GDP ratio, it would be useful to reread *Extensions in Theory 32-1*. The change in the debt-to-GDP ratio (Δd) depends on the value of the primary deficit as a percentage of GDP (x), the real rate of interest (r), the growth in real GDP (g), and d, the debt-to-GDP ratio. Using this equation, it is then possible to determine the conditions that are needed to stabilize the debt-to-GDP ratio.

Questions 6 to 9 are based on Figure 32-1.

Figure 32-1

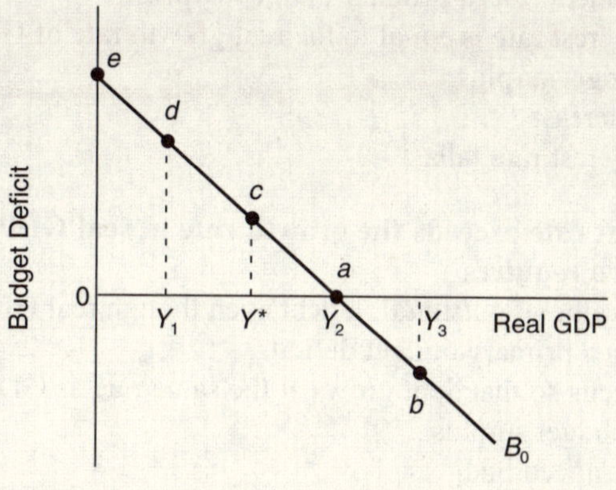

6. **Referring to the budget deficit function labelled B_0 which of the following points represents a budget surplus?**
(a) *e*.
(b) *a*.
(c) *b*.
(d) *c*.
(e) *d*.

7. **A movement from point *a* to point *d***
(a) represents an increase in the budget deficit because either government expenditures have increased or tax rates have been reduced.
(b) represents the creation of a budget surplus because government expenditures have been cut or tax rates have been increased.
(c) illustrates the creation of a budget surplus since tax revenues have fallen with the decline in real GDP.
(d) indicates that a budget deficit can be created as tax revenues fall with declines in real GDP.
(e) indicates that a budget surplus can be created as tax revenue fall with declines in real GDP.

8. **The cyclically adjusted deficit for budget deficit function B_0 is a**
(a) deficit of the distance Y^*c.
(b) deficit of the distance $0e$.
(c) balance at point *a*.
(d) surplus of the distance Y_3b.
(e) deficit of the distance Y_1d.

9. **If at every level of real GDP the budget deficit function shifted up, then**
(a) the value of the CAD increases.
(b) the stance of fiscal policy is expansionary.
(c) the stance of fiscal policy is contractionary.
(d) the value of the CAD decreases.
(e) the value of the CAD increases <u>and</u> the stance of fiscal policy is expansionary

10. **Which of the following events by itself increases the debt-to-GDP ratio?**
(a) The real interest rate exceeds the growth rate of real GDP.
(b) The government runs a primary budget surplus.
(c) The real interest rate is equal to the real growth rate of GDP and the government runs a primary budget surplus.
(d) Tax rates increase.
(e) The real interest rate falls.

11. **If the real interest rate exceeds the growth rate in real GDP, then the goal of a stable debt-to-GDP ratio requires**
(a) a constant value of outstanding debt even though real GDP is growing.
(b) an unchanged primary budget deficit.
(c) budget deficits so that debt grows at the same rate as GDP.
(d) a primary budget surplus.
(e) annually balanced budgets.

The Effects of Government Debt and Deficits

This section deals with the potential effects of government deficits (and surpluses). Two crowding-out effects are identified, the debate regarding the redistribution of resources away from future generations to current generations is outlined, and finally the efficacy of fiscal and monetary policy with lower or higher debt levels is discussed.

12. With a decrease in current taxes, consumers are likely to

(a) cause the *AD* curve to shift up and to the right in the short run since national saving decreases.
(b) have no effect on the *AD* curve since national saving is unaffected.
(c) cause the *AD* curve to shift down and to the left as they increase private saving by more than the decrease in government saving.
(d) have no effect on either the *AD* curve or real interest rates.
(e) cause the *AS* curve to shift down and to the right.

13. The "crowding out" effect of a larger government budget deficit in a closed economy refers to the outcome of

(a) higher interest rates and less private investment.
(b) higher interest rates and more saving.
(c) lower interest rates and more investment.
(d) lower interest rates and less saving.
(e) no change in national saving.

14. The "crowding out" effect of a larger government budget deficit in an open economy refers to the outcome of

(a) higher interest rates, an appreciation of the domestic currency, and increased net exports.
(b) higher interest rates, lower financial capital inflows and net exports.
(c) lower interest rates, more financial capital inflows, lower net exports.
(d) a depreciation of the domestic currency and an increase in net exports.
(e) higher interest rates, an appreciation of the domestic currency, and reduced net exports.

15. If a larger government budget deficit reduces the capital stock in the long run, then

(a) the current standard of living is likely to decline, but future standards of living will improve.
(b) the future standard of living is likely to decline.
(c) the current generation bears the burden of the debt.
(d) both the current and future standards of living will decline.
(e) future generations will be unaffected so long as consumption expenditure increases offset the effects of the deficit.

16. Some economists believe that a large and growing budget deficit

(a) reduces the government's flexibility to use fiscal policy as a stabilization tool.
(b) creates high interest payments, leaving less revenue for other public needs.
(c) may lead to a growing level of foreign indebtedness.
(d) erodes the competitiveness of the export sector as the exchange rate depreciates.
(e) All of the above.

Formal Fiscal Rules?

This section deals with two balanced-budget proposals. One requires governments to balance their budgets annually. Under this scheme, a predicted budget surplus would require governments to spend more or lower taxes. The second scheme requires governments to balance their budgets over the full course of a business cycle. In a growing economy, it is more sensible to focus on changes in the debt-to-GDP ratio than on balancing the budget annually or over the duration of a business cycle.

17. An annually balanced budget can be destabilizing because

(a) it can lead to too large a government sector and greater economic inefficiency.
(b) it can lead to too small a government sector and inadequate provision of public goods.
(c) aggregate demand could grow faster at all stages of the business cycle.
(d) government expenditure (hence, aggregate demand) could be increased in expansions and reduced in contractions.
(e) the debt to GDP ratio would increase through time.

18. A cyclically balanced budget would

(a) require increasing government expenditures when revenues are rising.
(b) require increasing taxes when revenues are falling.
(c) call for substantial government infrastructure investments in periods of economic boom.
(d) allow for the implementation of countercyclical policies without affecting the level of the national debt.
(e) allow for the implementation of countercyclical policies without affecting the debt-to-GDP ratio.

SHORT-ANSWER QUESTIONS

1. Explain the following concepts.

(a) Program spending, transfer spending, and spending on debt servicing.

(b) An actual budget deficit and a cyclically adjusted deficit.

2. The following table shows the actual budget deficit and the cyclically adjusted budget deficit (both as a percentage of GDP) for Canada from 1994 to 1999.

Budget Deficits, Percentage of GDP, Canada

Year	Actual Deficit	Cyclically Adjusted Deficit
1994	6.7	6.0
1995	5.3	4.8
1996	2.8	1.8
1997	–0.2	–0.8
1998	–0.1	–0.5
1999	–1.7	–1.4

(a) Over the period 1994–99, was fiscal policy contractionary or expansionary? Explain.

(b) Explain why the actual deficit was greater than the cyclically adjusted deficit in 1995.

(c) Explain why the cyclically adjusted surplus was greater than the actual surplus in 1997.

3. Explain why monetary and fiscal policy may be hampered in an economy that has a high debt-to-GDP ratio.

4. Comment on the following statement: "A responsible government should always try to keep a balanced budget. Therefore, it should reduce expenditures when running a budget deficit and decrease taxes when running a budget surplus."

EXERCISES

1. **Government Budget Deficit**
You are given the following data about the 2006 fiscal year of a government in a hypothetical economy. All data are in billions of the domestic currency.
   - Real GDP in 2006 and 2007 is constant at 200.
   - Government expenditure on goods and services during 2006 is 20.
   - Outstanding government debt at the beginning of 2006 is 100.
   - Net taxation revenue during 2006 is 25.
   - Interest on outstanding debt is 10 percent.

(a) Calculate the value of debt-service payments in 2006, assuming that the interest on any newly created debt in 2006 is not paid until 2007.

(b) What is the value of program spending during 2006?

(c) Calculate the value of the primary budget deficit. Calculate the value of the overall budget deficit.

(d) What is your estimate of the level of government borrowing required in 2006?

(e) Estimate the debt-to-GDP ratio at the beginning of 2006. At the end of 2006.

(f) What is the deficit-GDP ratio at the end of 2006?

2. **Budget Deficit and Economic Policy**

Suppose that the Minister of Finance tables her 2007 fiscal-year forecast in the House of Commons. The budget includes a graph of the budget deficit function labelled B_{2007} (see Figure 32-2). Reluctantly, she reveals an anticipated downturn in the economy such that the 2007 real income level will fall by $10 billion from the 2006 level of $160 billion (which is equal to potential GDP.) The government's 2007 fiscal policy measures, which will be outlined in detail at a later date, will not change the 2006 federal debt-to-GDP ratio of 60 percent.

Phillip Wong, an energetic member of one of the opposition parties, decides to do some serious homework to understand the 2007 budget and its relationship with last year's budget.

(a) He prepares the following checklist for the 2007 budget. Calculate the 2007 magnitudes for him and fill in the missing entries.

The forecast level of real national income: ______________.
The value of the output gap: ______________.
The forecast deficit-to-GDP ratio: ______________.
The tax rate as a percentage: ______________.
The estimated value of federal debt outstanding: ______________.
Best estimate of the level of government expenditure: ______________.
The value of the cyclically adjusted deficit: ______________.
[Use the formula, $B = 30 - 0.2Y^*$, where Y^* is potential GDP.]

Figure 32-2

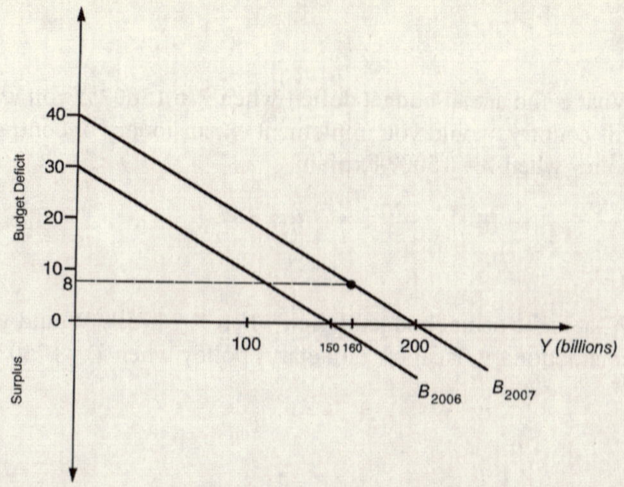

(b) Next, Wong retrieves 2006 budget information that included a graph of the budget deficit function (labelled as B_{2006} in Figure 32-2). Assuming that the function depicts actual values, calculate the 2006 values below and fill in the 2006 missing entries.

The level of real national income: ______________.

The value of the output gap: ______________.

The deficit-to-GDP ratio: ______________.

The tax rate as a percentage: ______________.

The value of federal government debt outstanding. ______________.

Best estimate of the level of government expenditure: ______________.

The value of the cyclically adjusted deficit: ______________.

[Use the formula, $B = 40 - 0.2Y^*$.]

(c) By comparing 2006 and 2007 figures, what should Wong conclude about the change in the fiscal policy stance of the government?

(d) During a question period, Wong asks the Minister why government policy for 2007 appears to be contractionary rather than expansionary. The Minister acknowledges that Wong's analysis is correct. However, she replies that, although her policies are painful in the short term, the economy is better off in the long run. Discuss this statement.

3. Calculation of the Budget Deficit

Consider the following data for a hypothetical economy:

$G = 300$

$T = -50 + 0.2\ Y$

$Y^* = 2000$

where G is government purchases, T is net tax revenues, and Y^* is potential real national income.

(a) What is the cyclically adjusted budget deficit for this economy?

(b) What is the actual budget deficit when $Y = 1500$? If you were the Minister of Finance of this country, would you implement expansionary or contractionary fiscal (or monetary) policy when $Y = 1500$? Explain.

(c) What is the actual budget deficit when $Y = 1750$? Would you implement expansionary or contractionary fiscal (or monetary) policy when $Y = 1750$? Explain.

(d) What is the actual budget deficit when $Y = 2250$? Would you implement expansionary or contractionary fiscal (or monetary) policy when $Y = 2250$? Explain.

(e) Would you implement expansionary or contractionary fiscal (or monetary) policy when $Y = 2000$? Explain.

4. **The Mathematics of the Change in the Debt-to-GDP Ratio**

Suppose that a hypothetical economy has a real interest of 4 percent, a growth rate of real GDP of 2 percent, a debt-to-GDP ratio of 50 percent and a primary budget deficit-to-GDP ratio of 1 percent.

(a) Calculate the change in the debt-to-GDP ratio. What does this value imply about government borrowing?

(b) Calculate the value of the primary budget deficit-to-GDP ratio that would be required to keep the debt-to-GDP ratio constant.

(c) Assuming a zero inflation rate, what annual budget deficit-to-GDP ratio is required to have a constant debt-to-GDP ratio of 50 percent?

(d) Recalculate your answers to parts (a), (b), and (c), assuming that the economy had a debt-to-GDP ratio of 60 percent; all other variables remain the same. What policy issues arise because of a higher debt-to-GDP ratio?

EXTENSION EXERCISES

E1. The Crowding-Out Effect

This exercise focuses on the crowding-out effect in a closed economy. The country of Alpha has a domestic market for financial funds (denominated in *zees*). In the past, all borrowing and lending have occurred exclusively in the private financial sector. The government of Alpha has played a completely passive role. It has made no expenditures, owes no debt, and has collected no taxes.

The supply of funds (S) arising from saving in the private sector is given by the equation $S = 30 + i$. The private-sector demand for funds for investment purposes (D) is $D = 60 - 5i$. Both curves represent demand and supply conditions each year. Thus, they are flow equations. Current GDP is 1000 and i ($= r$) is the percentage real/nominal interest rate.

(a) Plot the two curves in Figure 32-3 and determine the current equilibrium levels of the interest rate (i) and the total amount of private borrowing and saving (in *zees*).

Figure 32-3

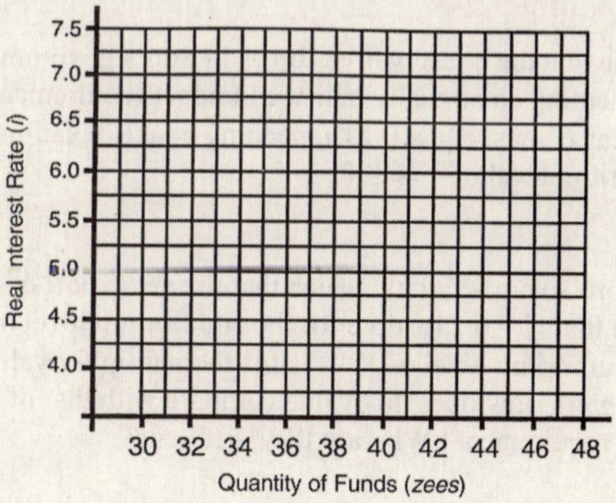

(b) For the first time, Alpha's government introduces, at the beginning of the current year, public spending programs that cost 6 *zees*. No tax programs are planned. For the purposes of this problem, suppose that the spending program has no effect on either GDP or the price level. Assuming the private-sector curve for funds is unaffected, determine the algebraic equation for national saving.

(c) Determine the new equilibrium levels of i and total investment either by plotting the national saving curve or by solving algebraically.

(d) How much "crowding out" of investment occurred?

E2. Short-Run Impact of an Annually Balanced Budget

Can an annually balanced budget be a short-run destabilizing force in the economy? The proof of this proposition involves showing that private-sector shocks have a greater multiplier effect with a balanced budget requirement than without it. Consider the following behavioural equations for the economy of Soo.

$C = 50 + 0.8(Y - T)$

$I = 100$

Government expenditure = G

$(X - IM) = 10 - 0.04Y$

$T = 0.2Y$

Potential GDP $(Y^*) = 800$

(a) If $G = 160$, what is the current equilibrium level of Soo's real national income? What is the current budget balance for Soo's government? What is the current value of the output gap?

(b) Now assume that Soo's exports fall by 2 such that the new net export function is $8 - 0.04Y$. Assume also that the price level, the exchange rate, and the interest rate in Soo are unaffected by this change. Determine the new equilibrium levels of Y and the government's budget position. What was the value of the (simple) multiplier? What is the value of the output gap?

(c) Suppose that the conservative forces in Soo's government had been successful in implementing an annually balanced budget requirement before exports fell. Hence, in each year G must equal $0.2Y$ (spending equals taxation revenue). Prove that the initial equilibrium level of Y is 800.

(d) As before, exports fall by 2 such that the net export equation becomes $8 - 0.04Y$. Using the fact that $G = 0.2Y$, solve for the equilibrium level of Y. What is the value of G at the new equilibrium level of Y? What is the multiplier value now? What is the value of the output gap? How does this value compare with that of having no annually balanced budget requirement? Why are they different?

ADDITIONAL MULTIPLE-CHOICE QUESTIONS

Use Figure 32-4 to answer Questions 1 through 3. Assume that potential real national income is 600 and that the curve labelled with the subscript 0 is the initial situation.

Figure 32-4

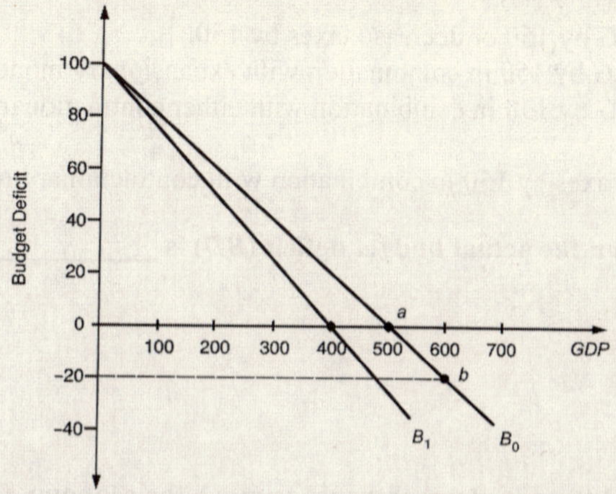

1. **Which one of the following statements is *not* true for the deficit function, B_0?**
   (a) The tax rate is equal to 20 percent.
   (b) The cyclically adjusted deficit is 20.
   (c) There is a balanced budget at $Y = 500$.
   (d) The cyclically adjusted deficit is –20; i.e., a surplus.
   (e) When $Y = 0$, the budget deficit is 100.

2. **For the curve B_0, which one of the following statements is true?**
   (a) A movement from point *a* to point *b* represents an increase in tax rates.
   (b) The decrease in the budget deficit depicted by a movement from point *b* to point *a* must have been caused by an increase in government expenditure.
   (c) Since the budget deficit increased when national income fell from 500 to 400, the government must have increased its discretionary spending.
   (d) Changes in discretionary fiscal policy are shown by movements along the budget deficit function.
   (e) Movements along the function represent the automatic stabilizing influence of the tax system.

*3. **If the budget deficit function changes to B_1, then**
   (a) the cyclically adjusted deficit increases to 50.
   (b) the tax rate increased from 20 to 25 percent.
   (c) the tax rate decreased from 20 to 15 percent.
   (d) government expenditures must have decreased at every level of national income.
   (e) the budget deficit decreases at every level of national income because the private saving ratio has increased.

Use the following information to answer Questions 4 to 7. Government purchases (G) is 400, net tax revenues (T) is tY (where $t = 0.25$ is the tax rate), and potential real national income (Y^*) is 1000.

*4. **If $Y = 800$, then the actual budget deficit (BD) is ___________________ and the cyclically adjusted budget deficit ($CABD$) is _________________.**
   (a) –200; –150
   (b) +200; –150
   (c) –200; +150
   (d) +200; +150
   (e) +150; +200

***5. If $Y = 800$ and the government wants to move the economy to the level of potential real national income while keeping a balanced budget, then the government could**

(a) decrease G by 200.
(b) increase G by 150 or decrease taxes by 150.
(c) decrease G by 150 in combination with expansionary monetary policy.
(d) increase G by 150 in combination with either contractionary or expansionary monetary policy.
(e) increase taxes by 150 in combination with contractionary monetary policy.

***6. If $Y = 1200$, then the actual budget deficit (BD) is ________________.**

(a) –150.
(b) –100.
(c) –200.
(d) +100.
(e) +150.

***7. If $Y = 1200$ and the government wants to move the economy to the level of potential real national income while keeping a balanced budget, then the government could**

(a) decrease G by 100.
(b) increase G by 150 or decrease taxes by 150.
(c) decrease G by 150 in combination with either expansionary or contractionary monetary policy.
(d) decrease G by 150 in combination with contractionary monetary policy.
(e) increase taxes by 150 in combination with contractionary monetary policy.

Answers Questions 8 to 13 by referring to the following table, which shows hypothetical data from year 2004 to 2006. The symbols as those defined by the textbook.

Year	x	r	g	d	Δd
2004	0	0.030	0.025	0.600	
2005	–0.010	0.028	0.025		
2006	–0.020	0.025	0.025		

8. The symbol g denotes

(a) the primary budget as a percentage of GDP.
(b) the debt-to-GDP ratio.
(c) the growth rate of real GDP.
(d) the rate of inflation.
(e) the real rate of interest.

9. Between 2004 and 2006, which of the following statements is true?

(a) The growth in real GDP increased.
(b) Real interest rates decreased.
(c) The primary budget balance became a budgetary deficit.
(d) The primary budget balance became a budgetary surplus.
(e) Both (b) and (d) are correct.

***10. The three-digit value of Δd for 2004 is**

(a) 0.033.
(b) –0.055.
(c) –0.005.
(d) +0.003.
(e) 0.055.

***11. Since *d* in 2005 is equal to *d* in 2004 plus Δ*d* in 2004, what is the three-digit value for *d* in 2005?**

(a) 0.603.
(b) 0.595.
(c) 0.597.
(d) 0.545.
(e) 0.595.

***12. The three-digit values of Δ*d* for 2005 and of *d* for 2006 are**

(a) 0, 0.600.
(b) −0.02, 0.595.
(c) −0.008, 0.595.
(d) −0.007, 0.589.
(e) None of the above.

13. Which of the following statements is true? Between 2004 and 2006,

(a) the budget surplus fell.
(b) the debt-to-GDP ratio fell.
(c) the real of interest increased.
(d) the change in the debt-to-GDP (Δ*d*) ratio became positive.
(e) All of the above are correct.

Questions 14 and 15 refer to Figure 32-5. The equilibrium initial situation for a closed economy is point E_0. Now suppose that the government increases its expenditures but keeps its net tax rate unchanged.

Figure 32-5

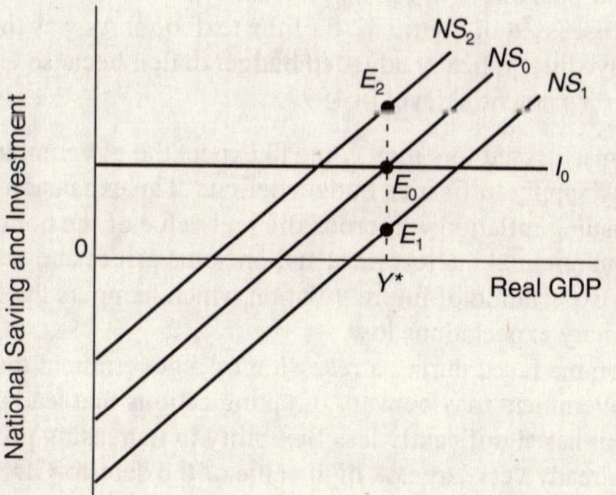

14. In the short run, we would expect this policy stance to

(a) create a budget surplus and a reduction in government borrowing.
(b) create an inflationary gap by shifting the national saving curve to NS_1.
(c) create a recessionary gap by shifting the national saving curve to NS_2.
(d) increase the measured unemployment beyond the NAIRU.
(e) shift the budget deficit function down and to the right.

***15. In the long run the effects of this policy stance are**

(a) the restoration of potential real GDP and a higher price level.
(b) higher interest rates triggered by increased demand for nominal money balances.
(c) a downward shift in the investment curve intersecting NS_1 at point E_1.
(d) leftward shifts in the *AS* curve as money wages are bid up.
(e) All of the above.

SOLUTIONS

Chapter Review

1.(a) **2.**(d) **3.**(c) **4.**(d) **5.**(e) **6.**(c) **7.**(d) **8.**(a) **9.**(e) **10.**(a) **11.**(d) **12.**(a) **13.**(a) **14.**(e) **15.**(b) **16.**(e) **17.**(d) **18.**(d)

Short-Answer Questions

1. **(a)** Program spending includes expenditures on goods and services that are required to provide social and economic programs to the public. Transfer payments are payments to households and firms such as subsidies, employment insurance, welfare, etc. In the textbook, these expenditures are subtracted from taxation revenue. The term T therefore represents net taxes (net of transfers.) If a government incurs debt, it must pay interest and principal payments to debt holders. These are called debt-service payments.

(b) An actual budget deficit is program and debt-servicing expenditures minus net taxation revenue. Since taxation revenue depends on the value of GDP, the actual budget deficit can change as GDP changes. If program and debt-servicing expenditure minus net taxation is positive, a deficit exists, and additional borrowing must occur. A cyclically adjusted budget deficit calculates taxation revenue only at potential GDP (Y^*). Hence, if the cyclically adjusted deficit increases, it implies that the stance of fiscal policy has changed either by reductions in the net tax rate or by increases in government expenditures.

2. **(a)** The stance of fiscal policy is judged only by changes in the cyclically adjusted deficit. The data clearly indicate that fiscal policy was contractionary. The budget deficit in 1994 progressively fell until a budget surplus of 1.4 in 1999 occurred.

(b) This matter is discussed in Figure 32-5 of the textbook. As was the case in 1995, the actual budget deficit was above the cyclically adjusted budget deficit because GDP was below its potential level.

(c) GDP was above its potential level in 1997.

3. Both foreign and domestic creditors may come to expect the government to put pressure on the central bank to increase the money supply to finance budget deficits. The expansion of the money supply causes higher inflation, and any ensuing inflation will erode the real value of the bonds held by creditors. These fears lead to upward pressure on nominal interest rates and on some prices and wages. Hence, a large government debt may lead to the expectation of future inflation which hampers the task of the central bank in keeping inflation and inflationary expectations low.

Consider the dilemma faced during a recession by a government that is considering an expansionary fiscal policy. The government may be wary of taking actions that lead to large increases in the debt-to-GDP ratio. The government has significantly less flexibility in increasing program spending if the stock of outstanding debt is already very large. A high value of the debt-to-GDP ratio (d) will increase quickly. Thus, any increase in the primary deficit runs the danger of generating increases in the debt-to-GDP ratio that may be viewed by creditors as unsustainable.

4. There is nothing intrinsically wrong (or right, for that matter) with budget deficits. During the business cycle it is expected that governments will run deficits during periods of recession and surpluses during periods of economic boom. Overall, it could be argued that governments should attempt to run a balanced budget over the business cycle where the surpluses of the boom years would offset the deficits of the recession years.

The proposition that governments should always run balanced budgets would have the effect of exacerbating a negative situation during periods of recession by further reducing aggregate demand when this one is already weak—i.e., it would result in the creation of more unemployment and greater excess productive capacity during recessions instead of contributing to their reduction. Similarly, it would have the effect of further increasing aggregate demand during periods of economic boom at a time when this one is already too strong—i.e., it would create further inflationary pressure in the economy.

This proposition has an ideological rather than an economic root—it aims to reduce the economic role of the state as much as possible. The claim is that government expenditure should be reduced in periods of recession to balance the budget, and taxes should be reduced in periods of economic boom for the same reason. The long-run result would be to minimize the economic and social role of the government.

The emergence of structural or cyclically adjusted budget deficits—i.e., deficits during both periods of recession and periods of economic boom—is a different story. Here it could be claimed that government deficits crowd out private investment. If that's the case, then the claim should be that governments should try to run balanced budgets over the business cycle period but not at all times.

In short, a deficit in any one year doesn't say much unless we look at it into the context of the business cycle. A deficit in a year of recession is something to be expected, and thus we should look at what the budget surplus (or deficit) might be at the level of potential real national income—the cyclically adjusted budget deficit. For instance, if at the level of potential output we determine that the government would be running a surplus, then the best policy for the government might be to use expansionary fiscal/monetary policy even if the budget deficit were to increase further in the short run.

Exercises

1. **(a)** $10 = (.10 \times 100)$.
(b) 20 = government spending on goods and services.
(c) A primary budget deficit of –5 (a surplus of 5). This value is obtained by subtracting 25 from 20. An overall budget deficit of 5 = a primary deficit (surplus) of –5 plus debt-service payments of 10.
(d) The overall budgetary deficit of 5 must be financed by borrowing.
(e) Fifty percent = (100/200 × 100 percent). 52.5 percent = (105/200 × 100 percent).
(f) Two and a half percent = (5/200 × 100 percent).

2. **(a)** \$150 billion; –10 (recessionary gap); 0; 20 percent; \$90 billion (60 percent of \$150 billion); \$30 billion (the vertical intercept value); \$2 billion surplus = (30 – 0.2 × 160).
(b) \$160 billion; 0; 5 percent (8/160); 20 percent; \$96 billion (60 percent of \$160 billion); \$40 billion (the vertical intercept value); Cyclically adjusted deficit of \$8 billion (40 – 32).
(c) Although the tax rate has not changed, government expenditures have fallen by \$10 billion from 2006 to 2007. This change in fiscal policy is best seen by noting that the government plans a cyclically adjusted surplus in 2007 (and reducing outstanding debt), while it ran a cyclically adjusted deficit in 2006. Also note that the change in fiscal policy stance is at a time when real national income is falling—i.e., fiscal policy is procyclical.
(d) The government appears to want to stabilize the debt-to-GDP ratio. Notice that the government ran a budget deficit in 2006 when the economy was at its potential level of output. With the downturn in the economy in 2007, tax revenues will be lost. If the government had continued its 2006 level of expenditures at \$40 billion in 2007, the deficit would have grown and the government would have had to increase the debt-to-GDP ratio. Future tax liabilities will be higher and possibly some of the crowding-out effects discussed in the text may cause declines in investment and exports.

3. **(a)** $CABD = G - T = 300 - (-50 + 0.2\ Y^*) = 350 - 0.2\ (2\ 000) = -50$.
(b) $BD = G - T = 300 - [-50 + 0.2\ (1500)] = 350 - 300 = 50$. Since $Y < Y^*$, it is rather expected that $BD > 0$. Moreover, $CABD < 0$, which indicates a structural budget surplus. The immediate concern would be to get the economy out of the recession and back to full-employment income, and thus expansionary fiscal policy (or a combination of expansionary fiscal and monetary policy) would be in order. However, as Y gets closer to Y^*, fiscal policy should be reviewed once again to ensure that the cyclically adjusted budget deficit does not turn positive.
(c) $BD = G - T = 300 - [-50 + 0.2\ (1750)] = 350 - 350 = 0$. Here the government is running a balanced budget but $Y < Y^*$. However, $CABD < 0$ which indicates a structural budget surplus. As in (a), the immediate concern should be to get the economy out of the recession and back to full-employment income, and thus expansionary fiscal policy would be in order. Again, as Y gets closer to Y^*, fiscal policy should be reviewed to ensure that the cyclically adjusted budget deficit does not turn positive.
(d) $BD = G - T = 300 - [-50 + 0.2\ (2250)] = 350 - 450 = -100$. Since $Y > Y^*$, it is rather expected that $BD < 0$. However, $CABD < 0$, which indicates a structural budget surplus. The immediate concern here should be to get the economy back to full-employment income through contractionary policy. Since contractionary fiscal policy would further increase the cyclically adjusted budget surplus, the use of contractionary monetary policy should be preferred. Moreover, since a parallel objective must be to eliminate the cyclically adjusted budget surplus, contractionary monetary policy should be complemented with slightly expansionary fiscal policy (e.g., a decrease in taxes).

(e) Here we have that $Y = Y^*$ but $BD < 0$. The objective then is to eliminate the budget surplus without changing the level of income. Therefore, a combination of expansionary fiscal policy (e.g., a decrease in taxes) and contractionary monetary policy should be in order.

4. (a) The change in the debt-to-GDP ratio is given by the formula $\Delta d = x + (r - g)d$. In this case, the change in the debt-to-GDP ratio is two percent = [0.01 + (0.04 – 0.02) × 0.50]. Since this value is positive, government borrowing increased.

(b) To obtain $\Delta d = 0$, then a primary surplus of 0.01 (a primary deficit of –0.01) is required to offset the growth in real debt-service payments of 0.01).

(c) The formula is given by deficit/GDP = $(\pi + g)$ times (debt/GDP). Since $\pi = 0$, then the deficit/GDP ratio is 1 percent = 0.02 times 0.50.

(d) The change in the debt-to-GDP ratio is 2.2 percent. The primary surplus required to keep $\Delta d = 0$ is 0.012. The new deficit/GDP ratio is 1.2 percent. One policy implication is that program spending must be reduced more than before because of a higher debt-to-GDP ratio. Hence, the flexibility in conducting counter-cyclical fiscal policy has been diminished.

Extension Exercises

E1. (a) $i = 5$ (percent) and total private saving borrowing (investment) = 35 *zees*.

Figure 32-6

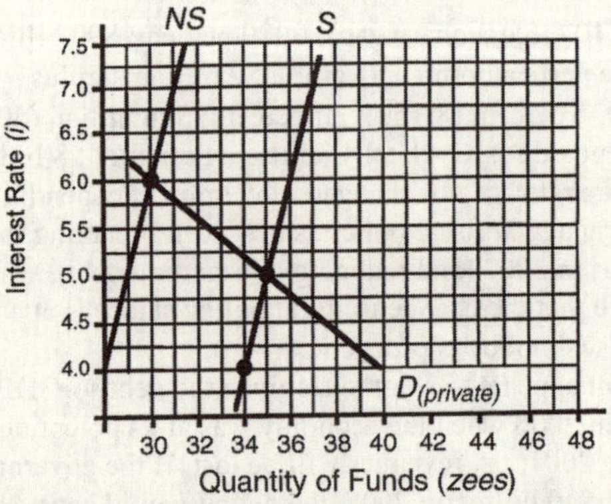

(b) National saving is equal to private saving plus public saving. In this case, public saving is –6 (the deficit). Hence, $NS = 30 + i - 6$, or $24 + i$. Since private saving was unaffected by the government's deficit, consumers were not Ricardian.

(c) The interest rate increases to 6% and total investment falls from 35 to 30 *zees*.

(d) From one equilibrium to another, 5 *zees* of investment were crowded out (decreased).

E2. (a) $AE = 50 + 0.8(Y - 0.2Y) + 100 + 160 + 10 - 0.04Y$. Using the equilibrium condition $Y = AE$, we obtain $Y = 800$. There is no output gap. The budget is balanced since total government spending equals total taxation revenue of 160.

(b) The new equilibrium GDP is 795. An export decline of 2 generated a decline in GDP of 5; hence the multiplier is 2.5. There is an output (recessionary) gap of –5 and the government deficit is 1.0.

(c) The expression for aggregate expenditure is now $50 + 0.8(Y - 0.2Y) + 100 + 0.2Y(= G) + 10 - 0.04Y$. As before, $Y = 800$.

(d) With the decline in net exports of 2, the new equilibrium GDP is 790. Since total taxation revenue is 158, G must also be 158. The multiplier value is 5 since a decline in net exports of 2 created a reduction of 10 in GDP. The output gap is now –10, which is greater than in part (b), which had no balanced budget requirement. The multiplier with an annually balanced budget requirement is larger because the recessionary gap automatically reduces tax revenue, which must be matched by an equal reduction in government spending. Thus, as the text suggests, an annually balanced budget serves as a *built-in destabilizer.*

Additional Multiple-Choice Questions

1.(b) **2.**(e) **3.**(b) **4.**(d) **5.**(c) **6.**(d) **7.**(c) **8.**(c) **9.**(e) **10.**(d) **11.**(a) **12.**(c) **13.**(b) **14.**(b) **15.**(e)

Explanations for the Asterisked Multiple-Choice Questions

3.(b) The slope of the budget deficit line has increased. The net tax rate increased from 20 percent to 25 percent as the diagram illustrates.

4.(d) $BD = G - T = 400 - 0.25\,Y = 400 - 0.25\,(800) = 400 - 200 = 200.$
$CABD = 400 - 0.25\,Y^* = 400 - 0.25\,(1000) = 400 - 250 = 150.$

5.(c) Since $CABD = 150$, either G must decrease by 150 or taxes must increase by 150 (e.g., by increasing t to 0.4). This contractionary fiscal policy will have the additional effect of moving equilibrium income further away from Y^*, and thus the government should complement this contractionary fiscal policy with expansionary monetary policy.

6.(d) $BD = G - T = 400 - 0.25\,Y = 400 - 0.25\,(1200) = 400 - 300 = 100.$

7.(c) Since $CABD = 150$, either G must decrease by 150 or taxes must increase by 150 (e.g., by increasing t to 0.4). This contractionary fiscal policy will have the additional effect of moving equilibrium income closer to Y^*. However, we don't know whether this would be enough to move the economy to Y^* or too much and move the economy to $Y < Y^*$. If Y remains greater than Y^*, then the government should complement this contractionary fiscal policy with contractionary monetary policy; if Y falls below Y^*, then the government should complement this contractionary fiscal policy with expansionary monetary policy.

10.(d) Using the formula, we obtain $\Delta d = 0 + (0.005) \times (0.60) = 0.003$.

11.(a) $0.600 + 0.003 = 0.603$.

12.(c) $\Delta d = -0.010 + (0.003) \times 0.603 = -0.008$. The value of d for 2006 is $0.603 - 0.008 = 0.595$.

15.(e) The national saving curve shifts to NS_1 and an inflationary gap situation is opened. As the price level rises, the nominal interest rate increases because the demand for money balances increases. Thus, the desired investment curve begins to shift down until it intersects the new NS curve at point E_1. Potential GDP is restored when money wage increases shift the AS curve leftward.

PART 12: CANADA IN THE GLOBAL ECONOMY

CHAPTER 33

THE GAINS FROM INTERNATIONAL TRADE

LO

LEARNING OBJECTIVES

In this chapter you will learn

1 why the gains from trade depend on the pattern of comparative advantage.

2 how factor endowments and climate can influence a country's comparative advantage.

3 about the law of one price.

4 why countries export some goods and import others.

CHAPTER OVERVIEW

This chapter explains how international trade makes possible a higher average standard of living for a country. A country benefits from buying goods abroad at a lower cost. A country is said to have **absolute advantage** in the production of a particular commodity when it can produce more of the good with a given amount of resources than can other countries. A country has a **comparative advantage** in producing a good when it has a lower opportunity cost in production than other countries. The **gains from trade** do not depend upon absolute advantage, but rather upon comparative advantage. Even if a country has an absolute advantage in the production of all goods, both trading partners can share in the gains from trade.

Comparative advantage can be attributed to differences in exogenous considerations such as factor endowments and climate. Today, there is widespread acceptance by economists that comparative advantage may also be acquired. International trade encourages countries to specialize in the production of goods where they have a comparative advantage as opposed to the costly product diversification associated with self-sufficiency. The gains from trade are likely to be even greater when countries can achieve economies of scale, or benefit from **learning-by-doing**.

When transportation costs are insignificant, a traded good will sell at the same price in all countries—this is the so-called *law of one price*. This price is referred to as the world price.

The division of the gains from trade between two countries depends upon the **terms of trade** which refers to the ratio of the price of exported goods to the price of imported goods. The terms of trade determine the quantity of imported goods that can be obtained per unit of exported good.

HINTS AND TIPS

The following may help you to avoid some of the most common errors on examinations.

✓ Learn that gains from trade depend only on comparative advantage. Comparative advantage promotes production specialization and gains from international trade.

- ✓ Understand that the basis for trade is differences in opportunity costs between countries. The opportunity cost of one good is measured by the forgone output of another good.
- ✓ Learn how to calculate opportunity costs from production possibilities information. In terms of a diagram, opportunity cost is measured by the slope of the country's production possibilities boundary.
- ✓ Learn how the law of one price determines the pattern of international trade. Countries export goods for which they are low-cost producers, and import goods for which they are high-cost producers.
- ✓ Learn that the terms of trade determine how the gains from trade are divided between trading partners. The terms of trade are measured by the ratio of the price of exports to the price of imports.

CHAPTER REVIEW

The Gains from Trade

After studying this section, you should recognize that international trade among countries involves basically the same principles of exchange that apply to trade among individuals. With trade, people (regions) can specialize in what they do well and satisfy other needs by trading. You will also learn that although gains from trade can occur even when production is fixed, further gains arise when nations specialize production in goods for which they have a comparative advantage. Comparative advantage arises from differences in production opportunity costs which are determined by factor endowments and climate but also by changing human skills and experience in production.

1. Country X has an absolute advantage over country Y in the production of widgets if

(a) more resources are required in X to produce a given quantity of widgets than in Y.
(b) a given amount of resources in X produces more widgets than the same amount of resources in Y.
(c) relative to Y, more widgets can be produced in X with fewer resources.
(d) relative to Y, fewer widgets can be produced in X with fewer resources.
(e) None of the above.

2. If, given the same amount of inputs, Canadian farmers produce 2 tons of rice per hectare while Japanese farmers produce 1 ton of rice per hectare, we can be certain that

(a) Canada will export rice to Japan.
(b) Canada has a comparative advantage in rice production.
(c) Canada has an absolute advantage in rice production.
(d) Japanese rice farmers must be paid twice as much as Canadian farmers.
(e) Japan should not produce any rice

3. Comparative advantage is said to exist whenever

(a) one country can produce a given level of output with fewer resources compared to another country.
(b) a given amount of resources produces more output in one country compared to another.
(c) one country has an absolute advantage over another country in the production of all goods.
(d) different countries have different opportunity costs in production.
(e) two countries are of different sizes.

4. **If there are two countries A and B, and two goods X and Y, and if A has a comparative advantage in the production of X, it necessarily follows that**
(a) A has an absolute advantage in the production of X.
(b) B has an absolute advantage in the production of X.
(c) A has a comparative disadvantage in the production of Y.
(d) B has an absolute advantage in the production of Y.
(e) B has a comparative disadvantage in the production of Y.

5. **Which of the following is *not* a source of comparative advantage?**
(a) Factor endowments.
(b) Climate.
(c) Country size.
(d) Acquiring human capital.
(e) None of the above.

6. **Gains from specialization can arise when**
(a) countries have different opportunity costs in production.
(b) there are economies of scale in production.
(c) experience gained via specialization lowers cost through learning by doing.
(d) trading partners have a different comparative advantage.
(e) All of the above.

7. **Free trade within the European Union led to**
(a) each member country specializing in specific products (e.g., furniture, cars, etc.).
(b) a large increase in product differentiation and intra-industry trade, with countries tending to specialize in subproduct lines (e.g., office furniture, household furniture, etc.).
(c) no perceptible alteration in production patterns.
(d) less trade among EU members.
(e) less product diversity.

8. **Economies of scale and learning by doing are different because**
(a) one refers to an increase in variable costs and the other to a decrease.
(b) economies of scale refer to a movement along the long-run average cost curve, whereas learning by doing shifts the long-run average cost curve.
(c) economies of scale affect variable costs, but learning by doing affects only fixed costs.
(d) learning by doing affects profits but not costs.
(e) economies of scale affect costs, whereas learning by doing affects revenue.

9. **According to the Hecksher-Ohlin theory,**
(a) resource-rich countries benefit the most from trade.
(b) different opportunity costs across countries can be explained by differences in factor endowments.
(c) different opportunity costs across countries can be explained by differences in production functions.
(d) low-wage countries gain the most from trade.
(e) countries with similar opportunity costs can gain the most from trade.

10. **The concept of dynamic comparative advantage is best characterized by**
(a) the importance of factor endowments in determining trade patterns.
(b) changes in a country's terms of trade due to depletion of natural resources.
(c) acquiring new areas of specialization through investment in human capital.
(d) changes in a country's variable costs due to economies of scale.
(e) greater specialization in resource-intensive industries.

The Determination of Trade Patterns

After reading this section, you will understand the law of one price and its implications for a country's imports and exports. Make certain that you understand the relationship between a country's comparative advantage and its no-trade price.

After studying this section you should be able to explain that the terms of trade, defined as the ratio of export prices to import prices, indicate how the gains from trade are divided between buyers and sellers. Changes in the terms of trade lead to changes in a country's consumption possibilities. You will also be able to distinguish an improvement in the terms of trade from a deterioration.

11. **The *law of one price* refers to**
(a) the idea that international cartels collude to charge a single price.
(b) federal statutes that regulate firms to charge the same price domestically and globally.
(c) the idea that when transportation costs are insignificant, a product will tend to have the same price worldwide.
(d) the international trade principle that export products cannot be subject to price discrimination.
(e) the assumption that average costs of production are equal in all countries.

12. **A single world price of oil is likely to exist if**
(a) oil can be transported easily from one country to another.
(b) each country produces all of its domestic consumption.
(c) all governments restrict exports of oil.
(d) demand for oil is the same in all countries.
(e) the cost of producing oil is the same in each country.

13. **Canada is a major exporter of nickel because at the world price**
(a) Canadian quantity demanded exceeds Canadian quantity supplied.
(b) Canadian quantity supplied exceeds Canadian quantity demanded.
(c) the quantity of nickel demanded by Canadians exceeds domestic production.
(d) Canada mines more nickel than any other country.
(e) domestic consumption and production are the same as they would be in the "no trade" equilibrium.

14. **The terms of trade**
(a) refer to the quantity of imported goods that can be obtained for a given amount of money.
(b) are measured by the product between the price of exports and the price of imports.
(c) determine the division of the gains from trade.
(d) are determined by the federal government.
(e) None of the above.

15. A rise in export prices as compared to import prices is considered a favourable change in the terms of trade since

(a) one can export more per unit of imported goods.
(b) employment in export industries will increase.
(c) one can acquire more imports per unit of exports.
(d) total exports will increase.
(e) All of the above.

16. Due to a labour strike by port workers, it is expected that this year beef exports will fall by 10 percent in the small country of Tacuarembó. As a result,

(a) the international price of beef will fall.
(b) the international price of beef will rise.
(c) the domestic price of beef will fall in Tacuarembó.
(d) Tacuarembó's supply curve for beef will shift to the left.
(e) Tacuarembó's supply curve for beef will shift to the right *and* the domestic price of beef will fall.

SHORT-ANSWER QUESTIONS

1. Distinguish between a country's constant cost production possibilities curve, the terms of trade, and its consumption possibilities curve.

2. Draw a rough diagram that illustrates a country importing a good for which the world price is below the domestic non-trade price of that good. What is the role of comparative advantage in this analysis?

3. Draw a rough diagram that illustrates a small country exporting a good for which the world price is above the domestic non-trade price of that good. Suppose now that a technological improvement takes place in the industry producing this good. Show the impact of this technological improvement in your diagram. What will be the impact of this technological improvement on both the domestic and international price of this good?

4. Identify the likely source of comparative advantage in each of the following trade relationships:
   (a) Canada exports apples to Honduras, and Honduras exports bananas to Canada.

   (b) Venezuela exports oil to Cuba, and Cuba exports medical services to Venezuela.

   (c) Canada exports financial services to China, and China exports shoes to Canada.

5. Explain the fact that while Canada exports cars to the U.S., the U.S. also exports cars to Canada.

EXERCISES

1. **Comparative and Absolute Advantage**

This exercise provides basic production data and requires you to calculate the opportunity cost of production. It then draws out the distinction between absolute and comparative advantage and the implications for trade.

For each of the following scenarios, determine the opportunity costs of producing each good in each country, and indicate which commodity each country should specialize its production with trade.

(a) One unit of resources can produce:

	Radios	*Cameras*
Japan	2	4
Indonesia	3	1

The opportunity costs are:

	1 Radio	*1 Camera*
Japan	______	______
Indonesia	______	______

Japan should specialize in the production of ________.
Indonesia should specialize in the production of ________.
Japan has an absolute advantage in the production of ________.
Indonesia has a comparative advantage in the production of ________.

(b) One unit of resources can produce:

	Radios	*Cameras*
Japan	2	4
Indonesia	1	3

The opportunity costs are:

	1 Radio	*1 Camera*
Japan	______	______
Indonesia	______	______

Japan should specialize in the production of ________.
Indonesia should specialize in the production of ________.
Indonesia has a comparative advantage in the production of ________.

(c) One unit of resources can produce:

	Radios	*Cameras*
Japan	2	4
Indonesia	1	2

The opportunity costs are:

	1 Radio	*1 Camera*
Japan	________	________
Indonesia	________	________

Japan should specialize in the production of ________.
Indonesia should specialize in the production of ________.

(d) Which scenario demonstrates that absolute advantage is not a sufficient condition for trade to occur? Explain.

(e) Which scenario suggests why a nation as technologically advanced as Japan can gain from trading with other countries with lower wages? Explain.

2. Opportunity Cost and Terms of Trade

Countries *A* and *B* each currently produce both watches and dairy products. Assume that country *A* gives up the opportunity to produce 100 litres of dairy products for each watch it makes, and *B* could produce one watch at a cost of 200 litres of dairy products.

(a) The opportunity cost of making watches (in terms of dairy products) is lower in country ________.

(b) The opportunity cost of making dairy products (in terms of watches) is lower in country ________.

(c) Country *B* should specialize in ________ and let country *A* produce ________.

(d) The terms of trade (the price of one product in terms of the other) would be somewhere between ________ and ________ litres of dairy products for one watch.

3. The Terms of Trade

The following table provides data on the index of merchandise export prices and the index of merchandise import prices for a hypothetical economy.

Year	Index of Export Prices	Index of Import Prices	Terms of Trade
1998	100.6	98.6	________
2000	103.3	102.3	________
2002	157.1	135.6	________
2004	176.6	157.9	________
2006	205.4	200.7	________

(a) Using the definition of the terms of trade that involves indexes, complete the table by calculating the terms of trade to one decimal place.

(b) What does an increase in the terms of trade signify?

(c) Would you classify the change in the terms of trade during the period 2000 to 2002 as favourable to this economy? Explain.

4. **The Production Possibility Curve and Trade**

The following table provides hypothetical data on the productivity of a single unit of resource in producing wheat and microchips in both Canada and Japan.

	One Unit of Resources Produces	
	Wheat (tons)	**Microchips**
Canada	50	20
Japan	2	12

(a) Which country has an absolute advantage in the production of wheat? Of microchips?

(b) What is the opportunity cost of producing a ton of wheat in Canada? In Japan?

(c) Which country has a comparative advantage in the production of wheat? Of microchips?

(d) Suppose that Canada is endowed with 2 units of this all-purpose resource while Japan is endowed with 10 units. Draw each country's production possibility boundary on the following grids. (Assume constant costs.)

Figure 33-1

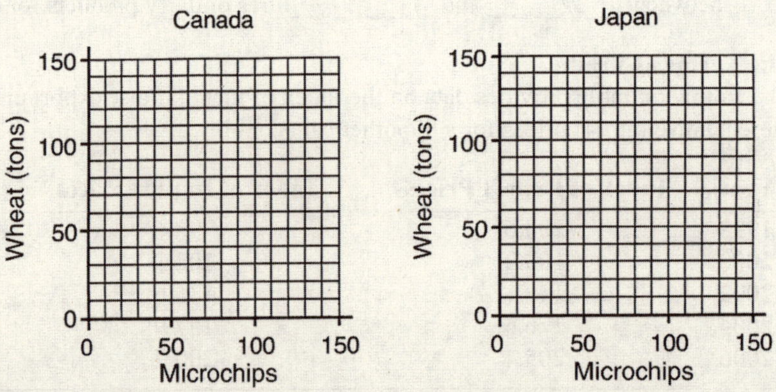

(e) Suppose that prior to trade, each country allocated half of its resource endowment to the production of each good. Indicate the production and consumption points of each country in the graphs (for simplicity, assume that these are the only two countries in the world).

(f) What is world output of each good?

(g) Indicate the production points of each country after trade, and determine world production levels.

(h) Suppose that the terms of trade are one microchip for one ton of wheat and that Canada consumes as much wheat after trade as it did before trade. Indicate the post-trade consumption points of each country and each country's imports and exports.

(i) If the terms of trade changed to two microchips for one ton of wheat, which country would benefit? Explain.

5. Imports and Exports

Figure 33-2 depicts Canadian domestic supply and demand curves, S_C and D_C, respectively, for a commodity in a market for which Canada is assumed to face a fixed world price.

Figure 33-2

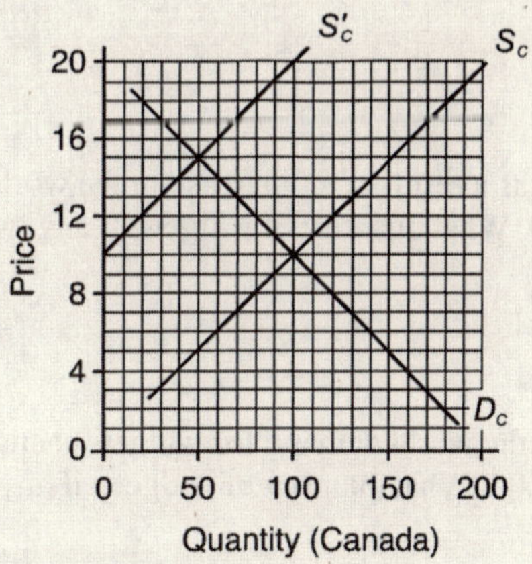

(a) At a world price of $5, Canadian producers sell __________ units, while Canadian consumers purchase __________ units. Canada therefore (imports/exports) __________ units of this commodity.

(b) If the world price increased from $5 to $12 per unit (assuming there was no tariff), Canadians would consume __________ units but produce __________ units. Thus Canada would (import/export) __________ units.

(c) Should domestic supply shift to S'_C while the world price remains at $12, domestic production would now be __________ units and domestic consumption __________ units. Canada would therefore be an (importer/exporter) of __________ units.

6. Imports and Exports

The table below shows the Canadian domestic demand schedule and the domestic supply schedule for widgets.

Price of Widgets	Quantity of Widgets Demanded (thousands)	Quantity of Widgets Supplied (thousands)
$10.00	1 000	10 000
9.50	1 500	9 000
9.00	2 000	8 000
8.50	2 500	7 000
8.00	3 000	6 000
7.50	3 500	5 000
7.00	4 000	4 000
6.50	4 500	3 000
6.00	5 000	2 000
5.50	5 500	1 000
5.00	6 000	0

(a) What are the equilibrium price and the equilibrium quantity of widgets under autarky?

(b) Suppose now that Canada—a relatively small producer of widgets—engages in international trade and that the world price of widgets is $6.00. What quantity of widgets, if any, will Canada export or import?

(c) Suppose that as a result of an increase in the world demand for widgets the world price rises to $8.00. What quantity of widgets, if any, will Canada now export or import?

(d) Suppose that the world demand for widgets changes once again causing the world price to drop to $7.00. What quantity of widgets, if any, will Canada now export or import?

7. Comparative Advantage and Specialization in Production

Italy and France produce only two goods, wine and wool, using a single input, labour. An Italian worker in an eight-hour day can produce 100 bottles of wine or 100 bales of wool, while a French worker can produce 75 bottles of wine or 25 bales of wool in an eight-hour day.

(a) In the absence of trade, what is the opportunity cost in Italy and in France of producing one unit of wine?

(b) If trade is opened up between the two countries, in which product will each of the countries specialize? Explain your answer.

(c) Suppose that labour productivity in both wine and wool production in France doubles. How does this change your answer in (b)? Explain.

(d) If mutually advantageous trade occurs between Italy and France, what will be the range of the international terms of trade between bales of wool and bottles of wine? Explain.

EXTENSION EXERCISES

E1. Production and Consumption Possibility Curves

The Republic of Canelones produces only two goods, wool and lumber. Given the current level of technology, 1 unit of resources can produce either 1 unit of wool or 2 units of lumber in this small country. Canelones has a total resource endowment of 1000 units.

(a) What is the opportunity cost of producing 1 unit of lumber in Canelones? And of producing 1 unit of wool?

(b) In a carefully labelled diagram, draw this country's production possibility curve measuring the quantity of lumber on the horizontal axis. What information does the slope of the production possibility curve give you? If Canelones is currently producing 800 units of lumber, how many units of wool might it be producing as well? Identify this point on your production possibility curve (point A).

(c) What is the consumption possibility curve of this country under autarky?

(d) Now Canelones starts trading in the world market where 1 unit of wool exchanges for 4 units of lumber. What good will this country sell (export) in the international market? Explain.

(e) Assuming that Canelones continues producing the output combination at point A, draw in your diagram the new consumption possibility curve. Given the new consumption possibilities open to this country, how many units of wool will Canelones end up consuming if it chooses to consume 1600 units of lumber? Identify this point on your consumption possibility curve (point B).

(f) Suppose now that Canelones changes its production bundle according to its comparative advantage. What combination of wool and lumber will it produce? Identify this point on your production possibility curve (point C).

(g) Given the new consumption possibilities open to this country, how many units of wool will Canelones end up consuming if it chooses to continue consuming 1600 units of lumber? Identify this point on your consumption possibility curve (point D).

The following exercise examines the tendency toward specialization with trade when production is characterized by increasing opportunity costs (i.e., production possibility curve is concave). A review of *Extensions in Theory 33-1*: *The Gains from Trade More Generally* will help you answer this exercise.

E2. International Trade and Opportunity Cost
The graph in Figure 33-3 depicts a country's production possibility curve between wool and lumber. Prior to trade, the country is producing and consuming at point *R*, which involves 10 units of wool and 10 units of lumber. Due to large increases in construction activity in this economy, the country now decides that it wishes to consume 14 units of lumber.

Figure 33-3

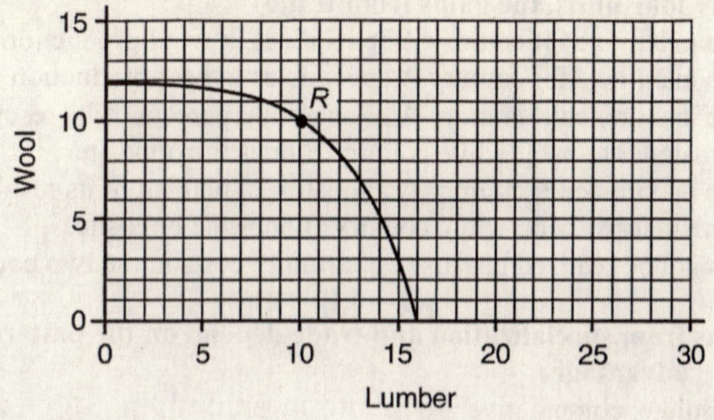

(a) How much wool must this country give up to obtain the additional four units of lumber in a no-trade environment? Explain.

(b) Suppose that the terms of trade in international markets are one unit of wool for two units of lumber. Assuming that production remains at *R,* how much wool would the country have to give up to obtain the additional four units of lumber if it engages in international trade? Explain.

ADDITIONAL MULTIPLE-CHOICE QUESTIONS

1. In a two-country and two-good model, gains from trade would not exist if

(a) one country had an absolute advantage in the production of both goods.
(b) a given amount of resources produced more of both goods in one country.
(c) one country was endowed with far more resources than the other.
(d) the countries had the same opportunity costs in the production of both goods.
(e) only one country had a comparative advantage in the production of one good.

2. Which of the following statements is *not* true about opportunity cost?

(a) Equal opportunity costs for pairs of commodities between two countries lead to gains from trade.
(b) Opportunity costs depend on relative production costs.
(c) Differences in opportunity costs across countries can enhance total output of both goods through trade and specialization.
(d) Comparative advantage can be expressed in terms of opportunity costs.
(e) Opportunity cost can be read as the slope of a tangent to a country's production possibility curve.

*3. **If production of each unit of wool in country A implies that beef production must be decreased by four units, while in country B each additional unit of beef decreases wool output by four units, the gains from trade**
(a) are maximized if country A specializes in wool production and country B in beef.
(b) are maximized if country A specializes in beef production and country B in wool.
(c) are maximized if country A allocates 80 percent of its resources to wool and the remainder to beef, while country B does the opposite.
(d) are maximized if country A allocates 20 percent of its resources to wool and the remainder to beef, while country B does the opposite.
(e) cannot be realized because opportunity costs in the two countries are the same.

4. **The gains from specialization and trade depend on the pattern of ________ advantage, not ________ advantage.**
(a) absolute; comparative
(b) monetary; non-monetary
(c) absolute; reciprocal
(d) comparative; absolute
(e) size; cost

*5. **By trading in international markets, countries**
(a) can consume beyond their production possibility boundary.
(b) will always produce the same commodity bundle as before trade.
(c) can produce outside of their production possibility boundary.
(d) must choose one of the intercepts on the production possibility boundary, indicating complete specialization.
(e) always produce and consume the same bundle of commodities.

Questions 6 to 11 refer to the data in the following table. You will find it useful to first calculate the opportunity costs of production for each commodity in each country.

	One Unit of Resource Can Produce	
Country	**Lumber (bd m)**	**Aluminium (kg)**
Australia	4	9
Canada	9	3
Brazil	3	2

6. **Considering just Australia and Canada,**
(a) Australia has an absolute advantage in lumber.
(b) Australia has an absolute advantage in aluminium.
(c) There are no possible gains from trade.
(d) Canada should specialize in aluminium production.
(e) Australia has a comparative advantage in lumber.

*7. **Considering just Canada and Brazil,**
(a) Brazil has an absolute advantage in lumber.
(b) Brazil has a comparative advantage in aluminium.
(c) Canada has an absolute advantage in only one commodity.
(d) there are no possible gains from trade.
(e) None of the above.

***8. Considering just Australia and Brazil,**

(a) Australia has an absolute advantage in lumber and Brazil in aluminium.
(b) Australia has an absolute advantage in aluminium and Brazil in lumber.
(c) Australia has a comparative advantage in lumber and Brazil in aluminium.
(d) Australia has an absolute advantage in lumber and a comparative advantage in aluminum.
(e) Australia has a comparative advantage in both lumber and aluminum.

***9. In Brazil, the opportunity cost of 1 kilogram of aluminum is**

(a) 0.67 bd m of lumber.
(b) 0.87 bd m of lumber.
(c) 1.25 bd m of lumber.
(d) 1.50 bd m of lumber.
(e) 1.30 bd m of lumber.

***10. In Australia, the opportunity cost of 1 board metre (bd m) of lumber is**

(a) 2.25 kg of aluminium.
(b) 0.44 kg of aluminium.
(c) 0.36 kg of aluminium.
(d) 3.60 kg of aluminium.
(e) 3.00 kg of aluminium.

11. In Canada, the opportunity cost of 1 kilogram of aluminium is

(a) 0.33 bd m of lumber.
(b) 2.70 bd m of lumber.
(c) 3.0 bd m of lumber.
(d) 3.33 bd m of lumber.
(e) 1.50 bd m of lumber.

12. For a country with one important export commodity such as coffee or oil,

(a) a rise in the commodity's price will improve the country's terms of trade.
(b) a fall in the commodity's price is a favourable change in its terms of trade.
(c) its terms of trade will improve only if it is able to increase the quantity of exports.
(d) its terms of trade will improve only if world demand for its exports is inelastic.
(e) its terms of trade improve only if the prices of imports decrease.

Use the following diagram to answer Questions 13 and 14.

Figure 33-4

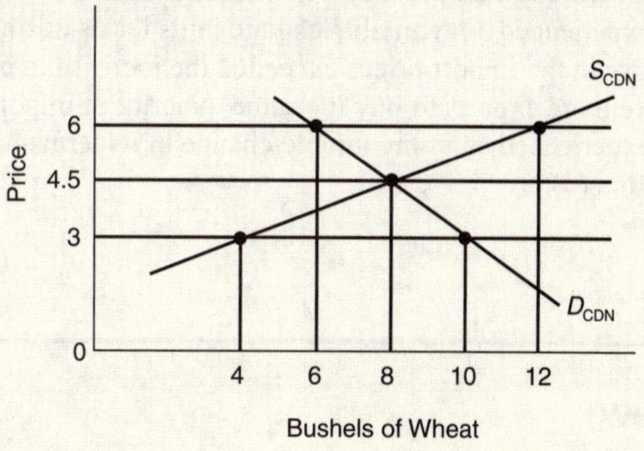

***13. At a world price of $3, Canada will**
- (a) produce 4 million bushels of wheat.
- (b) consume 10 million bushels of wheat.
- (c) import 6 million bushels of wheat.
- (d) consume more wheat than it produces.
- (e) All of the above are correct.

14. If the world price remains at $3, while the Canadian demand for wheat increases, the primary result would be
- (a) an increase in the Canadian production of wheat.
- (b) an increase in the price of wheat in Canada.
- (c) a decrease in Canadian wheat exports.
- (d) an increase in wheat imports into Canada.
- (e) a decrease in quantity supplied by Canadian producers.

***15. At a world price of $4.50, Canada will**
- (a) import 8 million bushels of wheat.
- (b) consume 8 million bushels of wheat.
- (c) import and consume 8 million bushels of wheat.
- (d) produce 8 million bushels of wheat.
- (e) produce and consume 8 million bushels of wheat.

***16. At a world price of $6.00, Canada will**
- (a) import 6 million and consume 12 million bushels of wheat.
- (b) import 6 million and consume 6 million bushels of wheat.
- (c) export 6 million and consume 6 million bushels of wheat.
- (d) produce 6 million and consume 6 million bushels of wheat.
- (e) export 12 million bushels of wheat.

***17. If the world price remains at $6.00, while the Canadian supply increases, the primary result would be**
- (a) a decrease in the price of wheat in Canada.
- (b) an increase in the Canadian consumption of wheat.
- (c) a decrease in Canadian wheat imports.
- (d) a decrease in the quantity demanded by Canadian consumers.
- (e) an increase in Canadian wheat export.

***18. Canada's terms of trade changed from 97.0 in the first quarter of 2002 to 105.1 in the first quarter of 2003. During this period, we conclude that**
- (a) Canada experienced a favourable change in its terms of trade.
- (b) the increase in the import prices exceeded the increase in export prices.
- (c) it will take more exports to buy the same quantity of imports.
- (d) Canada experienced an unfavourable change in its terms of trade.
- (e) Both (c) and (d).

SOLUTIONS

Chapter Review

1.(b) **2.**(c) **3.**(d) **4.**(c) **5.**(c) **6.**(e) **7.**(b) **8.**(b) **9.**(b) **10.**(c) **11.**(c) **12.**(a) **13.**(b) **14.**(c) **15.**(c) **16.**(c)

Short-Answer Questions

1. A constant cost production possibilities curve reflects the possible combinations of the production (and consumption) of two goods in a closed economy with a given endowment of resources. The two intercepts in a production possibilities diagram indicate the maximum production (consumption) levels if only one of the goods was produced. The slope of the production possibilities boundary indicates the opportunity costs of reallocating resources in order to increase the production of one good by decreasing the production of another. The terms of trade line reflects the relative price that one good can be traded for another. The relative price is constant and so the terms of trade line is linear. With constant costs, countries tend to completely specialize in production of one good (in a two-good world). The consumption possibilities curve is the line at which a country, specializing in one good, can consume some of the other good at the world's terms of trade. Hence, a country is able to consume combinations of two goods that are beyond its production possibilities curve.

2. Your rough sketch should resemble Figure 33-6 in the textbook. A country imports the goods of its trading partners because its opportunity costs are higher than the world price. The country will satisfy its total demand by importing goods from abroad at the lower world price. However, some domestic production will occur. Since its domestic opportunity costs are higher than the world price, the country has a comparative disadvantage.

3. Your rough sketch should resemble Figure 33-5 in the textbook. A country exports this good to its trading partners because its opportunity cost is lower than the world price. The country will produce in excess of what is required to satisfy the domestic demand at the world price and sell the rest in the world market. Technological improvement will allow this country to produce any quantity of this good at a lower cost than before, and thus the supply curve will shift down and to the right (i.e., the domestic supply will increase). Since this is a small country—i.e., a price-taker in the world market—the international price will not be affected by this country's increase in the production of this good. Therefore, the domestic price will not be affected either.

4. (a) In both cases, the most likely source of comparative advantage might be climatic differences.
   (b) In the case of Venezuela's exports of oil to Cuba, the most likely source of comparative advantage might be differences in natural resource endowments. In the case of and Cuba's exports of medical services to Venezuela, the most likely source of comparative advantages might be differences in human capital endowments.
   (c) In the case of Canada's exports of financial services to China, the most likely source of comparative advantage might be difference in technology and human capital endowments. In the case of China's exports of shoes to Canada, the most likely source of comparative advantage is differences in unskilled labour endowments.

5. This is the result of the existence of imperfectly competitive markets. Two basic assumptions of perfectly competitive markets are: (1) there is a large number of firms, and (2) these firms produce a homogeneous—i.e., undifferentiated—good. However, even if the assumption of a large number of producers were to be satisfied, only a few markets, if any, would satisfy today the latter strong assumption of producing an undifferentiated product. Indeed, virtually all of today's manufactured consumer goods are produced in a vast array of differentiated product lines. And it is this proliferation of differentiated products which allows different countries to specialize in different subproduct lines and to trade with each other—i.e., creating what is known as intra-industry trade.

Exercises

1. (a) Japan: 1 radio costs 2 cameras; 1 camera costs 1/2 radio.
   Indonesia: 1 radio costs 1/3 camera; 1 camera costs 3 radios.
   Japan should produce cameras. Indonesia should produce radios.
   Japan has an absolute advantage in the production of cameras.
   Indonesia has a comparative advantage in radios.
   (b) Japan: 1 radio costs 2 cameras; 1 camera costs 1/2 radio.
   Indonesia: 1 radio costs 3 cameras; 1 camera costs 1/3 radio.
   Japan should produce radios. Indonesia should produce cameras.
   Indonesia has a comparative advantage in cameras.

(c) Japan: 1 radio costs 2 cameras; 1 camera costs 1/2 radio.
Indonesia: 1 radio costs 2 cameras; 1 camera costs 1/2 radio.
Japan should produce both and Indonesia should produce both. There would be no gains from trade.

(d) Case (c) shows that even though Japan has an absolute advantage in producing both goods, no trade will occur because relative prices (or opportunity costs of production) are identical to those in Indonesia.

(e) Case (b) shows that even though Japanese workers are more productive in both industries (and therefore can expect to earn more than Indonesian workers), mutually beneficial trade can still occur if each country exports the good for which it has a comparative advantage.

2. **(a)** *A*.
(b) *B*.
(c) dairy products, watches.
(d) 100, 200.

3. **(a)** 102.0, 101.0, 115.9, 111.8, 102.3.
(b) An increase in the terms of trade means that fewer exports are required to pay for a given amount of imports.
(c) The terms of trade changed from 101.0 to 115.6; this was a favourable change in terms of trade for this economy. It cost fewer exports to buy the same imports, or for the same exports this economy received more imports.

4. **(a)** Canada has an absolute advantage in both goods.
(b) 0.4, 6.0.
(c) Canada, Japan.
(d) **Figure 33-5**

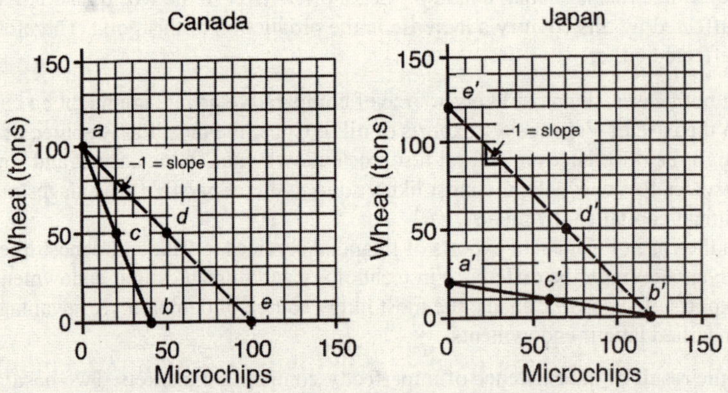

Canada's production possibility boundary is denoted *ab*, and Japan's is *a′b′*.

(e) Canada would be producing and consuming 50 tons of wheat and 20 microchips (point *c* in the diagram), and Japan would be producing and consuming 10 tons of wheat and 60 microchips (point *c′*).

(f) Assuming that these are the only countries making up the world, total output of wheat is 60 tons and world production of microchips is 80 units.

(g) Each country specializes in the commodity in which it has a comparative advantage. Thus Canada specializes completely in wheat production (see point *a*), and Japan specializes completely in microchip production (see point *b′*). World output is now 100 tons of wheat and 120 microchips.

(h) Terms of trade equal to one ton of wheat for one microchip mean that Canada can trade from its production point *a* to any point on its consumption possibility curve *ae* which has a slope of −1, representing the terms of trade. Similarly, Japan can trade from point *b′* to any point on its consumption possibility curve *b′e′*. Since it was assumed that Canada consumes the same amount of wheat both before and after trade, its consumption bundle is represented by point *d*, which contains 50 units of each good. Therefore, Canada is exporting 50 tons of wheat in return for imports of 50 microchips. Japan, having exported 50 microchips to Canada, has 70 remaining for its own consumption. When this is combined with its 50 tons of wheat imports, Japan consumes at point *d′*.

(i) The terms of trade lines in the graphs would become flatter with a slope of −1/2. Thus, Canada's consumption possibilities would increase (the new terms of trade line rotates outward on point *a*), while Japan's decrease (the new terms of trade line rotates inward on point *b*′). Thus, Canada would get a larger share of the gains from trade.

5. **(a)** 50; 150; imports; 100.
(b) 80; 120; exports; 40.
(c) 20; 80; importer; 60.

6. **(a)** \$7.00; 4000 thousand.
(b) Canada will produce 2000 thousand and consume 5000 thousand widgets at the world price of \$6.00. Hence, Canada will import 3000 thousand widgets to satisfy its domestic demand.
(c) Canada will produce 6000 thousand and consume 3000 thousand widgets at the world price of \$8.00. Hence, Canada will export 3000 thousand widgets.
(d) Canada will produce 4000 thousand and consume 4000 thousand widgets at the world price of \$7.00. Canada will produce just enough to satisfy the domestic demand and thus will neither export nor import widgets.

7. **(a)** In the absence of trade, the opportunity cost of 1 unit of wine is 1 bale of wool in Italy and 1/3 bale of wool in France.
(b) The opportunity cost of 1 unit of wine is lower in France than in Italy and thus France has a comparative advantage in the production of wine. Therefore, Italy has a comparative advantage in the production of wool. Indeed, the opportunity cost of 1 bale of wool is 1 unit of wine in Italy and 3 units of wine in France.
(c) There will be no change to the answer above. If labour productivity increases in the same proportion in the wine and wool industries in France, the opportunity cost of producing either good doesn't change.
(d) Since Italy has a comparative advantage in the production of wool, it will specialize in the production of wool and will export wool to France in exchange for wine. Before trade takes place, Italian wool producers would exchange 1 bale of wool for 1 unit of wine. Therefore, they will engage in trade if they can obtain from France more than 1 unit of wine for each bale of wool.

In turn, before trade takes place, French wine producers would exchange 3 units of wine for 1 bale of wool. Therefore, they will engage in trade if they can obtain from Italy 1 bale of wool for less than 3 units of wine.

→ 1Wool < 1 Wine < 3 Wool

Extension Exercises

E1. **(a)** The opportunity cost of producing 1 unit of lumber is 0.5 units of wool, while the opportunity cost of producing 1 unit of wool is 2 units of lumber in Canelones.
(b) The slope of the production possibility curve indicates the opportunity cost of producing an additional unit of lumber. Since Canelones must allocate 400 units of resources to produce 800 units of lumber, the remaining 600 units of resources will produce 600 units of wool—it will produce at point A.

Figure 33-6

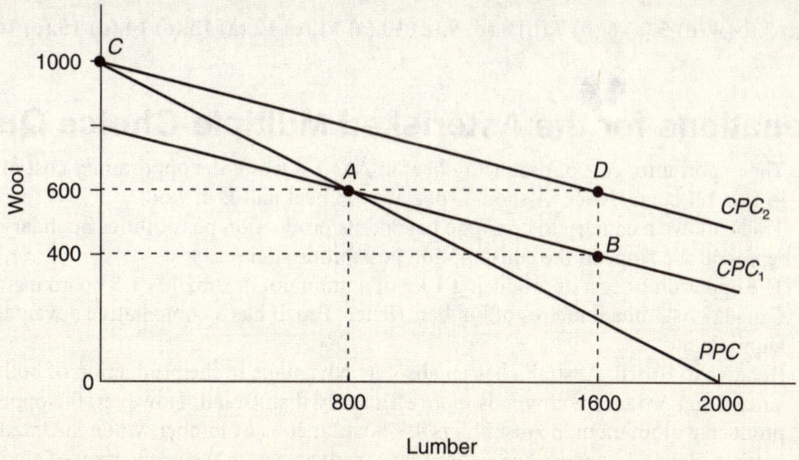

(c) In autarky, the consumption possibility curve coincides with the production possibility curve.

(d) The opportunity cost of producing 1 unit of wool is 2 units of lumber in Canelones, while the opportunity cost of obtaining 1 unit of wool in the international market is 4 units of lumber. Canelones has a comparative advantage in the production of wool and thus it will export wool and import lumber.

(e) The slope of the consumption possibility curve is now 0.25—flatter than the slope of the production possibility curve, which is 0.5. If Canelones continues to produce at point A—800 units of lumber and 600 units of wool—while consuming now 1600 units of lumber, then it will have to import 800 units of lumber—thus exporting 200 units of wool given that 1 unit of wool exchanges for 4 units of lumber in the world market. Therefore, it will now consume a combination of 400 units of wool and 1600 units of lumber (point B).

(f) Since Canelones has a comparative advantage in the production of wool, it will specialize in the production of wool. Moreover, since opportunity costs are constant, Canelones will produce only wool and import from the world market any quantity of lumber it will consume. Therefore, it will produce 1000 units of wool and 0 of lumber (point C).

(g) Canelones will need to export 400 units of wool to be able to import the 1600 units of lumber it desires to consume. Therefore, it will consume a combination of 600 units of wool and 1600 units of lumber (point D).

E2. **(a)** Five units. This requires a movement along the production possibility boundary from point *R* to point *A* in Figure 33-7.

Figure 33-7

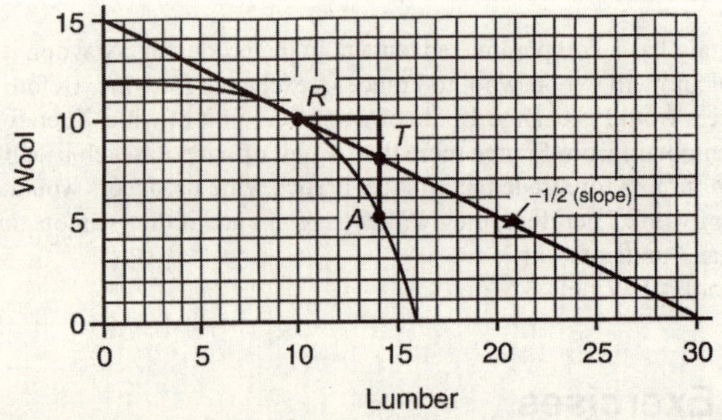

(b) Two units. The terms of trade line has a slope of –1/2 and is tangent to the production possibility curve at *R*. Thus, the economy can export two units of wool in return for imports of four units of lumber. This is represented by a movement from point *R* to point *T* on the graph.

Additional Multiple-Choice Questions

1.(d) **2.**(a) **3.**(b) **4.**(d) **5.**(a) **6.**(b) **7.**(b) **8.**(d) **9.**(d) **10.**(a) **11.**(c) **12.**(a) **13.**(e) **14.**(d) **15.**(e) **16.**(c) **17.**(e)

Explanations for the Asterisked Multiple-Choice Questions

3.(b) The opportunity cost of producing beef in A is 1/4 wool; the opportunity cost of the production of wool in B is 1/4 beef. Hence, A should specialize in beef and B in wool.

5.(a) Trade allows a country to consume beyond its production possibilities boundary. The terms of trade represent the slope of the consumption possibilities curve.

7.(b) The opportunity cost of producing 1 kg of aluminium in Brazil is 1.5 board metres of lumber, while in Canada it is 3 board metres of lumber. Hence, Brazil has a comparative advantage in the production of aluminium.

8.(d) Relative to Brazil, Australia has an absolute advantage in the production of both lumber and aluminium since it can produce both goods more efficiently than Brazil. However, the opportunity cost of producing aluminium in Australia is 4/9 board metres of lumber, while in Brazil is 1.5 board metres of lumber. Hence, Australia has a comparative advantage in the production of aluminium

9.(d) The table indicates that Brazil can produce either 3 board metres of lumber or 2 kg of aluminium with one unit of resources. Hence, the opportunity cost of producing 1 kg of aluminium in Brazil is 1.5 board metres of lumber.

10.(a) The table indicates that Australia can produce either 4 board metres of lumber or 9 kg of aluminium. Hence, the opportunity cost of 1 board metre of lumber is 2.25 kg of aluminium.

13.(e) Since the intersection of the domestic demand for and supply of wheat is above the world price of $3, this country has a comparative disadvantage in wheat. It would produce 4 bushels of wheat and satisfy the total demand of 10 bushels by importing 6 bushels at the world price of $3. Hence, trade allows the country to consume more wheat than it produces.

15.(e) Since the intersection of the domestic demand for and supply of wheat is at the world price of $4.50, the domestic quantity supplied of wheat will be just sufficient to satisfy the domestic quantity demanded and thus wheat will be neither imported into Canada nor exported abroad.

16.(c) Since the intersection of the domestic demand for and supply of wheat is below the world price of $6.00, this country has a comparative advantage in wheat. It would produce 12 bushels of wheat, satisfy the total domestic demand of 6 bushels, and export the other 6 bushels at the world price of $6.00. Hence, trade allows the country to produce more wheat than it consumes.

17.(e) Assuming Canada is a price-taker in the world market for wheat, the increase in the Canadian supply of wheat—i.e., a shift to the right of the domestic supply curve—will not affect the world price of wheat (i.e., the world price will remain at $6.00). However, a larger quantity of wheat will now be produced in Canada at the world price of $6.00 and, since the domestic quantity demanded will not change, a larger quantity of wheat will be exported.

18.(a) Canada's terms of trade improved. Canada can buy the same amount of imports with fewer exports in the first quarter of 2003.

CHAPTER 34

TRADE POLICY

LO LEARNING OBJECTIVES

In this chapter you will learn

1 the various situations in which a country may rationally choose to protect some industries.

2 the most common fallacious arguments in favour of protection.

3 the effects of a tariff or quota on imported goods.

4 why trade-remedy laws are sometimes just thinly disguised protection.

5 the distinction between trade creation and trade diversion.

6 the main features of the North American Free Trade Agreement.

CHAPTER OVERVIEW

This chapter examines the ways in which a government may intervene in markets to restrict international trade and demonstrates the resulting consequences. **Protectionist trade policy** usually takes one of two forms: **tariffs** that serve to raise import prices, and **nontariff barriers**—such as **import quotas** or **voluntary export restrictions**—that serve to reduce import quantities.

Free trade maximizes world output and living standards. Arguments for protection may rest on objectives other than maximizing living standards such as reducing fluctuations in national income or promoting economic diversification. Protectionism may also be advanced by a large country as a means of gaining a favourable improvement in the terms of trade, and thereby increasing national income. Several fallacious but widely employed arguments for protection are also discussed.

Since its inception in 1947, The **General Agreement on Trade and Tariffs** (GATT) has served to substantially reduce tariffs through a series of multilateral negotiations. The final round of trade agreements under GATT, the Uruguay Round, concluded in 1994 with an agreement in several important areas that served to promote more liberal trade. GATT was replaced by the **World Trade Organization** (WTO) in 1995.

There has been a sharp increase in the number and extent of regional trade-liberalizing agreements such as **free trade areas**, **customs unions**, and **common markets** since the early 1990s. The **North American Free Trade Agreement** (NAFTA) is the world's largest and most successful free trade area and the European Union is the world's largest and most successful common market. These regional agreements bring about efficiency gains through **trade creation**, but may also lead to efficiency losses from **trade diversion**.

HINTS AND TIPS

The following may help you to avoid some of the most common errors on examinations.

✓ Learn the economic considerations that might be used to refute the so-called fallacious arguments for protection.

✓ In order to analyze the effects of tariffs and quotas, refresh your understanding of the concepts of consumer surplus, producer surplus, and deadweight loss. Consumer surplus is the difference between the value that consumers place on a product and the payment they make to buy that product (Section 6.3 of the text) while producer surplus is the difference between the price that a producer receives and the lowest amount that the producer would be willing to accept for the sale of that product (Section 12.1 of the text).

✓ Learn the distinguishing features of a free-trade area, a customs union, and a common market.

✓ Learn some of the major features of NAFTA, including "national treatment," dispute settlement, and trade diversion and creation.

CHAPTER REVIEW

Free Trade or Protection?

After reading this section, you should be able to discuss the benefits and costs of protectionism versus freer international trade. You should begin to understand some of the valid arguments for trade policy that restricts trade and to recognize the fallacious arguments for protection.

1. Which of the following statements is *not* true of free trade?
(a) Free trade leads to a maximization of world output.
(b) Free trade maximizes world living standards.
(c) Free trade always makes each individual better off.
(d) Free trade can increase the average income in a country.
(e) Free trade encourages countries to specialize in production.

2. The infant industry argument for tariffs is
(a) only appropriate for industries where there are no economies of scale.
(b) an example of dynamic comparative advantage.
(c) theoretically valid if a new producer can sufficiently reduce average costs as output increases in the future.
(d) a proposal to earmark tariff revenues to finance day care facilities for infants.
(e) most applicable in developing countries because of their relative abundance of unskilled labour.

3. Protection against low-wage foreign labour is a fallacious protectionist argument because
(a) free trade benefits everyone.
(b) the gains from trade depend on comparative, not absolute, advantage.
(c) when the foreign country increases its exports to us, their wages will rise.
(d) the terms of trade are necessarily equal for low-wage and high-wage countries.
(e) low-wage labourers are necessarily less productive.

4. **If the objective of a government is to maximize national income, which of the following is the *least* valid reason for using tariff protection?**
   (a) To protect against unfair subsidization of foreign firms by their governments.
   (b) To protect against unfair low wages paid to foreign labour.
   (c) To protect newly developing industries.
   (d) To protect against dumping of foreign produced goods.
   (e) To improve its terms of trade.

5. **Which of the following is *not* a fallacious protectionist argument?**
   (a) Buy Canadian, and both the money and the goods stay at home.
   (b) Trade cannot be mutually advantageous if one of the trading partners is much larger than the other.
   (c) Too many imports lower Canadian living standards as our money is sent abroad.
   (d) A foreign firm, temporarily selling in Canada at a much lower price than in its own country, threatens the Canadian industry's existence.
   (e) A high-wage country such as Canada cannot effectively compete with a low-wage country such as Mexico.

6. **The main purpose served by a country's exports is**
   (a) to contribute toward the accumulation of foreign reserves.
   (b) to increase the country's GDP.
   (c) to increase the standard of living of its population.
   (d) to allow for higher levels of domestic consumption.
   (e) to provide the resources to purchase imports.

Methods of Protection

This section discusses protectionist trade policies that directly raise the price of imports or directly reduce the quantity of imports. A tariff or an import duty is a tax on imported goods. Quotas and voluntary export restrictions (VERs) restrict the quantity of an imported product. The chapter analyzes the "deadweight" loss of tariffs and quotas/VERs. Various trade-remedy laws and nontariff barriers are also discussed.

7. **Which of the following is an effect of imposing a tariff on an imported good?**
   (a) The domestic price of the imported product increases.
   (b) The quantity of domestic production increases.
   (c) The government receives customs revenues.
   (d) Domestic producers earn more because of increases in the domestic price and domestic production.
   (e) All of the above.

8. **Which of the following is an effect of imposing quotas and/or VERs on imported goods?**
   (a) Unlike tariffs, they lower domestic prices.
   (b) They decrease domestic production and consumption.
   (c) The deadweight loss for them is greater than that for an equivalent tariff.
   (d) All importers refuse to sell to the country that imposed the quotas.
   (e) In the case of VERs, the domestic government provides subsidies to exporters.

9. **Countervailing duties are attempts to maintain "a level playing ground" by**
   (a) retaliating against foreign tariffs.
   (b) raising or lowering tariffs multilaterally.
   (c) establishing a common tariff wall around customs union.
   (d) assessing tariffs that will offset foreign government subsidies.
   (e) subsidizing exports.

10. **Which of the following statements about nontariff barriers to trade (NTBs) is *incorrect*?**
   (a) The use of NTBs has been discontinued throughout the world.
   (b) The misuse of antidumping practices constitutes an increasingly important NTB.
   (c) Countervailing duties have become a covert method of protection.
   (d) Most NTBs are ostensibly levied for trade remedy purposes but end up being protectionist.
   (e) Environmental and labour standards can be used as disguised NTBs.

11. **Which of the following motivations for dumping can be of permanent benefit to the buying country?**
   (a) Predatory pricing.
   (b) Cyclical stabilization of sales.
   (c) Enabling foreign producers to achieve lower average costs and therefore price.
   (d) Altering the terms of trade.
   (e) All of the above.

Current Trade Policy

After reading this section you will have a better appreciation of the issues in multilateral, regional, and bilateral trade negotiations, and be able to discuss the important highlights of the NAFTA and its impact on the Canadian economy.

12. **Which of the following is an example of trade diversion?**
   (a) A government promotes diversification of a country's industries.
   (b) Liberalized trade encourages industries to specialize in subproduct lines.
   (c) NAFTA encourages more trade between low and high wage countries.
   (d) NAFTA encourages Canada to switch imports from low-wage nonmember countries to Mexico.
   (e) Publicized trade disputes divert attention from the gains from trade.

13. **A common market includes all but which of the following?**
   (a) Tariff-free trade among members.
   (b) A common trade policy with the rest of the world.
   (c) Rules of origin.
   (d) Free movement of labour.
   (e) Free movement of capital.

14. **The countries in a free trade area**
   (a) impose no tariffs on each other's goods.
   (b) each have an independent tariff structure with the rest of the world.
   (c) do not permit the free movement of labour across their borders.
   (d) do not have a common monetary policy.
   (e) All of the above.

15. **Which of the following was *not* one of the features of NAFTA?**
(a) Elimination of all tariffs between the U.S. and Canada by 1999.
(b) Elimination of countervailing duties between the two countries.
(c) Exemption of cultural industries.
(d) Continuance of quotas to support provincial supply management schemes.
(e) Provision for national treatment for most service industries.

16. **Which of the following was *not* an outcome of the Uruguay Round (1994) of GATT negotiations?**
(a) Major trade liberalization in agriculture.
(b) Replacement of the GATT with the World Trade Organization (WTO).
(c) A new dispute settlement mechanism.
(d) Reduction in world tariffs by approximately 40 percent.
(e) All of the above.

SHORT-ANSWER QUESTIONS

1. **Sketching the Effects of Various Trade Policies**
Case I: Demand Restriction
Figure 34-1 illustrates a country's demand and supply curves of commodity Z.
(a) According to the diagram, what are equilibrium values of price and quantity in a free market?

(b) Now, the government restricts importers to purchasing only half the quantity demanded at each price. Draw the new demand curve in Figure 34-1. What are the new equilibrium values for price and quantity?

Figure 34-1

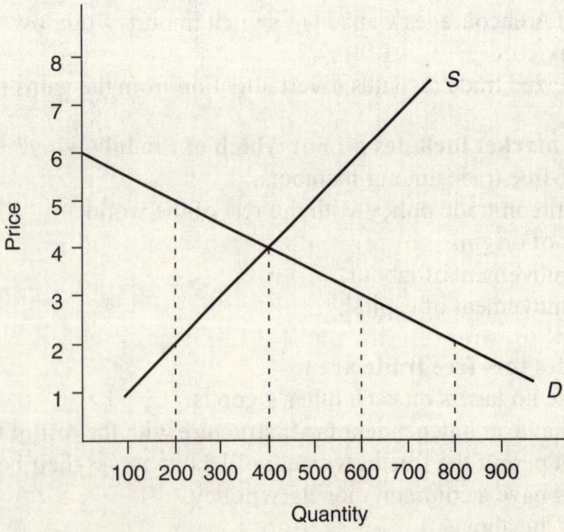

Case II: A Tariff

Figure 34-2 illustrates the domestic demand and supply curves of commodity *V*. The key assumption in this question is that the foreign (world) supply curve is horizontal at a world price of $2 for *V*.

Figure 34-2

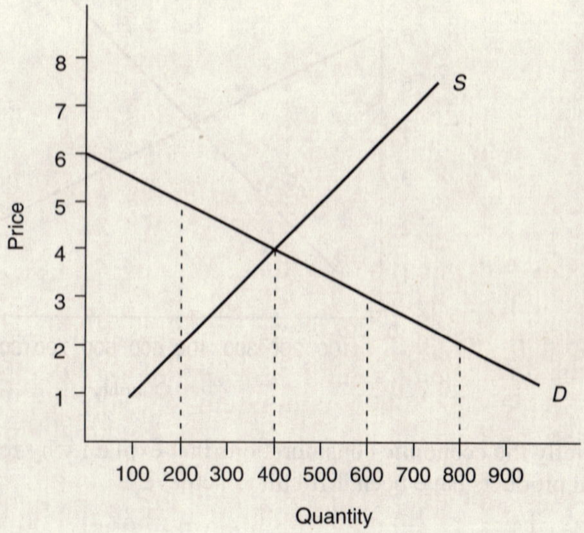

(a) At the world price, what is the total quantity of domestic supply? Domestic demand? What is the quantity of imports of *V* from foreign producers?

(b) Now, the government imposes a tariff of $1 per unit of *V* such that the domestic price (with the tariff) increases to $3/unit. Sketch this result, and estimate from the diagram what is the change in the quantity of imported *V*.

Case III: A Quota

Figure 34-3 illustrates the domestic demand and supply curves of commodity U. The world supply curve is horizontal at a price of $2 per unit of U. Now, the government wants to impose an import quota on commodity U of 300 units. The quota must satisfy domestic excess demand. Sketch this policy and indicate the new domestic price level of commodity U.

Figure 34-3

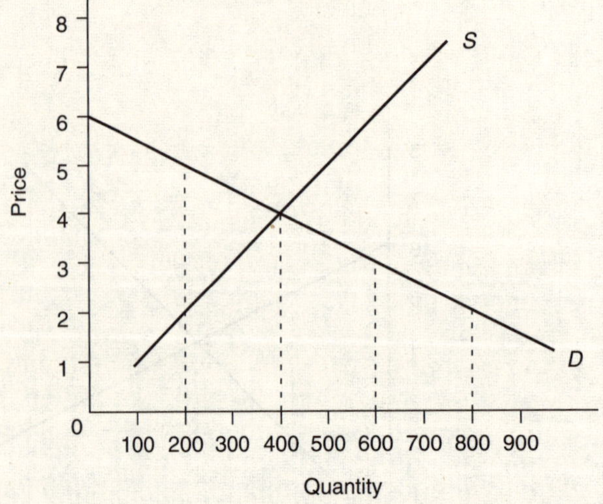

2. Explain briefly the economic considerations that explain why reductions in trade restrictions in agricultural products have been difficult to achieve.

3. A non-economist observes that wages in Mexico are considerably lower than wages in Canada, and concludes that there can be no gains from freer trade with Mexico. As an economist, how would you respond to this argument? Will Canada be able to export goods to Mexico? Explain.

4. In the second half of the 20th century, most developing countries adopted protectionist policies in order to develop their domestic industries. This was particularly the case among Latin American and East Asian countries. While the Latin American countries were still protecting their "infant industries" in the late 1970s, the East Asian countries had moved toward an export-oriented economic model. The distinct outcomes of these two different paths were also quite striking: while most Latin American economies remained stagnant, East Asian economies experienced an "economic miracle." What factors might have contributed to the realization of these two different economic outcomes?

5. Do you agree with the following statement about trade? Provide an explanation using a demand-supply diagram.

"When Canada imposes a tariff on an import, the government will earn tariff revenues; further, some Canadians will be better off and some will be worse off. The losses, however, will exceed the gains (including tariff revenues as a gain)."

EXERCISES

1. **The Economic Effects of a Tariff**

The hypothetical market for canned tuna in Canada is illustrated in Figure 34-4, where the foreign supply curve (S_f) is drawn as perfectly elastic (i.e., horizontal) at the world price of \$1.00, and the domestic demand and supply curves are denoted D_C and S_C, respectively.

The domestic curves are drawn using the following underlying algebraic equations:

Domestic demand: $D_C = 340 - 100P$
Domestic supply: $S_C = 20 + 100P$.

Figure 34-4

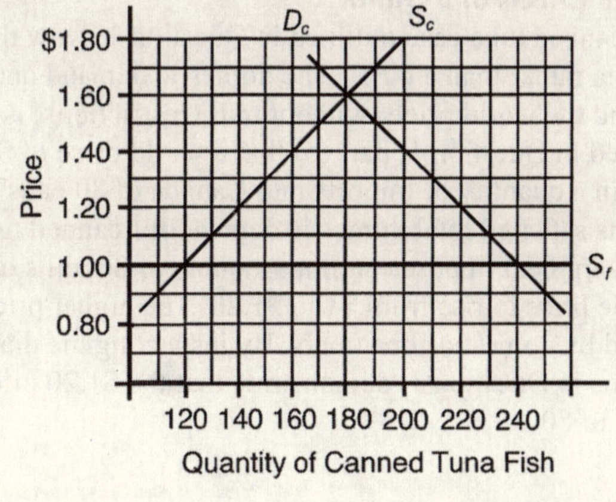

(a) Under free trade, what is the quantity of tuna consumed in Canada, the quantity supplied by Canadian producers, and the quantity supplied by foreign producers to Canadian consumers?

(b) Suppose that a 20 percent tariff is imposed such that new imported price on tuna is \$1.20 Calculate the consequent changes in domestic consumption, domestic production, and imports. Why is the change in imports greater than the change in domestic production?

(c) With the imposition of the 20 percent tariff on imported tuna, what is the quantitative change in consumer surplus? You might refer to Figure 34-1 in the textbook.

(d) With the imposition of the 20 percent tariff on imported tuna, what is the quantitative change in producer surplus? You might refer to Figure 34-1 in the textbook.

(e) What is the change in tariff revenue?

(f) What is the "deadweight" loss to Canada?

2. **The Economic Effects of a Quota**
Consider the canned tuna case outlined in Question 1. Now the government wishes to impose an import quota rather than a tariff. The domestic demand and supply curves are those in Question 1, and the world price (without trade restrictions) is \$1.

You learned in Question 1, part (b) that a world price of \$1.20 (including the 20 percent tax), resulted in a quantity of imports into Canada of 80 cans (220 – 140). Along with domestic supply, imports satisfied total domestic demand for canned tuna.

(a) The government imposes an import quota of 80 units of canned tuna, and allows the domestic price to rise from \$1 to \$1.20. The higher price is received by foreign producers and paid by domestic consumers. By inspecting the diagram or using the algebraic equations in Question 1, demonstrate that the \$1.20 price for canned tuna generates imports of 80.

(b) What quantitative change in consumer surplus is created by the introduction of the quota on canned tuna?

(c) What quantitative change in producer surplus is created by the introduction of the quota?

(d) What is the deadweight loss to Canada?

(e) How does this deadweight loss compare to that in Question 1?

3. **Impact of Free Trade and Government Subsidies**
Consider the following information: (1) corn production in the U.S. accounts for about 40 percent of world output and close to 70 percent of all corn exports; (2) American corn producers receive close to $10 billion a year in government subsidies; (3) in Mexico, the domestic price of corn was significantly higher than its world price at the outset of the NAFTA negotiations; and (4) U.S. corn exports to Mexico will have zero tariff after January 1, 2008.

(a) Draw a rough diagram that illustrates the situation in the Mexican corn market at the outset of the NAFTA negotiations. Show in your diagram the new domestic corn price when all tariffs are eliminated.

(b) Show in your diagram the effect of the change in domestic price on both the consumer surplus and the producer surplus.

(c) What role, if any, do U.S. government subsidies play in this outcome? What possible actions could the Mexican government undertake under NAFTA?

EXTENSION EXERCISE

E1. Improving the Terms of Trade

Suppose the country of Gill constitutes a large buyer of widgets. For simplicity, we will assume Gill represents the entire world demand. Production, however, takes place by both domestic and foreign firms. Gill's monetary unit is the dollar ($).

Gill's (and world's) demand curve is $Q_D = 1200 - 200P$;
Gill's domestic supply is $Q_S^G = 100P$;

Foreign supply is $Q_S^F = 300P$; [*Note:* The foreign supply is no longer horizontal, as was the case for the questions in Exercise 1.]

Total supply (domestic plus foreign): $Q_S^T = 400P$.

(a) Under free trade, what are the equilibrium values of world price and quantity demanded?

(b) At this world price, what is the level of Gill's consumption, imports, and production of widgets?

(c) Gill's government now seeks to improve its terms of trade by imposing a tariff on imported widgets. Suppose it levies a tariff of $2 per imported widget. Prove that the new foreign supply curve changes to $Q_S^F = -600 + 300P$. [*Hint:* What is the net price received by foreigners after paying the tariff?]

(d) What is the new world price? What are Gill's new levels of consumption, imports, and production of widgets?

(e) What price per widget do foreign firms receive after the tariff is imposed? What price per widget do domestic suppliers receive?

ADDITIONAL MULTIPLE-CHOICE QUESTIONS

***1. Which of the following trade practices is *not* specifically designed as a device to promote protectionism?**

(a) Tariffs.
(b) Voluntary export restrictions.
(c) Countervailing duties.
(d) Import quotas.
(e) Costly customs procedures.

2. Which of the following national objectives is a valid argument for some degree of protectionism?

(a) Concentration of national resources in a few specialized products.
(b) Increases in average incomes.
(c) Diversification of a small economy in order to reduce the risk associated with cyclical fluctuations in world prices.
(d) Ability of domestic firms to operate at minimum efficient scale.
(e) Maximization of the national standard of living.

***3. A large country may favourably alter its terms of trade by restricting domestic**

(a) demand and thereby reduce the price of imports for domestic consumers.
(b) demand and thereby reduce the price of imports received by foreign producers.
(c) supply and thereby reduce the price of imports for domestic consumers.
(d) supply and thereby reduce the price of imports for domestic consumers.
(e) demand and supply and thereby reduce imports.

4. _____________ serve to raise a country's standard of living only to the extent that they raise national income to permit the purchase of more _____________.

(a) Tariffs; imports
(b) Exports; imports
(c) Imports; strategic subsidies
(d) Imports; non-traded goods
(e) Exports; domestically produced goods

5. A large country, accounting for a significant share of world demand for an imported product, can increase its national income by

(a) encouraging domestic production.
(b) restricting domestic demand for the product, thereby decreasing its price and improving its terms of trade.
(c) imposing import quotas on the product.
(d) subsidizing imports of the good and thereby monopolize world consumption.
(e) negotiating voluntary export restrictions.

***6. The problem with restricting imports as a means of reducing domestic unemployment is that**

(a) it merely redistributes unemployment from import-competing industries to our export industries when trading partners retaliate.
(b) Canadians would rather do without than have to buy Canadian-produced goods.
(c) our import-competing industries are not labour-intensive.
(d) our import-competing industries are always fully employed.
(e) it will also reduce exports when the economy is in equilibrium.

7. Which of the following is *not* true of the EU's Common Agricultural Policy (CAP)?

(a) The CAP has led to agricultural surpluses in the EU.
(b) The CAP has turned the EU from a net importer in many agricultural products to self-sufficiency.
(c) The CAP leads the EU to heavily subsidize its agricultural exports.
(d) The CAP benefits agricultural producers in less developed countries.
(e) Quotas that support the CAP are being replaced with tariff equivalents.

8. The principle of national treatment that is embedded in the NAFTA means that Canada could, for example, introduce any product standards it likes, so long as

(a) they apply only to Canadian-produced goods.
(b) the standards are no more stringent than those existing in either Mexico or the United States.
(c) they apply equally to Canadian-, Mexican- and American-produced goods sold in Canada.
(d) they apply only to Canadian exports.
(e) they apply only to Canadian imports.

***9. A major effect of a tariff is to**

(a) redistribute income from consumers to domestic producers and the government.
(b) allow consumers to benefit at the expense of domestic producers.
(c) discourage domestic production.
(d) encourage consumers to buy more of the good.
(e) reduce government revenues.

10. A free trade agreement

(a) must include rules of origin.
(b) eliminates the need for customs controls on the movement of goods.
(c) allows for free cross-border movement of labour.
(d) erects a common tariff wall against nonmember countries.
(e) always contributes more to trade diversion than to trade creation

11. Which of the following is *not* a feature of the NAFTA?

(a) A common regime for antidumping and countervailing duties.
(b) The principle of national treatment.
(c) A dispute-settlement mechanism.
(d) Accession clause whereby other countries may join.
(e) Reduction in the barriers to trade in both goods and services among member countries.

Questions 12 to 18 refer to Figure 34-5, which illustrates the domestic demand and supply curves for a commodity as well as a horizontal world supply curve (P_w) at a constant price of \$6/unit.

Figure 34-5

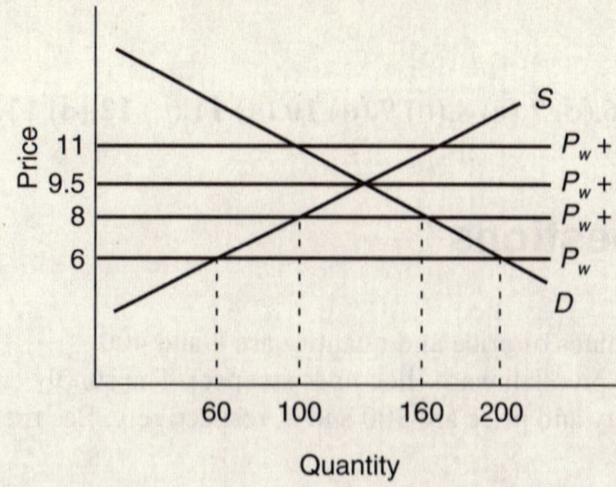

12. At a world price of $6, imports of this commodity into the domestic economy are
(a) 200.
(b) 160.
(c) 140.
(d) 60.
(e) 40.

***13. If a tariff of $2 is levied against imports of this commodity, domestic consumption and production would be**
(a) 200 and 60, respectively.
(b) 160 and 60, respectively.
(c) 200 and 100, respectively.
(d) 160 and 100, respectively.
(e) 160 and 40, respectively.

14. Given a tariff of $2, government tariff revenue would be
(a) $120.
(b) $320.
(c) $200.
(d) $1280.
(e) $800.

15. The tariff has ________ imports of this commodity by ________ units.
(a) reduced; 80
(b) reduced; 40
(c) reduced; 100
(d) increased; 40
(e) increased; 60

***16. The deadweight loss of the tariff is**
(a) $400.
(b) $120.
(c) $80.
(d) $160.
(e) $2.

***17. If a tariff of $3.50 is instead levied against imports of this commodity, government tariff revenue would be**
(a) $0.
(b) $45.
(c) $130.
(d) $195.
(e) $455.

***18. If a tariff of $5.00 is instead levied against imports of this commodity, domestic production would be**
(a) 0.
(b) 100.
(c) 130.
(d) 160.
(e) None of the above.

SOLUTIONS

Chapter Review

1.(c) **2.**(c) **3.**(b) **4.**(b) **5.**(d) **6.**(e) **7.**(e) **8.**(c) **9.**(d) **10.**(a) **11.**(c) **12.**(d) **13.**(c) **14.**(e) **15.**(b) **16.**(a)

Short-Answer Questions

1. *Case I:*

(a) The equilibrium values of price and quantity are 4 and 400.

(b) The demand curve pivots inward (becomes steeper). The supply curve doesn't change. The new equilibrium quantity and price are 300 and 3, respectively. See the following table that describes the new demand curve.

Price	Quantity
5	100
4	200
3	300
2	400

Case II:

(a) At a world price of $2, domestic supply is 200 while quantity demanded is 800. Imports are therefore 600.

(b) Draw a horizontal line at price equals $3. At this higher price, which includes the $1 tariff, the quantity supplied is 300 and the quantity demanded is 600. Therefore, imports have fallen to 300.

Case III:

An import quota of 300 can be achieved if the government allows the world price to increase to $3. Hence, draw a horizontal line at $3. Your diagram should indicate that domestic supply is 300 and the excess domestic demand of 300 is satisfied by a quota of 300 on imports.

2. Your explanation should discuss the unwillingness of governments to eliminate their supply-management policies. These have been a key feature of Canadian agricultural policy both at the federal and provincial level. The policies have been implemented mainly to stabilize farm income and protect domestic farmers from volatile price swings in international markets. They also serve to increase export competitiveness by subsidizing domestic production. The Canadian federal government has attempted to protect Canadian farmers by imposing quotas on imports or by levying tariffs.

3. Gains from trade are not determined by difference in absolute costs but rather by difference in opportunity costs. Freer trade with a low-wage country like Mexico will bring about a relocation of resources in Canada from unskilled labour-intensive to skilled labour-intensive industries. After a period of adjustment, therefore, Canada will end up importing unskilled labour-intensive goods from Mexico and exporting skilled labour-intensive goods to Mexico.

4. The "infant industry argument" justifies the introduction of protectionist measures when the government wants to foster the development of new industries with potential for economies of scale or learning by doing. This was the intention of both Latin American and East Asian countries when they first introduced these policies in the second half of the 20th century. In both groups of countries the objective was to protect their industries from foreign competition while they were growing up, and to gradually relax the level of protection as they became more competitive. This was what the East Asian governments did to a large extent—gradually reducing the level of protection in order to provide an incentive for firms to improve their degree of competitiveness in the international market. Latin American government, on the contrary, continued protecting their industries beyond the "infant" stage, thus providing the wrong incentive for firms to become complacence and inefficient.

5. The world price is P_w, and thus initially the domestic price is equal to the world price. The domestic quantity supplied is Q_S^1 and the domestic quantity demanded is Q_D^1, and thus imports are $Q_D^1 - Q_S^1$. When a tariff (t) is introduced, the domestic price becomes equal to the world price plus the tariff ($P_d = P_w + t$).

Now the domestic quantity supplied is Q_S^2 and the domestic quantity demanded is Q_D^2, and thus imports are now reduced to $Q_D^2 - Q_S^2$. This is shown in Figure 34-6.

Figure 34-6

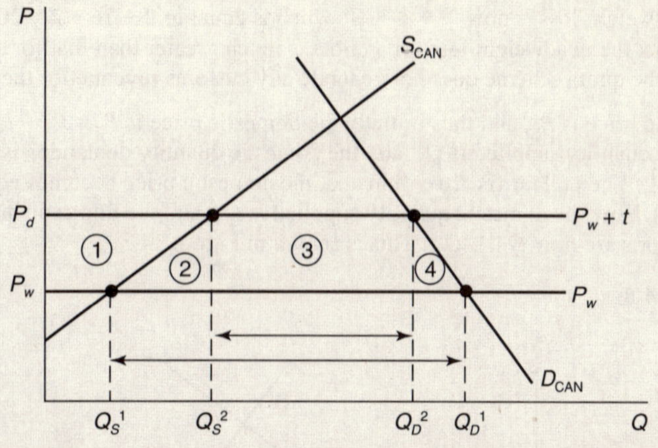

When the tariff is introduced and the domestic price increases, consumer surplus decreases. In the diagram, the decrease in consumer surplus is represented by the summation of the areas ① + ② + ③ + ④. At the same time, the increase in price causes the producer surplus to increase. In the diagram, the increase in producer surplus is represented by the area ①. The net loss between producers' gains and consumers' losses is thus represented by the sum of the areas ② + ③ + ④. However, since government tariff revenues are not a loss to society (area ③), the net welfare loss to society ("deadweight loss") is represented by the summation of the areas ② + ④.

Exercises

1. **(a)** Canadian production is 120, Canadian consumption is 240, and imports are 120.
   (b) Domestic production rises by 20, domestic consumption falls by 20, and imports fall by 40. Imports fall by more than domestic production rises due to the decline in total quantity demanded.

Figure 34-7

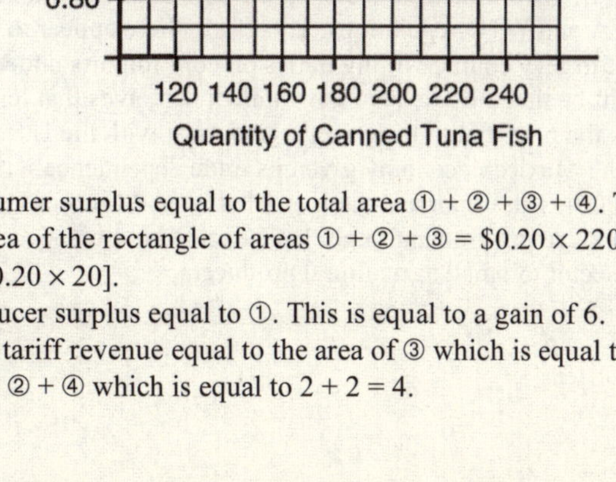

(c) There is a loss in consumer surplus equal to the total area ① + ② + ③ + ④. This is equal to a loss of $46. [*Hint:* Add the area of the rectangle of areas ① + ② + ③ = $0.20 × 220 to the area of the triangle (④) which equals 0.5[0.20 × 20].

(d) There is a gain in producer surplus equal to ①. This is equal to a gain of 6.

(e) There is an increase in tariff revenue equal to the area of ③ which is equal to $0.2 × 80 = 16.

(f) The deadweight loss is ② + ④ which is equal to 2 + 2 = 4.

2. **(a)** At a price of \$1.20, the total demand for canned tuna is 220. The domestic supply is 140. Hence, excess demand is 80, which can be met by allowing an import quota of 80.
(b) As was the case for question 1, part (c), the total loss in consumer surplus of \$46.
(c) The gain in producer surplus is 6.
(d) The deadweight loss is now ② + ③ + ④ which is equal to 2 + 16 + 2 = 20.
(e) Notice that the deadweight loss for a quota is much greater than that for an equivalent tariff. This is because the quota scheme does not generate any customs revenue for the government (area ③).

3. **(a)** The world price is P_w, and thus initially the domestic price is $P_d = P_w + t$, where t is the tariff. The domestic quantity supplied is Q_S^1 and the domestic quantity demanded is Q_D^1, and thus imports are $Q_D^1 - Q_S^1$. When all tariffs are eliminated, the domestic price becomes equal to the world price ($P_d = P_w$). Now the domestic quantity supplied is Q_S^2 and the domestic quantity demanded is Q_D^2, and thus imports are now $Q_D^2 - Q_S^2$. This is shown in Figure 34-8.

Figure 34-8

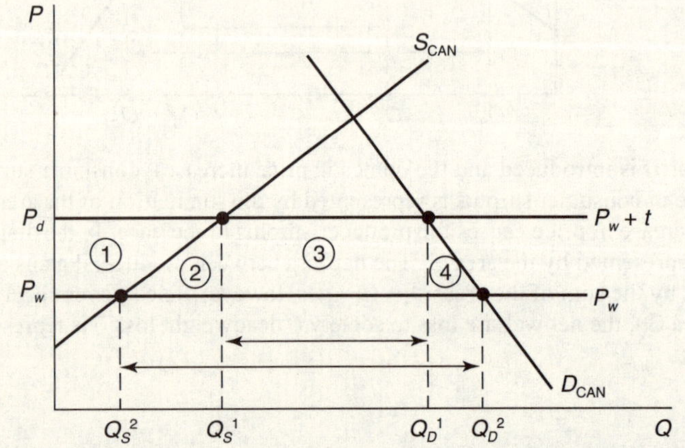

(b) When the tariff is eliminated and the domestic price falls to P_w, consumer surplus increases. In the diagram, the increase in consumer surplus is represented by the summation of the areas ① + ② + ③ + ④. At the same time, the fall in price causes the producer surplus to decrease. In the diagram, the decrease in producer surplus is represented by the area ①. Since government tariff revenues also decrease by the area ③, the net welfare gain to society ("deadweight gain") is represented by the summation of the areas ② + ④.
(c) If U.S. government subsidies to the corn sector were to be eliminated, corn production would significantly drop in the U.S. Given that the U.S. is the largest producer and exporter of corn in the world, the elimination of these subsidies would most likely cause a significant increase in the world price of corn. Therefore, these subsidies are responsible for the maintenance of an artificially low world price and represent, in the first place, a transfer from U.S. taxpayers to American corn producers and to corn consumers worldwide—including Mexican consumers. Second, these U.S. government subsidies are also ultimately responsible for a transfer from Mexican corn producers to Mexican corn consumers as shown in the diagram.

The U.S. government subsidies to the corn sector could be seen as unfair trade practice under both NAFTA and WTO regulations. Therefore, there appear to be grounds for the Mexican government to levy countervailing duties on corn imports under NAFTA. Why hasn't it done so? One reason might be that the Mexican government perceives that levying countervailing duties on corn imports has the potential of triggering a trade war with the U.S. with potentially enormous negative effects on the Mexican economy given its trade dependence with the U.S. A second reason might be that, since corn is an important staple in Mexico and low corn prices contribute to maintaining wages low, the Mexican government might have decided to pursue an industrial development strategy at a cost to the sector of small agricultural producers.

Extension Exercise

E1. **(a)** Equating total supply to demand, we obtain $P = \$2$ and a total quantity demanded of 800 widgets.

(b) At a world price of \$2, total demand is 800 widgets and domestic supply is 200 [100 × 2]. Hence, foreign supply is 600 = 300 × 2. This value represents the quantity of widget imports into Gill.

(c) The price received by foreigners after paying the tariff of \$2 per unit is $P - 2$. Substituting this value into the world supply equation, we obtain $Q_S^F = 300(P - 2)$ or $-600 + 300P$.

(d) The imposition of the tax has the effect of shifting the world supply upward. Equating the new total supply curve ($-600 + 400P$) with demand, we obtain a new world equilibrium price of \$3 and new quantity demanded of 600 widgets. Domestic production at the higher price increases to 300. Foreign supply (and imports) declines to 300.

(e) Domestic producers receive \$3 per widget. However, foreign firms receive a lower net price than before. They receive \$1 net after paying a \$2 tariff.

Additional Multiple-Choice Questions

1.(c) **2.**(c) **3.**(b) **4.**(b) **5.**(b) **6.**(a) **7.**(d) **8.**(c) **9.**(a) **10.**(a) **11.**(a) **12.**(c) **13.**(d) **14.**(a) **15.**(a) **16.**(c) **17.**(a) **18.**(c)

Explanations for the Asterisked Multiple-Choice Questions

1.(c) Although a counteracting duty may not be specifically designed as a device for protectionism, the textbook argues that it has the potential to be a thinly disguised trade barrier.

3.(b) The demand for imported products falls and the price received by foreign producers is reduced after they have paid the tariff/unit. Hence, the country's terms of trade have the potential to increase since import prices received by foreign producers fall.

6.(a) If foreigners impose countervailing tariffs, export industries in the domestic economy will be adversely affected. Employment will fall in these industries.

9.(a) A tariff increases the domestic price. Domestic suppliers gain, but consumers lose because they have to pay higher prices. The government gains by receiving tariff revenue.

13.(d) The tariff increases the price per unit by \$2. According to the diagram domestic supply is 100 and domestic demand is 160 at a price of \$8.

16.(c) As the textbook explains, the deadweight loss of a tariff is the sum of the areas of two triangles—one under the supply curve and one under the demand curve. The area of each is \$40, and so the deadweight loss is \$80.

17.(a) If a tariff of \$3.50 is levied against the import of this commodity, then the domestic price will be \$9.50—equal to the market price under autarky. Therefore, the quantity domestically supplied will be equal to the quantity demanded, and thus imports will be zero and so will be the government tariff revenue.

18.(c) A tariff that increases the domestic price of an imported commodity beyond the autarky market equilibrium price is ineffective since at the latter price imports are already zero. Therefore, the price of the commodity would be \$9.50 and the quantity domestically produced would be 130.

CHAPTER 35

EXCHANGE RATES AND THE BALANCE OF PAYMENTS

LEARNING OBJECTIVES

In this chapter you will learn

1 the components of Canada's balance of payments and why the balance of payments must always balance.

2 about the demand for and supply of foreign currency.

3 the various factors that cause fluctuations in the exchange rate.

4 why a current account deficit is not necessarily undesirable.

5 the theory of purchasing power parity (PPP) and its limitations.

6 how flexible exchange rates can dampen the effects of external shocks.

CHAPTER OVERVIEW

This chapter discusses the accounting framework for **balance-of-payments accounts** and how these international transactions determine the demand for and supply of foreign exchange. The balance of payments is divided into two major accounts: the current account (trade in goods, services, and net capital-service payments) and the capital account (trade in assets [direct and portfolio]). A *credit entry* results from the sale of a good or an asset to a foreigner; it represents extra demand for a country's currency or an extra supply of a foreign currency in the foreign-exchange market. A *debit entry* results from the purchase of a good or an asset from a foreigner; it represents extra supply of a country's currency or an extra demand for foreign currency in the exchange market.

Transactions that generate receipts for Canada in its balance of payments (Canadian exports, capital inflows into Canada, and firms, banks, and governments that want to increase their holdings of Canadian dollars by selling other foreign currencies) represent a supply of foreign currency and a demand for Canadian dollars. Conversely, payments to foreigners by Canadians (Canadian imports, capital outflows from Canada, and the firms, banks, and governments that want to decrease their holdings of Canadian dollars in order to buy other foreign currencies) represent a supply of Canadian dollars and a demand for foreign currency.

Exchange rates are determined in the foreign-exchange market. Two major types of exchange rate schemes are discussed. Under a **flexible exchange rate regime**, forces of demand and supply determine the equilibrium level of the exchange rate, with no intervention by the central bank. Important determinants of the equilibrium level of the exchange rate are relative inflation rates, relative interest rates, and structural changes in the domestic or foreign economies. At the equilibrium exchange rate, the sum of the current and capital accounts must be zero.

Under a **fixed exchange rate system**, the central bank may take steps to set an exchange rate that differs from the equilibrium value. A pegged rate that is set above the equilibrium exchange rate value implies that the sum of the domestic economy's current and capital accounts will be positive (a surplus). To maintain the pegged rate, the central bank increases its holdings of the foreign currency by selling domestic currency in the foreign-exchange market.

The chapter concludes by examining three important policy issues. (1) Is a current account deficit bad for Canada? (2) Is there a "correct" value for the Canadian dollar? and (3) Should Canada fix its exchange rate with the U.S. dollar? Purchasing-power-parity theory and the determination of the PPP exchange rate are important considerations for issue (2). Issue (3) deals with exchange-rate risk and the ability of flexible exchange rates to act as "shock absorbers."

HINTS AND TIPS

The following may help you to avoid some of the most common errors on examinations.

✓ Learn the international transactions that appear as credits and debits in the two sub-accounts of the Canadian balance of payment accounts. A payment by Canada is recorded as a debit; a receipt to Canada is a credit.

✓ Understand that the overall balance of payments (current plus capital) accounts must balance. However, individual sub-accounts (capital and current accounts) need not balance.

✓ Learn the determinants of the demand for and the supply of foreign currency. Movements along the demand and supply curve are caused by changes in the exchange rate. The curves shift if factors such as differential prices and interest rates change. For example, if foreign income increases, we expect the exchange rate to depreciate as the supply curve of foreign currency shifts to the right (because Canadian exports to foreigners increase).

✓ Understand the economic arguments for and against flexible exchange rate regimes.

CHAPTER REVIEW

The Balance of Payments

Understanding the difference between a *debit* and a *credit* is important for this section. Any transaction leads to two entries (one credit and one debit) in the balance of payments accounts. If a transaction is a receipt for Canada, it is recorded as a credit in Canada's accounts. If the transaction generates a payment for Canada, it is recorded as a debit in Canada's accounts. Hence, when both the current and the capital accounts are considered, the sum of all credits must equal the sum of all debits—e.g., the balance of payments must always balance. However, it is possible that one individual account may be in a deficit /surplus position. It follows that the other account is in a surplus/deficit position.

A deficit or surplus in the balance-of-payments refers to the combined net position of the current and capital accounts *excluding* the official financing account. Hence, the balance of payments can be in deficit or surplus only if the central bank changes its foreign-exchange reserves (this transaction appears in the official financing account). A "balance of payments deficit" refers to a situation where the Bank of Canada is selling foreign currency. A "balance of payments surplus" refers to a situation where the Bank of Canada is buying foreign currency.

Hence, the overall balance of payments is actually in balance.

1. **When Canadians purchase assets from abroad, these transactions are recorded as**
   (a) credits in the current account.
   (b) credits in the capital account.
   (c) debits in the capital account.
   (d) debits in the current account.
   (e) a credit in the official financing account.

2. **When the Bank of Canada sells foreign currency (and buys Canadian dollars) this transaction is recorded as a**
   (a) debit in the official financing account.
   (b) sale of a foreign asset to foreigners, and thus enters as a credit item in the balance of payments.
   (c) credit in the capital account.
   (d) debit in the capital account.
   (e) credit in the current account.

3. **Which of the following international transactions would be recorded as a credit in Canada's balance of payment accounts?**
   (a) Canadians buy U.S. bonds.
   (b) Canadians send cash gifts to their relatives in Italy.
   (c) Canadians receive dividend income from Germany.
   (d) Canadian firms pay New York consulting companies for their services.
   (e) The Bank of Canada purchases foreign currency (and sells Canadian dollars).

4. **Which international transaction would be recorded in France's current account?**
   (a) French banks receive interest payments from their holdings of German bonds.
   (b) French investors purchase stocks issued by Canadian companies.
   (c) A French investment group buys a mining company located in Bolivia.
   (d) The central bank of France adds to its holdings of U.S. dollars.
   (e) None of the above.

5. **Which international transaction would be recorded in Canada's capital account as a credit?**
   (a) Canadian sales of agricultural products to China.
   (b) Germans buy farm land in Saskatchewan.
   (c) Canadian investors receive interest payments from their U.S. bond holdings.
   (d) Japanese families take skiing trips to British Columbia.
   (e) The Bank of Canada increases its holdings of gold and/or foreign-currency reserves.

6. **If the Bank of Canada purchases foreign currency, then**
   (a) this transaction would be recorded as a credit in Canada's capital account.
   (b) this probably represents the Bank's effort to prevent a depreciation of the Canadian dollar.
   (c) the combined balance of Canada's current and capital accounts must be in a deficit position.
   (d) this transaction would be recorded as a debit in Canada's Official Financing Account.
   (e) there is a surplus in the capital account.

7. **If the Bank of Canada does not engage in any foreign-exchange transactions, then**
   (a) any deficit in Canada's current account must be matched by an equal and opposite deficit on Canada's capital account.
   (b) any surplus on Canada's capital account must be matched by an equal and opposite surplus on Canada's current account.
   (c) any deficit in Canada's current account must be matched by Canadians buying more foreign assets.
   (d) any deficit in Canada's capital account must be matched by an equal and opposite surplus on Canada's current account.
   (e) the combined balance of Canada's current and capital accounts could be either in a deficit or surplus position.

The Foreign-Exchange Market

The supply of foreign exchange arises from Canadian exports to foreign countries, capital inflows to Canada, and accumulation of Canadian dollar reserves by foreigners (they supply foreign currency). The theoretical bases for an upward-sloping supply curve for foreign exchange are discussed. If the exchange rate appreciates (the Canadian dollar depreciates), we would expect Canadian exports and purchases of Canadian assets by foreigners to increase.

If the exchange rate appreciates, we would expect the quantity demanded for foreign currency to decrease (imports into Canada and purchases of foreign assets by Canadians decrease). Hence, the demand curve for foreign exchange is downward-sloping. *Movements along* either the supply or demand curves for foreign exchange are caused *only* by changes in the value of the exchange rate.

8. **The exchange rate is defined as the**
   (a) ratio of exports to imports.
   (b) amount of domestic currency that must be given up in order to obtain one unit of foreign currency.
   (c) rate at which one country exchanges gold with another.
   (d) volume of foreign goods that can be obtained for one unit of domestic currency.
   (e) ratio of the price of imports to the price of exports.

9. **Suppose that one Swedish krona trades for 0.197 Canadian dollars. It follows that one Canadian dollar trades for**
   (a) 19.7 krona.
   (b) 1.97 krona.
   (c) 0.197 krona.
   (d) 197 krona.
   (e) 5.08 krona.

10. **Which of the following transactions between Canada and Japan constitutes a demand for Japanese currency (yen)?**
   (a) Japanese companies buy real estate in Calgary.
   (b) Ontario producers sell beef to Japan.
   (c) Japanese mutual fund companies buy Canadian securities.
   (d) The Bay (Canada) buys Japanese-produced cameras.
   (e) Canadians receive interest payments for their holdings of Japanese bonds.

11. **In the exchange market between Canadian dollars and Mexican pesos, a demander of dollars is also a**
   (a) supplier of dollars.
   (b) supplier of pesos.
   (c) demander of pesos.
   (d) Canadian exporter.
   (e) Canadian who is buying assets in Mexico.

The Determination of Exchange Rates

A flexible exchange rate system requires no intervention by the central bank. The equilibrium value of an exchange rate is determined by the equality between the supply of and the demand for foreign exchange arising from the capital and current accounts. When the central bank intervenes in the foreign-exchange market to "peg" the exchange rate at a particular value, there is said to be a fixed exchange rate. Between the two "pure" systems are a variety of intermediate cases, including a managed float.

You should understand how changes in foreign and domestic inflation rates, changes in interest rates and profit expectations, and structural changes in the economy *shift* either the supply and/or demand curves for foreign exchange, thereby causing either an appreciation or a depreciation of a flexible exchange rate. By reading *Applying Economic Concepts 35-2,* you will understand how changes in the equilibrium values of the exchange rate have potential policy implications for managing a fixed exchange rate.

Questions 12 through 19 refer to Figure 35-1. The two countries are Canada (the domestic country) and Japan (the foreign country). Recall that the currency of Japan is the yen.

Figure 35-1

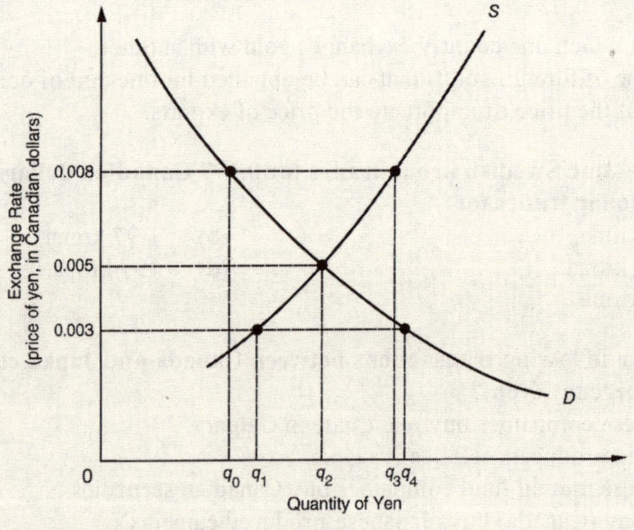

12. **A movement down the vertical scale means that**
   (a) the Canadian dollar is depreciating.
   (b) the yen is depreciating.
   (c) the Canadian dollar is fixed.
   (d) the yen is appreciating.
   (e) None of the above.

13. If the current exchange rate is 0.005,
(a) $200 trades for one yen.
(b) 0.005 yen trades for one Canadian dollar.
(c) one yen trades for 0.005 Canadian dollars.
(d) the quantity demanded of yen is less than the quantity supplied.
(e) the quantity supplied of yen is less than the quantity demanded.

14. At an exchange rate of 0.008,
(a) there is an excess demand of yen.
(b) there is an excess supply of yen.
(c) there is an excess supply of Canadian dollars.
(d) 0.008 yen trades for one Canadian dollar.
(e) one Canadian dollar trades for 1.25 yen.

15. At a current exchange rate of 0.003,
(a) the quantity demanded for yen is q_4 and the quantity supplied is q_1.
(b) one Canadian dollar trades for 33.33 yen.
(c) there is an excess demand for Canadian dollars of $q_4 - q_1$.
(d) the exchange rate has reached an equilibrium level.
(e) the Bank of Canada will buy a quantity $q_4 - q_1$ of yens.

16. Assuming that the initial exchange rate is 0.008 and no central bank intervention, market forces are likely to cause the
(a) Canadian dollar price of yen to rise.
(b) Canadian dollar to depreciate.
(c) yen to depreciate to 0.005.
(d) Canadian dollar to appreciate to 333.33 yen.
(e) quantity of demanded for Canadian dollars to increase and the quantity supplied of dollars to decrease.

17. As the exchange rate changes from 0.008 to 0.005,
(a) the quantity demanded for yen increases with the decline in the prices of Japanese goods in Canadian dollars.
(b) Japanese imports from Canada increase.
(c) the quantity demanded for Canadian dollars increases because Canadian exports rise.
(d) the prices of Canadian goods imported into Japan decrease.
(e) the Canadian dollar depreciates.

18. The supply curve of yen is upward sloping because
(a) as the dollar price of yen increases, the demand for Canadian exports will rise and Japanese customers will supply more yen.
(b) as the dollar price of yen decreases, the demand for Canadian exports will fall and Japanese customers will supply fewer yen.
(c) as the Canadian dollar appreciates (the yen depreciates), the Japanese demand for Canadian assets will decrease and Japanese investors will supply less yen.
(d) as the Canadian dollar depreciates (the yen appreciates), the Japanese demand for Canadian assets will increase and Japanese investors will supply more yen.
(e) All of the above.

19. **If the Bank of Canada's policy were to maintain a fixed (pegged) exchange rate of 0.008, then it must intervene in the exchange market by**
(a) buying yen and selling Canadian dollars.
(b) selling yen and buying Canadian dollars.
(c) buying gold and selling yen.
(d) increasing the Canadian interest rate.
(e) selling yen and increasing the Canadian interest rate.

20. **Assuming a flexible exchange rate regime, a lower inflation rate in Canada than in South Korea, other things being equal, is predicted to cause**
(a) the Canadian dollar price of Korean won to rise.
(b) the won price of dollars to fall.
(c) the demand curve for won and the supply curve of won to shift to the right, assuming that Canadian and South Korean goods are price elastic.
(d) a depreciation of the won in Canadian dollars.
(e) an increase in South Korean net exports to Canada.

21. **A desire by Canadians to invest more in European Union countries than before, other things being equal, will cause**
(a) the dollar price of euros to appreciate under a flexible exchange rate.
(b) the demand curve for euros to shift to the left.
(c) the supply curve of euros to shift to the right.
(d) both the demand and supply curves of euros to shift to the left.
(e) both the demand and supply curves of euros to shift to the right.

22. **If short-term interest rates in Canada increase relative to short-term U.S. interest rates, other things being equal, then**
(a) capital flows from the United States to Canada are likely to increase and the U.S. dollar will depreciate under a flexible exchange rate system.
(b) the supply curve of U.S. dollars will shift to the left.
(c) the demand curve for U.S. dollars will shift to the right.
(d) the Canadian dollar will depreciate under a flexible exchange rate system.
(e) capital flows from Canada to the United States will increase thereby causing the U.S. dollar to appreciate under a flexible exchange rate system.

23. **Which of the following is *not* likely to cause an appreciation of the Canadian dollar under a flexible exchange rate?**
(a) An increase in interest rates in Canada relative to rates elsewhere.
(b) A lower inflation rate in Canada relative to foreign rates, assuming all internationally traded goods are price elastic.
(c) Lower earnings expectations on Canadian assets relative to those elsewhere.
(d) Economic expansion in the economies of Canada's major trading partners.
(e) A higher propensity to buy Canadian produced goods in international markets.

24. **An increase in the world demand for a country's products**
(a) leads to an appreciation of that country's currency in a flexible exchange rate markets.
(b) leads to an appreciation of the currency of other countries in flexible exchange rate markets.
(c) leads to a depreciation of that country's currency under a flexible exchange rate system.
(d) signals that this country has a current account deficit.
(e) None of above.

25. If the Bank of Canada maintains an exchange rate between euros and the Canadian dollar which is higher than the equilibrium dollar price of euros, then

(a) the combined balance of Canada's current and capital accounts will be in a deficit position.
(b) the Bank will have to buy Canadian dollars by reducing its holdings of foreign exchange.
(c) the Bank will buy euros.
(d) the Bank might try to lower Canadian interest rates in order to increase the demand for Canadian dollars.
(e) the Bank will increase the interest rates and sell euros.

26. If the Canadian dollar appreciated with respect to the U.S. dollar, we would expect:

(a) an increase in Canadian exports to the United States and a decrease in imports from the United States.
(b) an increase in Canadian exports to the United States and an increase in imports from the United States.
(c) fewer Canadian tourists visiting Florida over the winter months and more American tourists visiting Toronto.
(d) a decrease in Canadian exports to the United States and an increase in imports from the United States.
(e) a decrease in Canadian exports to the United States and a decrease in imports from the United States.

Three Policy Issues

Is a current account deficit bad for Canada? The lesson to be learned from Chapter 33 is that the gains from trade depend on the volume of trade (both imports and exports) rather than the balance of trade. A current account deficit is created by changes in private saving, domestic investment, and the government's budget deficit. Hence, knowing the cause of the deficit is crucial to knowing whether the change in the current account is undesirable.

27. A current account deficit

(a) is viewed to be a "good" situation by Mercantilists.
(b) can be created by an increase in private saving.
(c) will increase if governments adopt budget surplus policies.
(d) can be created by increases in domestic investment.
(e) necessarily implies a capital account deficit.

Is there a "correct" value for the Canadian dollar? As forces of demand and supply for the Canadian dollar in foreign-exchange markets change, the "correct" value of the Canadian dollar is constantly changing. However, some economists argue that, whereas various shocks may cause the exchange rate to rise or fall in the short run, there exists some long-run purchasing-power-parity level to which it will return. According to the PPP theory, the relative price levels in the two countries determine the exchange rate between two countries' currencies. However, since countries produce different goods and not all goods are traded internationally, we must be extremely careful in selecting the price indices that are used when applying the PPP theory.

28. According to the purchasing power parity (PPP) hypothesis, if domestic inflation in country A exceeds that in country B by 10 percent, B's currency (in terms of A's currency) should

(a) increase by about 10 percent.
(b) not change, since any trade deficit will be offset by a capital inflow.
(c) not change, since the theory applies only to fixed or pegged exchange rate systems.
(d) decrease by about 10 percent.
(e) not change, since inflation rates are calculated on the basis of domestically produced goods and services.

Should Canada fix its exchange rate with the U.S. dollar? Advocates of a fixed exchange rate argue that exchange-rate fluctuations generate uncertainty for importers and exporters and thus increase the costs associated with trade which in turn decrease the potential gains from trade. On the other hand, advocates of flexible exchange rates stress the importance that changes in exchange rates play in absorbing the effects of international shocks, thereby reducing the impact of these shocks on the domestic economy's output and employment.

29. Suppose that the Liquor Control Board of Ontario (LCBO) agrees to pay 400 000 French francs for French champagne three months in the future. When the LCBO negotiates this deal, the dollar price of francs is $0.20 but when payment becomes due the dollar price of francs is $0.25. We observe that

(a) the French franc has depreciated.
(b) French champagne producers will receive larger franc payments.
(c) the costs of the transaction from the LCBO's perspective have increased.
(d) the LCBO is subject to an exchange-rate risk because the contract was in terms of a given number of French francs regardless of the level of the exchange rate.
(e) the LCBO is subject to an exchange-rate risk and the costs of the transaction have increased from its perspective.

30. If a Mexican fruit exporters agree that they will be paid $100 000 (Canadian) in four months by Canadian fruit importers, then

(a) the Mexican fruit exporters have accepted the possibility of an exchange-rate risk.
(b) Canadian importers will lose if the Canadian dollar falls between the period that the deal was negotiated and payment is made.
(c) Mexican fruit exporters will gain more Mexican pesos if the Canadian dollar price of the peso depreciates between the period that the deal was negotiated and payment is made.
(d) Canadian fruit importers have accepted the possibility of an exchange-rate risk.
(e) if the Canadian dollar price of the peso appreciate by the time the payment is made, the Canadian importer will pay a higher amount in Canadian dollars.

31. In terms of an *AD–AS* framework, a decrease in a country's exports will

(a) be shown as a shift to the left in the *AS* curve.
(b) cause the *AD* curve to shift to the right.
(c) result in a greater decrease in output and employment if the country has a flexible exchange rate rather than a fixed exchange rate.
(d) reflect an initial current account surplus.
(e) generate a smaller short-run recessionary gap when the country's currency depreciates with a flexible exchange rate.

SHORT-ANSWER QUESTIONS

1. Explain where the following international transactions appear in one of the three sub-accounts of the balance of payment accounts. Indicate whether the transactions are recorded as debits or credits.

(a) The central bank adds to its holdings of foreign reserves (gold plus foreign currency).

(b) A domestic fabrication firm makes a dividend payment to the owners of a manufacturing firm located in Korea.

(c) A domestic travel company opens up a chequing account in a Hong Kong bank.

2. Suppose that the exchange rate between Canadian dollars and Japanese yen is established in a flexible exchange market without any intervention by the Bank of Canada. For each of the following events, indicate whether the exchange rate (in this case the Canadian dollar price of yen) will tend to appreciate, depreciate, or remain unchanged. Explain your answer briefly and indicate whether the event is likely to affect the demand curve for yen (denoted by D_y), the supply curve of yen (denoted as S_y), or both.

(a) Japanese tourist trade doubles in Montreal.

(b) The rate of inflation in Canada increases relative to the Japanese inflation rate.

(c) Short-term interest rates rise in Japan relative to those in Canada.

(d) Prolonged Japanese economic expansion increases Canadian exports to Japan.

(e) Japanese investors buy several hotels in Alberta.

(f) Japanese construction companies expect U.S. lumber prices to increase more than Canadian lumber prices.

(g) Canadian firms reduce their holdings of Japanese yen.

3. Explain how flexible exchange rates serve as "shock absorbers" when there are large increases in imports from abroad. Compare the effects of this external shock with those that would occur if the country had pursued a fixed exchange rate policy.

4. Comment on the following statements: "For a country as a whole, the gains from trade are to be judged by the volume of trade rather than by the balance of trade."

5. Comment on the following statement: "If there is a decline in interest rates in the United States, with no change in the level of interest rates in Canada, Canada's exports to the United States will fall."

6. Explain how the sum of the balances in a country's current and capital accounts could be in a deficit position if the bookkeeping in the balance-of-payments must always balance.

EXERCISES

1. **The Domestic Market for Imports**
Figure 35-2 represents the hypothetical market for Canadian imports of Japanese cameras, with prices given in Canadian dollars.

Figure 35-2

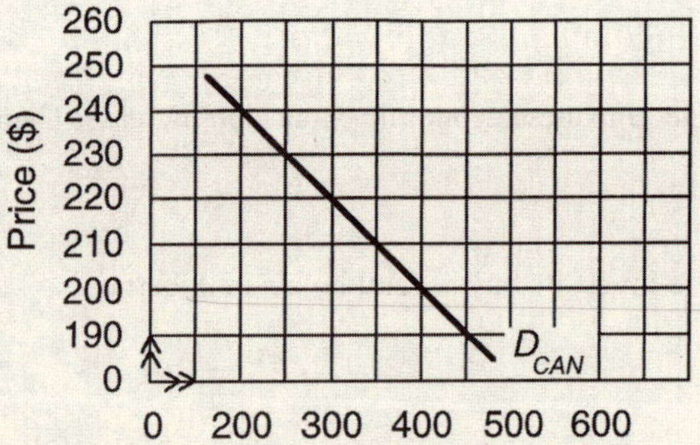

(a) The Canadian demand for imported Japanese cameras is shown in the diagram. The Japanese supply schedule for cameras is given below, with prices shown in yen (the Japanese currency). If Japanese producers quote yen prices to their Canadian buyers, determine what the supply schedule must be in terms of Canadian dollars if one Canadian dollar trades for 150 yen.

Quantity	Price in Yen	Price in Dollars
200	27 000	________
300	28 500	________
400	30 000	________
500	31 500	________
600	33 000	________

(b) In Figure 35-2, plot the supply curve in Canadian dollars and determine the equilibrium price and quantity of imported cameras.

2. **Flexible Exchange-Rate System**
You are given the demand for and supply of U.S. dollars at alternative prices in terms of Canadian dollars. Assume that the U.S. dollar changes without intervention from any central bank. The curves labelled D_0 and S_0 represent the initial case. The other curves represent changes in economic conditions between the two countries. Use them to answer (b) to (d).

Figure 35-3

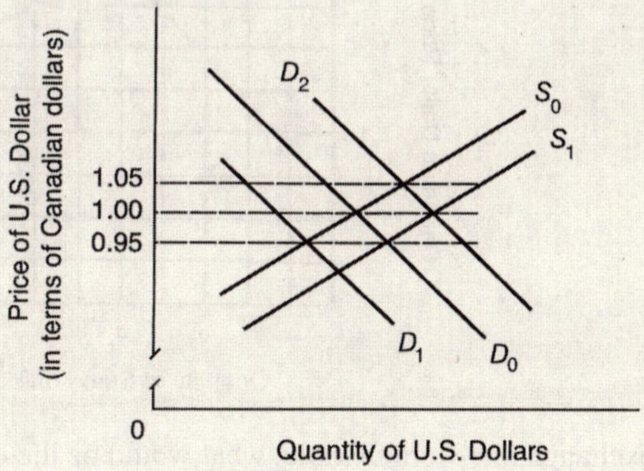

(a) Determine the equilibrium Canadian dollar price of the U.S. dollar, assuming that D_0 and S_0 apply.

(b) Suppose that there is a sizable increase in short-term capital flows from Canada to the United States, other things being equal. Which curves would shift and explain why? What will happen to the exchange rate (the Canadian dollar price of the U.S. dollar)?

(c) Which curve or curves would shift if Canadians imported significantly less from the United States? What will happen to the Canadian dollar price of the U.S. dollar?

(d) Suppose that Canadian exports to the United States increased significantly, other things being equal. Predict the effect on the price of the U.S. dollar.

3. **Maintaining a Fixed Exchange Rate**

Figure 35-4 represents the exchange market for euros. The horizontal axis denotes millions of euros, and the vertical axis is the Canadian dollar price of euros.

Figure 35-4

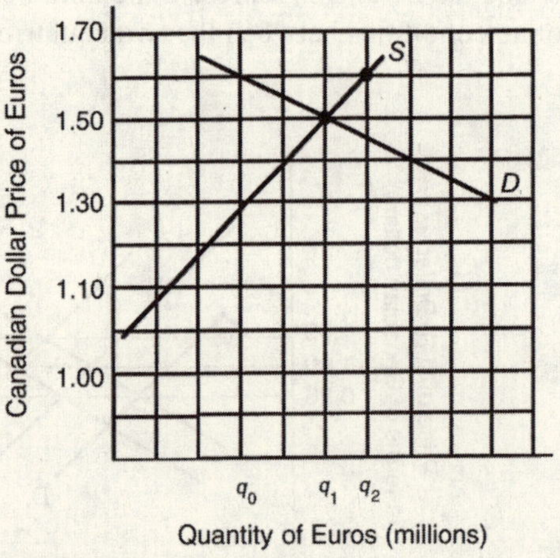

(a) If the exchange rate were flexible, what would be the equilibrium dollar price of euros?

(b) If the Bank of Canada wants to maintain a fixed value of $1.60 per euro, what foreign-exchange transactions must it conduct at the current market conditions depicted by the demand and supply curves? What will happen to the Bank of Canada's holdings of euros?

(c) What would happen in the foreign-exchange market if the European Union countries pursued a pegged value of 0.65 euros per Canadian dollar?

4. **Fixed Exchange Rate and Monetary Policy**
The central bank of Solimar has decided to peg its domestic currency, the peso, to the U.S. dollar.

(a) Provide a diagram of the foreign-exchange market in which the equilibrium occurs without any pressures on the foreign-exchange rate (i.e., within the fixed boundaries for the exchange rate). Suppose now that foreign investors become concerned about Solimar's economy and decide to withdraw substantial assets from Solimar. Use the diagram to show what the central bank of Solimar must do to maintain the exchange rate.

(b) Return to the original equilibrium (without pressures on the exchange rate). Suppose Solimar's economy is faltering, and the central bank decides to implement an expansionary monetary policy. Discuss the implications of this policy on the foreign-exchange market, and the ability to maintain the fixed exchange rate.

EXTENSION EXERCISES

E1. **The Revaluation of the Chinese Currency and the U.S. Current Account**
"The U.S. is experiencing significant macroeconomic imbalances: the federal government is running a record budget deficit while the current account deficit is at an all time high. The data also show that the U.S. trade deficit with China accounts for a significant portion of this current account deficit, while China's purchases of U.S. treasury bills account for a significant portion of the capital account surplus the U.S. is also experiencing. Some economists and policy advisers suggest that, in order to eliminate the current account deficit, the U.S. government should continue pressuring China to revalue its domestic currency."

Given the above scenario, what would be the impact of a significant revaluation of the Chinese currency on the balances of the U.S. current and capital accounts?

E2. **Exchange-Rate Risk**
One of the criticisms of a flexible exchange rate is that its volatility creates uncertainty or risk. Exchange-rate risk arises for individuals/institutions that have a liability/receivable in foreign currency sometime in the future when the future value of the foreign currency is uncertain. If the exchange rate changes between the period that a contract is arranged and payment is due,

the individual or business may gain or lose in terms of the amount of domestic currency that is actually received or must be paid relative to what receipt/payment was anticipated at the time the deal was made.

In each of the following cases, determine who is taking the exchange-rate risk and calculate the value of the gain or loss in terms of the payment in domestic currency at the time of payment/receipt versus the anticipated cost/earnings in domestic currency at the time when the contract was negotiated. Assume in each case that the individual/business taking the risk anticipates the exchange rate that prevails when the contract is signed will not change.

(a) Stacey, from Moose Jaw, agrees to pay 500 000 yen three months from now. At the time of signing the contract, the exchange rate was $0.10 dollars per yen. When payment is made three months thereafter, Stacey pays an exchange rate of $0.15 per yen.

(b) A hotel in Buffalo, New York agrees to be paid $25 000 Canadian for a June wedding reception booked by a Hamilton, Ontario couple. When the contract was signed in March, one U.S. dollar traded for $1.40 Canadian. Suppose that the exchange rate in June was $1.45 Canadian.

(c) As an investment strategy, Fritz from Sackville, New Brunswick buys a Florida condominium in 1997 for $60 000 (U.S.) at an exchange rate of 1.45 Canadian dollars. He intends to sell the condo in 1998 and use the earnings to buy Canadian securities. He sells the condo in 1998 for $63 000 (U.S.) to a couple from North Carolina, but pays $3000 (U.S.) for real estate and legal services. He then exchanges $60 000 (U.S.) at a rate of $1.51 (Canadian).

ADDITIONAL MULTIPLE-CHOICE QUESTIONS

Questions 1 through 8 refer to the balance-of-payment items for a particular country. Before attempting these questions, you should be familiar with the components of the capital and current accounts discussed in the text. All foreign currency purchases have been converted into millions of the domestic currency (assumed to be dollars) at a specified exchange rate value.

(1)	Long-term capital inflows	785
(2)	Merchandise exports	17 785
(3)	Exports of traded services	1 170
(4)	Short-term capital inflows	932
(5)	Debit on official reserves	7
(6)	Merchandise imports	15 556
(7)	Long-term capital outflows	814
(8)	Short-term capital outflows	1 158
(9)	Investment income receipts	545
(10)	Investment income payments	1 613
(11)	Net international transfer payments	721
(12)	Imports of traded services	1 348

***1. The balance on merchandise trade is a**

(a) credit (surplus) balance of $33 341.
(b) credit balance of $2229.
(c) debit (deficit) balance of $2229.
(d) debit balance of $33 341.
(e) credit balance of $1330.

2. Which of the following is not a credit item in the balance of payments accounts?

(a) Item 2.
(b) Item 4.
(c) Item 9.
(d) Item 7.
(e) Item 1.

***3. The value of the current account balance is a**

(a) credit balance of $262.
(b) deficit balance of $262.
(c) surplus of $983.
(d) surplus of $2051.
(e) None of the above.

4. Which of the following is not a capital account item?

(a) Item 8.
(b) Item 4.
(c) Item 1.
(d) Item 7.
(e) Item 9.

5. The value of the capital account balance, excluding changes to official reserves is

(a) a deficit of $255.
(b) a surplus of $255.
(c) a deficit of $262.
(d) a surplus of $777.
(e) None of the above.

***6. The sum of the current and capital accounts, ignoring the Official Financing Account, indicates a**

(a) surplus position of $7.
(b) deficit position of $517.
(c) deficit position of $7.
(d) surplus position of $517.
(e) balanced position.

7. If there had been no central bank intervention in the foreign-exchange market, the situation described in question 6, implies that

(a) this country's currency would ultimately appreciate.
(b) the exchange rate would ultimately depreciate.
(c) there is an excess supply of foreign currency or an excess demand for the country's currency at the current exchange rate.
(d) the country's balance of payments ultimately would be in balance at a lower exchange rate.
(e) All of the above.

***8. Given your answers to Questions 6 and 7, what central bank intervention is necessary to prevent the exchange rate changing from its current value?**

(a) The central bank would have to buy up the excess supply of the domestic currency of \$7 (millions) by reducing its official reserves.
(b) The central bank would have to supply the excess demand for the domestic currency of \$7 (millions) and add to its holdings of foreign currency.
(c) By increasing the domestic interest rate, the central bank could eliminate the surplus balance of \$7 (millions).
(d) By selling bonds to foreigners, the central bank would finance the deficit in the balance of payments of \$7 (millions).
(e) The central bank would have to buy up the excess supply of the domestic currency of \$517 by reducing its official reserves.

Questions 9 through 12 refer to the following exchange rates in Canadian dollars for two years:

Foreign Currency	2001	2002
Euro	\$1.387	\$1.483
Swedish krona	\$0.150	\$0.162
U.S. dollar	\$1.548	\$1.570
Japanese yen	\$0.0128	\$0.0126
South Korean won	\$0.0012	\$0.0013

9. Which of the following was *not* true in 2001? One Canadian dollar traded for

(a) 0.721 euros.
(b) 6.667 krona.
(c) \$1.548 U.S. dollars.
(d) 78.125 yen.
(e) 833.33 won.

10. Which of the following was *not* true in 2002? One Canadian dollar traded for

(a) 0.674 euros.
(b) 6.173 krona.
(c) 0.637 U.S. dollars.
(d) 79.365 yen.
(e) 833.33 won.

***11. Which of the following statements concerning exchange rate movements between 2001 and 2002 is true?**

(a) The European Union euro depreciated.
(b) The Japanese yen depreciated.
(c) The South Korean won depreciated.
(d) The U.S. dollar depreciated.
(e) The Swedish krona depreciated.

12. **Suppose that a week's skiing vacation (meals, ski tows, accommodations, but excluding travel) costs $1000 (U.S.) at U.S. resorts, 900 euros at French resorts, and 11 000 krona at Swedish resorts during this two-year period. Which of the following statements is *not* correct?**
(a) A Canadian paid $1548 (Canadian) in 2001 for a skiing vacation in the United States.
(b) A Canadian supplied approximately 1335 Canadian dollars and demanded 900 euros in 2002 for a skiing vacation in France.
(c) The Canadian dollar price of a skiing vacation in the United States decreased between 2001 and 2002.
(d) The Canadian dollar price of a skiing vacation in France increased between 2001 and 2002.
(e) A Canadian supplied 1782 Canadian dollars in 2002 to get 11 000 krona for a skiing vacation in Sweden.

13. **Which of the following events, by itself, will cause the Canadian dollar price of Mexican pesos to appreciate?**
(a) Canadians import fewer Mexican products.
(b) Canadians export more raw resources to Mexico.
(c) Price inflation in Mexico is less than inflation in Canada.
(d) Canadian interest rates rise while interest rates in Mexico remain constant.
(e) Canadians receive higher interest payments for their Mexican asset holdings.

14. **The short-run expansion of Canadian GDP and employment triggered by an increase in domestic investment will be less if**
(a) Canada operates on a flexible exchange-rate system.
(b) the *AS* curve is relatively flat.
(c) the exchange rate is fixed by the Bank of Canada.
(d) there is no "crowding-out" effect.
(e) None of the above.

15. **If an identical basket of goods in Canada has a price index of 110 and a price index of 200 in Germany, then the PPP exchange rate**
(a) equals 0.55 dollars.
(b) equals 90 dollars.
(c) equals 1.82 dollars.
(d) indicates that Canadian dollars are undervalued.
(e) cannot equal the actual exchange rate because the two indices are not equal.

*16. **What is the value of the current account if $S = 100$, $I = 50$ and $(T - G) = -24$?**
(a) A surplus of 150.
(b) A surplus of 76.
(c) A surplus of 26.
(d) A deficit of 26.
(e) A surplus of 126.

*17. **Which of the following would reduce (a smaller surplus or a greater deficit) the value of the current account balance that you calculated in question 16?**
(a) *S* increases from 100 to 110.
(b) *I* increases from 50 to 56.
(c) The government's budget deficit changes from –24 to –20.
(d) *S* increases from 100 to 110 and investment decreases from 50 to 40.
(e) All of the above.

18. Suppose Canada initially has both its current and capital accounts in balance (no surplus or deficit). Then Canadian firms increase the amount they import from Japan, financing that increase by borrowing from Japan. There will now be a current account ______________ and a capital account ______________.

(a) surplus; surplus
(b) surplus; deficit
(c) deficit; surplus
(d) deficit; deficit
(e) Both accounts will remain in balance.

19. Assume that Japan has a flexible foreign-exchange rate. Which one of the following statements would allow for a depreciation of the Japanese currency:

(a) Japanese exports to Australia increased.
(b) Brazil places new import restrictions on Japanese exports.
(c) More Asian visitors vacationed in Japan.
(d) More American parent companies have increased their foreign direct investment in subsidiaries in Japan.
(e) Japan levies an import tariff on American automobiles.

***20. The Canadian dollar would appreciate relative to the euro if**

(a) Canadians reduced their imports of French wine.
(b) More Canadians visited Spain.
(c) Canadians imported more snails from France.
(d) Italy stopped importing Canadians furs.
(e) Canadians buy German government bonds.

***21. Suppose that Thailand has a fixed foreign-exchange rate and that the sum of the current and capital accounts shows a deficit position. Which one of the following independent events would reduce this deficit?**

(a) Chinese exports to Thailand increased.
(b) Thailand increased short-term interest rates.
(c) China placed new restrictions on textile imports from Thailand.
(d) More residents of Thailand visited China.
(e) None of the preceding statements is correct.

***22. Consider the following hypothetical open economy: Domestic investment = 100; Private saving = 100; Current account balance = 10. The government budget deficit is**

(a) –20. (b) 20.
(c) –10. (d) 10.
(e) 30.

Question 23 refers to the following foreign-exchange rate model.

Country Alba has a demand curve for foreign currency given by $D = 6 - 2e$ and a supply curve given by $S = 0.5 + 3e$, where e is the amount of Alba's currency for one unit of foreign currency, and quantities are in millions.

***23. Which of the following statements is correct?**

(a) An increase in e increases the quantity demanded for foreign currency.
(b) An increase in e, decreases the quantity supplied of foreign currency.
(c) If Alba operates on a flexible exchange rate, the value of e is 1.1.
(d) The equilibrium quantity of the foreign exchange is 3.8 million.
(e) Both (c) and (d).

Questions 24 and 25 refer to the following foreign-exchange rate model.

Alba increases its interest rate with the result that the new demand curve for foreign currency is $D = 5.8 - 2e$ and the new supply curve of foreign currency is $S = 0.8 + 3e$.

***24. Which of the following statements is correct? Compared with question 23,**
(a) the new free-market value of *e* is higher.
(b) Alba's currency appreciates with a flexible exchange rate.
(c) Alba's currency depreciates with a flexible exchange rate.
(d) the demand for foreign exchange has increased.
(e) the supply of foreign exchange has decreased.

25. If the demand and supply curves were those described in Question 24, what foreign-exchange transactions must Alba's central bank conduct to maintain a pegged *e* value of 0.9?
(a) It must satisfy the excess demand for foreign currency by selling foreign currency and buying Alba's currency.
(b) It must satisfy the excess supply of foreign currency by buying foreign currency and selling Alba's currency.
(c) None since the pegged value is equal to the free market rate.
(d) None other than some minor adjustments to deal with seasonal fluctuations in trade flows.
(e) Both (c) and (d).

SOLUTIONS

Chapter Review

1.(c) **2.**(b) **3.**(c) **4.**(a) **5.**(b) **6.**(d) **7.**(d) **8.**(b) **9.**(e) **10.**(d) **11.**(b) **12.**(b) **13.**(c) **14.**(b) **15.**(a) **16.**(c) **17.**(a) **18.**(e) **19.**(a) **20.**(d) **21.**(a) **22.**(a) **23.**(c) **24.**(a) **25.**(c) **26.**(d) **27.**(d) **28.**(a) **29.**(e) **30.**(a) **31.**(e)

Short-Answer Questions

1. (a) The official financing account. This transaction indicates that the central bank is intervening in the foreign-exchange market by adding to its holdings of foreign reserves and by selling its domestic currency. The central bank is attempting to prevent the domestic currency from appreciating. The buying of foreign currency represents the purchase of assets from abroad, and thus enters as a debit item in the balance of payments.

(b) The current account. A dividend payment represents a capital-service transaction. Since the domestic firm is paying a foreigner, the dividend payment is recorded as a debit item in the balance of payments.

(c) The capital account. A Canadian company is purchasing a foreign asset (a deposit in a Hong Kong bank). This is an example of a capital outflow from the domestic economy. It is recorded as a debit in the balance of payments.

2. (a) When more Japanese tourists visit Montreal, Canadians are exporting more tourist services to Japan. Hence, S_y will shift to the right, with the result that the yen should depreciate.

(b) A greater inflation rate in Canada will decrease Canadian exports to Japan and increase imports from Japan. D_y will shift to the right (Canadian imports increase), and S_y will shift to the left (reduced Canadian exports to Japan). Both are likely to cause the Canadian dollar price of the yen to appreciate (the Canadian dollar depreciates).

(c) Japan is likely to experience more capital inflows from Canada, and less international capital will flow from Japan to Canada. Hence, both the demand and supply curves for yen are affected such that the yen will appreciate.

(d) S_y will shift to the right, and hence the yen will depreciate.
(e) These transactions constitute capital outflows from Japan. The supply curve for yen will shift to the right, and hence the yen will depreciate.
(f) The yen will depreciate (with respect to the Canadian dollar) as Japanese companies switch away from U.S. suppliers to Canadian suppliers.
(g) S_y will shift to the right, and the yen should depreciate.

3. An increase in imports will increase the demand for foreign currency. The *AD* curve will shift leftward and a short-run recessionary gap will be created. In time, wages and prices will fall thereby shifting the *AS* curve downward until potential GDP is restored. If the central bank operates a fixed exchange rate, it must satisfy the excess demand for foreign currency by supplying it and by buying domestic currency. The negative external shock still occurs, and the recessionary gap may be prolonged. However, with a flexible exchange rate, the excess demand for foreign currency will cause the domestic currency to depreciate. The lower domestic currency discourages imports and encourages exports. Hence, the negative aggregate demand shock is moderated, and the recessionary gap is likely to be less pronounced and perhaps shorter in duration.

4. The principle of comparative advantage shows that average living standards are maximized by having countries specialize in the things they produce comparatively best and then trading with other countries to obtain the things they produce comparatively worst. The more specialization there is, the more trade occurs. Therefore, if the objective is to promote the welfare and living standards of the population, having a surplus in the trade account does not serve that objective—it reduces the consumption possibilities of the population. On the other hand, a situation in which there is a large volume of trade even though the balance in the trade account is zero can be regarded as satisfactory.

5. A decline in the rate of interest in the U.S. relative to the rate of interest in Canada will cause a net inflow of capital into Canada, and thus the Canadian dollar will appreciate. The appreciation of the Canadian dollar will, in turn, make Canadian goods relatively more expensive in the international market and exports will fall and imports will rise. Therefore, the statement is correct: exports to the U.S. will fall.

6. If the exchange rate is not flexible, then the sum of the balances in the current and capital account does not need be zero. But the "overall" balance of payment will always be zero because the central bank will sell foreign currency to eliminate a deficit in the sum of the current and capital accounts or buy foreign currency to eliminate a surplus in the sum of the current and capital accounts.

Exercises

1. (a) Column entries are $180, $190, $200, $210, and $220.
(b) The equilibrium price is $200, and 400 cameras are sold.

2. (a) One Canadian dollar trades for one U.S. dollar.
(b) The demand curve for U.S. dollars will shift to the right (such as that labelled D_2). The U.S. dollar will appreciate to perhaps 1.05 Canadian dollars.
(c) The demand curve for U.S. dollars will shift to the left (such as that labelled D_1). The U.S. dollar will depreciate to perhaps $0.95 Canadian.
(d) The supply curve of U.S. dollars will shift to the right (such as that labelled S_1). The U.S. dollar will depreciate to perhaps $0.95 Canadian.

3. (a) $1.50 where $D = S$.
(b) At a fixed price of $1.60, there is an excess supply of euros (and an excess demand for dollars). Thus, the Bank must sell dollars and buy $q_2 - q_0$ euros in the exchange market. The Bank's holdings of euros (which may be held for reserves) will increase.
(c) Probably confusion, increased speculation, and destabilized exchange markets. The European Union peg of 0.65 translates into a dollar price of euros of $1.54, which is different from the Bank of Canada's target of $1.60.

4. **(a)** In the absence of any pressure in the foreign-exchange rate, the equilibrium value of the exchange rate is e_1 as shown in the diagram. An outflow of capital will increase the demand for foreign exchange (the U.S. dollar) and the demand curve for U.S. dollars will shift to *D'*. At the initial value of the exchange rate (e_1) there is now an excess demand equal to $Q_2 - Q_1$, which puts upward pressure on the value of the exchange rate. To prevent the exchange rate from appreciating, the central bank of Solimar will sell foreign currency to eliminate this excess demand.

Figure 35-5

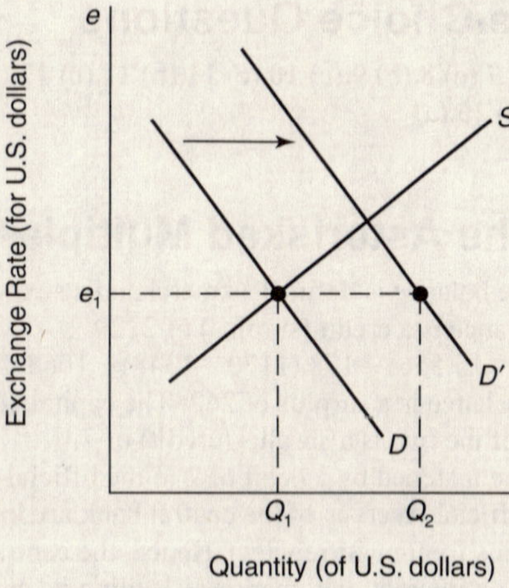

(b) Expansionary monetary policy by the central bank of Solimar will have an impact similar to the one examined in part (a). The decrease in domestic rate of interest in Solimar will cause an outflow of capital, and the demand curve for U.S. dollars will shift to *D'*. At the initial value of the exchange rate (e_1) there is now an excess demand equal to $Q_2 - Q_1$, which puts upward pressure on the value of the exchange rate. To prevent the exchange rate from appreciating, the central bank of Solimar will sell foreign currency to eliminate this excess demand.

There is a link, however, between the central bank intervention in the exchange market and the domestic supply of money. When the central bank sells foreign currency to eliminate a deficit in the foreign-exchange market, it receives payment in domestic currency and the central bank takes out of circulation this currency—i.e., the money supply decreases. Therefore, the central bank cannot implement monetary policy and fix the exchange rate at the same time; if it wants to decrease the rate of interest, the central bank must allow the exchange rate to float.

Extension Exercises

E1. A revaluation of the Chinese currency will make Chinese goods relatively more expensive and thus the U.S. trade account deficit with China will be reduced. This, however, will not guarantee a significant reduction in the overall U.S. current account deficit since other countries (e.g., Indonesia, Malaysia, etc.) will most likely start exporting to the U.S. what the U.S. was until now importing from China. Therefore, most likely the U.S. current account deficit will remain—at most, it will be marginally reduced.

What about the U.S. capital account? If China will no longer have a large trade account surplus with the U.S., it will not be able to continue accumulating reserves and buying U.S. treasury bills with it. Since there is no guarantee that the countries that will take the place of China as supplier of goods to the U.S. will invest their surplus in U.S. treasury bills, the demand for U.S. treasury bills will most likely decrease. This means that the U.S. surplus in the capital account will most likely decrease as well.

E2. (a) Stacey is taking the exchange-rate risk since her liability is in yen. The Japanese seller is guaranteed 500 000 yen. At the time the deal was made, Stacey anticipated paying $50 000 (Canadian) for 500 000 yen. However, at the time of payment, Stacey has to pay $75 000 (Canadian). Her loss is $25 000.

(b) The New York hotel is taking the exchange-rate risk since its receipt is in Canadian dollars. The Hamilton couple pay $25 000 (Canadian) regardless of the exchange rate value. When the hotel receives its payment in June, it converts \$25 000 (Canadian) into \$17 241 (U.S.). At the time the deal was signed, the hotel anticipated receiving \$17 857 (U.S.) at an exchange rate of 1.40. The loss is \$616 (U.S.).

(c) Fritz is taking the exchange-rate risk since his asset is valued in U.S. dollars. In 1997 he pays \$87 000 Canadian for the Florida condo. However, he receives \$90 600 (Canadian) in 1998. Although Fritz realized no net capital gain (in U.S. dollars) after deducting transactions costs on his Florida property, the appreciation of the U.S. dollar earned him a gain of \$3600 (Canadian).

Additional Multiple-Choice Questions

1.(b) **2.**(d) **3.**(a) **4.**(e) **5.**(a) **6.**(a) **7.**(e) **8.**(b) **9.**(c) **10.**(e) **11.**(b) **12.**(c) **13.**(c) **14.**(a) **15.**(a) **16.**(c) **17.**(b) **18.**(c) **19.**(b) **20.**(a) **21.**(b) **22.**(c) **23.**(e) **24.**(b) **25.**(a)

Explanations for the Asterisked Multiple-Choice Questions

1.(b) The merchandise trade balance is defined as merchandise exports minus merchandise imports. The merchandise trade balance is a credit (surplus) of 2229.

3.(a) +262 = 2229 (17 785 – 15 556) – 178 (1170 – 1348) – 1068 (545 – 1613) – 721.

6.(a) The current account balance is a surplus of 262. The capital account has a debit (deficit) position of 255. Hence, the sum of the two is a surplus (credit) of 7.

8.(b) The credit of 7 must be matched by a debit of 7 in the official financing account. A debit in this account reflects the fact that official reserves of the central bank are increasing. The central bank is buying foreign assets (gold plus foreign currencies). Hence, the central bank to satisfy the excess demand for its domestic currency on international markets is selling its currency and buying foreign reserves.

11.(b) The yen fell from 0.0128 to 0.0126 Canadian dollars. The Canadian dollar rose from 78.125 yen to 79.365 yen.

16.(c) $NX = (S - I) + (T - G) = 50 - 24 = +26$ (surplus).

17.(b) The textbook explains that the current account balance in any year is equal to the excess of national saving $[S + (T - G)]$ over domestic investment (I). An increase in investment reduces the current account surplus or generates a larger deficit. If Canadians do not save enough to finance domestic investment, the balance must be financed by foreign funds.

20.(a) A reduction in Canadian imports of French wine, all other things equal, will cause the demand for the euro to fall in the foreign-exchange market. Therefore, the euro will depreciate relative to the Canadian dollar (or the Canadian dollar will appreciate relative to the euro).

21.(b) An increase in the domestic rate of interest will make short-term investment in Thailand more attractive, and thus the demand for Thailand's currency (the baht) will increase—or, in other words, the supply of U.S. dollars will increase in the exchange market between the baht and the U.S. dollar. As a result, the deficit in the sum of the balances in Thailand's current and capital accounts will be reduced.

22.(c) The textbook explains that the current account balance in any year is equal to the excess of national saving $[S + (T - G)]$ over domestic investment (I), where $T - G$ is the government budget surplus (and thus $G - T$ is the government budget deficit):
$CUB = [S + (T - G)] - I \rightarrow G - T = S - I - CUB = 100 - 100 - 10 = -10$

23.(e) Equating $6 - 2e$ with $0.5 + 3e$, we obtain $e = 1.1$ and 3.8 million of foreign exchange traded.

24.(b) The new e value is 1.0. Hence, the foreign currency has depreciated while the domestic currency has appreciated.